HOW TO READ
THE CHINESE NOVEL

Princeton Library of Asian Translations

How to Read the

Chinese Novel

Edited by David L. Rolston

CONTRIBUTORS

Shuen-fu Lin	*David T. Roy*
Andrew H. Plaks	*John C.Y. Wang*
David L. Rolston	*Anthony C. Yu*

Princeton University Press

Princeton, New Jersey

Copyright © 1990 by Princeton University Press
Published by Princeton University Press, 41 William Street, Princeton,
New Jersey 08540
In the United Kingdom: Princeton University Press, Oxford

This book has been composed in Bembo and Goh Chinese Grotesk

Clothbound editions of Princeton University Press books are printed on
acid-free paper, and binding materials are chosen for strength and durability.
Paperbacks, although satisfactory for personal collections, are not usually
suitable for library rebinding

Printed in the United States of America by Princeton University Press,
Princeton, New Jersey

How to read the Chinese novel / edited by David L. Rolston;
    contributors, Shuen-fu Lin . . . [et al.].
        p.   cm.—(Princeton library of Asian translations)
    Bibliography: p.
    Includes index.
    ISBN 0-691-06753-8
    1. Chinese fiction—History and criticism.   I. Rolston, David L.,
    1952-   . II. Lin, Shuen-fu, 1943-   III. Series.
    PL2415.H66   1989
895.1'3'009—dc19   88-37900
                                                               CIP

CONTENTS

Appendixes

BIBLIOGRAPHICAL MATERIAL

LIST OF ABBREVIATIONS

AMB 　*All Men Are Brothers*, Pearl Buck, trans. (N.Y.: John Day, revised edition, 1937).

CPMTLHP 　*Chin P'ing Mei tzu-liao hui-pien* 金瓶梅資料滙編 (Collected Material on the *Chin P'ing Mei*), Hou Chung-i 侯忠義 and Wang Ju-mei 王汝梅, eds. (Peking: Pei-ching ta-hsüeh, 1985).

CST 　*Chin Sheng-t'an*, by John Ching-yu Wang (N.Y.: Twayne, 1972).

CSTCC 　*Chin Sheng-t'an ch'üan-chi* 金聖歎全集 (Complete Works of Chin Sheng-t'an), 4 vols. (Nanking: Chiang-su ku-chi, 1985).

CYCPYCC 　*Hsin-pien Shih-t'ou chi Chih-yen chai p'ing-yü chi-chiao* 新編石頭記脂硯齋評語輯校 (A Newly Edited Collation of Chih-yen chai Comments on the *Story of the Stone*), Ch'en Ch'ing-hao 陳慶浩, ed. (Taipei: Lien-ching ch'u-pan she, 1979).

CYY 　*P'ing-chu Chin-yü yüan* 評註金玉緣 (Annotated and Commentated Affinity of Gold and Jade; Taipei: Feng-huang ch'u-pan she, 1974).

HLMC 　*Hung-lou meng chüan* 紅樓夢卷 (Collection of Material on the *Hung-lou meng*), I-su 一粟, ed. (Shanghai: Chung-hua shu-chü, 1963).

HLMSL 　*Hung-lou meng shu-lu* 紅樓夢書錄 (Bibliography of Works on the *Hung-lou meng*), I-su 一粟, ed. (Shanghai: Shang-hai ku-chi, revised edition, 1981).

HLMTLHP 　*Hung-lou meng tzu-liao hui-pien* 紅樓夢資料彙編 (Collected Material on the *Hung-lou meng*), Chu I-hsüan 朱一玄, ed. (Tientsin: Nan-k'ai ta-hsüeh, 1985).

Hu Shih 　*Hu Shih lun Chung-kuo ku-tien hsiao-shuo* 胡適論中國古典小說 (Hu Shih on Classical Chinese Fiction), I

Chu-hsien 易竹賢, ed. (Wuhan: Ch'ang-chiang wen-i, 1987).

HYC   *Hsi-yu chi* 西遊記 (The Journey to the West; Peking: Tso-chia ch'u-pan she, 1954).

HYCTLHP   *Hsi-yu chi tzu-liao hui-pien* 西遊記資料彙編 (Collected Material on the *Hsi-yu chi*), Chu I-hsüan and Liu Yü-ch'en 劉毓忱, eds. (Cheng-chou: Chung-chou shu-hua she, 1983).

JLWS   *Ju-lin wai-shih* 儒林外史 (The Scholars; Peking: Jen-min wen-hsüeh, 1975).

JLWSHCHPP   *Ju-lin wai-shih hui-chiao hui-p'ing pen* 儒林外史會校會評本 (Variorum Edition of the *Ju-lin wai-shih* with Collected Commentary), Li Han-ch'iu 李漢秋, ed. (Shanghai: Shang-hai ku-chi, 1984).

JLWSYCTL   *Ju-lin wai-shih yen-chiu tzu-liao* 儒林外史研究資料 (Research Material on the *Ju-lin wai-shih*), Li Han-ch'iu, ed. (Shanghai: Shang-hai ku-chi, 1984).

JW   *The Journey to the West*, Anthony C. Yu, trans., 4 vols. (Chicago: University of Chicago Press, 1977–83).

Ku-chin   *Chung-kuo ku-tai chin-tai wen-hsüeh yen-chiu* 中國古代近代文學研究 (Studies in Ancient and Modern Chinese Literature), reprint series (Peking: Chinese People's University).

LCH   *Chung-kuo li-tai hsiao-shuo lun-chu hsüan* 中國歷代小說論著選 (Selection of Writings on Chinese Fiction Through the Ages), Huang Lin 黃霖 and Han T'ung-wen 韓同文, eds. (Nan-ch'ang: Chiang-hsi jen-min, vol. 1, 1982; vol. 2, 1985).

Needham   *Science and Civilisation in China*, Joseph Needham, et al., projected for 7 vols. (Cambridge: Cambridge University Press, 1954–).

Pan-pen   *Ku-tien hsiao-shuo pan-pen tzu-liao hsüan-pien* 古典小說版本資料選編 (Selected Material on the Publication of Classical [Chinese] Fiction), Chu I-hsüan, ed., vol. 1 (T'ai-yüan: Shan-hsi jen-min, 1986).

RTK   *Romance of the Three Kingdoms*, C.H. Brewitt-Taylor, trans., 2 vols. (Rutland, Vt.: Charles E. Tuttle, 1959).

Scholars	*The Scholars*, Yang Hsien-yi and Gladys Yang, trans. (Peking: Foreign Languages Press, 1957).
SHCHPP	*Shui-hu chuan hui-p'ing pen* 水滸傳會評本 (Variorum Commentary Edition of the *Shui-hu chuan*), Ch'en Hsi-chung 陳曦鐘 et al., eds. (Peking: Pei-ching ta-hsüeh, 1981).
SHCTLHP	*Shui-hu chuan tzu-liao hui-pien* 水滸傳資料彙編 (Collected Material on the *Shui-hu chuan*), Chu I-hsüan and Liu Yü-ch'en, eds. (Tientsin: Pai-hua wen-i, 1981).
SKYI	*Ch'üan-t'u hsiu-hsiang San-kuo yen-i* 全圖綉像三國演義 (Fully Illustrated *San-kuo yen-i*), 3 vols. (Huhehot: Nei-meng-ku jen-min, 1981).
Stone	*The Story of the Stone*, David Hawkes and John Minford, trans., 5 vols. (Harmondsworth: Penguin Books, 1973–86).
TGL	*The Golden Lotus*, Clement Egerton, trans., 4 vols. (London: Routledge and Kegan Paul, 1972).
The I Ching	*The I Ching or the Book of Changes*, by Richard Wilhelm, Cary F. Baynes, trans. (Princeton: Princeton University Press, 1967).
TICS	*Ti-i ch'i-shu* 第一奇書 (The Number One Marvelous Book), 5 vols. (Taipei: Li-jen shu-chü, 1981).

EDITOR'S PREFACE

The title of this volume is *How to Read the Chinese Novel*. It might seem that a book bearing such a title should contain a certain number of all-purpose prescriptive rules that would dictate the range of conventional approaches to be taken by the reader in his or her encounters with works of Chinese fiction of more than novella length. The truth of the matter is simultaneously less presumptuous and more complicated.

First, what do we mean by "the Chinese novel"? Behind this universalistic terminology rests a much more modest territorial claim. This book does not explicitly deal with the Chinese novel as a whole, but only with what has been referred to as "the classic Chinese novel" by C.T. Hsia in his book of that title, *The Classic Chinese Novel: A Critical Introduction* (New York: Columbia University Press, 1968). Two notions are involved in the word "classic": a certain removal in time (and perhaps mind-set) from our modern epoch and a level of artistic excellence justifying our continued interest no matter how much time intervenes between our age and theirs. Although the classic or traditional Chinese novel continues to have an influence on modern writers and recent years have seen the appearance of magazines featuring serialized formal imitations of traditional fiction, as a living art form it would appear that the traditional Chinese novel did not survive beyond the first two decades of this century. There is another point of similarity between Professor Hsia's book and this volume—both focus primarily on six novels: (1) *San-kuo yen-i* 三國演義 (The Romance of the Three Kingdoms), (2) *Shui-hu chuan* 水滸傳 (The Water Margin), (3) *Hsi-yu chi* 西遊記 (The Journey to the West), (4) *Chin P'ing Mei* 金瓶梅 (conventionally translated as "The Plum in the Golden Vase" or "The Golden Lotus," but the primary reference in the title is to the three most important female characters of the novel), (5) *Ju-lin wai-shih* 儒林外史 (The Scholars), and (6) *Hung-lou meng* 紅樓夢 (Dream of the Red Chamber; also known as the *Shih-t'ou chi* 石頭記, "Story of the Stone"). There is no coincidence here. On at least one level, this volume was designed to complement and supplement Professor Hsia's work, which remains the only general introduction to the traditional Chinese novel in English and is used as a basic text in courses in this field. Readers requiring information on the plots or textual histories of the six classic novels can find the answers to some of their questions in his book. However, it might be fitting to add a few words here about the authorship and dating of these six novels.

The earliest extant printed edition of any of the six novels is the 1522 printing of the *San-kuo yen-i*, but all printings agree in ascribing the authorship of the novel to a much earlier figure, Lo Kuan-chung 羅貫中 (fl. 1330–1400). Lo Kuan-chung was known in his lifetime primarily as a dramatist, and the only reliable biographical information on him comes from a work on drama and dramatists. Be that as it may, a rather prodigious number of traditional Chinese novels are attributed to him, most of them dealing with historical or pseudohistorical themes. An example of the latter is the *Shui-hu chuan* (first extant dated edition, 1589). The authorship for that novel is sometimes given to Lo Kuan-chung alone, sometimes it is shared with another figure (often described as Lo's teacher) named Shih Nai-an 施耐庵, or sometimes attributed to Shih Nai-an alone. Despite fervent efforts to provide a hometown and ancestors for Shih Nai-an in Kiangsu Province, many remain convinced that there never was such a person and that Shih Nai-an is just a pseudonym. Most scholars tend to agree in awarding the authorship of the *Hsi-yu chi* (first dated edition, 1592) to Wu Ch'eng-en 吳承恩 (ca. 1500–1582), primarily on the basis of notices to that effect in various local gazetteers, the earliest of them dating from the late Ming dynasty. The attribution, however, is not uncontested. In any case these three novels all represent, to a large extent, the reworking and expansion of pre-existent traditional material, and the editorial work of weaving together these sources may have been as important as any purely creative work undertaken by the individuals responsible for the final versions of the material in novel form.

The *Chin P'ing Mei* (earliest extant printed edition, 1617–1618) is generally acclaimed as a milestone in the development of the Chinese novel away from the earlier accretive, compilatory process of composition outlined above toward a more purely individual method of composition. Although the novel borrows heavily from other works of vernacular literature, most conspicuously from the *Shui-hu chuan* (from which the general outline of the plot and a number of the individual characters are derived), careful reading of the text reveals that the writing technique underlying the borrowing of this material tends to be ironic and is motivated by a consistent rhetorical strategy. The novel was published under a pseudonym, however, and the lack of incontrovertible evidence for any of the over twenty candidates proposed as authors by various scholars to date has prevented the development of a consensus on any single figure among them. Most prominent among the names mentioned for this honor are Li K'ai-hsien 李開先 (1502–1568), T'u Lung 屠隆 (1542–1605), and T'ang Hsien-tsu 湯顯祖 (1550–1616).

The problem of authorship for the last two novels is comparatively simple. Both rely rather heavily on autobiographical material, but neither in the case of the *Ju-lin wai-shih* (earliest extant edition, 1803) nor in that of the *Hung-lou meng* (first printed edition, 1791–1792; but prior to that circulated in manuscript copies several of which are still extant), does the author's name appear on the title page. The author of the *Hung-lou meng*, Ts'ao Hsüeh-ch'in 曹雪芹 (1715?–1763?), did work his name into the body of his novel, but he gave himself the status of editor and not author. Because Ts'ao Hsüeh-ch'in came from an extremely prominent family that lost imperial favor before he came of age, we know far more about his ancestors than about Ts'ao Hsüeh-ch'in himself. The author of the *Ju-lin wai-shih*, Wu Ching-tzu 吳敬梓 (1701–1754), also came from a prominent family only to end up in abject poverty, but the preservation of an earlier version of his collected works and the reminiscences of scholar friends allow us considerable insight into his life.

The words "how to read" in the title primarily represent a translation of the Chinese phrase *tu-fa* 讀法, a compound made from the verb "to read" and a noun meaning "law" or "method." Although this compound has wide usage with a variety of meanings depending on context, the specific reference intended in the title is to a kind of essay that appears in commentary editions of traditional Chinese novels. The history of this type of essay begins with the first example of the genre written by Chin Sheng-t'an 金聖歎 (1608–1661) as part of his commentary on the *Shui-hu chuan* and ends with the death of the traditional novel itself. The bulk of this volume consists of the translation into English of *tu-fa* essays for five of the six novels mentioned above. The first of those selected dates from sometime before 1644, while the latest was completed in 1850. They appear in the book in the order of their composition rather than in the order of the writing of the novels involved so that the reader can get some idea of the historical evolution of the genre and how the influence of earlier writers worked its effect, in both direct and indirect fashion, on those who came after. The essays themselves do deal with general problems involved in the reading of any work of fiction, such as the differing effects produced by swallowing the text whole in as short a time as possible or the other extreme of drawing out the experience by savoring to the full the implications of each and every word, but the majority of the comments are more narrowly focused on issues connected with the critic's evaluation of the characters in the novel or his reconstruction of the author's motives for inserting various features into the text. An alternative translation for *tu-fa* would be "principles for reading," which would emphasize the fact that *tu-fa* essays for Chinese novels are made up of numerous separate items, sometimes numbering over one hundred.

Often the items were numbered consecutively in the printing of the commentaries, as in the *tu-fa* essays for the *Shui-hu chuan* and the *Chin P'ing Mei*. For the convenience of citation, that practice is retained in the translation of those two essays and supplied for the other three as well.

Some novels have been the subject of more than one *tu-fa* essay. In the case of the *Ju-lin wai-shih* no *tu-fa* essay exists, so we have substituted instead the preface and chapter comments (also broken up into separate items) from the earliest edition of that novel. In this instance many of the more general pronouncements made in the commentary as a whole appear in the preface and the comments for the first several chapters, while most of the other chapter comments deal with specific incidents or characters appearing in that chapter.

The idea of producing a volume of translations of this material dates back to the conference on Chinese narrative held at Princeton University in 1974. The purpose behind the endeavor, whether then or now, was not to say that these traditional critics were infallible and hit their mark every time. The point to be made is rather different. Aside from the important facts that early critics had a direct influence on the writing of later novels and that the mere practice of publishing novels together with commentary eventually changed the mix of narrative voices in the traditional novel, we can turn to these traditional critics for help in avoiding, in our interpretations of these novels, the imposition of foreign frameworks and literary theory onto a tradition alien to them.

To place these translated essays in perspective, the first chapter contains four essays that apply four different approaches to the field of traditional Chinese fiction criticism. The first essay explores the sources for this branch of criticism; the second outlines its early history (up to the work of Chin Sheng-t'an); the third describes the formal structure of Chinese fiction commentaries, of which the *tu-fa* essays form just one part; while the last analyzes some of the more important and recurring terminology and interpretive strategies used by the critics. The translations of the *tu-fa* essays themselves are prefaced by brief introductions on the authors by this editor. The editor has also partially or wholly annotated these translations and has compiled three appendixes and a bibliography. Appendix 1 is a finding list for the occurrence of critical terms in the translations, appendix 2 deals with the problem of the fiction commentaries attributed to Li Chih 李贄 (1527–1602), appendix 3 is a conversion table showing the Wade-Giles and *pinyin* romanization systems of Chinese, and the multipart bibliography contains one section describing the various commentary editions for the six novels.

The number of first-rate traditional Chinese novels does not extend very far past the six in this volume. These few novels formed a select canon and they were read and reread with more concentration and fervor than most of us are inclined to give to individual works. Traditional Chinese fiction critics made rather severe demands on their readers, whom they expected to be very familiar with the text of the novel commented on. The critics also presumed that their readers would be able to extend their method of interpretation onto aspects of the novels not explicitly examined. Hopefully the annotations provided for the translations will be of some help in overcoming the inevitable gap between the commentator's ideal reader and today's general reader. On the other hand, it is sincerely hoped that this book will prove of interest to a wide range of readers with a variety of needs and that the measures taken to ensure the comfort of one type of reader are not found offensive by others who have no need for or interest in them.

Because this project was begun so long ago, the Wade-Giles system of romanization used in this volume is different from the *pinyin* system now used widely in the People's Republic of China, American newspapers and magazines, and (increasingly) Western Sinological works as well. For readers unfamiliar with the Wade-Giles system, a conversion chart is provided in appendix 3.

As editor, I would like to state here that this volume is the first of its kind in English. It is no doubt riddled with mistakes of fact and judgment that will not escape the eyes of present and future scholars. Some mistakes have been prevented from reaching a larger readership through the kind advice of various readers, chief among whom are Professor Robert E. Hegel of Washington University, whom I would like to thank for his close and critical reading of the manuscript as a whole; Professor Poon Ming-sun of the Chinese University of Hong Kong, for pointing out errors in the bibliographies; and students at the University of Michigan who participated in a seminar where this material was used. The contributors and I would also like to express our gratitude to the Committee on Studies of Chinese Civilization of the American Council of Learned Societies for the generous provision of funds that facilitated meetings among the contributors and the physical preparation of the manuscript. An earlier version of chapter IV appeared in *Renditions* 24 (Autumn 1985), published by the Chinese University of Hong Kong.

HOW TO READ
THE CHINESE NOVEL

徵求批評

此書前集四十回曾將與今本不同之點畧爲批出此後集四十回中之優點欲求閱者寄稿無論頂批總批祇求精意妙論一俟再版時即行加入茲定酬例如下

一等　每千字　十元

二等　每千字　六元

三等　每千字　三元

再前集四十回中批語過簡儻蒙賜批一例歡迎

再原稿概不寄還以免周折

上海望平街有正書局啓

Advertisement for someone willing to provide marginal comments for the last forty chapters and additions to the marginal comments for the first forty chapters of an eighty-chapter version of the *Hung-lou meng* (Dream of the Red Chamber). See page 469 of the descriptive bibliography.

CHAPTER I

Traditional Chinese Fiction Criticism

(a) Sources of Traditional Chinese Fiction Criticism

What Is P'ing-tien?

The bulk of traditional Chinese fiction criticism takes the form of commentary editions on individual works. Aside from prefaces and essays of a more general nature that appear as front matter, the commentaries themselves consist of comments attached as closely as possible to that section of the text to which they refer. This type of criticism is referred to in the titles of the commentary editions by a variety of terms usually consisting of combinations of the following words: *p'i* 批 (to add a remark to a document), *p'ing* 評 (to evaluate), *yüeh* 閱 (to read or peruse), and *tien* 點 (to add punctuation dots);[1] but it is the custom to refer to this general activity, whether applied in fiction criticism or in commentaries

---

[1] For the bulk of the first millenium A.D., *tien* also had the meaning of crossing out characters in a text by means of a circle. See the annotations of the phrase *mieh wei chih tien* 滅謂之點 in the early work on philology, *Erh-ya* 爾雅, by Kuo P'u 郭璞 (276–324) and Hsing Ping 邢昺 (932–1010), in *Shih-san ching chu-shu* 十三經注疏 (Annotated and Commentated Thirteen Classics; Taipei: Shih-chieh shu-chü, 1963), "Shih-ch'i" 釋器 section, p. 5/23a. *Tien* is used in this sense in item 67 of the "Wen-hsüeh" 文學 (Literature) chapter of the *Shih-shuo hsin-yü* 世說新語 (A New Account of Tales of the World) in reference to Juan Chi's 阮籍 (210–265) ability to compose without making corrections (see Richard Mather, trans., *A New Account of Tales of the World* [Minneapolis: University of Minnesota Press, 1976], p. 127) and in the "Tien-fan" 點煩 (Editing Prolixity) chapter of Liu Chih-chi's 劉知幾 (661–721) *Shih-t'ung* 史通 (Generalities of Historiography), which contains this passage: "where there are cases of prolixity, in all cases they are marked with a brush. All such marked characters should be completely excised." 有煩者皆以筆點其上. 凡字經點者盡宜去之. See the facsimile edition (Peking: Chung-hua shu-chü, 1961), p. 15/1a–b. Although fiction critics were not loath to do a little editing on the texts of the fictional works on which they were working, they were generally reluctant to admit this fact.

written for dramatic, poetic, or classical works, as *p'ing-tien* 評點. Although there are those who assert that the use of *tien* in this context refers more to the idea of "pointing out" something,[2] a sense that *tien* certainly has in such compounds as *tien-p'o* 點破 or *chih-tien* 指點, it is most certain that in this case the operative meaning is that listed above. This latter function of punctuating a text with reading marks, when spoken of alone, is called *ch'üan-tien* 圈點 (literally, adding circles and dots). Long neglected by scholars, this type of criticism has recently begun to enjoy a certain modicum of attention. Claims are now made for the worldwide uniqueness of *p'ing-tien* as a form of criticism,[3] which is certainly not true, but it would be safe to say that the strength and influence of this tradition in Chinese literature is in all probability without parallel in the literatures of the world.

The Historical Sources for P'ing-tien

The Classical Tradition of Lexical and Exegetical Commentaries   Sets of informative notes designed to clarify or amplify the meaning of a text rather than to add subjective, evaluative comments are not commonly included under the heading of *p'ing-tien*. Instead, they are referred to by a different set of names: *chuan* 傳, *chu* 注, *chieh* 解, *chu* 註, or *shu* 疏. There is no hard dividing line between the two and we can point to instances where terminology more commonly applied to one sphere is applied to the other.[4]

According to Liu Chih-chi 劉知幾 (661–721), *chuan* and *chu* 注 refer to the same thing and he glosses both as enabling the meaning of the text

---

[2] See, for instance, Pai Tun 白盾, "Shuo Chung-kuo hsiao-shuo p'ing-tien yang-shih" 說中國小說評點樣式 (On the Mode of Chinese Fiction *P'ing-tien*), in *Chung-kuo ku-tai hsiao-shuo li-lun yen-chiu* 中國古代小說理論研究 (Studies in Traditional Chinese Fiction Theory; Wu-ch'ang: Hua-chung kung-hsüeh yüan, 1985), pp. 95–104, p. 96.

[3] See Chang Pi-po 張碧波, "Shih-lun p'ing-tien p'ai tsai Chung-kuo wen-hsüeh shih shang ti li-shih ti-wei" 試論評點派在中國文學史上的歷史地位 (On the Historical Importance of the *P'ing-tien* School in Chinese Literature), in *Chung-kuo ku-tai hsiao-shuo li-lun yen-chiu*, pp. 79–94, p. 82; Liu Chien-fen 劉健芬, "Lüeh-t'an Chung-kuo ku-tien hsiao-shuo li-lun ti min-tsu t'e-se" 略談中國古典小說理論的民族特色 (On the Ethnic Characteristics of Classical Chinese Fiction Theory), *Ku-tai wen-hsüeh li-lun yen-chiu* 古代文學理論研究 (Studies in Ancient Literary Theory) 10:272–87 (1985), p. 283; and Han Chin-lien 韓進廉, *Hung-hsüeh shih-kao* 紅學史稿 (A Draft History of Redology [The Study of the *Hung-lou meng*]; Shih-chia-chuang: Ho-pei jen-min, 1981), p. 125.

[4] Toward the end of the Ch'ing dynasty (1644–1911), many editions of commentaries clearly in the genre of *p'ing-tien* were published with titles containing the words *p'ing-chu* 評註. Fiction commentators such as Liu I-ming 劉一明 (1734–1820+), who treated the novels that they worked on as esoteric texts, also use the word *chu-chieh* 注解 to refer to their work. See his "*Hsi-yu yüan-chih tu-fa*" 西遊原旨讀法 (How to Read the Original Intent of the *Journey to the West*), items 44 and 45, translated in chap. VI below.

to be transmitted without obstruction.[5] The basic idea of *chu* 注, *shu*, and *chieh* is all part of this metaphorical idea of removing obstructions so that the meaning will flow unhindered from the text to the reader. What kinds of obstructions have to be removed? There are problems in lexicology that arise when the language of the text and that used by the readers diverge more and more over time and through changes in usage. Sometimes a new work is not completely understandable even to the contemporaries of the author, as was the case with sections of the *Han-shu* 漢書 (History of the Han Dynasty) by Pan Ku 班固 (32–92); or the true meaning was never committed to paper, as was supposedly the case with Confucius's (551–479 B.C.) esoteric teaching (*wei-yen ta-i* 微言大義) on the *Ch'un-ch'iu* 春秋 (The Spring and Autumn Annals), transmitted orally to his disciples and reconstructed by later commentators.[6] With only a few exceptions, these commentaries circulated together with the texts of the classical works that they were designed to explicate.

Commentaries on classical texts tend to contain differing proportions of six general types of material: (1) linguistic glosses on the meaning and pronunciation of individual characters, (2) paraphrases of the original into the language of the reader,[7] (3) quotation from relevant supplemental material,[8] (4) interpretation of the meaning and/or significance of the text,[9] (5) identification and explication of allusions, and (6) literary analysis of the style and composition of the particular work. This last category develops comparatively late and will be treated separately below.

While the production of commentaries on early canonical texts and commentaries on earlier commentaries, in turn, continued unabated, there is a marked decrease in the compilation of this kind of commentary for works written after the Six Dynasties period (222–589). According

---

[5] The relevant section from his *Shih-t'ung*, "Pu-chu" 補注 (On Supplements and Commentaries), is quoted in Chang Hsüeh-ch'eng 章學誠 (1738–1801), *Wen-shih t'ung-i chiao-chu* 文史通義校注 (Collated and Annotated General Principles of Historiography; Peking: Chung-hua shu-chü, 1985), Yeh Ying 葉瑛, ed., "Shih-chu" 史注 (Historical Commentaries) chapter, p. 245, n. 38.

[6] These two examples are mentioned by Chang Hsüeh-ch'eng, *Wen-shih t'ung-i chiao-chu*, p. 237.

[7] The most prominent example is Chao Ch'i's 趙岐 (d. A.D. 201) *Meng Tzu chang-chü* 孟子章句 (Mencius by Paragraph and Sentence).

[8] Two examples of commentaries that favor this kind of material are Liu Chün's 劉峻 (462–521) annotated *Shih-shuo hsin-yü* 世說新語 (A New Account of Tales of the World) and P'ei Sung-chih's 裴松之 (372–451) *San-kuo chih chu* 三國志注 (Commentary on the Chronicle of the Three Kingdoms).

[9] I refer to the distinction between these two words outlined by J.D. Hirsch, Jr., *Validity in Interpretation* (New Haven: Yale University Press, 1967), p. 8.

to Chang Hsüeh-ch'eng 章學誠 (1734–1801), this was true in regard to historical works because the later writers used a long-winded and simple style without the hidden rhetorical techniques of the earlier works.[10] A similar situation also holds true for Neo-Confucian philosophy, especially as three of the most favored media for promulgating Neo-Confucian ideas were the writing of commentaries on the classics, the compiling of recorded conversations (*yü-lu* 語錄), and the preparation of anthologies, none of which afterward seemed to require secondary works to reveal their true meaning.

The interpretation of the classics in Chinese society, of course, was something that touched close to the center of state power. Wang An-shih 王安石 (1021–1069), Chu Hsi 朱熹 (1130–1200), and K'ang Yu-wei 康有為 (1858–1927) all tried to transform the China of their day through the rereading of the Confucian classics. The wide divergence between the surface meaning and what was held to be the underlying truth of the text in this type of interpretation is a phenomenon that occurs in fiction criticism and in the writing of fiction influenced by this tradition.

How do the concerns of the classical exegetical tradition manifest themselves in commentaries on works of fiction and drama? The provision of phonological and semantic glosses is fairly common in commentaries written for individual plays. The glosses were added after each section or collected and printed as an appendix,[11] but the Wang Hsi-lien 王希廉 (fl. 1832–1875) 1832 commentary on the *Hung-lou meng* 紅樓夢 (Dream of the Red Chamber) also contains a set of similar glosses.[12]

Commentaries on historical fiction, especially the most famous work in that genre, the *San-kuo yen-i* 三國演義 (The Romance of the Three Kingdoms), tend to contain informative comments designed to help the reader understand the language or the historical background of the text.

---

[10] *Wen-shih t'ung-i chiao-chu*, "Shih-chu," p. 237.

[11] An example of the former is the 1498 edition of the *Hsi-hsiang chi* 西廂記 (Romance of the Western Chamber) printed by Chin T'ai-yüeh 金臺岳 of Peking, full title *Hsin-k'an ta-tzu k'uei-pen ch'üan-hsiang ts'an-tseng ch'i-miao chu-shih Hsi-hsiang chi* 新刊大字魁本全相參增奇妙註釋西廂記 (Newly Printed, Large-Character, Large-Format, Fully Illustrated, Expanded, Marvelous, Annotated Romance of the Western Chamber), photo-reprint (Taipei: Shih-chieh shu-chü, 1976) under the title *Hsi-hsiang chi tsa-chü* 西廂記雜劇. An example of the latter type is the commentary attributed to Ch'en Chi-ju 陳繼儒 (1558–1639), *Ch'en Mei-kung p'i-p'ing P'i-p'a chi* 陳眉公批評琵琶記 (The Story of the Lute with Commentary by Ch'en Chi-ju; Peking: Wen-hsüeh ku-chi k'an-hsing she, 1954 reprint).

[12] The full title of the commentary is *Hsin-p'ing hsiu-hsiang Hung-lou meng ch'üan-chuan* 新評繡像紅樓夢全傳 (Newly Commentated, Illustrated, Complete Edition of the *Hung-lou meng*), printed by the Shuang-ch'ing hsien kuan of Suchou. Photo-reprinted (Taipei: Kuang-wen shu-chü, 1977) under the title *Wang Hsi-lien p'ing-pen Hsin-chüan ch'üan-pu hsiu-hsiang Hung-lou meng* 王希廉評本新鐫全部繡像紅樓夢 (Newly Cut, Completely Illustrated *Hung-lou meng* with Commentary by Wang Hsi-lien).

The earliest extant edition of that novel (preface dated 1522) contains notes identifying place names, vocabulary, and allusions among other things.[13] On the title page of a later (1591) edition of this novel the publisher, Chou Yüeh-chiao 周曰校, wrote the following advertisement:

> This book has already appeared in several different editions, all of them quite corrupt. I searched out old editions, employed famous scholars to compare the text against the standard chronological accounts [chien 鑑] and repeatedly collate textual variants; punctuation marks [ch'üan-tien 圈點] were added to distinguish the commas and periods of the sentences, difficult characters have been given glosses [yin-chu 音注], geographical terms have been given explanations [shih-i 釋義], allusions have been traced [k'ao-cheng 考證], and lacunae have been filled in....
>
> 是書也刻已數種, 悉皆譌舛. 輒購求古本, 敦請名士, 按鑑參考, 再三讐校, 俾句讀有圈點, 難字有音註, 地里有釋義, 典故有考證, 缺略有增補....[14]

Although much rarer, informative glosses can also be found in commentaries on nonhistorical fiction, where commentators explain linguistic puns in the text,[15] apprise the reader of the truthfulness of statements by characters,[16] or indirectly convey information by referring him to other parts of the novel.[17]

Eventually separate commentaries and reference works appeared,

---

[13] See the typeset reprint (Shanghai: Shang-hai ku-chi, 1980) of this edition, San-kuo chih t'ung-su yen-i 三國志通俗演義 (A Popularization of the Chronicle of the Three Kingdoms), pp. 61 (chüan 卷 4, tse 則 2), 9 (chüan 1, tse 2), and 427−28 (chüan 9, tse 6) for examples of the three categories of glosses mentioned.

[14] Quoted in Sun K'ai-ti 孫楷第, Chung-kuo t'ung-su hsiao-shuo shu-mu 中國通俗小說書目 (Bibliography of Chinese Popular Fiction; Peking: Jen-min wen-hsüeh, 1982), p. 36. The full title of this edition is Hsin-k'an chiao-cheng ku-pen ta-tzu yin-shih San-kuo chih-chuan t'ung-su yen-i 新刊校正古本大字音釋三國志傳通俗演義 (Newly Cut, Collated, Large-Character, Ancient Edition of the Popularization of the Chronicle of the Three Kingdoms with Phonetic Glosses and Explanations). In the text, the notes are often prefixed by headings such as Shih-i 釋義 (Explanation) or Pu-i 補遺 (Supplementary Material).

[15] See the marginal comment on p. 32/10b of the microfilm of a copy of the so-called "Ch'ung-chen" 崇禎 commentary to the Chin P'ing Mei held in the Tokyo Imperial University library. The same device (a pun where the true meaning is obtained by taking every third character) is explained less directly in the copy of the commentary held at Peking University, quoted in CPMTLHP, p. 307.

[16] See the double-column interlineal comment in which Chang Chu-p'o points out that P'an Chin-lien is lying when she talks about losing her shoe, TICS, 29/1b−2a.

[17] See the interlineal comment of the so-called "chia-hsü" 甲戌 (1754) version of the Chih-yen chai 脂硯齋 (Red Inkstone) commentary to the Hung-lou meng on the mention of Lin Tai-yü's former incarnation, Chiang-chu 絳珠, in Yü P'ing-po 俞平伯, ed., Chih-yen chai Hung-lou meng chi-p'ing 脂硯齋紅樓夢輯評 (Collected Chih-yen chai Comments on the Hung-lou meng; Hong Kong: T'ai-p'ing shu-chü, 1975), p. 5.83.

which took as their goal the provision of nothing but informative material to aid the reader in understanding the meaning of the novels involved. The earliest instance of a work of this type is Ch'eng Mu-heng's 程穆衡 *Shui-hu chuan chu-lüeh* 水滸傳注略 (Concise Annotations to the Water Margin; author's preface dated 1779, but not printed, in expanded form, until 1845). Keyed to the seventy-chapter version of that novel but without the entire text reprinted, the commentary proceeds chapter by chapter, lexical item by lexical item.[18] In a note made in 1868, Yang Mao-chien 楊懋建 mentioned that he had been working on a similar work, to be entitled *Hung-lou meng chu* 紅樓夢注 (Notes on the *Hunglou meng*), since adolescence and had already annotated more than two thousand items.[19] The work was unfinished at the time of the note and does not seem to have survived in any form, but a full-scale lexical commentary on a novel written in parallel prose, the *Yen-shan wai-shih* 燕山外史 (Informal History of Yen Mountain; by Ch'en Ch'iu 陳球, fl. 1808), became the most popular edition of that work. The bulk of that commentary consists of quotations of the original sources for the allusions used by Ch'en Ch'iu, but there are also informative notes of a more general nature as well.[20] Reference works collecting useful lists of characters and events, such as Yao Hsieh's 姚燮 (1805–1864) *Tu Hung-lou meng kang-ling* 讀紅樓夢綱領 (An Outline for Reading the *Hung-lou meng*; author's preface dated 1860) were also published.[21]

There was a growing feeling in some circles that certain novels were of such a high complexity of design and subtlety that they required exegetical commentary. This was especially the case first with the *Hsi-yu chi* 西遊記 (The Journey to the West) and then later with the *Hung-lou meng*. Since the latter half of the seventeenth century and the popular attribution of the authorship of the *Hsi-yu chi* to a Taoist patriarch, Ch'iu

---

[18] The entire text of this work is reprinted in Ma T'i-chi 馬蹄疾, ed., *Shui-hu tzu-liao hui-pien* 水滸資料彙編 (Collected Material on the *Shui-hu*; Peking: Chung-hua shu-chü, 1980), pp. 270–344 and *SHCTLHP*, pp. 429–93. Informative commentaries were also produced at an early date for the *Liao-chai chih-i* 聊齋誌異 (Strange Stories from Desultory Studio), a collection of short tales in classical Chinese by P'u Sung-ling 蒲松齡 (1640–1715), the earliest of which was by Lü Chan-en 呂湛恩, published without the text of the stories for the first time in 1825.

[19] The note is recorded in his *Meng-hua so-pu* 夢華瑣簿, quoted in K'ung Ling-ching 孔另境, ed., *Chung-kuo hsiao-shuo shih-liao* 中國小說史料 (Historical Material on Chinese Fiction; Shanghai: Shang-hai ku-chi, 1982 reprint), pp. 221–22.

[20] This commentary was published in 1879 under the title *Yen-shan wai-shih chu-shih* 燕山外史註釋 (*Yen-shan wai-shih* Annotated) and the commentator was Fu Sheng-ku 傅聲谷 (pseud. Jo-k'uei-tzu 若騤子).

[21] Published posthumously under the title of *Hung-lou meng lei-so* 紅樓夢類索 (An Index to Categories of Things in the *Hung-lou meng*; Shanghai: Chu-lin shu-tien, 1940).

Ch'u-chi 丘處機 (1148–1227), a series of commentators on the novel arose who treated the text as if it were scripture and objected to the idea of literary analysis of the novel as beside the point.[22] Another commentator on the same novel, Chang Shu-shen 張書紳 (fl. 18th century), took that work as an explication through parable of the meaning of the Four Books (*The Great Learning*, *The Doctrine of the Mean*, *The Confucian Analects*, and *The Mencius*) and provided a separate table of contents for his commentary in terms of which Confucian classic or which Confucian precept is treated in what part of his commentary.[23] This phenomenon is obviously related to the powerful influence of the official examination system on all spheres of literary life in traditional China, but we will treat that topic separately below. Chang Shu-shen's lead was followed in a commentary on the *Hung-lou meng* by Chang Hsin-chih 張新之 (fl. 1828–1850),[24] and the Chang Hsin-chih commentary is also an example of the use of the hexagrams of the *I Ching* 易經 (Book of Changes) to interpret the characters of a novel.[25]

The tendency to view some of the novels as romans à clef influenced some commentators to expend a lot of energy in ferreting out the supposed models for the literary characters, and advocates of this type of analysis for the *Hung-lou meng* characterized their commentary as "i chu-ching chih fa chu *Hung-lou*" 以注經之法注紅樓 (using the method of commentaries on the classics to do a commentary on the *Hung-lou meng*).[26] One writer excused the need for a commentary on the *Hung-lou meng* by saying that even the works of Confucius and Mencius contain topical references ("chiu-shih fa-yen chih ch'u" 就時發言之處) and recommended that commentators on the novel should emulate Li Shan's 李善 (630?–689) commentary on the *Wen-hsüan* 文選 (The Anthology of Refined Literature), and Liu Chün's 劉峻 (462–521) com-

---

[22] See especially, item 1 of Liu I-ming's *tu-fa* essay on the *Hsi-yu chi*, chap. VI below.

[23] "Hsin-shuo Hsi-yu chi ch'üan-pu ching-shu t'i-mu" 新說西遊記全部經書題目 (Topics from the Classics [Discussed in the Prechapter Comments] of the Entire New Explication of the *Hsi-yu chi*), in *Hsin-shuo Hsi-yu chi t'u-hsiang* 新說西遊記圖像 (Illustrated New Explication of the *Hsi-yu chi*; Peking: Chung-kuo shu-tien, 1985, reprint of 1888 edition), pp. 7b–9a of the table of contents.

[24] First appeared in manuscript form, completed in 1850, *Miao-fu hsüan p'ing Shih-t'ou chi* 妙復軒評石頭記 (Commentary on the *Story of the Stone* from Miao-fu Studio), copy held in the Peking Library.

[25] See items 26 and 27 in his *tu-fa* essay on the *Hung-lou meng*, chap. VII below. Other examples include item 24 of Liu I-ming's *tu-fa* essay on the *Hsi-yu chi*, chap. VI below, and an unnamed Manchu who reportedly used the hexagrams to explain features of the *Shui-hu chuan*. For the latter, see K'ung Ling-ching, ed., *Chung-kuo hsiao-shuo shih-liao*, p. 37.

[26] From the "Li-yen" 例言 (General Principles) of Wang Meng-juan 王夢阮, Shen P'ing-an 沈瓶庵, *Hung-lou meng so-yin* 紅樓夢索隱 (The Hidden Meaning of the *Hung-lou meng*; Shanghai: Chung-hua shu-chü, 1916).

mentary on the *Shih-shuo hsin-yü* 世說新語 (A New Account of Tales of the World).[27] Another critic presented the problem this way:

> Readers of the *Hung-lou meng* must not only be up on present affairs, they must also be fully conversant with the past. Attention to details is very important, but sharp perception is even more so. One should use Ho Cho's 何焯 [1661–1722] method of commenting on the *Shih-ch'i shih* 十七史 [Seventeen Official Histories] to comment on it. If you use Chin Sheng-t'an's 金聖歎 [1608–1661] method of commenting on the "Four Great Marvelous Books," the results will be very shallow.
>
> 閱紅樓夢者既要通今, 又要博古;既貴心細, 尤貴眼明. 當以何義門評十七史法評之. 若但以金聖歎評四大奇書法評之, 淺矣.[28]

Poetry Criticism   Works in rhyme such as the *Shih-ching* 詩經 (Classic of Poetry) were part of the classical canon and received their share of lexical annotation of the type discussed above. One of the earliest extant commentaries to punctuate its text into paragraphs and sentences is the *Ch'u-tz'u chang-chü* 楚辭章句 (Songs of Ch'u by Paragraph and Sentence) by Wang I 王逸 (89?–158), and other anthologies of poetry and belles-lettres became the subject of like activity over the ages.

Because of the importance of occasional poetry in the tradition, it soon became the practice for poets to indicate the nature of these occasions. The inclusion of lengthy titles, prefaces, or glosses identifying persons and places thus attempted to forestall the efforts of later scholars to define retroactively the circumstances that gave rise to the poem.

The canonization of the three hundred poems of the *Shih-ching* gave rise to a very interesting problem in interpretation. That collection contains some love poems that are perfectly easy to understand as such, but if one feels compelled to wring out a deeper and more "Confucian" meaning from them, a certain amount of interpretive violence has to be unleashed upon them, as was actually done. Embodied most prominently in the "Great Preface" (*Ta-hsü* 大序) for the work as a whole and the "Little Prefaces" (*hsiao-hsü* 小序) treating each poem individually, this kind of interpretation provided a political background and a moral for each of the poems. This trend also carried over into the interpretation of other poetic works, such as that applied to the poems in the *Wen-hsüan* in

---

[27] Ch'en T'ui 陳蛻, "Lieh *Shih-t'ou chi* yü tzu-pu shuo" 列石頭記於子部說 (On Classifying the *Story of the Stone* as a Work of Philosophy), published in 1914, quoted in *HLMC*, p. 270. The commentaries by Li Shan and Liu Chün (courtesy name Hsiao-piao 孝標) are known for the quantity of supplementary material quoted in them showing the linguistic and historical background of passages in the two works.

[28] Chou Ch'un 周春 (1729–1815), *Yüeh Hung-lou meng sui-pi* 閱紅樓夢隨筆 (Notes on Reading the *Hung-lou meng*), quoted in *HLMC*, p. 67.

the so-called "Five Officials" (Lü Yen-chi 呂延濟, Liu Liang 劉良, Chang Hsien 張銑, Lü Hsiang 呂向, and Li Chou-han 李周翰) annotated edition offered to the throne in A.D. 718. One of the main features of the mind-set behind this type of interpretation was the idea that the emperor is the final reader and the poet has the responsibility to nudge the ruler away from evil without getting his head chopped off for his impertinence. Hence the need for indirect means of expression, so as to encase the barb in an outwardly pleasing form (*mei tz'u* 美刺).

The Six Dynasties period and the T'ang dynasty that followed saw the appearance of separate works of poetry criticism, such as Chung Jung's 鍾嶸 (468–518?) *Shih-p'in* 詩品 (The Evaluation of Poetry; this work tries to place the poets that it deals with into patterns of filiation that are traced back ultimately to the *Shih-ching* or the *Ch'u-tz'u* 楚辭), and manuals to help novices learn the secrets of writing poetry, such as the *Shih-ko* 詩格 (Poetic Genres) and *Shih chung mi-chih* 詩中密旨 (Secrets of Poetry) by Wang Ch'ang-ling 王昌齡 (fl. 8th century).[29] However, the most influential genre of poetry criticism, *shih-hua* 詩話 (talks on poetry), only dates back to the eleventh century. The first example, Ou-yang Hsiu's 歐陽修 (1007–1072) *Liu-i shih-hua* 六一詩話 (Ou-yang Hsiu's Talks on Poetry), originally was simply titled *Shih-hua*. It and its later imitators consist of a sequence of short comments on poetry in general or on specific poems or lines of poems. All of these different forms of poetry criticism contain prescriptions on composition and rhetoric expressed in terminology that was later partially adopted in fiction criticism. The genre of *shih-hua* was later adapted to the criticism of the *tz'u* 詞 and *ch'ü* 曲 styles of poetry. These works are called, predictably enough, *tz'u-hua* and *ch'ü-hua*.[30]

Huang T'ing-chien 黃廷堅 (1045–1105) wanted to produce an edition of Tu Fu's 杜甫 (712–770) poetry with his own comments added,[31] but never accomplished the task. The earliest examples of *p'ing-tien* volumes of poetry seem to be commentary editions by Liu Ch'en-weng 劉辰翁 (1232–1297) of the collected poetry of Meng Hao-jan 孟浩然 (689–740), Wang Wei 王維 (701–761), Li Ho 李賀 (790–816), and Lu

---

[29] The authenticity of extant copies of these two works has been questioned, but it is beyond doubt that Wang Ch'ang-ling wrote two such works since they are quoted in *Bunkyō hifuron* 文鏡秘府論 (Scholastic Commentary on the Treasury of Marvels of the Literary Mirror) by Kūkai 空海 (774–835), a work compiled from several of these manuals with the intention of providing a primer for Japanese on how to write Chinese poetry.

[30] *Ch'ü-hua* can also refer to works of drama (*hsi-ch'ü* 戲曲) criticism.

[31] Lo Ken-tse 羅根澤, *Chung-kuo wen-hsüeh p'i-p'ing shih* 中國文學批評史 (History of Chinese Literary Criticism), 3 vols. (Shanghai: Shang-hai ku-chi, 1984), vol. 3, p. 362.

Yu 陸游 (1125–1210), plus a volume of Lu Yu's poetry edited by Lo I
羅椅 (fl. 13th century).[32] The innovation was primarily one of form
and not of substance. Ch'ien Chung-shu 錢鍾書, for instance, has maintained that a letter from Lu Yün 陸雲 (262–303) to his brother, Lu Chi
陸機 (261–303), discussing the poetry of the older man, contains in
embryo much of the language and concerns of later poetry p'ing-tien
without taking on the specific form associated with p'ing-tien.[33] The
main difference, in the end, is one of presentation and the consequent
effect on the reader who, in the case of p'ing-tien, can read both the
original work and comments on it all at once.[34]

Not long after Liu Ch'en-weng, Fang Hui 方回 (1227–1307) produced a very influential collection of regulated verse (lü-shih 律詩), Ying-
k'uei lü-sui 瀛奎律髓, with short comments and marks of emphasis (ch'üan-
tien) added to each poem.[35] Fang Hui used this collection to promulgate
through concrete examples the literary preferences of the particular
school of poetry to which he adhered, the so-called "Kiangsi school"
that took Huang T'ing-chien as its founding father. This school of poetry laid great stress on technique and the copying of earlier models;
therefore the p'ing-tien style of criticism was well suited to Fang Hui's
purpose. Toward the end of the Ming dynasty (1368–1644), Chung

---

[32] The Lo I and Liu Ch'en-weng collections of Lu Yu's poetry were printed together
and are available in the first series of the Ssu-pu ts'ung-k'an collection, where they are
referred to as the first and second collection (ch'ien-chi 前集, hou-chi 後集). Lo I's section
has only emphatic punctuation, while the Liu Ch'en-weng section also has comments,
almost all prefixed by the word p'i 批 (comment). The Liu Ch'en-weng commentary
edition of Wang Wei's poetry is also reprinted in the Ssu-pu ts'ung-k'an series. There is a
record of a Liu Ch'en-weng edition of Wang An-shih's poetry where the comments are
prefixed by the words p'ing-yüeh 評曰 (the comment says) carved in negative characters
(white in a field of black). See Fu Tseng-hsiang 傅增湘, Ts'ang-yüan ch'ün-shu ching-yen lu
藏園群書經眼錄 (Ts'ang-yüan's Notes on Books Seen; Peking: Chung-hua shu-chü,
1983), p. 1158.

[33] See his Kuan chui pien 管錐編 (Pipe and Awl Chapters; Peking: Chung-hua shu-chü,
1979), pp. 1215–17.

[34] There is an edition of the Hsi-hsiang chi purporting to contain commentary done by
Wang Shih-chen 王世貞 (1526–1590), but the truth is that a later editor has taken the
different comments on that play that appear in Wang's Ssu-pu kao 四部稿 (Draft in Four
Parts) and printed them next to the appropriate sections of the play. See Chiang Hsing-yü
蔣星煜, "Yüan-pen ch'u-hsiang Hsi-hsiang chi ti Wang Li ho-p'ing pen" 元本出像西廂
記的王李合評本 (The Combined Wang Shih-chen, Li Chih Commentary Edition of the
Yüan Edition Illustrated Romance of the Western Chamber), Chung-hua wen-shih lun-ts'ung
中華文史論叢 (Collected Articles on Chinese Literature and History), 1984. 1:119–36,
p. 133.

[35] Recently reprinted in an edition that preserves the comments added over the years
by more than ten other commentators, Ying-k'uei lü-sui hui-p'ing 瀛奎律髓彙評 (Collected Commentary on the Ying-k'uei lü-sui; Shanghai: Shang-hai ku-chi, 1986).

Hsing 鍾惺 (1547–1624) and T'an Yüan-ch'un 譚元春 (1586–1637) used
works of *p'ing-tien* criticism, *T'ang-shih kuei* 唐詩歸 (Repository of
T'ang Poetry) and *Ku-shih kuei* 古詩歸 (Repository of Ancient Poetry),
to advance their school of poetry, the Ching-ling school, named after
their native place. Even the most popular and influential of poetry collections, the *T'ang-shih san-pai shou* 唐詩三百首 (Three Hundred T'ang
Poems; compiled by Sun Chu 孫洙, 1751 *chin-shih* degree), circulated in
editions that contained not only annotations but also *p'ing-tien* style
criticism.[36]

Poetry and fiction are quite removed from each other in form and
function, as modern literary critics like M.M. Bakhtin are at pains to
point out.[37] Chinese poetry is also somewhat different from the poetry
of other nations in that narrative poems constitute only a very minor
part of the tradition. Be that as it may, fiction critics made use, often in
modified form, of many items of terminology developed in poetry
criticism. Critics more famous for their work on fiction and drama, such
as Chin Sheng-t'an and Li Yü 李漁 (1611–1680), also published works of
poetry criticism, and the concern with techniques of indirect presentation and with structuration in poetry criticism has its parallels in fiction
criticism.

Miscellaneous Arts—Painting, Chess, Horticulture   Art criticism, particularly the criticism of portrait and landscape painting, has a long and
strong tradition in China dating back to the Six Dynasties period and
before. Notions such as suggestion versus realism (*hsü-shih* 虛實), spatial
composition (*chang-fa* 章法), and subordination of elements (*pin-chu*
賓主) are prominent in works of art criticism and, in turn, have their
importance in fiction criticism, although in somewhat modified form. In

[36] Recent reprints of these kinds of editions include: *T'ang-shih san-pai shou chu-shu*
唐詩三百首注疏 (Annotated Three Hundred T'ang Poems; Hofei: An-hui jen-min, 1983
[original preface, 1835]), and *T'ang-shih san-pai shou* (Peking: Chung-hua shu-chü, 1978,
this is a reprint of *T'ang-shih san-pai shou pu-chu* 唐詩三百首補注 [Supplementary Annotation to Three Hundred T'ang Poems, ca. 1844]). The editor of an 1884 reprint of the
first volume objected to the use of the words *chu-shu* in the title which, according to him,
should be restricted to commentaries on the classics. He changed the last two words of the
title of his edition to *chu-shih* 注釋 (explanations). Although the main emphasis in these
works is on the explanation of allusions and lexical glosses, as can be seen from their titles,
a substantial amount of attention was also paid to pointing out more literary features in
the poems.

[37] Bakhtin consistently describes poetry as monologic (and thus, to him, of comparatively little interest), as opposed to the novel, which he conceived of as dialogic in nature.
See his *Discourse in the Novel*, more particularly the section entitled, "Discourse in Poetry
and Discourse in the Novel," translated in Michael Holquist, ed., *The Dialogic Imagination: Four Essays by M.M. Bakhtin* (Austin: University of Texas Press, 1981), pp. 275–300.

the case of some commentaries, such as the Chih-yen chai 脂硯齋 (Red Inkstone Studio) commentary on the *Hung-lou meng*, the majority of the critical vocabulary used comes from art criticism, and different techniques pointed out in the novel are explicitly labeled as painterly techniques. Anecdotes taken from the history of painting are also a part of the vocabulary of fiction criticism and are used to stress the importance of elements such as the imaginary identification of the artist with his subject[38] or attention to details capable of bringing out the spirit of the subject.[39]

It should also be kept in mind that from a certain point of view Chinese painting, particularly landscape painting, was conceived of as a narrative art form. It is true that in this case narrative flow was completely spatialized; the "reader" of the painting was free to direct his attention to any part of it in whatever sequence he wished within certain physical limitations due to the fact that lengthy landscape pictures were often rolled and unrolled during the viewing process. However, it may be precisely these differences between our classical idea of narrative and Chinese landscape painting tradition that may be of some aid in understanding divergences between the ways in which Chinese and Western fictional narrative unfold. For instance, neither landscape painting nor traditional Chinese fiction is structured around the use of the convention of fixed perspective or viewpoint so important in Western painting and fiction.

There are various manuals on individual arts such as garden landscaping, chess, and medicine that also contribute technical vocabulary and illuminating anecdotes to Chinese fiction criticism. There was a perceived similarity between, for instance, the spatial interplay involved in the placing of trees in a famous garden or the organic unity of the moves of a master at chess, on the one hand, and the balance of compositional elements in the work of literature, on the other.[40]

[38] There is an anecdote about how Chao Meng-fu 趙孟頫 (1254–1322), prior to painting a horse, first studied horses by imitation. He was so successful that his wife, finding him clothes off and on the floor one day, was startled to see so much horse in him. Chin Sheng-t'an uses this anecdote in his discussion of the author's portrayal of the tiger killed by Wu Sung in the *Shui-hu chuan*. See *SHCHPP*, p. 22.424, interlineal comment.

[39] The anecdote of Ku K'ai-chih 顧愷之 (ca. 344–406) adding three hairs to his portrait of P'ei K'ai to bring the whole thing to life is used in the chapter comment to chap. 11 (item 2) of the Wo-hsien ts'ao-t'ang edition of the *Ju-lin wai-shih*, translated in chap. v below.

[40] See Chiang Shun-i 江順怡 (fl. 19th century), *Pu Tz'u-p'in* 補詞品 (Addendum to The Evaluation of *Tz'u* Poetry), quoted in Chang Sheng-i 張聲怡 and Liu Chiu-chou 劉九州, eds., *Chung-kuo ku-tai hsieh-tso li-lun* 中國古代寫作理論 (Traditional Chinese Theories of Composition; Wu-ch'ang: Hua-chung kung-hsüeh yüan, 1985), pp. 169–70.

P'ing-tien *Criticism of the Confucian Classics*   While most scholars in the Sung dynasty (960–1279) and earlier took the Confucian classics as sacred texts that primarily posed problems of interpretation for the reader and scholars of the Ch'ing dynasty (1644–1911) began to study them as historical texts, in the Ming dynasty there is a pronounced trend to look upon them as models of literary style. This, of course, is partly a function of the passion for archaism (*fu-ku* 復古) in Ming literature, but we can find traces of this new way of regarding the classics back in the Sung dynasty. That dynasty saw the origin of publications designed to help candidates pass the official civil service examinations, an industry that greatly expanded in the Ming. As the candidate in the examinations, especially after the institution of the so-called "eight-legged essays" as the required form, was supposed·to "speak on behalf of the sages" (*tai sheng li yen* 代聖立言), this development surely favored giving more attention to the precise manner of expression used in the classics.

Some Sung dynasty writers, after acknowledging that the classics were written to convey a message and not to show off literary skills, saw them as the source from which all later writing proceeded,[41] while others sought to trace certain literary techniques back to examples in the classics.[42] Hu Ying-lin 胡應麟 (1551–1602) stated the matter in more emphatic terms:

> People say that there were no men of letters in antiquity, and there is no literary technique [*wen-fa* 文法] in the Six Classics. I say that there are no men of letters who surpass those of antiquity, and there is no literary technique that surpasses that of the Six Classics.

世謂三代無文人, 六經無文法. 吾以為文人無出三代, 文法無大六經.[43]

The earliest example of a *p'ing-tien* edition of one of the Confucian classics is *Su p'i Meng Tzu* 蘇批孟子 (The Su Hsün Commentary on *Mencius*). Although the attribution of the work to Su Hsün 蘇洵 (1009–1060) seems improbable in view of the fact that one edition is supposed to have quoted from Hung Mai 洪邁 (1123–1202) and the style of

[41] See Li T'u 李塗 (fl. 12th century), *Wen-chang ching-i* 文章精義 (The Essential Meaning of Literature), opening sentence quoted in Cheng Tien 鄭奠 and T'an Ch'üan-chi 譚全基, eds., *Ku Han-yü hsiu-tz'u hsüeh tzu-liao hui-pien* 古漢語修辭學資料匯編 (Collected Material on Ancient Chinese Rhetoric; Peking: Commercial Press, 1980), p. 226.

[42] See Ch'en K'uei 陳騤 (d. A.D. 1203), *Wen tse* 文則 (Literary Models), printed together with *Wen-chang ching-i* (Hong Kong: Commercial Press, 1977), especially "ting" sec., pp. 17–21 and Ch'en Shan 陳善 (fl. 12th century), *Men-shih hsin-hua* 捫蝨新話 (New Talks While Picking Lice), quoted in *Ku Han-yü hsiu-tz'u hsüeh tzu-liao hui-pien*, p. 206.

[43] Hu Ying-lin, *Shih-sou* 詩藪 (Thicket of Remarks on Poetry; Shanghai: Chung-hua shu-chü, 1958), p. 2.

punctuation in the volume was not in use while Su Hsün was alive, [44] it still predates other examples. The latter half of the Ming saw the production of a wide variety of *p'ing-tien* editions of the classics. Favorite choices for this treatment included the "T'an-kung" 檀弓 and "K'ao-kung" 考工 chapters of the *Li-chi* 禮記 (Book of Rites), the *Shu-ching* 書經 (Classic of History), the *Shih-ching*, the *Ch'un-ch'iu*, and the *Tso-chuan* 左傳 (The Tso Commentary); some of these were printed in opulent two-color editions. The names of the commentators as given on the title pages include Yang Shen 楊慎 (1488–1559), Mao K'un 茅坤 (1512–1601), Sun K'uang 孫鑛 (1542–1613), Ling Chih-lung 凌稚隆 (fl. 16th century),[45] Chung Hsing, and Ch'en Chi-ju 陳繼儒 (1558–1639).[46] Sun K'uang was the maternal grandfather of Lü T'ien-ch'eng 呂天成 (1580–1618), author of *Ch'ü-p'in* 曲品 (Ranking of the Dramas), and the ten prerequisites to writing good Southern-style dramas listed in the second half of that work are quoted from Sun K'uang.[47] Finally, the convergence of literary criticism on the Confucian classics with fiction criticism comes about in the early seventeenth century with the appearance of *Ssu-shu p'ing* 四書評 (Comments on the Four Books), attributed to Li Chih 李贄 (1527–1602), but most likely by Yeh Chou 葉畫 (fl. 1595–1624?).[48] Both of these men were involved in the first stages of the production of *p'ing-tien* editions of novels and plays. The influence of this

[44] These arguments, and others against the attribution, are made in Chi Yün 紀昀 (1724–1805), *Ssu-k'u ch'üan-shu tsung-mu t'i-yao* 四庫全書總目提要 (Annotated Catalogue of the Imperial Library; Shanghai: Ta-tung shu-chü, 1926), p. 8/22.

[45] Also involved in the publication of *p'ing-lin* 評林 (collected commentary) editions of the *Shih-chi* 史記 (Records of the Historian) and the *Han-shu* 漢書 (History of the Han Dynasty) that include comments on literary style.

[46] On Mao K'un and Sun K'uang's activities in this regard, see Kuo Shao-yü 郭紹虞, *Chung-kuo wen-hsüeh p'i-p'ing shih* 中國文學批評史 (A History of Chinese Literary Criticism; Shanghai: Shang-hai ku-chi, 1979), pp. 446–52.

[47] See *Chung-kuo ku-tien hsi-ch'ü lun-chu chi-ch'eng* 中國古典戲曲論著集成 (Compendium of Traditional Writings on Chinese Drama; Peking: Chung-hua hsi-chü, 1959), vol. 6, *Ch'ü-p'in*, p. 223. Ho Man-tzu 何滿子, "Chin Sheng-t'an" 金聖歎, in *Chung-kuo li-tai chu-ming wen-hsüeh chia p'ing-chuan* 中國歷代著名文學家評傳 (Critical Biographies of Famous Chinese Literary Figures through the Ages; Tsinan: Shan-tung chiao-yü, 1985), vol. 5, p. 29, asserts that all Chin Sheng-t'an actually did was "take the method of commentary of Sun K'uang in his *Sun Yüeh-feng p'ing-ching* 孫月峯評經 [Sun K'uang's Commentary on the Classics] and Mao K'un in his *T'ang-Sung pa ta-chia wen-ch'ao* 唐宋八大家文鈔 [Selections from the Eight Masters of the T'ang and Sung] and extend them to the realm of fiction and drama." Ho Man-tzu seems to be subsuming these two works under the heading of eight-legged essay criticism (a not entirely unreasonable assumption, see the discussion of prose and examination criticism below), as elsewhere in the same biography (p. 25) he says that the heart of Chin Sheng-t'an's criticism is nothing but examination essay techniques (*pa-ku chang-fa* 八股章法).

[48] On this question, see app. 2.

way of approaching the classics can also be seen in the third preface of
Chin Sheng-t'an's commentary on the *Shui-hu chuan* 水滸傳 (The Water
Margin), where he speaks of the fine construction (*chia kou* 佳構) of the
wording in the *Lun-yü* 論語 (The Confucian Analects).[49]

Fiction P'ing-tien *and Examination Essay Criticism*   Ever since Hu
Shih 胡適 (1891–1962) and others inaugurated the serious study of traditional vernacular fiction early in this century, fiction *p'ing-tien* has been
closely linked with that popularly detested literary form, the so-called
"eight-legged essay" (*pa-ku wen* 八股文), and more specifically with
eight-legged essay criticism and how-to manuals.[50] This development
occurred not long after the abolition of the old-style civil service examinations in which one's answers had to be written according to very strin-
gent formal rules and the content was restricted (in the lower-level
examinations) to rehashing Sung dynasty interpretations of the Four
Books. Originally presented more as a reason to ignore fiction *p'ing-tien*
than to further our understanding of it, such claims were never backed
up with either facts or interpretation. This attitude has persisted in the
older generation of scholars[51] and can be found in somewhat milder
form in the middle generations as well.[52] Some Chinese critics with
positive evaluations of fiction *p'ing-tien*, such as Yeh Lang 葉朗 of Peking
University, have tried to deny any connection between it and the examination essays,[53] but even he has had to admit the common pool of
terminology between the two.[54] Partisans of traditional fiction criticism
in the West who do not have an instinctive negative reaction toward the
examination essays as a literary form have been more open to examining
the mutual influence of these two bodies of criticism.[55]

[49] *SHCHPP*, p. 10.
[50] For instance, see Hu Shih on Chin Sheng-t'an, "*Shui-hu chuan* k'ao-cheng" 水滸傳
考證 (A Critical Study of the *Shui-hu chuan*), in *Chung-kuo chang-hui hsiao-shuo k'ao-cheng*
中國章回小說考證 (Critical Studies on Chinese Novels; Shanghai: Shang-hai shu-tien,
1979), p. 2.
[51] Ho Man-tzu, "Chin Sheng-t'an," p. 25.
[52] See *LCH*, vol. 1, p. 455, and Tseng Tsu-yin 曾祖蔭 et al., eds., *Chung-kuo li-tai hsiao-
shuo hsü-pa hsüan-chu* 中國歷代小說序跋選注 (Annotated Selections of Prefaces to Chinese Fiction through the Ages; Hsien-ning: Ch'ang-chiang wen-i, 1982), p. 52.
[53] *Chung-kuo hsiao-shuo mei-hsüeh* 中國小說美學 (The Aesthetics of Chinese Fiction;
Peking: Pei-ching ta-hsüeh, 1982), pp. 16–17.
[54] Ibid., p. 18. See also p. 45 on Chin Sheng-t'an.
[55] Andrew H. Plaks, in the prepublication version of "After the Fall: *Hsing-shih yin-
yüan chuan* and the Seventeenth-Century Chinese Novel," *Harvard Journal of Asiatic
Studies*, 45.2:543–80 (1985), p. 43, n.32, remarked, "I believe this critical interest in
matters of structural arrangement is also related to the predominance of *pa-ku* theory and
practice beginning from the end of the 15th century." Professor Plaks is also the author of

In Ming and Ch'ing dynasty China, learning to write examination essays was one of the main parts of every literate person's education, and success in the examinations was the only respected path to high office. Under these circumstances it is not surprising to find that masters of the examination essay were at the heart of literati culture and, conversely, the literati took the writing of examination essays very seriously. One of the earliest mentions of the *Shui-hu chuan* is in a work by Li K'ai-hsien 李開先 (1502–1568) entitled *Tz'u-nüeh* 詞謔 concerned mostly with drama.[56] In Li K'ai-hsien's list of names of those who rate that novel on a par with the *Shih-chi* 史記 (Records of the Historian) in narrative accomplishment are T'ang Shun-chih 唐順之 (1507–1560) and Wang Shen-chung 王慎中 (1509–1559). Both men were instrumental in the introduction of *ku-wen* 古文 (classical prose) style into examination essay writing and were as famous for their examination essays as for their other prose works which, for T'ang Shun-chih's part, included a *p'ing-tien* edition of selections from T'ang and Sung prose stylists. On the other hand, some of the early fiction commentators tried to distance themselves and their beloved fiction from the "eight-legged essays" and those who wrote them, but if we examine their remarks we find that their real targets are holders of the lowest degree in the examination system. In the commentary on the *Hsi-yu chi* attributed to Li Chih the commentator says: "This writing is the utmost in marvelousness and imagination. How can holders of the *hsiu-ts'ai* degree working on their examination essays come up with anything like this?"[57] Elsewhere, the same commentator jokes about old men who shave their beards to cover up their ages, so that they can sit for the preliminary examinations and try to gain *t'ung-sheng* 童生 (literally, child candidate) status.[58]

During the years 1616 to 1621 Chung Hsing published several collections of examination essays[59] and his name appears on the title page of several commentary editions of individual novels, but there is no reason to believe in the authenticity of these attributions. The situation is different with Chin Sheng-t'an. A biography of him by a contemporary

the essay on the eight-legged essay in William Nienhauser, Jr., ed., *The Indiana Companion to Traditional Chinese Literature* (Bloomington, Indiana: Indiana University Press, 1986), pp. 641–43.

[56] *Chung-kuo ku-tien hsi-ch'ü lun-chu chi-ch'eng*, vol. 3, *Tz'u nüeh*, p. 286.

[57] Microfilm of *Li Cho-wu hsien-sheng p'i-p'ing Hsi-yu chi* 李卓吾先生批評西遊記 (Commentary Edition of the *Hsi-yu chi* by Li Chih), original held in Japan, p. 30/16b, chapter comment.

[58] Ibid., p. 40/16a, chapter comment.

[59] See his biography in L. Carrington Goodrich and Chaoying Fang, eds., *Dictionary of Ming Biography*, 2 vols. (New York: Columbia University Press, 1976), vol. 1, p. 409.

states that a collection of examination essays with his commentary was in circulation,[60] but does not mention the name of the collection. The preface to a collection of classical prose with commentary by Chin Sheng-t'an, *T'ien-hsia ts'ai-tzu pi-tu shu* 天下才子必讀書 (Required Reading for the Geniuses of the World), mentions the title of the collection of examination essays as *Chih-i ts'ai-tzu shu* 制義才子書 (Geniuses of the Examination Essays),[61] but there is also extant a list of Chin Sheng-t'an's works that gives an alternate title with the same meaning, *Ch'eng-mo ts'ai-tzu* 程墨才子.[62] Although the existence of this collection of examination essays with commentary by Chin Sheng-t'an seems beyond doubt, there is no record that it is now extant.

The third preface (dated 1641) of Chin Sheng-t'an's commentary on the *Shui-hu chuan* is written as if it were a private letter to his son. He talks about his days in school reading the Four Books when he was the same age as his son (ten years old) and remembers saying to his fellow students, "I don't see why we are studying this stuff."[63] There are various rumors about how Chin Sheng-t'an was disrespectful to the examining officials in the wording of his examination essays and was several times expelled from the roster of registered students. In one version, he exults over the freedom he has gained by being expelled.[64] Some of his displeasure with the last act of the *Hsi-hsiang chi* 西廂記 (Romance of the Western Chamber) seems to be related to disapproval of the way the hero, Chang Chün-jui 張君瑞, wins success in the examination system and how this affects the other characters. Also, the Shun-chih emperor's (r. 1644–1661) remark about Chin Sheng-t'an, which was transmitted to Chin and clearly made him quite proud, praises him as an adept at classical prose (*ku-wen kao-shou* 古文高手) and cautions people not to judge him according to examination essay standards ("mo

[60] See the biography of Chin Sheng-t'an by Liao Yen 廖燕 (1644–1705), in his *Erh-shih-ch'i sung t'ang chi* 二十七松堂集 (Collection from the Hall of Twenty-seven Pines; Tokyo: Hakuetsu dō, 1862), pp. 14/5b–7b.

[61] See the original preface, by Hsü Tseng 徐增, reprinted by Shu-hsiang ch'u-pan she (Taipei, 1978), p. 2b.

[62] Liu Hsien-t'ing 劉獻廷 (1648–1695), ed., *Ch'en-yin lou shih-hsüan* 忱吟樓詩選 (Selected Poems of Chin Sheng-t'an), manuscript copy dated 1727 (Shanghai: Shang-hai ku-chi, 1979), pp. 155–56. The list, which includes published as well as unpublished works, also mentions a *Hsiao-t'i ts'ai-tzu* 小題才子 (Geniuses of the Small Topics), which might also be a collection of examination essays with commentary.

[63] *SHCHPP*, p. 8.

[64] For the details of several of these sometimes apocryphal stories, see Ch'en Wan-i 陳萬益, *Chin Sheng-t'an ti wen-hsüeh p'i-p'ing k'ao-shu* 金聖歎的文學批評考述 (Analysis and Description of the Literary Criticism of Chin Sheng-t'an; Taipei: College of Liberal Arts of National Taiwan University, 1976), pp. 5–6.

i shih-wen yen k'an t'a" 莫以時文眼看他).[65] As for the terminology used by Chin Sheng-t'an in his fiction and drama criticism, many of these terms are also used in examination essay criticism, but they have been adapted to the differing concerns of these two new media. We can also see the effect of Chin Sheng-t'an's fiction and drama criticism on examination essay criticism where some of the terminology popularized by him also shows up in p'ing-tien collections of examination essays.

Li Yü never wrote a major commentary on a work of fiction or any major piece of fiction criticism, but his dramatic theory as worked out in several chapters of his Hsien-ch'ing ou-chi 閑情偶寄 (Random Repository of Idle Thoughts) with its attention to structure, characterization, and stress on innovation was very influential on fiction criticism. Li Yü was a professional literary man who supported himself through publishing and performing his plays with his troupe of actors. He is supposed to have published volumes of examination essays with commentary, but no copies seem to have survived. Li Yü's fiction abounds with references to and metaphors from the whole process of taking the examinations and writing eight-legged essays,[66] and he continues this practice in the sections on drama in Hsien-ch'ing ou-chi.[67] Contrary to what one might expect, in his writing on drama Li Yü often points to the spirit of innovation in examination essay writing, rather than to any inherent conservatism. On further reflection, we realize that the intense competition and the high degree of sophistication in essay criticism over the years would certainly be a good incentive to innovation.

Mao Tsung-kang 毛宗崗 (fl. 17th century and author of a commentary on the San-kuo yen-i) makes comparatively few overt references to examination essays or to those involved in taking them or writing criticism on them. In the few examples that there are, he tends to restrict himself to mocking examination takers for copying the essays of others or trying to get by without real learning.[68] Various later commentators on fictional works relate the writing of fiction to the writing of examination essays[69] or use the terminology of the different sections of the eight-legged essay to identify the structural function of different sections

[65] The remark is related in the preface to a set of poems that Chin Sheng-t'an wrote to commemorate hearing this news, "Ch'un-kan pa-shou" 春感八首 (Spring Reflections, Eight Poems), Ch'en-yin lou shih-hsüan, in CSTCC, vol. 4, p. 585.

[66] The consistent use of this feature in the Jou p'u-t'uan 肉蒲團 (The Prayer Mat of Flesh) and in Li Yü's fiction is one reason for crediting the traditional attribution of this novel to Li Yü. The commentary to this novel is also probably by Li Yü.

[67] See Li Li-weng ch'ü-hua 李笠翁曲話 (Li Yü on Drama), Ch'en To 陳多, ed. (Ch'ang-sha: Hu-nan jen-min, 1981), pp. 4, 49, 102, 110, and 114.

[68] See SKYI, pp. 102.1022 and 113.1124, interlineal comments.

[69] See the San-chiang tiao-sou 三江釣叟 (pseud.) preface, T'ieh-hua hsien shih 鐵花仙史 (History of the Iron-Flower Immortal; Shenyang: Ch'un-feng wen-i, 1985).

in a novel.[70] Yet what is surely one of the most amusing examples of the joining of fiction and drama criticism with examination essay criticism occurs in the text of a novel, *Ch'i-lu teng* 歧路燈 (The Warning Light at the Crossroads) by Li Lü-yüan 李綠園 (1707–1790). Chapter 11 presents the example of a tutor using the *Hsi-hsiang chi* and the *Chin P'ing Mei* 金瓶梅 (The Plum in the Golden Vase) to teach his charge how to write winning examination essays.[71] Although not explicitly indicated, it is clear from the context and the tutor's remarks that the editions of these two books that he has in mind are those with commentary by Chin Sheng-t'an and Chang Chu-p'o 張竹坡 (1670–1698), respectively. The whole episode is treated by the author with palpable distaste for the very idea, but many of the commentaries on fiction repeatedly insist that if a young person can learn all the techniques of writing fiction pointed out by them he will have no trouble with other types of writing, including the examination essays. According to Chou Tso-jen 周作人 (1884–1969), his grandfather was a believer in this kind of pedagogy and had his students read novels such as the *Hsi-yu chi*, *Ju-lin wai-shih* 儒林外史 (The Scholars), and the *Ching-hua yüan* 鏡花緣 (The Fate of the Flowers in the Mirror) in preparation to learning how to write examination essays.[72]

The so-called "eight-legged essay" became the required form for many of the individual sessions of the civil service examinations around the middle of the Ming dynasty. Civil service examinations had become increasingly important in the selection of government officials starting from the T'ang dynasty, but the examination papers prior to the Ming had been written according to different formal rules and had also emphasized the ability to write poetry and rhyme prose (*fu* 賦). As can be seen from the name most often used to refer to this particular type of examination essay, "eight-legged essay," the formal requirements for the essays were considered, in popular perceptions of the genre, to be the main characterizing feature. It thus comes as somewhat of a disappointment to find that the formal requirements for these essays contained a substantial amount of flexibility. Although the structure of a model essay does tend to break up into eight parts, not all of these parts can be described as "legs" (*ku* 股, literally "thigh"), sections of the main body of the essay in which the argument is advanced through means of parallelism and whose actual number, although usually kept to four,[73] could be in-

---

[70] See item 1 of Wang Hsi-lien's "Tsung-p'ing" 總評 (General Remarks) for the *Hung-lou meng*, quoted in *CYY*, p. 21.

[71] *Ch'i-lu teng* (Cheng-chou: Chung-chou shu-hua she, 1980), pp. 11.120–21.

[72] Chou Tso-jen, "*Ching-hua yüan*," dated 1923, *Chih-t'ang shu-hua* 知堂書話 (Talks on Books by Chou Tso-jen; Ch'ang-sha: Yüeh-lu shu-she, 1986), p. 102.

[73] These four sections of the essay are most often labeled as *ch'i-ku* 起股 (opening leg), *hsü-ku* 虛股 (indirect statement leg), *chung-ku* 中股 (middle leg), and *hou-ku* 後股 (final

creased. There was also considerable historical change in the formal
requirements for the essays from their initial institution to their abolition
at the end of the Ch'ing dynasty. The particular form of the essays forced
the writer to present his argument from several points of view, usually in
pairs because of the requirement for parallelism, and thus encouraged
attention to the effect of rhetoric and structure in a very concrete way. In
any case, strict formal requirements are not insurmountable obstacles to
creative expression, per se, as was eloquently proven in the history of
Chinese "regulated verse."

Besides being an outgrowth of the forms used in previous civil service
examinations in the T'ang and the Sung,[74] the eight-legged essay was
traced back to sources in classical prose (ku-wen 古文) and drama. The
classical prose (literally, "archaic prose") movement associated with Han
Yü 韓愈 (768–824) is usually seen primarily as the championing of the
prose style of the Ch'in and Han dynasties in opposition to parallel prose
(p'ien-t'i wen 駢體文), which dominated prose writing in the Six Dynasties and the T'ang, and classical prose style is also usually taken to be a
radical freeing up of prose writing from the cumbersome strictures of
parallel prose. Nevertheless, the fact remains that classical prose as written
by Han Yü and those who came after him preserved a heavy bias toward
parallelism in the language of each section and toward balance between
the sections of the argument. Different writers, both ancient and modern, have pointed to individual pieces of classical prose writing by figures
such as Han Yü, Fan Chung-yen 范仲淹 (989–1052), and Wang An-shih
as stylistic sources for the eight-legged essay.[75]

---

leg) (see Maeno Naoaki 前野直彬, ed., Chung-kuo wen-hsüeh kai-lun 中國文學概論
[Survey of Chinese Literature], Hung Shun-lung 洪順隆, trans. [Taipei: Ch'eng-wen
ch'u-pan she, 1971], pp. 184–85), but the ku are also sometimes referred to as pi 比
(paired sections) and the two parallel parts of each section are then referred to as ku (as
opposed to being called shan 扇 [literally, "fan"] in the other terminology), thus bringing
to eight the total number of ku in a standard essay (see Li Yü's description, Li Li-weng
ch'ü-hua, p. 49).

[74] See the remarks on the origin of the eight-legged essay in the "Hsüan-chü chih"
選舉志 (Monograph on Civil Service Recruitment) of the Ming-shih 明史 (History of the
Ming Dynasty), Chang T'ing-yü 張廷玉 (1672–1755) et al., comps., quoted in Kuo Shao-
yü 郭紹虞, ed., Chung-kuo li-tai wen-lun hsüan 中國歷代文論選 (Selections in Traditional
Chinese Literary Theory), 4 vols. (Shanghai: Shang-hai ku-chi, 1980), vol. 3, p. 544, n. 16
and Maeno Naoaki, Chung-kuo wen-hsüeh kai-lun, p. 183.

[75] On Han Yü, see Maeno Naoaki, Chung-kuo wen-hsüeh kai-lun, p. 186. On Wang An-
shih, see p. 183 of the same work. As for Fan Chung-yen, in T'ien-hsia ts'ai-tzu pi-tu shu
Chin Sheng-t'an comments on a piece of prose by that writer, "Yen hsien-sheng tz'u-
t'ang chi" 嚴先生祠堂記 (A Record of Mr. Yen's Sacrificial Hall), "This is the source for
today's examination essays" ("tz'u chin-jih chih-i chih so ch'u yeh" 此今日制義之所
出也), p. 15/24a.

A new feature of the eight-legged essay was the custom that the candidate was supposed to express himself on behalf of the sages using their manner of expression ("tai ku-jen yü-ch'i wei chih" 代古人語氣爲 之).[76] Perhaps this is one of the reasons that a strong connection between Yüan dynasty drama and this form of examination essay is often felt to exist. The notion that the writing of arias was part of the Yüan dynasty examination system, undocumented but championed by such people as the editor of the most influential collection of Yüan plays, Tsang Mao-hsün 臧懋循 (1550–1620),[77] and portrayed on stage in scene eight of Ming dynasty versions of the *P'i-p'a chi* 琵琶記 (Story of the Lute), might have contributed to this view. The specific form that parallelism takes in the operas and the requirement to speak on behalf of others certainly have their relevance to the eight-legged essay. In any case, there were those who complained of the influence travelling the other way, from the essays to drama. Hsü Wei 徐渭 (1521–1593), in his *Nan-tz'u hsü-lu* 南詞叙錄 (A Record of Southern Drama), describes the fashion of writing dramas preaching Neo-Confucian ideals in very flowery language that began with the writing of *Hsiang-nang chi* 香囊記 (The Story of the Perfumed Bag) by Shao Ts'an 邵燦 (fl. 15th century) as writing plays as if they were essays ("i shih-wen wei Nan-ch'u" 以時文 爲南曲).[78]

Although it is now the fashion to view the examination system as a government instrument for controlling intellectuals and some officals admitted as much,[79] collections of examination essays were also pub-

[76] *Ming-shih*, "Hsüan-chü chih," quoted in *Chung-kuo li-tai wen-lun hsüan*, vol. 3, p. 544, n. 16.

[77] See his second preface to his *Yüan-ch'ü hsüan* 元曲選 (Anthology of Yüan Drama). This kind of link posited between Yüan drama and the contemporary examination system has similarities to the theory that the prominence of the classical tale in the T'ang dynasty was related to the alleged practice of examination candidates who used the tales to arouse the examiners' interest in them (*wen-chüan* 溫卷).

[78] *Chung-kuo ku-tien hsi-ch'ü lun-chu chi-ch'eng*, vol. 3, p. 243.

[79] "It's not that we don't know that the eight-legged essays are worthless, they are specifically good for co-opting men of ambition. For keeping control of the talented, no technique is better than this." 非不知八股爲無用, 特牢籠志士, 驅策英才, 其術莫善 於此. This statement was made by E Erh-t'ai 鄂爾泰 (1677–1745), and preserved in a work called *Man-Ch'ing pai-shih* 滿淸稗史 (Anecdotal History of the Ch'ing Dynasty). See Ch'en Mei-lin 陳美林, "Lun *Ju-lin wai-shih* ti feng-tz'u i-shu" 論儒林外史的諷刺 藝術 (On the Satiric Art of the *Ju-lin wai-shih*), in his *Wu Ching-tzu yen-chiu* 吳敬梓研究 (Studies on Wu Ching-tzu; Shanghai: Shang-hai ku-chi, 1984), p. 199. In an essay on the founding emperor of the Ming dynasty who was seen as the first ruler to institute the use of eight-legged essays in the examination system (*Ming T'ai-tsu lun* 明太祖論), Liao Yen says that that emperor achieved the same effect desired by the first emperor of the Ch'in dynasty (221–206 B.C.) when he burned the Confucian classics by the mere use of the examination system. This essay is included in his *Erh-shih-ch'i sung t'ang chi*, pp. 1/12a–14a.

lished by organizations usually seen as politically progressive, such as the Fu-she 復社 (Restoration Society), active at the end of the Ming dynasty.[80] The latter part of the Ming saw the development of a major industry devoted to the printing and circulation of examination essays with or without commentary centered in Suchou and Hangchou.[81] The way that these essays forced their writers to put themselves into the shoes of not only the sages but also the manner of men with whom the sages came into conflict, such as King Hui of Liang 梁惠王 (r. 370–335 B.C.), must have encouraged the practice of imaginative identification with characters (historical or not) different from oneself (*she-shen ch'u-ti* 設身處地), a facility so very important to creative work in fiction or drama.[82]

The rudiments of examination essay criticism come out of two main sources—the practice of examination candidates marking up examples of essays with punctuation marks and comments as part of their education in how to write essays[83] and the fact that part of the grading system of the examination papers involved the adding of emphatic punctuation and comments by the examining officials.[84] Apparently, friends also liked to add their comments to the copies of the examination papers taken home by the candidates,[85] to say nothing of how teachers marked the essays of their pupils. In the *Ju-lin wai-shih*, an essay by K'uang

[80] Maeno Naoaki, *Chung-kuo wen-hsüeh kai-lun*, p. 189.

[81] See the section on the printing of examination essays ("K'o shih-wen" 刻時文) in Chao I's 趙翼 (1727–1814) *Kai-yü ts'ung-k'ao* 陔餘叢考 (Collected Studies from Retirement), preface 1790, quoted in Ho Tse-han 何澤翰, *Ju-lin wai-shih jen-wu pen-shih k'ao-lüeh* 儒林外史人物本事考略 (Brief Study of the Models for the Characters of the *Ju-lin wai-shih*; Shanghai: Shang-hai ku-chi, 1985), p. 132.

[82] See T'an Chia-chien 譚家健, "Shen-mo chiao 'pa-ku wen'?" 甚麼叫八股文 (What is the "Eight-Legged Essay"?), *Wen-shih chih-shih* 文史知識 (Literary and Historical Knowledge), 1984.3:112–15; Chou Chen-fu 周振甫, *Wen-chang li-hua* 文章例話 (Prose Criticism with Examples; Peking: Chung-kuo ch'ing-nien, 1983), p. 91; and Andrew H. Plaks, *The Four Masterworks of the Ming Novel* (Princeton: Princeton University Press, 1987), pp. 33–34.

[83] For a fictional portrayal, see the description of Miss Lu in the *JLWS* marking her texts with different colored ink and writing comments in tiny characters, p. 11/2a.

[84] See Hsü K'o-wen 徐克文, "Shih-t'an Chung-kuo ch'uan-t'ung ti wen-hsüeh p'i-p'ing hsing-shih: p'ing-tien" 試談中國傳統的文學批評形式：評點 (On a Traditional Chinese Mode of Literary Criticism: P'ing-tien), reprinted in *Ku-chin*, 1983.6:211–14, p. 213. In *Ch'i-lu teng*, the reason for the rejection of Lou Chao's examination paper (two lines critical of the emperor) becomes clear from the fact that the reading punctuation of the examining official stops abruptly at that point (see p. 10.112).

[85] In Wen K'ang's 文康 (fl. 19th century) *Erh-nü ying-hsiung chuan* 兒女英雄傳 (Tales of Male and Female Heroes), An Hsüeh-hai 安學海 justifies not bringing home a copy of his essays because "even if people want to read them, they will only add on some consecutive circles [*mi-ch'üan* 密圈] to a couple of sentences and add a few lines of ready-made comments [*t'ung-t'ao p'i-yü* 通套批語]." (Peking: Jen-min wen-hsüeh, 1983), p. 1.15.

Ch'ao-jen is looked at by his mentor, Ma Ch'un-shang:

> He took the essay and put it on the desk. Taking up his brush and marking
> dots with it, he went through the essay from beginning to end, telling him
> all about techniques like the alternation of abstract and concrete [*hsü-shih*
> 虛實], indirect and direct [*fan-cheng* 反正], rhetorical hesitation [*t'un-t'u*
> 吞吐], and meaning through implication [*han-hsü* 含蓄].
>
> 將文章按在桌上, 拏筆點着, 從頭至尾, 講了許多虛實反正吞吐含蓄之法與
> 他.[86]

Ma Ch'un-shang, of course, makes his living by publishing his selections
with commentary of examination essays. In the *Ju-lin wai-shih* we also
get to hear his principles for writing these commentaries,[87] learn something of the financial arrangements between commentator and publisher,[88] and even get a glimpse of the actual stages of publication.[89]
Aside from the scattered remarks in commentary editions of essays and
in their prefaces, there are a few works that take examination essay
criticism as their topic. One of these, *Chih-i ts'ung-hua* 制義叢話 (Collected Comments on Examination Essays) by Liang Chang-chü 梁章鉅
(1775–1849), uses the same rambling format as *shih-hua* poetry criticism,
while the "Ching-i kai" 經義概 (Outline of the Examination Essay)
section of the *I-kai* 藝概 (Outline of the Arts) by Liu Hsi-tsai 劉熙載
(1813–1881) is more focused and organized.

　　Almost from the beginning, *p'ing-tien* criticism of classical prose was
tailored to the needs of examination candidates. This is not only the
opinion of later scholars,[90] but can be seen from the prefaces of the
works themselves. For instance, in Wang Shou-jen's 王守仁 (1472–1529)
preface to Hsieh Fang-te's 謝枋得 (1226–1289) *Wen-chang kuei-fan* 文章
軌範 (The Model for Prose), he says:

> Hsieh Fang-te of the Sung took examples of classical prose that were of use
> to one when taking the examinations... and by use of headings [*piao* 標]
> explicated each piece.... The mysteries of classical prose are not exhausted
> by this. This is designed solely for examination candidates.
>
> 宋謝枋得氏, 取古文有資於場屋者...標揭其篇. ...蓋古文之奧, 不止於是. 是
> 獨為舉業者設耳.[91]

[86] *JLWS*, p. 15/12a–b.
[87] Ibid., p. 13/7a.
[88] Ibid., p. 18/1a–b.
[89] See the story of Chu-ko T'ien-shen's hiring of Nanking literati to help him produce
a collection of essays, chaps. 28–29, esp. pp. 29/6a–b and 29/8b–9b. This material is
presented satirically, but the general details should be realistic enough.
[90] See, for instance, Lo Ken-tse, *Chung-kuo wen-hsüeh p'i-p'ing shih*, vol. 3, pp. 262–63.
[91] Kuang-wen shu-chü (Taipei, 1970) reprint of the *Wen-chang kuei-fan*. See also Lin
Yün-ming 林雲銘 (fl. 17th century), "Fan-li" 凡例 (General Principles) to his *Ku-wen*

This was true as well for later examples of this genre, such as the *Ku-wen pi-fa pai-p'ien* 古文筆法百篇 (Examples of Classical Prose Technique in One Hundred Selections).[92] One of the prefaces to this work claims that all of the great critics on classical prose of the Ming and Ch'ing dynasties such as Kuei Yu-kuang (1506–1571), T'ang Shun-chih, and Fang Pao 方苞 (1668–1749) treated classical prose as if it were examination essay prose ("i ku-wen wei shih-wen" 以古文為時文).[93] T'ang Shun-chih and Kuei Yu-kuang are generally credited with introducing classical prose stylistics into examination essay writing[94] and, in the T'ung-ch'eng school (*T'ung-ch'eng p'ai* 桐城派) founded by Fang Pao, there is also a close connection between classical prose and examination essay aesthetics.[95] Of course, there was also no lack of people who thought that the aspects of classical prose pointed out in these *p'ing-tien* collections for the use of students learning to write examination essays represented only a fraction of the marvels of that genre. We have already mentioned Wang Shou-jen's views on this subject, and he is seconded by Fang Pao and others.[96] Chin Sheng-t'an compiled a collection of short passages of classical prose with his comments, *T'ien-hsia ts'ai-tzu pi-tu shu*,[97] patterned on an earlier

hsi-i 古文析義 (Analysis of Classical Prose), where he maintains that other collections of classical prose do not contain selections from works such as the "T'an-kung" chapter of the *Li-chi* or the Kung-yang or Ku-liang commentaries to the *Ch'un-ch'iu* because "the editors think they are not very useful for [writing] examination essays" ("hsüan-chia wei i pu shen ch'ieh yü chih-i" 選家惟以不甚切於制義), pp. 3a–b of the Chin-chang t'u-shu edition (Shanghai, 1922).

[92] Compiled by Li Fu-chiu 李扶九 and Huang Jen-fu 黃仁黼. See the 1881 preface by the latter in the Yüeh-lu shu-she reprint (Ch'ang-sha, 1983).

[93] Ibid., Li Yüan-tu 李元度 preface, 1881. This collection also has an essay, "Lun hua ku-wen wei shih-wen ssu-tse" 論化古文為時文四則 (Four Points on Transforming Classical Prose into Examination Essays), left out of the reprint mentioned in the note above. In the editorial principles ("Fan-li" 凡例) to *Ch'in-ting ssu-shu wen* 欽定四書文 (Imperial Collection of Essays on the Four Books) in *Ssu-k'u ch'üan-shu chen-pen* 四庫全書珍本 (Rare Books from the Quadripartite Imperial Library), series 9, vols. 325–40 (Taipei: Commercial Press, 1979), vol. 325, item 1, p. 1a, Fang Pao himself said, "Writers of the Cheng-te [1506–1521] and Chia-ching [1522–1566] reign periods were the first to be able to use classical prose to write examination essays" 正嘉作者, 始能以古文為時文.

[94] Maeno Naoaki, *Chung-kuo wen-hsüeh kai-lun*, p. 187.

[95] David E. Pollard, *A Chinese Look at Literature: The Literary Values of Chou Tso-jen in Relation to the Tradition* (Berkeley: University of California Press, 1973), p. 155.

[96] See Fang Pao's "*Ku-wen yüeh-hsuan* hsü" 古文約選序 (Preface to the Concise Selection of Classical Prose), quoted in Kuo Shao-yü, ed., *Chung-kuo li-tai wen-lun hsüan*, vol. 3, p. 395. For Chang Hsüeh-ch'eng on this subject, see below, "Contemporary Evaluation of *P'ing-tien* Criticism."

[97] Reprinted under this title by Shu-hsiang ch'u-pan she (Taipei, 1978), and in typeset edition under the title *Chin Sheng-t'an p'i ts'ai-tzu ku-wen* 金聖歎批才子古文 (Classical Prose by Geniuses with Commentary by Chin Sheng-t'an), Chang Kuo-kuang 張國光, ed. (Wuhan: Hu-pei jen-min, 1986).

collection of the same type by Chang Nai 張鼐 (courtesy name, T'ung-ch'u 侗初), and Chin's work was in its turn the model for the most popular of all the collections in this genre, the *Ku-wen kuan-chih* 古文觀止 (Pinnacles in Classical Prose).[98]

Fiction was not an overly respectable genre in traditional China. Some of its most fervent advocates, such as Chang Chu-p'o, still used the word fiction as though it had negative connotations for them as well as for their audience.[99] Other fiction critics claimed that the examinations and poetry of the people who accused them of being overly interested in "base" literature were not even one ten-thousandth part as good as their novels,[100] but it was also common to use the readers' familiarity with the genre of the examination essay as an aid in describing certain features in drama and fiction. This is particularly the case in drama criticism,[101] but examples in fiction criticism also abound.[102] Some fiction critics claimed that the relationship was even closer than that. Chang Shu-shen 張書紳 (fl. 18th century), in his *Hsin-shuo Hsi-yu chi* 新說西遊記 (A New Explication of the *Hsi-yu chi*), claimed that after a certain amount of effort by the reader, he will realize that that novel is "just like a collection of provincial or metropolitan examination essays" ("ssu i pu hsiang-hui chih-i wen-tzu" 似一部鄉會制義文字).[103] The author of *Hai-shang hua lieh-chuan* 海上花列傳 (Biographies of the Flowers Adrift on the Sea), Han Pang-ch'ing 韓邦慶 (1856–1894), stated flatly, "The method of writing fiction is the same as that for examination essays" ("hsiao-

[98] The title of Chang T'ung-ch'u's collection is alternatively *Chang T'ung-ch'u hsien-sheng hui-chi pi-tu Ku-wen cheng-tsung* 張侗初先生彙輯必讀古文正宗 (The True Transmission of Classical Prose, Required Reading, Edited by Chang T'ung-ch'u) or *Tseng-ting* 增訂 (Expanded and Revised) *Ku-wen cheng-tsung*. The relationship between this collection and Chin Sheng-t'an's is discussed by him in item 14 of his "Tu *Ti-liu ts'ai-tzu shu Hsi-hsiang chi* fa" 讀第六才子書西廂記法 (How to Read The Sixth Work of Genius, The Romance of the Western Chamber), in *CSTCC*, vol. 3, p. 12. On the relationship between *Ts'ai-tzu ku-wen* and *Ku-wen kuan-chih*, see the introductory essay by Chang Kuo-kuang in *Chin Sheng-t'an p'i Ts'ai-tzu ku-wen*, pp. 1–11.

[99] See, for instance, item 37 of his *tu-fa* essay on the *Chin P'ing Mei*, chap. IV below.

[100] See item 18 of the "*Hsüeh Yüeh Mei* tu-fa" 雪月梅讀法 (How to Read the *Hsüeh Yüeh Mei*), by Tung Meng-fen 董孟汾 (fl. 18th century), *Hsüeh Yüeh Mei* (Tsinan: Ch'i Lu shu-she, 1986), p. 5.

[101] See *Li Li-weng ch'ü-hua*, "Pieh chieh wu-t'ou" 別解務頭 (An Alternative Explanation of "Wu-t'ou"), p. 77 and "Chia-men" 家門 (The Prologue), p. 99; and Wang Chi-te 王驥德 (d. 1623), *Wang Chi-te Ch'ü-lü* 王驥德曲律 (Wang Chi-te's Rules of Dramatic Prosody), Ch'en To and Yeh Ch'ang-hai 葉長海, eds. (Ch'ang-sha: Hu-nan jen-min, 1983), "T'ao-shu" 套數 (Song Sequences), p. 138.

[102] See, for instance, a comment by Chang Hsin-chih, *CYY*, p. 84.1099 (interlineal comment), and the chapter comments to chap. 1 of *T'ieh-hua hsien shih*, p. 1.10.

[103] See item 72 in his "Tsung-p'i" 總批 (General Comments), quoted in *HYCTLHP*, p. 235.

shuo tso-fa yü chih-i t'ung" 小說作法與制義同),[104] while Wang
Meng-juan 王夢阮 claimed that the author of the *Hung-lou meng*, judging from his fictional writing, must have been good at writing examination essays.[105] There are also anecdotes that tie fiction and drama
together with the examination essays, such as the one about Chou
Tso-jen's grandfather using novels as textbooks mentioned above and
the story that a person named Huang Chün-fu 黃君輔 was successful in
the examinations after intensive study of the famous play, *Mu-tan t'ing*
牡丹亭 (The Peony Pavilion).[106] On the other hand, for the writer
of the commentary in the Jung-yü t'ang edition of the *Shui-hu chuan*
attributed to Li Chih, passages in the text that incurred his wrath might
be compared to examination essays: "Saying it over and over again,
what's the difference between this and an examination essay?"[107]

Historiographical criticism, as exemplified in works such as Liu
Chih-chi's (661–721) *Shih-t'ung* 史通 (Generalities of Historiography),
was originally written for people engaged in writing history or interested in the problems of historiography. Although some of the critics'
attention was directed to the topic of literary style, the proportion was
not very great. During the Ming dynasty, editions of historical works
with *p'ing-tien* style criticism began to appear in increasing numbers.
Most prominent among these were editions of the *Shih-chi* with collected commentary, but other histories such as the *Han-shu* were also
treated in this way. The most important of the early *p'ing-tien* editions is
the *Shih-chi p'ing-lin* 史記評林 (Forest of Comments on the *Shih-chi*),
published by Ling Chih-lung with a 1576 preface by him. The total
number of commentators represented is said to be 146,[108] and that
number includes critics such as Liu Ch'en-weng, Yang Shen, and Mao
K'un, whom we have had occasion to mention above. Later expanded

[104] Han Pang-ch'ing, *Hai-shang hua lieh-chuan* (Peking: Jen-min wen-hsüeh, 1985),
"Li-yen" 例言 (General Principles), item 9, p. 3.

[105] "*Hung-lou meng so-yin* t'i-yao" 紅樓夢索隱提要 (Abstract of the *Hong-lou meng so-
yin*), quoted in *HLMC*, p. 295.

[106] Ch'ien Chung-lien 錢仲聯, "T'ung-ch'eng p'ai ku-wen yü shih-wen ti kuan-hsi
wen-t'i" 桐城派古文與時文的關係問題 (The Problem of the Relationship of the Classical Prose of the T'ung-ch'eng School to Examination Essays), *T'ung-ch'eng p'ai yen-chiu
lun-wen chi* 桐城派研究論文集 (Collected Research Papers on the T'ung-ch'eng School;
Hofei: An-hui jen-min, 1963), p. 152. For examples of other men who got inspiration or
technical help for their examination essays from reading the *Mu-tan t'ing* and the *Hsi-
hsiang chi*, see Ch'ien Chung-shu 錢鍾書, *T'an-i lu* 談藝錄 (A Record of Investigations
into the Arts; Peking: Chung-hua shu-chü, revised edition, 1984), "Fu-shuo ssu" 附說四
(app. 4), p. 33.

[107] *SHCHPP*, p. 67.1475, marginal comment.

[108] Hsü K'o-wen, "Shih-t'an Chung-kuo ch'uan-t'ung ti wen-hsüeh p'i-p'ing hsing-
shih: p'ing-tien," p. 213.

editions add the comments of people such as Chung Hsing and Li Chih. Ch'ing dynasty scholars such as Fang Tung-shu 方東樹 (1772–1851) thought that these collections were very similar to the annotated collections of examination essays,[109] but the relationship is spelled out explicitly in a commercial abbreviation of the *Shih-chi p'ing-lin* that appeared in 1591. At the head of the first chapter of this work, whose full title is *Hsin-ch'ieh T'ao hsien-sheng ching-hsüan Shih-chi sai-pao p'ing-lin* 新鍥陶先生精選史記賽寶評林 (Newly Cut, Precious Forest of Comments on the *Shih-chi*, Finely Edited by T'ao Wang-ling 陶望齡, 1562–1609), the editor and the commentator have put before their names the information that one was ranked first in the metropolitan examination and the other was number one in the provincial examination. In item five of the "Fan-li" 凡例 (General Principles) for the edition, they explain that the selections that they included were chosen with the requirements of the writing of examination essays in mind ("so ts'ui wei chü-yeh erh she" 所萃為舉業而設).[110]

In the sections above, we have shown that the examination essays and the body of criticism devoted to them were influential not only on traditional fiction and drama criticism, but also on the criticism of classical prose and history alike. As for the concrete manifestations of this influence in fiction criticism, that will have to be left for another time.

Dramatic Criticism   The very earliest examples of drama criticism in traditional China consist, for the most part, of little more than notes about performances, actors, or technical problems in prosody. Although drama flourished in the Yüan dynasty (1279–1368), we do not even have contemporary editions of complete scripts for any of those plays. In the Ming dynasty that situation changed. The earliest extant printed edition of the *Hsi-hsiang chi*, printed in 1498, has a wealth of prefatory material and lexical and phonetic glosses, but none of that material has very much to do with literary criticism. The rest of the Ming dynasty saw the publication of growing numbers of plays with *p'ing-tien* style commentary. The actual bulk of the comments in each of these editions remained rather small, even the comments after each act rarely exceeding a sentence or two, until the publication of Chin Sheng-t'an's commentary on the *Hsi-hsiang chi* in 1658. The real contribution of dramatic criticism to fiction criticism probably did not come from these commentary editions but from the tradition of publishing treatises on drama, a phenomenon unparalleled in fiction criticism.

[109] Quoted by Ch'ien Chung-lien, "T'ung-ch'eng p'ai ku-wen yü shih-wen ti kuan-hsi wen-t'i," p. 152.

[110] Copy held in Peking Library.

Drama criticism included a type of criticism similar to the *shih-hua* and *tz'u-hua* of poetry, known as *ch'ü-hua* 曲話. For the most part, that genre of criticism shared the rather random form of its models, but there are a couple of works whose breadth and organization almost put them into another class altogether. The two most impressive examples are Wang Chi-te's 王驥德 (d. 1623) *Ch'ü lü* 曲律 (Rules of Dramatic Prosody) and the appropriate sections of Li Yü's *Hsien-ch'ing ou-chi*. In the latter case in particular, the author has set himself the job of writing a manual for the dramatist that includes all stages of the art from scriptwriting to makeup. Leaving aside the technical sections that treat problems of interest only to dramatists, there are also sections on structure and characterization that are equally applicable to fiction. For instance, Li Yü's term *chu-nao* 主腦 (literally, the main brain) referring to the central incident or character upon which the whole play hinges was taken over by fiction critics as well as drama critics.

Li Yü praised Chin Sheng-t'an's commentary on the *Hsi-hsiang chi* for his thoroughness in ferreting out the secrets of its composition, but condemned the other man's ignorance of the performance side of drama.[111] Although Li Yü was perfectly correct to attack Chin Sheng-t'an for treating the *Hsi-hsiang chi* solely as a work of literature to be read rather than also as a play to be performed, the fact remains that there was a very strong trend at the time to write plays without thought of producing them and to read plays almost as if they were novels.[112] This is quite different from the very earliest edition of Yüan dramas, where the dialogue is missing or very sketchy. This partial convergence of drama and fiction encouraged the cross-fertilization of ideas and techniques between the two genres.

Contemporary Evaluation of P'ing-tien Criticism

Generally speaking, *p'ing-tien* criticism has a very bad name. This is true not only in modern times, but also in the period when it flourished as the most influential form of criticism. The most common complaint by Ming and Ch'ing writers is that only formal techniques that could be

---

[111] *Li Li-weng ch'ü-hua*, "T'ien-tz'u yü-lun" 填詞餘論 (Leftover Comments on Dramatic Writing), p. 103.

[112] The "Fan-li" (p. 5b) to the Ling Meng-ch'u 淩濛初 (1580–1644) edition of the *Hsi-hsiang chi* says, "This printing is really intended to provide refined entertainment and should be taken as a piece of writing. It should not be taken as a work of drama." In item 3 of the "Fan-li" for *Ch'ing-hui ko p'i-tien Mu-tan t'ing* 清暉閣批點牡丹亭 (Ch'ing-hui Lodge Commentary on the Peony Pavilion), the play is called *an-t'ou chih shu* 案頭之書 (a book to be read at home; as opposed to a playscript). See Mao Hsiao-t'ung 毛效同, ed., *T'ang Hsien-tsu yen-chiu tzu-liao hui-pien* 湯顯祖研究資料彙編 (Collected Research Material on T'ang Hsien-tsu; Shanghai: Shang-hai ku-chi, 1986), p. 858.

applied mechanically were to be learned from reading such works, while the true individuality of the works criticized got lost in the shuffle. In a letter Wu Ying-chi 吳應箕 (1594–1645) said:

> Most likely, the fact that the real spirit of the ancients has been lost is the fault of the commentator-editors [p'ing-hsüan-che 評選者]. I say that the commentating of examination essays by Chang T'ung-ch'u, the commentating of poetry by Chung Hsing, and the commentating of classical prose by Mao K'un are superbly able to bury the real spirit of the ancients, and that people on the contrary look up to them and are all in a hurry to emulate them is really a pity. They provide explanations and comments for every sentence and every character; every section and every paragraph have been marked off with emphatic punctuation [ch'üan-tien 圈點]. They themselves are convinced that they have captured the very marrow and essence of the ancients and have opened up the way for later people to emulate them. What they don't know is that their real crime against the ancients and their misleading of later people lies precisely there.

> 大抵古人精神不見於世者，皆評選者之過也. 弟嘗謂張侗初之評時義，鍾伯敬之評詩，茅鹿門之評古文，最能埋沒古人精神，而世反效慕恐後，可歎也. 彼其一字一句，皆有釋評，逐段逐節，皆為圈點，自謂得古人之精髓，開後人之法程，不知所以冤古人，誤後生者，正在此.[113]

Wang Fu-chih 王夫之 (1619–1692) also had harsh words to say about Mao K'un and his selections with commentary of T'ang and Sung classical prose stylists: "Once *Pa-ta chia wen-ch'ao* 八大家文鈔 [Selections from the Eight Masters] appeared, that spelled the end of writing [*wen* 文]. He thought that this was a good way to teach young students, but he did not see that he was leading the students right into a thicket of brambles."[114] The most eloquent attack on *p'ing-tien* and *p'ing-hsüan* came from Chang Hsüeh-ch'eng in two of the sections of his *Wen-shih t'ung-i* 文史通義 (General Principles of Historiography).[115] In the "Wen-li" 文理 (Principles of Writing) chapter of that work, he tells of seeing a copy of Kuei Yu-kuang's commentary on the *Shih-chi* done with five different colors of ink to show different levels of language and technique in that text. The copy is owned by a friend of his, who explains that his former reverence for the work as the source of the true transmission of the way of writing (he compares this to the transmission of the Way in Buddhism) has since changed, but although he no longer

---

[113] "Ta Ch'en Ting-sheng shu" 答陳定生書 (Reply to a Letter from Ch'en Ting-sheng), quoted in Kuo Shao-yü, ed., *Chung-kuo li-tai wen-lun hsüan*, vol. 3, p. 83.

[114] From his *Hsi-t'ang yung-jih hsü-lun wai-pien* 夕堂永日緒論外編, quoted in Kuo Shao-yü, ed., *Chung-kuo li-tai wen-lun hsüan*, vol. 3, p. 304, n. 22.

[115] For a summary of Chang Hsüeh-ch'eng on *p'ing-tien*, see Chou Chen-fu, *Wen-chang li-hua*, pp. 2–3.

treasures it, he feels that there are a few redeeming features about the work and so has preserved it. Chang Hsüeh-ch'eng remarks that Kuei Yu-kuang and T'ang Shun-chih have the same status in the history of the eight-legged essay as Ssu-ma Ch'ien 司馬遷 (b. 145 B.C.) in historiography and Han Yü in classical prose, and both took the *Shih-chi* as their guide. Unfortunately, according to him, what they grasped about the *Shih-chi* was only mere externals (*p'i-mao* 皮毛). To him, the compilation of *p'ing-tien* style books was of the least concern to writing (*wen chih mo-wu* 文之末務), not to be shown to others but only to aid one's own memory, to be passed down neither from father to son, nor from teacher to pupil. Why is that? "Because they are afraid to take the inexhaustible books of the ancients and put them on the procrustean bed of the limited perception of one man at any one point in time."[116]

In the other section of the *Wen-shih t'ung-i* that deals with this problem, "Ku-wen shih pi" 古文十弊 (Ten Faults in Classical Prose), Chang Hsüeh-ch'eng describes the genesis of *p'ing-tien* style criticism and its terminology:

> When instructors teach [their pupils] the style and meaning of the Four Books and how to write examination essays, the essays must have technique [*fa-tu* 法度] so as to comply with the formal requirements [*ch'eng-shih* 程式]. But technique is difficult to speak of abstractly, so they often use metaphors to teach their students. Comparing [the essays] to buildings, they speak of the framework [*chien-chia* 間架] and structure [*chieh-kou* 結構]; comparing [the essays] to the human body, they speak of the eyebrows and eyes [*mei mu* 眉目], tendons and joints [*chin-chieh* 筋節]; comparing [the essays] to painting, they talk of "filling in the pupils of the dragon" [*tien-ching* 點睛][117] and "adding the whiskers" [*t'ien-hao* 添毫];[118] and comparing [the essays] to geomancy, they speak of "lines of force" [*lai-lung* 來龍] and "convergence points" [*chieh-hsüeh* 結穴]. They make these up as they go, but it's all just for teaching elementary students, there is no help for it, so there is no need to upbraid them for it.

> 蓋塾師講授四書文義, 謂之時文, 必有法度以合程式; 而法度難以空言, 則往往取譬以示蒙學, 擬於房室, 則有所謂間架結構; 擬於身體, 則有所謂眉目筋節; 擬於繪畫, 則有所謂點睛添毫; 擬於形家, 則有所謂來龍結穴. 隨時取譬. 然為初學示法, 亦自不得不然, 無庸責也.[119]

---

[116] Chang Hsüeh-ch'eng, *Wen-shih t'ung-i chiao-chu*, pp. 286–88.

[117] Anecdote about the Six Dynasties period painter Chang Seng-yu 張僧繇, who painted four dragons without pupils. When he finally did fill in the pupils, the dragons flew away. This anecdote is used to refer to that final touch that brings life to a work of art.

[118] See n. 39 above.

[119] Chang Hsüeh-ch'eng, *Wen-shih t'ung-i chiao-chu*, "Ku-wen shih-pi," item 9, p. 509.

The real problem, according to Chang Hsüeh-ch'eng, is when this meth-od is directed toward classical prose. He is opposed to the influence of *p'ing-hsüan* on two grounds. One is historical—he accuses *p'ing-hsüan* critics of having only a very imperfect understanding of classical prose to begin with.[120] The other is theoretical—for him, theory or technique comes into being only after the event of creation (*wen ch'eng fa li* 文成法 立),[121] and thus always lags behind, making universal prescriptions useless. "Writing is always changing and no set law can encompass it" ("wen-chang pien-hua fei i-ch'eng chih fa so neng hsien yeh" 文章變化非 一成之法所能限也).[122] However, from the material from Chang Hsüeh-ch'eng introduced above, we can see that he was not against the formula-tion of laws of writing for the use of the student; what he was protesting against was mature writers allowing those very same laws to restrict their creativity. Critics in several fields of artistic endeavor in China called on their students to escape this trap by studying the various laws but apply-ing them flexibly and creatively to match the particular needs of the moment. "One cannot do without laws, but one cannot let oneself be stifled by them" ("pu wei wu-fa, tan pu k'o ni" 不爲無法, 但不可 泥).[123] "It is the case with all laws that the truly marvelous comes from transformation [of them]" ("fan fa miao tsai chuan" 凡法妙在轉).[124]

Speaking in their own defense, some in the industry of producing *p'ing-tien* volumes complained of sloppy reprints that distorted the texts of the comments.[125] Others confessed that the job of commenting on books was very difficult. Chang Shu-shen said:

> It is said that writing books is difficult, but people do not know that writing explications of books is also difficult. Why is this so? If you write too little, the meaning is not clear; if you write too much the meaning is obscured. The more you write the more mistakes, until one ends up going through with a fine-toothed comb looking for errors. They do not know how many

---

[120] Ibid., item 10, p. 509.

[121] Ibid., item 9, p. 508.

[122] Ibid., "Wen-li," p. 289.

[123] Li Tung-yang 李東陽 (1447–1516), *Lu-t'ang shih-hua* 麓堂詩話 (Lu-t'ang Talks on Poetry), quoted in Cheng Tien and T'an Ch'üan-chi, eds., *Ku Han-yü hsiu-tz'u hsüeh tzu-liao hui-pien*, p. 420.

[124] Lu Shih-yung 陸時雍, *Shih-ching tsung-lun* 詩鏡總論 (General Remarks from the Mirror of Poetry), quoted in Chang Pao-ch'üan 張葆全 and Chou Man-chiang 周滿江, eds., *Li-tai shih-hua hsüan-chu* 歷代詩話選注 (Annotated Selections from Talks on Poetry; Hsi-an: Shan-hsi jen-min, 1984), p. 258.

[125] See item 30 of the "Fan-li" to Yü Ch'eng 余誠, ed., *Ch'ung-ting ku-wen shih-i hsin-pien* 重訂古文釋義新編 (Revised, Newly Edited Classical Prose Explained; Wuhan: Wu-han ku-chi, 1986 reprint), p. 4b and item 7 of the "Fan-li" of *Ch'ing-hui ko p'i-tien Mu-tan t'ing*, quoted in Mao Hsiao-t'ung, ed., *T'ang Hsien-tsu yen-chiu tzu-liao hui-pien*, p. 859.

fine books have been buried in this way, how much marvelous writing has
been ruined through commentary. It's really too bad.

嘗言著書難, 殊不知解書亦不易. 何則？蓋少則不明, 多則反晦, 而言多語失,
以致吹毛求疵, 不知淹沒多少好書, 批壞無限奇文, 戻可惜也.126

A different commentator on the *Hsi-yu chi*, Chang Han-chang 張含章
(fl. 19th century), recognized the possible problems arising from his
commentarial procedure:

> As for how I have annotated the sentences and marked off the paragraphs
> in this volume, it is nothing more than unnatural manipulation [literally,
> making the ducks' feet long and the cranes' feet short], I have been forced
> into it, but it is a fact to be recognized. As for the breadth and depth of
> thought of the author and whether I have managed to capture it with my
> circumscribed vision, the book itself still remains, let the reader ponder it
> carefully. What need is there for me to say more?

則今之注句分章, 其續鳬斷鶴耶, 亦出于不得已也, 是亦不可不知者也. 至于
作者之弘深精詳, 與管見之是否, 全書具在, 請細玩之, 又何贅焉？127

Conclusion

The fact that traditional Chinese fiction criticism was so closely connected to several other types of literary and aesthetic criticism is simultaneously a source of strength and limitation. Much effort was surely saved
by the implementation of ready-made terminology, but at the same
time much confusion was engendered as a result of this practice due to
imprecision in the definition of terms and weakness for facile analogies.
In terms of the problem of the relatively low status of fictional composition in the vernacular language, the equation of fiction with other more
respected genres, such as classical prose and painting, no doubt had a
positive effect on some. However, the equally close association with
genres held in low esteem in some literati circles, such as the examination
essay and the whole practice of *p'ing-tien* itself, was liable in the end
(especially for the modern reader) to produce just the opposite effect.

---

[126] See item 75 in his "*Hsin-shuo Hsi-yu chi* tsung-p'i," quoted in *HYCTLHP*, p. 235.

[127] See the preface to his commentary on the *Hsi-yu chi*, *T'ung-I Hsi-yu cheng-chih*
通易西遊正旨 (The True Intent of the *Hsi-yu chi* Explained by Way of the *I Ching*),
quoted in *HYCTLHP*, p. 239.

(b) The Historical Development of Chinese Fiction Criticism Prior to Chin Sheng-t'an

Liu Ch'en-weng

In China the practice of writing *p'ing-tien* commentaries for works of fiction can be traced back to Liu Ch'en-weng's 劉辰翁 (1232–1297) commentary on the *Shih-shuo hsin-yü* 世說新語 (A New Account of Tales of the World) by Liu I-ch'ing 劉義慶 (403–444). That work, which is a collection of historical anecdotes, is not strictly speaking a work of fiction, but under traditional Chinese classification systems it was not placed with the standard historical works. Instead it was given pride of place near the beginning of lists of *hsiao-shuo* 小說 (usually translated as "fiction") in the *tzu* 子 or philosophy section. Six Dynasties fiction is usually divided into two main traditions, *chih-kuai* 志怪 (records of anomalies) and *chih-jen* 志人 (records of men). We can take Kan Pao's 干寶 (fl. A.D. 340) *Sou-shen chi* 搜神記 (A Record of Searching Out Spirits) as representative of the *chih-kuai* tradition and *Shih-shuo hsin-yü* as representative of the other. Both volumes put themselves forward as records of true events but were not accepted as history because of their subject matter, which was anecdotal rather than concerning itself with affairs of state. The anecdotes in *Shih-shuo hsin-yü* are arranged under more than thirty topical headings and are generally selected so that they point to a moral connected with their respective headings or reveal an aspect of the personality of the anecdote's main character.

Liu Ch'en-weng was a prolific writer of *p'ing-tien* commentaries for many different literary genres, but of all these it is only his *Shih-shuo hsin-yü* commentary and, to some extent, his work on the *Shih-chi* 史記 (Records of the Historian) that contain remarks dealing more specifically with the writing of fiction. The *Shih-shuo hsin-yü* commentary itself is very sketchy, but parts of it represent a very clear example of an important trend in traditional fiction criticism, the comparative evaluation of characters against each other. This concept is integral to the *Shih-shuo hsin-yü* itself as well as to other works of the Six Dynasties period such as Liu Shao's 劉邵 (fl. 3d century) *Jen-wu chih* 人物志, which was designed to help the ruler or the reader recognize human talent. One of the most common terms for this kind of comparative evaluation, *yüeh-tan* 月旦, also comes from this general time period, as does the institution of dividing the civil service into the so-called nine grades (*chiu-p'in* 九品). For instance, Liu Ch'en-weng draws attention to the implicit ranking of Kuan Ning (158–241), Hua Hsin (156–231), and Wang Lang (d. 228) in items eleven through thirteen in the first section of *Shih-shuo hsin-yü*, "Te-hsing" 德行 (Virtuous Conduct): "Kuan Ning is better than Hua Hsin, but Hua Hsin is better than Wang Lang. One cannot not discriminate between them."[1]

Li Chih

The next important figure in the development of traditional fiction criticism and fiction *p'ing-tien* was born almost three hundred years after Liu Ch'en-weng. It is true that, prior to or at approximately the same time as Li Chih 李贄 (1527–1602) was writing his commentary on the *Shui-hu chuan*, publishers such as Yü Hsiang-tou 余象斗 (ca. 1550–1637) were bringing out editions of longer-length fiction with commentary attached. Although these works are interesting for some of the attitudes toward fiction revealed obliquely in them, their comments do not generally extend beyond historical notes and subjective remarks on characters in the novels. In the case of the Yü Hsiang-tou editions of the *Shui-hu chuan* and the *San-kuo yen-i*, although the fact that they contain commentary is loudly proclaimed in the titles and a separate register is reserved in the top fourth of each page for the comments, it is fairly clear that the commentary was added to increase sales rather than project any particular interpretation of the texts. In addition, the commentator, usually identified as Yü Hsiang-tou himself, can never seem to set aside his identity as publisher of the work in his comments. Li Chih was a very different kind of figure and, like Liu Ch'en-weng, he had a great affection for the *Shih-shuo hsin-yü*.[2]

Li Chih was an iconoclastic figure whose dwelling was once burned by a mob and who, in the end, committed suicide in prison, where he was being held on charges based on complaints about his writings and style of life. His official career came to an end long before then. His highest appointment was Prefect of Yao-an in Yunnan Province, and it is reported that he was a good official who ruled through the force of

---

[1] Liu Ch'en-weng's comments are available in later editions of the work with commentary from several hands entitled *Shih-shuo hsin-yü pu* 世說新語補 (Supplement to a New Account of Tales of the World). His comments on Kuan Ning, etc., are quoted in *LCH*, vol. 1, p. 69.

[2] Li Chih's *Ch'u-t'an chi* 初潭集 (First Collection from Lung-t'an) contains his comments on the *Shih-shuo hsin-yü* and an updating of it by his friend Chiao Hung 焦竑 (1541–1610). Although its authenticity has been questioned, the *Shih-shuo hsin-yü pu* mentioned in n. 1 above also contains commentary by Li Chih and supplementary material by Chiao Hung, a preface by Chiao Hung mentioning Li Chih's commentary, as well as a preface and a "Statement of Editorial Principles" ("Fan-li" 凡例) signed Li Chih. If the latter piece is truly by Li Chih, then he was also responsible for the editing of that volume.

example. Be that as it may, one day he decided that he had had enough and, failing to get official permission, simply abandoned his post of office. The last several decades of his life were spent in writing his own works and writing commentaries on the works of others.

From his letters and the testimony of friends we know that Li Chih wrote a large number of commentaries on a variety of works that include fiction and drama as well as philosophy and belles-lettres. It is clear that he regarded some works of fiction and drama very highly, listing the *Shui-hu chuan* as part of a list of five great works that included the *Shih-chi* and the poetry of Tu Fu 杜甫 (712–770). Short remarks on four plays appear in the earliest published collection of his writing, the *Fen-shu* 焚書 (Book for Burning; first printing 1590). The commentary that receives the greatest amount of attention is one on the *Shui-hu chuan* which, if the testimony of Yüan Chung-tao 袁中道 (1570–1623) on the matter is to be believed, was in a state of completion justifying the making of a fair copy in 1592.[3] Even earlier, what is assumed to be the preface for this commentary appeared in the *Fen-shu*. Currently, however, the only major piece of writing on the *Shui-hu chuan* demonstrably attributable to Li Chih is just this preface. Although at least a half-dozen commentaries on that novel attributed to him are extant, there are reasons to be suspicious of them all; nevertheless, our suspicion should not lead us to rule out the idea that some of Li Chih's original commentary on the novel is partially preserved in one of these editions.[4] In terms of general interpretation, the extant "Li Chih" commentary on the *Shui-hu chuan* most in line with the preface preserved in the *Fen-shu* is that published by Yüan Wu-yai 袁無涯 in 1612 or slightly later. However, that interpretation, which takes Sung Chiang seriously as a nonproblematic example of a loyal servant of the state done wrong by petty men close to the throne, is rather disappointing in its lack of depth. That reading of the novel is also more similar to the preference for content over form expressed in his preface and elsewhere in his literary criticism, most particularly in "Tsa-shuo" 雜說 (Miscellaneous Remarks), which is included in *Fen-shu*. On the other hand, Li Chih is responsible for popularizing some important concepts, such as the difference between *hua-kung* 畫工 (artisanly achievement) and *hua-kung* 化工 (divine achievement) and the idea that literature is written to express resentment. He

---

[3] See his *Yu-chü Fei lu* 游居柿錄 (Travels in the Fei Region), relevant section quoted in *SHCTLHP*, p. 223.

[4] For a discussion of the authenticity of the commentaries on major novels attributed to Li Chih, see app. 2. For a review of recent scholarship on the problem, see the appendix in Andrew H. Plaks, *The Four Masterworks of the Ming Novel* (Princeton: Princeton University Press, 1987), pp. 513–17.

referred to this latter concept by borrowing a famous expression from Ssu-ma Ch'ien, *fa-fen chu-shu* 發憤著書 (express resentment through writing a book), or by the phrase "to t'a-jen chih chiu-pei chiao tzu-chi chih lei-k'uai" 奪他人之酒杯澆自己之壘塊 (borrow the other man's wine glass to assuage your own troubles).

In any case, for later commentators what seems to have been of the utmost importance in regard to Li Chih is the mere idea of such a well-known, albeit controversial, man spending his time writing them. The example was picked up by others, some of whom, such as Chin Sheng-t'an, attacked the "Li Chih" commentaries while at the same time being very indebted to them.

Yeh Chou

Besides the Yüan Wu-yai edition of the *Shui-hu chuan* with commentary mentioned above, the other most influential early commentary on a work of fiction is the Jung-yü t'ang edition of that novel, also with commentary attributed to Li Chih. That commentary was reprinted in 1610, but the date of the first edition is uncertain. Although conclusive evidence is lacking, scholarly opinion is now generally in agreement that this edition's commentary was by Yeh Chou 葉畫 (fl. 1595–1624).[5] He is also thought to be the author of commentaries on the *San-kuo yen-i* and the *Hsi-yu chi*. His name appears three times in the commentary on the *San-kuo yen-i*. In the words of one of his contemporaries: "He was always down on his luck but remained untrammeled. Although he was poor, he had a long-lasting fondness for wine. Sometimes he would sell the services of his pen to buy it."[6] He is supposed to have been beaten to death by the husband of a woman with whom he took up.[7] His contemporaries also claimed that he was the author of several commentaries on drama attributed to Li Chih, a number of which were also published by the Jung-yü t'ang of Hangchou.

Whether or not we need to take seriously the claim that Yeh Chou was the author of all of these commentaries, they do have a sort of family resemblance that seems to justify our taking them as the work of one

[5] For information concerning the evidence on Yeh Chou's connection with this commentary and others, see app. 2.

[6] Ch'ien Hsi-yen 錢希言, *Hsi-hsia* 戲瑕, *chüan* 3, "Yen-chi" 贋籍 (Forged Works), quoted in *SHCTLHP*, p. 151.

[7] See Sheng Yü-ssu 盛于斯, *Hsiu-an ying-yü* 修庵影語, and Chou Liang-kung 周亮工, *Yin-shu wu shu-ying* 因樹屋書影, quoted in Ts'ui Wen-yin 崔文印, "Yüan Wu-yai k'an-pen *Shui-hu* Li Chih p'ing pien-wei" 袁無涯刊本水滸李贄評辨偽 (On the Authenticity of the Li Chih Commentary on the *Shui-hu chuan* Printed by Yüan Wu-yai), *Chung-hua wen-shih lun-ts'ung* 中華文史論叢 (Collected Articles on Chinese Literature and History), 1980.2:311–17, p. 315.

man. Speaking in terms of style, we can point out a high proportion of lighthearted remarks in these commentaries. That proportion is estimated as seventy percent lighthearted to thirty percent serious in one of the prefatory pieces in the Jung-yü t'ang *Shui-hu chuan* commentary,[8] there is a similar remark in the "Fan-li" 凡例 (General Principles) of the *Hsi-yu chi* commentary,[9] and jokes and quips are much in evidence in the others as well. The commentator is also very critical toward the text he is commenting on, complaining about mistakes in grammar (see especially the early chapters in the *San-kuo yen-i* commentary), the poor quality of poetry included in the fiction (see the *Shui-hu chuan* commentary), and sections of the text that he considers not necessary. We can also point out shared vocabulary in these commentaries.

As for the content of the commentaries, there are a few recurring concepts. The commentator pays particular attention to discrepancies between the presentation of certain characters and what appears to be a different appraisal of their moral worth by the author, explaining some of these by attacking the text for being poorly written but interpreting others as examples of irony being turned against the characters. This is the case with several characters who are usually taken as nonproblematic in popular literature of the stage and the marketplace—Sung Chiang, Liu Pei, Chu-ko Liang, Tripitaka, etc. Part of this is connected with his dislike for *chia tao-hsüeh* 假道學 (moral hypocrisy). Although sometimes he seems to confuse the different properties of history and fiction,[10] he is generally supportive of the role of imaginative representation in fiction. Other topics of concern are the relationship between individual characters and types of character and the employment of different literary techniques.

Chung Hsing, Ch'en Chi-ju, and T'ang Hsien-tsu

Shortly after the appearance of the commentaries that we have speculated might be from the hand of Yeh Chou, a number of commentaries were published where it seems that, not only was the name of the commentator on the title page purloined, but substantial portions of the

---

[8] See item 2 of "P'i-p'ing *Shui-hu chuan* shu-yü" 批評水滸傳述語 (Recorded Remarks on Commenting on the *Shui-hu chuan*), quoted in *SHCTLHP*, p. 208.

[9] See p. 3a–b of the "Fan-li."

[10] See the prefatory material to the commentary on the *San-kuo yen-i*, quoted in Chu I-hsüan and Liu Yü-ch'en, eds., *San-kuo yen-i tzu-liao hui-pien* 三國演義資料彙編 (Collected Material on the *San-kuo yen-i*; Tientsin: Pai-hua wen-i, 1983), pp. 276–84; quotation of Yeh Chou's remarks on the *Shui-hu chuan* by Sheng Yü-ssu, quoted in *SHCTLHP*, p. 350; and comments on that novel in *Shu-chai man-lu* 樗齋漫錄 (Leisurely Notes from Useless Wood Studio), thought to have been written by Yeh Chou for Hsü Tzu-ch'ang 許自昌 (fl. 1596–1623), quoted in *SHCTLHP*, pp. 215–16.

commentary were as well. This is the case with the commentary on the
Shui-hu chuan attributed to Chung Hsing 鍾惺 (1574–1625)[11] and
dramatic commentaries attributed to Ch'en Chi-ju 陳繼儒 (1558–1639)
for six of the plays with commentary associated with Yeh Chou.[12]
Chung Hsing was famous for commentary editions of poetry and prose
such as *Ku-shih kuei* 古詩歸 (The Repository of Ancient Poetry), but it is
extremely unlikely that either the *Shui-hu chuan* commentary, or another
for the *San-kuo yen-i* attributed to him, or any of the third-rate historical
novels that appeared under his name have anything to do with him. The
San-kuo yen-i commentary is all new material, but substantial portions of
the prefatory matter and chapter comments in the *Shui-hu chuan* commentary have been borrowed without attribution from the Jung-yü
t'ang edition. As for Ch'en Chi-ju, there is a not particularly interesting
commentary under his name on an early version of the *Lieh-kuo chih*
列國志 (Romance of the Feudal States) with a preface dated 1615 that
might indeed be from his hand, but the dramatic commentaries are little
more than slightly expanded versions of the earlier commentaries.

T'ang Hsien-tsu 湯顯祖 (1550–1616) and Yüan Hung-tao 袁宏道
(1568–1610) were highly influential writers of the time, the former
known particularly for his dramatic works and the latter for his poetry
and prose. Commentary editions of plays and historical novels under
their names appeared after their deaths, but either the attributions are too
shaky or the content too prosaic to interest us.

Feng Meng-lung

Feng Meng-lung 馮夢龍 (1574–1646) is mainly known for his compilation of a total of 120 short stories collectively known as the *San-yen* 三言
(each of the titles of the three collections ends in the word *yen*), for which
he wrote the prefaces and brief comments; he never wrote a commentary on a novel. He did, however, leave a lasting mark on the novel of
his day through his rewriting of earlier works (such as the *P'ing-yao chuan*
平妖傳 [Pacification of the Demons] and the *Lieh-kuo chih*) and his connection with the publication (and editing) of other novels (such as the
Yüan Wu-yai edition of the *Shui-hu chuan*[13] and the first printing of the

---

[11] There is a microfilm of the Ssu-chih kuan edition (original held in the Bibliothèque
nationale, Paris) in the Gest Oriental Library of Princeton University.

[12] These six plays with commentary were later printed as a set with superb illustrations
under the general title, *Liu-ho t'ung ch'un* 六和同春 (Everywhere Spring), copy in Peking
University Library.

[13] See the remarks in the *Shu-chai man-lu* on his participation in the preparation of this
edition, *SHCTLHP*, p. 217.

Chin P'ing Mei[14]). Feng Meng-lung had very definite and generally archaic notions on the form according to which fiction should be written. He put those notions into practice in his rewriting of preexistent fiction, whether of novel or short story length, and verbalized them to some extent in his prefaces.

As for the history of Chinese fiction criticism in its maturity, that would take as its primary subject the history of the work of its major practitioners, six of whom are introduced to the reader in this volume by means of translations of representative samples of their work and brief introductions to their careers. The next two essays in this chapter will present a description of the formal features of this type of criticism and a discussion of the major concepts employed by traditional Chinese fiction critics.

[14] See the section in Shen Te-fu's 沈德符 (1578–1642) *Yeh-huo pien* 野獲編, quoted in *CPMTLHP*, p. 222. Many have speculated that Feng Meng-lung played a more pivotal part in the publication of this edition than Shen Te-fu's account indicates.

(c) Formal Aspects of Fiction Criticism and Commentary in China

From Private to Public Practice

This essay will describe briefly the main forms that traditional fiction criticism took in China, with particular emphasis on the commentarial tradition. As we have seen in the preceding essays, it is a time-honored and widespread practice in China for the reader to write in punctuation markings and add appreciative or substantive comments in the margins of his personal copy of a literary work to enhance his own mastery of the text. This routine was conceived of both as an aid for future reading and as a way of increasing the benefit derived by the reader in his initial encounter with the text by forcing him to take an active rather than passive stand toward the work.[1] It was possible to extend some of these benefits to other readers by marking the text with them in mind. This practice was used by teachers, who could test their students' understanding by having them mark the texts and then correct their markings or could guide the students through a text already marked in this manner.[2]

---

[1] Mao Tse-tung is supposed to have once said, "If you don't put your pen into action, it cannot really be considered reading." ("Pu tung pi-mo pu k'an shu" 不動筆墨不看書) Quoted in an anonymous article, "Tu-shu fang-fa man-t'an" 讀書方法漫談 (Leisurely Talks on Methods of Reading), pt. 2 of a series, Hsin-shu pao 新書報 (New Books), 5/28/1986, p. 4. This type of idea was extended explicitly to fiction by another writer: "Reading fiction is not as good as commenting on fiction, because only if he is going to make comments on it will the reader apply himself and read with care; only then will the reading have flavor. Otherwise, no matter how many times he reads it, the reader will not get any benefit from it." 讀小說不如評小說, 以欲評小說, 才肯用心細細讀, 方有趣味. 不然任他讀了若干遍, 未得一點好處. This unattributed comment is quoted in Liu Tao-en 劉道恩, "Wo-kuo ku-tai pi-chiao hsiao-shuo hsüeh yin-lun" 我國古代比較小說學引論 (An Introduction to Ancient Chinese Comparative Fiction Criticism), reprinted in Ku-chin, 1984.22:156–60, p. 160.

[2] The earliest mention of this type of practice occurs in the Li-chi 禮記 (Book of Rites), where it is called li-ching pieh-chih 離經別志. For a discussion of this passage, see Sun Te-ch'ien 孫德謙, Ku-shu tu-fa lüeh-li 古書讀法略例 (Brief Examples of How to Read Ancient Texts; Shanghai: Shang-hai shu-tien, 1983 reprint of 1936 Commercial Press original), p. 208 and Hsü K'o-wen 徐克文, "Shih-t'an Chung-kuo ch'uan-t'ung ti wen-hsüeh p'i-p'ing hsing-shih: p'ing-tien" 試談中國傳統的文學批評形式:評點 (On a Traditional Chinese Mode of Literary Criticism: P'ing-tien), reprinted in Ku-chin, 1983.6: 211–14, p. 212. Sun Te-ch'ien also mentions Tseng Kuo-fan's 曾國藩 (1811–1872) instruction that his family members be taught by this method, Ku-shu tu-fa lüeh-li, p. 207. For glimpses of this practice in Chinese fiction, see Ch'i-lu teng 歧路燈 (The Warning Light at the Crossroads; Cheng-chou: Chung-chou shu-she, 1980), p. 11.120 and Ching-hua yüan 鏡花緣 (The Fate of the Flowers in the Mirror; Peking: Jen-min wen-hsüeh, 1984), p. 22.154.

As printing and publishing expanded in China, the market for mass-produced, premarked texts of the type we are talking about also expanded. By the Ming dynasty (1368–1644), it was possible for literary figures to become famous through the publication of editions with their added textual markings (*ch'üan-tien* 圈點) and commentary (*p'i-p'ing* 批評). The preparation of editions of literary works with commentary and punctuation thus extends from a very personal level designed for private consumption all the way to a highly professionalized degree of commentary writing and diversification in terms of markets.

Informational Commentaries

The earliest commentaries written for public consumption dealt with classical texts and concentrated on presenting authoritative information to the reader. Some of these commentaries, such as the three early works on the *Ch'un-ch'iu* 春秋 (The Spring and Autumn Annals)—the *Kung-yang chuan* 公羊傳 (The Kung-yang Commentary), the *Ku-liang chuan* 穀梁傳 (The Ku-liang Commentary), and the *Tso-chuan* 左傳 (The Tso Commentary)—were eventually to gain the status of Confucian classics themselves and to become, in turn, the subject matter of other commentaries. This type of informational commentary was designed to meet the needs of readers unlucky enough not to have heard the Master (Confucius) or his disciples give the true interpretation of the classics. It was also designed to help the later reader bridge the gulf between the archaic language of the original texts and the language of the reader's time, a gap that could become quite severe in a relatively short period of time. In his commentary on *The Mencius, Meng Tzu chang-chü* 孟子章句 (Mencius by Paragraph and Sentence),[3] Chao Ch'i 趙岐 (d. A.D. 201) felt it necessary to include an almost complete paraphrase of the original using the grammar and vocabulary of his own day. The punctuation of the text into sentences is reinforced by Chao Ch'i's insertion of commentary at practically every break in the flow of Mencius's exposition.

The practical concerns in these informational commentaries can be broken down under several headings. At the most immediate level (following directly upon the quotation of the original text) are glosses on the pronunciation and meaning of obscure words along with help with difficult grammar and phrasing. What is aimed at here is an understanding on a linguistic and lexical level of what the text is saying, rather than appreciation or interpretation by commentator or reader. Some commentators also seek to improve the reader's understanding of a passage

---

[3] Included in the edition of the Thirteen Classics with commentary edited by Juan Yüan 阮元 (1764–1849), *Shih-san ching chu-shu* 十三經注疏.

through the quotation of supplementary material. The most famous examples of this type are probably P'ei Sung-chih's 裴松之 (372–451) commentary on the *San-kuo chih* 三國志 (Chronicle of the Three Kingdoms) and Li Shan's 李善 (630?–689) annotations to the *Wen-hsüan* 文選 (The Anthology of Refined Literature). Another feature at this level is the provision of textual variants.

A second level in these commentaries, sometimes standing at some remove from the letter of the text itself, is concerned primarily with matters of interpretation. This level is most striking and takes on the most importance when the text is not easily perceived as conveying any particular moral message. This is the case with a fair proportion of the commentary on the *Ch'un-chiu* and the love songs recorded in the "Kuo-feng" 國風 (Airs of the States) section of the *Shih-ching* 詩經 (Classic of Poetry).

The major differences between classical, informative commentaries of the type discussed above and the fiction commentaries that are the real focus of this volume are at least two in number: the fiction commentaries are little, if at all, concerned with lexical meaning or textual variants while, on the other hand, they are almost all concerned with questions of style and composition, something originally ignored in classical commentaries. Although modern readers often find themselves brought up short in old vernacular fiction before obscure expressions that have dropped out of currency, the idea that in vernacular fiction the language itself could cause problems for the reader is rarely given credence by writers or commentators. At the same time, the relative fullness of the narrative exposition when compared to the treatment of similar material in the historical or classical tradition also helps to eliminate the need for supplementary material to round out the picture.

Although less needed, informational commentaries on Chinese vernacular fiction do exist. The earliest extant edition of a full-length work of fiction, the *San-kuo chih t'ung-su yen-i* 三國志通俗演義 (A Popularization of the Chronicle of the Three Kingdoms; preface 1522), contains notes that quote from supplementary material and give information on items such as the contemporary names for archaic place names mentioned in the story. This novel was written in a simplified form of the literary language and was also able to lay claim to a certain amount of prestige through its avowed connection with esteemed historical texts. Such prestige was rarely accorded to novels or stories not promoted as popularizations of classical works and written in a more vernacular style. It was not until the eighteenth century that an annotated commentary for a novel of this latter type appeared—Ch'eng Mu-heng's 程穆衡 *Shui-hu chuan chu-lüeh* 水滸傳注略 (Concise Annotations to the

Water Margin; author's preface, 1779).[4] The existence of such a commentary for this particular novel is surely the product of the interest and respect won for the *Shui-hu chuan* by Chin Sheng-t'an, whose edition of the novel was enormously successful and influential.[5] At the same time, it also reflects the distance that readers of Ch'eng Mu-heng's day probably felt toward a novel they thought was composed some four hundred years before their time.

Stylistic Commentaries

The concern for style and compositional techniques found in fiction commentary also distinguishes it from classical commentary. This lack of attention to style in commentaries on the classics began to change in the middle of the Ming dynasty, perhaps under the combined weight of the interest in formal technique both in *ku-wen* 古文 (classical prose) and in examination essay criticism and the heavy current of archaism in Ming literature. Kuo Shao-yü has remarked that while scholars in the Ch'ing dynasty (1644–1911) viewed the Confucian classics primarily as historical documents, one could say that in the Ming dynasty the classics were taken primarily as literature.[6] According to him, the idea of writing stylistic commentaries on the classics dates from Mao K'un 茅坤 (1512–1601), although the most influential practitioner was Sun K'uang 孫鑛 (style Yüeh-feng 月峰).[7]

We can point out many instances of commentaries written in the latter part of the Ming dynasty that treat the Confucian classics as models of style and even go as far as to say that reading the classics is like reading popular fiction.[8] It is only by taking into account this new idea of

---

[4] The entire text of this work, which is keyed to the Chin Sheng-t'an 70-chapter edition but published without the text of the novel, is quoted in *SHCTLHP*, pp. 429–93, with additional entries by Wang K'ai-wo 王開沃 added in 1845.

[5] Wang T'ao 王韜 (1828–1897), in a preface to a late Ch'ing edition (1888) of the *Shui-hu chuan*, went so far as to say that the novel was not even well known before Chin Sheng-t'an. See *SHCTLHP*, p. 373 for a quotation of the entire preface.

[6] Kuo Shao-yü 郭紹虞, *Chung-kuo wen-hsüeh p'i-p'ing shih* 中國文學批評史 (A History of Chinese Literary Criticism; Shanghai: Hsin wen-i, 1955), p. 389.

[7] Ibid., pp. 389–90.

[8] For instance, there is the commentary in the *Ssu-shu p'ing* 四書評 (Comments on the Four Books) attributed to Li Chih but claimed for Yeh Chou 葉晝 (fl. 1595–1624) by contemporary writers such as Sheng Yü-ssu 盛于斯 (see the item "*Hsi-yu chi* wu" 西遊記誤 [Correction of an Error on the *Hsi-yu chi*]) in his *Hsiu-an ying-yü* 休庵影語, quoted in *HYCTLHP*, pp. 214–15. A modern reprint of the *Ssu-shu p'ing* was brought out in 1975 by the Jen-min ch'u-pan she in Shanghai. In a general comment on the eighteenth book of the *Confucian Analects* (*Lun-yü* 論語, "Wei-tzu" 微子), the commentator says that reading this section is just like reading popular fiction (p. 156 of the Shanghai edition).

viewing the classics not only as the source of societal values but also as models of composition that we can understand why Chin Sheng-t'an justifies his meticulous and sometimes very formalistic attention to stylistics in his commentary on the *Shui-hi chuan* by reference to devices he finds in the Confucian classics.[9]

A recognition of the eventual fluidity and lack of absolute boundaries between the different categories of commentary and their mutual cross-fertilization should not prevent us from seeing that, for practical purposes, a distinction between the methods and goals of commentaries on classical literature and those on fiction remained a part of the rhetoric of the commentators on fiction. On the one hand, the prestige of the classical commentaries was a source of envy to those working with less-respected materials. Calls for fiction commentaries that followed the model of commentaries on classical works contain at least two interesting assumptions about fiction made by those supporting such demands. First, some fictional works are of such value and importance as to merit such treatment, and second, fictional works are not as transparent in meaning as they were often taken to be. For instance, the Yu T'ung 尤侗 (1618–1704) preface to Mao Lun's commentary on the *P'i-p'a chi* 琵琶記 (Story of the Lute) places Mao Lun's name among the ranks of commentators on the *Chuang Tzu* 莊子 (by Chuang Chou, 369?–286? B.C.), the *Li-sao* 離騷 (Encountering Sorrow; by Ch'ü Yüan, 340?–278? B.C.), the *Shih-chi* 史記 (Records of the Historian; by Ssu-ma Ch'ien, b. 145 B.C.), and the poetry of Tu Fu 杜甫 (712–770).[10] A comparison of Mao Lun's work with that of the other commentators mentioned, however, shows him to be little indebted to their examples. On the other hand, writers on the *Hung-lou meng* argue that veiled topical references in that work require the broad learning and technical methods of classical commentators such as Li Shan and Liu Chün 劉峻 (462–521, author of a widely respected commentary to the *Shih-shuo hsin-yü* 世說新語 [A New Account of Tales of the World] which quotes a large amount of supplementary material).[11]

Control of Punctuation by Commentators

Commentators on Chinese fiction often made themselves responsible for more than just adding their comments to their editions of works of

---

[9] See the preface addressed to his son and dated 1641 in his *Shui-hu chuan* commentary, quoted in *SHCHPP*, p. 10.

[10] *Ti-ch'i ts'ai-tzu shu* 第七才子書 (The Seventh Work of Genius; n.p.: Ta-wen t'ang, 1735 reprint), Yu T'ung preface, dated 1665, p. 4b.

[11] Ch'en T'ui 陳蛻, "Lieh *Shih-t'ou chi* yü tzu-pu shuo" 列石頭記於子部說 (On Classifying the *Story of the Stone* as a Work of Philosophy), published in 1914 and quoted in *HLMC*, pp. 270–71.

fiction. They also supplied marks of punctuation and did some editing of their texts as well. The more concrete of these is the problem of punctuation, which we will take up first.

What we are referring to as punctuation actually involves a little more than the English word implies. As important as indicating reading pauses in the text by the insertion of commas and periods (*tou-tien* 讀點) was, in the Chinese editions marking certain sections for emphasis (by such techniques as placing boldface lines or symbols next to the sections involved) and providing other aids for the reader also played a role.

Some of the more theoretical aspects of this type of punctuation and the commentator's control of it are discussed in the last essay of this introductory section. Here we will restrict ourselves to a few remarks on some of the formal features of this practice.

Originally, Chinese texts were published without punctuation indicating pauses between clauses or sentences. A reader would often add marks (usually commas or circles) as he read to indicate these divisions for himself. Informal, private punctuation of this sort can often be found in old private copies of works later acquired by libraries. The marking of a text for reading and emphasis was called *ch'üan-tien* 圈點 (adding circles and dots) and the idea of "worth marking for emphasis" (*k'o-ch'üan k'o-tien* 可圈可點) exists as a common saying with fairly broad application.

This kind of punctuation and marking for emphasis is quite old. Early classical commentaries divided their texts up into paragraphs (*chang* 章) and sentences (*chü* 句) and the names of the commentaries often contained these two characters in their titles, as is the case with Chao Ch'i's *Meng Tzu chang-chü* mentioned above. In the T'ang dynasty (618–907) there is mention of the use of different colored inks (black and red) to mark the different kinds of emphasis and punctuation.[12] Editions of Chinese fiction and drama often have statements of editorial principles (*fan-li* 凡例) prefixed to them explaining unusual or new uses of punctuation in that particular edition. Sometimes the different marks were supposed to indicate what feature in the text was being highlighted according to a code explained in the *fan-li*. In the "Fan-li" written for the late Ming novel *Ch'an-chen i-shih* 禪真逸史 (The Unofficial History of the True Way), transitional passages are supposed to be marked with an open-centered comma (𝕯), "delightful" parts with open-centered circles (○), and powerful sections capable of providing warnings to

[12] Liu T'ui 劉蛻 (fl. first half of the 9th century), "Wen-ch'üan-tzu chi" 文泉子集. See Ch'ien Chung-lien 錢仲聯, "T'ung-ch'eng p'ai ku-wen yü shih-wen ti kuan-hsi wen-t'i" 桐城派古文與時文的關係問題 (The Problem of the Relationship of the Classical Prose of the T'ung-ch'eng School to Examination Essays) in *T'ung-ch'eng p'ai yen-chiu lun-wen chi* 桐城派研究論文集 (Collected Research Papers on the T'ung-ch'eng School; Hofei: An-hui jen-min, 1963), pp. 153–54.

the reader are to be marked with a solid comma (🌢).[13] According to
the "Fan-li" of an edition of selections of classical prose with commentary by Lin Yün-ming 林雲銘 (1658 chin-shih), places of central importance (chu-nao ch'u 主腦處) and summation (chieh-hsüeh ch'u 結穴處) are
marked with concentric circles (◎) and elements of forward and
retroactive projection (mai-fu 埋伏, chao-ying 照應) are indicated with
elongated commas, while other sections worthy of note are marked with
open-centered circles.[14]

Punctuation could also be used by the editor or commentator to set
off other features of the text. For instance, in the *Ch'en Mei-kung hsien-
sheng p'i-p'ing Ch'un-ch'iu Lieh-kuo chih-chuan* 陳眉公先生批評春秋列國
志傳 (The Romance of the Contending States of the Ch'un-ch'iu
Period, with Commentary by Ch'en Chi-ju; preface 1615), the names of
the various states and kingdoms mentioned in the text are circled and
personal names are underlined.[15]

Not everyone was satisfied with having the texts of novels marked
up in this way. In one section of the *Hung-lou meng tu-fa* essay, Chang
Hsin-chih said that there was no need for all these odd marks of emphasis
because a good commentary would clearly point out these features to the
reader.[16] However, the commentator's control over emphasis and punctuation was a powerful tool that could be used to condition the reader's
response to the text. Chin Sheng-t'an, in particular, seems to have taken
great pleasure in tinkering with the punctuation in the *Shui-hu chuan*. At
worst, the effect is merely distracting, but when well done it has the
beneficial result of forcing the reader to slow up and appreciate some of
the nuances in the text.

We should note here in passing that although it was usually the
commentator's responsibility to do some of the punctuation of the text
of the fictional work that he was working on,[17] his commentary itself
was often published in unpunctuated form. Sometimes, in the original

---

[13] This "Fan-li" is quoted in *LCH*, vol. 1, p. 274.

[14] *Ku-wen hsi-i* 古文析義 (Analysis of Classical Prose; n.p., preface dated 1716, copy
held in the Far Eastern Library, University of Chicago).

[15] In other commentaries, the circling of characters was also used for emphasis. Some
Chinese characters have different meanings according to which tone the character is read
with. Sometimes small circles are placed at one of the corners of a character to indicate an
unusual reading of the character.

[16] See chap. VII below, item 28.

[17] For representative statements by commentators indicating their responsibility for
adding punctuation and emphasis, see item 2 of the "Fan-li" 凡例 (General Principles) of
Chang Chu-p'o's commentary on the *Chin P'ing Mei*, quoted in *CPMTLHP*, p. 1, and
the *tu-fa* essay in Qasbuu's (Chinese transliteration: Ha-ssu-pao 哈斯寶) translation with
commentary of the *Hung-lou meng* into Mongolian (Chinese title: *Hsin-i Hung-lou meng*
新譯紅樓夢), translated by I Lin-chen 亦鄰真 and quoted in *HLMTLHP*, p. 772.

edition, the commentary itself was punctuated, but later editions dropped the punctuation.[18] It is also sometimes the case that not only the
commentary but the text of the novel itself is printed without punctuation, as is true of the Wo-hsien ts'ao-t'ang edition of the *Ju-lin wai-shih*.
In this text, as well as in some others, interlineal comments such as the
single word *chü* 句 (sentence) are occasionally inserted to guide the reader
through important or tricky breaks between sentences. Chang Chu-p'o
uses a similar technique to break up the speech of some of the characters
in the *Chin P'ing Mei* when they are making love so as to better simulate
their out-of-breath condition and to add a touch of realism to the depiction.[19]

Western-style punctuation for editions of traditional Chinese novels
was first introduced by the Oriental Book Company in Shanghai after
World War I. The editor of these volumes, Wang Yüan-fang 汪原放,
also took the bold step of removing all the old commentaries from his
editions and was praised on both accounts by the "father" of the Chinese
"Cultural Renaissance," Hu Shih 胡適 (1891–1962).[20]

Indications of Subdivisions in the Text

Chinese texts are not divided into paragraphs, and in novels the smallest
subdivision used is the chapter (called variously: *hui* 回, *chüan* 卷, or
tse 則). Commentators and editors were aware of the difficulties that
this presents to the reader[21] and developed many strategies to point out
subchapter divisions to the reader. In editions from Fukien (so-called
Min-pen 閩本) which ran illustrations across the top third of each page,
the captions of the illustrations are usually a good indication of the
content of the text below. This same idea, but without the illustrations, is
used in Hsiung Ch'ing-po's 熊清波 *San-kuo ch'üan-chuan* 三國全傳
(Complete Story of the Three Kingdoms), dated 1596, which runs a six-
character heading at the top of each page to refer to the most important
event treated on that page.

The physical separation of the text into paragraphs (*chang* 章) on the

[18] According to Liu Fu's 劉復 (1891–1934) 1934 preface to a reprint of Chin Sheng-
t'an's *Shui-hu chuan*, this was the case with some of the later editions of that work. The
preface is quoted in the San-min shu-chü (Taipei) 1961 photo-reprint of an early edition
of the Chin Sheng-t'an commentary.

[19] See, for example, a double-column interlineal comment on p. 61/10a of the reprint
of the 1695 Tsai-tzu t'ang 在茲堂 edition of the *Chin P'ing Mei*, TICS.

[20] See his "*Shui-hu chuan* k'ao-cheng" 水滸傳考證 (A Critical Study of the *Shui-hu
chuan*), first printed in the 1920 Oriental Book Company edition of that novel. The essay
is collected in Hu Shih 胡適, *Chung-kuo chang-hui hsiao-shuo k'ao-cheng* 中國章回小說
考證 (Critical Studies on Chinese Novels; Shanghai: Shang-hai shu-tien, 1979), pp. 1–63.
See esp. p. 1.

[21] See chap. VII below, item 14 of the *Hung-lou meng tu-fa* essay.

model of classical commentaries such as Chu Hsi's 朱熹 (1130–1200) editions of the Four Books, where all of the paragraphs are numbered sequentially, never became an important part of the fiction commentary tradition. A variant of it was used by Chin Sheng-t'an in his commentary on the *Hsi-hsiang chi* 西廂記 (Romance of the Western Chamber), in which he divides and numbers the text of each scene of the play into so many *chieh* 節 (sections). As part of his campaign to discredit the fifth act of the play, he complains in this last part of not being able to find the joints between the sections.[22]

In most of the fiction commentaries, the reader's attention is drawn to subdivisions in the text by interlineal and marginal comments that point them out on the page or by their being listed in the chapter comments at the beginning or the end of the chapter.[23] Some commentators who pay particular attention to this aspect of criticism are Chin Sheng-t'an, Chang Chu-p'o, Wang Hsi-lien 王希廉 (fl. 1832–1875), and Chang Hsin-chih.

Marking for Excision

In our discussion of the adding of marks of emphasis by the commentators above, we did not mention that they also had at their disposal ways to indicate graphically their displeasure with specific sections of the text. This was called *t'u-mo* 塗抹 (blotting or crossing out) and was conceived to be the opposite of *ch'üan-tien*.[24] In private life, when a teacher cor-

---

[22] In the rest of the commentary, each of his "postsection" comments is always prefixed by the words, "above is section number x," but in the last act he makes such comments as "This seems to be a section, but since it is not really connected to or separate from what follows, it is hard to be sure." See *Ti-liu ts'ai-tzu Hsi-hsiang chi* 第六才子 西廂記 (Sixth Work of Genius, Romance of the Western Chamber; Taipei: Wen-kuang t'u-shu, 1978), p. 290 (act 5, scene 1). This is a photo-reprint of a 1720 reprint of the original with added commentary.

[23] The practice of marking off sections of the text with small wedges to the left of the last character, used frequently in examination essay and classical prose criticism, does not seem to figure in fiction criticism, except in the case of the thirty *chüan* "Li Chih" commentaries on the *Shui-hu chuan*, where such markers are the only indicators of chapter divisions. Oddly enough, the tendency of some critics such as Chin Sheng-t'an and Chang Chu-p'o to break the text up into fragments for the purpose of discussion has its parallel in Roland Barthes's technique of dividing a text into "lexias," as in his *S/Z* (trans. Richard Miller, New York: Hill and Wang, 1974), a very detailed commentary on Balzac's novella *Sarrazine*.

[24] The two terms are used in this way in the seventh item of the "Fan-li" to Mao Tsung-kang's edition of the *San-kuo yen-i*. At an early time, *mo* 抹 indicated elongated strokes of ink placed next to a character for emphasis, a practice that actually seems to predate the circles and dots used later, but I have come across no examples of this kind of *mo* used to express displeasure with the characters that it accompanies.

rected his students' compositions or an editor prepared drafts for publication, it was indeed the practice to cross out sections of the text to be
deleted or changed.[25] The texts were not, however, published with
sections crossed out, so when we are dealing with a printed edition with
commentary it is a slightly different practice that is meant by the words
t'u-mo. On the one hand, it refers to the physical marking off of sections
with brackets and underlining ([_____]), accompanied usually by
derogatory comments or, on the other, to the practice of deleting the
offending passages before publication.

Li Chih (1527–1602) used the words *t'u-mo* when talking about his
work on the plays *Hsi-hsiang chi* and *P'i-p'a chi*: "The commentary on
the *Shui-hu chuan* turned out quite well, but the deletions (*t'u-mo* 塗抹)
and changes (*kai-ts'uan* 改竄) I made in the *Hsi-hsiang chi* and the *P'i-p'a
chi* turned out even more marvelously."[26] An examination of the extant
editions of these two plays with commentary attributed to Li Chih does
not turn up any indication that the texts have been heavily edited over
previous versions. Instead, we find numerous passages boxed off on three
sides with comments usually ending in the word *shan* 刪 (cut!). All of the
Jung-yü t'ang 容與堂 editions of fiction and drama with commentary
attributed to Li Chih use this kind of device liberally to point out
sections of the text the commentator would like to see removed, as do
editions with commentary based on them, such as the drama commentaries attributed to Ch'en Chi-ju.

Why not just cut the passages before the woodblocks for the editions
were prepared? In these types of editions the commentator seems to get a
certain amount of satisfaction from pointing out negative as well as
positive features in his text. In effect, the commentator is saying that he
could have done a better job than the author himself. In these early
editions of fiction and drama with commentary, it is also the case that the
commentary is more of a supplement to than a main part of the total
text. The amount of thought, time, and effort put into these editions
seems to have been quite small. If they were indeed prepared by a hired
pen such as Yeh Chou 葉晝 (fl. 1595–1624), it is understandable that such
a person would not invest too much time in the project. In any case,
these commentators did not have the problem of publishers of more
formal and respected genres where any editorial changes would be noticed

[25] This practice can easily be seen in the *Ch'ien-lung ch'ao-pen pai-nien hui Hung-lou meng
kao* 乾隆抄本百廿回紅樓夢稿 (The Ch'ien-lung 120-Chapter Manuscript Draft of the
Hung-lou meng; Shanghai: Shang-hai ku-chi, 1984 photo-reprint of the original).

[26] Li Chih 李贄, letter to Chiao Hung 焦竑 (1541–1620), included in *Hsü Fen-shu*
續焚書 (Book for Burning, Continued; Peking: Chung-hua shu-chü, 1959), pp. 34–35
and quoted in *SHCTLHP*, p. 191.

and protested against. Fang Pao 方苞 (1668–1749), "founder" of the
T'ung-ch'eng school of classical prose writing, found it necessary to
adopt the less intrusive device of marking the texts in his selection of
classical prose, *Ku-wen yüeh-hsüan* 古文約選 (Concise Selection of Classical Prose), rather than taking the scissors in hand and cutting out
offending passages. In his "Fan-li" to the collection he said:

> Although they [the texts] have been passed down and recited for genera-
> tions, it is perhaps unavoidable that there are digressions or superfluous
> expressions in them. However, it is not quite fitting to rashly chop these
> out, so I have merely marked these passages with lines at one side, so as to
> allow freedom for the reader to make up his own mind.

> 雖舉世傳誦之文, 義枝辭冗者, 或不免矣. 未便削去, 姑鈎划於旁, 俾觀者別擇
> 焉.[27]

Commentators and Editorial Changes

Beginning perhaps with the Yüan Wu-yai 袁無涯 and Chin Sheng-t'an
editions of the *Shui-hu chuan*, some commentators not only took on
editorial responsibilities, but also sat down and extensively rewrote sections of their texts. It was still felt to be necessary, however, to attribute
such changes to an earlier edition of the text (*ku-pen* 古本) that had come
into the hands of the commentator and was superior (i.e., closer to the
author's original version) to the popular editions (*fang-pen* 坊本, *su-pen*
俗本). In this the fiction commentators were carrying on a Ming dynasty
literary tradition. For instance Yang Shen 楊慎 (1488–1559), a very
respected literary figure praised by Li Chih among others, whose works
are a source for poetry used in commentary editions of novels,[28] changed
the text of a Tu Mu 杜牧 (803–852) poem to suit his own ideas of how
it should read, asserting that the popular editions were wrong.[29]

　　The importance of this editing activity in the seventeenth century has
been pointed out by Robert E. Hegel in his *The Novel in Seventeenth-
Century China*. He states that although few of the novels written during
that century attained prominence, it was the recensions of the *San-kuo
yen-i*, the *Shui-hu chuan*, the *Hsi-yu chi*, and the *Chin P'ing Mei* produced

---

[27] Quoted in Chou Chen-fu 周振甫, *Wen-chang li-hua* 文章例話 (Prose Criticism with
Examples; Peking: Chung-kuo ch'ing-nien, 1983), p. 392. However, examination of
editions of the *Ku-wen yüeh-hsüan* reveals only a very sparing use of this technique.

[28] The opening poem in Mao Tsung-kang's edition of the *San-kuo yen-i* comes from
Yang Shen's *Nien-wu shih t'an-tz'u* 念五史彈詞 (The Twenty-five Standard Histories in
Verse and Prose), sec. 3. See *Nien-wu shih t'an-tz'u chi-chu* 念五史彈詞輯註 (The Twenty-
five Standard Histories in Verse and Prose with Collected Annotations; Shanghai: Ch'iu-
ku chai shu-t'ieh she, 1918), p. 3/1a.

[29] See Chou Chen-fu 周振甫, *Shih-tz'u li-hua* 詩詞例話 (Poetry Criticism with Examples; Peking: Chung-kuo ch'ing-nien, 1962), pp. 52–53.

in that century that became the most popular and influential examples of the genre.[30] The commentators were often quite proud of their work in this connection, calling attention to the changes with fatherly pride, even as they energetically denied their paternity.

As time passed, it became possible to forego the ruse of having discovered an old edition that had all of one's editorial corrections already in it. Ts'ai Ao 蔡奡 (courtesy name Yüan-fang 元放), a rather pedestrian but extremely prolific commentator on Chinese fiction in the last half of the eighteenth century, also greatly reworked the texts of the novels for which he produced commentaries—the *Lieh-kuo chih* 列國志 (Romance of the Feudal States), the *Shui-hu hou-chuan* 水滸後傳 (Continuation of the *Shui-hu chuan*), and the *Hsi-yu chi*.[31] He apparently did not feel the need to spend too much time justifying the changes he made. By the end of the nineteenth century, when Yü Yüeh 俞樾 (1821–1907) published his heavily edited version of *San-hsia wu-i* 三俠五義 (Three Knights and Five Stalwarts), he could say in the preface: "Why should I be afraid of making changes? When the spirit moved me I made changes. There is no need to act like Chin Sheng-t'an and attribute every change to an 'old edition.'"[32] The editor of the Ch'i-hsing t'ang 齊省堂 edition (1874) of the *Ju-lin wai-shih* is very forthright about the changes made in the original text and in the chapter comments taken over from the Wo-hsien ts'ao-t'ang edition.[33]

Placement of Comments

In printed editions of Chinese fiction the most convenient place for a reader or commentator to start to add his own comments is on the margins at the top of the page, on the last page of each chapter, and, in a pinch, between the lines of the text. The texts of Chinese woodblock editions are surrounded on four sides (before the sheets are folded to produce a recto and verso side) by solid lines (*pien-lan* 邊欄) that delineate the margins. The upper margin is usually quite substantial, and comments written there are called *mei-p'i* 眉批 (literally, eyebrow notes, but translated as marginal comments in this volume). In some editions, such as the *Li Li-weng p'ing-yüeh San-kuo chih* 李笠翁評閱三國志 (*San-kuo yen-i* with Commentary by Li Yü), the only type of comment used is the

---

[30] *The Novel in Seventeenth-Century China* (New York: Columbia University Press, 1981), p. 227.

[31] For an analysis of Ts'ai Ao's revision of the *Shui-hu hou-chuan*, see Ellen Widmer, *The Margins of Utopia* (Cambridge, Mass.: Harvard University Press, 1987).

[32] See his 1884 preface to the *Ch'i-hsia wu-i* 七俠五義 (Seven Knights and Five Stalwarts), quoted in *LCH*, vol. 1, p. 631.

[33] See the "Li-yen" 例言 to this edition, quoted in *JLWSYCTL*, pp. 132–33.

marginal comment. In that edition the marginal comments are separated
from the text by the usual solid lines, but above and to either side are
thinner dark lines enclosing them, thus creating a separate register for the
marginal comments with a clean margin above them. A separate upper
register reserved for marginal comments is also used in the Yü Hsiang-
tou 余象斗 (ca. 1550–1637) editions of the *Shui-hu chuan* and the *San-kuo
yen-i*.

Marginal Comments   Because the marginal comment is written above
the text at some distance from the passage to which it refers there is a
potential for confusion as to what the comment is annotating. Again, as
ample as some of the margins might be, there is really no room to
indicate in detail the context of the comment. A technique commonly
used to avoid ambiguity and questions as to which marginal comment
refers to what in the text involves placing the comment over the passage
referred to and highlighting that passage in the text by adding circles or
other marks of emphasis such as underlining (since the text actually reads
from top to bottom, the underlining is placed to the right of the characters and is called underlining here by analogy rather than as a description of where the lines are placed). Another technique used in the Yü
Hsiang-tou editions mentioned above is to prefix the comments with
short phrases, such as "comment on_____" (*p'ing*_____ 評 _____),
where the blank portion is the name of the character or incident commented on.

Some editions break up the material contained in the marginal comments into categories and print them in two different registers above the
text. In such cases the outermost layer of marginal comments usually
deals with more general topics not necessarily keyed to a specific passage
on the page on which they appear. Comments of this type (usually called
ting-p'i 頂批)[34] are often very similar to chapter comments in terms of
content and style.

When an edition with marginal comments is republished or re-
copied, it is common to convert these comments into double-column

---

[34] For an example of a commentary edition that uses both *ting-p'i* and regular *mei-p'i*,
see Li Fu-chiu 李夫九 and Huang Jen-fu 黃仁黼, eds., *Ku-wen pi-fa pai-p'ien* 古文筆法百篇
(Examples of Classical Prose Technique in One hundred Selections; Ch'ang-sha: Yüeh-
lu shu-she, 1983), typeset reprint of 1882 edition. A similar arrangement is used when
there are multiple commentators, such as in the *p'ing-lin* 評林 (Forest of Comments)
editions of the *Shih-chi* 史記 (Records of the Historian) and the *Han-shu* 漢書 (History of
the Han Dynasty) of the late Ming. One late Ch'ing edition of the Mao Tsung-kang
commentary on the *San-kuo yen-i* (1890, Shang-hai shu-chü) printed the chapter comments as *ting-p'i*.

interlineal comments (*shuang-hang chia-p'i* 雙行夾批) inserted into the text immediately after the passage to which they refer. This, of course, leaves the upper margin free for new comments. This process of accretion is very evident in the various manuscript copies of the *Hung-lou meng* with commentary by Chih-yen chai 脂硯齋 (Red Inkstone Studio).

Interlineal Comments   A similar process occurs in the case of comments written in between the lines of the text, referred to as *p'ang-p'i* 旁批 or *ts'e-p'i* 側批 and translated in this volume as single-column interlineal comments. These comments are necessarily quite short because of the extreme lack of space and are usually restricted to brief, formulaic interjections. They are not a favored form in printed texts, appearing with greater frequency in manuscripts.[35] Occasionally these types of comments are written in between marks of emphasis (circles or commas) or set into the underlining of important sections of the text.

Chapter Comments   There are often a couple of lines of blank space on the last page of each chapter in a Chinese novel, and in editions that always start the next chapter on the recto side of the page, there is often a whole empty page that can be used to record comments. It is therefore understandable that chapter comments (*hui-p'i* 回批 or *hui tsung-p'i* 回總批) of short to moderate length tend to be appended at the end of the chapters rather than being placed at the beginning. The most notable exceptions to this rule are those commentators whose chapter comments are very prolix, such as Chin Sheng-t'an, Mao Tsung-kang, and Chang Chu-p'o. As for the early commentaries, such as those attributed to Li Chih on the *Shui-hu chuan* and other novels, the end of the chapter is the favored place for chapter comments. The economic aspects behind this are particularly evident in the edition of the *Shui-hu chuan* with commentary attributed to Chung Hsing 鍾惺 (courtesy name Po-ching 伯敬, 1574–1625). At the end of some of the chapters there is not enough blank space for even the quite abbreviated chapter comments of this edition, so the comments are cut in double columns of reduced size in order to squeeze them onto the page.

Ordinarily, the chapter comments are printed in characters the same size as those in the text and are indented a couple of characters from the

[35] Similar to this kind of comment are those written in any available blank space in the body of the text, such as at the end of an indented section. This kind of comment occurs in manuscript copies (such as the Chih-yen chai commentary on the *Hung-lou meng*) and printed editions (such as the Jung-yü t'ang edition of the *Shui-hu chuan*) and has been labeled *t'e-p'i* 特批 (special comment) by Ch'en Ch'ing-hao 陳慶浩 in the introduction to his edited collection of Chih-yen chai comments, *CYCPYCC*.

top of the page. They are prefixed by such headings as *tsung-p'i* 總批, *tsung-p'ing* 總評, or presented as a quotation (i.e., *Li Cho-wu yüeh* 李卓吾曰, "Li Chih says"). Sometimes several separate comments are involved in the chapter comment as a whole. They can be set off from each other by prefixing a heading (*yu-yüeh* 又曰) or by merely starting the new comment at the top of the next line. Chapter comments tend to deal with the more general subjects that interlineal or marginal comments do not have the space to handle.

Chapter comments that are placed before the chapter tend to be more developed and run for a page or two in length in the Chin Sheng-t'an edition of the *Shui-hu chuan* and the Mao Tsung-kang edition of the *San-kuo yen-i*. As is the case with chapter comments placed at the end of the chapter, discussion of separate topics is broken up into paragraphs. Some editions, such as Chang Shu-shen's 張書紳 *Hsin-shuo Hsi-yu chi* 新說西遊記 (A New Explication of the *Hsi-yu chi*) and some of the manuscript versions of the Chih-yen chai commentary on the *Hung-lou meng*, use chapter comments both before and after the chapters, but this is rather rare.

From one point of view, it seems more natural to place the chapter comments after the chapter, so that the reader will have the contents of the chapter fresh in his mind when he reads the comments. When the chapter comments precede the text and deal with a great amount of detail, as happens with Chin Sheng-t'an in particular, it seems unlikely that a first-time reader would get very much from such comments. However, the implied reader that emerges from between the lines of most of the extended commentaries is a person who is assumed to have already read the novel at least once and to have a respectable degree of control over the text. The effect of reading chapter comments before or after the chapter itself is, of course, very different. The feeling of placing one's sensibilities in the hands of the commentator when one reads the commentary before the text can be quite pronounced. It is perhaps for this reason that Liu I-ming in his *tu-fa* essay on the *Hsi-yu chi* warns the beginning student against turning to the commentaries before spending a lot of time with the novel itself.[36]

The material treated in chapter comments varies greatly from novel to novel and from commentator to commentator. Some writers are primarily interested in chronology and logical consistency in the narrative. In a separate work on the *Hung-lou meng*, the *Tu Hung-lou meng kang-ling* 讀紅樓夢綱領, Yao Hsieh 姚燮 (1805–1864) treated such topics extensively; the chapter comments he wrote for the novel published in

---

[36] See items 44 and 45 in chap. VI below.

the series of texts entitled *Tseng-p'ing pu-t'u Shih-t'ou chi* 增評補圖石頭記 (*Story of the Stone* with Added Commentary and Illustrations) are also confined almost entirely to such subjects. In some commentaries, such as that attributed to Chung Hsing on the *Shui-hu chuan* (*Chung Po-ching hsien-sheng p'i-p'ing Shui-hu chung-i chuan* 鍾伯敬先生批評水滸忠義傳), the chapter comments are really little more than a few lines of evaluation of the characters and incidents treated in the chapter and pay no attention to composition or language. One of the preferred topics dealt with by more structurally oriented critics like Chin Sheng-t'an, Mao Tsung-kang, and Chang Chu-p'o is the way that the chapter about to be read relates to the one immediately preceding it, while other critics such as Wang Hsi-lien and Chang Hsin-chih are more interested in how particular chapters fit into structural divisions that encompass several chapters at a time. Finally, there are commentators such as Chin Sheng-t'an who take advantage of the reader's attention and indulgence to work all kinds of extraneous and only tangentially related material into their chapter comments.[37]

To summarize, the main categories of comments to be found accompanying the text of each chapter are chapter, marginal, and interlineal comments. The interlineal comments can be further broken down into double- and single-column interlineal comments. In some editions the inserted double-column interlineal comments can take up almost as much space on the page as the text proper, but the amount of material that can be written in single-column interlineal comments is quite limited and amounts to a mere fraction of the total number of characters on any one page.

Other Material: Prefaces

Aside from the commentary for each chapter printed alongside the text of the novel, one also has to consider the variety of essays, prefaces, and other kinds of material printed before and after the fictional text begins and ends. The first of these to be encountered by the reader is usually the preface (*hsü* 序).

Under primary consideration here are prefaces written by the commentator or by persons acquainted with him. Two general kinds of material are treated in prefaces written by the commentator himself.

---

[37] One of the most striking of these is surely his short essay on an artist whose performance consists of making an enormous variety of noises with his mouth while hidden behind a screen ("K'ou-chi" 口技), which is inserted into the chapter comments on chap. 65 of the *Shui-hu chuan* (*SHCHPP*, p. 1191). Equally extravagant is his list of "pleasurable things" in the prescene comments to scene 2 of act 4 of the *Hsi-hsiang chi* (Wen-kuang t'u-shu edition), pp. 250–54.

Sometimes the commentator's preface is almost entirely concerned with presenting the genesis and history of the project of writing the commentary, as is the case with Chang Hsin-chih's preface to his commentary on the *Hung-lou meng*.[38] For other writers, the preface is an opportunity to present their general point of view on the piece of fiction that concerns them or to justify their own commentary. In brief, these prefaces try to establish that fiction in general is worthy of serious consideration and that among all the famous works of fiction the particular piece picked by the commentator is superior to the rest for the variety of reasons cited. The commentator may try to establish that his work of fiction is universally superior to the others or is so at least in certain aspects. This seems to be the primary concern in the Li Yü preface to the commentary edition on the *San-kuo yen-i* attributed to him and in Wang Hsi-lien's preface to his own commentary on the *Hung-lou meng*. Sometimes in his preface the commentator is eager to clarify how his commentary surpasses or builds upon earlier commentaries written on the same piece of fiction. For instance, in Liu I-ming's first preface to his *Hsi-yu yüan-chih* 西遊原旨 (The Original Intent of the *Hsi-yu chi*) he criticizes the commentary of Wang Hsiang-hsü 汪象旭 (fl. 1605–1668) and claims to be following the work of Ch'en Shih-pin 陳士斌, whose commentary on the novel is titled *Hsi-yu chen-ch'üan* 西遊真詮 (The True Explication of the *Hsi-yu chi*; preface 1696).

The most prolific and complicated preface writer among our commentators is Chin Sheng-t'an, who wrote three separate prefaces for his edition of the *Shui-hu chuan* and composed a fourth preface in the name of Shih Nai-an 施耐庵, championed by him as the author of the real *Shui-hu chuan*. There is a division of labor among the first three prefaces as well as stylistic differences among them. The first preface is a long and convoluted argument in which he ends up comparing the expected effect of the abolition of private unauthorized writing of books through the publication of his commentary with the effect of the burning of books by the first emperor of the Ch'in dynasty (r. 221–210 B.C.). The second preface deals with the problem of the morality of the novel (which tends to lionize brigands and thieves), while the third preface changes tack again. This preface is addressed to his son and recommends the reading of the book and commentary as a beneficial pedagogical experience.

---

[38] Quoted in *HLMC*, pp. 34–35. Other examples include Ts'ai Ao's 蔡昇 preface to the *Hsi-yu cheng-tao ch'i-shu* 西遊證道奇書 (The Extraordinary Book of the Way of Enlightenment through the *Hsi-yu chi*), microfilm of the prefatory matter of this edition held in the Gest Oriental Library, Princeton University; Chang Shu-shen's 張書紳 preface to his *Hsin-shuo Hsi-yu chi* 新說西遊記, quoted in *HYCTLHP*, p. 221; and Liu I-ming's two prefaces to his *Hsi-yu yüan-chih*, quoted in *HYCTLHP*, pp. 244–45, 254.

Many editions of fiction with commentary also contain prefaces by persons other than the commentator. These tend to present supplementary material on the commentator and his commentary.[39] Some of these prefaces end up being little more than endorsements by famous literary men or powerful patrons. Although the "Chin Sheng-t'an" preface included in some of the Mao Tsung-kang editions of the *San-kuo yen-i* is a forgery, it presents a full-blown example of this type. After first elevating the status of the novel to the rank of "number one work of genius" (directly contradicting Chin Sheng-t'an's appraisal of it in the *Shui-hu chuan tu-fa* essay, item six), "Chin Sheng-t'an" introduces "Mr. Mao" to the reading audience and recommends his work as a worthy substitute for the commentary that he himself had planned to write but was forced to put off because of illness. This fictional concoction illustrates the outlines of this type of preface very nicely, but legitimate examples also abound.[40]

Statements of Editorial or Commentarial Principles

The *fan-li* 凡例 or *li-yen* 例言 is a standard feature of Chinese editions in which the editor or commentator explains unusual features of the volume or makes clear his stand on certain issues concerning editorial or commentarial practice treated item by item. The more interesting documents of this type occurring in commentarial editions of the six most famous Chinese novels are the "P'i-p'ing *Shui-hu chuan* shu-yü" 批評 水滸傳述語 (Recorded Remarks on Commenting on the *Shui-hu chuan*) in the Jung-yü t'ang edition of the *Shui-hu chuan*, purporting to be based on the words of Li Chih written down by his monk friend, Huai-lin 懷林; the "Fa-fan" 發凡 of the Yüan Wu-yai edition of the *Shui-hu chuan*; the "Fan-li" of Mao Tsung-kang's edition of the *San-kuo yen-i*; the "Fan-li" in some of the editions of Chang Chu-p'o's commentary on the *Chin P'ing Mei*; the "Fan-li" in *Li Cho-wu hsien-sheng p'i-p'ing Hsi-yu chi* 李卓吾先生批評西遊記 (Commentary Edition of the *Hsi-yu chi* by Li Chih); the "Li-yen" in the Ch'i-hsing t'ang edition of the *Ju-lin wai-shih*; and the "Fan-li" of the so-called "chia-hsü" 甲戌 (1754) manuscript copy of the Chih-yen chai commentary on the *Hung-lou meng*.

[39] The Wu-kuei shan-jen 五桂山人 and Yüan-hu Yüeh-ch'ih-tzu 鴛湖月痴子 prefaces to the Chang Hsin-chih *Hung-lou meng* commentary concentrate respectively on the actual writing of the commentary and on the methods and philosophic underpinning of Chang Hsin-chih's commentary. They are quoted in *HLMC*, pp. 35–36, 36–37.

[40] See, for example, the Tzu-lang shan-jen 紫琅山人 preface to the Chang Hsin-chih commentary (*HLMC*, pp. 37–38). For further discussion of the "Chin Sheng-t'an" preface and its relationship to a preface signed Li Yü and dated 1679, see the introduction to chap. III below.

Many revealing statements are made in these documents, but they have to be taken with a grain of salt as they are often part of an attempt to increase sales of the book through less than honest practices, such as attributing the commentary to a famous figure or claiming that the text of the edition is based on an old and rare copy of the novel. The latter claim is made in the "Fa-fan" mentioned above and in Mao Tsung-kang's "Fan-li," both of which labor to point out the strengths of their emendations while simultaneously trying to justify them as already existent in a rare edition available to them. The straightforward account of the changes made in the received text of the novel and chapter comments in the "Li-yen" of the Ch'i-hsing t'ang edition of the *Ju-lin wai-shih* is, by contrast, very open and aboveboard, even if rather pedestrian in thought and logic.[41]

The "Fan-li" in Chang Chu-p'o's commentary discusses his motivation for writing the commentary and some of the circumstances behind its writing. The commentary's style is also contrasted with that of Chin Sheng-t'an. Other *fan-li*, such as the one in the "Li Chih" commentary edition of the *Hsi-yu chi*, set forth some of the conventions operating in the commentary. That "Fan-li" has five items that discuss in turn the use of the phrases *cho-yen* 着眼 (pay attention), *hou* 猴 (monkey), *ch'ü* 趣 (interesting), and the idea of chapter comments (*tsung-p'ing* 總評) and individual comments (*sui-p'ing* 碎評). In other cases some of the functions more often treated in *fan-li* are covered in other types of writing, such as prefaces or *tu-fa* essays.[42] In the outside gutter (*pan-k'ou* 版口 or *pan-hsin* 版心) of the *tu-fa* essay in the Te-hsüeh t'ang edition of the novel *Hsüeh Yüeh Mei* 雪月梅 (preface 1775), the essay is labeled as a *fan-li*, although the title at its head is clearly given as "*Hsüeh Yüeh Mei* tu-fa."

"How to Read" Essays

The most extended genre used by the critics to set forth their reading of their texts is the *tu-fa* 讀法 or "how to read" essay. *Tu-fa* essays by Chin Sheng-t'an, Mao Tsung-kang, Chang Chu-p'o, Liu I-ming, and Chang Hsin-chih are translated in this volume, so the reader can easily get an idea of the main outlines of this form of criticism. The essays are made up of separate items, some of which are extremely brief and light-hearted, while others are long and involved. This same basic form of prefatory essay is called *tsung-p'ing* 總評 in Wang Hsi-lien's and Yao Hsieh's commentaries and *tsung-p'i* 總批 by Chang Shu-shen in his *Hsin-*

---

[41] See esp. items 1–3, quoted in *JLWSYCTL*, p. 132.

[42] See items 28 and 30 in the *Hung-lou meng tu-fa* essay, chap. VII below.

shuo Hsi-yu chi. Other *tu-fa* essays worthy of note are those by Ts'ai Ao for his versions of the *Lieh-kuo chih*, the *Shui-hu hou-chuan*, and the *Hsi-yu chi* and the "Tu *Liao-chai* tsa-shuo" 讀聊齋雜說 (Random Words on How to Read the *Liao-chai chih-i*; dated 1818) by Feng Chen-luan 馮鎮鸞.

The organization of the *tu-fa* essay is rather loose. At first glance it appears to be nothing more than a jumble of random comments. Although certain patterns of argument can almost always be found in them (attention to the genesis of the work, evaluation of characters, etc.), it is still the freedom of the form that is most outstanding.

Prefatory Essays

The commentaries also contain prefatory essays on particular subjects. The essay evaluating the characters of the *Shui-hu chuan* in the Jung-yü t'ang edition (entitled "Liang-shan-po i-pai tan-pa jen yu-lieh" 梁山泊一百單八人優劣) is cannibalized and expanded in the "Chung Hsing" commentary edition (where it is entitled "*Shui-hu chuan* jen-p'in p'ing" 水滸傳人品評). The most prolific writer of essays on separate, specific topics is Chang Chu-p'o. His commentary contains essays on the layout of Hsi-men Ch'ing's household ("Hsi-men Ch'ing fang-wu" 西門慶房屋),[43] allegory in the novel ("*Chin P'ing Mei* yü-i shuo" 金瓶梅寓意說), the play of "hot" and "cold" in the work ("Leng-je chin-chen" 冷熱金針), a defense of the novel against the charge of obscenity ("*Ti-i ch'i-shu* fei yin-shu lun" 第一奇書非淫書論), and two essays of miscellaneous content ("Tsa-lu hsiao-yin" 雜錄小引 and "Chu-p'o hsien-hua" 竹坡閒話).[44]

The dialogue form is also used in some of the prefatory essays included in commentary editions of Chinese fiction. They are labeled "Wen-ta" 問答 (Question and Response) or "Huo-wen" 或問 (Someone Asked), and examples are found in the 120-chapter "Li Chih" commentary edition of the *San-kuo yen-i* (the essay is entitled "Tu San-kuo shih ta-wen" 讀三國史答問) and in the Wang Hsi-lien and late Ch'ing commentary editions of the *Hung-lou meng*. The last-mentioned piece is variously titled "Huo-wen" or "*Hung-lou meng* wen-ta" 紅樓夢問答 and is by T'u Ying 涂瀛 (fl. early 19th century). Both of these types of essays fulfill some of the functions of the *tu-fa* essay, while the dialogue form is

---

[43] There is a slightly similar, anonymous essay on the Grand Prospect Garden, "Ta-kuan yüan t'u-shuo" 大觀園圖說, that first appeared in the Wang Hsi-lien edition of the *Hung-lou meng* and was reprinted in most of the late Ch'ing editions with commentary.

[44] The essays "Leng-je chin-chen" and "*Ti-i ch'i-shu* fei yin-shu lun" do not appear in all editions of the commentary, and their authenticity, as well as that of the "Fan-li" mentioned above, has been questioned. See the introduction to chap. IV below.

also used in some of the items in the regular *tu-fa* essays, such as items four and six in Chin Sheng-t'an's essay on the *Shui-hu chuan*.[45]

General comments on the work of fiction are also sometimes cast in the form of a long poem included in the prefatory section of the edition. It seems that the oldest example of this practice dates to 1522 and the Chang Shang-te 張尚德 (style Hsiu-jan-tzu 修髯子) preface to the *San-kuo chih t'ung-su yen-i*. Chang Shang-te, however, did not write any commentary on the novel itself. The first commentator to use this form might be Liu I-ming, who in his *Hsi-yu yüan-chih* added a long poem of the sort discussed here, entitled "*Hsi-yu yüan-chih ko*" 西遊原旨歌 (Song of the *Hsi-yu yüan-chih*), which takes its place in his overall strategy of explicating the hidden meaning of that novel.

Charts and Lists

Some of the editions of Chinese novels with commentary contain a variety of charts and lists designed to help the reader keep track of the invariably multitudinous cast of characters, often numbering above two hundred, that makes its appearance in these novels. The first chart of this type actually appeared long before the vogue for editions with commentary began. This is the "*San-kuo chih* tsung-liao" 三國志宗僚, first found in the 1522 *San-kuo chih t'ung-su yen-i* and clearly modeled on the tables of contents of standard histories with the addition of some biographical material for each character listed. The persons named in the chart are divided among the Three Kingdoms (Shu, Wei, and Wu) and classified according to social status and rank. The chart was retained in many of the later editions of the *San-kuo yen-i* and similar charts appear in the Yüan Wu-yai and *Ying-hsiung p'u* 英雄譜 (The Roster of Heroes) editions of the *Shui-hu chuan*.[46] The latter chart includes the names of the enemies of as well as the members of the Shui-hu band. Chang Chu-p'o provides four separate lists of classes of characters in the *Chin P'ing Mei*: the names of the Hsi-men household servants, the servants' wives, the amorous conquests of Hsi-men Ch'ing, and the objects of P'an Chin-lien's sexual desire.

Quotations from Historical Works

For the convenience of the reader and perhaps to raise the general tone of the project, in editions of fiction with commentary it is also common to quote from historical or classical sources. The Yüan Wu-yai edition of

[45] See chap. II, *Shui-hu chuan tu-fa* essay below. See also item 17 of the *Hung-lou meng tu-fa* essay, chap. VII below.

[46] The chart in the Yüan Wu-yai edition is briefly discussed in item 9 of the "Fa-fan" in the same edition, *SHCHPP*, p. 32.

the *Shui-hu chuan* quotes the section from the *Hsüan-ho i-shih* 宣和遺事 (Anecdotes from the Hsüan-ho Reign Period) which treats Sung Chiang and his band, while Chin Sheng-t'an's edition quotes from a continuation of Chu Hsi's *Tzu-chih t'ung-chien kang-mu* 資治通鑑綱目 (Outline and Explanation of the Comprehensive Mirror for Aid in Government) on the capture of the historical (or one of them, anyway) Sung Chiang. Two of the editions of the *Hsi-yu chi* (*Hsi-yu cheng-tao shu* 西遊證道書 [The Way to Enlightenment through the *Hsi-yu chi*] and *Hsi-yu yüan-chih*) contain biographies of the reputed author of the novel, Ch'iu Ch'u-chi 丘處機 (1148–1227), compiled from classical sources. The *Hsi-yu cheng-tao shu* also contains a short essay based on historical sources on the real Hsüan-tsang (596–664), on whom the character Tripitaka is loosely based.

Lists of Vocabulary or Interesting Sayings

As we saw in the first essay of this introductory section, the genre of fiction commentary in China was greatly influenced by drama criticism. Drama criticism as a whole was more technically oriented than fiction criticism. This was perhaps because of the rather strict and complicated rules of prosody to be followed in the writing of the all-important arias that were the most prestigious part of the dramatists' craft. The pronunciation and rhyme category of words in the text was a matter of great importance. Therefore glosses giving this type of information were a staple feature in commentaries on dramatic works. These glosses were sometimes given on the page where the glossed word appears, or they might be collected together and printed at the end of the act or the volume. A collected list of glosses of this latter type appears in the Wang Hsi-lien edition of the *Hung-lou meng* (entitled "Yin-shih" 音釋, Explanation of Pronunciation). Related to this is a list of spicy sayings culled by Chang Chu-p'o from the text of the *Chin P'ing Mei* and included in the prefatory material to his commentary on that novel. The list is entitled "*Chin P'ing Mei* ch'ü-t'an" 金瓶梅趣談 (Interesting Sayings from the *Chin P'ing Mei*).

Variations on the Standard Form for Tables of Contents

A table of contents listing the titular couplets for each chapter is a standard feature of traditional Chinese novels, but there are a couple of variations on this form as well to be found in the commentary editions of novels. Chin Sheng-t'an put his table of contents (which consists of the titular couplets alone without chapter or *chüan* numbers) at the very end of the prologue ("Hsieh-tzu" 楔子) that he concocted out of the introductory section ("Yin-shou" 引首) and first chapter of the editions of the *Shui-hu chuan* that appeared before his. In the earliest published form (1905) of the *Nieh-hai hua* 孽海花 (Flowers on a Sea of Sin) a similar device was used to introduce the table of contents in the form of a list of the projected titular couplets for the remaining chapters of the book.[47] Chang Chu-p'o's edition of the *Chin P'ing Mei* has an unusual table of contents. Instead of the standard form listing the chapter titles, Chang Chu-p'o has provided an analytical table of contents that uses a pair of two-character phrases to remind the reader of the content of each chapter. Underneath, in short notes, Chang Chu-p'o indicates the place of these chapters in the flow and overall structure of the book.

Poetry in Fiction Commentaries

Occasional poetry had an important place in Chinese culture as a whole, and it also shows up in commentary editions of Chinese fiction. Poems written for the publication of an edition of a work of fiction (*t'i-shih* 題詩 or *t'i-tz'u* 題詞) became more and more common in new works from the middle of the Ch'ing to the end of the dynasty. These poems were written by the commentators, editors, and their friends and patrons. Beyond commemorating the appearance of the edition per se, these poems often fulfill some of the functions of the prefaces, such as helping to explain some of the history of the work of criticism at hand[48] or recommending the work to the general audience. Poems that take the work of fiction itself as their topic rather than using as a subject the enterprise of producing a commentary are also to be found.

Postfaces and Final Comments

Commemorative or commendatory poems of the sort mentioned above are often appended to the end of the volume when they do not follow directly after the prefaces. Also to be found at the back of the volume are postfaces (*pa* 跋) and, less frequently, concluding remarks (*tsung-chieh* 總結). The postfaces are, for the most part, very similar to prefaces. Sun T'ung-sheng 孫桐生 (1852 *chin-shih*), editor of the first printed version of Chang Hsin-chih's commentary on the *Hung-lou meng*, wrote both a preface and a postface for that edition.[49] There is considerable overlap in

---

[47] This version was published in 25 chapters in 1905. The first nine are reprinted in A-ying 阿英, ed., *Wan-Ch'ing wen-hsüeh ts'ung-ch'ao* 晚清文學叢抄 (Compendium of Late Ch'ing Literature), *Hsiao-shuo erh-chüan* 小說二卷 (Second Volume of Fiction; Peking: Chung-hua shu-chü, 1960), pp. 484–551.

[48] This is the case with the poems by Chang Hsin-chih commemorating the completion of his commentary, *HLMC*, pp. 506–7.

[49] See *HLMC*, pp. 39–41.

topic and treatment between the two. Some works, such as the 1819–1820 edition of Liu I-ming's *Hsi-yu yüan-chih*, contain a large number of postfaces. In Liu I-ming's case the majority are by his disciples and contain important information on Liu I-ming and his approach to the *Hsi-yu chi*.

A postface of considerable interest is that by Huang T'ai-hung 黃太鴻 (personal name Chou-hsing 周星, 1611–1680) attached to the end of the *Hsi-yu cheng-tao shu* brought out by him and Wang Hsiang-hsü. This postface follows directly upon the last chapter of the novel, much as if it was a postchapter comment. In the postface, Huang T'ai-hung discusses the differences between his edition of the novel (based on an inevitable old edition only available to him) and those commonly read.

The chapter comments of the final chapter of a novel often try to sum up what the commentator takes to be the main import of the work. In at least one case, Chang Shu-shen's *Hsin-shuo Hsi-yu chi*, this summation is divided from the rest of the chapter comment and given a separate heading, "Tsung-chieh" (General Summation).

A Paradigm of the Complete Commentary Edition

We can conclude the discussion of the different forms of commentarial material found in the various commentaries presented above by outlining a paradigm of a commentary edition of a novel in its fullest possible form as follows:

I. Prefatory material

  A. Prefaces (*hsü* 序)
    1. Prefaces by the commentator
    2. Prefaces by his friends or patrons
    3. Concocted prefaces (such as the "Yü Chi" 虞集 preface in the *Hsi-yu cheng-tao shu*, the "Shih Nai-an" preface in *Ti-wu ts'ai-tzu shu* 第五才子書, and the "Chin Sheng-t'an" preface to the *San-kuo yen-i*)
  B. Statements of general principles (*fan-li* 凡例, *li-yen* 例言)
  C. General essays dealing with the overall theme of the book, treated item by item (*tu-fa* 讀法, *tsung-p'ing* 總評, *tsung-p'i* 總批, *tsung-lun* 總論, *lun-lüeh* 論略)
  D. General essay in dialogue or question-and-answer form (*wen-ta* 問答, *huo-wen* 或問)
  E. Essays on specific topics (*chuan-lun* 專論)
    1. Evaluation of characters
    2. Physical settings
    3. Stylistics
    4. Miscellaneous

    F. Quotation of documents
       1. Biographies of reputed author
       2. Biographies of models for characters
       3. Historical sources
    G. Charts and lists of characters broken into categories (*piao* 表)
    H. Lists of vocabulary (with or without glosses)
    I. Commemorative poems (*t'i-shih* 題詩, *t'i-tz'u* 題詞)
    J. Analytical table of contents

II. Text of the novel chapter by chapter

    A. Prechapter comments (*hui-ch'ien tsung-p'i* 回前總批)
    B. Marginal comments
       1. Ordinary (*mei-p'i* 眉批)
       2. Chapter comment type (*ting-p'i* 頂批)
    C. Interlineal comments
       1. Double-column (*shuang-hang chia-p'i* 雙行夾批)
       2. Single-column (*p'ang-p'i* 旁批, *ts'e-p'i* 側批)
    D. Postchapter comments (*hui-hou tsung-p'i* 回後總批)
    E. Emphatic punctuation
       1. Positive (ch'üan-tien 圈點)
       2. Negative (*t'u-mo* 塗抹)

III. Appended material

    A. Concluding remarks (*tsung-chieh* 總結)
    B. Postfaces (*pa* 跋)
    C. More commemorative poems

The actual distribution of these types of material in the major commentary editions of the six novels that are the focus of this volume can be seen in the description of those commentaries in the annotated bibliography.

Commentaries Printed without the Full Texts of the Novels

To be sure, not all of the important criticism on Chinese fiction was included in commentary editions of the texts. Besides various independent forms in which fiction criticism was written, dealt with below, some commentaries were published without the text of the work of fiction on which they were commenting. In cases where the commentary included interlineal comments, cues of a sentence or so in length are given to enable the reader to find the appropriate place in an ordinary edition. This was the case with the Pao-wen ko 寶文閣 1885 edition of the *Ju-lin wai-shih p'ing* 儒林外史評 (Commentary on the *Ju-lin wai-shih*). The preface to that edition by Huang An-chin 黃安謹 explains the reason for not including the full text of the novel:

The original text of the *Ju-lin wai-shih* is quite long and it was not feasible to copy in the entire text. Therefore we selectively printed the indispensable parts in large characters and printed the comments in double columns as notes in order to save on expenses.

外史原文繁, 不勝全載, 節錄其要大書, 評語雙行作注, 以省費.[50]

Chang Ch'i-hsin 張其信 had originally thought to publish an edition of the *Hung-lou meng* with his comments on each section and chapter added in the margins for the convenience of the reader, but he was forced to abandon the idea because of the cost, among other reasons. His comments were published in 1877 under the title *Hung-lou meng ou-p'ing* 紅樓夢偶評 (Random Comments on the *Hung-lou meng*) and contained brief headings or quotations from the novel to help the reader find the proper place in the original.[51] It is also the case that Chang Hsin-chih's *Miao-fu hsüan p'ing Shih-t'ou chi* 妙復軒評石頭記 (Commentary on the *Story of the Stone* from Miao-fu Studio) and perhaps Liu I-ming's *Hsi-yu yüan-chih* once circulated in editions without the texts of their respective novels.[52] Modern collections of comments from commentary editions compiled for the convenience of scholars without access to the originals have often taken the form of the editions mentioned above. In order to save money and space, only as much of the novel is given as is necessary to locate the original placement of the comment. This is the form of Yü P'ing-po's 俞平伯 collection of Chih-yen chai comments (*Chih-yen chai Hung-lou meng chi-p'ing* 脂硯齋紅樓夢輯評, first published in 1954) and the revision of that work by Ch'en Ch'ing-hao 陳慶浩 (first published in 1972 in Hong Kong under the title *Hung-lou meng Chih-yen chai p'ing-yü chi-chiao* 紅樓夢脂硯齋評語輯校).

Some commentators never published their work, and all we have today is the original commentator's copy plus perhaps a few manuscript copies. This is the case for a commentary on the *Hung-lou meng* by Ch'en Ch'i-t'ai 陳其泰 published recently for the first time under the title *T'ung-hua feng ko p'ing Hung-lou meng chi-lu* 桐花鳳閣評紅樓夢輯錄 (Edited and Collected Ch'en Ch'i-t'ai Commentary on the *Hung-lou meng*).[53]

[50] This preface is quoted in *JLWSYCTL*, p. 136.

[51] An abridged version of this work is included in *HLMC*, pp. 214–18. See p. 214 for his original publication plans.

[52] The Peking Library manuscript copy of Chang Hsin-chih's commentary takes this form. Sun K'ai-ti 孫楷第, in his *Chung-kuo t'ung-su hsiao-shuo shu-mu* 中國通俗小說書目 (Bibliography of Popular Chinese Fiction; Peking: Jen-min wen-hsüeh, 1982), p. 192, says that he once saw such an edition of the *Hsi-yu yüan-chih*.

[53] Published without the text of the novel using a format similar to the Chih-yen chai comment collections, Liu Ts'ao-nan 劉操南, ed. (Tientsin: T'ien-chin jen-min, 1981).

Cumulative and Collective Commentary Editions

From the scattered remarks in various commentaries we can get an idea of how some of the commentators went about their work. Some of the commentaries were finished in a very short time, such as Chang Chu-p'o's (by his testimony, done in less than a month),[54] while the Chih-yen chai commentary contains signed and dated comments that stretch over twenty years' time. Some commentators did their work very systematically, while others proceeded in a more leisurely and less organized fashion. In commentaries where some of the comments are dated, such as the Chih-yen chai commentary, we can see a process of accretion and sedimentation at work. One very interesting comment by Chih-yen chai himself describes the method he used:

> My comments repeat themselves. While reading this book, if an insight comes to me, then I record it with my pen. I didn't read it [the novel] through from beginning to end and then go back to the beginning and start adding my comments. Therefore, occasionally there is duplication in them [my comments].... Later, whenever I read through a place, I always come up with a new phrase or two, which I add on as another layer next to the old....

> 余批重出. 余閱此書偶有所得即筆錄之, 非從首至尾閱過, 復從首加批者, 故偶有復處.... 後每一閱亦必有一語半言, 重加批於側....[55]

In commentaries that were written over extended periods of time, the commentator sometimes came to disagree with his earlier statements. Such disagreement was usually cleaned up before publication, but we can find evidence of this phenomenon in manuscript versions that preserve these different layers.[56]

Some commentary editions contain the comments of a number of different contributors. Sometimes these men were collaborators, as is the case in the original edition (1711) of the Nü-hsien wai-shih 女仙外史 (Informal History of the Female Immortal), which contains signed chapter comments by such famous literati as Hung Sheng 洪昇 (1645–1704),

---

[54] See Wu Kan 吳敢, "Chang Chu-p'o sheng-p'ing shu-lüeh" 張竹坡生平述略 (A Brief Account of Chang Chu-p'o's Life), Hsü-chou shih-fan hsüeh-yüan hsüeh-pao, 1984. 3:77. See also item 1 of the "Fan-li" of the Chang Chu-p'o Chin P'ing Mei commentary, quoted in CPMTLHP, p. 1.

[55] See CYCPYCC, p. 2.31, marginal comment.

[56] For examples of this see the Chih-yen chai Hung-lou meng commentary (which as a composite and collaborative work, also contains disagreements among the various commentators), CYCPYCC, p. 1.10 (chia-hsü copy marginal comment), p. 26.433 (keng-ch'en copy interlineal comment), and p. 27.384 (keng-ch'en copy marginal comment); and Ch'en Ch'i-t'ai's commentary on the same nove, T'ung-hua feng ko p'ing Hung-lou meng chi-lu, pp. 112.342–43, where he says, "I was wrong, I was wrong!"

Wang Shih-chen 王士禎 (1634–1711), Liu T'ing-chi 劉廷璣 (1653–1715+), and Chu Ta 朱耷 (1626–1706?), all friends of the author, Lü Hsiung 呂熊 (c. 1640–c. 1722). On the other hand, in the comments that Wang Wang-ju 王望如 added to his edition (1657) of Chin Sheng-t'an's *Shui-hu chuan*, he turned his attention to his predecessor's remarks almost as often as to the novel itself. Although not an example of fiction criticism, in an eighteenth-century reprint with added comments of Chin Sheng-t'an's commentary on the *Hsi-hsiang chi*,[57] the anonymous commentator treats Chin Sheng-t'an's essays as if they themselves were examples of exemplary writing and uses the whole gamut of stylistic terminology to dissect them, turning only a very small portion of his energy toward the play itself.

The Balance of Different Interests in Fiction Commentaries

Since fiction commentary in China was a comparatively fluid and unorganized genre, there was plenty of room for individual styles and for modulation of tone even within individual commentaries. Feng Chen-luan helpfully laid out five categories of comments in his commentary on the *Liao-chai chih-i*, first written in 1818 but not published until 1891, along with the comments of three other commentators. The five categories are: (1) comments on style (*lun-wen* 論文), (2) comments on content (*lun-shih* 論事), (3) identification of persons, places, and things in the text (*k'ao-chü* 考據), (4) supplementary or contrastive material (*p'ang-cheng* 旁證), and (5) jokes and puns (*yu-hsi* 游戲).[58] This list could be used to cover most of the other Chinese fiction commentators' preoccupations as well, although the proportion of comments belonging to each category varies widely.

Lighthearted comments were an important part of the tradition from the beginning. In early commentaries we are even told what ratio of serious to playful remarks is to be found.[59] Such a playful approach was

---

[57] Reprinted as *Ti-liu ts'ai-tzu Hsi-hsiang chi*. See n. 22 above.

[58] See his "Tu *Liao-chai* tsa-shuo" 讀聊齋雜說 (Random Words on How to Read the *Liao-chai chih-i*) included in Chang Yu-ho 張友鶴, ed., *Liao-chai chih-i hui-chiao hui-chu hui-p'ing pen* 聊齋誌異會校會注會評本 (Collated Edition of the *Liao-chai chih-i* with Collected Annotation and Commentary; Peking: Chung-hua shu-chü, 1962), p. 11.

[59] In the "P'i-p'ing *Shui-hu chuan* shu-yü" 批評水滸傳述語 attributed to Huai-lin in the Jung-yü t'ang edition of the *Shui-hu chuan* we are told, "In Li Chih's commentary on the *Shui-hu chuan*, seventy percent is irresponsible (*wan-shih* 玩世) and thirty percent is responsible (*ch'ih-shih* 持世). But even the irresponsible comments reveal responsible concern, it is only that it is expressed in an irresponsible manner. The truly perceptive will be able to grasp this between the lines." See *SHCHPP*, p. 25 for the text. There is a very similar comment in the "Fan-li" to the "Li Chih" commentary edition of the *Hsi-yu chi*, p. 3a–b, where the reader is told that whether he takes a particular comment seriously or

not, however, always well received. One of Liu I-ming's main criticisms of Wang Hsiang-hsü is that the other man's commentary on the *Hsi-yu chi* contained too much silliness and too many irresponsible comments.[60]

Commentator as Author/Collaborator

Some of the commentary on Chinese fiction was written by the authors of the original works or by persons having privileged information or even input into the composition of the work. In some cases the fact that the author was going to add his own commentary seems to have influenced the composition of the fictional work. For instance, one of the original components of vernacular Chinese fiction was the commentarial mode usually voiced through the narrator of the story.[61] In Tung Yüeh's (1620–1686) *Hsi-yu pu* 西遊補 (Supplement to the *Hsi-yu chi*) the commentarial mode is less pronounced than in earlier works and we can hypothesize that Tung Yüeh experimented in this way because of the use to which he planned to put his prefatory essay and chapter comments.[62] Other examples of commentary written by the author of the work and published at the same time are the *Shui-hu hou-chuan* 水滸後傳 (Continuation of the *Shui-hu chuan*) by Ch'en Ch'en 陳忱 (1614–1666+)[63] and *Lao Ts'an yu-chi* 老殘遊記 (The Travels of Lao Ts'an) by Liu E 劉鶚 (1857–1909).

The most prominent example of a commentary written by persons

---

not is entirely up to him. Also, the Li Yün-hsiang 李雲翔 preface to the "Chung Hsing" commentary edition of the *Feng-shen yen-i* 封神演義 (The Investiture of the Gods) describes the chapter comments as containing ironic (*fan-shuo* 反說) and mocking (*ch'ao-nüeh* 嘲謔) comments as well as straightforward ones (*cheng-tz'u* 正詞). This preface is quoted in Sun K'ai-ti, *Jih-pen Tung-ching so-chien hsiao-shuo shu-mu* 日本東京所見小說書目 (Bibliography of Fiction Seen in Tokyo, Japan; Peking: Jen-min wen-hsüeh, 1981), pp. 89–90.

[60] See Liu I-ming's first preface to the *Hsi-yu yüan-chih*, *HYCTLHP*, p. 245.

[61] For a definition of the concept of a "commentarial mode" in Chinese vernacular fiction, see Patrick Hanan, "The Early Chinese Short Story: A Critical Theory in Outline," in *Studies in Chinese Literary Genres*, Cyril Birch, ed. (Berkeley: University of California Press, 1974), p. 305.

[62] The long-established attribution of the authorship of this novel has been recently contested by Kao Hung-chün 高洪鈞, "*Hsi-yu pu* tso-che shih shui?" 西遊補作者是誰 (Who Is the Author of the *Hsi-yu pu*?), *T'ien-chin shih-ta hsüeh-pao* 天津師大學報 (Academic Journal of Tientsin Normal University), 1985. 6:81–84, who also contends that the bulk of the work was written by Tung Yüeh's father, Tung Ssu-chang 董斯張 (d. 1628), whose studio name appears not only at the end of one of the prefatory pieces of the earliest edition of the novel, but who is also identified as the author of the novel through the appearance of this studio name at the beginning of chap. 1.

[63] For a discussion of how Ch'en Ch'en's commentary interacts with his novel, see Ellen Widmer, *The Margins of Utopia*, especially pp. 109–56.

who participated in the composition of the novel is the Chih-yen chai commentary on the *Hung-lou meng*. Although the identities of those commentators included under the name Chih-yen chai have not been conclusively determined, it is clear that they were close friends and/or relatives of the author, Ts'ao Hsüeh-ch'in 曹雪芹 (1715?–1763?).

Re-creation of Past Works, Influence on New Works

Some commentators, such as Chang Chu-p'o, saw the composition of a work of fiction and the writing of a detailed commentary on that work to be a roughly equivalent activity in terms of difficulty and impor-tance.[64] Chang Chu-p'o's remarks to this effect are quite believable in light of the fact that he held that the commentator's job (and the reader's as well) was to retrace the author's steps and actively reconstruct the completed work by probing and asking searching questions at every bend in the road, no matter how inconspicuous.[65]

At the same time, it is clear that preexisting commentary influenced the composition of new fiction. On a very mundane level, the author of *Tang-k'ou chih* 蕩寇志 (Suppression of the Bandits), Yü Wan-ch'un 俞萬春 (1794–1849), wrote at the beginning of his novel that Chin Sheng-t'an had shown the real meaning of the *Shui-hu chuan* in his commentary on it, and that his own novel was an extension of Chin Sheng-t'an's conception.[66] Yü Wan-ch'un's reading of Chin Sheng-t'an was not overly subtle, but the critical tradition embodied in commen-taries on Chinese fiction had many different and truly subtle effects on later novels and surely had a hand in the production of major works in the genre such as the *Hung-lou meng* and the *Ju-lin wai-shih*.

Comprehensiveness versus Implication

The commentators developed a variety of strategies to deal with the problem of balance between text and commentary. How detailed does a commentary have to be? Is it good for a reader to be told everything the commentator knows, or is it better to make the reader do some of the work himself? As bulky as some of the commentaries are, the predomi-nant response to questions like these would seem to be that it is more important to develop in the reader a technique for reading that he can

---

[64] See his "Chu-p'o hsien-hua" 竹坡閒話 (Idle Talk from Chu-p'o), in his *Chin P'ing Mei* commentary, 1695 editions, p. 4a–b.

[65] See chap. IV below, items 40–42 in his *Chin P'ing Mei tu-fa* essay, for a concise statement of this view.

[66] See the prologue to the novel in the 1985 Jen-min wen-hsüeh (Peking) reprint, "Chieh *Shui-hu ch'üan-chuan*" 結水滸全傳 (Concluding the Complete Tale of the *Shui-hu*), p. 1. Also quoted in *SHCTLHP*, p. 579.

use on his own rather than remaining a passive receptor. Chang Hsin-chih said:

> [My commentary] was not written without method; if that were the case, the commenting would never come to an end. What is needed is for the reader to be able to take a hint and fill in the rest, to understand intuitively.

非隨意填寫者, 奈批不勝批. 是在閱者一隅三反, 神而明之, 可也.[67]

Chang Wen-hu 張文虎 (1808–1885), who also did a commentary on the *Ju-lin wai-shih*, was once told by a friend that the commentary in the original edition of the *Hsi-yu pu* was not comprehensive enough, and he agreed to supplement it with his own remarks. After finishing that project, Chang Wen-hu showed the commentary to his friend, who objected that it was not up to the level of comprehensiveness of Ch'en Shih-pin (author of a commentary on the *Hsi-yu chi*, *Hsi-yu chen-ch'üan*). Chang Wen-hu refused to add any more comments, telling his friend that the implications in the novel were infinite and that it was vain to try to exhaust these through commentary.[68]

At first some of the advice to the reader in the commentaries seems to be contradictory, but this confusion tends to disappear as soon as we remember that fiction is basically a multidimensional phenomenon and that one of the main drives behind the production of the commentaries is a desire to get the reader to perceive this multidimensionality. Thus, when in one place Chang Chu-p'o stresses the importance of reading carefully character by character, savoring to the full all the nuances of each,[69] and in another place he says that you need to take a long-range view in order to appreciate the full effect of the novel,[70] it is not a matter of either/or, but of the simple fact that multidimensionality cannot be perceived from any one point of view, no matter how penetrating or expansive.[71]

---

[67] *CYY*, p. 42.563, chapter comment.

[68] See his preface to his edition of the *Hsi-yu pu*, dated 1853. The preface is quoted in Tseng Tsu-yin 曾祖蔭 et al., eds., *Chung-kuo li-tai hsiao-shuo hsü-pa hsüan-chu* 中國歷代小說序跋選注 (Annotated Selections of Prefaces to Chinese Fiction through the Ages; Hsien-ning: Ch'ang-chiang wen-i, 1982), pp. 232–33.

[69] See chap. IV below, item 71 of the *Chin P'ing Mei tu-fa* essay.

[70] See chap. IV below, item 38 of the *Chin P'ing Mei tu-fa* essay.

[71] Two similar demands, "You ought to read character by character and sentence by sentence," and "You should also take in the whole book in a single gulp," occur within a single item in the "*Chuang Tzu* tsa-shuo" 莊子雜說 (Miscellaneous Remarks on the *Chuang Tzu*) section in the "Tu *Chuang Tzu* fa" 讀莊子法 (How to Read the *Chuang Tzu*) by Lin Yün-ming 林雲銘 included in the *Chao-tai ts'ung-shu* 昭代叢書 (Collectanea of This Illustrious Age), Chang Ch'ao 張潮 (1650–ca. 1703) et al., comps. See p. 19/7a of

Conclusion

This volume concentrates primarily on editions of Chinese fiction with commentary attached because that is the tradition with the most extensive influence. By comparison, the other forms in which we can find fiction criticism (prefaces and postfaces to regular editions, essays on particular works of fiction, and scattered comments in the *sui-pi* 隨筆 [random notes] tradition) cannot compare either in importance or bulk until late in the Ch'ing dynasty, when critical writings on the *Hung-lou meng* took every form imaginable.[72] Among these other forms of Chinese fiction criticism, the material contained in prefaces and postfaces is perhaps the most interesting, but we are familiar with this type of writing from the discussion above. Several collections of prefaces and postfaces from editions of fiction have been compiled since 1980, so this kind of material is now quite readily available.[73] A further reason for temporarily neglecting the other forms of Chinese fiction criticism outside of commentary is the fact that the latter is perhaps most unfamiliar to the Western reader and has no real literary parallel.

From the May Fourth period until about the beginning of the present decade, the traditional form of commentary on literary works (*p'ing-tien* 評點) was very much in disfavor. Some of the criticism leveled at *p'ing-tien* commentaries in premodern China has already been examined in the first essay in the introductory section above. Modern critics had their own interpretations of and uses for traditional novels, and they seem to have resented interference from the old commentators. At present, however, this type of commentary is not only enjoying a sharp rise in scholarly attention in China and abroad, but is also being employed in many new works of criticism now being published. This trend perhaps began sooner in Taiwan, which has already seen the appearance of two full-length commentaries on traditional novels, the

---

the *chia* 甲 section of the 1833 Shih-k'ai t'ang edition. This essay was clearly influenced by fiction criticism. In a different item in the same section of the essay Lin Yün-ming also says, "You ought to seek out the differences between similar passages and seek out the unity in passages that diverge from each other" (ibid., p. 19/6a). "*Chuang Tzu tsa-shuo*" also occurs in editions of Lin Yün-ming's commentary on the *Chuang Tzu, Chuang Tzu yin* 莊子因. There is a 1968 Kuang-wen shu-chü (Taipei) reprint: *Tseng-chu Chuang Tzu yin* 增註莊子因 (*Chuang Tzu yin* with Added Annotations).

[72] Quotations from and descriptions of some of the more representative critical works on that novel are available in *HLMC* and *HLMSL*.

[73] Collections of prefaces and postfaces or compilations that contain them include: *Chung-kuo li-tai hsiao-shuo hsü-pa hsüan-chu, Ming-Ch'ing hsiao-shuo hsü-pa hsüan* 明清小説 序跋選 (Selected Prefaces and Postfaces to Ming-Ch'ing Works of Fiction; Shenyang: Ch'un-feng wen-i, 1983), and *LCH*.

Hsi-yu chi and *Lao Ts'an yu-chi*.[74] Both of these novels are interpreted as expositions of esoteric philosophical traditions (Taoism and T'ai-chou school syncretism, respectively), but the same *p'ing-tien* style of commentary has already been used by modern writers to deal with chapters from traditional novels in China[75] as well as selections of classical prose.[76]

[74] Ch'en Tun-fu 陳敦甫, *Hsi-yu chi shih-i—Lung-men hsin-ch'uan* 西遊記釋義：龍門心傳 (Explication of the *Hsi-yu chi*—the Secret Teaching of Patriarch Ch'iu; Taipei: Ch'üan-chen ch'u-pan she, 1976), and Leng-ning jen 冷凝人 (pseud.) comment., Lü Tzu-yang 呂自揚, annot., *Mei-p'i hsiang-chu Lao Ts'an yu-chi* 眉批詳注老殘遊記 (The Travels of Lao Ts'an with Marginal Commentary and Extensive Annotation; Taipei: Ho-p'an ch'u-pan she, 1979). Six chapters of an annotated and commentated version of the *Shui-hu chuan* were prepared in 1965 by the Jen-min wen-hsüeh Publishing House in Peking, but the project was aborted. See Ma T'i-chi 馬蹄疾, *Shui-hu shu-lu* 水滸書錄 (Bibliography of Works on the *Shui-hu chuan*; Shanghai: Shang-hai ku-chi, 1986), p. 168.

[75] Treatments of the first five chapters of the *Hung-lou meng* by Chao Ching-yü 趙景瑜 complete with chapter comments, section comments (*tuan-p'ing* 段評), and interlineal comments have appeared in *Ming-tso hsin-shang* 名作欣賞 (Appreciation of Famous Works), 1981–82. Chaps. 75 and 76 of the *Chin P'ing Mei* have been treated in similar fashion in Yung-jen 邕人 (pseud.), "Wu Yüeh-niang P'an Chin-lien ho-ch'i tou-k'ou: *Chin P'ing Mei tz'u-hua* ti ch'i-shih-wu hui, ch'i-shih-liu hui p'ing-tien" 吳月娘潘金蓮合氣鬥口：金瓶梅詞話第七十五回，七十六回評點 (Wu Yüeh-niang and P'an Chin-lien Argue Up a Storm: Commentary on Chapters 75 and 76 of the *Chin P'ing Mei tz'u-hua*), in *Ku-tien hsiao-shuo hsi-ch'ü t'an-i lu* 古典小說戲曲探藝錄 (Explorations in the Art of Classical Fiction and Drama; Tientsin: T'ien-chin jen-min, 1982), pp. 330–42.

[76] Chang Yü-hui 張玉惠 et al., eds., *Ku-wen pai-p'ien p'ing-tien chin-i* 古文百篇評點今譯 (One Hundred Selections of Classic Prose with Commentary and Translations into Modern Chinese; Ch'ang-ch'un: Chi-lin jen-min, 1983).

(d) Terminology and Central Concepts

In this final introductory essay, we will examine the recurring terminology of traditional Chinese fiction criticism in order to define some of the central aesthetic concepts underpinning the Ming-Ch'ing novel. In view of the particular course of historical development of this critical medium and the specific formats in which the materials appear (as described in the previous essays), one could scarcely expect writings of such varied approach and provenance to project a unified theory of Chinese fiction. Certainly, it must be admitted at the outset that a large portion of the sort of materials under consideration here never quite cross the shadowy boundary from the prosaic world of textual commentary to the lofty heights of literary criticism proper. Yet a sufficient proportion of the discussion does move beyond isolated subjective remarks into the area of serious inquiry into the art of fiction writing to enable us to perceive, within this amorphous body of writings, the outlines of a more or less dominant set of aesthetic norms and compositional techniques governing the genres of extended vernacular prose fiction in late imperial China. In the prefatory and textual comments of the best of the critics represented in this volume—Chin Sheng-t'an, Mao Tsung-kang, and Chang Chu-p'o—we do in fact have something that comes close to a systematic poetics of the Chinese novel. But even in the rather random, fragmentary quips and stabs that comprise the bulk of the tradition, we can observe the workings of certain basic critical assumptions ostensibly shared by leading figures of the Ming-Ch'ing literary milieu, that may remain valid irrespective of the degree of persuasiveness of a given critic's specific readings and interpretive arguments.

As we have seen, the most valuable pieces of Chinese fiction criticism—those which take up, directly or obliquely, some of these basic principles of narrative composition and thus form the subject matter of this volume—tend to appear not as independent critical essays, but rather in the form of marginal or interlineal commentary and prefatory essays attached to the texts themselves. This fact alone may help to explain the wide range of variation in both the critical stance and the interpretive value of the materials, since in the field of exegesis per se we find a somewhat random mixture of exegetical functions: the hermeneutic, the evaluative, and the heuristic, among others. For the purposes of the following analysis, we will therefore divide the critical materials under investigation into several categories—informational, impressionistic, comparative, compositional, and interpretive—although of course no such distinctions exist in the original writings.

We should note before proceeding further that the particular terminology used by each of the Ming-Ch'ing fiction critics, whether borrowed, modified, or invented, is in some ways basically inseparable from the critical and interpretive strategies that each critic is employing in his overall approach to the work on which he is commenting. That is to say, all of the terms are primarily defined and redefined contextually according to the individual usage of the various critics and the changing subject matter elucidated. Consequently, there is a certain lack of consistency not only among the critics as a whole, but also in the work of the individual writers. This section of our introductory essay, however, must necessarily treat the material at a rather high level of synthesis and abstraction. It is hoped that the schematic and systematic outline presented here will be used by the reader in conjunction with the particular examples of usage that appear in the translations of the critical essays in this volume (please consult the finding list provided in appendix 1) and citations of usage made in the notes to this essay.

Before moving on to a more detailed inquiry into the compositional principles underlying the art of the Chinese novelist, let us begin by considering the less substantive categories of fiction commentary. In the first category, that of material which adduces additional information to elucidate a particular passage of a text, we may include the large amount of comments that are in effect no more than footnotes, commentary that should not rightly be termed *p'i-p'ing* 批評 (criticism) although it occasionally appears under that rubric in bibliographical designations. The seemingly straightforward nature of these informational remarks may at times be deceptive, since in Chinese as in Western exegesis, the glossing of a piece of text may often entail serious interpretive issues that the commentator attempts to solve through textual revision or through redefinition. The Chinese commentators assert that the encoding of a hidden and deeper meaning beneath the surface level of the text through the use of a system of precise and graded terminology exists in their texts and this feature is referred to by them as *Ch'un-ch'iu tzu-fa* 春秋字法 (control of diction as in *The Spring and Autumn Annals*).[1] The commen-

---

[1] This technique is also known as *Ch'un-ch'iu pi* 春秋筆 (style of *The Spring and Autumn Annals*) and *p'i-li yang-ch'iu* 皮裏陽秋 (hidden *Spring and Autumn Annals* style; *yang* 陽 is a substitution for the character *ch'un* 春) and is related to ideas such as *shih-pi* 史筆 (the style of the histories) and *ch'ü-pi* 曲筆 (indirect style). Almost all of the critics use this idea or variations of it as one of their critical tools. Its genesis comes from early commentaries on the *Ch'un-ch'iu* such as the *Ku-liang chuan* 穀梁傳 and the *Kung-yang chuan* 公羊傳, which try to find deep meaning in the exceedingly sparse and dry text of the *Ch'un-ch'iu*. The idea that there is indeed a consistent use of terminology to convey the judgments of the author of the *Ch'un-ch'iu* (traditionally held to be Confucius himself) is questioned by George Kennedy, "The Interpretation of the *Ch'un-ch'iu*," included in *Selected Works of George A. Kennedy*, Li T'ien-i, ed. (New Haven: Far Eastern Publications, 1964), pp. 79–103.

tator's job here is not so much to point out the lexical meaning of the terminology as to indicate the effects intended by the usage.

The function of identifying particular personages, place names, dates, events, unfamiliar objects, etc., referred to in a text is especially relevant in the various subgenres of historical fiction and especially in works treating more remote historical periods. In addition to the simple function of explaining the proper reading and meaning of difficult expressions, such commentary could also be said to be part of a strategy to buttress the illusion of historicity aimed for in some of the works in the *yen-i* 演義 tradition, where historical materials have been seriously reworked. Editions of some of these historical novels claim that their texts have been "collated according to the *Tzu-chih t'ung-chien*" (*an-chien* 按鑑).[2] In those texts where concern over the illusion of documentary authenticity gives way to concern for the mimetic credibility of a fabricated world, this type of commentary may also include information regarding the composition or publication of the text provided by the critic, allegedly based on personal acquaintance with the author or his associates, the most obvious example being the Chih-yen chai 脂硯齋 (Red Inkstone Studio) notes attached to the earliest manuscript versions of the *Hung-lou meng* 紅樓夢 (Dream of the Red Chamber).[3]

Our second category of traditional commentary, the impressionistic, is quantitatively the most numerous but for the most part of perhaps

[2] The *Tzu-chih t'ung-chien* 資治通鑑 (Comprehensive Mirror for Aid in Government) by Ssu-ma Kuang 司馬光 (1019–1068) is the standard chronological history of China up to the founding of the Sung dynasty (A.D. 960).

[3] For theories regarding the identification of Chih-yen chai and his co-commentators and their possible relationships to the author of the *Hung-lou meng*, see Wu Shih-ch'ang, *On the Red Chamber Dream* (Oxford: Oxford University Press, 1961); Chao Kang 趙岡 and Ch'en Chung-i 陳鍾毅, *Hung-lou meng hsin-t'an* 紅樓夢新探 (A New Investigation of the *Hung-lou meng*; Hong Kong: Wen-i shu-wu, 1970); Chan Hing-ho, *Le Hung-lou meng et les commentaires de Zhiyanzhai* (Paris: College de France, 1982); and Sun Hsün 孫遜, *Hung-lou meng Chih-p'ing ch'u-t'an* 紅樓夢脂評初探 (A Preliminary Investigation of the Chih-yen chai Commentary on the *Hung-lou meng*; Shanghai: Shang-hai ku-chi, 1981). The so-called Chih-yen chai commentary contains the signed comments of a fairly large number of people, besides the person using Chih-yen chai as his nom de plume. The various comments have been collected into a very convenient volume, *CYCPYCC*. All references to Chih-yen chai comments will be to this work, which has superseded the earlier collection of the comments by Yü P'ing-po 俞平伯.

Another example of this type of "criticism" is the debate over the authorship of the *Chin P'ing Mei* carried on in numerous diaries, letters, and *pi-chi* 筆記 of the late Ming and Ch'ing period. For some of the basic documents of this debate, see K'ung Ling-ching 孔另境, *Chung-kuo hsiao-shuo shih-liao* 中國小說史料 (Historical Material on Chinese Fiction; Shanghai: Shang-hai ku-chi, 1982 reprint), pp. 82–88 and Chiang Jui-tsao 蔣瑞藻, *Hsiao-shuo k'ao-cheng* 小說考証 (Studies in [Chinese] Fiction; Taipei: Commercial Press, 1975 reprint), pp. 52–55. See also the *Chin P'ing Mei tu-fa* essay, items 36 and 37, translated below, chap. IV.

dubious value in terms of critical content; this fact might help explain why the editors of reprints of the major works of fiction eliminated criticism of this type from nearly all of the modern typeset editions until very recently. These materials consist mainly of subjective reactions to turns of events in the plot, revelations of character, ideas expressed in dialogue, or the general tone or mood of a given passage, supposedly jotted down in the margins of the commentator's copy of the work during the course of close reading and later incorporated into a subsequent printing of the text. Theoretically, such comments may be either appreciative or derogatory toward the work itself, although in actual practice, the very fact that the critic has undertaken an extremely laborious and time-consuming task, nearly always a labor of love, renders the occurrence of the latter sort minimal.[4]

Because these remarks are intended to appear in a position immediately contiguous to the piece of text in question, there is in general no need for the critic to rehearse the textual basis for his response, with the result that such material may often be abbreviated to an absolute minimum. In the most extreme form of abbreviation, the critical "comment" consists of nothing more than the insertion of a line of dots or other marks[5] alongside of the line of the text to which the commentator wishes to draw the reader's attention, the equivalent of underlining in our own academic milieu. But whereas the underlining of books today is at best tolerated as a private convenience and at worst abhorred as an undergraduate abuse of the sanctity of the printed page, in the literary heritage of the Ming-Ch'ing critics the practice of inserting "critical dotting" (*p'ing-tien* 評點, *p'i-tien* 批點, *p'i-yüeh* 批閱, etc.) was elevated to the status of a serious intellectual pursuit, although Kuo Shao-yü perhaps overstates this point when he refers to a "school of critical dotting" (*p'ing-tien chih hsüeh* 評點之學) as a significant trend in late Ming literary theory.[6] In certain cases the thematic or structural signifi-

---

[4] In the early stages of the production of commentaries on fiction and drama, derogatory remarks aimed at the author played a far greater role. After the scale of the commentaries escalated beyond their original rudimentary nature and after the commentators began to appropriate to themselves a kind of responsibility for the texts they published with their commentary (which in some cases led them to edit the texts heavily), derogatory remarks began to dwindle dramatically.

[5] Other marks used are rows of small circles (*ch'üan* 圈), enlarged commas, or, occasionally, small triangles. See item 28 of the *Hung-lou meng tu-fa* essay translated below, chap. VII. This practice is directly related to the traditional habit of writing corrections and comments on calligraphy, painting, and essays produced by the student. At times, the custom of using red ink for such corrections or comments is transferred to fiction criticism as well, as in certain copies of the Chih-yen chai commentary.

[6] Kuo Shao-yü 郭紹虞, *Chung-kuo wen-hsüeh p'i-p'ing shih* 中國文學批評史 (A History of Chinese Literary Criticism; Shanghai: Hsin wen-i, 1955), pp. 389–94.

cance or the stylistic brilliance of a particular "dotted" line or passage may be clear enough—such as is the case with a cutting remark in the dialogue, a high point in the plot, or an original turn of phrase. More often than not, and especially when confronted with an extended section of the text marked in this way, the modern reader is at a loss to account for why, exactly, the critic has taken pains to highlight a given piece of text.

Fortunately, some of the traditional critics saw fit to make their intentions somewhat clearer by inserting into the margins of the text certain one- or two-character expressions in praise (or ridicule) of the contiguous passage. In the final analysis, however, such minimal remarks as "wonderful" (*miao* 妙), "marvelous" (*ch'i* 奇), "important" (*yao-chin* 要緊), or "beautiful" (*hao-k'an* 好看) generally add nothing to our understanding of the critic's response and may perhaps be viewed simply as a further extension of the practice of "critical dotting." Once a particular expression has appeared in the margins of a text, its usage tends to become formulaic, studding the pages of the book in a perfunctory manner at every point at which the same sort of response is evoked. In the commentaries attributed to Li Chih 李贄 (1527–1602) this practice is frequently seen, and it is carried one step further in the critical edition of the *Hsi-yu chi* ascribed to his name, by the provision in a prefatory section ("Fan-li" 凡例) of guidelines behind the systematic use in the commentary of such one-word comments as "monkey" (*hou* 猴) and "interesting" (*ch'ü* 趣).[7] This last expression is particularly associated with the literary theories of Yüan Hung-tao 袁宏道 (1568–1610), who was greatly influenced by Li Chih. The "Fan-li" directs the reader to the collected works of Yüan Hung-tao to obtain a clearer understanding of the import of this concept.

Of course, even the briefest of marginal comments do more often function to describe the passage in question in slightly more substantive terms. Among the relatively more descriptive formulas, we find various expressions of delight—"worth the telling" (*k'o-shu* 可述), "well done" (*shuang-k'uai* 爽快), etc.; or incredulity—"who would have thought" (*pu-hsiang* 不想), "unforeseeable" (*ch'uai-mo pu-ch'u* 揣摩不出), etc.; approval—"serves him right" (*chih-te* 值得), "what else could he do?"

---

[7] *Li Cho-wu hsien-sheng p'i-p'ing Hsi-yu chi* 李卓吾先生批評西遊記 (Commentary Edition of the *Hsi-yu chi* by Li Chih), microfilm of Naikaku Bunko original, "Fan-li" 凡例. Recently, two separate copies of this edition without the "Fan-li" were discovered in China. See Liao Nan 蓼南, "Kuo-nei fa-hsien Ming-k'an Li Cho-wu p'ing *Hsi-yu chi*" 國內發現明刊李卓吾評西遊記 (Ming Editions of the Li Chih Commentary on the *Hsi-yu chi* Found in China), *Wen-hsüeh i-ch'an*, 1980. 2:34. A facsimile edition based on these finds has been published (Cheng-chou: Chung-chou shu-hua she, 1983) and a typeset version is forthcoming.

(*nai-ho* 奈何), etc.; as well as numerous exclamations concerning the reader's response to the text—"heartrending" (*tuan-ch'ang* 斷腸), "laughable" (*k'o-hsiao* 可笑), "one could strike the table and shout with amazement" (*p'ai-an chiao-ch'i* 拍案叫奇), "makes one want to spit out his rice all over the table" (*p'en fan man an* 噴飯滿案), etc. With regard to the portrayal of individual characters, the critics may offer us a simple label for the ideal figure—"true hero" (*hao-han* 好漢), "sage" (*sheng-jen* 聖人), etc.; or his converse—"unscrupulous hero" (*chien-hsiung* 奸雄), "bandit" (*tsei* 賊), etc.; or may provide succinct appreciation of a figure's admirable or damnable qualities—"knightly valor" (*hsia-ch'i* 俠氣), "extremely righteous" (*i-shen* 義甚), "too cruel" (*t'ai-tu* 太毒), "doltish" (*ch'un* 蠢), etc. Similar formulas may at times be applied to the dominant mood of a given scene—"how exciting" (*je-nao* 熱鬧), "how desolate" (*ch'i-liang* 淒涼), etc.; or in praise of an author's vision—"what insight" (*yu yen-li* 有眼力), "vast vision" (*ta-t'ung* 大通), etc. When it is an idea expressed in dialogue that is at issue, a critic may express his own personal opinion (e.g., "but I say..." *yü-wei...* 余謂 ...), or make a comparison to current practice ("nowadays..." *ju-chin...* 如今 ...); express approval ("right!" *shih* 是, "a universal principle" *t'ien-li* 天理, etc.), or express disapproval ("what foolishness" *hao tai-hua* 好呆話, "just breaking wind" *fang p'i* 放屁, etc.).

This sort of marginal commentary comes closer to serious criticism when it is directed not at the content level of the text, but rather at the style or rhetoric of the language. Here too, however, the terminology used can tend toward the formulaic expression of delight or disgust, often offering little insight into the basis for a particular judgment even when taken in conjunction with the passage to which it is appended. This, of course, is perfectly in keeping with the tantalizing imprecision that remains a characteristic feature of Chinese literary criticism in general, and the criticism on poetry contained in the *shih-hua* 詩話 and *tz'u-hua* 詞話 tradition of poetics in particular.[8] By reviewing a large amount of such terms borrowed from poetry, drama, and classical prose criticism for application to the fiction texts, we can, however, isolate a certain number of evaluative criteria—or at least variables—that occur widely in the Ming-Ch'ing commentaries. For example, the critics most typically offer praise for such literary qualities as suggestiveness (*han-hsü* 含蓄, *han-hsü* 涵蓄, etc.), tight control (*i pi pu luan* 一筆不亂, *pi-li chin-chiu* 筆力

[8] *Shih-hua* 詩話 and *tz'u-hua* 詞話 are collections of critical remarks on *shih* (lyric verse) and *tz'u* (lyric verse in meter). Their organization is very loose and the arguments are primarily subjective. Although the name dates from later, the practice of writing *shih-hua* dates back to the T'ang dynasty (618–907), while *tz'u-hua* began to be written in the following Sung dynasty (960–1279).

勁救, etc.), economy or precision (*pu fei-pi* 不費筆, *pu shu-lou* 不疏漏, *sheng-pi* 省筆, etc.), suppleness (*wen-jou i-ni* 溫柔旖旎), unhurried elegance (*hsien-hsien ya-ya* 閒閒雅雅), forcefulness (*yu pi-li* 有筆力, *chuang-shen* 壯甚, etc.), and indirection (*wen-pi wo-hsüan* 文筆斡旋, *yin-yin yüeh-yüeh* 隱隱躍躍, etc.); while faulting such things as disunity (*jung-tsa* 冗雜, *fen-fen pu-i* 紛紛不一, etc.), contrived plot (*niu-nieh* 扭捏), artificiality (*yu tso-tso* 有做作), blandness (*ju chiao-la* 如嚼蠟), poor timing (*t'ai-chi* 太急, *cho-mang* 着忙, etc.), and disjointedness ("*pu pu-ch'eng ti p'o-pien wen-tzu*" 補不成的破編文字). It may be noted that some of the above values are mutually contradictory, as for example forcefulness versus suggestiveness, or tightness versus looseness of narrative pace. Within the overall context of Chinese aesthetics, however, such examples may better be viewed as instances of paired concepts conceived as axes of variation rather than polar opposites.

One additional criterion of evaluation that emerges in the cryptic remarks of the marginal commentaries is that of originality of conception, as indicated in such expressions as "startling use of language" (*ching-jen wen-tzu* 驚人文字) and "amazing writing" (*huan-pi* 幻筆). In keeping with the fact that in premodern China (as in pre-Romantic Europe) sheer novelty was rarely elevated into a major critical canon, although it might have been a selling point with publishers and readers, such comments as these more often refer to a specific turn of phrase than to the overall conception of a fictional work. On the other hand, such pejoratives as "stereotyped mold" (*k'o-chiu* 窠臼) or "the same old pattern" (*chiu-t'ao* 舊套, *hsi-t'ao* 習套) tend to refer to somewhat broader configurations of structure and characterization.

Of greater interest to us here is a final subgroup of comments of a subjective nature in which specific advice is offered to the reader as to how to react to a given passage. Some of the most common of these simply direct the reader to "pay attention" (*cho-yen* 着眼, *chü-yen* 具眼) or not to pass over in haste ("ch'ieh wu ts'ao-ts'ao fang-kuo" 切勿草草放過) or misread ("mo-tso...k'an-kuo" 莫作...看過) certain key points in the text. More striking expressions may urge the reader to, "having read up to this point, close the book and try to guess what will happen" ("tu chih tz'u shih yen-chüan ts'ai chih" 讀至此試掩卷猜之); or may warn him to take his time (*ch'ieh-man* 且慢), to beware of being taken in by the author's misleading surface ("wu pei tso-che man-kuo" 勿被作者瞞過) and thus miss the underlying meaning.

In categorizing critical discussions of traditional Chinese fiction, we may also mention those items involving comparisons drawn between the text under scrutiny and any number of other texts of the Chinese literary corpus. Although the majority of such comments amount to little more than the championing of one work at the expense of another, so that to call them "comparative" may be rather misleading, in other cases the point at issue may suggest certain implicit assumptions as to the generic boundaries of vernacular fiction. For example, a good deal of such comments draw an analogy between the ideas and issues expressed in the fictional text and those of the classical tradition, whether these be canonic texts such as the Four Books or the *I Ching* 易經 (Book of Changes) or the major volumes of official historiography, notably the *Shih-chi* 史記 (Records of the Historian) and the *Han-shu* 漢書 (History of the Han Dynasty).[9] These discussions are important not only because they reflect the desire of the critics to defend the seriousness of their favorite works of vernacular fiction, but also because they invariably argue for the acceptance of fiction writing as a subclass of the larger category of prose in the literary language of the high tradition, in terms of both its overall purposes and its specific artistic devices. Significantly, such discussions rarely trouble themselves with the distinction between varying uses of vernacular and classical diction as the basic narrative medium, a point which seems to indicate that in the intellectual milieu of Ming-Ch'ing fiction this was a less than crucial aspect of the definition of the novel form.

At the same time, however, it must be noted that some of these same critics continue to use the term *hsiao-shuo* 小說 (fiction) in a pejorative vein, referring to the faults (use of stereotypes and unbridled fantasies, etc.) of the ordinary fiction writer (*hsiao-shuo chia* 小說家), above which their own chosen texts have risen. Within this context the expression *pai-kuan* 稗官, supposedly derived from an ancient institution whereby collectors of local anecdotes were employed by the imperial court to keep tabs on public opinion[10] and later extended as a euphemism for the vernacular fiction writer, is frequently used in a derogatory sense.[11] In

---

[9] For comparative remarks concerning vernacular fiction and classical texts, see chap. II below, items 1, 66, and 68 of the *Shui-hu chuan tu-fa* essay; chap. III below, items 2–3, 11, 21, and 23 of the *San-kuo yen-i tu-fa* essay; chap. IV below, items 34–35, 37, 48, 53, 69, 71, and 81 of the *Chin P'ing Mei tu-fa* essay; chap. V below, chapter comments 1.1, 2.6, 4.4, 22.2, 24.3, 26.3, 30.3, 33.2, 34.1, 35.1, 36.2, 40.2, 50.1, and 56.1 to the *Ju-lin wai-shih*; chap. VI below, items 4 and 24 of the *Hsi-yu chi tu-fa* essay; and chap. VII below, items 2–4, 6–9, 21, and 26–27 of the *Hung-lou meng tu-fa* essay.

[10] This idea is most prominently expressed in the "I-wen chih" 藝文志 (Monograph on Literature) chapter in Pan Ku's 班固 (32–92) *Han-shu* 漢書 (History of the Han Dynasty; Peking: Chung-hua shu-chü, 1975), p. 30.1745.

[11] The innumerable examples of this kind include the 1791 Kao E 高鶚 preface to the *Hung-lou meng*, quoted in *HLMC*, pp. 31–32; item 44 of the Ts'ai Ao 蔡奡 (courtesy name Yüan-fang 元放) *tu-fa* essay for the *Tung-Chou Lieh-kuo chih* 東周列國志 (Chronicle of the Contending States of the Eastern Chou Dynasty), quoted in *LCH*, vol. 1, p.

works of historical fiction, on the other hand, the related term *pai-shih*
稗史, taken to indicate any of the various subgenres along the continuum
from unofficial historiography to historical fiction, generally functions as
a positive designation that the critics take great pains to defend in prefaces
and colophons.[12] When arguing for the acceptance of works of *yen-i*
fiction as serious endeavors on a par with texts of official historiography,
writers frequently made the claim that the text under consideration was
equal to, or even superior to, the historical narratives of Ssu-ma Ch'ien
司馬遷 (b. 145 B.C.). In the majority of cases, however, it is the narrative
skill of Ssu-ma Ch'ien as shown in the best-known passages of the *Shih-
chi*, rather than the historical veracity or methodology of his work, on
which such remarks are based, and it is the function of that text as
relatively "popular" narrative literature (viz. its inclusion as one of Chin
Sheng-t'an's "works of genius," *ts'ai-tzu shu* 才子書) that might have
given rise to the comparison in the first place.[13]

The frequent practice of drawing up lists of favorite reading matter—the *ts'ai-tzu shu*, *ch'i-shu* 奇書 (marvelous works), etc.—may be
cited here as a further indication of what we may term an intertextual, if
not a generic or comparative focus of Ming-Ch'ing fiction criticism.
Chin Sheng-t'an's original notion of *ts'ai-tzu shu* was, of course, based on
aesthetic and pedagogic rather than generic considerations, but as such
designations became more and more conventional additions to book
titles during the Ch'ing period, they began to take on a specific generic

---

416; item 41 of an introductory essay ("Tsung-p'i" 總批) by Chang Shu-shen 張書紳 in
his *Hsin-shuo Hsi-yu chi* 新說西遊記 (A New Explication of the *Hsi-yu chi*); chapter
comment (100/48a) in the 1858 Lien-yüan-ko edition of the *Ching-hua yüan* 鏡花緣 (The
Fate of the Flowers in the Mirror); comments appended to story number one in the Shui-
hsiang chi-chiu 睡鄉祭酒 commentary edition of *Shih-erh lou* 十二樓 (Twelve Towers)
held in École des Langues Orientales, Paris; and the second Chin Sheng-t'an preface to the
Shui-hu chuan, quoted in *SHCHPP*, p. 8.

[12] See for example, the Yü-ming t'ang 玉茗堂 edition preface to the *Ts'an-T'ang Wu-
tai shih yen-i chuan* 殘唐五代史演義傳 (Romance of the Late T'ang and Five Dynasties
Period); item 5 of Ts'ai Yüan-fang's *tu-fa* essay in the *Hsi-yu cheng-tao ch'i-shu* 西遊證道
奇書 (The Extraordinary Book of the Way of Enlightenment through the *Hsi-yu chi*);
and item 1 of the "Fan-li" of the Pu-ching hsien-sheng 不經先生 commentary edition of
the *Sui Yang-ti yen-shih* 隋煬帝艷史 (The Merry Adventures of Emperor Yang of the
Sui).

[13] For references to the *Shih-chi* or Ssu-ma Ch'ien in the essays translated below, see
chap. II, items 1, 7, 10, 66, and 68 of the *Shui-hu chuan tu-fa* essay; chap. III, item 14 of the
San-kuo yen-i tu-fa essay; chap. IV, items 34–35, 37, 48, 53, 77, and 81 of the *Chin P'ing
Mei tu-fa* essay; and chap. V, chapter comments 1.1, 5.1, 22.2, 35.1, 36.2, and 56.1 to the
Ju-lin wai-shih. Interestingly enough, there is some disagreement among the critics as to
whether the task of the fiction writer is more or less difficult than that of Ssu-ma Ch'ien.

cast in that they came to refer, for the most part, to texts of extended vernacular prose fiction, that is, to the traditional Chinese novel.[14]

By far the most significant category of materials under investigation here is that which we have termed the compositional or structural. Here the traditional critics go beyond the level of random subjective remarks to set forth a wide range of technical principles of the writer's craft upon which their judgments of value, whether explicitly stated or simply implicit in their choice of a text for commentary, are ultimately based. In the following pages we will consider these more substantive terms and discussions in greater detail, since it is to these that our argument regarding the possibility of reconstructing a poetics of the Chinese novel refer.

[14] Chin Sheng-t'an's list of *ts'ai-tzu shu* was preceded by an earlier list of "five great works" (*wu ta pu wen-chang* 五大部文章) attributed to Li Chih in a late Ming work, Chou Hui 周暉, *Chin-ling so-shih* 金陵瑣事 (Nanking Trivia). The passage is quoted in *SHCTLHP*, p. 227. Both lists contain a variety of genres. A 1679 preface signed Li Yü to what appears to be the earliest datable edition of the Mao Tsung-kang commentary to the *San-kuo yen-i* records two lists of "four great marvelous works" (*ssu ta ch'i-shu* 四大奇書): an earlier one by Wang Shih-chen 王世貞 (1526–1590) includes the *Shih-chi*, the *Chuang Tzu* 莊子, the *Shui-hu chuan*, and the *Hsi-hsiang chi* 西廂記 (Romance of the Western Chamber) and a later one by Feng Meng-lung 馮夢龍 (1574–1646) that consists only of novels (the *San-kuo yen-i*, *Shui-hu chuan*, *Hsi-yu chi*, and *Chin P'ing Mei*). The 1679 preface is only found in the personal copy of the Tsui-keng t'ang edition owned by Ogawa Tamaki 小川環樹 (the section containing the two lists is translated into Japanese by him in his "Sankoku engi no Mō Seizan hihyōbon to Ri Ryūō bon" 三国演義の毛声山批評本と李笠翁本 [The Mao Sheng-shan Commentary Edition of the *San-kuo yen-i* and the Li Yü Edition], in his *Chūgoku shōsetsu shi no kenkyū* 中国小説史の研究 [Studies in the History of Chinese Fiction; Tokyo: Iwanami shoten, 1968], p. 157). The Li Yü preface to his own edition of the novel only mentions Feng Meng-lung's list of *ch'i-shu*.

Prior to this, Mao Lun's commentary on the *P'i-p'a chi* 琵琶記 (The Story of the Lute; a southern-style drama) proclaimed itself the "Seventh Work of Genius" (*Ti-ch'i ts'ai-tzu shu* 第七才子書), thus presenting itself as an appendage to Chin Sheng-t'an's list of six. The Tsui-keng t'ang edition of the *San-kuo yen-i*, however, took for itself the title of "First of the Four Great Marvelous Works" (*Ssu ta ch'i-shu ti-i chung* 四大奇書第一種), but later editions contain a fabricated preface attributed to Chin Sheng-t'an that gives the title of "First Work of Genius" to the novel. Chang Chu-p'o then claimed the title of "Number One Marvelous Work" (*Ti-i ch'i-shu* 第一奇書) for the *Chin P'ing Mei*.

In the eighteenth century and later, numerous works were published as "works of genius." They included: *San ts'ai-tzu shu Yü Chiao Li* 三才子書玉嬌梨 (Third Work of Genius *Yü Chiao Li*), *Ssu ts'ai-tzu shu P'ing Shan Leng Yen* 四才子書平山冷燕 (Fourth Work of Genius *P'ing Shan Leng Yen*), *Ch'i ts'ai-tzu shu* 七才子書 (Seventh Work of Genius; a combined edition of the above two works), *Ti-pa ts'ai-tzu shu Pai-kuei chih* 第八才子書白圭志 (Eighth Work of Genius, Chronicle of the White Jade; also later published as the Tenth Work of Genius), and *Ti-chiu ts'ai-tzu shu Chan-kuei chuan* 第九才子書斬鬼傳 (Ninth Work of Genius, The Execution of the Demons). These novels, together with the *San-kuo yen-i* (First Work of Genius), the *Shui-hu chuan* (Fifth Work of Genius), and the *Hsi-hsiang chi* (Sixth Work of Genius), make up a fairly complete list,

In view of the recent emphasis on the concept of "structure" as a central analytical framework for the study of a variety of cultural forms, it is worth noting that an aspect of the art of fiction writing to which we may readily apply this term seems to have also preoccupied the Ming-Ch'ing critics. As a matter of fact the same expression that is used as the standard equivalent of the term "structure" today (*chieh-kou* 結構) appears in the writings of a number of the major literary figures of the period.[15] It is true that in a variety of alternate expressions (*ko-chü* 格局, *pu-chih* 布置, *chü-mien* 局面, *kou-chü* 構局, *p'u-hsü* 鋪序, etc.), and particularly in the term *chang-fa* 章法 used by Chin Sheng-t'an, Mao

---

which with the exception of the last-mentioned work, all belong to the genre of full-length fiction. The words *ts'ai-tzu* were also used for books centering on talented females such as *Nü ts'ai-tzu shu* 女才子書 (Book of Women Geniuses) and, in an alternate title for the *Pai-kuei chih*, *Ti-i ts'ai-nü chuan* 第一才女傳 (The Story of the Number One Talented Woman), usages bound to call Chin Sheng-t'an's list of *ts'ai-tzu shu* to mind.

The late additions to the list of *ts'ai-tzu shu* are primarily romantic tales belonging to the genre of *ts'ai-tzu chia-jen hsiao-shuo* 才子佳人小說 (tales of young geniuses and talented beauties), which began to be written in the late Ming and flourished in the Ch'ing dynasty. This was the case also for works calling themselves *hsü ts'ai-tzu shu* 續才子書 (Secondary Works of Genius) such as *Feng-huang ch'ih* 鳳凰池 (The Phoenix Pool; ranked number four) and *Wu-feng yin* 五鳳吟 (Song of the Five Phoenixes; ranked number six), as well as for a number of minor works published with the words *ch'i-shu* 奇書 (marvelous work) in their titles: *Lin Lan Hsiang* 林蘭香 (ranked number two marvelous work), *Hsüeh Yüeh Mei* 雪月梅 (ranked number one), *Yeh-sou p'u-yen* 野叟曝言 (The Old Man's Wild Words; also ranked number one), *Ju-i chün chuan* 如意君傳 (Mr. As You Like It; ranked number one "pleasing" [*k'uai-huo* 快活] *ch'i-shu*, not the same as the erotic work with the same title), and *Lien-tzu p'ing yen-i* 蓮子瓶演義 (Romance of the Lotus-Shaped Vase; called the Later T'ang *ch'i-shu* 後唐奇書). Some of these novels, such as *Lin Lan Hsiang*, *Hsüeh Yüeh Mei*, and *Yeh-sou p'u-yen*, were only influenced by *ts'ai-tzu chia-jen* fiction conventions and cannot be considered representative of that genre. In the titles of some of the *ts'ai-tzu chia-jen* novels mentioned above, the words *ts'ai-tzu* also refer to the young "geniuses" portrayed in the novels, thus the *P'ing Shan Leng Yen* can be taken as the Fourth Work of Genius or the Book of the Four Geniuses. The title of the novel is made up from a character from each of the names of the four geniuses.

A list of eleven *ts'ai-tzu shu* for texts of the Cantonese metrical narrative form known as *mu-yü shu* 木魚書 included versions of material labeled *ts'ai-tzu shu* in other genres, such as the *San-kuo yen-i*, *Yü Chiao Li*, *P'ing Shan Leng Yen*, *Hsi-hsiang chi*, and *P'i-p'a chi*, as well as two works that became famous for their treatment in the *mu-yü shu* genre: *Ti-pa ts'ai-tzu shu Hua-chien chi* 第八才子書花箋記 (Eighth Work of Genius, The Elegant Letter) and *Ti-chiu ts'ai-tzu shu Erh ho-hua shih* 第九才子書二荷花史 (Ninth Work of Genius, History of the Double Lotuses).

[15] For examples of the use of this expression, see chap. III below, item 13 of the *San-kuo yen-i tu-fa* essay; chap. V below, chapter comment 33.3 to the *Ju-lin wai-shih*; and chap. VII below, items 23 and 25 of the *Hung-lou meng tu-fa* essay. The term appears in the heading of the first section of Li Yü's collected comments on dramatics, *Li Li-weng ch'ü-hua* 李笠翁曲話 (Li Yü on Drama), Ch'en To 陳多, ed. (Ch'ang-sha: Hu-nan jen-min, 1981), pp. 1–13, and appears as well in Chang Hsüeh-ch'eng's (1738–1801) exploration of classical

Tsung-kang, and Chang Chu-p'o,[16] it is more a sense of compositional arrangement than structural ordering, strictly speaking, which is at issue. Nevertheless, we do find a number of discussions in which the metaphor of architectural construction is emphasized in order to explain the conception of narrative in terms of the articulation and assembling of constituent elements to form a fully integrated textual edifice. Li Yü 李漁 (1611–1680), for example, after explaining his conception of structure in drama in terms of the integration of body tissues in the human anatomy, elaborates at considerable length on the construction metaphor:

> It is the same when a master builder constructs a house. After first leveling the foundation, but before raising the construction frame, he first calculates where he will build the main hall, where he will put in doors, what type of lumber he needs for the beams and what type for the rafters. He always waits until the layout is perfectly clear before ever raising pick and ax.

> 工師之建宅亦然: 基址初平, 間架未立, 先籌何處建廳, 何方開戶, 棟需何木, 梁用何材; 必俟成局了然, 始可揮斤運斧.[17]

---

prose art in his *Wen-shih t'ung-i* 文史通義 (General Principles of Historiography; Taipei: Commercial Press, 1967), p. 138. Additional examples may be found in the Chang Wu-chiu 張無咎 preface to the *P'ing-yao chuan* 平妖傳 (Pacification of the Demons; quoted in *LCH*, vol. 1, p. 234); item 5 of Ts'ai Yüan-fang's *Hsi-yu cheng-tao ch'i-shu tu-fa* essay and item 39 of his *Shui-hu hou-chuan* 水滸後傳 (Continuation of the *Shui-hu chuan*) *tu-fa* essay (for the latter, see *SHCTLHP*, p. 575); Mao Tsung-kang chapter comments for chaps. 92 and 107 (see *SKYI*, pp. 92.910 and 107.1066), and comments in minor texts such as *Hsin-hua ch'un-meng chi* 新華春夢記 (Spring Dream of New China; 1917 edition in the Tōyō Bunko, Tokyo), pp. 5/62 and 8/116; and item 6 of the "*Hsüeh Yüeh Mei tu-fa*" 雪月梅 讀法 (How to Read the *Hsüeh Yüeh Mei*) by Tung Meng-fen 董孟汾 (Te-hsüeh t'ang edition, 1775), p. 1b.

[16] Examples of the use of this term appear below in chap. II item 18 of the *Shui-hu chuan tu-fa* essay; chap. IV item 7 of the *Chin P'ing Mei tu-fa* essay; and chap. VII item 16 of the *Hung-lou meng tu-fa* essay. The sixteenth section of Wang Chi-te's 王驥德 (d. 1623) *Ch'ü-lü* 曲律 (Rules of Dramatic Prosody) deals with *chang-fa* 章法 or the organization of textual sections larger than the sentence, whether paragraphs or dramatic acts.

[17] *Li Li-weng ch'ü-hua*, section on *chieh-kou* 結構, p. 7. This famous passage might have been influenced by a similar one in Wang Chi-te's *Ch'ü-lü*. See *Wang Chi-te Ch'ü-lü* 王驥德曲律, Ch'en To 陳多 and Yeh Ch'ang-hai 葉長海, eds. (Ch'ang-sha: Hu-nan jen-min, 1983), p. 121. One or both of these passages might be behind the restatement of this idea in chapter comment 33.3 to the *Ju-lin wai-shih* (see chap. V below). Probably the first person to use this construction metaphor and the tailoring metaphor also quoted from *Li Li-weng ch'ü-hua* below (n. 21) was Liu Hsieh 劉勰 (465?–520?) in the "Fu-hui" 附會 (Organization) chapter of his *Wen-hsin tiao-lung* 文心雕龍. See the annotated edition by Fan Wen-lan 范文瀾, *Wen-hsin tiao-lung chu* 文心雕龍註 (Peking: Jen-min wen-hsüeh, 1979), p. 43.650. The passage is translated in Vincent Yu-chung Shih, *The Literary Mind and the Carving of Dragons* (Taipei: Chung Hwa Book Co., 1961), p. 321: "It [organization] may be compared to the role of the foundation in the building of a house and the tailor's pattern in the making of a dress" ("Jo chu shih chih hsü chi-kou, ts'ai-i chih tai feng-ch'i i" 若築室之須基構, 裁衣之待縫緝矣).

The term "construction frame" (*chien-chia* 間架) derives from the language of classical prose criticism, appearing as early as Lü Tsu-ch'ien's 呂祖謙 (1137–1181) *Ku-wen kuan-chien* 古文關鍵 (Crucial Aspects of Classical Prose), and it figures in the fiction criticism of both Chang Chu-p'o and Chih-yen chai.[18]

Beyond these explicit descriptions of the "construction" of the narrative text, however, we must look for principles of coherency in structural design more often as merely implicit in the discussion of certain related topics without being fully verbalized. It may perhaps appear unnecessary to pursue so relentlessly the concept of structure in Chinese critical writings, but in view of the common impression of Chinese fiction among modern readers as an incorrigibly "episodic" medium—that is, given to the loose stringing together of incidents with little apparent regard for compositional integrity—it is of major significance that the traditional critics did, in fact, have an eye out for structural unity in their texts. The desideratum of structural integrity surfaces most explicitly in the praise variously offered for the quality of internal consistency (*i-kuan* 一貫, *lien-kuan* 聯貫, *kuan-ch'uan* 貫串, *i-ch'uan* 一串, etc.) and is made even clearer in such lines as "the entire work reads like a single sentence" ("*i-p'ien ju i-chü*" 一篇如一句).[19] In a more tenuous sense, of course, the notion of overall structure is also implied whenever critics make reference to the entire text (*t'ung-pu* 通部, *i-pu* 一部, *ch'üan-shu* 全書, etc.) with which they are working, or make comments that direct the reader to consider what he has just read in the light of other sections of the work or note patterns that recur in every chapter.

The fact that the traditional critics were interested in viewing works of fiction from an overall structural perspective may also be demonstrated by their frequent mention of those points at which an author may attempt to sum up, or otherwise pull together, material that has already appeared—in other words, the attempt to reintegrate earlier narrative elements into continuing patterns of the text. A wide variety of terminology is used to designate this particular function, ranging from the technical terms of the formal essay (*kuan-ho* 關合, *tsung-chieh* 總結, etc.) to certain theatrical jargon referring to the end of a sequence (*shou-k'o* 收科, *shou-ch'ang* 收場, etc.) and other general expressions for summation (*shou-lung* 收攏, *pao-lo* 包羅, *she-tsung* 攝總, etc.). By the same token, the common practice of calling the reader's attention to passages that pro-

---

[18] See Lü Tsu-ch'ien 呂祖謙, *Ku-wen kuan-chien* 古文關鍵 (Crucial Aspects of Classical Prose; Taipei: Kuang-wen shu-chü, 1970), interlineal comment, p. 56. The term also appears in item 12 of the *Chin P'ing Mei tu-fa* essay (see chap. IV below), and a Chih-yen chai marginal comment, *CYCPYCC*, p. 1.9 (chap. I, p. 9).

[19] See chap. III below, item 18 of the *San-kuo yen-i tu-fa* essay, and Mao Tsung-kang chapter comment, *SKYI* 57.564.

vide a "key" to the interpretation of an entire work, as indicated by such expressions as *kuan-chien* 關鍵, *kuan-mu* 關目, *t'i-kang* 提綱, *ta kuan-so ch'u* 大關鎖處, *ta-chih* 大旨, *tsung-chih* 宗旨, *kang-niu* 綱紐, *shu-lieh* 樞柝, *ta-kang* 大綱, etc., also carries the obvious implication of at least a sufficient degree of overall structural (or thematic) unity to allow such "keys" to be meaningful. One term of particular interest is the notion of "[setting up] the controlling conception or feature" ([*li*]*chu-nao* [立] 主腦), with its underlying assumption of a unitary focus at the very inception of the creative process. Li Yü devotes an entire section of his treatise on dramatic structure to this concept, which he says has reference to both the plot structure of a play and the taking of central characters as the backbone of a drama. In most fiction criticism, this expression is used more or less interchangeably with the other terms for the "key" to a text cited above.[20]

As a rule, however, the traditional Chinese fiction critics tend to spend less time on such aspects of overall structural unity than they do in the articulation and ordering of smaller sections and units of the narrative text. This orientation need present no difficulty since, after all, it is precisely such a view of the act of subdividing and rearranging human experience into meaningful patterns of sequence that we now understand to be the essence of the art of narration in any cultural context. Li Yü, again, provides us with a sophisticated discussion of this principle:

> Writing plays is something like the tailoring of clothing. In the beginning one cuts up whole cloth into pieces, and then one proceeds to piece together the cut fragments. Cutting something up into fragments is easy; it is piecing these back together that is difficult. The artistry of piecing together lies completely in the fineness of the stitching: if a given section happens to be too loosely connected, then holes in the composition [lit. "split seams"] will appear throughout the piece.

> 編戲有如縫衣, 其初則以完全者剪碎, 其後又以剪碎者湊成; 剪碎易, 湊成難; 湊成之工全在針線緊密; 一節偶疎, 全篇之破綻出矣.[21]

[20] For Li Yü's remarks on this term, see *Li Li-weng ch'ü-hua*, pp. 19–20. Prior to Li Yü, Wang Chi-te used *chu-i* 主意 (main idea) and *ta t'ou-nao* 大頭腦 (controlling center) to talk about the thematic and plot aspects, respectively, of what Li Yü called *chu-nao*. See *Wang Chi-te Ch'ü-lü*, pp. 138, 154. Occurrences of the term in fiction criticism per se include the Tung-kuan ko 東觀閣 edition of the *Hung-lou meng*, p. 2/7a; *Ju-lin wai-shih p'ing* 儒林外史評 (Commentary on the *Ju-lin wai-shih*; Pao-wen ko 1885 edition), p. 54/56a; chapter comment 2.1 to the *Ju-lin wai-shih* (chap. v below); and the preface to the *Hung-lou meng ying* 紅樓夢影 (Shadows of the *Hung-lou meng*), by Hsi-hu san-jen 西湖散人 (pseud.), quoted in *HLMC*, p. 55.

[21] *Li Li-weng ch'ü-hua*, "Mi chen-hsien" 密針線 (Fine Stitching) section, p. 26. A similar discussion of the piecing together of smaller units of a text appears in *Li Li-weng p'ing-yüeh San-kuo chih* 李笠翁評閱三國志 (*San-kuo yen-i* with Commentary by Li Yü; microfilm held in Gest Oriental Library, Princeton University, of original held in the Bibliothèque nationale, Paris), pp. 38/4b, 5b, marginal comments.

Often it appears that the critic's conception of his duties in connection with the tailoring together of smaller narrative units consisted of nothing more than drawing the reader's attention to those points at which the various sections of a text are joined together. These sections can be larger or smaller than the chapter divisions supplied by the author (or publisher).[22] What at first sight may seem to be a completely mechanical analysis in certain cases involves some rather penetrating insights into the makeup of the fictional text, as for example in the *tu-fa* 讀法 essays on the *San-kuo yen-i* and the *Hung-lou meng* contained in this volume.[23] The precise order of magnitude of the units isolated in such discussions may vary considerably, from entire halves of a text (*shang-hsia pan-chieh* 上下半截), suprachapter sequences (*chih* 支), or discrete episodes (*shih-chieh* 事節, *tuan-lo* 段落, *tuan* 段, *kung-an* 公案, etc.), to elements of less than chapter length. Chih-yen chai, for example, points out the manner in which chapter divisions in the *Hung-lou meng* may break down into smaller subsections, and a commentator of an edition of the *San-kuo yen-i* attributed to Li Yü notes certain recurring elements that signal the closure of chapter units.[24] In addition, a number of critics cite what they regard as capsule biographies (*hsiao-chuan* 小傳, *hsing-*

[22] The texts of premodern Chinese novels within each chapter were not further broken up by the author or publisher into paragraphs or subsections divided by headings or spaces. As for units larger than the chapter, it was not the custom to divide the novels, some of which were quite lengthy, into parts or volumes in an explicit fashion, as was done in Europe at the same time. The physical divisions of the printed editions of some of the novels did point to thematic or plot divisions in the work (such as the structuring of the *Chin P'ing Mei* into decades of chapters), but these physical divisions were neither self-explanatory nor consistently maintained in later editions. Therefore it was up to the commentator to point out for the reader the parameters of intelligible sections in the text sometimes marked off in Western printing through paragraphs, subsections, headings, and suprachapter divisions.

It should also be noted that the chapter divisions and their content in the more or less standard versions of the major novels are often at considerable variance with earlier editions, as in the case of the *San-kuo yen-i* (originally broken into 240 *tse* 則 subsections but later divided into 120 *hui* 回 or chapters), the *Chin P'ing Mei* (here the chapter divisions are basically the same but the content differs between editions), and the *Shui-hu chuan* (cut to seventy chapters and otherwise reedited by Chin Sheng-t'an).

[23] See Mao Tsung-kang's enumeration of the various "beginnings" (*ch'i* 起) and "conclusions" (*chieh* 結) in item 6 of the *San-kuo yen-i tu-fa* essay (chap. III below), and the discussion of the major sections of the text of the *Hung-lou meng* in items 13–14 and 23 of the *tu-fa* essay on that novel in chap. VII below.

[24] See *Li Li-weng p'ing-yüeh San-kuo chih*, marginal comment, pp. 4/9a–b and 48/7b–8a. For information on this text and its relationship to the early Mao Tsung-kang editions, from which it borrows both commentary and portions of the text of the novel as edited by Mao Tsung-kang (and/or his father Mao Lun), see Ogawa Tamaki, "*Sankoku engi* no Mō Seizan hihyōbon to Ri Ryūō bon," pp. 153–62.

chuang 行狀) as another type of narrative unit that does not coincide
with chapter divisions.

In considering the segmentation of the narrative continuum into
meaningful units of text, the traditional commentators pay a good deal
of attention to those units that they can identify as the beginnings and
endings of either smaller sections or the entire structure of a given work.
As in the case of Aristotle and his critical descendants in the West, the
Ming-Ch'ing critics seem to have accepted the assumption that to a large
extent it is these two points that determine overall structural coherence,
not only in the simple sense of enclosing the narrative sequence but also
in conditioning its pace and general shape throughout an entire composition.[25] In addition to simply applying conventional labels to opening
and concluding sections, using terminology borrowed from classical
prose criticism—"beginning" (*k'ai-tuan* 開端, *mao-t'ou* 冒頭) and "ending" (*shou-wei* 收尾), etc.—or dramaturgy—"prologue" (*hsieh-tzu* 楔子)
or "finale" (*fang-ch'ang* 放場), etc.—the relevant comments may also
go on to point out further nuances in the handling of this aspect of
narrative structure. Mao Tsung-kang's illuminating discussion of the
manner in which the denouement of the *San-kuo yen-i* manipulates the
aesthetic and emotional expectations of the reader to conform to certain
deterministic patterns of events in the universe is one such example.[26] In
his marginal commentary on the text itself, Mao Tsung-kang also provides interesting discussions of such related points as the appearance at
the very beginning and at the very end of the massive work before him
of the word "emptiness" (*k'ung* 空),[27] from which he derives a substantive point of interpretation; and the elucidation of the manner in which
the concluding scenes of the novel bear out narrative threads planted at
the start of the book.[28] A favorite metaphor employed by numerous
critics to describe this sort of resonance between beginning, middle, and
end is the "Ch'ang-shan snake formation" (*Ch'ang-shan she chen* 常山
蛇陣), a battle line whose ranks are able to close in or spread out with
perfect coordination in response to an attack at any given point.[29]

[25] See Aristotle, *The Poetics* (New York: Loeb Classical Library, 1927), p. 31.

[26] See chap. III below, item 8 of the *San-kuo yen-i tu-fa* essay.

[27] *SKYI* 120.1191, interlineal comment. Mao himself added the final motif in his own
edition.

[28] Chapter comment (*SKYI* 114.1126–27) and interlineal comment (*SKYI* 120.1190).

[29] See, for example, chap. VII below, item 25 of the *Hung-lou meng tu-fa* essay. The
expression also occurs in a section of Mao Tsung-kang's chapter comment cited below
from chap. 94 (*SKYI* 94.929), as well as a comment attributed to Ch'en Chi-ju 陳繼儒
(1558–1639) on the *Ch'un-ch'iu Lieh-kuo chih chuan* 春秋列國志傳 (The Contending
States of the Ch'un-ch'iu Period; preface 1615), p. 1/84a, section comment. The expression seems to originate from the 1st millenium B.C. text on military strategy, the *Sun Tzu*

After having taken due note of the structural significance of major segments of the narrative texts, the next obvious aspect of textual arrangement is the order of incidents presented in a particular fictional sequence, an aspect referred to by such terms as *tz'u-hsü* 次序, *tz'u-ti* 次第, *p'ai-lieh* 排列, *p'u-hsü* 鋪敍, etc. At numerous points the critics call the reader's attention to the fact that a given incident must appear before or after another, with special interest devoted to instances of deliberate reversal or alteration of the "historical" or "natural" order for a desired literary effect. With reference to military scenes in the *San-kuo yen-i*, for example, Mao Tsung-kang makes the point that the narrative focus purposely manipulates the relation between material presented before a given battle scene and the representation of the fighting itself.[30] In describing this sort of tampering with narrative time, the critics frequently distinguish between "forward" or "backward" (*shun* 順 versus *tao* 倒 or *ni* 逆) direction of narrative flow, and identify such devices as "advance insertion" (*tao-ch'a fa* 倒插法) or "passages inserted into the middle of other passages" ("heng-chien tsai chung che" 橫間在中者) as major elements of the fiction writer's craft. At worst, these techniques tend merely to shuffle the narrative material for the purpose of variety, but at other times they may function to create narrative suspense by deliberately withholding information or anticipated actions at one point (e.g., "liu tsai hou-wen shih chien..." 留在後文始見...) in order to leave the "filling in " (*pu* 補) of the expected material for a later point in the text. This leaves considerable room for provisional gap filling on the part of the reader.[31]

In connection with both the segmentation of the narrative continuum and the reordering of the resulting segments into meaningful sequences, key importance falls to the particular points of transition or change of situation since, in the final analysis, it is the perception of such change of focus or direction that is responsible for the apprehension of narrative units in the first place. This, at least, is the assumption underlying Aristotle's famous emphasis of the two elements "reversal" (*peripeteia*) and "discovery" (*anagnorisis*) as the central determinants of narrative shape.[32] With regard to this aspect of structural analysis, the traditional Chinese critics distinguish between points of sudden reversal and techniques of gradual shading off from one narrative tack to another. As

---

孫子, and occurs in several variations: *Ch'ang-shan chih she* 常山之蛇, *ch'ang-she chen fa* 長蛇陣法, and *Ch'ang-shan she yao* 常山蛇腰.

[30] Mao Tsung-kang chapter comment (*SKYI* 48.477).

[31] Hence the frequent enjoinders to the reader to "guess" what is about to happen.

[32] See Aristotle, *The Poetics*, pp. 39, 59.

examples of the former alternative we find frequent use of terms borrowed from classical essay technique to describe a deliberate change of
direction of argument (*chuan* 轉, *huan* 換, etc.), as well as numerous
expressions of surprise or delight at the abruptness of the change (*tun-ts'o*
頓挫, *i-che* 一折, *hu-jan* 忽然, etc.) or the clean break made with what has
gone before (*t'o-hsieh* 脫卸, *pieh k'ai sheng-mien* 別開生面, *ch'ien-hou t'o-
hsien* 前後脫線, etc.).[33] It was part of the conventional rhetoric of the
simulated oral narrator in Chinese vernacular fiction to signal to the
reader any shifting of narratorial point of view or focus when such
occurred. The quotation of poetry by the narrator was also used to
accentuate narrative divisions. As these devices became less important in
later fiction and later editions of earlier works, some of this function was
taken over by the commentators.

    On the other hand, however, critical approbation is regularly
awarded to the contriving of a smooth transition from one narrative unit
to another, such that one incident appears to follow on the heels of
another in a manner that leaves a minimal impression of the joining of
two discrete sections. This impression is described through a variety of
metaphoric expressions, such as the invisible stitchwork referred to in the
Ch'an term "secret transmission of the golden needle" (*chin-chen an-tu*
金針暗度),[34] Chin Sheng-t'an's somewhat original figure of the "otter's
tail" (*t'a-wei fa* 獺尾法),[35] or frequent praise for narrative junctions that
leave no scar or trace (*wu-hen* 無痕, *wu-chi* 無迹, etc.). By the same token,
fiction writers may often be faulted for joints between sections that are
too abrupt (*t'u-jan* 突然), too obtrusive (*lou* 露), or remind the critic of
"split seams" (*p'o-chan* 破綻).

    As is already quite evident by this point, the traditional Chinese
fiction critics, while demonstrably concerned with the question of overall
structural models and the ordering of major constituent units, were far
more interested in the fine interweaving of narrative units on a smaller
scale. In passing over at this point into the area of this smaller order of
magnitude, it may be more correct to say that in the following discussions we will be dealing not with the structure but with the texture of
narrative discourse, that is, with the interweaving of discrete narrative

---

[33] See *Li Li-weng p'ing-yüeh San-kuo chih*, "the technique of leaving aside one thread of
the plot for the moment" ("an-hsia i-t'ou chih fa" 按下一頭之法), p. 2/6b–7a, and Mao
Tsung-kang chapter comments (*SKYI* 64.637, 69.684).

[34] For the origin of this term, see Isshū Miura and Ruth Fuller Sasaki, *The Zen Kōan*
(New York: Harcourt, Brace & World, 1965), p. 108, n. 154. In the Chih-yen chai
commentary, the variation *t'ou tu chin-chen* 偷渡金針 is used (*CYCPYCC* 8.167, marginal comment). See also chap. IV below, item 48 of the *Chin P'ing Mei tu-fa* essay.

[35] See chap. II below, item 58 of the *Shui-hu chuan tu-fa* essay.

elements to compose a dense fabric of mimetic substance. Of course, when we speak here of "texture," "fabric" or "interweaving" we are clearly indulging in a sort of metaphorics that may tend to obscure the true nature of the aesthetic issues involved. But in this case the indulgence may be at least partly justified by the fact that this same kind of heavily metaphorical description occupies a central place in the writings of the Chinese critics as well. We have already cited one extended example of the needlework metaphor in the Li Yü passage on fine stitching above, and similar expressions derived from the craft of sewing and tailoring appear quite frequently in the traditional commentaries, especially such terms as "needle and thread" (*chen-hsien* 針線), "brocade" (*chin* 錦), "sewing of seams" (*feng* 縫), etc. Mao Tsung-kang's discussion of what he calls "the technique of inserting additional threads to fill out the figure and adjusting the needlework to balance the pattern" ("t'ien-ssu pu-chin, i-chen yün-hsiu chih miao" 添絲補錦, 移針勻繡 之妙) represents but another, more extended version of the same metaphorical reference.[36] Moreover, this same essential conception of the narrative function of the piecing together, or overlapping, of contiguous chunks of text may also be expressed in a variety of other sets of metaphors derived from such fields as horticulture—"places where the leaves and branches are grafted on" ("kuo-chih chieh-yeh ch'u" 過枝接葉處), "transplanting of flowers and trees" ("i-hua chieh-mu fa" 移花接木法), etc.; descriptions of natural landscape—"sharp overlapping of distinct peaks" (*ying-tieh ch'i-feng* 硬疊奇峯); music—"the technique of interrupting drums with woodwinds and interspersing strings among the bells" ("sheng-hsiao chia ku, ch'in-se chien chung chih miao" 笙簫夾鼓, 琴瑟間鐘之妙); meteorology—"the technique of making sleet appear when it is about to snow and thunder reverberate when it is about to rain" ("chiang hsüeh chien hsien, chiang yü wen lei chih miao" 將雪 見霰, 將雨聞雷之妙), "the technique of making the stars move and the dipper revolve and causing rain to inundate things and wind to overturn them" ("hsing-i tou-chuan, yü-fu feng-fan chih miao" 星移斗轉, 雨覆 風翻之妙), etc.;[37] or medicine—various references to "pulse" (*lo-mai* 落脈), "veins" (*mai-lo* 脉絡), etc.

[36] See chap. III below, item 18 of the *San-kuo yen-i tu-fa* essay.

[37] The expression *kuo-chih chieh-yeh* 過枝接葉 may be found in a Mao Tsung-kang chapter comment (*SKYI* 81.800) and numerous interlineal comments (*SKYI* 10.90, 28.282, 38.379), while the expression *i-hua chieh-mu* 移花接木 is used by Ts'ai Yüan-fang in item 37 of the *Shui-hu hou-chuan tu-fa* essay (*SHCTLHP* 575). The expression *ying-tieh ch'i-feng* 硬疊奇峯 is used in a chapter comment to chap. 12 of an edition of the *Jou p'u-t'uan* 肉蒲團 (The Prayer Mat of Flesh) held in the Diet Library, Tokyo. For the last three terms, see chap. III below, items 16, 13, and 11 of the *San-kuo yen-i tu-fa* essay.

One metaphor of particular relevance to our investigation of Chinese narrative theory is that of the joiner's technique of mortise and tenon or "tongue and groove" insertion of one plank into another, as indicated by usages of the character *sun* 筍 or 笋 (one or the other of these homophones appears almost without exception in place of the more correct, but unfamiliar, graph 榫). Occurrences of this term merit our special attention not only because they provide a good example of the sort of construction metaphors discussed earlier, but also because they convey a rather useful description of the manner in which the Chinese critics saw the contours of the next narrative unit taken up or evoked in the unit preceding it. Perhaps the fullest treatment of this metaphor is found in Chang Chu-p'o's references to "the point at which the tenon is inserted" (*ju-sun ch'u* 入筍處),[38] but a number of other compounds using the same basic term (*chieh-sun* 接筍, *ch'u-sun* 出筍, *ho-sun* 合筍, and particularly *tou-sun* 斗筍) are widely current both before and after his time.[39] In the final analysis the tenor of this metaphor is in most cases practically indistinguishable from that of the "seam" (*feng* 縫), and in fact the two characters are practically interchangeable in many of the above compounds and even appear together in various combined phrases (e.g., *tou-sun ho-feng* 斗筍合縫, *hao sun-feng* 好筍縫, etc.).[40] A further example of this latter sort of combined usage, in a collection of commentary on the *Ju-lin wai-shih*, gives a more detailed idea of the conception of this particular narrative technique:

> In the midst of Wang Hui's talk about how he is fated to succeed in the examinations, the section in which Chou Chin corrects the student's composition is dovetailed or patched into [*tou-sun chieh-feng* 鬭筍接縫] the narrative. As one might think it [the transition] too abrupt, Wang Hui's instructions to his servant are inserted to slow down the pace.

正說着鼎元, 鬭筍接縫批做一節. 意嫌太促, 故夾入吩咐家人以緩之.[41]

[38] See chap. IV below, item 13 of the *Chin P'ing Mei tu-fa* essay.

[39] For an example of the use of the term *chieh-sun* 接筍, see *SKYI* 42.423, interlineal comment; for *ho-sun* 合筍, see *SHCHPP* 8.189, Chin Sheng-t'an interlineal comment; for *ch'u-sun* 出筍, see the "Ch'ung-chen" edition of the *Chin P'ing Mei*, *Hsin-k'o hsiu-hsiang p'i-p'ing Chin P'ing Mei* 新刻繡像批評金瓶梅 (Newly Cut, Illustrated, and Commented *Chin P'ing Mei*), p. 10/37a, marginal comment. Mao Tsung-kang discusses the term *tou-sun* 斗筍 in a chapter comment (*SKYI* 113.1118). *Tou-sun* 斗筍 is probably the same in meaning as *tou-sun* 逗筍. For an example of the latter orthography, see Chang Hsin-chih interlineal comment, *CYY* 24.340. 斗 also appears as 鬭.

[40] For an example of the use of the term *tou-sun ho-feng* 斗筍合縫, see *SHCHPP* 16.314, Chin Sheng-t'an interlineal comment. *Hao sun-feng* 好筍縫 is found in a marginal comment on story six of the *P'ai-an ching-ch'i* 拍案驚奇 (Slapping the Table in Astonishment), Li T'ien-i 李田意, ed. (Hong Kong: Yu-lien ch'u-pan she, 1966), p. 119.

[41] *Ju-lin wai-shih p'ing*, p. 2/6a. For the section of the novel referred to, see *JLWS*, p. 2/12b–13a.

Additional ways of expressing the same concept of textural linkage include references to the insertion of interludes (*ch'uan-ch'a* 穿插)[42] or the use of various metaphors of veinlike interweaving (*mai-lo* 脉絡) to describe the density of overlapping at issue. In the language of classical prose and poetry criticism, the fixed terms "introduction" (*ch'i* 起) and "development" (*ch'eng* 承) are modified to describe the manner in which a given textual unit may both take up a point introduced earlier and simultaneously lead in a new direction (*ch'eng-shang ch'i-hsia* 承上 起下), that is, in terms of the function of interconnecting contiguous narrative units.[43]

While all of the above discussions, both metaphorical and otherwise, deal technically with the manner in which contiguous sections of a text are joined together, another group of related metaphors turns the critical focus to structural arrangements whereby discontinuous and noncontiguous sections of a text link up to form a recurring pattern, which in turn serves as a framework for the perception of structural relations. A variety of figurative expressions are used by the traditional critics to refer to this aspect of narrative art, most notably the notion of cross-reflection or, more accurately, "projection and reflection" (*chao-ying* 照應, *ying-chao* 映照, *ying-she* 映射, etc.). Here again, the order of magnitude of the textual units under analysis may vary widely. For example, when Chin Sheng-t'an speaks of the narrative technique he terms "snake in the grass or [discontinuous] chalk line" (*ts'ao-she hui-hsien* 草蛇灰線),[44] he is talking about the repetition, at scattered points in the *Shui-hu chuan* text, of specific figures or even single words that serve to join the parts of the work together into a unity. Other critics including Mao Tsung-kang, Chih-yen chai, and the commentators on certain late Ch'ing editions of the novels *Ching-hua yüan* 鏡花緣 and *Hua-yüeh hen* 花月痕 use this same expression to describe the recurrence of relatively extended textual units.[45] In all cases, however, the point at issue is the ability of the master narrator to arrange his narrative details so as to impart to his text the impression of a tight web of interrelated elements, each of which takes on its full significance only in the total context of all the other narrative

[42] See chap. IV below, item 39 of the *Chin P'ing Mei tu-fa* essay, and item 3 of the "Li-yen" 例言 (General Principles) of *Hai-shang hua lieh-chuan* 海上花列傳 (Biographies of the Flowers Adrift on the Sea), quoted in *LCH*, vol. I, p. 634.

[43] There is an explicit discussion of this sort of application of classical essay terminology in a marginal comment in the Yüan Wu-yai 袁無涯 edition of the *Shui-hu chuan*, pp. 22/ 12a and 13a, not reprinted in *SHCHPP*.

[44] See chap. II below, item 53 of the *Shui-hu chuan tu-fa* essay.

[45] See Chih-yen chai interlineal comment (*CYCPYCC* 26.426); chapter comments to the *Ching-hua yüan* (1/5a, 2/11b); and *Hua-yüeh hen* 花月痕 (Fu-chou: Fu-chien jen-min, 1981), p. 5.35, chapter comment.

units brought together in his coordinated structure, as in the "Ch'ang-shan snake" figure cited above. In fact, the ultimate signification of numerous references to the "head" and "tail" (*shou-wei* 首尾) of a narrative sequence most often lies in this critical canon of coordinated cross-reflection, rather than in a literal designation of the beginning and ending of a piece. Mao Tsung-kang provides a rather comprehensive summation of this conception of narrative structure in the following textual comment:

> When the reader of *San-kuo* reaches this chapter, he then realizes that separate parts of the text have been placed in anticipation of one another, that earlier and later sections are mutually reliant, to the extent that ten-odd *chüan*[46] taken together are just like a single integrated piece of writing, in fact just like a single sentence.... The text is like a Ch'ang-shan snake formation such that when attacked at the head its tail responds, when attacked at the tail its head responds, and when attacked in the middle both head and tail respond. Is this not a case of absolute mastery of narrative structure?

> 讀三國者, 讀至此卷而知文之彼此相伏, 前後相因, 殆合十數卷而只如一篇只如一句也.... 文如常山蛇然, 擊首則尾應, 擊尾則首應, 擊中則首尾皆應. 豈非結構之至妙者哉?[47]

It may be convenient for us to distinguish here between two possible directions of thrust within this central critical category of cross-reflection. In the first type of construction, we are asked to admire the manner in which material introduced earlier in a text reflects forward or projects (*chao* 照) to later occurrences of the same textual configuration. To a certain extent, of course, this function is governed by the closing of the bracket, i.e. the later appearance of the second half of the equation reflecting back on the first intimations of the pattern. But in a tradition in which narrative suspense is generally based more on certainty of denouement than on the fascination of the unknown, the aesthetic function of forward reflection can be seen to operate even before the full pattern of recurrence has been formed sufficiently to bear out the expectations of the reader.

There are various expressions that literally direct the reader's attention forward (e.g., "this connects to..." [*chih chu tao*... 直注到 ...], "this sets up..." [*wei hsia-wen*... 爲下文 ...], etc.), but the most common set of terms for indicating this structural function makes use of combina-

---

[46] Some of the Mao Tsung-kang editions divide the 120 chapters of the novel into 60 *chüan* 卷 with two chapters each, others have nineteen uneven *chüan*. It is possible that Mao Tsung-kang has in mind here earlier editions of the novel that were divided into twleve *chüan*.

[47] Mao Tsung-kang chapter comment (*SKYI* 94.929).

tions where the main verb is *fu* 伏, "to hide or conceal as in an ambush,"[48] in the sense of deliberately planting narrative threads to be taken up later at one or a series of points and worked into the continuing patterns of recurrence that make up the texture of the work. Other critics may draw upon the terminology of the prose essay to describe the manner in which one section or point leads into another (e.g., *ch'i* 起, *yin* 引, etc.)[49] or may substitute such expressions as "stirs up what follows" (*chen hsia-wen* 振下文), "provoke" (*tou-ch'u* 逗出), etc.[50]

One particular critical term that closely approximates our own notion of "planting" hints and threads in a text is that of "sowing seeds a year in advance" (*ko-nien hsia-chung* 隔年下種). Mao Tsung-kang elaborates on this principle in item seventeen of his *tu-fa* essay translated below and explains, in one interlineal comment on the *San-kuo yen-i*, that by this concept he understands the technique of "leaving ample space in an earlier part of the text to reflect what is to come" ("ch'ien-wen liu-pu i ying-hou" 前文留步以應後).[51] A later commentator on the *Hsi-yu chi* further specifies that:

Whenever *Hsi-yu chi* treats a specific topic, its origins and organic connections must be planted [*fu* 伏] in the two preceding chapters [*chang* 章]. This is what is meant by the "technique of sowing seeds a year in advance."

西遊每寫一題, 源脉必伏於前二章, 此乃隔年下種之法.[52]

When commentators point out that an earlier occurrence of a certain representation of character or events is intended to serve as a "model" or "standard" for later portions of the text (*chang-pen* 張本, *yang-tzu* 樣子, *pang-yang* 榜樣, *hua-yang* 花樣, *fa-pen* 法本, etc.), that function is occasionally indicated also by extended usage of the term for the prologue section in drama (*hsieh-tzu* 楔子).[53] In both cases it is the same aesthetic principle of forward projection that is at issue.

As we have already pointed out, in most cases reference to advance

---

[48] I.e., *fu-pi* 伏筆, *fu-hsien* 伏線, *mai-fu* 埋伏, *fu-mai* 伏埋, etc.

[49] See chap. II below, item 57 of the *Shui-hu chuan tu-fa* essay.

[50] For *chen hsia-wen* see *Hua-yüeh hen* (Shanghai: Hui-wen t'ang, 1933), marginal comment, p. 11.77. For *tou-ch'u* see *Tung Chieh-yüan Hsi-hsiang* 董解元西厢 (Master Tung's Romance of the Western Chamber; Taipei: Commercial Press, 1970), 2/35a (p. 133), marginal comment.

[51] See chap. III below, item 17 of the *San-kuo yen-i tu-fa* essay. Mao Tsung-kang refers to this same principle in a chapter comment (*SKYI* 27.260) as well.

[52] See *Hsin-shuo Hsi-yu chi*, General Comments ("Tsung-p'i" 總批), item 67.

[53] See chap. V below, chapter comment 1.1 to the *Ju-lin wai-shih*. For a full treatment of the use of the *hsieh-tzu* technique in Chinese fiction, see Chuang Yin 莊因, *Hua-pen hsieh-tzu hui-shuo* 話本楔子彙說 (Taipei: National Taiwan University College of Liberal Arts, 1965).

reflection implies the presence of the follow-up function as well, so that the same terminology (e.g., *chao-ying* 照應) may be cited to refer to both the former and the latter phases of this pattern. In fact, Chin Sheng-t'an's discussion of advance insertion (*tao-ch'a fa* 倒插法), for example, which might at first glance seem to describe the follow-up function, actually deals with the advance planting of narrative threads.[54] On the other hand, a number of critical expressions do refer more specifically to the functioning of echoing or repeating a motif, that is, completing rather than initiating a pattern of recurrence. The term "shadow" (*ying-tzu* 影子), for example, frequently refers to this sort of narrative reflection, as do such explicit remarks as "looks back to an earlier passage" (*hui-ku ch'ien-wen* 回顧前文), "once again we have a case of..." (*yu shih i fan...* 又是一番...), "follow-up narration" (*chui-hsü* 追敍), etc. In addition, the notion of a ripple effect of incidents, as in such expressions as "after-ripples" (*yü-po* 餘波), "has repercussions" (*yu po-lan* 有波瀾), "back waves" (*ni-po* 逆波), etc.,[55] may in certain places refer more to the echo or follow-through on a narrative pattern than to the idea of "shading off" the original narrative sequence or providing an "aftertaste" for the treatment of a specific motif. At any rate, Mao Tsung-kang's elaboration of the ripple metaphor in his discussion of the item he calls " the technique of making ripples follow in the wake of waves and drizzle continue after rain" ("lang-hou po-wen, yü-hou mo-mu chih miao" 浪後波紋, 雨後霡霖之妙) clearly refers to the former type of construction.[56]

One of the most common, but at the same time most troublesome, of the critical terms used in traditional commentaries, one which also appears in the language of poetry, painting, and classical prose criticism, is the notion of "lining" or "padding" (*ch'en* 襯). This term is also used in *ch'ü* 曲 prosody, where it refers to "padding words." Within the context of narrative structure the term is employed in a number of combinations (e.g., *p'ei-ch'en* 陪襯, *ch'en-t'ieh* 襯貼, *ch'en-ying* 襯映, etc.) to describe the manner in which one piece of text supports or "fleshes out" another incidence of the same recurring pattern that might otherwise remain insufficiently developed. Sometimes the term is even used for the first half of the cross-reflection bracket, to refer to the adumbration of something to come rather than a later corroboration of the model (we will return to the question of textual adumbration in a subsequent section of this introduction). By the same token, this sense of the later completion

---

[54] See chap. II below, item 51 of the *Shui-hu chuan tu-fa* essay. Mao Tsung-kang also treats the notion of simultaneous forward and backward reflection in a chapter comment (*SKYI* 72.719).

[55] For *ni-po* 逆波, see Chih-yen chai, *CYCPYCC* 2.37 and 8.151.

[56] See chap. III below, item 14 of the *San-kuo yen-i tu-fa* essay.

of a pattern initiated earlier may also be indicated by the related term *pu*
(補, "to fill in" or "mend"), perhaps most clearly in Mao Tsung-kang's extended discussion of "the technique of inserting additional threads to fill
out the figure and adjusting the needlework to balance the pattern" ("t'ien-
ssu pu-chin, i-chen yün-hsiu chih miao" 添絲補錦, 移針勻繡之妙).[57]

Chang Chu-p'o takes the concept of motival recurrence one step
further in his discussion of the technique that has been rendered below as
"incremental repetition" ("chia i-pei hsieh fa" 加一倍寫法).[58] Mao
Tsung-kang also makes use of this term in his commentary:

> This is an example of the type of writing in which narration presented in
> the later phases of a text is employed to highlight [*ch'en-jan* 襯染]with
> heightened intensity [*chia-pei* 加倍] an earlier segment.
>
> 文有敘事在後幅而適爲前篇加倍襯染者, 此類是也.[59]

A number of other critics writing during the Ming-Ch'ing period also
utilize the term.[60] These discussions may, in addition, be interpreted as
examples of the principle of follow-up reflection in narrative composition, although in this case the implication of a gradual buildup of inten-
sity or clarity entails a somewhat different aesthetic pattern from that of
recurrence alone. Other examples of critical attention paid to patterns
with this sort of logical direction include Chih-yen chai's description of
his author's tendency to arrange his narration "from smaller to larger
scale" (*yu hsiao chih ta* 由小至大) or "from the superficial to the more
profound" (*yu ch'ien chih shen* 由淺至深).[61]

Quite obviously, nearly all of the above patterns of forward and
backward reflection between narrative units are ultimately reducible to
instances of the simple perception of analogous outlines of character or
incident at noncontiguous points of a textual continuum. In fact, this
marked feature of Chinese narrative art—the seemingly interminable

[57] See chap. III below, item 18 of the *San-kuo yen-i tu-fa* essay.

[58] See chap. IV below, item 25 of the *Chin P'ing Mei tu-fa* essay.

[59] Mao Tsung-kang chapter comment (*SKYI* 21.199). Elsewhere in the chapter in an
interlineal comment, Mao Tsung-kang associates this technique with the idea of *ts'ao-she
hui-hsien* 草蛇灰線 and *hui-ku ch'ien-wen* 回顧前文 (*SKYI* 21.205).

[60] For additional usages of the term "chia i-pei hsieh fa" 加一倍寫法, see *Hua-yüeh hen*
(1858 copy in Diet Library, Japan), p.8/37a; and item 31 of the *Shui-hu hou-chuan tu-fa*
essay (*SHCTLHP* 573). Sometimes, however, the words *chia-pei* are just used as an
intensifier and do not have any connotation of recurrence—as is the case in the last item
above and a Chin Sheng-t'an chapter comment (*SHCHPP* 40.750).

[61] See Chih-yen chai, prechapter comment, *CYCPYCC* 2.29–30. For a similar expression, see ibid., 27.456, marginal comment. For the latter term, see *Hsiu-hsiang Ti-pa ts'ai-
tzu shu Hua-chien chi* 繡像第八才子書花箋記 (n.d., copy held in Gest Oriental Library,
Princeton University), "General Introduction" ("Tsung-lun" 總論), p. 5b.

repetition of the same type of events and figures with what at first seems to be little more than a change of name—is particularly troubling to the modern reader. Uninspired, nearly identical repetitions of narrative units in the texts under consideration are, of course, faulted by the critics,[62] who do sometimes point out subtlety and significance in patterns of repetition that might also be taken as uninspired at first glance. The writers of traditional Chinese fiction were deeply concerned with the evocation of a rhythm of recurrence as the essential ground for the representation of reality in fiction, but the recognition of difference within identity was just as important to them as its contrary. The critics point to this dialectic of difference and identity directly,[63] or figuratively, as in item ten of Mao Tsung-kang's *tu-fa* essay on the *San-kuo yen-i*.[64]

Such discussions of identity and difference can be framed in the terminology of parallelism borrowed from other fields of Chinese aesthetics. For example, the use of such terms as "mutual reflection" (*tui-chao* 對照), "contrastive reflection" (*fan-chao* 反照), and particularly "reflection between opposites" (*cheng-fan hsiang-tui* 正反相對) in the context of fiction criticism usually refers precisely to this sort of presentation of analogous yet different patterns in the narrative text, as opposed to the tonal, lexical, or semantic categories of meaning most central to these terms when they are applied to the function of parallelism in poetics. But just as in the field of poetics, critical discussion of parallelism is often more interested in the subtle nuances of differentiation conveyed when abstract and concrete figures are juxtaposed in parallel constructions, or when true parallelism gives way to complex devices of pseudo-parallelism; here too attention is focused both on the disjunctive and the conjunctive functions of such structures. There remains a certain ambiguity, however, when this technique is referred to by terms prefixed by the character *fan* 反 —for example, *fan-chi fa* 反激法, *fan-ch'en* 反襯, *fan-ying* 反映, etc.—since such expressions may refer either to the "backward" thrust of the pattern of reflection or to the sort of "contrastive" parallelism under discussion here.[65]

[62] Expressions like *lei-t'ung chih ping* 雷同之病 and *ho-chang chih ping* 合掌之病 are used to disparage such writing.

[63] The commentator in the Jung-yü t'ang 容與堂 edition of the *Shui-hu chuan* praises his text for clearly delineating between different and identical features in the personalities of the characters ("t'ung erh pu-t'ung yu pien" 同而不同有辨) and this idea was picked up by Chin Sheng-t'an and used in item 24 of his *Shui-hu chuan tu-fa* essay (see chap. II below). Similar arguments are used in chapter comments by Mao Tsung-k'ang (*SKYI* 45.447 and 51.507) and in the preface to the Li Yü commentary to the same novel, p. 4a.

[64] See chap. III below. Chin Sheng-t'an expresses himself in a similar fashion in a chapter comment (*SHCHPP* 19.361).

[65] For a full discussion of direct and contrastive parallelism (*cheng-tui* 正對, *fan-tui* 反對), see chap. III below, item 20 of the *San-kuo yen-i tu-fa* essay.

One important term of classical literary criticism adopted for application to the structures of recurrence in vernacular fiction is that of the "violation" (*fan* 犯) of the general rule against redundancy. In fiction criticism the focus quickly changed to how well and for what purpose the "redundancy" was employed, rather than the objective violation of a general rule, even though this added spice and danger to the game. This sense of the word is behind the use of such phrases as "deliberate violation that is not a violation" (*t'e fan pu fan* 特犯不犯),[66] "violates but does not really violate" (*fan yü pu fan* 犯與不犯),[67] etc. Chin Sheng-t'an draws a further distinction between "full" and "partial" repetitions of narrative detail (*cheng-fan fa* 正犯法, *lüeh-fan fa* 略犯法), citing both of these possibilities as valid devices of fiction writing; and Mao Tsung-kang also offers praise for both the skillful avoidance and the skillful commission (*shan-pi* 善避, *shan-fan* 善犯) of textual redundancy.[68]

As in the other branches of Chinese aesthetics, the significant function of parallelism in fiction composition lies neither in achieving mechanical balance and rhythm nor even in prescribing a precise relation of similarity and difference in a given parallel construction, but rather in the attempt of the artist to set up the coordinates of his world along each of a number of axes of time, space, and various perceptual or abstract correlatives. When a writer devotes considerable creative effort to setting up such coordinates by framing figures and scenes involving analogous-yet-contrastive categories of conception, what he is in effect driving at is a certain dualistic vision predicated upon the complementary interrelation of paired concepts—a vision within which the aesthetic impulse toward mutual implication or cyclical alternation of apparent "opposites" outweighs the surface impression of dialectical opposition. The Ming-Ch'ing fiction critics seem to have been quite conscious of this aesthetic principle, and their discussions of certain polar coordinates of particular relevance to narrative structure frequently turn upon the sort of conceptual models under consideration here.

One such set of coordinates which appears in a wide range of critical writings is that of cold and heat (*leng-je* 冷熱). As an example of the terminology of fiction criticism, this axis generally refers not to literal temperature variation, but rather to "heat" and "cold" in the sphere of human action, that is, to the contrasting qualities of feverish activity or

---

[66] For an example, see Chih-yen chai, *CYCPYCC* 18.282, interlineal comment.

[67] See item 25 in the *Shui-hu hou-chuan tu-fa* essay (*SHCTLHP* 572). For the use of a similar term, see item 18 of the same essay (*SHCTLHP* 570).

[68] See chap. III below, item 10 of the *San-kuo yen-i tu-fa* essay. For Chin Sheng-t'an on *cheng-fan fa* 正犯法 and *lüeh-fan fa* 略犯法, see chap. II below, items 59 and 60 of the *Shui-hu chuan tu-fa* essay and his chapter comments for chap. 11 (*SHCHPP* 11.232–33). Mao Tsung-kang also takes up the same issue in a chapter comment (*SKYI* 113.1117).

excitement (*je-nao* 熱鬧) and the corresponding "coolness" of tranquility, loneliness, or unreality. For example, Chang Chu-p'o's discussion of the "hot" and "cold" halves of the *Chin P'ing Mei* seems to penetrate the brilliant interweaving in that text of the pattern of rise and fall in Hsi-men Ch'ing's own career with parallel and opposite patterns of rise and fall of temperature and related imagery.[69] A similar contrast is involved in Mao Tsung-kang's explanation of "the technique of introducing cold ice to break the heat and cool breezes to sweep away the dust" ("han-ping p'o-je, liang-feng sao-ch'en chih miao" 寒冰破熱, 涼風掃塵之妙), wherein he makes specific reference to the alternation of scenes of activity in the mundane world with scenes involving intimations of a different sphere of life on a more tranquil and transcendent level.[70] In a valuable chapter comment, Mao Tsung-kang gives further clarification as to what he has in mind. He is discussing the differences between the outlook of the hermits in the novel and those who come to ask their advice:

> The highest mastery of prose writing lies in introducing a cold figure into the narration at the hottest point of action or a scene of calm idleness right in the midst of the most intense activity.... They [the hermits] may be extremely calm [at heart] but the heart of the visitor is extremely agitated; they [the hermits] may be extremely "cold" [at heart] but the heart of the visitor is extremely "heated up."

> 文章之妙, 妙在極熱時寫一冷人, 極忙中寫一閒影.... 彼雖極閒而見者之心極忙, 彼雖極冷而見者之心極熱.[71]

In the above passage, Mao Tsung-kang's use of the terms "agitated" and "calm" (*mang-hsien* 忙閒) provides an example of an alternate set of expressions for referring to the same sort of critical analysis. Chih-yen chai is particularly conscious of this dimension of structural significance

---

[69] See chap. IV below, items 10, 25, 71, 83, and 88 of the *Chin P'ing Mei tu-fa* essay. The concept is also used by him in two separate pieces included in the prefatory material to his commentary: an essay entitled "Leng-je chin-chen" 冷熱金針 (The Secret of Hot and Cold) and an analytical table of contents.

[70] See chap. III below, item 15 of the *San-kuo yen-i tu-fa* essay.

[71] Mao Tsung-kang, chapter comment (*SKYI* 89.877). For additional discussions of the "hot" and "cold" motifs, see *Li Cho-wu hsien-sheng p'i-p'ing San-kuo yen-i* 李卓吾先生批評三國演義 (Li Chih Commentary Edition of the *San-kuo yen-i*; 1687 preface 120-chapter edition), marginal comments, p. 69/2b; Chih-yen chai, prechapter comment (*CYCPYCC* 2.29) and interlineal comment (ibid., 63.578); *Shih-erh lou*, comment on the ninth story (p. 5/31a); *Ching-hua yüan*, chapter comment (3/31b); *Ch'un-ch'iu Lieh-kuo chih* comments (pp. 1/64a, 3/56b); etc. See also item 33 of the *Shui-hu hou-chuan tu-fa* essay (*SHCTLHP* 574) on the term "shui chung t'u-yen fa" 水中吐焰法 (spitting fire from the middle of water).

which plays so central a role in the composition of the *Hung-lou meng* and speaks repeatedly of such features as "casual insertion in the midst of feverish activity" (*mang-chung hsien-pi* 忙中閒筆), etc., in accounting for the manifest greatness of that work.[72] Along the same lines of analysis, numerous commentators point out the manner in which writers contrive to introduce a change of pace or direction "in the midst of feverish activity" (*pai-mang chung...* 百忙中 ...), something which we may view as an example of the sort of contrastive transition between narrative units discussed earlier. Further variations on the same idea are expressed through the use of such correlative terms as "action and repose" (*tung-ching* 動靜), or "urgency and ease" (*chi-huan* 急緩, *chin-k'uan* 緊寬, etc.).[73] A commentator on the *Ching-hua yüan*, for example, explains that the difficulty of literary writing lies in the following pitfall:

> If it is too "loose" [*k'uan* 寬], then it easily loses its sense of direction, if it is too "tight" [*chin* 緊], then it easily becomes forced. To avoid excessive adherence [to fixed patterns] and excessive departure from them is the mark of the master [writer].
>
> 寬則易泛, 緊則易逼, 不粘不脫, 斯稱妙手.[74]

In addition to the above examples of paired terms used by the traditional commentators to describe major structural patterns employed in plotting the texts of the Chinese novel, many writers draw upon the language of drama criticism to discuss the alternating patterns of "union and separation" (*li-ho* 離合) and "joy and sorrow" (*pei-huan* 悲歡), etc., which comprise the essential framework of so many works of the vernacular tradition. Significantly, a number of critics take these categories of analysis beyond the level of simple thematic description to consider their functioning as models of the aesthetics of recurrence at the heart of both the fictional and the dramatic modes. The same commentator on the *Ching-hua yüan*, for example, provides an interesting discussion of the former set of correlatives in a later chapter comment:

> All works of drama and fiction are reducible to the two terms "union" and "separation" as the central hinge of the entire composition. At points of union it is consistently difficult to achieve naturalness, while at points of separation it is easy to lapse into stiffness. . . .

[72] See also the variant term, "mang-li t'ou-hsien fa" 忙裏偷閒法 (sneaking a bit of calmness amidst agitation) in item 27 of the *Shui-hu hou-chuan tu-fa* essay (*SHCTLHP* 572).

[73] See, for example, Mao Tsung-kang chapter comment (*SKYI* 9.77) and marginal comment to chap. 18 of the Yüan Wu-yai edition of the *Shui-hu chuan* (*SHCHPP* 17.331).

[74] *Ching-hua yüan*, chapter comment, p. 1/7b.

凡傳奇說部不過以離合二字為通篇樞板, 合處固難自然, 而離處易於生硬....[75]

Similarly, a Ch'ing critic offers his praise for the author of the *Hung-lou meng* on the basis of his handling of this same structural dimension:

> In general, the structure of fictional works moves from sorrow to joy, from separation to union. This book, however, proceeds from joy to sorrow, from union to separation, thus giving the impression of something totally unique.
>
> 小說家結構大抵由悲而歡, 由離而合. 是書則由歡而悲, 由合而離, 逐覺壁壘之新.[76]

One final pair of correlative terms that presents particular difficulties of interpretation is that of the characters *shih* 實 and *hsü* 虛. Sometimes these terms are used simply to designate truth or fabrication, respectively, as in Chang Hsüeh-ch'eng's (1738–1801) well–known appraisal of the *San-kuo yen-i* as seven parts fact and three parts fiction.[77] But in numerous other occurrences, this pair of terms refers to a more purely aesthetic category—the direct (*shih*) or indirect (*hsü*) mimesis of action in a work of fiction. Mao Tsung-kang is particularly fond of this distinction, for which he employs the terms "direct" and "indirect narration" (*shih-hsü* 實敍, *hsü-hsü* 虛敍) in a large number of places. On the other hand, these same terms may also be brought in to refer more specifically to the structural function of advance projection and subsequent textual fulfillment, as in the expression "first indirectly, later directly" (*ch'ien-hsü hou-shih* 前虛後實) or the more graphic "a light knock and a solid answer" (*hsü-ch'iao shih-ying* 虛敲實應).[78]

---

[75] Ibid., chapter comment, p. 5/34a–b. See also a similar discussion in the first preface to the *Hua-yüeh hen* by Mien-ho chu-jen 眠鶴主人.

[76] This remark first appeared in Erh-chih tao-jen 二知道人 (pseud.), *Hung-lou meng shuo meng* 紅樓夢說夢 (Dream Talk on the *Hung-lou meng*), printed in 1812. It is reproduced in *HLMC*, pp. 83–103 (see p. 86 for the translated section). This and several other remarks from this work are quoted (most with direct attribution) at the end of a piece called "Ming-chai chu-jen tsung-p'ing" 明齋主人總評 (General Remarks by the Owner of Ming Studio), which appears in popular editions of the *Hung-lou meng* with commentary (see *CYY*, p. 28 for the translated section). This latter piece seems to be the same as Chu Lien 諸聯 (style Ming-chai), *Hung-lou p'ing meng* 紅樓評夢 (Commentary on the Dream from the Red Chamber), quoted in abridged form in *HLMC*, pp. 117–21.

[77] In *Ping-ch'en cha-chi* 丙辰劄記 (Notes Made in 1796), in *Chü-hsüeh hsüan ts'ung-shu* 聚學軒叢書 (Chü-hsüeh Studio Collectanea; preface 1903), Liu Shih-heng 劉世珩, ed., 30 vols. (Taipei: I-wen yin-shu kuan, n.d.), vol. 16, p. 63b. Quoted in K'ung Ling-ching, *Chung-kuo hsiao-shuo shih-liao*, p. 45.

[78] The latter term appears in Chih-yen chai, *CYCPYCC* 27.460, postchapter comment, and ibid., 27.456, marginal comment.

All of the above critical discussions of the aesthetics of overlapping, cross-reflection, and parallel recurrence in Chinese fiction writing also carry the implication of concern for the problem of narrative pace or rhythm, that is, the spacing of intervals in the interconnection of narrative units. The traditional Chinese fiction critics demonstrate their consciousness of this issue in their penetrating treatment of sudden and gradual transitions between narrative units, as well as the complex interrelation of patterns of action and nonaction (*mang-hsien* 忙閒, *leng-je* 冷熱, *tung-ching* 動靜, etc.), and occasionally make explicit reference to the question of narrative speed with such terms as "technique of expansion and contraction" (*shen-so fa* 伸縮法), "alternation of fast and slow" (*i su i ch'ih* 一速一遲), etc.[79]

With regard to the overall flow of the narrative continuum, the critics pay particular attention to the modulation of narrative time in order to create an impression of regulated rhythm (*yu ts'eng-tz'u* 有層次, *yu pu-tsou* 有步驟, etc.). What such expressions refer to is not the maintenance of a smooth fixed pace, but rather the careful handling of frequent interruptions and rhythmic fluctuations (e.g., *ts'en-tz'u yu chih* 參差有致, *ch'i-fu* 起伏, *ts'o-tsung* 錯綜, etc.)[80] without losing the sense of close artistic control. Devices pointed out by the critics, such as "insertion of passages" (*ch'a-ju* 插入), "peripheral narration" (*chia-tai* 夾帶), "simultaneous narration" (*chien-hsü* 兼敍), etc., must be understood to be grounded in concern over the various patterns of textural linking discussed earlier. Of particular interest to us here are the numerous discussions in which the commentators borrow the critical terms "continuity" and "disjunction" (*lien* 連, *tuan* 斷) from classical poetics to describe this aspect of narrative structuration. As in most other variables of Chinese aesthetics, the Ming-Ch'ing critics condemn both of the hypothetical "poles" of this conceptual pair, citing as serious faults both disjointed structure and monotonous regularity. Instead, the thrust of such discussions almost invariably goes in the direction of advocating the complementary alternation of both possibilities, as may be clearly seen in the borrowing of painting terms such as "technique of clouds cutting the mountains in half" ("heng-yün tuan-ling chih miao" 橫雲斷嶺之妙) and "continuous mountains, broken mountain ranges" (*lien-shan tuan-shan* 連山斷山) by Chin Sheng-t'an, Mao Tsung-kang, and others to describe the manner in which the artist can convey a sense of continuity and

[79] The former usage can be found in a comment to the *Hsin-hua ch'un-meng chi*, p. 8/116. The latter term appears in a Mao Tsung-kang interlineal comment (*SKYI* 106.1057).

[80] For a discussion of the term *ch'i-fu* 起伏, see Susan Bush, "Lung-mo, K'ai-ho, and Ch'i-fu," *Oriental Art*, n.s. 7: 120, 127 (1962).

discontinuity at the same time through coordinated patterns of segmentation and linkage.[81]

Another major area of narrative technique which may be singled out for critical scrutiny is that of the representation of human character in the fictional text. But just as Henry James was to maintain two or three centuries later in his often quoted statement regarding the identity of character and incident, the Ming-Ch'ing critics felt no need for a conceptual separation between actor and act, so that nearly all of the above principles of textual structuration may apply to either character or events as narrative units. The narrative device of figural redundancy (*fan* 犯), for example, seems to be used to refer more often to the recurrent type of character than to the configurations of events in which they manifest their attributes, while the majority of Mao Tsung-kang's "masterful devices" (*miao* 妙) are exemplified in his discussions primarily by individual figures instead of actions.

We do find, however, a limited number of critical comments in which it is clearly the specific conception of character that is at issue. Within the context of the aesthetics of recurrence that constitutes one of the central underpinnings of the narrative tradition, it is perhaps natural to expect that more creative energy would be expended on exploring recurrent patterns of human behavior than in delineating the uniqueness of the individual figure. When practiced excessively or with insufficient imagination, this technique may at times result in the monotonous repetitiveness that has troubled many readers of the classic Chinese novel, among them an early commentator on the *San-kuo yen-i*, who said:

> Why do you suppose the reader begins to doze off whenever he gets to this point? It can only be because all of this has been said before; the story is stretched out over and over again with only the names of the characters changed. It is really insufferable. Is this why it is called the "novel" of the *San-kuo chih* [Chronicle of the Three Kingdoms; puns with "pass through it three times" 三過之]? My little joke.

---

[81] See chap. II below, item 64 of the *Shui-hu chuan tu-fa* essay; chap. III below, item 12 of the *San-kuo yen-i tu-fa* essay; and Mao Tsung-kang chapter comment (*SKYI* 64.637). See also Chih-yen chai, *CYCPYCC* 27.456, marginal and interlineal comments. The same sense of coordinated disjunction and linkage underlies Chin Sheng-t'an's use of the term *ts'ao-she hui-hsien* 草蛇灰線, see chap. II below, item 53 of the *Shui-hu chuan tu-fa* essay; and also Mao Tsung-kang's discussion of the interspersal of feminine motifs into the predominantly masculine *San-kuo yen-i* (see Chap. III below, item 16 of his *tu-fa* essay). For a penetrating treatment of the aesthetics of continuity and discontinuity in Chinese poetics, see Yu-kung Kao and Tsu-lin Mei, "Syntax, Diction, and Imagery in T'ang Poetry," *Harvard Journal of Asiatic Studies* 31:51−136 (1971).

讀演義至此, 惟有打盹而已何也？只因前面都已說過, 改換姓名重疊敷演云耳. 真可厭也. 此其所以為三國志演義乎？一笑.⁸²

On the other hand, the traditional commentators point out the ways in which the great novelists turn this feature to more subtle purposes. One of these consists in the attempt to focus on both the individual figure and his or her relationship to other figures as a technique to produce rounded characters. Numerous commentators draw the reader's atttention to the use of both separate (*fen-hsü* 分敍) and joint (*ho-hsü* 合敍, *tsung-hsü* 總敍) treatment of the characters, a practice that they see as deriving from the narrative techniques employed by Ssu-ma Ch'ien in the *Shih-chi*.⁸³ On the other hand, certain critics go on to identify those cases in which individual figures can be seen to be components of a single "character" (e.g., "shih i pu shih erh" 是一不是二, *san-jen i-shen* 三人一身, *san-jen i-t'i* 三人一體, etc.).⁸⁴

Perhaps the most interesting treatments of this aspect of characterization in Chinese fiction criticism are those that apply the analytical tools of parallelism to the portrayal of figures, since the use of such terms as "parallelism at a distance" (*yao-tui* 遙對), "contrastive reflection" (*fan-chao* 反照), "contrastive parallelism" (*fan-tui* 反對), etc., immediately directs the reader's attention to the subtle nuances of difference within sameness, as we have seen in the above discussion. The most common use of this idea in characterization is the employment of one character as a foil to set off a second character through direct or subtle contrast. Chin Sheng-t'an and Chih-yen chai refer to this technique by the expression "whitening the background [to bring out the foreground]" ("pen-mien p'u [fu] fen" 背面鋪 [傅] 粉).⁸⁵ Mao Tsung-kang and others use the con-

⁸² *Li Cho-wu hsien-sheng p'i-p'ing San-kuo yen-i*, chapter comment (p. 112/10a–b). A similar discussion appears on p. 113/10b in a marginal comment. The earliest generation of commentators were far more ready to make remarks like these than Chin Sheng-t'an or Mao Tsung-kang were.

⁸³ For example, the expression "Lung-men ho-chuan fa" 龍門合傳法 (the technique of combined biographies of Ssu-ma Ch'ien) appears in *Hua-yüeh hen* (1981 edition), chapter comment (p. 2.10). Ssu-ma Ch'ien wrote both separate and composite biographies. Furthermore, he dispersed material on particular individuals among several chapters, producing a kind of stereographic effect (this is the so-called *hu-chien fa* 互見法 technique of cross-reflection).

⁸⁴ See for example, Mao Tsung-kang chapter comment on Chi P'ing and Hua T'o (*SKYI* 75.745); *Li Cho-wu hsien-sheng p'i-p'ing San-kuo yen-i*, chapter comment, 69/12a; and item 12 of the *Shui-hu hou-chuan tu-fa* essay (*SHCTLHP* 568). Chih-yen chai expresses more or less the same idea with the geopolitical term *ting-li* 鼎立 (like the legs of a tripod), *CYCPYCC* 5.94, marginal comment.

⁸⁵ See chap. II below, item 56 of the *Shui-hu chuan tu-fa* essay and Chih-yen chai, *CYCPYCC* 1.10, marginal comment, and ibid., 24.395, interlineal comment.

ventional pair of terms "guest and host" (*pin-chu* 賓主) with the emphasis more on mutual reflection than on a contrast between primary and secondary figures,[86] while the use of the term "shadows" (*ying-tzu* 影子), as in the *tu-fa* essay on the *Hung-lou meng* translated below, often conveys a greater sense of disparate levels of importance between the members of the pairs or the series of related figures.[87] One additional set of terms used to indicate the contrastive parallelism between pairs of fictional characters includes such expressions as "act as foil" (*p'ei* 陪) or "adjunct" (*t'ieh* 貼), as well as various combinations of these words with the term "padding" (*ch'en* 襯) discussed earlier. In such expressions we can gain a clearer understanding of the precise usage of this latter term in fiction criticism —that is, to describe the manner in which one narrative unit or figure is both supported and set off by the appearance of another one of analogous or contrasting configuration, which is somewhat at variance with the uses of this term in other branches of Chinese criticism.

Further examples of ways of talking about characterization include the subjective identification of specific character types as discussed above, as well as the use of names for the role categories of the Chinese stage to classify the dramatis personae of prose fiction.[88] One additional technique of particular interest to the modern student is an aspect of the presentation of character corresponding fairly closely to the notion of "point of view" that has gained a somewhat disproportionate fascination for theorists of narrative fiction of late. The Chinese critics frequently point out that certain information or an idea has been expressed through the mouth of a particular person (... *k'ou-chung shuo-ch'u* ... 口中說出) or seen through the eyes of such and such a person (... *yen-chung k'an* ... 眼中看), thus shifting attention from the object of perception itself to its transmitter or perceiver.[89] Finally, we may include in this section on characterization the discussion of ways to introduce characters into the

---

[86] See chap. III below, item 9 of the *San-kuo yen-i tu-fa* essay.

[87] See chap. VII below, item 16 of the *Hung-lou meng tu-fa* essay.

[88] The word *t'ieh* 貼 is a common abbreviation for the term *t'ieh-tan* 貼旦 (supporting female role), and some of this sense of the meaning of the word is probably carried over into compounds such as *ch'en-t'ieh* 襯貼 found in fiction criticism. For examples of the use of dramatic role-category terminology, see *Jou p'u-t'uan*, chapter comment (p. 2/16a); *Hsi-yu cheng-tao shu* 西遊證道書 (The Way to Enlightenment through the *Hsi-yu chi*; microfilm held in Gest Oriental Library, Princeton University, of original in Naikaku Bunko, Japan), chapter comment (p. 9/1a–b); and Chang Hsin-chih interlineal comment, *CYY* 4/12a (p. 119).

[89] Comments pointing out this use of "point of view" are legion, but it will suffice here to mention a passage of the *Shui-hu chuan* changed by Chin Sheng-t'an so as to more clearly reflect the consciousness of the main character of the action. This occurs in the description of Li K'uei's night attack on Lo Chen-jen (*SHCHPP* 52.978).

action of the novel, such as Mao Tsung-kang's "first he relates their character and then their names" ("hsien hsü ch'i jen-p'in hou hsiang ch'i hsing-shih" 先敍其人品後詳其姓氏) or "first he relates their names and then their character" ("hsien hsü ch'i hsing-shih hou hsiang ch'i jen-p'in" 先敍其姓氏後詳其人品).[90] The twin devices of revealing a character's name and social identity only long after the reader has had a chance to observe the character in action, while the entrances of other characters are carefully prepared beforehand by discussions of the newcomer's person by other characters or the narrator, is carried to a high degree of development in the *San-kuo yen-i* and the *Ju-lin wai-shih*.

A final grouping of concepts of a compositional orientation may include the analysis of narrative techniques concerned with questions of rhetoric, or what has been called "narrative stance." One of these features of Chinese fiction writing to which the traditional critics pay considerable attention is the continuum ranging from extreme fullness of treatment, leaving no detail unaccounted for, to the opposite pole of extreme economy of treatment, conveying the desired impression with a minimum of direct statement and maximum use of suggestive language, structural cross-reflection, or character foils. Fullness is praised for its "thoroughness" (*chou-chih* 周緻) and called "detailed and extended narration" (*ta lo-mo fa* 大落墨法), but such things as "subtle divulgence" (*wei-lou* 微露), the cutting of extraneous material (*chien-ts'ai* 剪裁) or polysemy (*i-pi san-yung* 一筆三用) are also praised in their place. By the same token, the fiction critics may find fault with writing which is too "dense" (*fan* 繁) and express their appreciation of an author's deliberate avoidance of verbosity (*pi-fan* 避繁) or structural entanglements (*pi-nan fa* 避難法).[91]

As we have already seen in connection with several other variables of Chinese narrative aesthetics, for the traditional critics it was not a question of general preference for one possibility over the other, rather what was important was the alternation of both and the suitability of either pole for use with particular narrative material. We find expressions such as "moving back and forth between detailed and abbreviated treatment" (*i-hsiang i-lüeh* 一詳一略) and "both dense and sparse" (*yu mi yu sheng* 又密又省). As for the common term *sheng* 省 ("economy") that ap-

---

[90] See Mao Tsung-kang, interlineal comment (*SKYI* 106.1061); and *Li Li-weng p'ing-yüeh San-kuo chih*, marginal comments (10/7a–b, 15/14a, 106/9b). The device of introducing a character by name long before bringing him out onto the stage of the novel has been observed by critics to be a major technique in the Japanese classic, *Genji monogatari* (The Tale of Genji).

[91] See Chih-yen chai, marginal comment (*CYCPYCC* 27.448) and interlineal comment (ibid., 16.241).

pears in numerous critical writings and refers to the elimination of unnecessary narrative detail, Chin Sheng-t'an characteristically presents
as equally valid narrative techniques both "extreme narrative frugality"
(*chi sheng fa* 極省法) and "extreme avoidance of narrative frugality" (*chi
pu-sheng fa* 極不省法).[92] This range of variation is presented forcefully in
the following passage from a Chih-yen chai comment on the *Hung-lou
meng*:

> This is what is meant by saying that this book has points of narrative
> complexity rendered even more complex and instances of further economy
> on top of economy; it also has examples in which [the author] does not
> worry about the complexity on top of complexity but just strives to achieve
> a sense of simplicity within complexity; while by the same token he shows
> no fear of economy on top of economy, but only strives to achieve a sense
> of solidity within economy.

所謂此書有繁處愈繁, 省中愈省; 又有不怕繁中繁, 只要繁中虛, 不畏省中省,
只要省中實.[93]

Another way of looking at what is in effect the same critical issue
appears in various discussions of foreground and background or, more
accurately, center stage versus side actions and digressions in the narrative text. Within the context of the conventional rhetoric of the Chinese
vernacular fiction genres—that is, the simulated pose of the oral storyteller in sophisticated non-oral literary forms—the intrusion of the narrator's persona into the text in the form of asides, digressions, and particularly as simulated repartee between narrator and audience exercises a
significant function in terms of narrative focus, as well as obviously
retarding the narrative pace. In dealing with this type of rhetorical
manipulation, the traditional commentators frequently point out the
presence of passages deliberately inserted to shift the narrative focus
from center stage to the wings (*ch'uan-ch'a* 穿插, *p'ang-wen* 旁文, *sui-pi*
隨筆, etc.) and often draw upon the terminology of prose essay criticism
to distinguish between direct narration (*chih-pi* 直筆) or focused treatment (*chuan-hsieh* 專寫) and various types of circuitous (*ch'ü-pi* 曲筆) or
seemingly inconsequential discourse (*hsien-wen* 閒文). Mao Tsung-
kang's discussion of "the technique of interrupting drums with woodwinds and interspersing strings among the bells" ("sheng-hsiao chia ku,
ch'in-se chien chung chih miao" 笙簫夾鼓, 琴瑟間鐘之妙), for example,

---

[92] See chap. II below, items 61 and 62 of the *Shui-hu chuan tu-fa* essay. Similar discussions appear in the *Hsin-k'o hsiu-hsiang p'i-p'ing Chin P'ing Mei*, p. 1/13a; *Ju-lin wai-shih
p'ing*, p. 7/19a; and *Hsin-hua ch'un-meng chi*, p. 5/35.

[93] Chih-yen chai marginal comment (*CYCPYCC* 4.85). See also a similar remark in
another marginal comment (ibid., 7.131).

deals specifically with the relation between the main plot focus and narrative tangents in the *San-kuo yen-i*.[94]

Once again, however, it is the maintenance of a subtle interplay between these two aspects of narrative discourse rather than the determination of fixed critical criteria that remains uppermost in the minds of the commentators. We have already considered such expressions as "busy" and "idle" (*mang-hsien* 忙閒) or "solid" and "empty" (*shih-hsü* 實虛) above in connection with problems of structure, and often these same terms are employed to refer to this particular variable of direct versus indirect narration in a manner that emphasizes the validity of both approaches (e.g., *i-shih i-hsü* 一實一虛, etc.). Another set of terms frequently adopted to convey the same sort of meaning is that of "explicit" and "implicit" (*ming-an* 明暗) statement. Chih-yen chai uses an historical allusion from the founding of the Han dynasty, "making an explicit show of repairing the mountain bridges while secretly crossing by way of Ch'en-ts'ang" ("ming-hsiu chan-tao, an-tu Ch'en-ts'ang" 明修棧道, 暗渡陳倉), to describe this aspect of the narrative technique of the *Hunglou meng*;[95] and a late Ch'ing commentator on the novel *Hua-yüeh hen* combines several of these usages in a single item:

> He uses the alternation of explicit and implicit narration, of direct and indirect statement ... and moreover employs explicitness within implicitness, implicitness within explicitness, directness within indirection, and indirection within directness, as well as the techniques of the "snake in the grass or chalk line" or the "horses' hoofprints, threads of gossamer...."
>
> 用一明一暗, 一正一側...更用暗中之明, 明中之暗, 正中之側, 側中之正, 草蛇灰線, 馬迹蛛絲....[96]

When treating indirection or suggestiveness, the Ming-Ch'ing critics borrowed from the field of painting a variety of technical terms, most of which can be rendered as "adumbration" (e.g., *hung-jan* 烘染, *tien-jan* 點染, *hsüan-jan* 縉染, *ts'un-jan* 皴染, etc.). In the majority of such expressions, the landscape painter's technique of applying ink wash of varying thickness or the combination of the ink wash with other more sharply defined brushstrokes in order to evoke the presence of images not directly depicted is transferred to the field of fiction criticism to describe the manner in which the narrator may evoke specific impressions and responses through the various devices of indirection discussed above. This sort of usage is perhaps most clear in the expression "touching in the

---

[94] See chap. III below, item 16 of the *San-kuo yen-i tu-fa* essay.

[95] Chih-yen chai marginal comment (*CYCPYCC* 1.10).

[96] *Hua-yüeh hen*, chapter comment, p. 5.35 (1981 edition). A similar discussion appears in item 23 of the *Shui-hu hou-chuan tu-fa* essay (*SHCTLHP* 571).

clouds to adumbrate the moon" (hung-yün t'o-yüeh 烘雲托月),[97] a term
that appears so often in the critical commentary on vernacular fiction as
to become a stock cliché meaning at times perhaps nothing more than
that a given passage has suggestive overtones. It is interesting to note that
the character ch'en 襯 also appears in a number of combinations in the
terminology borrowed from the criticism of painting. Here it seems to
describe the sort of devices a writer may use to strengthen or support an
impression he wishes to evoke through indirect suggestion rather than
direct narration. One additional term that may be derived from the field
of painting, but comes to be widely used in nearly all the branches of
Chinese literary criticism as well, is the technique of "dotting and
connecting" (tien-chui 點綴). In the context of commentary on particular passages of vernacular fiction, this expression seems to refer most
often to an author's attention to a filling in of background details that
both sets the stage for the main action at hand and also contributes to the
illusion of reality evoked through painstaking representation of quotid-
ian detail.

This last technique of narrative composition brings us to an aspect of
the craft of fiction writing that comprises a favored topic for the traditional critics. This is the obvious fascination felt by the Ming-Ch'ing
commentators for the maintenance of an impression of convincing
verisimilitude within the unabashed fabrication of a fictional mode.
Notwithstanding the fact that the penchant for realistic depiction of
detail in Chinese narrative was never elevated to the status of a full-
fledged critical canon of realism, the margins of the fictional texts are
studded with admiring comments on a given writer's ability to create
lifelike images of "real" people and events. We may note, for example,
such expressions as "convincingly real" (pi-chen 逼真), "lifelike" (huo-
hsiang 活像), "like a picture" (ju-hua 如畫), "I can see it with my eyes"
(tsai mu-chung 在目中), "an identical image" (hsiao-hsiang 肖像), or
"how very like" (hsiang 像, wan-jan 宛然, etc.), as well as various references to an author's skill at depicting (miao-hsieh 描寫, hsing-jung 形容,
etc.) characters and events in his text. Of course, the generally abstract
canons of Chinese painting theory never rule out the practice of painstaking imitation of reality in certain genres (e.g., birds and flowers,
etc.). But we may be closer to the truth if by the many references to
verisimilitude in fiction criticism we understand not any attempt at
trompe l'oeil illusion, but rather the mimetic representation of the
complementary dimensions of substantiality and insubstantiality, mass

[97] For examples of this usage, see items 29 and 30 of the Shui-hu hou-chuan tu-fa essay
(SHCTLHP 573); Ching-hua yüan, marginal comment (p. 1/5b) and chapter comment (p.
4/27a); Hsin-hua ch'un-meng chi, marginal comment (p. 10/152); and Hua-yüeh hen (1981
edition), chapter comment (p. 3.19).

and void, action and repose, that make up the traditional Chinese conception of the "real world." This vision of complementarity, at least, seems to be behind the frequent use of the terms *shih* 實 and *hsü* 虛 in a variety of critical discussions to indicate two mutually supporting aspects of a broader view of reality, and is related to the use of these two terms to evaluate the "truth value" of varying combinations of fact and fabrication in historical fiction.

In the specific field of prose narrative, the issue of verisimilitude takes on an additional dimension of meaning in connection with the impression of plausibility in sequences of events or credibility of motivation in the sphere of character portrayal—that is, those aspects by which the fictional text may "make sense" according to one frame of reference or another. Although it has been argued by some that traditional Chinese fiction writers display considerably less interest in logical structure than their Western counterparts, they of course share fully in the central aim of all narrative art to recreate an intelligible world through the devices of fictional mimesis.[98] At certain points, the critics take the trouble to point out the manner in which their authors arrange to explain or justify a particular piece of text or to question the logical necessity of a given narrative unit. Mao Tsung-kang spends perhaps the most effort in this regard, as in his lengthy discussion of the chain of necessity that requires that the *San-kuo yen-i* open long before the start of the Three Kingdoms period proper.[99]

In general, however, the Ming-Ch'ing critics rarely enter into a detailed analysis of the workings of textual causality. To some extent, this might be due to the centrality of the element of coincidence rather than causality in Chinese philosophy, as evidenced in the *I Ching*. Such stock expressions as "without coincidence there would be no story" ("wu ch'iao pu-ch'eng shu" 無巧不成書) or various storyteller's tag phrases emphasizing the role of fortuitous circumstances (*ts'ou-ch'iao* 湊巧, *ch'ia-hao* 恰好, etc.) reflect this sort of attitude, but they usually occur at a fairly "naive" or surface level of the text in serious Chinese fiction. The traditional critics do not make causality into an overriding desideratum; instead, they praise examples in which both causality and coincidence are present at the same time (e.g., "wu-yin erh yu-yin" 無因而有因). In his *tu-fa* essay on the *San-kuo yen-i*, Mao Tsung-kang provides a good exam-

---

[98] See, for example, Jonathan Culler, "The Poetics of the Novel," in *Structuralist Poetics* (Ithaca: Cornell University Press, 1975), pp. 189–248; Georg Lukács, *The Theory of the Novel* (Cambridge, Mass.: MIT Press, 1971); and Ralph Freedman, "The Possibility of a Theory of the Novel," in *Disciplines of Criticism*, Peter Demetz, ed. (New Haven: Yale University Press, 1968), pp. 57–77.

[99] See chap. III below, item 7 of the *San-kuo yen-i tu-fa* essay. See also Mao Tsung-kang chapter comment (*SKYI* 120.1179).

ple of this critical attitude when he cites both reasoned predictability and tantalizing unpredictability as factors responsible for the greatness of the novel.[100] Similarly, in Chin Sheng-t'an's discussion of the terms "extreme narrative frugality" (*chi sheng fa* 極省法) and "extreme avoidance of narrative frugality" (*chi pu-sheng fa* 極不省法), it is clear that both techniques are concerned in their own way with causality, but its expression is handled in a different way because of the complexity or dramatic importance of a segment or because of the need to alternate the use of narrative techniques to achieve variety.[101]

In our final category of fiction criticism, what we have designated as "interpretive comments," we may consider the quantitatively significant portion of the commentaries on fiction that treat intellectual issues arising in connection with one or another narrative text. Obviously, the profundity of interpretation is for the most part conditioned by the seriousness and depth of the work under consideration, so that the interpretive commentary on the *Hsi-yu chi* and the *Hung-lou meng*, for example, is far more substantial than that on a second-rate novel such as *P'ing Shan Leng Yen* 平山冷燕. By the same token, we also find a wide range of variation between those comments that present penetrating critical insight and the many others that may be quite farfetched. What is at issue in our own study of these materials, however, is not the validity or persuasiveness of a given commentator's specific interpretations, but rather the general attitudes among the Ming-Ch'ing critics regarding the susceptibility of the fictional texts to serious interpretation in the first place. On this point we observe a predominant seriousness of approach to the major narrative texts which at times might perhaps be unfounded, but which has resulted in the production of interpretive commentaries of great potential value to the modern reader, not only for their specific attempts at the explication of individual difficult texts, but also for the reflection of broader intellectual trends in late Ming and Ch'ing China.

In terms of format, we find that the more substantive interpretive materials generally appear in essay form (e.g., prefaces and colophons [*hsü-pa* 序跋], general remarks on the novel as a whole or on specific chapters [*tsung-p'i* 總批, *tsung-p'ing* 總評], *tu-fa* essays and essays on particular topics) or separate critical writings, instead of in marginal and interlineal commentary. This seems to be due not simply to reasons of space, but also to the fact that the interpretation of narrative literature, as a rule, demands an overview of the entire work and is therefore not quite suited to line-by-line commentary. In this introductory essay we will be forced to pass over somewhat summarily these extremely valuable mate-

---

[100] See chap. III below, item 11 of the *San-kuo yen-i tu-fa* essay.

[101] See chap. II below, items 61 and 62 of the *Shui-hu chuan tu-fa* essay.

rials, since they tend to bring in issues of Chinese civilization that would take us far beyond the scope of our volume. Instead, we will simply review here several of the most common interpretive approaches that appear in the critical corpus.

One type of substantive discussion that accounts for a large portion of these materials occurs when the critics indulge in heated polemics regarding specific political-historical issues. Such discussions are of course most relevant to works of historical substance, such as *yen-i* fiction, with its unavoidable analogies between past and present dynasties. Mao Tsung-kang, for example, devotes the lengthy first section of his *tu-fa* essay to a consideration of the problem of legitimate succession in the Three Kingdoms period, which is by no means innocently academic, but fairly bristles with controversial implications given the political situation in the mid-seventeenth century after the imposition of Manchu rule. Similarly, Chin Sheng-t'an's rather caustic remarks on the nature of the rebels in certain of the items toward the beginning of his *tu-fa* essay are at striking variance with the tone of sophisticated urbanity that dominates the remainder of the essay and seem to reflect his bitter reaction to the conditions that brought on the fall of the Ming.

On a more personal level, a number of critics become embroiled in polemics over the seriousness of texts to which they feel an intense commitment despite the fact that those texts have been seen by others as nothing more than exercises in popular entertainment, or worse. This is especially true in the case of the *Chin P'ing Mei*, a novel whose particularly engrossing mimetic surface has led centuries of readers to overlook the depth of seriousness behind its structural brilliance and penetrating view of the human condition. In addition to several important items of his *tu-fa* essay in which he carefully threads his way around the problem of the effect that the book might have on some of its readers, Chang Chu-p'o devotes the entire space of a separate essay to outlining his conviction that the *Chin P'ing Mei* is much more than an obscene book.[102] Contrary to what the modern reader might think, the same argument seems to have been necessary for the *Hung-lou meng*. Numerous critical essays from the Ch'ing period engage in the same sort of defense of it against charges of obscenity or frivolousness.[103]

---

[102] The essay is entitled "*Ti-i ch'i-shu* fei yin-shu lun" 第一奇書非淫書論 (The Number One Marvelous Book Is Not an Obscene Book) and appears in the front matter of Chang Chu-p'o's commentary to the novel.

[103] For examples of such arguments regarding the *Hung-lou meng*, see the Wu-kuei shan-jen 五桂山人 preface to the Chang Hsin-chih commentary on the novel (*HLMC* 35); the Tzu-lang shan-jen 紫琅山人 preface to the same work (*HLMC* 37–38); *Tu Hung-lou meng tsa-chi* 讀紅樓夢雜記 (Miscellaneous Notes on Reading the *Hung-lou meng*; *HLMC* 205); and chap. VII below, item I of the *Hung-lou meng tu-fa* essay.

A second type of interpretive approach to the masterworks of traditional Chinese fiction is the allegorical reading of works involving particularly multilayered surface texture. Given the strong genetic links that tie fiction criticism to the long-standing tradition of classical exegesis in China, it is natural to expect that the development of textual hermeneutics, as in the West, would give rise to the literary pastimes of allegorical composition and allegorical reading of prose fiction as well. At times this sort of commentary is limited to the ad hoc exegesis of individual words or lines in terms of various preexisting schemes of analysis (such as "five phases" theory) or the insistence on reading some works as romans à clef and trotting out "proof" from the text that such-and-such a character is really an historical figure lightly disguised (as in certain readings of the *Ju-lin wai-shih* or *so-yin* 索隱 interpretations of the *Hung-lou meng*); however, in certain cases the critics do commit themselves to fully articulated allegorical readings of an entire text. Of course, the number of works that support this sort of rigorous allegorical interpretation is very small, in the Chinese as in the European literary tradition, but by the same token this select group includes some of the greatest works in the respective literatures.

The one work of Chinese fiction that lends itself most completely to allegorical interpretation is the *Hsi-yu chi*. From the time that this text was first circulated in the sixteenth century, critical commentators accepted the novel as a serious allegory and proceeded to offer their own suggestions for its proper interpretation, whether that be in terms of the Buddhist and Taoist figures dominating the surface of the text or various schemes of *san-chiao* 三教 (Confucianism, Taoism, and Buddhism) syncretism. Beginning with the late Ming commentary attributed to Li Chih (already including a number of stabs at allegorical exegesis of such figures as the "exile of the mind" [*fang-hsin* 放心]), the list of allegorical interpretations includes those of the Ch'ing commentators Wang Hsiang-hsü 汪象旭, Ch'en Shih-pin 陳士斌, Chang Shu-shen 張書紳 (whose Neo-Confucian scheme of interpretation is of particular interest), and Liu I-ming 劉一明 (whose *tu-fa* essay is translated in this volume).[104] Unfortunately, the majority of modern students of the *Hsi-yu chi* seem to have followed Hu Shih's lead in rejecting all such traditional readings as examples of unscientific subjective interpretation. That position may perhaps be justified in connection with some of the more outlandish readings, but it certainly throws the baby out with the bathwater as far as

[104] The titles of the editions in question, respectively, are *Hsi-yu cheng-tao shu; Hsi-yu chen-ch'üan* 西遊真詮 (The True Explication of the *Hsi-yu chi*), preface 1696; *Hsin-shuo Hsi-yu chi* 新說西遊記 (A New Explication of the *Hsi-yu chi*), preface 1749; and *Hsi-yu yüan-chih* 西遊原旨 (The Original Intent of the *Hsi-yu chi*), first edition 1810.

some of the valuable critical materials contained in many of these editions is concerned.

The question of whether or not the *Hung-lou meng* was intended to comprise an allegorical representation of the human condition in an enclosed garden of earthly delights may perhaps be an open one,[105] but a good majority of the Ch'ing readers of the novel who felt moved to set brush to paper in defense of their own particular understanding of the text provide us with clear examples of possible allegorical interpretations of the work as a whole.[106] Perhaps the strongest argument for serious treatment of this sort of interpretation lies in the fact that the commentators now collectively known as Chih-yen chai, whose personal relationships to the author lend a heightened degree of credibility to their remarks, indulge in allegorical readings at numerous points.

Even a work such as the *Chin P'ing Mei*, in which the creative energies of the author seemingly concentrated on mimesis of everyday life, has inspired serious allegorical interpretation. At first sight Chang Chu-p'o's essay, "*Chin P'ing Mei* yü-i shuo" 金瓶梅寓意說 (Allegorical Meaning in the *Chin P'ing Mei*),[107] seems to be somewhat superficial, as it concentrates almost entirely on what kind of allegorical meanings can be found from an examination of the characters' names.[108] However

---

[105] See Andrew H. Plaks, *Archetype and Allegory in the Dream of the Red Chamber* (Princeton: Princeton University Press, 1976), chaps. 5–7; and Andrew H. Plaks, "Allegory in *Hsi-yu chi* and *Hung-lou meng*," in *Chinese Narrative: Critical and Theoretical Essays*, pp. 187–202.

[106] Some of the most valuable of the allegorical interpretations of the *Hung-lou meng* include: the Tzu-lang shan-jen preface to the Chang Hsin-chih commentary to the novel (*HLMC* 37–38); Chou Ch'un 周春, *Yüeh Hung-lou meng sui-pi* 閱紅樓夢隨筆 (Notes on Reading the *Hung-lou meng*; *HLMC* 66–77); Erh-chih tao-jen, *Hung-lou meng shuo meng* (*HLMC* 83–103); Chang Ch'i-hsin 張其信, *Hung-lou meng ou-p'ing* 紅樓夢偶評 (Random Comments on the *Hung-lou meng*; *HLMC* 215–18); Meng-ch'ih hsüeh-jen 夢痴學人, *Meng-ch'ih shuo meng* 夢痴說夢 (Dream Talk from Dream-Crazy; *HLMC* 218–27); and Hsü Yeh-fen 許葉芬, *Hung-lou meng pien* 紅樓夢辨 (On the *Hung-lou meng*; *HLMC* 227–32). Also of interest are the Ch'i Liao-sheng 戚蓼生 preface to the novel (*HLMC* 27–28); Hua-shih chu-jen 話石主人, *Hung-lou meng pen-i yüeh-pien* 紅樓夢本義約編 (The Basic Meaning of the *Hung-lou meng*; *HLMC* 179–83); and Chieh-an chü-shih 解盦居士, *Shih-t'ou i-shuo* 石頭臆說 (My Thoughts on the *Story of the Stone*; *HLMC* 184–97).

[107] This essay is included in the prefatory material in Chang Chu-p'o's commentary on the *Chin P'ing Mei*.

[108] The practice of using names that convey insight into the personalities of the characters or into the main concerns of the work through puns or association is a technique widely used in Chinese fiction and is somewhat similar to the naming of characters such as Thwackum in Henry Fielding's *Tom Jones* or to Charles Dickens's many suggestively named characters. In Chinese fiction, this usage seems to be not as restricted to minor characters as in the West; furthermore, the polysemic nature of the Chinese language and the overabundance of homophones makes it difficult for the commentators to stop pursuing such leads before the bounds of reason are already crossed.

limited in scope it might be, the main aim of the essay is to warn the reader against becoming infatuated with the mimetic surface of the novel. Such warnings are all the more valuable for Western readers, accustomed to expecting "realistic" depiction of the world in novels of social manners.

By far the most common type of interpretive commentary in Chinese fiction criticism centers on the evaluative judgment of figures and ideas presented in the narrative works, as is to be expected from the overwhelmingly didactic tone of the Chinese literary tradition as a whole. With regard to the judgment of specific characters in fiction, we have already noted in the first part of this essay the frequency of brief subjective comments that express succinctly and sometimes quite baldly the critics' assessment of a character. This same impulse to provide an evaluation of character may be seen in the frequent practice of compos-ing sets of evaluative pieces (*tsan* 贊, *yung* 詠, etc.) for the entire cast of characters of certain works (notably the *Hung-lou meng*)[109] or in the campaign undertaken by some of the critics to reverse the received evaluation of certain fictional characters (e.g., Chin Sheng-t'an's con-demnation of Sung Chiang, Chang Chu-p'o's attack on Wu Yüeh-niang, or even the contempt directed toward either Hsüeh Pao-ch'ai or Lin Tai-yü by supporters of the one or the other of the two heroines of the *Hung-lou meng*).[110]

In general, however, it may be said that the Chinese fiction critics resist the temptation toward easy labeling of figures and demonstrate considerable flexibility in their judgment of major characters, even of those whose images are predominantly negative in the popular tradition. For example, Mao Tsung-kang is quick to point out in numerous textual comments instances of the treachery by which Ts'ao Ts'ao gains and keeps power, but in other places he is also perfectly willing to give proper credit to Ts'ao Ts'ao's admirable qualities—his wiliness, resourcefulness, and particularly his ability to attract and hold the loyalty of worthy followers. In many comments the expression "unscrupulous hero" (*chien-hsiung* 奸雄) does double duty, conveying both the fascinating and the menacing aspects of this sort of figure, so that this concept becomes another cliché of the fiction criticism tradition, later applied in the Chih-yen chai commentary to the role of Wang Hsi-feng in the *Hung-lou*

[109] See for instance, Tu-hua chu-jen 讀花主人 (pseud. of T'u Ying 涂瀛), "*Hung-lou meng* lun-tsan" 紅樓夢論贊 (Evaluations of the Characters of the *Hung-lou meng*; *HLMC* 125–42), which contains over seventy evaluations and was reprinted in most of the late Ch'ing editions of the *Hung-lou meng* with commentary.

[110] See chap. III below, items 2, 3, and 22 of the *Shui-hu chuan tu-fa* essay and chap. IV below, item 24 of the *Chin P'ing Mei tu-fa* essay.

meng.[111] Even more interesting are comments in the Mao Tsung-kang and "Li Chih" commentaries on the *San-kuo yen-i*, which show that they did not shrink from severe criticism of even such a revered figure as Chu-ko Liang,[112] although they also express unreserved admiration for him in those passages in which they feel it is merited. The modern reader ought not to take this as simple inconsistency of judgment, but rather as a function of the sort of flexibility or fluidity inherent in the fictional representation of character in the Chinese tradition.

The above type of critical evaluations, of course, grow directly out of the tradition of Chinese historiography and more particularly the format of the official biography with its concluding evaluative comments (set off from the narrative itself by such terms as *T'ai-shih kung yüeh* 太史公曰, *p'ing-yüeh* 評曰, *lun-yüeh* 論曰, *tsan-yüeh* 贊曰, etc.). In fact, it might be argued that the historical development of many of the genres of Chinese fiction both began with, and remained inextricably linked to, the prototypes of biographical narrative forged in Ssu-ma Ch'ien's *Shih-chi*. In fiction criticism, the recurrent criteria of historical judgments, such as the proper maintenance of the ruler–ruled relation, the proper correspondence between the micro- and macrocosm, and the need for the restoration of equilibrium in the human sphere, are applied to fictional worlds as well, even those that appear at first sight to be totally removed from historical considerations. The most serious attention of all is paid to instances in which figures are forced by circumstance to act against their own wills or face an insoluble contradiction between individual inclinations and universal principles. At their most serious level, these raise the issue of the disjunction between traditional affirmation of a principle of moral justice inherent in the universe and the evidence that contradicts the rule of such a moral order, or the issue of what can be attained by individual action in such a situation and whether the true motives of one's actions, often doomed to failure, can be understood by others. The problem of the conflict betwen individual expectations of what can be accomplished and elements of determinism that seem to control our lives is treated by Mao Tsung-kang in item eight of his *tu-fa* essay on the *San-kuo yen-i*. The problem of whether later men will understand the true motives behind personal action is, of course, fundamental to the whole enterprise of writing commentaries on works of fiction. Almost all of the commentators consider themselves to be able

---

[111] *CYCPYCC* 68.590. This prechapter comment is found in the Yu-cheng 有正 filiations but not in earlier manuscripts, and compares her to Duke Chuang of Cheng (r. 743–701 B.C.) and Ts'ao Ts'ao.

[112] Mao Tsung-kang chapter comment (*SKYI* 97.961), and *Li Cho-wu hsien-sheng p'i-p'ing San-kuo yen-i*, chapter comment (p. 102/10a).

in some way or other to cross the boundaries of time and space to become the intimate friends (*chih-chi* 知己) of the often anonymous authors.

When concerned with texts that seem to merit it, the Chinese fiction critics sometimes move beyond the historical frame of reference into the metaphysical dimension to consider certain abstract philosophical issues. The treatment of such issues in traditional criticism is unfortunately somewhat clouded by the particular terminology of Buddhist, Taoist, or Confucian origin in terms of which they are presented in the majority of the texts themselves—a surface ideology of popular wisdom, often expressed through what appear to be rather shallow notions of retribution, withdrawal, or conventional morality. It should be noted to the credit of the best of the Ming-Ch'ing critics, however, that they often go beyond this level to pursue some of the deeper issues of their intellectual milieu as they appear in various fictional transformations. This is of course particularly true in criticism of those novels that focus on serious problems of this sort, a set of works that certainly includes the six novels treated in the *tu-fa* material translated in this volume. Here we find discussions of such central concepts as mind (*hsin* 心), attachment (*ch'ing* 情), enlightenment (*wu* 悟), the Tao, and the Void (*k'ung* 空), which transcend the common use of these terms as linguistic placeholders nearly devoid of meaning.

Before concluding, let us recall our observation that the great majority of the critical terms employed by the traditional fiction commentators were not invented for the purpose, but were borrowed either unaltered or in modified form from the existing body of critical vocabulary developed over the centuries in the areas of classical poetry and prose, drama, and painting theory. We have seen that in quite a few cases (e.g., *ch'en* 襯) the meaning of such terms in their new context may differ substantially from what they may have signified in the old. The precise source of a given term, on the other hand, may be of significance for our understanding of the critical concept involved. For example, the use of the terminology of parallelism with reference to narrative structure can only be fully understood when compared with the unique aesthetics of correlative parallelism that comprises a central principle of Chinese poetics, particularly in the genre of *lü-shih* 律詩 (regulated verse). The extensive borrowing of terms developed in connection with landscape painting, moreover, may help to explain the emphasis on various models of spatial relations—that is, nontemporal, overlapping patterns of simultaneous juxtaposition—at the heart of the Chinese novel form.

By far the most significant source for the terminology of fiction criticism can be identified as the vocabulary of the theory and practice of the classical prose essay. This critical tradition goes back at least as far as the Six Dynasties and T'ang periods (e.g., certain chapters on narrative structure and rhetoric in Liu Chih-chi's 劉知幾 [661–721] *Shih-t'ung* 史通 [Generalities of Historiography]) and is fully articulated in the Sung period in works such as Lü Tsu-ch'ien's *Ku-wen kuan-chien*, where we find a number of the same terms we have considered in this introduction: *chien-chia* 間架, *chieh-kou* 結構, *tun-ts'o* 頓挫, *i-mai kuo-chieh* 一脉過接, *p'u-hsü* 鋪敍, *shou-wei hsiang-ying* 首尾相應, etc.[113] By the Ming and Ch'ing periods the theory and technique of the prose essay took on even greater importance with the revival and redefinition of the *ku-wen* movement and preoccupation with the examination essay as the stepping-stone to government office. Of primary significance here is not simply the appropriation from one classical genre to a vernacular medium of a wide range of structural and rhetorical devices, but also the conviction with which fiction critics argued for the inherent commensurability of prose written in both media with respect to their seriousness and validity as vehicles for the discussion of important cultural issues. That is, when the Ming–Ch'ing critics speak of fiction as equivalent to formal prose, dub the authors of the vernacular novels as literati (*wen-jen* 文人), and praise the literary style (*wen-pi* 文筆) and devices (*wen-fa* 文法) found in their work, it is more the subtlety and deftness of expression associated with the more formal genres than merely the borrowed devices themselves that they most often have in mind.[114]

We have taken the trouble to point out the sources of the terminology of Chinese fiction criticism, not only because it can help us to understand more fully the new usages to which they were put, but also because the interchangeability of the critical terminology of the various fields reflects a very important aspect of the intellectual milieu of Ming–Ch'ing culture. In this period the enterprise of criticism and connoisseurship in all fields, from poetry, painting, drama, and the prose essay to historiography and such "minor" pursuits as gardening, antiques, and interior designing,[115] had become a very central preoccupation of Chinese literati culture. Not only can we trace the influences of writings

[113] Lü Tsu-ch'ien, *Ku-wen kuan-chien*. See also Liu Chih-chi, *Shih-t'ung hsüeh-fan chu* 史通削繁注 (Annotated and Abridged *Shih-t'ung*), Chi Yün 紀昀, ed. (Taipei: Kuang-wen shu-chü, 1963), pp. 64–72, "Hsü-shih" 敍事 (Narration of Events) section.

[114] For a discussion of the relationship of the examination essay and fiction writing, see item 49 of the "General Remarks" ("Tsung-p'i" 總批) of the *Hsin-shuo Hsi-yu chi*.

[115] Li Yü, for example, ranges from structural criticism of drama to chapters on interior design, rockery, and cooking in his *Hsien-ch'ing ou-chi* 閒情偶寄 (Random Repository of Idle Thoughts), vol. 5 of *Li Yü ch'üan-chi* 李漁全集 (The Collected Works of Li Yü), Helmut Martin, ed., 15 vols. (Taipei: Ch'eng-wen, 1970). For an example of late Ming garden criticism, see Chi Ch'eng 計成, *Yüan yeh* 園冶, in *Hsi-yung hsüan ts'ung-shu* 喜咏軒 叢書 (Hsi-yung Studio Collectanea), T'ao Hsiang 陶湘, ed. (Wu-chin: She-yüan, 1927–31), collection 5 (*wu* 戊), vol. 5.

in one field of thought on another, but in many cases the artists and critics in question actually knew one another, travelled in the same circles, and lived in the same geographical areas.[116] In addition, a large percentage of the fiction critics whose writings we have considered in this chapter actually worked in more than one field of aesthetics—fiction, poetry, painting, and drama,[117] so that their critical writings show a high degree of cross-fertilization between the separate art forms.[118] The rigid division of fiction and drama in a volume such as this, although undertaken primarily because of convenience, tends to obscure what was actually a very close and mutually fertile relationship between these two fields of endeavor and the body of criticism that developed around them. Beginning in the late Ming this relationship became all the closer with the rise of dramatic texts written primarily for the reading table (*an-t'ou chü-pen* 案頭劇本) rather than for performance on stage. The implications of this overlapping of media are particularly great for the field of vernacular fiction, in that the theoretical and technical points described here were intended to serve as practical guides for fiction writers as well as aids for armchair readers and fellow critics. Hopefully, the entire question of the role of criticism in all its many manifestations in late imperial Chinese civilization will become the subject for more comprehensive investigation, with particular attention paid to the overlapping and cross-fertilization of the aesthetics of the various fields, an aim toward which this volume is but a first step.

It is extremely suggestive to note, in conclusion, that the precise coincidence of the flourishing of extended vernacular fiction with the development of this critical perspective of sixteenth- through eighteenth-century thought in China parallels closely some of the developments in European intellectual life in the same period that form the groundwork for the rise of the Western novel form.[119] If there is any truth to the argument of recent Western theorists to the effect that the

[116] For discussions of the backgrounds of these interlocking circles of artists and critics, see David T. Roy, "Chang Chu-p'o's Commentary on the *Chin P'ing Mei*," and Robert E. Hegel, "*Sui-T'ang yen-i* and the Aesthetics of the Seventeenth-Century Suchou Elite," in *Chinese Narrative: Critical and Theoretical Essays*, pp. 115–23 and 124–62.

[117] To name only the two most obvious examples, Chin Sheng-t'an and Mao Tsung-kang (along with his father, Mao Lun) were as well known at one time for their commentaries on dramatic works (i.e., the *Hsi-hsiang chi* and the *P'i-p'a chi*, respectively) as for their work on full-length fiction.

[118] By the same token, many of the leading figures in the late Ming and early Ch'ing Chinese intellectual world, such as Li Yü, Tung Ch'i-ch'ang 董其昌 (1555–1636), and Ch'en Chi-ju, etc., worked in more than one field of aesthetics.

[119] See, for instance, the role of such figures as Samuel Johnson, the Schlegel brothers, and Madame de Stael, etc., in the development of the European novel form.

novel is first and foremost an outgrowth of this new critical vision—that the contribution of the novel to modern civilization lies precisely in its capacity to recreate its world *critically*[120]—then this is equally valid for the literary developments in China during the same centuries. Thus, while some of the critical assumptions of Chinese fictional art—the emphasis on textural linkage, figural parallelism, structures of recurrence, etc.—reflect certain special predispositions of traditional Chinese aesthetics, we also find considerable areas of overlap with Western theory regarding structuration, characterization, and interpretation. In view of the fact that a number of the directions of recent Western fiction criticism and practice appear curiously compatible with the critical assumptions of the Chinese tradition as formulated in the writings of the Ming-Ch'ing commentators, we may now be in a better position to incorporate these valuable materials into the construction of general models of narrative theory.

[120] Georg Lukács, *The Theory of the Novel*, esp. chap. 4, "The Inner Form of the Novel," and chap. 5, "The Historico-Philosophical Conditioning of the Novel and Its Significance," pp. 70–83 and 84–93.

Chin Sheng-t'an on How to Read the *Shui-hu chuan* (The Water Margin)

INTRODUCTION:
Chin Sheng-t'an and His "Tu *Ti-wu ts'ai-tzu shu* fa" (How to Read *The Fifth Book of Genius*)

Chin Sheng-t'an 金聖歎 (1608–1661, personal name originally Ts'ai 采, courtesy name Jo-ts'ai 若采) is an extremely important and pivotal figure in the history of traditional Chinese fiction and fiction criticism. Even though the elevation of fiction and drama to an equal position with classical literature was already championed by figures like Li Chih 李贄 (1527–1602) and Yüan Hung-tao 袁宏道 (1568–1610), we can attribute a large portion of the eventual success of this endeavor to Chin Sheng-t'an. He provided later commentators with an almost larger-than-life image of a practicing fiction commentator and left readers with a new method of reading Chinese fiction. His importance as a model lasted into the twentieth century when almost all of the traditional commentaries were sacrificed on the altar of modernization and Westernization by Hu Shih 胡適 (1891–1962) and others.

Commentators on fiction and drama prior to Chin Sheng-t'an are a shadowy group who used pseudonyms or attributed their commentaries to famous literary figures such as Li Chih, Ch'en Chi-ju 陳繼儒 (1558–1639), or Chung Hsing 鍾惺 (1574–1625).[1] The most active of these figures appears to have been Yeh Chou 葉晝 (fl. 1595–1624), who has recently been honored with separate treatment in a monograph on the aesthetics of the traditional Chinese novel.[2] Although it seems clear that Yeh Chou depended mainly on writing commentaries for financial sup-

---

[1] On the problem of the "Li Chih" commentaries, see app. 2.
[2] Yeh Lang 葉朗, *Chung-kuo hsiao-shuo mei-hsüeh* 中國小說美學 (The Aesthetics of Chinese Fiction; Peking: Pei-ching ta-hsüeh, 1982).

port, his relationship to his texts is diametrically opposed to that of Chin Sheng-t'an. From what we know, people like Yeh Chou were hired to do commentaries by publishing houses on a piecemeal basis. They expressed their frustration through often acerbic remarks on the texts for which they provided commentaries. In effect, they tried to elevate their own status by denigrating the texts before them. As we will see, Chin Sheng-t'an's practice was very different.

Chin Sheng-t'an was born and spent his whole life in Suchou, one of the main cultural centers of South China. From maturity on, he seems to have devoted the greater part of his energy to writing commentaries on a variety of literary works. His original plans were quite ambitious. He devised a list of "books by and for geniuses" (ts'ai-tzu shu 才子書), including both classical literature (the Chuang Tzu 莊子 by Chuang Chou 莊周, 369?–286? B.C.; the Li-sao 離騷 [Encountering Sorrow] by Ch'ü Yüan 屈原, 340?–278? B.C.; the Shih-chi 史記 [Records of the Historian] by Ssu-ma Ch'ien 司馬遷, b. 145 B.C.; and the poetry of Tu Fu 杜甫, 712–770) and vernacular works (the Shui-hu chuan 水滸傳 [The Water Margin] and the Hsi-hsiang chi 西廂記 [Romance of the Western Chamber]),[3] for which he planned to provide his own editions with commentary. The Shui-hu chuan was called "The Fifth Book of Genius" because it was fifth on this list. Of the books on the list, Chin Sheng-t'an only managed to complete the commentaries on the Shui-hu chuan and the Hsi-hsiang chi[4] and partially finish the one on Tu Fu's poetry.[5] He also prepared an anthology, with brief commentary, of short selections of prose in the classical language, T'ien-hsia ts'ai-tzu pi-tu shu 天下才子必讀書 (Required Reading for the Geniuses of the World).[6] Posthumous

---

[3] See the first preface of his edition of the Shui-hu chuan, quoted in SHCHPP, p. 6.

[4] There is a photo-reprint of a 1720 edition with added commentary, Ti-liu ts'ai-tzu Hsi-hsiang chi 第六才子西廂記 (Sixth Work of Genius, Romance of the Western Chamber; Taipei: Wen-kuang t'u-shu, 1978), as well as a collated and annotated typeset edition, Chin Sheng-t'an p'i-pen Hsi-hsiang chi 金聖歎批本西廂記 (Chin Sheng-t'an Commentary Edition of the Hsi-hsiang chi), Chang Kuo-kuang 張國光, ed. (Shanghai: Shanghai ku-chi, 1986). This commentary, as well as almost all of Chin Sheng-t'an's extant writings (commentary or otherwise), is also available in typeset form as part of CSTCC. The major additions to this collection over previous versions is the inclusion of Chin Sheng-t'an's poetry (see n. 7 below) and his anthology with commentary of classical prose (see n. 6 below).

[5] Preface by his cousin, Chin Ch'ang 金昌, dated 1659. Included in CSTCC.

[6] Photo-reprint under the same title, 2 vols. (Taipei: Shu-hsiang ch'u-pan she, 1978); plus a typeset reprint, Chin Sheng-t'an p'i ts'ai-tzu ku-wen 金聖歎批才子古文 (Classical Prose by Geniuses with Commentary by Chin Sheng-t'an), Chang Kuo-kuang 張國光, ed. (Wuhan: Hu-pei jen-min, 1986). This volume also contains a biography of Chin Sheng-t'an by the editor, pp. 587–93.

collections of his prose (essays and miscellaneous commentaries) and
poetry are still extant.[7] There is some evidence that he compiled an
anthology of examination essays, *Ch'eng-mo ts'ai-tzu* 程墨才子 (Geniuses
of the Examination Essay).[8]

In Chin Sheng-t'an's commentaries his personality looms large and
at times commands more attention than the text itself. To some extent,
his commentaries are dialogues with the reader in which the literary
work is but a pretext. The personal element in his writing seems to have
encouraged a variety of what seem to be legendary anecdotes about him.
In any case, the image of Chin Sheng-t'an had more impact than the real
person.[9] Some say that he was originally surnamed Chang 張 but changed
to Chin to inherit his uncle's line or claim that he changed his name to
avoid a ban on his participation in the civil service examinations.[10] He
did change his personal name from Ts'ai 采 to Jen-jui 人瑞 after the fall
of the Ming dynasty in 1644, according to some for patriotic reasons.[11]
Sheng-t'an is the pen name he used for his commentaries. By his selection of that name he compared himself to Tseng Tien 曾點, one of
Confucius's (551–479 B.C.) more carefree and unconventional disciples.[12]

[7] For his essays and miscellaneous commentaries, see *CSTCC* and earlier editions of his
collected works. His poetry was not readily available until the 1979 photo-reprint (Shang-
hai: Shang-hai ku-chi) of a rare manuscript copy, *Ch'en-yin lou shih-hsüan* 沉吟樓詩選
(Selected Poems of Chin Sheng-t'an), Liu Hsien-t'ing 劉獻廷 (1648–1695), ed., which is
included in *CSTCC*.

[8] See the list of Chin Sheng-t'an's posthumous works appended to the manuscript copy
of the *Ch'en-yin lou shih-hsüan*, pp. 155–56.

[9] His life and work are the subject of *CST*.

[10] See sources quoted in Ch'en Hsiang 陳香, "Lun Chin Sheng-t'an ti p'i-p'ing fang-
fa" 論金聖歎的批評方法 (On Chin Sheng-t'an's Method of Criticism), pt. 3, *Shu-p'ing
shu-mu* 19:59–66 (1974) and Wu Chien-i 吳監益, *Chin Sheng-t'an ti wen-hsüeh p'i-p'ing
k'ao-shu* 金聖歎的文學批評考述 (Analysis and Description of the Literary Criticism of
Chin Sheng-t'an; Taipei: College of Liberal Arts of National Taiwan University, 1976),
p. 12, n. 1. These stories are refuted by Ch'en Hung 陳洪 in his "Chin Sheng-t'an 'Chang
hsing shuo' pien-i" 金聖歎張姓說辨疑 (A Refutation of the Theory that Chin Sheng-
t'an was Surnamed Chang), *Chiang Hai hsüeh-k'an*, 1983.5:98. Huang Lin 黃霖, however, has come out in support of the idea that Chin Sheng-t'an once changed his surname
to Chang for the purpose of taking the civil service examinations. See his "Chin Sheng-
t'an 'hsiang hsing Chang' pien" 金聖歎庠姓張辨 (On the Question of Chin Sheng-t'an's
Changing His Name to Chang for Examination Purposes), *Chiang Hai hsüeh-k'an*, 1985.
1:52–54.

[11] See Chang Kuo-kuang 張國光, *Shui-hu yü Chin Sheng-t'an yen-chiu* 水滸與金聖歎
研究 (Studies on the *Shui-hu chuan* and Chin Sheng-t'an; Honan: Chung-chou shu-hua
she, 1981), p. 91 and Chao Ching-shen's 趙景深 preface to *CSTCC*. This idea seems to
have originated in Liao Yen's 廖燕 (1644–1701) biography of Chin Sheng-t'an in his *Erh-
shih-ch'i sung t'ang chi* 二十七松堂集 (Collection from the Hall of Twenty-seven Pines;
Tokyo: Hakuetsudō, 1862), pp. 14/5b–7b. Chin Sheng-t'an also used the name Wei 謂.

[12] See *CST*, pp. 37–38, 133–34 n. 69.

There are numerous stories of his being kicked out of the civil service examinations for outrageous conduct. He obtained only the lowest civil service degree, never held public office, and ceased to participate in the examination system after the fall of the Ming.

The Shun-chih emperor (r. 1644–1661) is reported to have praised Chin Sheng-t'an's literary ability[13] and there is some controversy as to what his reaction was on hearing of this and whether he had hopes of appointment to an offical post. His execution as one of the instigators of a protest against harsh local officials on the occasion of official mourning ceremonies for the Shun-chih emperor in 1661 was misconstrued by later scholars, including the influential Lu Hsün 魯迅 (1881–1936), as primarily an act of sincere grief at the passing of the emperor.[14]

Since Chin Sheng-t'an first became famous, assessment of his commentarial method and in particular his work on the *Shui-hu chuan* has ranged from praise to damnation. Moralists accused him of contributing to the spread of banditry through his promotion of the novel.[15] Even among those who were sympathetic, he was sometimes criticized for focusing too much attention on purely formal features of the text. On the other hand, his example was the standard against which all later commentators had to compete, and his influence is implicit in their commentaries whether their personal reaction to him was negative or positive.

Up until very recently, the twentieth century has not been kind to Chin Sheng-t'an. One of his staunchest supporters, Chang Kuo-kuang 張國光 (who often overstates his case), has classified post-1949 judgments of Chin Sheng-t'an and his commentary on the *Shui-hu chuan* into five classes: (1) he is considered a reactionary member of the literati, (2) a rebel against Chinese feudal culture (this is Chang Kuo-kuang's own position), (3) a sympathizer with the Liang-shan outlaws who opposes their surrender to the throne or co-optation (*chao-an* 招安), (4) a contradictory figure both sympathetic and antagonistic to the rebels, and (5) a supporter of feudalism but with nationalistic (anti-Manchu) feelings.[16] Chang Kuo-kuang's list focuses on problems of content and ideology. As

[13] We know this from the preface that he wrote for his "Ch'un-kan pa-shou" 春感八首 (Spring Reflections, Eight Poems), in *Ch'en-yin lou shih-hsüan* (*CSTCC*, vol. 4, p. 585).

[14] See Hsü T'ao 徐濤, "Lüeh-lun Lu Hsün hsien-sheng tui Chin Sheng-t'an ti p'i-p'ing chi ch'i-t'a" 略論魯迅先生對金聖歎的批評及其他 (A Brief Discussion of Lu Hsün's Criticism of Chin Sheng-t'an and Other Matters), *Shui-hu cheng-ming* 1: 255–66 (1983), p. 260.

[15] See *CST*, pp. 120–21.

[16] *Shui-hu yü Chin Sheng-t'an yen-chiu*, pp. 339–55. See also *CST*, p. 60.

for the question of his style of literary criticism, many critics in this century have condemned him for the infraction of numerous laws of accepted critical practice, such as respect for the original text.[17]

Chin Sheng-t'an's identification with the authors of the texts he commented on was very deep and intense. He took the audacious step of making himself responsible for providing a positive explanation for all the features of each of the texts. In the case of the *Shui-hu chuan*, he made his job easier by cutting out those portions of the text that he was not prepared to defend and adding new sections of his own invention. He justified this by claiming to have found in the studio (Kuan-hua t'ang 貫華堂) of a friend an old edition that represented the original form of the novel as it came from the pen of the author. Chin Sheng-t'an attributed objectionable parts of the text to persons other than the original author.[18] Even though some of his contemporaries immediately saw through his ruse, Chin Sheng-t'an's edition won out over all the others to such an extent that scholars at the beginning of the twentieth century were unaware of the existence of the older versions and of the part that Chin Sheng-t'an had played in the fabrication of his seventy-chapter version.[19] The publication of a variorum edition of the novel under the general editorship of Cheng Chen-to 鄭振鐸 (1898–1958)[20] now makes comparison of the various editions an easy and convenient task.

Chin Sheng-t'an's edition has three different prefaces, all from his own hand. The first establishes, in a somewhat backhanded fashion, the

---

[17] The most developed attack of this type is found in the articles by Ch'en Hsiang 陳香 in *Shu-p'ing shu-mu* 11:30–36, 17:39–48, 18:80–86, 19:59–66, 20:51–61 (1974).

[18] For instance, the last third of the 100- and 120-chapter versions of the novel were attributed by him to Lo Kuan-chung 羅貫中 (fl. 1364), while minor discrepancies were blamed on redactors who produced debased, popular editions.

[19] For instance, a note on the title page of the 1664 first edition of the *Shui-hu hou-chuan* 水滸後傳 (Continuation of the *Shui-hu chuan*) accuses Chin Sheng-t'an of cutting and changing (*shan-kai* 刪改) the *Shui-hu chuan*. For the Chinese text, see Liu Ts'un-jen 柳存仁, *Lun-tun so-chien Chung-kuo hsiao-shuo shu-mu t'i-yao* 倫敦所見中國小說書目提要 (Annotated Bibliography of Chinese Fiction Seen in London; Peking: Shu-mu wen-hsien, 1982), p. 170. For translation, see Ellen Widmer, *The Margins of Utopia* (Cambridge, Mass.: Harvard University Press, 1987), pp. 8, 214. Although the majority of scholars see the seventy-chapter version as a product of Chin Sheng-t'an's editing, there do exist those who argue that the original version of the novel did have seventy chapters complete with the nightmare sequence at the end. For an example, see Lo Erh-kang 羅爾綱, "Ts'ung Lo Kuan-chung *San Sui p'ing-yao chuan* k'an *Shui-hu chuan* chu-che ho yüan-pen wen-t'i" 從羅貫中三遂平妖傳看水滸傳著者和原本問題 (Looking at the Problem of the Authorship and Original Text of the *Shui-hu chuan* from Lo Kuan-chung's *San Sui p'ing-yao chuan*), *Hsüeh-shu yüeh-k'an*, 1984. 10:22–32. The evidence presented does not support his assertions.

[20] *Shui-hu ch'üan-chuan* 水滸全傳 (Complete *Shui-hu chuan*; Peking: Jen-min wen-hsüeh, 1954).

right of the author to write the novel and Chin's own right to publish a commentary on it. The second preface stresses the moral value of the novel while refuting previous interpretations of it as a panegyric to the Liang-shan rebels. The third preface is addressed to his young son and written in a very personal tone. It deals with his relationship to the novel over the years and his method of interpreting it. There is a consistent attempt here to raise the status of the novel by comparing it to canonical texts. This last preface is dated 1641.[21] Following the prefaces is an essay that quotes the heading (*kang* 綱) and text (*mu* 目) of an official account of the surrender to government forces of the historical Sung Chiang.[22] Comments following the heading and the text place the blame for banditry on the emperor and condone the pacification of bandits.[23] The essay entitled "How to Read *The Fifth Book of Genius*" and translated below follows next. Finally there is the fabricated preface attributed to Shih Nai-an 施耐庵, which attempts to defuse the controversial nature of the novel.[24] The text of the novel itself is punctuated by Chin Sheng-t'an's prechapter comments, double-column interlineal comments, and marginal comments (comparatively rare).

In the notes for the translation of the *tu-fa* essay below, where Chin Sheng-t'an cites incidents in the novel as examples, the reader will be referred to the relevant passages in the Chinese text and to an English translation. It is hoped that this will help the reader gain a deeper understanding of the particular issues involved and lead him back to the novel itself. The Chinese text of the novel used is that included in the recent variorum commentary edition edited by Ch'en Hsi-chung 陳曦鐘 and others, cited in the notes and abbreviated as *SHCHPP*. This work includes the entire text of Chin Sheng-t'an's edition as well as collated commentaries from various other editions that precede and follow his.

[21] Portions of this preface are translated in *CST*, pp. 25, 46, 50.

[22] The *kang* and the *mu* are identical to the corresponding entries in the *Yü-p'i Tzu-chih t'ung-chien kang-mu* 御批資治通鑑綱目 (Imperially Sanctioned Outline and Explanation of the Comprehensive Mirror for Aid in Government; 1476 preface by the Ch'eng-hua emperor [r. 1464–1487]), *Ssu-k'u ch'üan-shu chen-pen* 四庫全書珍本, sixth series, vol. 167 (Taipei: Commercial Press, 1977), "Hsü-pien" 續編 (Continuation), p. 10/45a.

[23] The comments are prefaced by the words, *shih-ch'en tuan yüeh* 史臣斷曰 (the official historian says), which resembles the terminology used in the "Hsü-pien" of the *T'ung-chien kang-mu* for quotation from the standard histories. See ibid., vol. 162, "Fan-li" 凡例 (Editorial Principles), 1a. However, I have been unable to locate a source for these comments, so perhaps they are by Chin Sheng-t'an. At the very least, his publication of them implies some acceptance of responsibility for their content.

[24] The preface is translated in its entirety by Pearl Buck in *AMB* and partially in Lin Yutang, *The Importance of Living* (New York: John Day, 1937), pp. 218–19. *The Importance of Living* also contains translated selections from Chin Sheng-t'an's other writings, pp. 131–36, 334–38.

Use of this edition encourages the comparison of Chin Sheng-t'an's commentary with that of his predecessors and provides graphic proof of the contention that in his shorter interlineal comments he was heavily influenced by them.[25] The text of the *tu-fa* essay translated below is based on this edition and has been collated with photo-reprint copies of early editions of the novel with Chin Sheng-t'an's commentary. The most complete translation of the Chin Sheng-t'an edition currently available is that by Pearl S. Buck, published under the title *All Men Are Brothers*.[26] Although the recent translation of the novel in one hundred chapters by Sidney Shapiro claims to use Chin Sheng-t'an's version as its main text for the first seventy chapters,[27] it is likely that he used one of the typeset editions published since 1949 and edited to remove "objectionable" material. In his translation he also follows the chapter divisions of the longer version, which greatly obscures some of the formal features of the original design of Chin Sheng-t'an's edition and makes citation cumbersome. Neither of these translations includes the dream sequence added by Chin Sheng-t'an at the end of his version. There is an extremely abbreviated rendering of that ending in the translation by J.H. Jackson.[28] Although Pearl Buck's translation reads rather awkwardly and is riddled with errors of interpretation and transcription, reference to it still has value for the reader unable to read Chinese who wishes to fill in the context of Chin Sheng-t'an's remarks.

[25] Ch'en Chin-chao 陳錦釗 estimates that about half of the comments attributed to Li Chih in the Yang Ting-chien 楊定見 preface edition of the novel published by Yüan Wu-yai 袁無涯 (ca. 1612) are echoed in Chin Sheng-t'an's comments and that his edition follows many of the editorial changes of the Yüan Wu-yai edition. See his *Li-Chih chih wen-lun* 李贄之文論 (Li Chih on Literature; Taipei: Chia-hsin shui-ni kung-ssu, 1974), p. 124.

[26] Revised edition, 2 vols. (New York: John Day, 1937).

[27] *Outlaws of the Marsh*, 3 vols. (Peking: Foreign Languages Press, 1980), "Translator's Preface," p. viii.

[28] *Water Margin*, 2 vols. (Hong Kong: Commercial Press, 1963), vol. 2, p. 917.

How to Read *The Fifth Book of Genius*

Translated by JOHN C.Y. WANG
Annotation by DAVID L. ROLSTON

1. When reading a book the first thing to be taken into account is the state of mind of the author when he wrote it. For example, the *Shih-chi* [Records of the Historian] was the product of Ssu-ma Ch'ien's [b. 145 B.C.] bellyful of stored-up resentment.[1] Therefore he poured [his emotions] into the writing of the collective biographies of the knights-errant and the money-makers.[2] Even in the other biographies, whenever he comes to accounts of great generosity or assassination, he cannot stop his exclamations of admiration. The whole *Shih-chi* can be summed up by the phrase "people all have their moments of crisis,"[3] and this is the main concern of Ssu-ma Ch'ien's lifetime of writing. The *Shui-hu chuan*, on the other hand, is a different matter. Its author, Shih Nai-an,[4] had no bellyful of stored-up resentment he needed to let out.[5] Well-fed, warm, and without anything else to do, carefree at heart, he spread out paper and picked up a brush, selected a topic [*t'i-mu* 題目], and then wrote out his fine thoughts and polished phrases [*chin-hsin hsiu-k'ou* 錦心繡口]. There-

[1] Ssu-ma Ch'ien was Grand Historian at the court of Emperor Wu (r. 141–87 B.C.) and was castrated (98 B.C.) for offending the emperor. In the last chapter of his *Shih-chi* 史記 (Peking: Chung-hua shu-chü, 1959), p. 130.3300, translated by Burton Watson in his *Ssu-ma Ch'ien: Grand Historian of China* (New York: Columbia University Press, 1958), pp. 54–55, Ssu-ma Ch'ien put forth the theory that great literature is written to relieve the author's pent-up resentment over personal misfortune.

[2] Chaps. 124 and 129 of the *Shih-chi*. Translated in Burton Watson, *Records of the Grand Historian of China*, 2 vols. (New York: Columbia University Press, 1961), vol. 2, pp. 452–61, 476–99.

[3] This phrase is found (with slight variation) in Ssu-ma Ch'ien's introductory remarks to the collective biographies of the knights-errant, *Shih-chi* 124.3182. See *Records of the Grand Historian of China*, vol. 2, p. 453.

[4] Although clan records discovered in this century claim that Shih Nai-an was the founder of a branch of the Shih family in Pai-chü ch'ang 白駒場 in Kiangsu, the truth of this claim has not yet been established. For a review of this material and its authenticity, see Liu Shih-te 劉世德, "Shih Nai-an wen-wu shih-liao pien-hsi" 施耐庵文物史料辨析 (An Analysis of the Authenticity of the Archaeological Finds and Historical Materials on Shih Nai-an), *Chung-kuo she-hui k'o-hsüeh* 中國社會科學 (Chinese Social Science), 1982.6, reprinted in *Shih Nai-an yen-chiu* 施耐庵研究 (Studies on Shih Nai-an; Nanking: Chiang-su ku-chi, 1984), pp. 214–60. Chin Sheng-t'an claimed that Shih Nai-an was the author of an old edition of the novel, in seventy chapters, that he found in the studio of a friend.

[5] Since elsewhere in his commentary (*SHCHPP*, P.38, prologue comment; 6.167, interlineal comment; 14.274, 278, interlineal comments; and 18.342, chapter comment), Chin Sheng-t'an says precisely the opposite, it is possible that his comments here are part of a smoke screen designed to deflect criticism of the unorthodox content of the novel.

fore his judgments do not go against those of the sages.[6] People of later times[7] were unaware of this and went so far as to add the characters for "loyal" [*chung* 忠] and "righteous" [*i* 義] to the title and considered its writing to be similar to Ssu-ma Ch'ien's writing of the *Shih-chi* to express his resentment [*fa-fen chu-shu* 發憤著書]. This is precisely what ought not to be done.

2. The *Shui-hu chuan* contains substantial sections of serious writing, but the author hates Sung Chiang with a passion and portrays him so that, on seeing him, readers will scorn him as much as if he were a piece of meat that neither dog nor swine would come near. However, this is something others have not noticed up to now.[8]

3. The reason the *Shui-hu chuan* singles out Sung Chiang for detestation is because it intends to destroy the chief rebel. The rest [of the rebel band] are forgiven.

4. Someone may ask: "When Shih Nai-an was looking for a topic [*t'i-mu* 題目] on which to write out his fine thoughts and polished phrases, there were all the topics in the world available to him. Why did he go and choose this one?" The answer is: "He was tempted by the fact that just as there are thirty-six major heroes,[9] there are thirty-six different personalities [*hsing-ko* 性格]. Out of these a fine story could be concocted [*chieh-chuan* 結撰]."

5. The topic [*t'i-mu* 題目] is the most important thing when writing a book. As long as the topic is a good one, the book will be well done.

6. Someone may ask: "How about the topics [*t'i-mu* 題目] of books such as the *Hsi-yu chi* 西遊記 [The Journey to the West] and the *San-kuo yen-i* 三國演義 [The Romance of the Three Kingdoms]?" The answer is: "Neither of them is any good. In the standard history of the Three Kingdoms period [220–280] there are too many characters and events and too much conversation. The author's pen cannot move or turn at will. It is just like an official sending a message through his attendant. The latter can only use his voice to transmit what he has been told. Indeed, how dare he add or subtract a word? The *Hsi-yu chi*, on the other

---

[6] This is a reference to the criticism of Ssu-ma Ch'ien in his biography in Pan Ku's 班固 (32–92) *Han-shu* 漢書 (Peking: Chung-hua shu-chü, 1962), p. 62.2737. See also *Ssu-ma Ch'ien: Grand Historian of China*, p. 68.

[7] This most certainly refers to Li Chih's 李贄 (1527–1602) preface to the novel collected in his *Fen-shu* 焚書 (Book for Burning) and included in the Jung-yü t'ang and Yüan Wu-yai editions of the *Shui-hu chuan* published prior to Chin Sheng-t'an's.

[8] Actually it was Chin Sheng-t'an himself who, through editorial revisions and his comments, substantially changed the attitude of the text toward Sung Chiang.

[9] The rebel band in the novel has thirty-six major heroes and seventy-two minor ones, plus Ch'ao Kai, who dies early and is not counted in these lists.

hand, is too fantastic. The author just made it up paragraph by paragraph. It is like setting off fireworks on New Year's Eve—they explode one group after another with no connecting link [*kuan-ch'uan* 貫串] between. When we read it, we can stop at any place."

7. All the literary devices used in the *Shui-hu chuan* are taken from the *Shih-chi*, yet the former surpasses the latter in many places. As for the very best aspects of the *Shih-chi*, they can all be found in the *Shui-hu chuan*.

8. When you read a book, you should widen and deepen your range of vision. For example, if you take them in at a single glance, the seventy chapters of the *Shui-hu chuan*, which cover more than two thousand pages, really constitute a single composition. The various events and devices in those pages are used as methods to begin [*ch'i* 起], continue [*ch'eng* 承], change direction [*chuan* 轉], and sum up [*ho* 合] the composition. However, if read over too drawn out a period of time, these devices cannot be detected by the reader.

9. The *Shui-hu chuan* was not written carelessly. We need only note that Sung Chiang's name does not appear until chapter 17[10] to realize that the author must have thought the matter over more than a hundred times. If the book had been written carelessly, then Sung Chiang would certainly have been treated from the beginning in chapter 1, but then the text would be nothing but a straightforward accounting, with no play in it.

10. I have said that the *Shui-hu chuan* is superior to the *Shih-chi*, but nobody believes me. Really, I wasn't talking nonsense. The truth is that in the *Shih-chi* words are used to carry events [*i-wen yün-shih* 以文運事], while in the *Shui-hu chuan* events are produced from the words [*yin-wen sheng-shih* 因文生事]. When you use words to carry events, you first have events that have taken place in such-and-such a way, and then you must figure out a piece of narrative for them. To use words to produce events, on the other hand, is quite different. All you have to do is follow where your pen leads. To cut down what is tall and make tall what is short is all up to you.

11. The author of the *Shui-hu chuan* was a man of surpassing intelligence. As for his book, it is going to portray 108 bandits, yet it begins with the portrait of a filial son as a frontispiece [*men-mien* 門面]. This is the first proof of the author's surpassing intelligence. Of the thirty-six bandits who are incarnations of heavenly stars and the seventy-two bandits

---

[10] *SHCHPP* 17.329, *AMB* 1.17.287. In references to *AMB*, the first digit indicates the volume number.

who are incarnations of earthly stars, it is three earthly stars who are the first to become bandits.[11] Clearly, this shows that they are acting against the will of Heaven.[12] This is the second proof. The chief of the bandits is Sung Chiang, yet the author purposely does not let him take this position right away. Instead he creates Ch'ao Kai to "cover" [*kai* 蓋] him.[13] This is proof number three. Both the heavenly and earthly stars are relegated to a secondary position and are not allowed to appear at the very beginning.[14] This is proof number four. The book ends with the words "peace under Heaven."[15] This is the fifth proof of the author's surpassing intelligence.

12. The words "stone tablet" [*shih-chieh* 石碣] appear three times and each occurrence marks a major section of the *Shui-hu chuan*.[16]

13. The *Shui-hu chuan* does not talk about ghosts, spirits, or other strange and exotic matters.[17] This is where its power surpasses other books. In the *Hsi-yu chi*, whenever the author is at a loss as to what to do, the Bodhisattva Kuan-yin of the Southern Seas comes to the rescue.

14. The *Shui-hu chuan* does not contain literary language particles like *chih* 之, *hu* 乎, *che* 者, and *yeh* 也.[18] Each individual character is made to speak in his own individual way. This is truly marvelous skill!

15. For every character who appears in the *Shui-hu chuan* a clear-cut

Notso see ch.4?

[11] *SHCHPP* 1.71 and *AMB* 1.1.34. They are Chu Wu, Ch'en Ta, and Yang Ch'un. Chu Wu is ranked first among the earthly stars.

[12] The slogan of the rebel band, "Act on behalf of Heaven" (*t'i-t'ien hsing-tao* 替天行道) is here turned on its head by Chin Sheng-t'an (*ni-t'ien erh-hsing* 逆天而行).

[13] The *kai* in Ch'ao Kai's name means to cover. He dies in chap. 59, after which Sung Chiang takes over the leadership of the band.

[14] This statement is rather vague, but it seems to refer to the fact that the heroes do not appear in the narrative until after the story of Wang Chin and Kao Ch'iu.

[15] *SHCHPP* 70.1273. Not translated by Buck. This is part of the ending added by Chin Sheng-t'an himself. There is a very abbreviated translation of this ending in J. H. Jackson, trans., *Water Margin*, 2 vols. (Hong Kong: Commercial Press, 1963), vol. 2, p. 917. The same phrase also occurs at the end of the prologue rewritten by Chin Sheng-t'an, *SHCHPP* P.50 and *AMB* 1.P.15.

[16] The words occur in the prologue and the last chapter, where they refer to a tablet with the names of the 108 heroes on it. In the first instance, Chin Sheng-t'an has changed the word "stele" (*pei* 碑) to "tablet" (*chieh* 碣). See Cheng Chen-to 鄭振鐸, ed., *Shui-hu ch'üan-chuan* 水滸全傳 (The Complete *Shui-hu chuan*; Peking: Jen-min wen-hsüeh, 1954), p. 1.13, n. 70. The third instance is Stone Tablet Village (Shih-chieh ts'un 石碣村) where the Juan brothers live and where Ch'ao Kai and the others first fight openly against government troops in chap. 18.

[17] Chin Sheng-t'an might be echoing a famous statement in the *Confucian Analects* (*Lun-yü* 論語), XX.20. For Chinese text and translation, see James Legge, trans., *The Chinese Classics*, 5 vols. (Hong Kong: Hong Kong University Press, 1960), vol. 1, p. 201.

[18] The *Shui-hu chuan*, unlike the *San-kuo yen-i*, is written in vernacular Chinese and does not use these literary language particles.

biography [*lieh-chuan* 列傳][19] is provided. As for the events contained within them, each section further forms an independent unit in itself. Sometimes two or three chapters will form such a unit. Sometimes it takes just five or six sentences.

16. Other books you read through once and stop, but one never tires of reading the *Shui-hu chuan* because it succeeds completely in describing the different personalities [*hsing-ko* 性格] of all 108 people.

17. When the *Shui-hu chuan* describes the personalities of 108 persons, there are truly 108 different personalities. In other books, the people they describe all look the same, be they as many as a thousand or as few as two.

18. In the *Shui-hu chuan* each chapter has its principle of organization [*chang-fa* 章法], so does each sentence [*chü-fa* 句法] and each word [*tzu-fa* 字法]. As soon as a young person can read a little, he should be taught to read the book carefully over and over again. If he can appreciate all the fine points in the *Shui-hu chuan*, reading other books will be as easy as splitting bamboo.

19. The account of the rescue of Sung Chiang from the execution ground in Chiang-chou is already extremely unusual,[20] but later on there is the account of the rescue of Lu Chün-i from the execution ground in Ta-ming fu which is even more unusual.[21] The account of P'an Chin-lien's adultery with Hsi-men Ch'ing is already extremely unusual,[22] but later on there is the account of P'an Ch'iao-yün's adultery with P'ei Ju-hai which is even more unusual.[23] The account of Wu Sung's fight with the tiger on Ching-yang Ridge is already extremely unusual,[24] but later on there is the account of the killing of the tigers at the I River by Li K'uei which is even more unusual.[25] Truly, the author's genius is unfathomable.

20. The rescue of someone from an execution ground, adultery, and fighting with tigers are all extremely difficult topics [*t'i-mu* 題目]. One almost feels that there is no way to begin. Yet the author was not only undaunted, he even insisted on giving two accounts of each.

21. The *Hsüan-ho i-shih* 宣和遺事 [Anecdotes from the Hsüan-ho

---

[19] *Lieh-chuan* (here translated as biography) is a genre invented by Ssu-ma Ch'ien and used in the latter half of his *Shih-chi*. Although mostly comprised of individual and collective biographies, treatises on foreign countries are also included.

[20] Chap. 39.

[21] Chaps. 61–62. There is an unsuccessful attempt by Shih Hsiu in chap. 61.

[22] Chaps. 23–25. This story was later expanded into the novel *Chin P'ing Mei*.

[23] Chaps. 44–45.

[24] Chap. 22.

[25] Chap. 42.

Reign Period][26] records the names of all thirty-six major heroes. We can see then that these thirty-six people did exist. We must be aware, however, that many events within the seventy chapters were made up out of thin air [*p'ing-k'ung tsao-huang* 憑空造謊] by the author. Yet, after reading the seventy chapters we have become acquainted with the thirty-six characters. Just mention any one of them, and we feel we have known him well for a long time. Such is the power of the author's pen!

22. Of the 108 heroes, Wu Sung must be rated as belonging to the upper-high [*shang-shang* 上上] category of character.[27] Shih Ch'ien and Sung Chiang, being the same sort of person, must both be rated as belonging to the lower-low [*hsia-hsia* 下下] category of character.[28]

23. Lu Chih-shen is of course a character of the upper-high [*shang-shang* 上上] category. He is shown to have an honest heart and an imposing physique. As for roughness, he is indeed a little rough. As for meticulosity, he is also quite meticulous. Yet, for some reason I feel that there are many places where he is not the equal of Wu Sung. If Lu Chih-shen is already a pinnacle among men, then Wu Sung must simply be a heavenly god, standing high above the others.

24. Just in the description of rough men alone, the *Shui-hu chuan* uses many methods of description. For example, the roughness of Lu Chih-shen is that of a man of hasty temperament, that of Shih Chin the impulsiveness of youth, that of Li K'uei wildness; the roughness of Wu Sung is that of an untrammeled hero; the roughness of Juan the Seventh comes from his pent-up sorrow and anger; and the roughness of Chiao T'ing is simply his bad temper.

25. Li K'uei is a character of the upper-high [*shang-shang* 上上] category. He is shown as a creature of great simplicity without a speck of guile in his body. It would seem that in his eyes none of the other 107 leaders in the mountain lair are worthy of his approval. Mencius's say-

[26] A semifictional work, dating probably from the beginning of the Yüan dynasty (1279–1368), treating the fall of the Northern Sung dynasty (960–1127). The list of the thirty-six heroes is not completely the same as in the *Shui-hu chuan*. The relevant section has been translated by Richard G. Irwin, *The Evolution of a Chinese Novel* (Cambridge, Mass.: Harvard University Press, 1953), pp. 26–31. The entire work has been translated by William O. Hennessey, *Proclaiming Harmony* (Ann Arbor: University of Michigan Center for Chinese Studies, 1981).

[27] This rating system dates back at least as far as the "Ku-chin jen piao" 古今人表 (A Chart of the Notables through the Ages), chap. 20 in the *Han-shu*, and uses two ranges with three terms each (upper, middle, lower and high, middle, low) to produce nine categories from upper-high to lower-low.

[28] Shih Ch'ien is a professional thief whose theft of a chicken starts off a war between the Liang-shan band and the Chu Family Village in chap. 45. To pair Sung Chiang with him can be seen as part of Chin Sheng-t'an's campaign against Sung Chiang.

ing, "Wealth and honor cannot lead him to immoderation, poverty and obscurity cannot change his purpose, external authority cannot force him to kneel down,"[29] applies to him exactly.

26. It seems that in writing a composition, one must first have in mind a reason [*yüan-ku* 緣故] for writing. If there is a reason behind it, no matter what one writes about, it will turn out to be excellent writing. If there is no reason behind it, there is no way to write. Even if one can produce something, it will be as dry and unpleasant as chewing wax.

27. Just take the portrayal of Li K'uei. Isn't it true that every episode about him is absolutely marvelous writing? Yet few notice that all these episodes come right after events dealing with Sung Chiang, and this is why they are so unspeakably marvelous. Because the author vehemently hates Sung Chiang's deceitfulness, after each episode about him there always follows another one about Li K'uei's guilelessness to form an unflattering contrast [*hsing-chi* 形擊]. Although the author's purpose was to reveal the wickedness of Sung Chiang, he has unexpectedly brought out the wonderfulness of Li K'uei. This is like stabbing with a spear— your main purpose is to kill someone, and yet in the process you display the technique of your school of spear fighting.

28. Recently there was someone who did not grasp the author's intention in pairing Sung Chiang and Li K'uei. He selected out all the passages about Li K'uei into a separate volume called *Shou-chang wen-chi* 壽張文集 [The Collected Writings of the Magistrate of Shou-chang].[30] He indeed can be said to be one who eats human excrement—not a very good dog.

29. In the portrayal of Li K'uei, every feature is incomparable. The author truly possesses a most natural [*hua-kung* 化工] and lifelike [*hsiao-wu* 肖物] style. Leaving aside the rest, just consider the fact that Li K'uei has an elder brother Li Ta and thus must be the second eldest in his family. However, all his life he insists on calling himself Li the First. Not until an emergency arises and he must change his name does he finally

---

[29] *Mencius*, IIIB.2. See James Legge, *The Chinese Classics*, vol. 2, p. 265.

[30] Not now extant. The full title seems to have been *Shou-chang hsien-ling Hei-hsüan-feng chi* 壽張縣令黑旋風集 (The Collected Works of the Black Whirlwind, Magistrate of Shou-chang). In chap. 74 of the longer versions of the *Shui-hu chuan*, Li K'uei is the magistrate of the neighboring Shou-chang hsien for one day. Ch'ien Hsi-yen 錢希言 (fl. 1596–1622) identified the compiler of this work as his contemporary and acquaintance, Yeh Chou 葉畫, and said that the work was quite funny. Quoted in *SHCTLHP*, p. 151. The work is mentioned in the preface attributed to Li Chih's friend, Huai-lin 懷林, in the Jung-yü t'ang edition of the *Shui-hu chuan* (reprinted in 1610), which also promises a forthcoming sequel centered on one of the other heroes of the novel, Hua Jung (quoted in *SHCTLHP*, p. 208). For more references to *Shou-chang wen-chi*, see *SHCTLHP*, pp. 37, 149.

call himself Li the Second.[31] You might say he is quick-witted, but stop and think how foreign such matters really are to him.

30. Even a truly great and heroic man can sometimes be induced by money to agree to something. Only Li K'uei cannot be bought by any amount of silver. You must wait until he is willing to do the thing of his own accord. He is truly in a class by himself.

31. Lin Ch'ung is, of course, a character belonging to the upper-high [*shang-shang* 上上] category, but he is made to appear too ruthless. He can anticipate, he can endure, he can control himself firmly, he can do things thoroughly; all this makes one afraid of him. Such a person will certainly be able to make his way in the world, but he will also harm his physical constitution a great deal.

32. Wu Yung must be considered an upper-high [*shang-shang* 上上] character. He is as tricky as Sung Chiang, but he has a more upright heart than Sung does.

33. Sung Chiang relies solely on trickery to get people to do his bidding, but Wu Yung's direction of the band's efforts is out in the open and aboveboard. He is appropriate as a military commander.

34. The difference between Wu Yung and Sung Chiang is that the former is willing openly to call himself the "Star of Wisdom" [*chih-to hsing* 智多星] while the latter always speaks of himself as sincere and unrefined.

35. Sung Chiang thinks that he has Wu Yung in the palm of his hand when actually it is Wu Yung who has Sung Chiang under his thumb. Both know this within their hearts, and yet on the outside both pretend not to know anything of it. Truly fascinating writing!

36. Hua Jung naturally belongs to the upper-high [*shang-shang* 上上] category. He is portrayed as being so cultured and refined!

37. Juan the Seventh belongs to the upper-high [*shang-shang* 上上] category. He is shown to be of an altogether different complexion from the rest. Of the 108 characters, he must be considered the most straightforward. He thinks straightforwardly and speaks straightforwardly. Meeting up with him, all pollution melts away.

38. Both Yang Chih and Kuan Sheng are of the upper-high [*shang-shang* 上上] category of character. Yang Chih is portrayed as the scion of an old family, while Kuan Sheng is presented as the veritable incarnation of Kuan Yü.[32]

---

[31] *SHCHPP* 52.982, and *AMB* 2.52.961.

[32] Yang Chih claims to be descended from Yang Yeh 楊業 (d. 986), the founder of the famous Yang family of generals (*SHCHPP* 11.233 and *AMB* 1.11.195). Kuan Yü 關羽 (160–219) was a famous general later deified as the personification of loyalty. Kuan Sheng shares with Kuan Yü the same surname and many other attributes as well.

39. Ch'in Ming and So Ch'ao are both characters of the middle-high [*shang-chung* 上中] category.

40. Shih Chin can only be ranked in the middle-high [*shang-chung* 上中] category because the second part of his story is not well done.

41. The author expended a lot of effort on Hu-yen Cho, but he is only a character of the middle-high [*shang-chung* 上中] category.

42. Lu Chün-i and Ch'ai Chin are only characters of the middle-high [*shang-chung* 上中] category. In the story of Lu Chün-i, the author has done his best to create the image of an heroic man of social standing. In the end, however, Lu Chün-i is not without a certain awkwardness. It's like painting a camel—although it is an imposing creature, when we look at it we feel that it is not very handsome. Ch'ai Chin doesn't have anything to recommend him except his hospitality.

43. Between Chu T'ung and Lei Heng, Chu T'ung comes off better, but both are just in the middle-high [*shang-chung* 上中] category of characters.

44. Between Yang Hsiung and Shih Hsiu, Shih Hsiu comes off better. While Shih Hsiu is in the upper-middle [*chung-shang* 中上] category of characters, Yang Hsiung can only be placed in the lower-middle [*chung-hsia* 中下] category.

45. Kung-sun Sheng is just an upper-middle [*chung-shang* 中上] character, functioning only as a reserve player.

46. Li Ying is just a character of the upper-middle [*chung-shang* 中上] category. This ranking, however, is based on considerations of status and precedence, not on how he is actually portrayed.[33]

47. Juan the Second, Juan the Fifth, Chang Heng, and Chang Shun are all upper-middle [*chung-shang* 中上] characters, as are Yen Ch'ing, Liu T'ang, Hsü Ning, and Tung P'ing.

48. Tai Tsung is a lower-middle [*chung-hsia* 中下] character. Except for his ability to travel at superhuman speed, he doesn't have anything else to recommend him.

49. I hate those young people who, when they read, ignore the art of writing itself. As long as they can remember a few incidents from the book, they consider themselves to have read it. Since even the *Chan-kuo ts'e* 戰國策 [Intrigues of the Warring States][34] and the *Shih-chi* are passed

---

[33] Li Ying is a village head before joining the rebel band. He does his best to prevent the war between the band and Chu Family Village, and eventually is forced to join the band, chaps. 46–49.

[34] This collection of rhetorical persuasions, probably compiled in its present form in the first century B.C., contains many pieces of fiction, but it was traditionally considered as a work of history.

over as nothing but collections of incidents, how much more so is this the fate of the *Shui-hu chuan*?

50. The *Shui-hu chuan* contains a lot of literary devices that cannot be found in other books. In what follows, I will point out just a few of them.[35]

51. Advance insertion [*tao-ch'a fa* 倒插法]. This means that things or people that will be important in a later part of the book are inconspicuously inserted into the narrative ahead of the place where they take on real importance. Examples of this are the first mention of the Father and Son Inn next door to the smithy in the village at the foot of Mt. Wu-t'ai,[36] [the first mention of] the vegetable garden of the Great Hsiang-kuo Monastery adjacent to the Temple of the Eastern Peak,[37] P'an Chin-lien's mention of going with Dame Wang to see the tiger,[38] and Li K'uei's recruitment of T'ang Lung into the band when he was out buying dates.[39]

52. Simultaneous narration [*chia-hsü fa* 夾敍法]. This means that two people in great haste want to speak at the same time. It cannot be that after one has finished speaking, the other then begins. The author must write the speeches with one stroke of the pen [so that they seem to be simultaneous]. For example, in the Wa-kuan Monastery Ts'ui Tao-ch'eng says, "Calm down, Brother Monk, and let me . . ." and Lu Chih-shen says, "Out with it! Out with it! Speak!"[40]

53. Snake in the grass or [discontinuous] chalk line ["ts'ao-she hui-

---

[35] For further discussion of these techniques, see Richard G. Irwin, *The Evolution of a Chinese Novel*, p. 93; *CST*, pp. 68–74; and Ellen Widmer, *The Margins of Utopia*, pp. 91–103, 113–19.

[36] The inn is lightly inserted into the narration of Lu Chih-shen's first trip to the village, *SHCHPP* 3.113 and *AMB* 1.3.80. He later stays in the inn after he has been sent away from the monastery on the mountain, *SHCHPP* 4.124 and *AMB* 1.4.89.

[37] The temple is first mentioned in connection with Wang Chin's story, *SHCHPP* 1.62 and *AMB* 1.1.25, but the garden is not mentioned until *SHCHPP* 5.155, *AMB* 1.5.118. Both the garden and the temple figure prominently in the story of Lin Ch'ung in chaps. 5–6.

[38] Dame Wang's name is offhandedly brought into the text (*SHCHPP* 23.433 and *AMB* 1.23.393) some time before she herself appears in the narration (*SHCHPP* 23.434 and *AMB* 1.23.393), and quite a while before she becomes central to the story of Wu Ta's murder.

[39] *SHCHPP* 53.990–92 and *AMB* 2.53.966–68. The recruitment has no immediate consequences, but in chap. 55 it is he who persuades Hsü Ning to join the band, which in turn sets up the crucial victory over the government troops in chap. 56.

[40] *SHCHPP* 5.146 and *AMB* 1.5.110. This technique was written into the novel by Chin Sheng-t'an himself, although he claimed that it was used in the old edition of the novel that he found.

hsien fa" 草蛇灰線法].[41] Examples of this are the frequent mention of the word "club" [*shao-pang* 哨棒] when Wu Sung crosses Ching-yang Ridge,[42] and the continual appearance of the word "curtain" [*lien-tzu* 簾子] in the passages set [in P'an Chin-lien and Wu Ta's home] on Amethyst Street.[43] Read in haste, there seems to be nothing there, but a closer look reveals a connecting thread [*hsien-so* 線索] which, if pulled, draws the whole sequence together.

54. Detailed and extended narration [*ta lo-mo fa* 大落墨法]. Examples of this are Wu Yung's persuasion of the three Juan brothers,[44] Yang Chih's contest in arms in the Northern Capital [Ta-ming fu],[45] Dame Wang's persuasion of Hsi-men Ch'ing,[46] Wu Sung's fight with the tiger,[47] the besieging of Sung Chiang in Huan-tao Village,[48] and the second attack on the Chu Family Village.[49]

55. Needles wrapped in cotton and thorns hidden in the mud ["mien-chen ni-tz'u fa" 綿針泥刺法]. One example is Sung Chiang's refusal

[41] It is common to translate this phrase as "the faint line of the grass-snake," taking the "line" referred to as either the movement of the snake in the grass or faint lines on the body of the snake itself. The translation here takes the phrase as a combined metaphor in which the first two characters present the image of a snake moving through the grass and the last two characters refer to the discontinuous line formed when a carpenter's chalk line is used on an uneven surface. This reading is reinforced by the fact that some commentators reversed the order of the two phrases or used them separately.

[42] Chin Sheng-t'an counts eighteen occurrences of the word, *SHCHPP* 22.417–25 and *AMB* 1.22.378–85, beginning with Wu Sung's departure from Ch'ai Chin's manor through the killing of the tiger on the ridge. The text of the novel and the interlineal commentary on it from occurrence number nine to number eighteen are translated in *CST*, pp. 75–80.

[43] Chin Sheng-t'an points out nine casual mentions of this word up to the point where P'an Chin-lien accidentally hits Hsi-men Ch'ing on the head with a pole while putting up the curtain (*SHCHPP* 23.433–48 and *AMB* 1.23.393–406). A variant of this technique is identified by Chin Sheng-t'an in chap. 1 where every occurrence of the words "mother" and "son" is pointed out and counted (total of nineteen) in order to emphasize Wang Chin's filiality (*SHCHPP* 1.61–69 and *AMB* 1.1.24–33). It would seem then that this technique has both plot and thematic functions.

[44] *SHCHPP* 14.272–82 and *AMB* 1.14.234–45. This passage is carefully sequenced and narrated in great detail.

[45] *SHCHPP* 11–12.242–54 and *AMB* 1.11–12.204–15. Again, this sequence is carefully plotted so as to reach a climax slowly and is told in great detail.

[46] *SHCHPP* 23.450–68 and *AMB* 1.23.410–16. Dame Wang carefully manipulates Hsi-men Ch'ing until she has him hooked. Then she goes on to lay out a ten-step plan to seduce P'an Chin-lien.

[47] Chap. 22.

[48] *SHCHPP* 41.774–82 and *AMB* 1.41.738–47. It is during this section that he receives a heavenly book from the Dark Goddess of the Nine Heavens.

[49] Chap. 47.

to take off his cangue when asked to do so by Hua Jung.[50] Another example is that each time Ch'ao Kai wants to leave the mountain lair, Sung Chiang exhorts him not to, but the last time he doesn't do this.[51] From somewhere beyond the actual words comes a sharp knife which sticks into its target.

56. Whitening the background to bring out the foreground ["pei-mien p'u-fen fa" 背面鋪粉法]. For example, in order to set off Sung Chiang's deceitfulness, the author unobtrusively portrays Li K'uei's straightforwardness; and to set off Shih Hsiu's sharpness, he unobtrusively portrays Yang Hsiung's dullness.

57. Displaying the bait [*nung-yin fa* 弄引法]. This means that when there is an important section of writing it is best not to start in abruptly; rather, a passage of minor interest should be used to lead into it. For example, before Yang Chih fights So Ch'ao he first fights Chou Chin.[52] Before Dame Wang lays out the ten-step plan for seducing P'an Chin-lien, she first enumerates the five prerequisites for the successful seducer.[53] The *Chuang Tzu* 莊子 says, "The wind begins at the tips of the green duckweed and becomes strong at the mouth of the big cave."[54] The *Li-chi* 禮記 [Book of Rites] states, "When the people of Lu want to make sacrifice to Mt. T'ai, they must first make sacrifice to the P'ei Woods."[55]

58. The otter's tail [*t'a-wei fa* 獺尾法]. At the end of an important section things should not come to a sudden stop; rather, after-ripples [*yü-po* 餘波] from the main story are used to bring about a gradual tapering

---

[50] What Chin Sheng-t'an seems to have in mind is understated satire, usually brought out through contradictions between a character's actions in different situations. Sung Chiang first loudly stands on principle and refuses to allow the cangue to be removed (*SHCHPP* 35.662 and *AMB* 1.35.625), but shortly after he lightly allows it to be taken off (*SHCHPP* 36.677 and *AMB* 1.36.637).

[51] *SHCHPP* 59.1090 and *AMB* 2.59.1073. Chin Sheng-t'an deleted Sung Chiang's exhorting Ch'ao Kai not to leave the camp here so as to put the blame on Sung Chiang for Ch'ao Kai's death.

[52] *SHCHPP* 11–12.243–53, *AMB* 1.11–12.205–14.

[53] *SHCHPP* 23.454–58, *AMB* 1.23.412–15.

[54] This line does not occur in *Chuang Tzu*, but it is very similar to a line in Sung Yü's 宋玉 (fl. 3d century B.C.) rhyme prose on the wind ("Feng fu" 風賦). See *Wen-hsüan* (The Anthology of Refined Literature; Shanghai: Shang-hai ku-chi, 1986), p. 13.582. This section of the "Feng fu" is translated in Burton Watson, *Chinese Rhyme-Prose* (New York: Columbia University Press, 1971), p. 22.

[55] See *Shih-san ching ching-wen* 十三經經文 (Text of the Thirteen Classics; Taipei: K'ai-ming shu-tien, 1955), *Li-chi* 禮記 (Book of Rites), sec. 24 of the "Li-ch'i" 禮器 chapter (p. 49), and James Legge, trans., *Li Chi: The Book of Rites*, 2 vols. (New Hyde Park, N.Y.: University Books, 1967), vol. 1, p. 407. The state of Lu 魯 is a mistake for the name of the neighboring state, Ch'i 齊.

off [*yen-yang* 演漾]. For example, after Imperial Delegate Liang returns
from the tournament held outside the eastern city wall, the magistrate of
Yün-ch'eng hsien, Shih Wen-pin, presides in his yamen.[56] After Wu
Sung kills the tiger, he meets two hunters [dressed in tiger skins] on his
way down the ridge.[57] Again, after the massacre in the Hall of the
Mandarin Ducks, there is the mention of the moonlight over the moat
around the city wall.[58]

59. Direct repetition of topic [*cheng-fan fa* 正犯法]. For example,
after the account of Wu Sung's fight with the tiger, there are accounts of
Li K'uei's killing of four tigers and of the quarrel between the two Hsieh
brothers and the Mao family over a tiger.[59] After the story of P'an Chin-
lien's adultery with Hsi-men Ch'ing, there is that of P'an Ch'iao-yün
with P'ei Ju-hai.[60] After the rescue of Sung Chiang from the execution
ground at Chiang-chou, there is that of Lu Chün-i in Ta-ming fu.[61]
After the account of Ho T'ao's attempt to capture the robbers, there is
that of Huang An's trying to capture the same robbers.[62] After the story
of Lin Ch'ung's exile, there is that of Lu Chün-i's exile.[63] Also, after the
release of Ch'ao Kai by Chu T'ung and Lei Heng, there is the release of
Sung Chiang by the same pair.[64] This means that the author, for his
amusement, deliberately repeats [*fan* 犯] the topic [*t'i-mu* 題目] and yet
has the ability not to borrow any detail or stroke from the previous
treatment. Truly, he is bursting with methods and techniques.

60. Incomplete repetition of topic [*lüeh-fan fa* 略犯法]. Examples are
Lin Ch'ung's purchase of a sword followed by Yang Chih's selling of a
sword,[65] the parts played by the urchins T'ang Niu-erh and Yün-ko,[66]
the beating of Butcher Cheng in his butcher shop and the beating of
"Door God" Chiang in K'uai-huo Forest,[67] and Lu Chih-shen's trying

---

[56] *SHCHPP* 12.254–56 and *AMB* 1.12.215–18. After the tournament, Liang discusses
with his wife the problem of sending birthday presents to her father. The previous year
the presents were stolen by thieves. The narrative switches to Magistrate Shih, who
implements new measures to protect against thieves.

[57] *SHCHPP* 22.425, *AMB* 1.22.385.

[58] *SHCHPP* 30.575 and *AMB* 1.30.528. This is the last in a series of mentions of
moonlight during this episode which are all pointed out by Chin Sheng-t'an.

[59] Chaps. 22, 42, and 48.

[60] Chaps. 22–23 and 44.

[61] Chaps. 39 and 61.

[62] Chaps. 16–17 and 19.

[63] Chaps. 7 and 61.

[64] Chaps. 17 and 21.

[65] Chaps. 6 and 11.

[66] Chaps. 20 and 23. In both cases the urchins fight with go-between figures.

[67] Chaps. 2 and 28.

out his monk's staff at Wa-kuan Monastery and Wu Sung's trying out his monk's dagger on top of Centipede Ridge.[68]

61. Extreme avoidance of narrative frugality [*chi pu-sheng fa* 極不省法]. For example, in order to make Sung Chiang commit a crime, the author first arranges to put the gold into his document bag. Prior to this, he sets up Yen P'o-hsi's affair with Chang Wen-yüan, and even before that he mentions Sung Chiang's taking of Yen P'o-hsi as his concubine and his donation of a coffin to the Yen family. However, all of these things are not part of the main story.[69]

62. Extreme narrative frugality [*chi sheng fa* 極省法]. For example, after Wu Sung is given a hero's welcome in Yang-ku hsien, he runs into Wu Ta, who just happens to have moved into the same town.[70] Another example is Sung Chiang's eating fish soup at the Lute Pavilion and suffering an upset stomach for several days on end.[71]

63. Introducing new twists into the narrative just as you are about to bring it to a close ["yü-ho ku-tsung fa" 欲合故縱法].[72] For example, after the rescue boats under Li Chün, the two Chang brothers, the two T'ung brothers, and the two Mu brothers have already arrived at the White Dragon Temple, Li K'uei wants to fight his way back into the city.[73] After both Chao Neng and Chao Te have left the Temple of the Dark Goddess of the Nine Heavens in Huan-tao Village, soldiers trip on the root of a tree and call out.[74] The reader is thus given an extra fright at the end of the narrative sequence.

64. Clouds cutting the mountains in half ["heng-yün tuan shan fa" 橫雲斷山法]. For example, after the second attack on the Chu Family Village, there is suddenly inserted the story of Hsieh Chen and Hsieh Pao's quarrel with Squire Mao over the carcass of a tiger and their subsequent jailbreak.[75] Another example is that during the siege of Ta-ming fu there is suddenly inserted the episode of the robbery and murder

---

[68] Chaps. 5 and 30.

[69] Chaps. 19–20. All of these steps are necessary to set up the climactic scene where Yen P'o-hsi tries to blackmail Sung Chiang with evidence she finds in the document bag and Sung Chiang is forced to kill her.

[70] Chap. 23.

[71] *SHCHPP* 38.715 and *AMB* 2.38.674. According to Chin Sheng-t'an, because Sung Chiang's illness keeps him from going out, the author is spared the task of describing his meeting with his new friends in Chiang-chou prior to his getting drunk and writing a seditious poem a couple of days later (*SHCHPP* 38.715, interlineal comment).

[72] *SHCHPP* 21 has accidentally omitted the character *ku* 故.

[73] *SHCHHP* 39.748, *AMB* 2.39.212–13.

[74] *SHCHPP* 41.777, *AMB* 2.41.740.

[75] Chap. 48. The joining of the band by the Hsieh brothers is crucial to the third and successful attack on the Chu Family Village.

committed by "River Hopping Devil" Chang Wang and "Slippery Loach" Sun the Fifth.[76] This is because when an episode is too long, it may seem tiresome [to the reader]. Therefore the author inserts a passage into the middle of the episode so as to separate it into two parts.

65. Joining a broken zither string with glue ["luan-chiao hsü-hsien fa" 鸞膠續絃法]. For example, on his way to Liang-shan-po to inform Sung Chiang of Lu Chün-i's arrest, Yen Ch'ing comes upon Yang Hsiung and Shih Hsiu. The two parties do not know each other. Moreover, since they are travelling on out-of-the-way roads between Liang-shan-po and Ta-ming fu, how could they happen to be on the same road? The author casually brings about the first coincidence by using Yen Ch'ing's shooting of the magpie with his lucky arrow to divine the fate of his master to lead him to Yang Hsiung and Shih Hsiu. Then Yen Ch'ing fells Shih Hsiu with one blow of the fist and Yen Ch'ing's name is revealed in the ensuing tussle.[77] All this is meticulously planned.

66. Formerly when young people read the *Shui-hu chuan* they learned many irrelevant matters from it. Although the punctuation and commentary [*tien-yüeh* 點閱] of my edition is only rough and incomplete, after the young people read it, they will have learned many literary devices. They will not only know that there are numerous literary devices in the *Shui-hu chuan*, they will also be able to detect even the literary devices in the *Chan-kuo ts'e* and the *Shih-chi*. Formerly, when young people read the *Chan-kuo ts'e* and the *Shih-chi*, they would only pay attention to the irrelevant matters. This is really laughable.

67. The *Shui-hu chuan* is, after all, only a work of fiction. Young people are anxious to read it. Once they have read it, unexpectedly it will cause them to learn a number of literary methods.

68. Once young people have learned these literary methods, they will want to read without stopping such works as the *Chan-kuo ts'e* and the *Shih-chi*. The benefit of the *Shui-hu chuan* to young people is great.

69. Formerly the *Shui-hu chuan* was read even by peddlers and yamen runners. Although not a word has been added or subtracted in this version, it is not destined for petty people. Only those with refined thoughts and feelings can appreciate it.

[76] Chap. 64.
[77] *SHCHPP* 61.1140–41, *AMB* 2.61.1123–24.

CHAPTER III

Mao Tsung-kang on How to Read the *San-kuo yen-i* (The Romance of the Three Kingdoms)

INTRODUCTION:
Mao Tsung-kang and His "Tu *San-kuo chih* fa"
(How to Read *The Romance of the Three Kingdoms*)

Mao Tsung-kang 毛宗崗 and his father, Mao Lun 毛綸, are a literary team similar to that of Ssu-ma Ch'ien 司馬遷 (b. 145 B.C.) and his father, Ssu-ma T'an 司馬談 (d. 106 B.C.), the authors of the *Shih-chi* 史記 (Records of the Historian). The credit for the authorship of the *Shih-chi* is almost always given to the son alone, and Mao Tsung-kang is likewise given primacy over his father more often than not. Together they completed two projects, a commentary on the *P'i-p'a chi* 琵琶記 (Story of the Lute; a Southern-style play by Kao Ming 高明, fl. 14th century) and one on the *San-kuo yen-i* 三國演義 (The Romance of the Three Kingdoms). Their manner of collaboration is much easier to make out in the case of the commentary on the *P'i-p'a chi*.

The prefaces in the *P'i-p'a chi* commentary are dated 1665 (Yu T'ung 尤侗, 1618–1704) and 1666 (Fu-yün k'o-tzu 浮雲客子). From the prefatory material we learn that although Mao Lun (style Te-yin 德音, later changed to Sheng-shan 聲山) was an adolescent when he first got the idea to do a commentary on the play, it was not until thirty to forty years later that this wish came true.[1] He presents the writing of commentaries on this play and *The Romance of the Three Kingdoms* as a leisure activity of no great importance that he did not get around to until after he went blind. The commentaries were dictated by the blind father to his

---

[1] *Ti-ch'i ts'ai-tzu shu* 第七才子書 (The Seventh Work of Genius), reprint with preface dated 1735 (Suchou: Ta-wen t'ang), "Tsung-lun" 總論 (General Remarks), p. 1/19b. Estimating from these figures, Mao Lun's birth date should be in the first decade of the seventeenth century. Father and son were natives of a section of present-day Suchou called Ch'ang-chou 長洲.

son, Mao Tsung-kang (courtesy name Chieh-an 子庵, style Hsü-shih
序始).[2] One of the essays in the prefatory material to the *P'i-p'a chi*
commentary, the "Ts'an-lun" 參論 (Supplementary Remarks), is solely
the work of Mao Tsung-kang.

The main thrust of the commentary on the *P'i-p'a chi* is that Kao
Ming wrote the play to criticize an acquaintance of his, Wang the Fourth
王四. Not even the slightest bit of objective evidence is presented to back
up this assertion and no small amount of sophistry is required to use this
approach to interpret all of the features of the play. This theory did not
originate with Mao Lun nor did it disappear with him, but the unfortunate choice of this critical strategy was criticized by many of his
contemporaries, including Li Yü 李漁 (1611–1680)[3] and Chang Chu-p'o
張竹坡 (1670–1698).[4]

Both the commentary for the *P'i-p'a chi* and that for *The Romance of
the Three Kingdoms* were undertaken in reference to Chin Sheng-t'an's
commentaries on the *Shui-hu chuan* 水滸傳 (The Water Margin) and the
Hsi-hsiang chi 西廂記 (Romance of the Western Chamber). These four
works, easily among the most influential in the entire vernacular tradition, form two pairs. In the *P'i-p'a chi* and *The Romance of the Three
Kingdoms* conventional morality is perhaps questioned, but ultimately
affirmed. The *Shui-hu chuan* and the *Hsi-hsiang chi*, on the other hand, are
more subversive in nature. The former tends to uphold the right to rebel
against the state, while the latter praises romantic love. The two Maos
emphasize the moral correctness of their texts.[5] In the *P'i-p'a chi* com-

[2] Basing himself on the fact that in Mao Tsung-kang's preface to the *keng* 庚 collection
of Ch'u Jen-huo's 褚人獲 (ca. 1630–1705) *Chien-hu chi* 堅瓠集 (Hard Gourd Collectanea)
he refers to himself as Ch'u Jen-huo's *t'ung-hsüeh* 同學 (classmate), Robert E. Hegel
conjectures that Mao Tsung-kang was also born around 1630 at the earliest. See his "*Sui-
T'ang yen-i* and the Aesthetics of the Seventeenth-Century Suchou Elite," in *Chinese
Narrative: Critical and Theoretical Essays*, p. 144, n. 44. *Chien-hu chi* is a good source for
information on Mao Lun and his son, particularly the item entitled "Wang Hsiao-yin
chu-shou shih" 汪嘯尹祝壽詩 (Birthday Poems [for Mao Lun] by Wang Hsiao-yin) of
the *Pu-chi* 補集 (Supplementary Collection). See the reprint of the Po-hsiang shu-wu
edition (Hangchou: Che-chiang jen-min, 1986), *Pu-chi*, p. 2/12b. Mao Tsung-kang was
still alive in 1700, when his entire collection of books was lost in a fire. See ibid., *Pu-chi*,
p. 5/14a.
[3] See *Li Li-weng ch'ü-hua* 李笠翁曲話 (Li Yü on Drama), Ch'en To 陳多, ed. (Ch'ang-
sha: Hu-nan jen-min, 1980), "Chieh feng-tz'u" 戒諷刺 (Avoid Personal Satire), pp. 14–19.
[4] See chap. IV below, item 36 of his *Chin P'ing Mei tu-fa* essay.
[5] It has been suggested recently that the Maos' vehement attack against the legitimacy
of the Wei government is really anti-Manchu in nature. See, for instance, Huang Chung-
mo 黃中模, "Lun Mao Tsung-kang p'ing-kai *San-kuo yen-i* ti chu-yao ssu-hsiang i-i"
論毛宗崗評改三國演義的主要思想意義 (On the Fundamental Thought behind Mao
Tsung-kang's Commentating on and Editing of the *San-kuo yen-i*), *Ming-Ch'ing hsiao-
shuo yen-chiu* 3:283–96 (1986).

mentary Chin Sheng-t'an is never referred to by name, although he is
once mentioned by implication as the author of the prefaces to the *Shui-
hu chuan*.[6] Yu T'ung's preface presents precisely the opposite point of
view from Chin Sheng-t'an's on the question of the endings of the *Shui-
hu chuan* and the *Hsi-hsiang chi* and glaringly leaves out his name from a
list of famous commentators.[7] Be that as it may, the title of the Mao
edition of the play, *The Seventh Work of Genius*, adds it to Chin Sheng-
t'an's list of six; in addition, the Maos' reliance on a mysterious "old
edition" to justify their textual emendations in both the *P'i-p'a chi* and
The Romance of the Three Kingdoms replicates Chin Sheng-t'an's way of
handling the same problem.[8] The Maos and Chin Sheng-t'an were all
residents of Suchou and a letter from Chin Sheng-t'an to the younger
Mao has been preserved.[9]

In the "Tsung-lun" 總論 (General Remarks; p. 18b) of the *P'i-p'a chi*
commentary, Mao Lun says:

> Formerly Mr. Lo Kuan-chung composed the *T'ung-su San-kuo chih* 通俗三國志
> [Popularized Chronicle of the Three Kingdoms] in 120 *chüan* 卷 [chapters].
> As for the marvelousness of his narration of incidents, he holds his own with
> Ssu-ma Ch'ien, but his book was changed for the worse by village know-it-
> alls, which I thought a great pity. Two years ago I got the chance to read a
> copy of the original text. I edited and collated it and, despite my inadequacies,
> divided up the text into sections and added my comments [on them]. I also
> wrote a few paragraphs of general comments before each chapter. Aside from
> this, I let my son add his comments at the end of them [the chapter comments]
> and participate in the completion of the project. After the draft was finished,
> someone from Nanking read and admired it. He was interested in publishing
> it, but unexpectedly one of my own students turned against me and wanted
> to pass the book off as his own. Because of this, plans to publish [the com-
> mentary on the novel] were put aside. The whole affair is quite vexing. After
> publishing the present commentary [on the *P'i-p'a chi*], I ought to be able to
> follow up with the publication of the commentary on *The Romance of the
> Three Kingdoms*.

It is unclear to what extent the present editions with commentary ascribed
to Mao Tsung-kang are really the work of the father or the son.

The earliest extant copy of a Mao edition of *The Romance of the Three*

---

[6] *Ti-ch'i ts'ai-tzu shu*, Mao Lun's preface, p. 2b.

[7] Ibid., Yu T'ung preface, p. 4b.

[8] See the introductory remarks to chap. II.

[9] See *T'ang ts'ai-tzu shih* 唐才子詩 (Poetic Geniuses of the T'ang Dynasty), *CSTCC*,
vol. 4, p. 56. The authenticity of the "Chin Sheng-t'an" preface to the Mao commentary
on the novel will be taken up below.

Kingdoms has a preface signed by Li Yü, dated 1679.[10] In another preface to an edition of the novel printed by Li Yü's own publishing house, the Chieh-tzu yüan 芥子園, also signed Li Yü, the writer mentions that he once wrote a preface for an edition of the novel by the Maos, so perhaps there is no reason to doubt the authenticity of the 1679 Li Yü preface to the Tsui-keng t'ang edition.[11] Later editions contain a reworked version of the 1679 preface and it is in this fashion that the "Chin Sheng-t'an" preface to the popular editions of the novel with commentary ascribed to Mao Tsung-kang came into existence. Ninety percent of the original text of the Li Yü preface was retained in the new reworked versions,[12] but Chin Sheng-t'an's name and a date in 1644 were added at the end of the preface. The last paragraph was also changed so as to relate how "Chin Sheng-t'an" came to know of "Mr. Mao" and his commentary. Some editions also add Chin Sheng-t'an's name to the title page or attribute the entire commentary to him.[13] This led later scholars such as Lu Hsün 魯迅 to speak occasionally of Chin Sheng-t'an as the author of a commentary on *The Romance of the Three Kingdoms*. Another name that frequently appears on the title pages or at the beginning of the text of Mao commentary editions of the *San-kuo yen-i* is that of Hang Yung-

[10] The edition was published by the Tsui-keng t'ang 醉耕堂. See Ogawa Tamaki 小川環樹, "*Sankoku engi* no Mō Seizan hihyōbon to Ri Ryūō bon" 三国演義の毛声山批評本と李笠翁本 (The Mao Sheng-shan Commentary Edition of the *San-kuo yen-i* and the Li Yü Edition), in his *Chūgoku shōsetsu shi no kenkyū* 中国小説史の研究 (Studies in the History of Chinese Fiction; Tokyo: Iwanami shoten, 1968), p. 156.

[11] Ibid., p. 155. Toward the end of the Chieh-tzu yüan preface, the writer says, "At the head of Mao Lun's commentary on the novel, I have already made so bold as to write a preface [for the novel]" 余于聲山所評傳首, 已僭為之序矣. He goes on to say that although Chin Sheng-t'an rated the *Shih-chi* as the first work of genius, he never produced a commentary on it. He lists the good points of *The Romance of the Three Kingdoms*, saying in conclusion, "Truly, it is [worthy to be called] *The First Work of Genius*. Therefore, I made a reprint of it so as to share it with other lovers of antiquity." 誠哉第一才子書也. 因再梓以公諸好古者. The Chieh-tzu yüan edition uses the words "First Work of Genius" in its title, while the Tsui-keng t'ang edition calls itself the "First of the Four Great Marvelous Works" (*Ssu ta ch'i-shu ti-i chung* 四大奇書第一種). See the bibliographical appendix to this volume for more information on the relationship of the "Li Yü" and Mao Tsung-kang editions of the novel. The sections of the Chieh-tzu yüan preface translated above are from pages 5a–b of a microfilm of the Paris copy of this rare edition held in the Gest Oriental Library of Princeton University.

[12] Ogawa Tamaki, "*Sankoku engi* no Mō Seizan hihyōbon to Ri Ryūō bon," p. 161, n. 2.

[13] Ogawa Tamaki, ibid., p. 158, describes an edition held in the Center for Humanistic Studies in Kyoto University whose title page says the original commentary is by Chin Sheng-t'an. Princeton University possesses an 1820 reprint by the Yung-an t'ang 永安堂 that attributes the commentary to Chin Sheng-t'an on the title page. Even a 1977 Shanghai yin-shu kuan (Hong Kong) edition of the novel gives some credit for the commentary to Chin Sheng-t'an.

nien 杭永年. He was a native of Suchou, sometimes mentioned as the author of a commentary on the *San-kuo yen-i*. In editions that include his name, the commentary (*p'ing* 評) is attributed to Mao Tsung-kang while some sort of unspecified editorial work (*ting* 定) is attributed to Hang Yung-nien. Huang Lin 黃霖 has speculated that Hang Yung-nien was the wayward disciple who prevented the publication of the commentary prior to that of the *P'i-p'a chi* and that the appearance of his name on the printed version represents an accommodation towards his power and influence.[14]

The Mao editions of *The Romance of the Three Kingdoms* are also prefaced by a helpful "Fan-li" 凡例 (General Principles) which outlines a lot of the editorial changes made in the text of the novel for the new edition. This "Fan-li"[15] lists such changes as the improvement of the writing style, deletion of historical material, addition of new historical material, addition of historical documents and set pieces, revision of the chapter titles, removal of commentary attributed to Li Chih 李贄 (1527–1602), changes in the use of emphatic punctuation and the deletion of inferior poems and insertion of higher-quality T'ang dynasty (618–907) poems.[16] These changes are all justified as being in accord with the text of an "old edition" free of the textual corruptions of the popular versions of the novel. It seems fairly clear that the base text that was in fact used was one of those containing commentary ascribed to Li Chih,[17] which

[14] See Huang Lin 黃霖, "Yu-kuan Mao-pen *San-kuo yen-i* ti jo-kan wen-t'i" 有關毛本 三國演義的若干問題 (Concerning Some Problems with the Mao Commentary on the *San-kuo yen-i*), in *San-kuo yen-i yen-chiu chi* 三國演義研究集 (Collected Articles on the *San-kuo yen-i*; Ch'eng-tu: Ssu-ch'uan sheng she-hui k'o-hsüeh yen-chiu yüan, 1983), p. 328.

[15] It has been translated by Andrew Hing-bun Lo in his "*San-kuo chih yen-i* and *Shui-hu chuan* in the Context of Historiography: An Interpretative Study," Ph.D. dissertation, Princeton University, Princeton, 1981, pp. 27–34.

[16] T'ang poems are held up as important models for literary composition at several points in the *P'i-p'a chi* commentary. See *Ti-ch'i ts'ai-tzu shu*, "Ts'an-lun," p. 36a and pre-act comments, first act, p. 2/5a.

[17] There are a couple of types of editions of the novel with commentary attributed to Li Chih, the most influential being one in 240 *tse* 則 (items) in 12 *chüan* 卷 edited by Cheng I-chen 鄭以楨 and one in 120 chapters loosely retaining a 12-*chüan* division edited by Wu Kuan-ming 吳觀明 (see the entries in the bibliography for details). Although the Cheng I-chen edition has been put forward as the base text used by the Maos, that edition is very rare and not available for examination at present. Examination of the 120-chapter version, however, reveals it to fulfill all the conditions set forth in the "Fan-li." Furthermore, some of the commentary in the Mao editions seems to be based on that of the 120-chapter version (compare, for instance, the chapter comments to chap. 6 in both), besides numerous examples of textual similarities shared by the two editions but not to be found in the 1522 *San-kuo chih t'ung-su yen-i* edition. For further discussion of this issue, see Huang Lin, "Yu-kuan Mao-pen *San-kuo yen-i* ti jo-kan wen-t'i," p. 335, and Wu Chien-i

already represented to some extent an intermediate stage between the Mao editions and the earliest known version of the novel, the *San-kuo chih t'ung-su yen-i* 三國志通俗演義 (A Popularization of the Chronicle of the Three Kingdoms; preface 1522).[18]

The Mao commentary to *The Romance of the Three Kingdoms* is made up of the essay "How to Read *The Romance of the Three Kingdoms*," supplemented by prechapter and interlineal comments. It has been estimated that the commentarial sections of the Mao edition are almost two-thirds as large in bulk as the text of the novel itself.[19]

As in the case of Chin Sheng-t'an's version of the *Shui-hu chuan*, the recension of the text of *The Romance of the Three Kingdoms* produced by the Maos became the accepted version of the novel, completely eclipsing all of its rivals. References to the Chinese text of the novel in the translation of the essay below will be to a typeset edition of the Mao version of the novel complete with their commentary.[20] The translation of the *tu-fa* essay itself is also based on the text as included in this edition, with corrections indicated in the notes. The only complete translation of the novel into English is that by C.H. Brewitt-Taylor[21] originally published in 1925. As in the case of Pearl S. Buck's translation of the *Shui-hu chuan*, Brewitt-Taylor's translation is rife with errors of interpretation and transcription, but the translator does appear to have diligently tried to produce a complete version of the novel, even to the extent of translating most of the incidental poetry usually left out by translators of Chinese novels.[22]

吳監益, "*San-kuo yen-i* k'ao-shu" 三國演義考述 (Analysis and Description of *The Romance of the Three Kingdoms*), Master's Thesis, Soochow University, Taipei, 1976, p. 22.

[18] There is a photo-reprint edition (Peking: Jen-min wen-hsüeh, 1975) and a typeset version (Shanghai: Shang-hai ku-chi, 1980) under this same title.

[19] See Wu Chien-i, "*San-kuo yen-i* k'ao-shu," p. 22.

[20] *SKYI*. The modern-style punctuation of this edition has drawn criticism, but the text itself, apart from minor errors, seems basically sound. See Wen Wei 聞畏, "Pu-k'an tsu-tu ti *Ch'üan-t'u hsiu-hsiang San-kuo yen-i*" 不堪卒讀的全圖绣像三國演義 (A *Fully Illustrated Romance of the Three Kingdoms* That Is Hard to Read to the End), in *Tu-shu*, 1984.10:149–51.

[21] *RTK*.

[22] A new and complete translation of the Mao Tsung-kang edition of the novel by Moss Roberts is in progress.

How to Read *The Romance of the Three Kingdoms*

Translated and Annotated by DAVID T. ROY
Additional Annotation by DAVID L. ROLSTON

1. Readers of the *Chronicle of the Three Kingdoms*[1] should be aware of the distinction between states that rule by legitimate succession, those that rule during an intercalary period, and those that rule illegitimately. Which state was a legitimate regime? The state of Shu-Han [221–263]. Which states were illegitimate regimes? The states of Wu [222–280] and Wei [220–265]. Which state is an example of an intercalary regime? The Western Chin dynasty [265–317].

Why should the state of Wei not be accorded legitimacy? According to territorial criteria, control of the Central Plain might be sufficient to establish legitimacy; but according to the criterion of principle, legitimacy should be accorded to the Liu clan [the ruling house of the Han dynasty, 202 B.C.–220 A.D.]. The criterion of principle ought to take precedence over territorial considerations. Thus Ssu-ma Kuang [1019–1068] is wrong to have accorded legitimacy to the state of Wei in his *Tzu-chih t'ung-chien* [Comprehensive Mirror for Aid in Government], and Chu Hsi [1130–1200] is correct to have accorded it to the state of Shu-Han in his *Tzu-chih t'ung-chien kang-mu* [Outline and Explanation of the Comprehensive Mirror for Aid in Government].[2] In the latter work, at the end of the Chien-an reign period [196–220] of Emperor Hsien [r. 189–220] of the Han dynasty, there is written in large characters, "The first year of the Chang-wu reign period [221] of Emperor Chao-lieh[3] [r. 221–223] of the Later Han dynasty," and the relevant information about the reign periods of the kingdoms of Wu and Wei is placed after the notice of which year it is according to the Shu-Han reign period.[4]

---

[1] In this essay both the novel the *San-kuo yen-i* 三國演義 (The Romance of the Three Kingdoms) and the standard history of the period, the *San-kuo chih* 三國志 (Chronicle of the Three Kingdoms) by Ch'en Shou 陳壽 (233–297), are referred to by the same title, *San-kuo chih* (or sometimes just *San-kuo*). The translator has had to rely on his own sense of whether it is the novel or the historical work that is being referred to in any particular instance and the translation reflects these decisions.

[2] Chu Hsi's 朱熹 work is a rearrangement of Ssu-ma Kuang's 司馬光 chronological history of China according to the model of the *Ch'un-ch'iu* 春秋 (The Spring and Autumn Annals) and commentaries on it so as to make the recording of history embody and teach by example certain Confucian moral principles.

[3] Chao-lieh is the posthumous title of Liu Pei (161–223), founder of the kingdom of Shu-Han.

[4] According to the rules giving priority to legitimate states listed in its general principles, the *T'ung-chien kang-mu* labels the first year of the Wei dynasty (220) as the twenty-fifth year of the Chien-an reign period (see *Yü-p'i Tzu-chih t'ung-chien kang-mu* 御批資治

Thus he accords [*yü* 予] legitimacy to the state of Shu-Han because its founder was a descendant of the imperial house of Han and denies [*to* 奪] it to the state of Wei because its founder had usurped the throne. For the same reason the text states prior to this that Liu Pei [161–223] raised an army in Hsü-chou in order to "chastise" [*t'ao* 討] Ts'ao Ts'ao [155–220][5] and later states that the Han chancellor, Chu-ko Liang [181–234], launched a "punitive expedition" [*fa* 伐] against Wei.[6] By this choice of terminology he makes the cause of right manifest for all time.

As long as the Liu clan had not yet perished and the state of Wei had not succeeded in unifying the country it is obvious that the state of Wei should not be accorded legitimacy. But when the Liu clan had been deposed [263] and the Chin dynasty succeeded in unifying the country [280], why should it not be accorded legitimacy? The reason is that the Western Chin dynasty was established by regicide and is thus no better than the state of Wei. Furthermore, after the reign of its first emperor its years were numbered, so it can only be regarded as an intercalary regime and cannot be accorded legitimacy. The Eastern Chin [317–420], which established a truncated regime in South China and whose founder was the bastard son of a man named Niu rather than the heir of the Ssu-ma family,[7] has even less claim to legitimacy.

Thus the amalgamation of the Three Kingdoms by the Western Chin dynasty is comparable to that of the Six Warring States by the Ch'in dynasty [221–207 B.C.] and that of the Anterior Five Dynasties[8] into the Sui dynasty [589–618]. The Ch'in dynasty did no more than

---

通鑑綱目, *Ssu-k'u ch'üan-shu chen-pen* 四庫全書珍本, sixth series, vols. 133–72 [Taipei: Commercial Press, 1977], vol. 8, "Cheng-p'ien" 正篇 [Main Section], p. 14/51a), and the following year is given as the first year of the Chang-wu reign period (ibid., p. 14/57b). Starting from this point, the reign periods first of Wei, then later Wu as well, are listed using smaller characters below the Shu-Han reign period dates (cf. ibid., p. 14/67b).

[5] Ibid., p. 13/50a.

[6] The exact phrasing used here is not in the *T'ung-chien kang-mu*. However, the word *fa* 伐 (punitive expedition) is used several times in the large-character headings in reference to Chu-ko Liang's campaigns against Wei (cf. ibid., vol. 8, pp. 15/1a, 6a, 8a). The 1522 *San-kuo chih t'ung-su yen-i* uses the word *fan* 犯 (invade) to refer to Chu-ko Liang's campaigns against Wei while the Mao edition uses the word *fa* 伐 (make a punitive expedition).

[7] Ssu-ma Jui (276–322), first emperor of the Eastern Chin, is alleged to have been the bastard son of a minor functionary surnamed Niu in his biography in the *Chin-shu* 晉書 (History of the Chin Dynasty; Peking: Chung-hua shu-chü, 1974), 6.157–58. A summary of the conflicting evidence on this point can be found in Wu Shih-chien 吳士鑑 and Liu Ch'eng-kan 劉承幹, *Chin-shu chiao-chu* 晉書斠注 (Collated and Annotated Edition of the *Chin-shu*; Nanking, 1928), vol. 2, p. 6/21b.

[8] The states of the Anterior Five Dynasties (420–618) and the Posterior Five Dynasties (907–960) are listed by the author of the essay at the end of this paragraph.

prepare the way for the Han dynasty, and the Sui dynasty performed the same service for the T'ang dynasty [618–907]. The legitimate succession in the earlier period must be accorded to the Han dynasty and the claims of the Ch'in, Wei, and Chin dynasties must be denied, just as the legitimate succession in the later period must be accorded to the T'ang and Sung [960–1279] dynasties, while the claims of the Liu Sung [420–479], Ch'i [479–502], Liang [502–557], Ch'en [557–589], and Sui dynasties and the Liang [907–923], T'ang [923–936], Chin [936–946], Han [947–950], and Chou [950–960] dynasties must be denied.

Moreover, not only are the Wei and Chin dynasties less legitimate than the Han, but this is true even of the T'ang and Sung dynasties.

Emperor Yang of the Sui dynasty [r. 604–618] was an unprincipled ruler and it is appropriate that he should have lost his throne to the T'ang. However, it is to be regretted that this transition was not as clear-cut as that between the Shang [trad. dates 1765–1122 B.C.] and Chou [1122–256 B.C.] dynasties and that the founder of the T'ang dynasty chose to follow the evil precedents of the Wei and Chin dynasties in declaring himself Prince of T'ang and having the Nine Distinctions conferred upon himself.[9] Thus the T'ang dynasty's acquisition of the empire was not as legitimate as that of the Han dynasty.

The Sung dynasty was established on the basis of loyalty and integrity and saw the emergence of many renowned officials and great scholars, therefore those who discourse on past worthies regard it as legitimate; but it was never able to regain the possession of the sixteen prefectures on the northern frontier and was thus restricted to a smaller scale than the T'ang dynasty. Moreover, when the imperial robe was thrust upon its founder during the mutiny at Ch'en-ch'iao, he took the empire from the hands of a widow and a fatherless child. Thus the Sung dynasty's acquisition of the empire was also not as legitimate as that of the Han dynasty.

If even the T'ang and Sung dynasties are less legitimate than the Han, how can one consider the claims of the Wei and Chin dynasties? Emperor Kao-tsu of the Han dynasty [r. 202–195 B.C.] rose to power by destroying the harsh rule of Ch'in and defeating Hsiang Yü [232–202 B.C.], the murderer of Emperor I of Ch'u [r. 208–206 B.C.]. Emperor Kuang-wu [r. 25–57] eliminated Wang Mang [r. 9–23] and restored the

---

[9] The founder of the T'ang dynasty, Li Yüan (566–635), entered the Sui capital in 617 and assumed the title of prince (*wang* 王, not *kung* 公 as the text has it) of T'ang. The following year he had the Nine Distinctions conferred upon him. Both of these are part of the traditional preliminaries to "legitimate" usurpation of the throne. The novel itself contains a list and description of the Nine Distinctions in Chap. 61. See *SKYI*, p. 61.612, and *RTK*, p. 2.61.8. Volume number is only indicated for the English translation. The other two figures indicate chapter and page number, respectively.

Han dynasty to power, and Liu Pei attacked Ts'ao Ts'ao and continued the rule of the Han in Szechwan. The founder of the dynasty was legitimate, and those descendents who enabled it to continue were also legitimate. We cannot accord legitimacy to Emperor Kuang-wu because he succeeded in reunifying the empire and deny it to Liu Pei because he was able to gain control of only a remote portion of the empire.

If Liu Pei is legitimate, then why can we not also accord legitimacy to Liu Yü [r. 420–422, founder of the Liu Sung dynasty] and Liu Chih-yüan [r. 947–948, founder of the Later Han dynasty], both of whom were descendants of the Liu clan? The answer is that their affiliation with the house of Han was too distant and lacked proof, whereas Liu Pei's descent from Liu Sheng, Prince Ching of Chung-shan [r. 154–113 B.C.], was close in time and could be substantiated. Moreover, Liu Yü and Liu Chih-yüan obtained the throne by regicide and usurpation, so they cannot be compared with Liu Pei.

Why can we not accord legitimacy to Li Ts'un-hsü [r. 923–926, founder of the Later T'ang dynasty]? The answer is that his family was not originally named Li, that surname having been conferred on his father. His case is not very different from those of the first emperor of the Ch'in dynasty [r. 221–210 B.C.] who was the bastard son of Lü Pu-wei [d. 235 B.C.], and Emperor Yüan [Ssu-ma Jui, r. 317–322] of the Eastern Chin dynasty, who was the bastard son of a man named Niu. Thus, Li Ts'un-hsü also cannot be compared with Liu Pei.

Why can we not accept the claim of Li Pien[10] [r. 937–943, founder of the Southern T'ang dynasty] to have succeeded legitimately to the T'ang dynasty? The answer is that his claimed affiliation with the house of T'ang was so attentuated as to make his case comparable to those of Liu Yü and Liu Chih-yüan. Thus he too cannot be compared with Liu Pei.

If the claim of Liu Pien[11] of the Southern T'ang dynasty must be disallowed, why should we recognize the claim of Emperor Kao-tsung [r. 1127–1162] of the Southern Sung [1127–1279] to have legitimately continued the Sung dynasty? Emperor Kao-tsung's claim to the throne was based on his status as a descendant of the dynastic founder and his desire to perpetuate the dynasty. That is why his legitimacy is recognized. Even though Emperor Kao-tsung killed Yüeh Fei [1103–1141], gave power to Ch'in Kuei [1090–1155], and disregarded his responsibility to his predecessors,[12] historians have accorded legitimacy to him

[10] Read *pien* 昪 for *sheng* 昇.

[11] Read *pien* 昪 for *sheng* 昇.

[12] The last and penultimate emperors of the Northern Sung dynasty were captured and taken north by invading troops of the Chin dynasty (1115–1234) in 1127. They died in captivity.

because he perpetuated the dynasty. How much more should this principle apply in the case of Liu Pei, who cooperated with his chief minister, Chu-ko Liang, in single-minded devotion to the cause of extirpating the usurpers of the Han?

For these reasons, Liu Pei's legitimacy is all the more beyond doubt. Ch'en Shou's [233–297] *Chronicle of the Three Kingdoms* does not make this clear. I have therefore taken some of the views expressed by Chu Hsi in his *Tzu-chih t'ung-chien kang-mu* and inserted them into the text of *The Romance of the Three Kingdoms*.[13]

2. There are many histories of former times, but people are especially fond of reading the *Chronicle of the Three Kingdoms* because there is no other period in which so many talents flourished at the same time. There is nothing remarkable to be seen in the contest between a talented man and an untalented one. It is remarkable, however, to see one man of talent contend against another. When talents are pitted against each other, it is not so remarkable to see a single talented man hold his own against a combination of talented men. But it is truly remarkable, in such circumstances, when a combination of talented men are forced to yield before the superiority of a single man of talent.

I believe that there are three remarkable men from the period of the Three Kingdoms who may be said to be without peer. Chu-ko Liang is one. Kuan Yü [160–219] is another. And Ts'ao Ts'ao is the third.

A survey of the historical record would reveal a host of worthy chief ministers, yet for all-time preeminence none is a match for Chu-ko Liang. Before he enters public life, he plays the *ch'in* or sits with arms around his knees, exemplifying the casual elegance of a recluse. When he emerges from seclusion, he affects a feathered fan and silken headdress, retaining his air of cultured refinement. While still in his thatched hut, he foresees the tripartite division of the empire, thus revealing his thorough

---

[13] The earliest extant version of the novel (preface dated 1522) is already basically in accord with the judgments of the *T'ung-chien kang-mu*. In fact, Andrew Hing-bun Lo has shown that the *tse* 則 (section) titles of the earliest edition of the novel seem to have been modeled on the large-character headings (*kang* 綱) in that work. See his "*San-kuo chih yen-i* and *Shui-hu chuan* in the Context of Historiography: An Interpretative Study," Ph.D. dissertation, Princeton University, Princeton, 1981 and his entry on the novel in William Nienhauser, Jr., ed., *Indiana Companion to Traditional Chinese Literature* (Bloomington, Indiana: Indiana University Press, 1986), pp. 668–71. Although Mao Tsung-kang and his father further revised the novel in regard to some of the details of the handling of Ts'ao Ts'ao and Liu Pei, for instance, the real departure of the Mao edition from the earlier editions is in the addition of a detailed and highly didactic commentary that stresses political legitimacy and moral righteousness. One can, however, easily point out features like the omission of a mention of the Wei reign period (*SKYI* 91.903) as fully in accord with Chu Hsi's rules for handling such matters.

understanding of the times. Having accepted the heavy responsibility of Liu Pei's testamentary charge,[14] he mounts six campaigns against the state of Wei through the Ch'i Mountains,[15] thus carrying out his obligations to the full. However, his seven captures of Meng Huo,[16] his eight-fold battle formation,[17] and his invention of the wooden oxen and running mechanical horses[18] show him to be so unfathomable in his designs as to make you doubt whether he is not a demon or a god. He gives his utmost, devoting himself to his chosen cause until death, ever striving to fulfill his obligations as minister and son. He surpasses Kuan Chung [d. 645 B.C.] and Yüeh I [fl. 3d century B.C.] and combines the virtues of I Yin and Lü Shang.[19] Surely he is the most remarkable among the worthy chief ministers of all time.

A survey of the historical record would reveal as many famous generals as there are clouds in the sky, yet for peerless supremacy none is a match for Kuan Yü. His perusal of the histories by lamplight[20] fully reveals the cultivation of a scholar. The ardor of his heart matches the redness of his face[21] and reveals his heroic nature. For his holding the candle all night long,[22] he is taken as the standard for scrupulous conduct. For attending the conference with nothing to protect him but his sword,[23] the world acknowledges him to be awe inspiring. All by him-

[14] *SKYI* 85.842, *RTK* 2.85.258.

[15] Chaps. 93–104.

[16] Chaps. 87–90.

[17] *SKYI* 84.835–36, *RTK* 2.84.251–53.

[18] *SKYI* 102.1020–21, *RTK* 2.102.446.

[19] The latter two men were, respectively, the founding statesmen of the Shang (trad. dates 1766–1123 B.C.) and Chou (1122–256 B.C.) dynasties.

[20] This phrase comes from a couplet hung in a temple dedicated to Kuan Yü which is quoted in the novel (*SKYI* 77.766, *RTK* 2.77.180). In the novel itself, Kuan Yü is shown reading only once (*SKYI* 27.267, *RTK* 1.27.286–87) where the book is unspecified. In the popular culture of China, he is always conceived of as spending his leisure time reading historical works like the *Ch'un-ch'iu*, and he is so portrayed on the stage in traditional plays like *Ku-ch'eng hui* 古城會 (The Meeting of the Sworn Brothers at Ku-ch'eng). Ts'ao Ts'ao also mentions the fact that Kuan Yü is well versed in the *Ch'un-ch'iu* (*SKYI* 50.503, *RTK* 1.50.524).

[21] In the novel, Kuan Yü's face is originally spoken of as being red-brown (*chung-tsao* 重棗, *SKYI* 1.6, *RTK* 1.1.5) in color, but it is also frequently said to be red (*ch'ih* 赤). It seems that the practice of painting the face of the actor portraying him red dates back at least as far as the Yüan dynasty (1279–1368). See Ch'i Ju-shan 齊如山, *Kuo-chü t'u-p'u* 國劇圖譜 (Collected Illustrations of Peking Opera; Taipei: Yu-shih wen-hua, 1977), p. 84.

[22] Trying to compromise Kuan Yü, Ts'ao Ts'ao forced him to spend the night with Liu Pei's two wives. Kuan Yü, however, stands outside the ladies' apartment with candle in hand until the dawn (*SKYI* 25.246, *RTK* 1.25.263).

[23] *SKYI* 66.622–24, *RTK* 2.66.61–63.

self he travels a thousand *li*,[24] so firm is his resolve to requite his master. He lets Ts'ao Ts'ao escape at Hua-jung,[25] so seriously does he take the obligation to repay a kindness. His own conduct is like the white sun in a blue sky. His treatment of others is like the bright breeze under a clear moon. His heart is even more open and fearless than that of Chao Pien [1008–1084], who each night, after burning incense, would make a frank report of his conduct that day to Heaven.[26] His standards are even more uncompromising than those of Juan Chi [210–263], who revealed his contempt for others by showing them the whites of his eyes.[27] Surely he is the most remarkable among the famous generals of all time.

A survey of the historical record would reveal so many unscrupulous heroes [*chien-hsiung* 奸雄] that they tread on one another's heels, yet for cunning sufficient to control men of talent and deceive the world, none is a match for Ts'ao Ts'ao. He accepts Hsün Yü's [163–212] advice to support the imperial cause[28] and compares himself to King Wen of the Chou dynasty,[29] thereby seeming to be loyal. He repudiates Yüan Shu [d. 199] for illegitimately assuming the imperial title and is content to accept enfeoffment as a marquis, thereby seeming to show proper allegiance. He spares the life of Ch'en Lin [d. 217] out of admiration for his talent,[30] thereby seeming to be tolerant and accommodating. By not pursuing Kuan Yü[31] he allows him to realize his ambitions, thereby seeming to be chivalrous. In his ability to attract men to his service he surpasses Wang Tun [266–324], who was unable to make use of Kuo P'u [276–324].[32] In his ability to judge character he surpasses Huan Wen [312–373], who failed to appreciate Wang Meng [325–375].[33] Although

[24] Chap. 27.

[25] *SKYI* 50.503, *RTK* 1.50.524–25.

[26] See his biography in the *Sung shih* 宋史 (History of the Sung Dynasty; Peking: Chung-hua shu-chü, 1977), 316.10325. Read *t'ien* 天 for *ti* 帝.

[27] Juan Chi reserved the pupils of his eyes for his friends and those he respected. Faced with vulgar aristocrats and office holders, he would avert his pupils and only show the whites of his eyes. See his biography in the *Chin-shu*, 49.1361.

[28] *SKYI* 14.125, *RTK* 1.14.135.

[29] *SKYI* 78.777, *RTK* 2.78.190.

[30] *SKYI* 32.323, *RTK* 1.32.345.

[31] *SKYI* 27.261, *RTK* 1.27.279.

[32] Wang Tun killed Kuo P'u when the latter predicted (accurately as it later turned out) the defeat of Wang Tun's planned usurpation of the throne. See Kuo P'u's biography in the *Chin-shu*, 72.1909–10.

[33] Actually, Huan Wen offered to take Wang Meng into his service and give him a post, but he was not able to convince the latter to accept the offer. See Wang Meng's biography in the *Chin-shu*, 114.2930. Wang Meng later became a powerful minister under Fu Chien 苻堅 (338–385), emperor of the Anterior Ch'in dynasty (r. 357–384).

Li Lin-fu [d. 752] was able to restrain An Lu-shan [d. 757], this accomplishment is not the equal of Ts'ao Ts'ao's campaign against the Wuhuan beyond the borders.[34] Although Han T'o-chou [1151–1207] was able to bring about posthumous sanctions against Ch'in Kuei [d. 1155],[35] this accomplishment is not the equal of Ts'ao Ts'ao's punitive campaign against Tung Cho [d. 192][36] while the latter was still alive. To have usurped the power of the state and yet preserve it in name is not the same thing as Wang Mang's open regicide. To have left the task of formally changing the mandate to his son is superior to Liu Yü's haste to usurp the Eastern Chin dynasty. Surely he is the most remarkable among the unscrupulous heroes of all time.

Three such remarkable men as these are not to be found in the histories of other times, before or since. Therefore, the reading through of all the other histories will only serve to strengthen one's predilection for the *Chronicle of the Three Kingdoms*.

3. But even if we leave aside these three paragons, what do we find if we survey the histories of the periods that come before and after the Three Kingdoms?

How many control the fortunes of battle by the calculations they perform within their tents as effectively as do Hsü Shu and P'ang T'ung [177–214]? How many direct their armies and employ their military forces as effectively as do Chou Yü [175–210], Lu Hsün [183–245], and Ssu-ma I [179–251]? How many anticipate the deeds of men and the outcome of events as accurately as Kuo Chia [170–207], Ch'eng Yü [143–222], Hsün Yü, Chia Hsü [148–224], Pu Chih [d. 247], Yü Fan [164–233], Ku Yung [168–243], and Chang Chao [156–236]? How many surpass their contemporaries in military accomplishments and generalship as do Chang Fei [d. 221], Chao Yün [d. 229], Huang Chung [d. 220], Yen Yen, Chang Liao [171–221], Hsü Sheng, and Chu Huan [177–238]? How many fight so bravely when they find themselves endangered that no one can withstand them as do Ma Ch'ao [176–222], Ma Tai, Kuan Hsing, Chang Pao, Hsü Ch'u, Tien Wei [d. 197], Chang Ho [d. 231], Hsia-hou Tun [d. 220], Huang Kai, Chou T'ai, Kan Ning, T'ai-shih Tz'u [166–206], and Ting Feng [d. 271]? How often do men of talent and worth encounter their peers as do Chiang Wei [202–264]

---

[34] *SKYI* 33.331–33, *RTK* 1.33.353–55.

[35] Ch'in Kuei, scorned in Chinese history as a traitor and murderer of the famous general, Yüeh Fei (1103–1141), was stripped of his title of prince and given the posthumous epithet *miu-ch'ou* 謬醜 (Benighted and Unsightly). See his biography in the *Sung shih*, 473.13765.

[36] Chaps. 4–6.

and Teng Ai [197–264], who are equals in intelligence and courage; or Yang Hu [221–278] and Lu K'ang [226–274], who defend their borders against each other with such grace and style? How many periods can boast such exemplars of scholarship as Ma Jung [79–166] and Cheng Hsüan [127–200], such exemplars of literature as Ts'ai Yung [132–192] and Wang Ts'an [177–217], such exemplars of quick-wittedness as Ts'ao Chih [192–232] and Yang Hsiu [178–220], such exemplars of precocity as Chu-ko K'o [203–253] and Chung Hui [225–264], such exemplars of ready eloquence as Ch'in Mi [d. 226] and Chang Sung [d. 213], such exemplars of disputation as Li Hui [d. 226] and K'an Tse [d. 227], such exemplars of successful diplomacy as Chao Tzu and Teng Chih [d. 251], such exemplars of the art of drafting declarations as Ch'en Lin and Juan Yü [d. 212], such exemplars of able administration as Chiang Wan [d. 245] and Tung Yün [d. 245], such exemplars of rapid rise to fame as Ma Liang [d. 222] and Hsün Shuang [128–190], such an exemplar of devotion to antiquity as Tu Yü [222–284], or such an exemplar of broad erudition as Chang Hua [232–300]? It would be hard to find examples of all these talents in any other work.

But we marvel also at the perspicacity of Ssu-ma Hui [d. 208] in recognizing men of worth; the loftiness of Kuan Ning [158–241] in exemplifying high moral standards; the unconstraint of Ts'ui Chou-p'ing, Shih Kuang-yüan, and Meng Kung-wei in their lives of reclusion; the rectitude with which K'ung Jung [153–208] defies tyranny; the forthrightness with which Chao Yen attacks corruption; the heroism with which Mi Heng [171–196] denounces evil; the stalwartness with which Chi P'ing [d. 218] curses the usurper; the worthiness of Tung Ch'eng [d. 200] and Fu Wan [d. 209], who die for their country; the integrity of Keng Chi [d. 218] and Wei Huang [d. 218], who sacrifice their lives; the filiality of Liu Ch'en [d. 263] and Kuan P'ing [d. 219], who die for their fathers; the loyalty of Chu-ko Chan [227–263] and Chu-ko Shang [d. 263], who die for their rulers; and the chivalry of Chao Lei and Chou Ts'ang, who die for their commanding officer.

In addition there are such exemplars of foresight as T'ien Feng [d. 200], such exemplars of remonstration as Wang Lei, such exemplars of fidelity as Chu Shou, such exemplars of indomitability as Chang Jen [d. 213], such exemplars of unstinting friendship as Lu Su [171–217], such exemplars of unswerving loyalty as Chu-ko Chin [174–241], such exemplars of undauntedness as Ch'en T'ai [d. 260], such an exemplar of the courage to face death with equanimity as Wang Ching [d. 260], and such an exemplar of scrupulous adherence to principle as Ssu-ma Fu [180–272].

The brilliant accomplishments of these men illuminate the pages of history. Their deeds are comparable to those of their predecessors such as the three heroes of the Feng-P'ei region,[37] the four graybeards of Shang-shan,[38] the twenty-eight generals whose portraits adorned the Cloud Tower,[39] and Yen Kuang [37 B.C.–43 A.D.], the "guest star" of Fu-ch'un;[40] or those of their successors such as the eighteen scholars immortalized by the founder of the T'ang dynasty in 621, the eleven meritorious officials depicted in the Unicorn Pavilion,[41] the regional commander Li Sheng [727–793] who could forget a grudge over a cup of wine, or Wen T'ien-hsiang [1236–1282], the prime minister who died for his country at Ch'ai-shih.[42]

But instances such as these are scattered over thousands of years, whereas those of the Three Kingdoms are all concentrated in one period. Is it not a veritable metropolis, teeming with human talent? One has the sensation of trying to select the finest timber from Teng Forest[43] or catching sight of the piles of jade in the garden atop K'un-lun Mountain.[44] There is more than one can absorb or have the time to take account of. When I contemplate the period of the Three Kingdoms, I sigh with the feeling that this is a vision that cannot be surpassed.

[37] This probably refers to Hsiao Ho 蕭何 (d. 193 B.C.), Chou Po 周勃 (d. 169 B.C.), and Fan K'uai 樊噲 (d. 189 B.C.), who were all born in the Feng-P'ei region of what is now Kiangsu province and helped their fellow countryman Liu Pang (256–195 B.C.) found the Han dynasty.

[38] These four men were recluses of great fame who helped avert a succession crisis in the early years of the Han dynasty by supporting the cause of the heir apparent. See the *Shih-chi* 史記 (Records of the Historian; Peking: Chung-hua shu-chü, 1959), pp. 55.2044–47 and Burton Watson, trans., *Records of The Grand Historian of China*, 2 vols. (New York: Columbia University Press, 1961), vol. 1, pp. 145–49.

[39] The twenty-eight generals helped restore the Han dynasty in 25 A.D. Their portraits were painted and hung in this tower to memorialize their merit.

[40] Yen Kuang was acquainted with Liu Hsiu (6–57), the founder of the Eastern Han dynasty. Liu Hsiu asked him to take a post in the administration, but Yen Kuang refused him. However, on one visit to the new emperor, Yen Kuang made himself so at home as to lie on the same couch with him and rest his feet on the emperor's stomach. The next day the court astrologer reported that the night before the *k'o-hsing* 客星 (guest star) had encroached upon the emperor's star. See Yen Kuang's biography in the *Hou Han-shu* 後漢書 (History of the Later Han Dynasty; Shanghai: Chung-hua shu-chü, 1973), 83.2764.

[41] The portraits were hung by Emperor Hsüan (r. 74–49 B.C.) of the Western Han dynasty to commemorate Huo Kuang 霍光 (d. 68 B.C.) and others who helped the dynasty through a succession crisis.

[42] Read *ch'ai* 柴 for *chai* 砦.

[43] This forest is mentioned in the *Shan-hai ching* 山海經 (The Classic of the Mountains and Seas), *Ssu-pu ts'ung-k'an* 四部叢刊, first series, vol. 27 (Taipei: Commercial Press, 1965), p. 8/2a–b.

[44] According to tradition, the garden on this remote mountain to the west of China communicated with Heaven and abounded in jade.

4. *The Romance of the Three Kingdoms* is a most remarkable example of literary composition. Its subject is the Three Kingdoms, but rather than beginning with them, it traces their origins back to the reigns of Emperors Huan [r. 146–167] and Ling [r. 167–189] of the Han dynasty. Its subject is the Three Kingdoms but, rather than ending with them, it follows their fortunes through their final culmination in the Chin dynasty.

But this is not all. Liu Pei takes advantage of his royal descent to carry on the legitimate succession, but there are other imperial clansmen such as Liu Piao [144–208], Liu Chang, Liu Yu, Liu P'i, and so forth, to serve as his foils [*p'ei* 陪]. Ts'ao Ts'ao takes advantage of his position as a powerful minister to seize control of the government, but there are figures such as Tung Cho, who deposes one emperor in order to set up another;[45] and Li Chüeh [d. 198] and Kuo Ssu [d. 197], who wreak havoc in the state,[46] to serve as his foils. Sun Ch'üan [182–252] takes advantage of his position as a local magnate to become ruler of one of the Three Kingdoms, but there are also Yüan Shu, who illegitimately assumes the imperial title,[47] Yüan Shao [d. 202], who establishes a claim to power, and Lü Pu [d. 198], Kung-sun Tsan [d. 199], Chang Yang [d. 199], Chang Miao [d. 196], Chang Lu [fl. 190–220], Chang Hsiu [d. 207], and so forth, who carve out their own domains, to serve as his foils.

Liu Pei and Ts'ao Ts'ao appear in chapter 1, but Sun Ch'üan does not appear until chapter 7. Ts'ao Ts'ao establishes his capital at Hsü-ch'ang in chapter 11 and the Sun brothers gain control of Chiang-tung in chapter 15,[48] but Liu Pei's conquest of Szechwan does not take place until after chapter 60.

If an author of the present day were to create a novel [*pai-kuan* 稗官] with the subject of the history of three such kingdoms, he would surely begin his narrative with an account of the three rulers and how each gained control of his realm. Who among them would have the genius to set the foundation for some things beforehand and to reveal some things only after the event, skillfully interweaving several matters at once? By preserving the natural periodic variations [*po-lan* 波瀾] and configurations [*ts'eng-che* 層折] in the narration of these ancient events, the author has produced an incomparable literary masterpiece. That is why reading *The Romance of the Three Kingdoms* is truly superior to reading any number of ordinary novels [*pai-kuan* 稗官].

5. If we consider the founders of the Three Kingdoms, every one

---

[45] *SKYI* 4.32–33, *RTK* 1.4.35.
[46] Chaps. 9–17.
[47] *SKYI* 17.162, *RTK* 1.17.174.
[48] Read *wu* 五 for *erh* 二.

knows that they are Liu Pei, Sun Ch'üan, and Ts'ao Ts'ao, but not everyone may be aware of the differences between them.

Both Liu Pei and Ts'ao Ts'ao are the creators of their own regimes, whereas Sun Ch'üan benefits from the efforts of his father and elder brother. This is the first difference.

Both Liu Pei and Sun Ch'üan assume the emperorship in person, whereas Ts'ao Ts'ao does not, leaving this task to his son and grandsons. This is the second difference.

The ruler of Wei is the first of the rulers of the Three Kingdoms to declare himself emperor [220][49] whereas the ruler of Shu declares himself emperor [221][50] after Ts'ao Ts'ao is dead and Ts'ao P'i [187–226] has ascended the throne [220], and the ruler of Wu declares himself emperor [229][51] after Liu Pei is dead and Liu Shan [207–271] has ascended the throne [223]. This is the third difference.

In the struggle for supremacy among the Three Kingdoms, Wu is a neighbor to Shu while Wei is Shu's enemy. Shu and Wu are sometimes at peace and sometimes at war with one another, whereas Shu and Wei are always at war and never at peace with one another. Wu and Shu are more often at peace than at war with one another, whereas Wu and Wei are more often at war than at peace with each other. This is the fourth difference.

So far as the royal successions of the Three Kingdoms are concerned, that of Shu lasts for only two generations, whereas there are five rulers of Wei from Ts'ao P'i to Ts'ao Huan [r. 260–265] and four rulers of Wu from Sun Ch'üan to Sun Hao [r. 264–280]. This is the fifth difference.

As for the durations of the Three Kingdoms, Wu comes to an end last [280],[52] preceded by Shu [263][53] and then Wei [265].[54] The throne of Wei is usurped by one of its ministers, whereas Wu and Shu are annexed by their enemies. This is the sixth difference.

But these are not the only differences. In the case of Sun Ts'e [175–200] and Sun Ch'üan, when the elder brother dies he is succeeded by his younger brother.[55] In the case of Ts'ao P'i and Ts'ao Chih, the younger brother is rejected in favor of the older.[56] In the case of Liu Pei and Liu Shan, the father becomes emperor but the son ends his career as a captive. In the case of Ts'ao Ts'ao and Ts'ao P'i, the father serves as a

[49] *SKYI* 80.793–94, *RTK* 2.80.207–8.
[50] *SKYI* 80.796–97, *RTK* 2.80.211.
[51] *SKYI* 98.976, *RTK* 2.98.401.
[52] *SKYI* 120.1189, *RTK* 2.120.621.
[53] *SKYI* 118.1162, *RTK* 2.118.591.
[54] *SKYI* 119.1177, *RTK* 2.119.608.
[55] *SKYI* 29.290, *RTK* 1.29.309.
[56] *SKYI* 68.685, *RTK* 2.68.86.

minister but the son becomes a ruler. These events could certainly be described as heterogeneous and variegated, inexhaustible in the number of their variations.

Nowadays when unskillful painters portray two different people they look the same. When unskillful singers perform two different songs they sound alike. The similarity [*ho-chang* 合掌] between literary works is often just as pronounced. This is because, although the events that occurred to the men of former times were never exactly alike [*lei-t'ung* 雷同], the writers of our day choose to produce works that are scarcely distinguishable from each other. Why not read this version of *The Romance of the Three Kingdoms* on which I have written my commentary [*p'i* 批] instead?

6. In *The Romance of the Three Kingdoms*, between the initial beginning [*tsung-ch'i* 總起] and the final conclusion [*tsung-chieh* 總結] there are six other significant beginnings [*ch'i* 起] and conclusions [*chieh* 結].

The narrative of the career of Emperor Hsien of the Han dynasty begins [*ch'i* 起] when Tung Cho deposes his predecessor to set him up as emperor [189][57] and concludes [*chieh* 結] when Ts'ao P'i usurps the throne [220].[58]

The narrative of the state of Shu begins when Liu Pei declares himself emperor in Ch'eng-tu [221][59] and concludes when Liu Shan surrenders after the loss of Mien-chu [263].[60]

The narrative of the relationship between Liu Pei, Kuan Yü, and Chang Fei begins with their oath of brotherhood in the peach garden[61] and concludes when Liu Pei entrusts his heir to Chu-ko Liang at Pai-ti [223].[62]

The narrative of the career of Chu-ko Liang begins with Liu Pei's three visits to his thatched cottage [207][63] and concludes with his sixth campaign through the Ch'i Mountains [234].[64]

The narrative of the state of Wei begins with the adoption of the new reign title Huang-ch'u [220][65] and concludes with Ssu-ma Yen's [r. 265–290] acceptance of Ts'ao Huan's abdication [265].[66]

The narrative of the state of Wu begins when Sun Chien [157–193]

---

[57] *SKYI* 4.32–33, *RTK* 1.4.35–36.
[58] *SKYI* 80.793–94, *RTK* 2.80.207–8.
[59] *SKYI* 80.796–97, *RTK* 2.80.211.
[60] *SKYI* 117.1162, *RTK* 2.117.591.
[61] *SKYI* 1. 6, *RTK* 1.1.5–6.
[62] *SKYI* 85.842, *RTK* 2.85.258.
[63] Chaps. 37–38.
[64] Chap. 104.
[65] *SKYI* 80.794, *RTK* 2.80.208.
[66] *SKYI* 119.1177, *RTK* 2.119.608.

secretes the Great Seal of State [191][67] and concludes with the surrender of Sun Hao [280].[68]

All these narrative strands are interwoven so skillfully that no sooner does one of them begin than another is concluded and before it is concluded, yet another one begins. While reading, one is scarcely aware of the way in which they are interrupted or resumed [*tuan-hsü* 斷續], but if one looks more closely, there are structural principles [*chang-fa* 章法] that can be discerned.

7. One of the marvels of *The Romance of the Three Kingdoms* is the technique of tracing things to their roots and divulging their sources ["*chui-pen chiu-yüan chih miao*" 追本究源之妙].

The tripartite division of the empire arises out of the struggle for power between the regional warlords. The struggle for power between the regional warlords arises out of the havoc wreaked by Tung Cho. The havoc wreaked by Tung Cho arises out of Ho Chin's [d. 189] decision to summon provincial armies to the capital [189].[69] Ho Chin's decision to summon provincial armies to the capital arises out of the monopoly of power by the Ten Constant Attendants.[70] Therefore the narrative of the Three Kingdoms must begin with the Ten Constant Attendants.

Liu Pei does not get his start as one of the regional warlords, but as a freebooter in the wilds. Now the fact that heroes congregate in the wilds and warlords mobilize for war arises from the rebellion of the Yellow Turbans [184]. Therefore the narrative of the Three Kingdoms must begin with the Yellow Turbans.

But before the revolt of the Yellow Turbans, Heaven sends down disasters and prodigies as a warning, and loyal and astute ministers prophesy the dangers to come in straightforward and outspoken remonstrances.[71] If the rulers of that time had been able to apprehend the benevolence of Heaven's intent and to accept the wise counsel of their loyal ministers by eliminating the Ten Constant Attendants from court, the Yellow Turbans need never have revolted, heroes need never have arisen in the wilds, the warlords need never have mobilized for war, and the tripartite division of the empire need never have taken place. Therefore the fact that the narrative of the Three Kingdoms traces its roots back to the reigns of Emperors Huan and Ling is like the fact that the Yellow River has its source in the Lake of Stars.[72]

[67] *SKYI* 6.56, *RTK* 1.6.59–60.

[68] *SKYI* 120.1189, *RTK* 2.120.621.

[69] *SKYI* 3.22, *RTK* 1.3.23.

[70] *SKYI* 1.3, *RTK* 1.1.2.

[71] *SKYI* 1.2–3, *RTK* 1.1.1–2.

[72] This lake is in modern Ch'ing-hai Province and was formerly thought to be the source of the Yellow River.

8. One of the marvels of *The Romance of the Three Kingdoms* is the technique of artful disposition and mysterious consummation ["ch'iao-shou huan-chieh chih miao" 巧收幻結之妙].

If the state of Wei had been annexed by the state of Shu, everyone would consider this a consummation to be devoutly wished. If the state of Shu had perished and the state of Wei had succeeded in reuniting the empire, everyone would consider this a consummation to be greatly abhorred. But it was the will of Heaven neither to grant to man the consummation he so devoutly wished, nor to inflict upon him an outcome he so greatly abhorred, but rather to avail itself of the Chin dynasty to complete the task of unification. This is an example of the mysterious consummation wrought by the Creator himself.

But if Heaven could no longer confer its blessing on the Han dynasty and likewise withheld it from the state of Wei, why did it not avail itself of the state of Wu rather than the Chin dynasty?

It goes without saying that the state of Wei was a traitor to the Han dynasty. But the state of Wu killed Kuan Yü, seized Ching-chou, and collaborated with Wei in attacking Shu. Thus, it was also a traitor to the Han dynasty. As for the usurpation of the state of Wei by the Chin dynasty, it is almost as though it were an act of retribution [*pao-ch'ou* 報仇] for the usurpation of the Han dynasty by the state of Wei. Therefore, rather than leaving the task of unification to the state of Wu, it was more fitting to leave it to the Chin dynasty.

Moreover, the state of Wu was an enemy of the state of Wei, whereas the founders of the Chin dynasty had been subjects of Wei. The fact that the state of Wei was founded by an act of usurpation and suffered retribution [*pao* 報] in the form of a like act of usurpation by the founder of the Chin dynasty serves as a warning to future generations. Thus it would have been less satisfying if the state of Wei had been taken over by its enemy than it is that it was taken over by its own subjects.

This is an example of the artful dispositions of the Creator. Though his mysteries are beyond human imagination, his artistry can be imitated by us. The Creator can indeed be said to be a master of the literary arts. When the writers of our day set pen to paper they command neither such mystery nor such art. If this is so, we would do better to study the spontaneous patterns of the Creator himself rather than to peruse the literary works dreamed up by our contemporaries.

9. One of the marvels of *The Romance of the Three Kingdoms* is the technique of using the guest as a foil for the host ["i pin ch'en chu chih miao" 以賓襯主之妙].

For example, before the account of the three heroes who swear

brotherhood in the peach garden[73] comes an account of the three brothers who lead the revolt of the Yellow Turbans.[74] The story of the oath in
the peach garden is the host [*chu* 主] and that of the leaders of the Yellow
Turbans is the guest [*pin* 賓].

Before the statement that Liu Pei is a descendant of Liu Sheng, Prince
Ching of Chung-shan,[75] we are told that Liu Yen [d. 194] is a descendant of Liu Yü [r. 154–129 B.C.], Prince Kung of Lu.[76] The statement
about Prince Ching of Chung-shan is the host and that about Prince
Kung of Lu is the the guest.

Before the story of Ho Chin[77] comes the story of Ch'en Fan [d. 168]
and Tou Wu [d. 168].[78] The story of Ho Chin is the host and that of
Ch'en Fan and Tou Wu is the guest.

The description of the outstanding qualities of Liu Pei, Kuan Yü, and
Chang Fei, on the one hand, and of Ts'ao Ts'ao and Sun Chien, on the
other, brings out the lack of ability of the various regional authorities.
The description of Liu Pei, Ts'ao Ts'ao, and Sun Chien is the host and
that of the various regional authorities is the guest.

When Liu Pei is about to meet Chu-ko Liang, he first meets Ssu-ma
Hui, Ts'ui Chou-p'ing, Shih Kuang-yüan, and Meng Kung-wei.[79] The
story of his meeting with Chu-ko Liang is the host and that of his
encounters with Ssu-ma Hui and the rest is the guest.

The account of Chu-ko Liang's service under two successive reigns
also includes the careers of Hsü Shu, who joins and leaves Liu Pei before
Chu-ko Liang enters his service,[80] and of P'ang T'ung, who joins up
later but dies earlier than Chu-ko Liang does.[81] The story of Chu-ko
Liang is the host and those of Hsü Shu and P'ang T'ung are the guests.

Chao Yün first serves under Kung-sun Tsan,[82] Huang Chung first
serves under Han Hsüan,[83] Ma Ch'ao first serves under Chang Lu,[84] Fa
Cheng [176–220] and Yen Yen first serve under Liu Chang,[85] but all of

---

[73] *SKYI* 1.6, *RTK* 1.1.5–6.

[74] *SKYI* 1.3, *RTK* 1.1.2–3.

[75] *SKYI* 1.4–5, *RTK* 1.1.4.

[76] *SKYI* 1.4, *RTK* 1.1.4.

[77] *SKYI* 1.4, *RTK* 1.1.3.

[78] *SKYI* 1.2, *RTK* 1.1.1. These men all tried, unsuccessfully, to break the power of the
eunuchs in the central government.

[79] Chaps. 35–37.

[80] *SKYI* 35–36.351–60, *RTK* 1.35–36.373–83.

[81] *SKYI* 57–63.568–629, *RTK* 1.57.594–2.63.26.

[82] Chap. 7.

[83] *SKYI* 53.527, *RTK* 1.53.548.

[84] *SKYI* 64.645, *RTK* 2.64.44.

[85] *SKYI* 60.599, 63.635; *RTK* 1.60.631, 2.63.29.

them end up in the service of Liu Pei. The story of Liu Pei is the host and those of Kung-sun Tsan, Han Hsüan, Chang Lu, and Liu Chang are the guests.

T'ai-shih Tz'u first serves under Liu Yu but later gives his allegiance to Sun Ts'e,[86] and Kan Ning first serves under Huang Tsu [d. 208] but later gives his allegiance to Sun Ch'üan.[87] Chang Liao first serves under Lü Pu, Hsü Huang first serves under Yang Feng [d. 197], Chang Ho first serves under Yüan Shao, Chia Hsü first serves under Li Chüeh and Chang Hsiu, but all of them end up in the service of Ts'ao Ts'ao. The stories of the Sun brothers and Ts'ao Ts'ao are the hosts and those of Liu Yu, Huang Tsu, Lü Pu, Yang Feng, and the others are the guests.

The prophecy, "That which replaces the Han will be tall and face the road," is fulfilled by the founding of the state of Wei [which means here the city gate that faces the main road], but Yüan Shu mistakenly takes it to refer to himself.[88] The account of the founding of the state of Wei is the host and that of the abortive ambitions of Yüan Shu is the guest.

The dream in which Ts'ao Ts'ao sees three horses feeding out of the same trough is fulfilled by the usurpation of the Wei by the Ssu-ma clan [the character *ma* 馬 in the surname Ssu-ma 司馬 means "horse"], but Ts'ao Ts'ao mistakenly understands it to refer to Ma T'eng [d. 212] and his sons.[89] The account of the usurpation by the Ssu-ma clan is the host and that of Ma T'eng and his sons is the guest.

Li Su [d. 192] invents the construction of the altar for the abdication ceremony in order to deceive Tung Cho,[90] but it turns out to be true for Ts'ao P'i[91] and again for Ssu-ma Yen.[92] The narrative about Ts'ao P'i and Ssu-ma Yen is the host and that about Tung Cho is the guest.

Moreover, this technique of using the guest as a foil for the host is applied not only to men but also to places.

In those segments of the narrative in which the site of Emperor

---

[86] *SKYI* 15.143, *RTK* 1.15.155–56.

[87] *SKYI* 38.382–83, *RTK* 1.38.405–6.

[88] *SKYI* 17.162, *RTK* 1.17.175. His personal name, Shu, and his courtesy name, Kung-lu, both can mean "high road," and he misconstrues the prophecy to mean "that which replaces the Han will be high mud road." This prophecy also appears in a short piece of fiction probably from the Six Dynasties period, *Han Wu ku-shih* 漢武故事 (The Story of Emperor Wu of the Han), see Lu Hsün 魯迅, ed., *Ku hsiao-shuo kou-ch'en* 古小說鉤沉 (Recovered Ancient Fiction; Peking; Jen-min wen-hsüeh, 1951), p. 354, as well as orthodox historical accounts such as the biography of Yüan Shu, *Hou Han-shu*, 75.2439.

[89] *SKYI* 78.777, *RTK* 2.78.191.

[90] *SKYI* 9.80, *RTK* 1.9.85.

[91] *SKYI* 80.793–94, *RTK* 2.80.207.

[92] *SKYI* 119.1177, *RTK* 2.119.608.

Hsien's capital is moved from Lo-yang to Ch'ang-an [190],[93] then back to Lo-yang again [196],[94] and finally to Hsü-ch'ang [196],[95] Hsü-ch'ang is the host and Ch'ang-an and Lo-yang are the guests.

In those segments of the narrative in which Liu Pei loses control of Hsü-chou[96] and gains control of Ching-chou,[97] Ching-chou is the host and Hsü-chou is the guest. Whereas in those segments of the narrative in which he gains control of both regions of Szechwan[98] but loses control of Ching-chou,[99] Szechwan is the host and Ching-chou is the guest.

In the segment of the narrative in which Chu-ko Liang is preparing to launch a northern expedition against the Central Plain he first subdues the aboriginal regions to the south.[100] In so doing his attention is not focused on the aboriginal regions but on the Central Plain. Hence the Central Plain is the host and the aboriginal regions are the guest.

This technique of using the guest as a foil for the host is applied not only to places but also to objects.

In the incident in which Li Ju presents poisoned wine, a dagger, and a sash of white silk to Emperor Shao of the Han dynasty [r. 189],[101] the poisoned wine is the host and the dagger and the sash of white silk are the guests.

In the narrative of the hunt at Hsü-t'ien,[102] the description of Ts'ao Ts'ao's shooting the deer is preceded by that of Liu Pei's shooting the rabbit. The deer is the host and the rabbit is the guest.

In the narrative leading up to the battle at the Red Cliffs [208],[103] the description of Chu-ko Liang's borrowing the east wind[104] is preceded by that of his borrowing the arrows.[105] The east wind is the host and the arrows are the guest.

In the incident in which Tung Ch'eng receives the jade girdle from Emperor Hsien of the Han dynasty, that gift is accompanied by the gift of a brocade robe.[106] The girdle is the host and the robe is the guest.

[93] *SKYI* 6.53, *RTK* 1.6.57.
[94] *SKYI* 14.125, *RTK* 1.14.134.
[95] *SKYI* 14.130, *RTK* 1.14.140.
[96] *SKYI* 24.238–39, *RTK* 1.24.257.
[97] *SKYI* 51.513, *RTK* 1.51.535.
[98] *SKYI* 65.655, *RTK* 2.65.55.
[99] Chaps. 75–77.
[100] Chaps. 87–90.
[101] *SKYI* 4.34, *RTK* 1.4.36.
[102] *SKYI* 20.193, *RTK* 1.20.209–11.
[103] Chaps. 43–49.
[104] Chap. 49.
[105] Chap. 46.
[106] *SKYI* 20.194–95, *RTK* 1.20.211–13.

In that segment of the narrative in which Kuan Yü bows to Ts'ao Ts'ao in return for the gift of the prize steed, Red Hare,[107] he also receives gifts of money, a seal of office, and a red robe. The horse is the host and the money, seal, and other gifts are the guest.

In that segment of the narrative in which Ts'ao Ts'ao unearths the copper sparrow and erects a tower in honor of the event, the tower is flanked by lesser structures named Jade Dragon and Golden Phoenix.[108] The sparrow is the host and the dragon and the phoenix are the guests.

Instances of this kind are too numerous to be listed in full. Those who give the book a careful reading will be able to discern in examples such as these the structural principles governing the use of guest and host in literary composition.

10. One of the marvels of *The Romance of the Three Kingdoms* is the technique of portraying different branches growing on the same tree, different leaves stemming from the same branch, different flowers blooming on the same leaf, and different fruits developing from the same flower ["t'ung-shu i-chih, t'ung-chih i-yeh, t'ung-yeh i-hua, t'ung-hua i-kuo chih miao" 同樹異枝、同枝異葉、同葉異花、同花異果之妙].

Writers take pride in their skill at avoiding [*pi* 避] [duplication], but they also take pride in their skillful use of duplication [*fan* 犯]. If a writer wishes to avoid [duplication] by never duplicating [*fan* 犯] himself, his skill at avoiding [duplication] will not be apparent. It is only when he avoids [duplication] in the process of duplicating himself that his skill at avoiding [duplication] becomes manifest.

For example, in describing life in the palace, the author depicts the Empress Dowager Ho [d. 189][109] and then proceeds to depict the Empress Dowager Tung [d. 189].[110] He depicts Empress Fu [d. 214][111] and then proceeds to depict Empress Ts'ao [d. 260].[112] He depicts the Imperial Favorite T'ang[113] and then proceeds to depict the Imperial Favorite Tung.[114] He depicts the ladies Kan and Mi[115] and then proceeds to depict Lady Sun[116] and the consort of the Prince of Pei-ti.[117] He depicts

---

[107] *SKYI* 25.247, *RTK* 1.25.265.
[108] *SKYI* 34.336, *RTK* 1.34.358.
[109] *SKYI* 2.19, *RTK* 1.2.18.
[110] *SKYI* 2.19, *RTK* 1.2.18.
[111] *SKYI* 66.665–67, *RTK* 2.66.64–67.
[112] *SKYI* 80.791, *RTK* 2.80.204.
[113] *SKYI* 4.33, *RTK* 1.4.36–37.
[114] *SKYI* 24.235, *RTK* 1.24.253–54.
[115] Chap. 27.
[116] Chaps. 54–55, 61.
[117] *SKYI* 118.1162–63, *RTK* 2.118.592.

Empress Chen [183−221][118] and Empress Mao [d. 237][119] of the state of Wei and then proceeds to depict Empress Chang of the state of Shu.[120] Yet in his description of all these persons not so much as a single word is the same.

In describing the careers of the relatives of the imperial family by marriage, the author first depicts Ho Chin[121] and then proceeds to depict Tung Ch'eng.[122] After depicting Tung Ch'eng he proceeds to depict Fu Wan.[123] Having depicted Chang Ch'i [d. 254] of the state of Wei[124] he proceeds to depict Ch'üan Shang [d. 258] of the state of Wu.[125] Yet in his descriptions of all these persons not so much as a single word is the same.

In describing powerful ministers, the author first depicts Tung Cho and then proceeds to depict Li Chüeh and Kuo Ssu. After depicting Li Chüeh and Kuo Ssu, he proceeds to depict Ts'ao Ts'ao. After depicting Ts'ao Ts'ao, he proceeds to depict Ts'ao P'i. After depicting Ts'ao P'i, he proceeds to depict Ssu-ma I. After depicting Ssu-ma I, he proceeds to depict the brothers Ssu-ma Shih [208−255] and Ssu-ma Chao [211−265]. After depicting Ssu-ma Shih and Ssu-ma Chao, he proceeds to depict Ssu-ma Yen and even to devote some peripheral attention [*p'ang-hsieh* 旁寫] to Sun Lin [231−259] of the state of Wu. Yet in his descriptions of all these persons not so much as a single word is the same.

Moreover, in the author's depiction of brothers, Yüan T'an [d. 205] and Yüan Shang [d. 207] do not get along with each other,[126] Liu Ch'i [d. 209] and Liu Ts'ung do not get along with each other,[127] and Ts'ao P'i and Ts'ao Chih also do not get along with each other.[128] Yet in these conflicts, Yüan T'an and Yüan Shang both die,[129] Liu Ts'ung dies while Liu Ch'i remains alive,[130] and neither Ts'ao P'i nor Ts'ao Chih dies. Are not these events very different?

In the author's descriptions of marriage alliances, Tung Cho seeks a

[118] *SKYI* 33.326−27, *RTK* 1.33.346.
[119] *SKYI* 105.1054, *RTK* 2.105.480.
[120] *SKYI* 109.1087−89, *RTK* 2.109.516−18.
[121] *SKYI* 2.18, *RTK* 1.2.18.
[122] Chaps. 20−24.
[123] *SKYI* 66.665−67, *RTK* 2.66.64−65.
[124] *SKYI* 109.1087−89, *RTK* 2.109.516−17.
[125] *SKYI* 113.1119−20, *RTK* 2.113.547. Read *ch'üan* 全 for *ch'ien* 錢.
[126] Chaps. 31−33.
[127] Chaps. 34−41.
[128] Chaps. 34, 79.
[129] *SKYI* 33.351, 356; *RTK* 1.33.329, 333.
[130] *SKYI* 41.410, *RTK* 1.41.432.

marriage alliance with Sun Chien,[131] Yüan Shu agrees to a marriage alliance with Lü Pu,[132] Ts'ao Ts'ao agrees to a marriage alliance with Yüan T'an,[133] while Sun Ch'üan forms a marriage alliance with Liu Pei[134] and seeks one with Kuan Yü.[135] But these alliances are variously rejected and never consented to, or consented to and subsequently rejected, or agreed to under false pretenses but consummated nevertheless, or wholeheartedly agreed to but never consummated. Are not these events very different?

Moreover, both Wang Yün [137–192] and Chou Yü resort to plots that depend on the seductiveness of women,[136] but they differ in that one succeeds and the other does not.

Tung Cho and Lü Pu become enemies[137] and Li Chüeh and Kuo Ssu do likewise,[138] but they differ in that in the second case they are [eventually] reconciled and in the first they are not.

There are two occasions on which Emperor Hsien issues secret edicts, but the first is kept secret[139] and the second becomes known.[140] There are also two occasions when Ma T'eng leads troops against usurpers of state power,[141] but the first time he acts openly while the second time he tries to hide his intentions. Such are the differences between them.

There are two occasions on which Lü Pu kills an adopted father, but the first is motivated by greed[142] and the second by lust.[143] In the first case his private desires cause him to disregard the public good, whereas in the second case he is able to act in the name of the public good in order to accomplish his private desires. Such are the differences between them.

There are two occasions on which Chao Yün saves the life of his infant master, Liu Shan, but the first occurs on land[144] and the second on water.[145] In the first case he receives his charge from the hands of one of his master's wives, Lady Mi,[146] and in the second he wrests him from the

[131] *SKYI* 6.52, *RTK* 1.6.55.
[132] *SKYI* 16.153–54, *RTK* 1.16.164.
[133] *SKYI* 32.320, *RTK* 1.32.340.
[134] Chaps. 54–61.
[135] *SKYI* 73.731–32, *RTK* 2.73.140.
[136] Chaps. 8–9, 54–55.
[137] Chaps. 8–9.
[138] Chap. 13.
[139] *SKYI* 10.88, *RTK* 1.10.93.
[140] Chaps. 20–21.
[141] *SKYI* 10.88–90, 57.570–72; *RTK* 1.10.93–94, 1.57.597–600.
[142] *SKYI* 3.29, *RTK* 1.3.32.
[143] *SKYI* 9.82, *RTK* 1.9.86.
[144] *SKYI* 41–42.415–19, *RTK* 1.41–42.437–39.
[145] *SKYI* 61.609–11, *RTK* 2.61.4–6.
[146] *SKYI* 41.414, *RTK* 1.41.437.

breast of another of his master's wives, Lady Sun.[147] Such are the differences between them.

As for the description of events that hinge on the deployment of water or fire in battle, the author does not stop short with a single instance in either case. Ts'ao Ts'ao resorts to the use of water at Hsia-p'ei[148] and again at Chi-chou.[149] Kuan Yü resorts to the use of water at Pai-ho[150] and again at Tseng-k'ou ch'uan.[151] Lü Pu resorts to the use of fire at P'u-yang,[152] Ts'ao Ts'ao resorts to the use of fire at Wu-ch'ao,[153] Chou Yü resorts to the use of fire at the Red Cliffs,[154] Lu Hsün resorts to the use of fire at Hsiao-t'ing,[155] Hsü Sheng resorts to the use of fire at Nan-hsü,[156] and Chu-ko Liang resorts to the use of fire at Po-wang[157] and Hsin-yeh[158] and then again at P'an-she Valley[159] and Shang-fang Valley.[160] In all of these instances, from first to last, is there the slightest duplication?

Even more remarkably, Meng Huo is captured seven times,[161] Chu-ko Liang mounts six campaigns through the Ch'i Mountains,[162] and Chiang Wei launches nine punitive expeditions against the Central Plain.[163] Yet in the descriptions of all of these events one cannot find so much as a single instance of verbal duplication.

This kind of writing is marvelous indeed. It is like a tree with branches, leaves, and flowers like any other tree that nevertheless plants its roots, puts forth its stems, bursts into bloom, and bears fruit in such a way that it produces a profusion of colors, no shade of which is like any other. From this the reader may awaken to the fact that in literature there is not only a technique for avoiding [duplication] but also one for employing duplication.

11. One of the marvels of *The Romance of the Three Kingdoms* is the

---

[147] *SKYI* 61.610, *RTK* 2.61.5.
[148] *SKYI* 19.186, *RTK* 1.19.202.
[149] *SKYI* 32.322, *RTK* 1.32.344.
[150] *SKYI* 40.403, *RTK* 1.40.426.
[151] *SKYI* 74.742–43, *RTK* 2.74.153.
[152] *SKYI* 12.106–7, *RTK* 1.12.113–14.
[153] *SKYI* 30.301, *RTK* 1.30.321.
[154] Chaps. 49–50.
[155] *SKYI* 84.832–33, *RTK* 2.84.247–48.
[156] *SKYI* 86.857, *RTK* 2.86.275.
[157] *SKYI* 39.393–94, *RTK* 1.39.416.
[158] *SKYI* 40.402–3, *RTK* 1.40.425–26.
[159] *SKYI* 90.894–96, *RTK* 2.90.316–20.
[160] *SKYI* 103.1030, *RTK* 2.103.455.
[161] Chaps. 87–90.
[162] Chaps. 92–104.
[163] Chaps. 107–19.

technique of making the stars move and the dipper revolve and causing rain to inundate things and wind to overturn them ["hsing-i tou-chuan, yü-fu feng-fan chih miao" 星移斗轉, 雨覆風翻之妙].

There is a poem by Tu Fu [712–770] that says, "The floating clouds in the sky are like white garments, / But in a moment they have changed to gray dogs."[164] These lines allude to the unpredictability of events in this world. The writing in *The Romance of the Three Kingdoms* is of the same nature.

At first Ho Chin plots to eliminate the eunuchs,[165] but in the end the eunuchs kill Ho Chin,[166] which is a reversal [*pien* 變].

At first Lü Pu is an adherent of Ting Yüan [d. 189], but in the end Lü Pu kills Ting Yüan,[167] which is a reversal.

At first Tung Cho attracts Lü Pu into his service,[168] but in the end Lü Pu kills Tung Cho,[169] which is a reversal.

At first Ch'en Kung [d. 199] releases Ts'ao Ts'ao,[170] but in the end Ch'en Kung is tempted to kill Ts'ao Ts'ao,[171] which is a reversal.

Ch'en Kung does not kill Ts'ao Ts'ao,[172] but in the end Ts'ao Ts'ao kills Ch'en Kung,[173] which is a reversal.

At first Wang Yün refuses to pardon Li Chüeh and Kuo Ssu,[174] but in the end Li Chüeh and Kuo Ssu kill Wang Yün,[175] which is a reversal.

At first Sun Chien becomes disenchanted with Yüan Shu,[176] but in the end Yüan Shu sends Sun Chien the letter that leads to his death,[177] which is a reversal.

At first Liu Piao seeks the aid of Yüan Shao,[178] but in the end Liu Piao kills Sun Chien,[179] which is a reversal.

At first Liu Pei joins Yüan Shao in order to attack Tung Cho,[180] but

---

[164] The complete text of this poem can be found in *A Concordance to the Poems of Tu Fu*, 3 vols. (Peiping: Harvard-Yenching Institute, 1940), vol. 2, p. 191.20.

[165] *SKYI* 2.18, *RTK* 1.2.19.

[166] *SKYI* 3.24, *RTK* 1.3.25.

[167] *SKYI* 3.29, *RTK* 1.3.32.

[168] *SKYI* 3.29, *RTK* 1.3.31.

[169] *SKYI* 9.82, *RTK* 1.9.86.

[170] *SKYI* 4.38, *RTK* 1.4.41.

[171] *SKYI* 4–5.39–41, *RTK* 1.4–5. 42–43.

[172] *SKYI* 4.41, *RTK* 1.5.43.

[173] *SKYI* 19.188, *RTK* 1.19.204–5.

[174] *SKYI* 9.83, *RTK* 1.9.88.

[175] *SKYI* 9.86, *RTK* 1.9.91.

[176] *SKYI* 5.45, *RTK* 1.5.48.

[177] *SKYI* 7.64, *RTK* 1.7.68.

[178] *SKYI* 7.65, *RTK* 1.7.71.

[179] *SKYI* 7.66, *RTK* 1.7.71.

[180] *SKYI* 5.46, *RTK* 1.5.45.

in the end he helps Kung-sun Tsan to attack Yüan Shao,[181] which is a reversal.

At first Liu Pei relieves the siege of Hsü-chou,[182] but in the end he gets control of Hsü-chou,[183] which is a reversal.

At first Lü Pu is going to attack Liu Pei,[184] but in the end he offers a welcome to Liu Pei,[185] which is a reversal.

At first Lü Pu severs relations with Yüan Shu,[186] but in the end he seeks the aid of Yüan Shu,[187] which is a reversal.

At first Liu Pei helps Lü Pu to attack Yüan Shu,[188] but in the end he encourages Ts'ao Ts'ao to kill Lü Pu,[189] which is a reversal.

At first Liu Pei joins forces with Ts'ao Ts'ao,[190] but in the end he attacks Ts'ao Ts'ao,[191] which is a reversal.

At first Liu Pei attacks Yüan Shao,[192] but in the end he seeks refuge with Yüan Shao,[193] which is a reversal.

At first Liu Pei helps Yüan Shao to attack Ts'ao Ts'ao,[194] but in the end Kuan Yü helps Ts'ao Ts'ao to attack Yüan Shao,[195] which is a reversal.

At first Kuan Yü sets out to find Liu Pei,[196] but in the end Chang Fei wants to kill Kuan Yü,[197] which is a reversal.

At first Kuan Yü wants to kill Ts'ao Ts'ao at Hsü-t'ien,[198] but in the end he lets Ts'ao Ts'ao escape on the Hua-jung road,[199] which is a reversal.

At first Ts'ao Ts'ao pursues Liu Pei,[200] but in the end Liu Pei allies himself with Sun Ch'üan and defeats Ts'ao Ts'ao,[201] which is a reversal.

---

[181] *SKYI* 7.63, *RTK* 1.7.67.
[182] *SKYI* 11.99–101, *RTK* 1.11.103–6.
[183] *SKYI* 12.108, *RTK* 1.12.116.
[184] *SKYI* 15.136, *RTK* 1.15.147.
[185] *SKYI* 15.136–37, *RTK* 1.15.147–48.
[186] *SKYI* 16.158, *RTK* 1.16.173.
[187] *SKYI* 19.84, *RTK* 1.19.199.
[188] *SKYI* 17.164, *RTK* 1.17.177–78.
[189] *SKYI* 19.189, *RTK* 1.19.205.
[190] *SKYI* 17.163, *RTK* 1.17.179.
[191] *SKYI* 31.310, *RTK* 1.31.329–30.
[192] *SKYI* 7.63, *RTK* 1.7.67.
[193] *SKYI* 24.238–39, *RTK* 1.24.257–58.
[194] *SKYI* 24.238, *RTK* 1.24.257–58.
[195] *SKYI* 25–26.250–59, *RTK* 1.25–26.268–77.
[196] *SKYI* 26.259, *RTK* 1.26.277.
[197] *SKYI* 28.276–77, *RTK* 1.28.295.
[198] *SKYI* 20.193, *RTK* 1.20.210.
[199] *SKYI* 50.503, *RTK* 1.50.525.
[200] Chaps. 39–42.
[201] Chaps. 43–50.

At first Sun Ch'üan is an enemy of Liu Piao's,[202] but in the end Lu Su proffers his condolences after the deaths of Liu Piao[203] and Liu Ch'i,[204] which is a reversal.

At first Chu-ko Liang offers to help Chou Yü,[205] but in the end Chou Yü wants to kill Chu-ko Liang,[206] which is a reversal.

At first Chou Yü wants to kill Liu Pei,[207] but in the end Sun Ch'üan makes a marriage alliance with Liu Pei,[208] which is a reversal.

At first it is intended that Lady Sun be used to control Liu Pei,[209] but in the end Lady Sun helps Liu Pei,[210] which is a reversal.

At first Chu-ko Liang so infuriates Chou Yü that he kills him,[211] but in the end he weeps over the loss of Chou Yü,[212] which is a reversal.

At first Liu Pei refuses to accept Ching-chou when it is offered to him by Liu Piao,[213] but in the end he borrows Ching-chou from Wu,[214] which is a reversal.

At first Liu Chang wants to make an alliance with Ts'ao Ts'ao,[215] but in the end he invites Liu Pei into his territory,[216] which is a reversal.

At first Liu Chang invites Liu Pei into his territory,[217] but in the end Liu Pei seizes control of his territory,[218] which is a reversal.

At first Liu Pei offers to divide up the territory of Ching-chou,[219] but in the end Lü Meng [178–219] attacks Ching-chou,[220] which is a reversal.

At first Liu Pei inflicts a setback upon the forces of Sun Ch'üan,[221] but in the end Lu Hsün defeats Liu Pei,[222] which is a reversal.

---

[202] *SKYI* 7.66, *RTK* 1.7.70–71.

[203] *SKYI* 42.423, *RTK* 1.42.445.

[204] *SKYI* 53.533, *RTK* 1.53.557.

[205] Chaps. 43–49.

[206] *SKYI* 49.490–91, *RTK* 1.49.511–12.

[207] *SKYI* 45.451–52, *RTK* 1.45.471.

[208] Chap. 54.

[209] Chap. 54.

[210] Chap. 55.

[211] *SKYI* 57.565, *RTK* 1.57.590.

[212] *SKYI* 57.565–66, *RTK* 1.57.591–92.

[213] *SKYI* 39.388–99, 40.398; *RTK* 1.39.410, 40.420.

[214] *SKYI* 54.536–37, *RTK* 1.54.561.

[215] *SKYI* 60.594–97, *RTK* 1.60.623–27.

[216] *SKYI* 60.601, *RTK* 1.60.633.

[217] *SKYI* 60.601, *RTK* 1.60.633.

[218] *SKYI* 65.655, *RTK* 2.65.55.

[219] *SKYI* 66.660, *RTK* 2.66.59.

[220] *SKYI* 75.751, *RTK* 2.75.163.

[221] Chaps. 83–84.

[222] *SKYI* 84.832–33, *RTK* 2.84.247–49.

At first Sun Ch'üan seeks the aid of Ts'ao P'i,[223] but in the end Ts'ao P'i wants to attack Sun Ch'üan,[224] which is a reversal.

At first Liu Pei feels enmity toward Wu,[225] but in the end Chu-ko Liang makes an alliance with Wu,[226] which is a reversal.

At first Liu Feng [d. 220] pays heed to Meng Ta [d. 228],[227] but in the end he attacks Meng Ta,[228] which is a reversal.

At first Meng Ta deserts the cause of Liu Pei,[229] but in the end he wants to give his allegiance to Chu-ko Liang,[230] which is a reversal.

At first Ma T'eng and Liu Pei are coconspirators,[231] but in the end his son, Ma Ch'ao, attacks Liu Pei,[232] which is a reversal.

At first Ma Ch'ao comes to the aid of Liu Chang,[233] but in the end he gives his allegiance to Liu Pei,[234] which is a reversal.

At first Chiang Wei opposes Chu-ko Liang,[235] but in the end he helps Chu-ko Liang,[236] which is a reversal.

At first Hsia-hou Pa serves under Ssu-ma I, but in the end he serves under Chiang Wei,[237] which is a reversal.

At first Chung Hui wants to neutralize Teng Ai,[238] but in the end it is Wei Kuan [220–291] who has Teng Ai killed,[239] which is a reversal.

At first Chung Hui is tricked by Chiang Wei,[240] but in the end he is killed by his own officers,[241] which is a reversal.

At first Yang Hu deals amicably with Lu K'ang,[242] but in the end he proposes a punitive expedition against Sun Hao,[243] which is a reversal.

At first Yang Hu proposes a punitive expedition against the state of

---

[223] *SKYI* 82.810, *RTK* 2.82.224.
[224] *SKYI* 85.839, *RTK* 2.85.255.
[225] *SKYI* 78.773, *RTK* 2.78.186.
[226] *SKYI* 86.850–54, *RTK* 2.86.266–70.
[227] *SKYI* 76.759–60, *RTK* 2.76.173.
[228] *SKYI* 79.787, *RTK* 2.79.201.
[229] *SKYI* 79.785, *RTK* 2.79.199.
[230] *SKYI* 94.934–37, *RTK* 2.94.359–63.
[231] Chaps. 20–21.
[232] *SKYI* 64.645, *RTK* 2.64.44.
[233] *SKYI* 64.645, *RTK* 2.64.44.
[234] *SKYI* 65.653, *RTK* 2.65.52.
[235] *SKYI* 92–93.917–23, *RTK* 2.92–93.341–46.
[236] *SKYI* 92.923–24, *RTK* 2.92.346–47.
[237] *SKYI* 107.1071, *RTK* 2.107.499.
[238] Chaps. 117–19.
[239] *SKYI* 119.1173, *RTK* 2.119.603.
[240] *SKYI* 118–19.1164–73, *RTK* 2.118–19.594–603.
[241] *SKYI* 119.1173, *RTK* 2.119.602.
[242] *SKYI* 120.1182–83, *RTK* 2.120.612–13.
[243] *SKYI* 120.1184, *RTK* 2.120.614.

Wu,[244] but in the end the task is undertaken by Tu Yü and Wang Chün [206–285],[245] which is a reversal.

On the one hand, the component parts of this work are interrelated [*hu-ying* 呼應] in such a way that one cannot read the beginning without some presentiment of the end; yet, on the other hand, the reversals that characterize it are so unpredictable that one cannot anticipate what will happen from one passage to the next. The fact that such presentiments arise shows that the writing in *The Romance of the Three Kingdoms* is finely wrought, while the fact that the reader cannot anticipate what will happen next shows that it is also magical in its effects.

12. One of the marvels of *The Romance of the Three Kingdoms* is the technique of intersecting mountain ranges with clouds and interlacing streams with bridges ["heng-yün tuan shan, heng-ch'iao so hsi chih miao" 橫雲斷山, 橫橋鎖溪之妙].

There are some kinds of literary material that benefit from consecutive [*lien* 連] treatment and some that benefit from nonconsecutive [*tuan* 斷] treatment.

For instance, Kuan Yü's slaying of the generals in command of the five barriers,[246] Liu Pei's three visits to the thatched cottage of Chu-ko Liang,[247] and Chu-ko Liang's seven captures of Meng Huo[248] are examples of kinds of literary material that benefit from consecutive treatment. Whereas the three occasions on which Chu-ko Liang infuriates Chou Yü,[249] his six campaigns through the Ch'i Mountains,[250] and Chiang Wei's nine punitive expeditions against the Central Plain[251] are examples of kinds of literary material that benefit from nonconsecutive treatment.

This is due to the fact that short passages, if they are not treated consecutively [*lien-hsü* 連敘], will seem disconnected, whereas long passages, if they are treated consecutively [*lien-hsü* 連敘], will run the danger of becoming tedious. Therefore other matters must be interpolated into the account of these events in order to obtain a rich narrative texture [*ts'o-tsung* 錯綜] and fulfill to the utmost the possibilities inherent in the material. Few of the novelists [*pai-kuan chia* 稗官家] of later times have been able to measure up to the achievements of the author in this regard.

[244] *SKYI* 120.1184, *RTK* 2.120.614.
[245] *SKYI* 120.1185–89, *RTK* 2.120.615–20.
[246] Chap. 27.
[247] Chaps. 37–38.
[248] Chaps. 87–90.
[249] Chaps. 51, 55, and 56.
[250] Chaps. 92–104.
[251] Chaps. 107–19.

13. One of the marvels of *The Romance of the Three Kingdoms* is the technique of making sleet appear when it is about to snow and thunder reverberate when it is about to rain ["chiang hsüeh chien hsien, chiang yü wen lei chih miao" 將雪見霰, 將雨聞雷之妙].

Every significant passage [*cheng-wen* 正文] is preceded by an inconsequential one [*hsien-wen* 閑文] that serves to lead up to it. Every major passage [*ta-wen* 大文] is preceded by a minor passage [*hsiao-wen* 小文] that serves to inaugurate it.

For example, before describing Ts'ao Ts'ao's defeat by fire at P'u-yang,[252] the author first inserts an inconsequential passage about the fire in the house of Mi Chu[253] in order to lead up to it.

Before describing K'ung Jung's request for aid from Liu Pei,[254] the author first inserts an inconsequential passage about the way in which K'ung Jung gained entrée to Li Ying [110–169][255] in order to lead up to it.

Before embarking on the major passage describing the burning of Ts'ao Ts'ao's fleet at the battle of the Red Cliffs,[256] the author first inserts two minor passages about the use of fire in the battles at Po-wang[257] and Hsin-yeh[258] in order to lead up to it.

Before embarking on the major passage describing Chu-ko Liang's six campaigns through the Ch'i Mountains,[259] the author first inserts a minor passage about his seven captures of Meng Huo[260] in order to lead up to it.

"When the men of the state of Lu were about to perform a ceremony dedicated to the Sovereign on High they would always first perform a ceremony in the ducal school."[261] The marvels produced by literary artistry are of the same kind.

14. One of the marvels of *The Romance of the Three Kingdoms* is the technique of making ripples follow in the wake of waves and drizzle

[252] *SKYI* 12.106–7, *RTK* 1.12.113–14.
[253] *SKYI* 11.95–96, *RTK* 1.11.100.
[254] *SKYI* 11.97, *RTK* 1.11.103.
[255] *SKYI* 11.96, *RTK* 1.11.100–101. Read *ying* 膺 for *hung* 弘.
[256] Chaps. 49–50.
[257] *SKYI* 39.393–94, *RTK* 1.39.415–16.
[258] *SKYI* 40.402–3, *RTK* 1.40.425–26.
[259] Chaps. 92–104.
[260] Chaps. 87–90.
[261] This quotation is from the *Li-chi* 禮記 (Book of Rites) and appears immediately prior to the quotation made by Chin Sheng-t'an in his "How to Read the *Fifth Book of Genius*," item 57, chap. II above. See *Shih-san ching ching-wen* 十三經文 (Text of the Thirteen Classics; Taipei: K'ai-ming shu-tien, 1955), "Li-ch'i" 禮器 chapter of the *Li-chi*, p. 49, sec. 24, translated by James Legge in his *Li Chi: The Book of Rites*, 2 vols. (New Hyde Park, N.Y.: University Books, 1967), vol. 1, p. 407. Read *p'an* 頖 for *p'in* 頻.

continue after rain ["lang-hou po-wen, yü-hou mo-mu chih miao" 浪後波紋, 雨後霢霂之妙].

Every passage of unusually fine writing is preceded by a prelude [*hsien-sheng* 先聲] and succeeded by a postlude [*yü-shih* 餘勢].

For example, the story of Tung Cho[262] is continued [*chi* 繼] by that of the scoundrels who had been his subordinates.[263]

The story of the Yellow Turbans[264] is supplemented [*yen* 衍] by that of their surviving remnants.[265]

The story of Liu Pei's three visits to Chu-ko Liang's thatched cottage[266] is enhanced [*ying-tai* 映帶] by the subsequent passage describing Liu Ch'i thrice requesting help from Chu-ko Liang.[267]

The major passage describing Chu-ko Liang's campaigns[268] is re-echoed [*tang-yang* 蕩漾] in the passage describing Chiang Wei's expeditions against the state of Wei.[269]

Examples of this kind are not to be found in other books.

15. One of the marvels of *The Romance of the Three Kingdoms* is the technique of introducing cold ice to break the heat and cool breezes to sweep away the dust ["han-ping p'o-je, liang-feng sao-ch'en chih miao" 寒冰破熱, 涼風掃塵之妙].

For example, just as Kuan Yü is engaged in slaying the generals in command of the five barriers there suddenly occurs the passage describing his encounter with the abbot, P'u-ching, in the Chen-kuo Temple.[270]

No sooner does Liu Pei escape from his enemies by successfully leaping across T'an Stream on horseback[271] than there occurs the passage describing his encounter with Ssu-ma Hui in his Water Mirror Hermitage.[272]

Just as Sun Ts'e is consolidating his regime in the Southeast there suddenly occurs the passage describing his encounter with the Taoist necromancer, Yü Chi.[273]

Just as Ts'ao Ts'ao is being enfeoffed as Prince of Wei there suddenly

[262] Chaps. 1–9.
[263] Chaps. 9–17.
[264] Chap. 1.
[265] *SKYI* 2.13–14, *RTK* 1.2.13–14.
[266] Chaps. 37–38.
[267] *SKYI* 39.389–90, *RTK* 1.39.410–12.
[268] Chaps. 92–104.
[269] Chaps. 107–19.
[270] *SKYI* 27.265–66, *RTK* 1.27.284–86.
[271] *SKYI* 34.342–43, *RTK* 1.34.366–67.
[272] *SKYI* 35.347–49, *RTK* 1.35.369–72.
[273] *SKYI* 29.286–90, *RTK* 1.29.304–8.

occurs the passage describing his encounter with the magician Tso Tz'u.[274]

In the course of Liu Pei's three visits to the thatched hut of Chu-ko Liang there suddenly occurs the passage describing his encounter with Ts'ui Chou-p'ing, during which they sit down and have an idle chat.[275]

Soon after Kuan Yü has flooded the seven armies[276] there suddenly occurs the passage describing the enlightenment of his departed spirit on a moonlit night at Yü-ch'üan Mountain.[277]

Furthermore, there are such episodes as that in which Chu-ko Liang, in the course of his campaign against the southern aborigines,[278] suddenly encounters Meng Chieh[279] and that in which Lu Hsün, in pursuit of Liu Pei's army, suddenly meets Huang Ch'eng-yen.[280] There are such episodes as that in which Chang Jen, on the verge of meeting the enemy in battle, suddenly asks to have his future foretold by Tzu-hsü Shang-jen [The Priest Purple Void][281] and that in which Liu Pei, as he is about to launch his punitive campaign against the state of Wu, suddenly asks to have his future foretold by Li I, the Old Man of Ch'ing-ch'eng.[282]

The advice of all these persons, whether they be Buddhists, Taoists, hermits, or recluses, is always requested at moments of crisis in the story. Such passages have the effect of suddenly stilling the anxious mind and completely cleansing the troubled breast.

16. One of the marvels of *The Romance of the Three Kingdoms* is the technique of interrupting drums with woodwinds and interspersing strings among the bells ["sheng-hsiao chia ku, ch'in-se chien chung chih miao" 笙簫夾鼓, 琴瑟間鐘之妙].

For example, in the course of describing the havoc wrought by the Yellow Turbans, the author suddenly inserts the passage about the quarrel between the Empress Dowagers Ho and Tung.[283]

In the course of describing the depredations of Tung Cho, the author suddenly inserts the passage about Tiao-ch'an's rendezvous with Lü Pu in the Feng-i Pavilion.[284]

In the course of describing the rampages of Li Chüeh and Kuo Ssu,

---

[274] *SKYI* 68–69.685–90, *RTK* 2.68–69.88–92.
[275] *SKYI* 37.367, *RTK* 1.37.390–91.
[276] *SKYI* 74.742–43, *RTK* 2.74.153–54.
[277] *SKYI* 77.765–66, *RTK* 2.77.179–80.
[278] Chaps. 87–90.
[279] *SKYI* 89.883–84, *RTK* 2.89.304–5.
[280] *SKYI* 84.836, *RTK* 2.84.252.
[281] *SKYI* 62.621, *RTK* 2.62.17–18. Read *shang* 上 for *chang* 丈.
[282] *SKYI* 81.804–5, *RTK* 2.81.218–19.
[283] *SKYI* 2.19–20, *RTK* 1.2.20.
[284] *SKYI* 8.74–76, *RTK* 1.8.79–80.

the author suddenly inserts the passage about the relationship between the wives of Yang Piao [142–225] and Kuo Ssu.[285]

In the course of describing the battle of Hsia-p'ei, the author suddenly inserts the passage about Lü Pu's attempt to deliver his daughter to Yüan Shu[286] and his affectionate concern for the safety of his wife, née Yen.[287]

In the course of describing the battle at Chi-chou, the author suddenly inserts the passage about Yüan T'an's loss of his promised bride[288] and Ts'ao P'i's marriage to the wife of Yüan Hsi, née Chen [183–221].[289]

In the course of describing the coup d'état in Ching-chou following the death of Liu Piao, the author suddenly inserts the passage about the advocacy by his widow, Lady Ts'ai, of the course of surrender to Ts'ao Ts'ao.[290]

In the course of describing the events leading up to the battle of the Red Cliffs,[291] the author suddenly inserts the passage about Ts'ao Ts'ao's desire to obtain possession of the two Ch'iao sisters.[292]

In the course of describing the battle at Wan-ch'eng, the author suddenly inserts the passage about the affair between Ts'ao Ts'ao and Chang Chi's [d. 196] widow, née Tsou.[293]

In the course of describing Chao Yün's seizure of Kuei-yang, the author suddenly inserts the passage about Chao Fan's widowed sister-in-law, née Fan, serving him with wine.[294]

In the course of describing Liu Pei's struggle for control of Ching-chou, the author suddenly inserts the passage about his marriage to Sun Ch'üan's sister, Lady Sun.[295]

In the course of describing Sun Ch'üan's battle with Huang Tsu, the author suddenly inserts the passage about Sun I's [184–204] wife, née Hsü, avenging the death of her husband.[296]

In the course of describing Ssu-ma I's elimination of Ts'ao Shuang [d. 249], the author suddenly inserts the passage about Hsin Hsien-ying's [191–269] advice to her younger brother, Hsin Ch'ang.[297]

[285] *SKYI* 13.115–16, *RTK* 1.13.124–25.
[286] *SKYI* 19.185, *RTK* 1.19.201.
[287] *SKYI* 19.183, *RTK* 1.19.198–99.
[288] *SKYI* 32–33.320–28, *RTK* 1.32–33.340–49.
[289] *SKYI* 33.326–27, *RTK* 1.33.347.
[290] *SKYI* 40.398–400, *RTK* 1.40.422–23.
[291] Chaps. 49–50.
[292] *SKYI* 48.480, *RTK* 1.48.502.
[293] *SKYI* 16.156, *RTK* 1.16.170–71.
[294] *SKYI* 52.522, *RTK* 1.52.544.
[295] Chap. 54.
[296] *SKYI* 38.380–81, *RTK* 1.38.403–4.
[297] *SKYI* 107.1067, *RTK* 2.107.493.

In addition, there is more than one instance where the author refers in passing to the erudition of Cheng Hsüan's maidservants while describing Yüan Shao's attack on Ts'ao Ts'ao[298] or where he mentions the story of Ts'ai Yung's daughter, Ts'ai Yen, in the course of describing Ts'ao Ts'ao's expedition to save Han-chung.[299]

Everyone knows that *The Romance of the Three Kingdoms* is about the struggles for power of dragons and tigers, but not everyone realizes that it is also replete with the deeds of lady phoenixes, orioles, and swallows. As a result, the reader periodically catches a glimpse of a red skirt through the phalanxes of marching men or spots a powdered face in the shadow of the battle pennants. This effect is achieved by presenting stories of heroic men and tales of beautiful women in a single book.

17. One of the marvels of *The Romance of the Three Kingdoms* is the technique of sowing seeds a year in advance and making preliminary moves to set up later strategies ["ko-nien hsia-chung, hsien-shih fu-cho chih miao" 隔年下種, 先時伏著之妙].

Good gardeners sow their seeds in the ground and wait for them to come up at the proper time. Good players of encirclement chess make seemingly inconsequential moves many plays in advance, the significance of which only becomes apparent many moves later. The art of literary narrative is analogous to this.

For example, Liu Chang, whose power base is in western Szechwan, is the son of Liu Yen. Therefore the author in the very first chapter, before introducing Liu Pei, first introduces Liu Yen[300] in order to fore-shadow [*fu-hsia i-pi* 伏下一筆] Liu Pei's later conquest of western Szechwan.[301]

In the course of describing the defeats Liu Pei inflicts on the Yellow Turbans, the author first introduces Ts'ao Ts'ao[302] and then Tung Cho,[303] in order to foreshadow Tung Cho's later disruption of the state[304] and Ts'ao Ts'ao's subsequent monopoly of power.[305]

Chao Yün does not give his allegiance to Liu Pei until the reunion of the heroes at Ku-ch'eng,[306] but long before this point the author describes Liu Pei's first meeting with Chao Yün during the battle between

---

[298] *SKYI* 22.211, *RTK* 1.22.228.

[299] *SKYI* 71.710, *RTK* 2.71.116.

[300] *SKYI* 1.4, *RTK* 1.1.4.

[301] *SKYI* 65.655, *RTK* 2.65.55.

[302] *SKYI* 1.8–9, *RTK* 1.1.8–9.

[303] *SKYI* 1.10, *RTK* 1.1.10.

[304] Chaps. 3–9.

[305] Chaps. 20–78.

[306] *SKYI* 28.280–81, *RTK* 1.28.300.

Yüan Shao and Kung-sun Tsan at the P'an River[307] in order to fore-shadow this subsequent development.

Ma Ch'ao does not give his allegiance to Liu Pei until after his battle with Chang Fei at Chia-meng Pass,[308] but long before this point the author describes Liu Pei's fellowship with Ma Ch'ao's father, Ma T'eng, when Tung Ch'eng receives the secret edict from the emperor,[309] in order to foreshadow this subsequent development.

P'ang T'ung does not give his allegiance to Liu Pei until after the death of Chou Yü,[310] but long before this point the author has Ssu-ma Hui's servant mention P'ang T'ung's name to Liu Pei at the Water Mirror Hermitage[311] in order to foreshadow this subsequent development.

Chu-ko Liang does not repine over the fact that "man proposes, but Heaven disposes" until after the rain puts out the fire he has set to trap Ssu-ma I at Shang-fang Valley,[312] but long before this point the au-thor inserts Ssu-ma Hui's remark that Chu-ko Liang has not been born at the right time[313] and Ts'ui Chou-p'ing's statement that Heaven cannot be coerced[314] during his description of Liu Pei's three visits to Chu-ko Liang's thatched hut in order to foreshadow this subsequent development.

The end of Liu Shan's reign of more than forty years as emperor of the state of Shu-Han does not come until after chapter 110,[315] but long before this point the author describes the omen of the crane that screeches more than forty times on the night of his birth in Hsin-yeh[316] in order to foreshadow this subsequent development.

Chiang Wei's nine punitive expeditions against the Central Plain do not occur until after chapter 105, but long before this point the author describes Chu-ko Liang's recruitment of Chiang Wei during his first expedition through the Ch'i Mountains[317] in order to foreshadow this subsequent development.

Chiang Wei does not encounter Teng Ai until his fifth punitive expedition against the Central Plain and does not encounter Chung Hui

[307] *SKYI* 7.63, *RTK* 1.7.67.
[308] *SKYI* 65.650–53, *RTK* 2.65.47–50.
[309] *SKYI* 20–21.197–201, *RTK* 1.20–21.216–19.
[310] *SKYI* 57.568, *RTK* 1.57.594.
[311] *SKYI* 35.347, *RTK* 1.35.369.
[312] *SKYI* 103.1030, *RTK* 2.103.455.
[313] *SKYI* 37.366, *RTK* 1.37.388.
[314] *SKYI* 37.367, *RTK* 1.37.390.
[315] *SKYI* 118.1162, *RTK* 2.118.591.
[316] *SKYI* 34.338, *RTK* 1.34.360.
[317] *SKYI* 92–93.917–23, *RTK* 2.92–93.341–46.

until after his ninth punitive expedition against the Central Plain,[318] but long before these campaigns occur the author has Hsia-hou Pa mention their two names to him[319] in order to foreshadow subsequent developments.

Ts'ao P'i does not usurp the throne of the Han dynasty until chapter 80,[320] but long before this point, at the end of chapter 32,[321] the author mentions the auspicious omen of the blue and purple clouds that had appeared over the house at the time of his birth in order to foreshadow this subsequent development.

Sun Ch'üan does not assume the prerogative of declaring a reign period of his own [222] until the beginning of chapter 86,[322] but long before this point, in chapter 38,[323] the author relates the omen that his mother, Lady Wu [d. 207], dreamed that the sun entered her bosom on the day of his birth, in order to foreshadow this subsequent development.

The Ssu-ma family does not usurp the throne of the state of Wei until chapter 119,[324] but long before this point, in chapter 78,[325] the author relates Ts'ao Ts'ao's dream in which he saw three horses [the character *ma* 馬 in the surname Ssu-ma means "horse"] feeding out of the same trough, in order to forshadow this subsequent development.

In addition to those mentioned here, further examples of this device of foreshadowing [*fu-pi* 伏筆] are too numerous to count.

I have often observed that the novelists [*pai-kuan chia* 稗官家] of recent years, whenever they find themselves in inextricable difficulties, solve the problem by producing a new character out of thin air or by creating an incident out of whole cloth, with the result that what follows seems cut off and unrelated to what comes before. If they were required to read *The Romance of the Three Kingdoms* how could they avoid perspiring with shame?

18. One of the marvels of *The Romance of the Three Kingdoms* is the technique of inserting additional threads to fill out the figure and adjusting the needlework to balance the pattern ["t'ien-ssu pu-chin, i-chen yün-hsiu chih miao" 添絲補錦, 移針勻繡之妙].

Effective narrative [*hsü-shih* 敍事] technique demands that what is omitted in one passage should be supplied in another and that when

---

318 *SKYI* 112.1114, *RTK* 2.112.544. Read *wu* 五 for *san* 三.

319 *SKYI* 107.1071–72, *RTK* 2.107.499.

320 *SKYI* 80.793–94, *RTK* 2.80.206–8.

321 *SKYI* 32.323, *RTK* 1.32.346.

322 *SKYI* 86.849, *RTK* 2.86.265.

323 *SKYI* 38.382, *RTK* 1.38.405.

324 *SKYI* 119.1177, *RTK* 2.119.608–9.

325 *SKYI* 78.777, *RTK* 2.78.191. Read *ch'i-shih-pa* 七十八 for *wu-shih-ch'i* 五十七.

there is too much material in one place it should be redistributed else-where. This will have the effect not only of avoiding diffuseness [*t'a-t'o* 沓拖] in earlier passages, but also of preventing any danger of insuffi-ciency [*chi-mo* 寂寞] in later ones. Not only will no earlier events go unaccounted for, but later events will be further enhanced [*hsüan-jan* 縉染]. Such is the practice of the best historians.

For example, Lü Pu's marriage to Ts'ao Pao's [d. 196] daughter actually occurs before his seizure of Hsü-chou,[326] but the author relates the details of it at the time when he is hard pressed at Hsia-p'ei.[327]

Ts'ao Ts'ao's ruse to slake the thirst of his men by pretending to sight a grove of plum trees in the distance actually occurs during his campaign against Chang Hsiu, but the author has him relate it to Liu Pei on the occasion when he invites him to enjoy fresh plums and newly brewed wine.[328]

The incident in which Kuan Ning cuts in two the mat that he has been sharing with Hua Hsin [157–231] and insists on sitting apart from him actually occurs before Hua Hsin assumes office, but the author relates it at the time when Hua Hsin breaks down the wall and drags out Empress Fu.[329]

Lady Wu's dream that the moon enters her bosom actually occurs when she is about to give birth to Sun Ts'e, but the author has her describe it as she is issuing her final injunctions on her deathbed.[330]

Chu-ko Liang's choice of Huang Ch'eng-yen's daughter as his wife actually occurs before he leaves his thatched cottage,[331] but we are not told about her until just prior to the death of her son, Chu-ko Chan, in battle.[332]

Further examples of this device are also too numerous to count.

Earlier passages leave room for subsequent development ["liu-pu i ying-hou" 留步以應後] and later passages shed retroactive light on earlier ones ["hui-chao i ying-ch'ien" 回照以應前]. As a result, the reader feels that the individual episodes of which the work is composed are as closely interrelated as the individual sentences in an essay ["i-p'ien ju i-chü" 一篇如一句].

19. One of the marvels of *The Romance of the Three Kingdoms* is the technique of meticulously rendering the hills in the foreground and

[326] *SKYI* 14.134, *RTK* 1.14.145.
[327] *SKYI* 16.152, *RTK* 1.16.165.
[328] *SKYI* 21.202, *RTK* 1.21.219–20.
[329] *SKYI* 66.666, *RTK* 2.66.66.
[330] *SKYI* 38.382, *RTK* 1.38.405.
[331] *SKYI* 37.371, *RTK* 1.37.395.
[332] *SKYI* 117.1156–59, *RTK* 2.117.585–88.

lightly sketching the trees in the distance ["chin-shan nung-mo, yüan-shu ch'ing-miao chih miao" 近山濃墨, 遠樹輕描之妙].

One of the techniques of the great painters is to render the hills and trees in the foreground meticulously and fully and the hills and trees in the distance lightly and sketchily. If this were not the case, the wooded hills that stretch into the distance and the misty peaks that pile on top of one another could scarcely be represented with equal fidelity on a square foot of silk or paper. Literary composition is also like this.

For example, we learn of Huang-fu Sung's defeat of the Yellow Turbans only through the report of Chu Chün's [d. 195] scout.[333]

We learn of Yüan Shao's elimination of Kung-sun Tsan only through the report of Ts'ao Ts'ao's envoy, Man Ch'ung [d. 242].[334]

We learn of Chao Yün's seizure of Nan-chün, Kuan Yü's seizure of Hsiang-yang, and Chang Fei's seizure of Ching-chou only through the eyes and ears of Chou Yü ["yen-chung, erh-chung t'ing-lai" 眼中耳中 聽來].[335]

We learn of Liu Pei's elimination of Yang Feng and Han Hsien [d. 197] only from his own report of this event [*k'ou-chung hsü-lai* 口中 敍來].[336]

We learn of Chang Fei's seizure of Ku-ch'eng through the ears of Kuan Yü [*erh-chung t'ing-lai* 耳中聽來].[337]

We learn that Chien Yung [168–243] has entered the service of Yüan Shao from Liu Pei's remark to that effect [*k'ou-chung hsü-lai* 口中 敍來].[338]

In the episode in which Ts'ao P'i sends three armies to attack the state of Wu all three are defeated, but only one defeat is described directly [*shih-hsieh* 實寫], while the other two are described indirectly [*hsü-hsieh* 虛寫].[339]

In the episode in which Chu-ko Liang repels the five armies that Ts'ao P'i has launched against the state of Shu, only the device of sending Teng Chih as an emissary to the state of Wu is described directly,[340] while the means by which the other four armies are repelled are described indirectly.[341]

Further examples of this device are also too numerous to count.

[333] *SKYI* 2.13, *RTK* 1.2.12.
[334] *SKYI* 21.204–5, *RTK* 1.21.222.
[335] *SKYI* 51.513–14, *RTK* 1.51.535.
[336] *SKYI* 17.165, *RTK* 1.17.179.
[337] *SKYI* 28.275–76, *RTK* 1.28.294.
[338] *SKYI* 28.279, *RTK* 1.28.298.
[339] *SKYI* 85.839–40, *RTK* 2.85.255–56.
[340] *SKYI* 85–86.847–54, *RTK* 2.85–86.264–70.
[341] *SKYI* 85–86.843–54, *RTK* 2.85–86.260–70.

In this way a mere sentence or two may be used to convey a great deal of information while at the same time saving [*sheng-ch'üeh* 省却] a great deal of ink.

20. One of the marvels of *The Romance of the Three Kingdoms* is the technique of balancing one striking peak against another and placing brocade screens face-to-face ["ch'i-feng tui-ch'a, chin-p'ing tui-chih chih miao" 奇峯對插, 錦屏對峙之妙].[342]

In this technique things may be juxtaposed either to bring out their similarities [*cheng-tui* 正對] or to emphasize their differences [*fan-tui* 反對]. In some cases they parallel each other [*tzu wei tui* 自爲對] in the same chapter, and in others they may parallel each other at a distance [*yao wei tui* 遙爲對] across several tens of intervening chapters.

For example, even in his youth Liu Pei is ambitious, whereas even in his youth Ts'ao Ts'ao is devious.[343]

Chang Fei is consistently impetuous, whereas Ho Chin is consistently lackadaisical.[344]

In proposing to depose the emperor during the meeting at the Wen-ming Palace, Tung Cho disregards his duty to his sovereign, whereas in murdering Ting Yüan, Lü Pu disregards his duty to his adopted father.[345]

In Yüan Shao's battle at the P'an River the fortunes of war prove to be inconstant, whereas in Sun Chien's engagement at Hsien Mountain life and death prove to be unpredictable.[346]

Ma T'eng is unsuccessful in his attempt to rescue the fortunes of the imperial house, but his loyalty does not falter, whereas although Ts'ao Ts'ao tries to revenge his father's death, he does not succeed in being filial.[347]

K'ung Jung's recommendation of Mi Heng is motivated by admiration for his worth like that which inspired the ode "Tzu-i," whereas Mi Heng's denunciation of Ts'ao Ts'ao is motivated by hatred for evil like that which inspired the ode "Hsiang-po."[348]

[342] Read *chih* 峙 for *ch'i* 崎.

[343] Chap. 1.

[344] Chap. 2.

[345] Chap. 3.

[346] Chap. 7.

[347] Chap. 10.

[348] For Chinese text and translation of these two odes from the *Shih-ching* 詩經 (Classic of Poetry), see James Legge, trans., *The Chinese Classics*, 5 vols. (Hong Kong: Hong Kong University Press, 1960), vol. 4, pp. 124–25, 346–49. The two odes are also discussed in the same terms as used in the essay in the *Li-chi* (Book of Rites). See *Shih-san ching ching-wen, Li-chi*, "Tzu-i" 緇衣 (Black Garments) chapter, sec. 2, p. 115, and James Legge, trans., *Li Chi: Book of Rites*, vol. 2, p. 352.

Liu Pei's meeting with Ssu-ma Hui is a case of an accidental encounter, whereas Hsü Shu's[349] visit to Hsin-yeh is a case of a deliberate self-introduction.[350]

Ts'ao P'i's cruel oppression of the living Ts'ao Chih[351] is a case of conflict between brothers of the same blood, whereas Liu Pei's grievous lamentation over the dead Kuan Yü[352] is a case of brotherly love between men of different surnames.

The fire is extinguished at Shang-fang Valley because Ssu-ma I is fated to survive, whereas the lamp goes out at Wu-chang Plateau because Chu-ko Liang is destined to die.[353]

Examples such as those enumerated above, some of which are analogous [*cheng-tui* 正對] and some of which are contrasting [*fan-tui* 反對], all parallel each other [*tzu wei tui* 自為對] within a single chapter.

In addition, Ho Chin is a relative of the imperial family by marriage who eliminates another such relative, Tung Chung [d. 189].[354] Fu Wan, however, is a relative of the imperial house by marriage who recommends another such relative, Tung Ch'eng.[355]

When Li Su persuades Lü Pu to murder Ting Yüan,[356] he uses his intelligence to tempt Lü Pu to evil. However, when Wang Yün leads on Lü Pu to murder Tung Cho,[357] he uses his cleverness to induce Lü Pu's loyalty.

When Chang Fei loses control of Hsü-chou it is his drinking that leads him to bungle his responsibilities.[358] However, when Lü Pu is trapped at Hsia-p'ei it is his prohibition of drinking that brings about his downfall.[359]

In drinking Lu Su's wine Kuan Yü is divinely majestic,[360] whereas in drinking Lu K'ang's wine Yang Hu is utterly serene.[361]

Chu-ko Liang's refusal to kill Meng Huo[362] is an instance of a benevolent man's magnanimity, whereas Ssu-ma I's insistence on killing

---

[349] The text refers here to Hsü Shu by his assumed name, Shan Fu.
[350] Chap. 35.
[351] *SKYI* 79.783–84, *RTK* 2.79.196–98.
[352] *SKYI* 78.773, *RTK* 2.78.186.
[353] Chap. 103.
[354] *SKYI* 2.20, *RTK* 1.2.21.
[355] *SKYI* 20.194, *RTK* 1.20.211.
[356] *SKYI* 3.27–29, *RTK* 1.3.30–32.
[357] *SKYI* 9.79–80, *RTK* 1.9.83–84.
[358] *SKYI* 14.133–34, *RTK* 1.14.144–45.
[359] *SKYI* 19.186, *RTK* 1.19.202.
[360] *SKYI* 66.662–64, *RTK* 2.66.61–63.
[361] *SKYI* 120.1183, *RTK* 2.120.613.
[362] Chaps. 87–90.

Kung-sun Yüan [d. 238][363] is an instance of an unscrupulous hero's [*chien-hsiung* 奸雄] harshness.

Kuan Yü chivalrously releases Ts'ao Ts'ao[364] in order to repay him for his former kindness, whereas Chang Fei chivalrously releases Yen Yen[365] in the hope of gaining his future services.

Chu-ko Liang's rejection of the plan to attack Ch'ang-an by way of Tzu-wu Valley[366] is a case of adopting a conservative strategy in order to ensure complete victory, whereas Teng Ai's refusal to be deterred by the perils of crossing the Yin-p'ing Range[367] is a case of adopting a risky strategy that leads to a lucky success.

Ts'ao Ts'ao is feeling poorly when a reading of Ch'en Lin's denunciation causes him to recover.[368] Wang Lang [d. 228], however, is perfectly healthy when Chu-ko Liang's denunciation precipitates his death.[369]

Lady Sun's love of weapons and armor[370] makes her a hero among women, whereas Ssu-ma I's acceptance of the scarf and bonnet[371] makes him a woman among men.

When Ssu-ma I takes Shang-yung after a march of only eight days,[372] it is a feat miraculous for the speed with which it is accomplished, whereas when he requires a hundred days to take Hsiang-p'ing,[373] his success depends upon his refusal to be hurried.

Chu-ko Liang establishes military colonies on the banks of the Wei River[374] in order to provide logistical support for offensive operations, whereas Chiang Wei establishes military colonies in T'a-chung as a means of avoiding trouble at court.[375]

When Ts'ao Ts'ao accepts the Nine Distinctions conferred on him by the ruler of the Han dynasty[376] he shows himself to be no true minister, whereas when Sun Ch'üan accepts the Nine Distinctions conferred upon

---

[363] *SKYI* 106.1060, *RTK* 2.106.486.

[364] *SKYI* 50.503, *RTK* 1.50.525.

[365] *SKYI* 63.635, *RTK* 2.63.33.

[366] *SKYI* 92.911, *RTK* 2.92.333.

[367] *SKYI* 117.1153–54, *RTK* 2.117.582–84.

[368] *SKYI* 22.216, *RTK* 1.22.234.

[369] *SKYI* 93.927, *RTK* 2.93.350–51.

[370] *SKYI* 54.537,543, 55.545; *RTK* 1.54.561, 568, 55.569.

[371] *SKYI* 103.1031, *RTK* 2.103.457.

[372] *SKYI* 94.936–37, *RTK* 2.94.362–63.

[373] *SKYI* 106.1057–60, *RTK* 2.106.482–86.

[374] *SKYI* 103.1027, *RTK* 2.103.452.

[375] *SKYI* 115.1139, *RTK* 2.115.568.

[376] *SKYI* 61.612–13, *RTK* 2.61.8.

him by the ruler of the state of Wei[377] he shows himself to be no true sovereign.

Ts'ao Ts'ao's shooting of the deer[378] is a violation of the proper relationship between ruler and minister, whereas Ts'ao P'i's shooting of a deer[379] awakens his son, Ts'ao Jui's [205–239], feelings for his mother.

Yang I [d. 235] and Wei Yen [d. 234] contend with one another as their armies withdraw from the field.[380] Teng Ai and Chung Hui, however, become jealous of each other as their armies take the offensive.[381]

Chiang Wei wishes to realize Chu-ko Liang's ambition[382] but his human efforts cannot prevail against the will of Heaven, whereas Tu Yü succeeds in carrying out Yang Hu's plan[383] because his human endeavors are opportune and coincide with the will of Heaven.

Examples such as those enumerated above, some of which are analogous and some of which are contrasting, do not occur in the same chapter but parallel each other at a distance [*yao-hsiang wei tui* 遙相爲對].

If the reader compares and evaluates ["chiao-liang erh pi-kuan" 較量 而比觀] such parallels, it cannot fail to enhance his taste for the study of the past and enrich his capacity for communing with the ancients.

21. In *The Romance of the Three Kingdoms* there are passages at the beginning and the end [*shou-wei* 首尾] of the work that are significantly correlated [*ta chao-ying* 大照應] and in between there are others that serve to link them significantly together [*ta kuan-so ch'u* 大關鎖處].

For example, in the opening chapter a motif is introduced [*ch'i* 起] with the formation of the eunuch clique known as the Ten Constant Attendants, and in the closing chapters this motif is concluded [*chieh* 結] first with the story of Liu Shan's favoritism for the eunuch, Huang Hao,[384] and is then concluded a second time with the story of Sun Hao's favoritism for the eunuch Ts'en Hun [d. 280].[385] This is an example of such significant correlation [*ta chao-ying* 大照應].

As another example, in the opening chapter a motif is introduced with the sorcery practiced by the Yellow Turbans,[386] and in the closing

---

[377] *SKYI* 82.810, *RTK* 2.82.226.

[378] *SKYI* 20.193, *RTK* 1.20.210.

[379] *SKYI* 91.903, *RTK* 2.91.325.

[380] *SKYI* 104–5.1043–46, *RTK* 2.104–5.469–70.

[381] Chaps. 117–19.

[382] Chaps. 104–19.

[383] *SKYI* 120.1185–89, *RTK* 2.120.615–20.

[384] Chaps. 113–18.

[385] *SKYI* 120.1181–89, *RTK* 2.120.610–21.

[386] *SKYI* 1.9, *RTK* 1.1.9.

chapters this motif is concluded first with the story of Liu Shan's faith in the predictions of a shamaness,[387] and is then concluded again with the story of Sun Hao's faith in the predictions of the necromancer, Shang Kuang.[388] This is another example of such significant correlation.

Even though there are such correlations [*chao-ying* 照應] between the beginning and the end [*shou-wei* 首尾] of the work, if there were no passages to link them together [*kuan-ho* 關合] in the more than a hundred chapters that lie in between, it would not be a successful composition [*chang-fa* 章法]. Consequently the author has inserted the passages in which Fu Wan entrusts the letter to the eunuch, Mu Shun,[389] and Sun Liang [243–260] catches a eunuch stealing honey[390] in order to link together examples of this motif that come before and after them. He has also inserted the passages describing Li Chüeh's predilection for shamanesses[391] and Chang Lu's reliance on heterodox doctrines[392] in order to link together examples of this motif that come before and after them.

All such devices succeed, in a natural way, in giving structure [*chieh-kou* 結構] to the whole work.

But there is more to it than this. Even more important to the author than the exposure of the roles played by eunuchs and black magic is the severe condemnation of disloyal ministers and rebellious sons, for he wishes his work to have the same kind of significance as the *Ch'un-ch'iu* 春秋 [The Spring and Autumn Annals].[393] Therefore his book records many instances of the loyalty of those who attack traitors and the evil of those who commit regicide. He ends the first chapter with Chang Fei angrily determined to kill Tung Cho[394] and ends the last chapter with Sun Hao indirectly expressing his desire to kill Chia Ch'ung [217–282].[395]

Looked at from this point of view, although *The Romance of the Three Kingdoms* is called a novel [*yen-i* 演義], it can really be considered a worthy successor of the *Ch'un-ch'iu*.

22. The narrative [*hsü-shih* 敍事] artistry of *The Romance of the Three*

---

[387] *SKYI* 116.1145, *RTK* 2.116.573.

[388] *SKYI* 120.1181, *RTK* 2.120.611.

[389] *SKYI* 66.665, *RTK* 2.66.65.

[390] *SKYI* 113.1119, *RTK* 2.113.546.

[391] *SKYI* 13.117–18, *RTK* 1.13.127.

[392] *SKYI* 59.591, *RTK* 1.59.621.

[393] This work is a chronicle of the state of Lu for the years 722–481 B.C., attributed to Confucius (551–479 B.C.). According to the commentators, Confucius showed his moral evaluation of the events recorded in the text by the use of precise and subtle terminology.

[394] *SKYI* 1.10, *RTK* 1.1.10.

[395] *SKYI* 120.1190, *RTK* 2.120.622.

Kingdoms is comparable to that of the *Shih-chi* 史記 [Records of the Historian], but the difficulties involved in composing its narrative [*hsü-shih* 敍事] were twice as difficult as those involved in the case of the *Shih-chi*.

In the *Shih-chi* each state and each individual is given separate treatment, with the result that the material is divided up into separate categories of basic annals [*pen-chi* 本紀], hereditary houses [*shih-chia* 世家], and biographies [*lieh-chuan* 列傳]. This is not so in the case of *The Romance of the Three Kingdoms*, where the basic annals, hereditary houses, and biographies are combined to form a single composite work. When things are treated separately, the text of each section is short and it is easy to exercise artistic control, whereas when things are combined, the text becomes long and artistic success is more difficult to achieve.

23. *The Romance of the Three Kingdoms* is superior to the *Lieh-kuo chih* 列國志 [Romance of the Feudal States].[396]

The *Tso-chuan* 左傳 [The Tso Commentary] and the *Kuo-yü* 國語 [Conversations of the States][397] are certainly among the finest of literary works, but the *Tso-chuan* was written as a commentary to the *Ch'un-ch'iu*. Since each of the sections of that classic constitutes an independent literary entity, the commentary adopts the same format, with a resultant loss of continuity. The *Kuo-yü* stands independent of the *Ch'un-chiu* as a self-contained work, so that it could have adopted a continuous format. But the author chose to treat the events of the Eastern Chou court and the states of Lu, Chin, Cheng, Ch'i, Ch'u, Wu, and Yüeh in eight separate sections so that it, too, lacks continuity.

Later authors have combined the subject matter of the *Tso-chuan* and the *Kuo-yü* to produce the *Lieh-kuo chih*, but the states are so many and the subject matter is so diffuse that, in the final analysis, they were unable to connect the individual segments of the narrative together [*kuan-ch'uan* 貫串] effectively.

One can read *The Romance of the Three Kingdoms* from one end to the other without finding any break in its continuity. Thus it is superior to the *Lieh-kuo chih*.

24. *The Romance of the Three Kingdoms* is superior to the *Hsi-yu chi* 西遊記 [The Journey to the West].

The *Hsi-yu chi* creates ex nihilo a world of monsters and magic that is fantastic and uncanonical, but this feat is not as impressive as that of *The*

[396] This historical novel is a popularization of portions of the history of the Chou dynasty (1122–221 B.C.), attributed to the reputed author of *The Romance of the Three Kingdoms*, Lo Kuan-chung 羅貫中 (fl. 1364).

[397] These two works were traditionally attributed to a contemporary of Confucius, Tso Ch'iu-ming 左丘明.

Romance of the Three Kingdoms, which faithfully relates [*shih-hsü* 實敍] a tale of emperors and kings that is true and verifiable.

Moreover, all the best features of the *Hsi-yu chi* are already to be found in *The Romance of the Three Kingdoms*. For example, what is there to choose between such wonders as the Dumb Spring,[398] Black Spring,[399] and so forth on the one hand and the Procreation River and Abortion Spring[400] on the other? What is there to choose between such names as King Flower-Thought [*To-ssu*],[401] King Wood-Deer [*Mu-lu*],[402] and so forth on the one hand and the Bull Monster King [*Niu-mo wang*], Deer-Strength Immortal [*Lu-li hsien*], Gold-Horn Demon [*Chin-chiao kuai*], and Silver-Horn Demon [*Yin-chiao kuai*] on the other?[403] What is there to choose between the epiphany of Ma Yüan [14 B.C.–A.D. 49],[404] the revelations of the Mountain Spirit,[405] and so forth on the one hand and the acts of salvation performed by the Bodhisattva Kuan-yin of the Southern Seas on the other? The section of *The Romance of the Three Kingdoms* devoted to the story of Chu-ko Liang's expedition against the southern aborigines[406] is by itself a match for the whole of the *Hsi-yu chi*.

And if we consider such episodes as that in Chen-kuo Temple in which Kuan Yü escapes calamity thanks to a glance at the abbot P'u-ching's consecrated blade[407] and that on Yü-ch'üan Mountain when he attains enlightenment on hearing the few words that P'u-ching addresses to him from the void,[408] what need is there to mull over such phrases as the "Holy Terrace in the Square Inch" [*ling-t'ai fang-ts'un* 靈臺方寸] or the "Slanting Moon and Three Stars" [*hsieh-yüeh san-hsing* 斜月三星][409] in order to awaken the contemplative mind?

[398] *SKYI* 89.881–84, *RTK* 2.89.301–5.

[399] *SKYI* 89.881–84, *RTK* 2.89.301–5.

[400] These two places figure in chap. 53 of *The Journey to the West*, where Tripitaka becomes pregnant after drinking the water of the river and is saved from this unwanted predicament with the aid of water from the spring.

[401] *SKYI* 89–90.880–89, *RTK* 2.89–90.300–311.

[402] *SKYI* 90.888–92, *RTK* 2.90.310–14.

[403] The Bull Monster King figures prominently in chaps. 59–61 of *The Journey to the West*. The Deer-Strength, Tiger-Strength, and Goat-Strength Immortals appear in chaps. 44–46, and the Gold-Horn and Silver-Horn Demons are major figures in chaps. 32–35 of the same novel.

[404] *SKYI* 89.882–83, *RTK* 2.89.302–4.

[405] *SKYI* 89.882–83, *RTK* 2.89.303–4.

[406] Chaps. 87–90.

[407] *SKYI* 27.266, *RTK* 1.27.285. Read *tsai* 災 for *huo* 火.

[408] *SKYI* 77.766, *RTK* 2.77.180.

[409] Sun Wu-k'ung's teacher, Subhodi, lives in the Mountain of Heart and Mind ("Ling-t'ai fang-ts'un shan" 靈臺方寸山) in the Cave of Slanting Moon and Three Stars

25. *The Romance of the Three Kingdoms* is superior to the *Shui-hu chuan* 水滸傳 [The Water Margin].

The realism of the *Shui-hu chuan* is to be preferred to the fantasy of the *Hsi-yu chi*. Nevertheless, because the author was free to create his material ex nihilo and to manipulate his plot at will, as a feat of literary craftsmanship his achievement was not as difficult as that of the author of *The Romance of the Three Kingdoms*, who succeeded in giving artistic form to predetermined material that would not admit of alteration.[410]

Moreover, the multitude of brilliant men of the era of the Three Kingdoms are individually brought to life in this novel far more effectively than are Wu Yung, Kung-sun Sheng, and the like in the *Shui-hu chuan*.

I contend that in any list of the "books of genius" [*ts'ai-tzu shu* 才子書][411] *The Romance of the Three Kingdoms* should occupy first place.

("Hsieh-yüeh san-hsing tung" 斜月三星洞). *Ling-t'ai* and *fang-ts'un* are euphemisms for the heart and mind, while the other phrase is a riddle that, if read correctly, produces the character for heart, *hsin* 心. See *HYC*, p. 1.9, and the corresponding passage in *JW*, p. 1.1.79–80.

[410] There is a very similar comparison of these two novels in Mao Lun's *Ti-ch'i ts'ai-tzu shu* 第七才子書, reprint with preface dated 1735 (Suchou: Ta-wen t'ang), "Tsung-lun" section, p. 18a–b.

[411] See essay d in chap. I and the introduction to the *Shui-hu chuan tu-fa* essay in chap. II above for discussion of Chin Sheng-t'an's list of books of genius and later permutations of this idea.

CHAPTER IV

(1670-1698)

Chang Chu-p'o on How to Read the *Chin P'ing Mei* (The Plum in the Golden Vase)

INTRODUCTION:
Chang Chu-p'o and His "*Chin P'ing Mei* tu-fa" (How to Read the *Chin P'ing Mei*)

Until quite recently, information concerning the life and career of Chang Chu-p'o 張竹坡 was not readily accessible. His personal name (Chu-p'o is his style), for instance, was not widely known. Aside from his extensive commentary on the *Chin P'ing Mei* (of which the *tu-fa* essay forms the lengthiest section), only scattered comments attributed to him in works such as the *Yu-meng ying* 幽夢影 (Quiet Dream Visions) compiled by Chang Ch'ao 張潮 (1650–ca. 1703)[1] and the *Tung-yu chi* 東遊記 (Journey to the East)[2] plus various letters and poems were available to the scholarly community.[3] This situation radically changed in 1984 with

---

[1] Chang Chu-p'o's comments to this work have been conveniently reprinted in *CPMTLHP*, pp. 197–207. Three other collections of material on the *Chin P'ing Mei* have already been published, two of which are identical in title to *CPMTLHP*. See the list of general reference works at the end of the *Chin P'ing Mei* section of the bibliography.

[2] For Chang Chu-p'o's comments to this work, see *CPMTLHP*, pp. 208–10.

[3] Some of Chang Chu-p'o's poetry has long been available (although sometimes wrongly attributed) in such works as *Hsü-chou shih-cheng* 徐州詩徵 (The Poetry of Hsü-chou; published 1891) and *Wan-ch'ing i shih-hui* 晚晴簃詩彙 (Poetry Collection from Late Clearing Sky Loft; comp. 1929). His full name is recorded in those works as well as in the official local history of his hometown in Hsü-chou, *T'ung-shan hsien-chih* 桐山縣志, compiled in 1919 and published in 1926. Three letters written by Chang Chu-p'o to Chang Ch'ao in 1696 are preserved in the *hsin* 辛 section of Chang Ch'ao's *Yu-sheng hou-chi* 友聲後集 (Voices of Friends, Latter Collection). These letters, as well as the local history entry and the poems recorded in *Wan-ch'ing i shih-hui* are available in *CPMTLHP*, pp. 195–96, 210, 196–97, respectively. For the rest of Chang Chu-p'o's extant poems and prose, see Wu Kan 吳敢, "Hsin fa-hsien ti *Chin P'ing Mei* p'ing-che Chang Chu-p'o tsu-p'u shu-k'ao, fu Chang Chu-p'o chuan yü ch'i shih-wen" 新發現的

the independent discovery of previously neglected material by Wu Kan
吳敢 and by scholars going through a collection of papers and books
owned by Shih Yu-heng 時有恒 (1906–1982) and donated to the library
of Hsü-chou Teachers' College, located in Chang Chu-p'o's hometown
of Hsü-chou 徐州 in Kiangsu.[4]

The most important part of this material is a genealogy of the Hsü-
chou branch of the Chang family with a preface by Chang Chu-p'o's
brother dated 1721. According to the biography of Chang Chu-p'o in
this version of the genealogy written by the same brother,[5] Chang Chu-
p'o's personal name was Tao-shen 道深 and his courtesy name Tzu-te
自德. He came from a locally prominent family that included holders of
military and civil degrees. His father, however, was not as successful,
careerwise, as other members of his generation, and Chang Chu-p'o
himself complains about his poverty and lack of success in several places
in the newly found material. Like sentiments can also be found in his
commentary on the *Chin P'ing Mei*.

According to the genealogy, Chang Chu-p'o was born in 1670 and
died in 1698. This is in accord with the fragmentary information we
have about Chang Chu-p'o's dates from other sources, such as the mention of his present age as twenty-six in the essay, "*Ti-i ch'i-shu* fei yin-shu
lun" 第一奇書非淫書論 (The Number One Marvelous Book Is Not an
Obscene Book) included in some of the editions of his commentary[6] and
the statement that he did not live long after the publication of his
commentary, made by Liu T'ing-chi 劉廷璣 (b. 1653) in his *Tsai-yüan
tsa-chih* 在園雜志.[7] The newly discovered material contains one of

金瓶梅評者張竹坡族譜述考, 附張竹坡傳與其詩文 (An Investigation of the Newly
Discovered Family Genealogy of the Commentator on the *Chin P'ing Mei*, Chang Chu-
p'o, with the Biography of Chang Chu-p'o and His Poetry and Prose Appended), *Wen-
hsien*, 1985.3:18–33.

[4] For details of these discoveries see the Wu Kan article cited above, pp. 18–19, and an
unpublished article by Li Shih-jen 李時人 of Hsü-chou Teachers' College, "I-p'i yu-kuan
Chang Chu-p'o ti chung-yao tzu-liao chien-chieh" 一批有關張竹坡的重要資料簡介 (A
Brief Introduction to a Collection of Important Material concerning Chang Chu-p'o),
photocopy courtesy of Andrew H. Plaks.

[5] This biography is quoted in full in the Wu Kan article cited in n. 3 above. The
brother's name was Chang Tao-yüan 張道淵, born only two years after Chang Chu-p'o.

[6] This essay is not included in all editions of the commentary, and its authenticity (as
well as that of two other essays not found in all editions) has been questioned by Huang
Lin 黃霖, "Chang Chu-p'o chi ch'i *Chin P'ing Mei* p'ing-pen" 張竹坡及其金瓶梅評本
(Chang Chu-p'o and His Commentary Edition of the *Chin P'ing Mei*), in *Chung-kuo ku-
tien wen-hsüeh ts'ung-k'ao* 中國古典文學叢考 (Collected Studies on Classical Chinese
Literature: Shanghai: Fu-tan ta-hsüeh, 1985), vol. 1, pp. 262–83.

[7] Liu T'ing-chi's notes on Chang Chu-p'o can be found in *CPMTLHP*, p. 213. *Tsai-
yüan tsa-chih* was published in 1715 and the item in question has been dated to 1712.

Chang Chu-p'o's poems entitled, "Playfully Written on the Evening of the Lantern Festival, 1695" ("I-hai yüan-yeh hsi-tso" 乙亥元夜戲作), in which he mentions that he is already over twenty-five years old. The genealogy also provides information on Chang Chu-p'o's literary and official career. We are told, for instance, that he achieved the lowest degree but failed the provincial civil service examination (*hsiang-shih* 鄉試) five times. Even prior to the publication of his commentary on the *Chin P'ing Mei*, successful participation in poetry circles during a brief stay in Peking won for him the name of Chu-p'o the Genius (*Chu-p'o ts'ai-tzu* 竹坡才子).

The commentary itself seems to have taken surprisingly little time to write. The section in his biography that treats his writing and publication of it reads as follows:

> My brother read books as quickly as if he were reading ten lines of text with every glance. Occasionally I would see him browsing through works of fiction like the *Shui-hu chuan* and the *Chin P'ing Mei*; the leaves of the book would turn as quickly as fallen leaves blown by the wind. Before much time had passed, he would already be finished with his reading. He once said to me: "The *Chin P'ing Mei* is a very finely constructed work (*chen-hsien chen-mi* 針綫縝密), but since the death of Chin Sheng-t'an there are few alive who know about this. I am going to pick out all its fine points and make them manifest." Thereupon he closeted himself in his room and in a little more than ten days his commentary was finished. Someone said to him, "If you sell your manuscript to a book publisher, you could get a very good price for it." My brother said: "Do you think that I did this for the sake of money? I intend to have it published so that all the people of the realm can also enjoy the beauty of its composition. Is this not a good enough reason?" Therefore, he had the blocks cut and then took them to Nanking. People came from far and near to purchase a copy and his fame spread widely. Of the famous literary men who came to Nanking, the number of them who paid visits to my brother in a single day could be counted by the tens. My brother was by nature very fond of society, and even though he was staying in rented lodgings, his parlor was always full of guests. However, his daily income was just enough to cover his expenses. One day he exclaimed, "How can a real man allow himself to be tied down like this!" He then turned over the woodblocks for the edition to his landlord and set out for the North empty-handed.[8]

[8] For the Chinese text, see *CPMTLHP*, pp. 211–12, and Wu Kan, *Wen-hsien*, 1985. 3:27–28. Liu T'ing-chi says in his *Tsai-yüan tsa-chih* that after Chang Chu-p'o's death the blocks were given to Wang T'ien-yü 汪天與 (courtesy name Ts'ang-fu 蒼孚) as repayment for an outstanding debt, and that Wang later burned them. It is not immediately clear whether Liu T'ing-chi's account is garbled or only incomplete. For instance, if the landlord of the biography subsequently gave the woodblocks to Wang T'ien-yü, then there would be no conflict between the two accounts and they could be seen as supple-

Chang Chu-p'o stayed for a while in Yangchou, where he made the acquaintance of Chang Ch'ao. Later, he went to Hopei and found a small post with the bureau concerned with river control, but shortly afterward fell ill and died.[9]

After the death in 1742 of the brother who wrote his biography, later compilers of the family genealogy took a different attitude toward Chang Chu-p'o and his activities. A revision of the family genealogy published in 1825 leaves out the poems and two essays by Chang Chu-p'o included in the earlier version, but more striking is the fact that all reference to the *Chin P'ing Mei* is excised from Chang Chu-p'o's biography. An 1849 revision of the genealogy that exists only in manuscript form reincludes the poems and essays but excises Chang Chu-p'o's biography. Chang Hsiang-hsien 張象賢 (1796–1857), the compiler of this revision, makes the following comments on Chang Chu-p'o: "Relying on his talent, Chang Chu-p'o looked down on others. He wrote a commentary on the *Chin P'ing Mei* that is full of hidden allusions and satiric remarks and violates the clan code of behavior. This is surely an improper use of his talents! That he died early and that his descendants have not prospered is surely not without cause."[10] Finally, an 1880 revision toned down some of Chang Hsiang-hsien's remarks but retained his concep-

mentary to each other. As for why someone would want to burn the woodblocks for printing this novel, Liang Kung-ch'en 梁恭辰 in his *Ch'üan-chieh ssu-lu* 勸戒四錄 (Four Records of Cautionary Anecdotes; 19th century) records the story of two publishers of the novel, one in Suchou and the other in Yangchou. The Suchou publisher was talked into burning his blocks and prospered thereafter. The Yangchou publisher, however, refused to do so and ended up dying a horrible death. The passage is reprinted in Chu I-hsüan 朱一玄, ed., *Chin P'ing Mei tzu-liao hui-pien* 金瓶梅資料彙編 (Collection of Material on the *Chin P'ing Mei*; Tientsin: Nan-k'ai ta-hsüeh, 1985), pp. 373–74. As for the idea that the commentary was finished in ten or so days, item one of the "Fan-li" 凡例 (General Principles) found in most of the Chang Chu-p'o commentary editions also states that the writing of the commentary only took slightly more than ten days, although there is the mention of adding a few short comments (*hsiao-p'i* 小批) at a later date in the following item of the "Fan-li." The "Fan-li" is reprinted in *CPMTLHP*, p. 1.

[9] Year-by-year biographies of Chang Chu-p'o compiled by Wu Kan are available in concise ("Chang Chu-p'o nien-p'u chien-pien" 張竹坡年譜簡編, *Hsü-chou shih-fan hsüeh-yüan hsüeh-pao*, 1985. 1:68–77) and full format (*Chin P'ing Mei p'ing-tien chia Chang Chu-p'o nien-p'u* 金瓶梅評點家張竹坡年譜 [Shenyang: Liao-ning jen-min, 1987]).

[10] Information on this and later versions of the genealogy can be found in Wu Kan, "Chang Chu-p'o nien-p'u chien-pien," under the appropriate year of compilation or publication. A recent article by the same author, "Chang Tao-yüan yü t'a ti liang-p'ien 'Chung-hsiung Chu-p'o chuan'" 張道淵與他的兩篇仲兄竹坡傳 (Chang Tao-yüan and the Two Versions of His "Biography of My Elder Brother, Chu-p'o"), in Hsü Shuo-fang 徐朔方 and Liu Hui 劉輝, eds., *Chin P'ing Mei lun-chi* 金瓶梅論集 (Collected Essays on the *Chin P'ing Mei*; Peking: Jen-min wen-hsüeh, 1986), contains the texts of the original and the 1825 revised version of Chang Chu-p'o's biography by his brother.

tion of Chang Chu-p'o as a black sheep of whom the family should not be proud. It was in this fashion that the valuable and interesting information on Chang Chu-p'o preserved mostly by his brother came to be lost and forgotten.

One of the other poems by Chang Chu-p'o quoted in the genealogy states that by the time he was twenty his writing was known throughout the land. Whether or not that was so, it is for his commentary on the *Chin P'ing Mei* that Chang Chu-p'o is of interest to us today. Besides the essay "How to Read the *Chin P'ing Mei*," the commentary contains several lists of different types of characters appearing in the novel, a list of interesting sayings taken from the novel, an analytical table of contents, and several essays of varying length on a variety of topics such as whether or not the book is obscene, allegorical meaning behind the names of the characters, filiality and the composition of the work, the importance of the physical layout of the dwellings described, and the interplay of "heat" (*je* 熱) and "cold" (*leng* 冷) in the novel.[11] Besides this prefatory material (a total of fifteen separate pieces not counting the preface signed Hsieh I 謝頤), the rest of the commentary consists of prechapter, interlineal, and marginal comments.[12] Although he was, in many ways, indebted to a previous commentator on the *Chin P'ing Mei*[13] and to Chin Sheng-t'an (the most influential critic of vernacular

[11] Some of Chang Chu-p'o's remarks from various of the prefatory pieces to his commentary have been translated by David T. Roy, "Chang Chu-p'o's Commentary on the *Chin P'ing Mei*," in *Chinese Narrative: Critical and Theoretical Essays*, pp. 115–23.

[12] Which of the extant printings of Chang Chu-p'o's commentary comes closest to the original edition is a complicated question. In some editions the Hsieh I preface (and sometimes the title page as well) is dated 1695, in other editions it is dated 1747 or even 1816. Hsieh I is almost certainly a made-up name. The majority of scholars think that the preface was really written by Chang Ch'ao, because a letter from Chang Chu-p'o to Chang Ch'ao thanks the older man for a preface to a commentary (see *CPMTLHP*, p. 195), but as far as we know, Chang Chu-p'o first made the acquaintance of Chang Ch'ao only after the printing of the first edition. Also, two earlier letters to Chang Ch'ao, written after his arrival in Yangchou, make no mention of the preface. Another possibility is that Chang Chu-p'o wrote the preface himself, assuming not only a false name but also a false persona, much as Chin Sheng-t'an did when he wrote his "Shih Nai-an" preface to the *Shui-hu chuan*. Some editions lack up to three of the prefatory essays, while some editions lack prechapter comments. In some editions a particular comment is printed in the margins, while in other editions the same comment might appear in double columns imbedded in the text of the novel. For more information on different editions of the commentary, see the descriptive bibliography.

[13] This is the so-called Ch'ung-chen (1628–1644) commentary. The comments from one edition of it are included in *CPMTLHP*, pp. 224–456. For differences in editions, see the descriptive bibliography. On Chang Chu-p'o's indebtedness to this earlier commentary, see Andrew H. Plaks, "The Chongzhen Commentary on the *Jin Ping Mei*: Gems amidst the Dross," *CLEAR* 8.1–2: 19–30 (1986).

fiction), Chang Chu-p'o's develo[...] of their ideas plus the injection of his own brought Chinese fiction [...] achievement.

Over the years there have bee[n...] Chin P'ing Mei, but they can be divided into two [...] one hand there are the editions with prefaces da[ted 1617–1618...] other textual line of filiation is said to date back t[o the Ch'ung-chen reign] period (1628–1644) and includes the edition that Chang Chu-p'o used.[15] Critical opinion holds that the first set of editions is far closer to the author's original conception of the novel,[16] but by Chang Chu-p'o's time those editions had become exceedingly rare and were apparently unavailable to him. Even though certain features of the text are distorted in the edition used by Chang Chu-p'o, as long as we bear in mind that these emendations and deletions are extremely valuable in our study of the changes in fiction writing and reading between the time of the original composition of the novel and the subsequent editing, this may lessen some of our disappointment over the unfortunate fact that Chang Chu-p'o used what appears to be an inferior edition for his commentary.

The translation of the "Chin P'ing Mei tu-fa" below is based on a collation of the texts of the essay from several editions. References to the text of the novel are to the large character Tsai-tzu t'ang edition, dated 1695, of Chang Chu-p'o's commentary, recently reprinted in Taiwan.[17] The reader is also referred to the corresponding sections of the translation of this version of the novel by Clement Egerton.[18]

[14] The "A" editions in Patrick Hanan's terminology. See his "The Text of the Chin P'ing Mei," Asia Major, n.s. 9.1 : 1–57 (1962).

[15] These editions are labeled "B" and "C" in Hanan's terminology. See n. 14 above.

[16] The idea that there was an original edition dating from around 1610 not identical to any of the types of editions discussed above was championed by Lu Hsün 魯迅 (1881–1936) and represented the dominant opinion on the matter for many years. Recently, a reexamination of the available evidence has led many scholars to the conclusion that it is most likely that the 1617–18 preface edition was the original printing mentioned by Shen Te-fu 沈德符 (1578–1642; see CPMTLHP, p. 222). For a representative statement of this argument, see Li Shih-jen, "T'an Chin P'ing Mei ti ch'u-k'o-pen" 談金瓶梅的初刻本 (On the First Printing of the Chin P'ing Mei), Wen-hsüeh i-ch'an, 1985. 2 : 115–18.

[17] An edition that seems to be an impression from the same blocks was reprinted in Hong Kong by the Hui-wen shu-tien in 1975 in the collection entitled Liang-chung Chu-p'o p'ing-tien ho-k'an T'ien-hsia ti-i ch'i-shu Chin P'ing Mei 兩種竹坡評點合刊天下第一奇書金瓶梅 (Combined Edition of Two Versions of the World's Number One Marvelous Book, the Chin P'ing Mei, with Commentary by Chang Chu-p'o). The Chinese text of the tu-fa essay is also available in CPMTLHP, pp. 24–46.

[18] The Golden Lotus, 4 vols. (London: Routledge & Kegan Paul, 1972). A translation into French of the type "A" edition (Chin P'ing Mei tz'u-hua 金瓶梅詞話) was recently completed by André Lévy under the title, Fleur en fiole d'or, 2 vols. (Paris: Editions Gallimard, 1985), and a complete English translation of the same type of edition by David T. Roy, translator of the tu-fa essay below, is currently in progress.

to Read the *Chin P'ing Mei*

Translated and Annotated by DAVID T. ROY
Additional Annotation by DAVID L. ROLSTON

1. The author has invented [*p'i-k'ung chuan-ch'u* 劈空撰出] the three characters [whose names make up the title], P'an *Chin* 金-lien, Li *P'ing* 瓶-erh, and Ch'un-*mei* 梅. Notice how he brings them together into one place and then disperses them again. In the first half [*ch'ien pan-pu* 前半部] of his work the focus is on P'an Chin-lien and Li P'ing-erh, but in the second half [*hou pan-pu* 後半部] it is on Ch'un-mei. In the first half Hsi-men Ch'ing manages, by hook and by crook, to obtain for himself the gold [*Chin* 金-lien] and the vase [*P'ing* 瓶-erh] that had belonged to other men; but in the second half the plum blossom [Ch'un-*mei* 梅] which was his to begin with falls easily into the hands of another man.

2. The action begins in the Yü-huang miao [Temple of the Jade Emperor][1] and ends in the Yung-fu ssu [Temple of Eternal Felicity],[2] and both these temples are introduced in the first chapter.[3] These two are places of pivotal importance [*kuan-chien ch'u* 關鍵處] in the book.

3. First Wu Shen-hsien [Wu the Immortal] surveys Hsi-men Ch'ing's household at its height,[4] then Huang Chen-jen [His Holiness Huang] sustains it somewhat in its decline,[5] and finally Master P'u-ching purges the sins of the main characters.[6] The way in which these episodes are correlated [*chao-ying* 照應] is highly significant.

4. Wu Shen-hsien's mirrorlike forecast of the fates of the members of Hsi-men Ch'ing's household[7] is a kind of summation [*chieh-shu* 結束], but Ch'en Ching-chi is conspicuously absent. P'an Chin-lien is not present when her fellow ladies lightheartedly have their fortunes told by means of the tortoise,[8] but she makes good the deficiency by what she says when she comes on the scene immediately afterward,[9] so she is not really left out. It is only Hsi-men Ch'ing and Ch'un-mei who are not

---

[1] *TICS* 1/10b–18a. Citations indicate chapter and page number. For an English translation of this passage, see *TGL*, 1.1.11–20. Citations for this translation will indicate volume, chapter, and page number.

[2] *TICS* 100/11a–17b, *TGL* 4.100.367–74.

[3] *TICS* 1/10b, *TGL* 4.1.11–12.

[4] Chap. 29.

[5] Chap. 66.

[6] Chap. 100.

[7] Chap. 29.

[8] *TICS* 46/14b–17a, *TGL* 2.46.262–65.

[9] *TICS* 46/17a, *TGL* 2.46.265.

included here, but Li P'ing-erh's two appearances in Hsi-men Ch'ing's dreams[10] supply the missing data for him. It is not until Ch'en Ching-chi is physiognomized by Yeh T'ou-t'o [Yeh the Ascetic],[11] however, that his final fortune is foretold.

5. Before introducing P'an Chin-lien,[12] the author introduces Li P'ing-erh.[13] Only after Hsi-men Ch'ing takes P'an Chin-lien into his household[14] does the author introduce Ch'un-mei.[15] However, before Hsi-men Ch'ing takes P'an Chin-lien into his household, he first marries Meng Yü-lou.[16] Again, before Hsi-men Ch'ing takes Li P'ing-erh into his household,[17] the author introduces Ch'en Ching-chi.[18] The skill with which these elements of the plot are dovetailed [*ch'uan-ch'a* 穿插] cannot be described in words. But the way in which the author goes on to weave in [*chia-hsieh* 夾寫] the stories of Sung Hui-lien, Wang Liu-erh, Pen the Fourth's wife, Ju-i, and the rest only demonstrates once again that he has mastered the creative skills of Heaven [*t'ien-kung* 天工] itself.

6. Those who really know how to read the *Chin P'ing Mei* appreciate the second half [*hsia pan-pu* 下半部], yet it is also only those who really know how to read it who prefer the first half [*shang pan-pu* 上半部]. You can only understand this after having fully savored scenes, of which there are too many to enumerate, such as those where the play about Han Hsiang-tzu's quest for his uncle, Han Yü, is performed,[19] and where the song "Alas! Life Is like a Dream" is called for[20] during the celebrations that mark the birth of Kuan-ko and Hsi-men Ch'ing's appointment to office.

7. The *Chin P'ing Mei* exhibits certain structural devices ["*pan-ting ta chang-fa*" 板定大章法]. For example, whenever P'an Chin-lien gets angry about something, the author arranges to have Meng Yü-lou at her side. This is done without any variation each time and is a seasoned stylistic technique [*chang-fa lao-ch'u* 章法老處]. Another example is the way that every time Hsi-men Ch'ing is about to go out drinking at someone else's place, some guest or official turns up for a visit and he has to delay his departure in order to entertain him. This is a major

[10] *TICS* 67/17b–18a, 71/6b–7b; *TGL* 3.67.221–22, 3.71.293–94.
[11] *TICS* 96/11b–12b, *TGL* 4.96.317–18.
[12] *TICS* 1/22b, *TGL* 1.1.25.
[13] *TICS* 1/10b–11a, *TGL* 1.1.12.
[14] *TICS* 9/1b, *TGL* 1.9.122.
[15] *TICS* 9/2a, *TGL* 1.9.122.
[16] *TICS* 7/12b, *TGL* 1.7.107–8.
[17] *TICS* 19/12a–b, *TGL* 1.19.271–72.
[18] *TICS* 17/3a–b, *TGL* 1.17.234.
[19] *TICS* 32/3a, *TGL* 2.32.60.
[20] *TICS* 31/13b, *TGL* 2.31.55.

structural device [*chang-fa* 章法] used in the chapters after the birth of Kuan-ko and Hsi-men Ch'ing's appointment to office.

8. Each of the hundred chapters of the *Chin P'ing Mei* is constructed by means of the structural device of juxtaposing two episodes [*liang-tui chang-fa* 兩對章法], so that there are two hundred episodes in all. However, there are some chapters in which the transition [*kuo-chieh* 過節] between the two episodes is effected by means of a single expression, while there are others in which the two episodes are mortised [*kuo-hsia* 過下] by a hidden tenon [*sun* 筍]. For example, Chao Yüan-t'an's tiger performs this function in chapter 1.[21]

There are some chapters in which the two episodes are further subdivided, the author narrating the first half of the first episode, shifting to the first half of the second, then going back to finish off the first, and only then going on to complete the second episode. There are some chapters in which the two episodes are completely intermingled [*san-wu ts'o-tsung* 參伍錯綜], and there are some in which the treatment of other matters is inserted into the narration of the two main episodes. In short, the two episodes form the framework [*t'iao-kan* 條幹] of each chapter. If you savor carefully the way in which they are handled from one chapter to another, you will know what I mean.

9. It is true that two episodes are juxtaposed [*tso-tui* 作對] in every chapter of the *Chin P'ing Mei* but there are also cases of episodes in different chapters that parallel each other at a distance [*yao-tui* 遙對]. Examples of this include the parallel episodes [*tui* 對] of P'an Chin-lien playing the p'i-p'a[22] and Li P'ing-erh playing elephant chess[23] and the paired episodes [*tui* 對] of the hiding of the wine pot[24] and the theft of the gold bracelet.[25] I could go on, but there are too many to enumerate fully.

10. In the first half [*ch'ien-pan* 前半] of the book, the motif of "cold" [*leng* 冷] is repeated so effectively that one can hardly bear to read on, whereas in the second half [*hou-pan* 後半] the motif of "heat" [*je* 熱] recurs but is not readily apparent to the reader. In the first half the motif of "cold" occurs where the greatest "heat" is being described. If you savor these passages you will know what I mean. The way that the motif of "heat" occurs in the second half can be seen in the description of

---

[21] *TICS* 1/14b, *TGL* 1.1.16. Talk about a tiger portrayed in a painting of Chao Yüan-t'an leads to mention of a man-eating tiger that is presently terrorizing the countryside. The tiger is killed by Wu Sung, who figures in the latter half of the chapter.

[22] *TICS* 38/9a–12b, *TGL* 2.38.161–65.

[23] *TICS* 44/5a–7a, *TGL* 2.44.234–35.

[24] Chap. 31.

[25] Chaps. 43–44.

Meng Yü-lou's visit to Hsi-men Ch'ing's grave where the author provides an elaborate description of the beauties of spring on the Ch'ing-ming Festival.[26]

11. In this book there are examples of the most dubious and unimportant characters who nevertheless play significant roles, such as Han Ai-chieh. Innumerable women appear in the work, but why does the author choose to end it with the example of Han Ai-chieh's integrity?[27] He has a profound reason for doing so. Han Ai-chieh's mother, Wang Liu-erh, becomes a prostitute, and Han Ai-chieh herself, after her return from the Eastern Capital, also engages in this profession,[28] but as soon as she becomes interested in Ch'en Ching-chi, she remains faithful to him until death.[29] If we compare this with the way in which Li P'ing-erh and Ch'un-mei treat their husbands, Hua Tzu-hsü and Chou Hsiu, it certainly puts them to shame. If we compare P'an Ch'in-lien's conduct after meeting Hsi-men Ch'ing with that of Han Ai-chieh after meeting Ch'en Ching-chi, we see that she is unfaithful first with Hsi-men Ch'ing,[30] then with Ch'en Ching-chi,[31] and finally even with Wang Ch'ao, so that she is not even the equal of a repentant prostitute. Thus the author concludes [*chieh* 結] his book with Han Ai-chieh in order to put to shame the other female characters and to emphasize the contrast between a repentant prostitute who can preserve her integrity and those who not only fail to correct their faults while living in luxury but, abandoning all integrity and shame, go unrepentant to their deaths.

12. In reading the *Chin P'ing Mei* we must pay attention to the significant features of the spatial setting [*ta chien-chia ch'u* 大間架處]. These include the location of P'an Ch'in-lien and Ch'un-mei in one place and Li P'ing-erh in another and the placing of all three of them in the single larger setting of the front garden. The fact that P'an Chin-lien and Ch'un-mei are placed together accentuates the isolation of Li P'ing-erh. The fact that P'an Chin-lien and Li P'ing-erh live close to each other in the garden allows their jealousy to flourish, while the fact that Wu Yüeh-niang lives far removed from them gives Ch'en Ching-chi his chance to get at P'an Chin-lien.

13. In reading the *Chin P'ing Mei* we must pay attention to the points at which one element in the narrative is used to lead into another [*ju-sun*

---

[26] *TICS* 89/3b–4a, *TGL* 4.89.212–13.

[27] *TICS* 99/10a–12b, 100/1a–9b; *TGL* 4.99–100.353–65.

[28] *TICS* 98/8a (the text of this edition is defective here), *TGL* 4.98.338.

[29] *TICS* 100/9a–b, *TGL* 4.100.365.

[30] Chap. 12.

[31] Chap. 53.

[32] *TICS* 86/12b–13b, *TGL* 4.86.178–79.

ch'u 入笥處]. For example, the theme of slaying a tiger is introduced [*ch'a-ju* 插入] amid the joking in the Yü-huang miao.[33] The fact that Hua Tzu-hsü is Hsi-men Ch'ing's next-door neighbor is introduced when he is proposed for membership in the brotherhood.[34] In chapter 8, when P'an Chin-lien is suffering from the heat, during her tirade at Tai-an the information that Hsi-men Ch'ing has taken Meng Yü-lou into his household is introduced.[35] Li Kuei-chieh is brought out [*ch'a ch'u* 插出] when Hsi-men Ch'ing asks Ying Po-chüeh where he has been the last few days.[36] Ch'en Ching-chi's establishment of intimacy with P'an Chin-lien is introduced on the occasion of the completion of the summer-house.[37] Wang Liu-erh's submission to Hsi-men Ch'ing's demands is introduced as a result of Chai Ch'ien's request for a concubine.[38] Li P'ing-erh's pregnancy is introduced in the course of her bout with Hsi-men Ch'ing in the Fei-ts'ui hsüan [Kingfisher Pavilion].[39] The origin of Li P'ing-erh's illness is introduced with the trial of the Indian monk's medicine.[40] The monk P'u-ching is introduced into the story as a result of the events in the Pi-hsia kung [Temple of the Goddess of the Iridescent Clouds].[41] Li Kung-pi is introduced on the occasion of the visit to Hsi-men Ch'ing's grave,[42] and the first indication that there is anything going on between Tai-an and Hsiao-yü is introduced when he is sent home for the fur coats.[43] Such examples of the author's ability to accomplish his aims without leaving a trace are innumerable. This is due to the skill with which he employs indirect [*ch'ü-pi* 曲筆] and unexpected [*ni-pi* 逆筆] techniques to tell his story. He is not willing to start a new narrative thread [*t'ou-hsü* 頭緒] from scratch or to use direct [*chih-pi* 直筆] or straightforward [*shun-pi* 順筆] techniques to tell his story. There is no end to the separate narrative threads in this book, and if each of them were started from scratch, one could not even count them. When I take up my brush I also try to use indirect and unexpected techniques but, unlike the author, I am unable to be indirect [*ch'ü* 曲] without leaving traces or to be unexpected [*ni* 逆] without tipping my hand. This is what makes his book so marvelous.

[33] *TICS* 1/14b–15b, *TGL* 1.1.16–17.
[34] *TICS* 1/9b–10a, *TGL* 1.1.11.
[35] *TICS* 8/3b, *TGL* 1.8.111. Read *pa* 八 for *liu* 六.
[36] *TICS* 1/8b, *TGL* 1.1.10.
[37] *TICS* 18/12b–13b, *TGL* 1.18.258–59.
[38] Chap. 37.
[39] *TICS* 27/4b, *TGL* 1.27.378.
[40] *TICS* 50/9a–11a, *TGL* 2.50.321–22.
[41] Chap. 84.
[42] Chaps. 89–90.
[43] *TICS* 46/6b–11b, *TGL* 2.46.252–57.

14. There are many episodes in the *Chin P'ing Mei* in which the clandestine activities of some of the characters are disclosed [*p'o-chan* 破綻] to others. For example, Hsi-men Ch'ing's sexual intercourse with P'an Chin-lien during the funeral service for her husband is overheard by the monks outside the window;[44] P'an Chin-lien's affair with Ch'in-t'ung is discovered by Sun Hsüeh-o, and the even more incriminating perfume sachet that P'an Chin-lien has given him is also found on Ch'in-t'ung's person;[45] P'an Chin-lien discovers Hsi-men Ch'ing's secret assignations with Li P'ing-erh over the garden wall[46] and stumbles upon Sung Hui-lien's affair with Hsi-men Ch'ing;[47] Li P'ing-erh's remarks in the Fei-ts'ui hsüan are overheard by P'an Chin-lien,[48] but her own antics in the grape arbor are witnessed by T'ieh-kun;[49] no sooner does Hsi-men Ch'ing accept the bribe of stolen goods from Miao Ch'ing than he incurs the wrath of the regional inspector;[50] no sooner does Wu Yüeh-niang implore the aid of the magistrate in her suit against Ch'en Ching-chi[51] than P'ing-an gives false testimony against her in the court of Wu Tien-en;[52] immediately after P'an Chin-lien's affair with Ch'en Ching-chi is first consummated, Hsi-men Ch'ing actually touches the evidence without realizing it,[53] and when Hsi-men Ch'ing burns moxa on Wang Liu-erh's pudendum, Hu Hsiu is an unseen witness to the scene.[54] Examples of this kind are too many to enumerate. In general, the author uses this risky technique [*hsien-pi* 險筆] in order to show the predicaments to which human emotions can lead. But even more remarkable is the way in which he enables the characters whose clandestine activities are disclosed to cover their tracks with plausible alibis so that he does not have to waste his energy on tedious explanations. This is why his technique is so miraculous [*hua-pi* 化筆].

15. There are instances in the *Chin P'ing Mei* in which the author seems to have deliberately created episodes or characters that appear from nowhere and disappear for no apparent reason [*wu-wei* 無謂]. Shu-t'ung is an example. Who knows how much planning went into the author's creation of this single character? It goes without saying that he

---

[44] *TICS* 8/11a, *TGL* 1.8.120.
[45] *TICS* 12/6b–8a, *TGL* 1.12.161–63.
[46] *TICS* 13/7a–10a, *TGL* 1.13.183–86.
[47] *TICS* 22/4a–b, *TGL* 1.22.313–14.
[48] *TICS* 27/4a–b, *TGL* 1.27.378.
[49] *TICS* 28/5a–b, *TGL* 2.28.5.
[50] Chaps. 47–48.
[51] *TICS* 92/14b–15b, *TGL* 4.92.262–63.
[52] *TICS* 95/4a–b, *TGL* 4.95.295.
[53] *TICS* 53/3b–4a, *TGL* 2.53.370–71.
[54] *TICS* 61/5a–6a, *TGL* 3.61.103.

serves the purpose of depicting Hsi-men Ch'ing's depravity and poly-
morphous promiscuity, but it is not so apparent that the author has
created Shu-t'ung in order to prepare the ground for the departure of
another character from Hsi-men Ch'ing's household. What is the explanation for this? Li P'ing-erh and Wu Yüeh-niang start out estranged but
end up on intimate terms. P'an Chin-lien and Wu Yüeh-niang start out
on intimate terms but end up estranged. Although the rift between them
develops over the expulsion of Lai Chao[55] and the banishment of Lai
Wang,[56] it need never have been as serious as it becomes when P'an
Chin-lien throws her tantrum.[57] This tantrum is precipitated by Yü-
hsiao's willingness to repeat every word of Wu Yüeh-niang's private
conversation to P'an Chin-lien.[58] Why should Yü-hsiao tell her everything? Because she has accepted her three conditions.[59] Why does she
accept these three conditions? Because P'an Chin-lien discovers her affair
with Shu-t'ung.[60] The author does not want to have to account for the
affair between Yü-hsiao and Shu-t'ung from scratch at this point in the
narative, so he describes the hiding of the wine pot and the ill will it
engenders at an earlier point.[61] But the reason why the author goes to
such pains [*yao-yao hsieh lai* 遙遙寫來] is because he needs P'an Chin-lien
to have her tantrum. Why is this? The [tantrum] episode is needed to
account for the fact that when P'an Chin-lien has to depart from the
household, Wu Yüeh-niang abandons her to her fate without the
slightest regret and P'an Chin-lien's downfall is complete.[62] How can
anyone say that there is a single example of irrelevant [*wu-wei* 無謂]
writing in the *Chin P'ing Mei*?

16. In the *Chin P'ing Mei* the author devotes serious attention to the
description [*cheng-ching hsieh* 正經寫] of six women, and of these he
really concentrates on only four, that is, Wu Yüeh-niang, Meng Yü-lou,
P'an Chin-lien, and Li P'ing-erh. But he describes Wu Yüeh-niang only
because of the requirements of the plot [*ta-kang* 大綱] and uses different
techniques to depict Meng Yü-lou because she is a person of superior
gifts who resents her unjust neglect. Thus he describes Wu Yüeh-niang
only because he has to and is unwilling to describe Meng Yü-lou the way
he does his other characters. Neither one of them is given full treatment
[*cheng hsieh* 正寫]. The full treatment is reserved for Li P'ing-erh and

[55] *TICS* 29/4a, *TGL* 2.29.15.
[56] *TICS* 26/9a–10b, *TGL* 1.26.364–65.
[57] *TICS* 75/22a–24b, *TGL* 3.75.375–77.
[58] *TICS* 75/14b–15b, 21a–22a; *TGL* 3.75.368–70, 375.
[59] *TICS* 64/2b–4a, *TGL* 3.64.167–68.
[60] *TICS* 64/2b–4a, *TGL* 3.64.167–68.
[61] *TICS* 31/7b–10b, *TGL* 2.31.47–52.
[62] *TICS* 86/8a–12b, *TGL* 4.86.174–78.

P'an Chin-lien. But again, he describes Li P'ing-erh by what he does not say about her, which is to say, he describes her while keeping his focus [*hsieh-ch'u* 寫處] elsewhere. This is because the focus of his description is always on P'an Chin-lien. Because he always concentrates [*tan-hsieh* 單寫] on P'an Chin-lien, it is no wonder that she emerges as the most vicious of all his characters. Such, indeed, is the awesome power of the writer's brush.

17. There are two characters in the *Chin P'ing Mei* to whom the author devotes special attention and whose final fates are also note-worthy: Ch'un-mei and Tai-an. While she is still only one of the maid-servants, the author indicates in numerous passages that Ch'un-mei possesses a sense of self-esteem and ambition that sets her apart from the others. While he is still only one among the many manservants, Tai-an is described by the author in passage after passage as being adept at pleasing people in everything he does. Why does the author insist on having Ch'un-mei become a lady of rank[63] and Tai-an a man of wealth and position[64] at the end of the book? In order that his novel on the theme of "heat and cold" [*yen-liang* 炎涼] should illustrate the reversal of fortunes [*fan-an* 翻案]. Notice how the other characters can only see that the Ch'un-mei before them is merely a maidservant—they have no idea that later she will become a lady of rank. Notice how they only see that the Tai-an before them is merely a manservant—they have no idea that later he will become a man of wealth and position. When their status changes, not only do others look upon Ch'un-mei and Tai-an in a new light and pay court to them, even Wu Yüeh-niang has to look on them differ-ently, treating Ch'un-mei as her social superior[65] and placing herself under Tai-an's protection after the decline of the Hsi-men family.[66] Of what utility then is judging people according to transitory social status [*yen-liang* 炎涼]? The author's acupuncture [*chen-pien* 針砭] uses satiric barbs instead of regular needles. In order to make the later reversal of their fortunes plausible, the author must first demonstrate the special qualities of Ch'un-mei and Tai-an.

18. What need does the author have for the characters Li Chiao-erh and Sun Hsüeh-o? He uses Li Chiao-erh to imply that even before Hsi-men Ch'ing meets P'an Chin-lien or Li P'ing-erh he is already a dissolute wastrel who is capable of any crime. In his treatment of P'an Chin-lien and Li P'ing-erh, he describes certain of Hsi-men Ch'ing's crimes in full [*shih-hsieh* 實寫], whereas in his treatment of Li Chiao-erh he describes others of Hsi-men Ch'ing's crimes by implication [*hsü-hsieh* 虛寫]. If the

[63] *TICS* 95/6b, *TGL* 4.95.297–98.
[64] *TICS* 100/18a, *TGL* 4.100.374.
[65] Chap. 96.
[66] *TICS* 100/18a, *TGL* 4.100.374.

Does the author like 報報?

actually described are as bad as they are, those that are not
~~travel leave~~ us free to wonder how many other indescribable crimes
he ~~has committed~~ in the past. How deep is the author's hatred of Hsi-
men Ch'ing!

As for Sun Hsüeh-o, why should the author devote the space he does
to this person of humble origins whose status is only that of a maidservant who has been seduced by her master? This is an example of the
author's Bodhisattva-like compassion. How could the retribution [*pao
報*] due a character as vicious as Hsi-men Ch'ing be complete without
his wife's becoming a prostitute?[67] But since the author has already
decided to handle Wu Yüeh-niang in a different way, he certainly could
never bring himself to reduce her to this. Meng Yü-lou is an innocent
victim of Hsi-men Ch'ing's depravity, so the author could scarcely
endure to expose her to any additional suffering for the sake of punishing
Hsi-men Ch'ing. Li Chiao-erh is a prostitute to begin with. Li P'ing-erh
is destined to play a role in Hsi-men Ch'ing's retribution while he is still
alive. As for P'an Chin-lien, not only does she have a nemesis of her
own, but even if she were to become a prostitute, it would not harm
Hsi-men Ch'ing and might even be beneficial to P'an Chin-lien, who
would probably be nothing loath. How could this be called retribution?
Thus the author describes Sun Hsüeh-o as being reduced to prostitution[68] in order to accentuate the retribution visited upon Hsi-men
Ch'ing and at the same time unobtrusively to bring to a conclusion [*an-
chieh* 暗結] the case of Sung Hui-lien.[69] As for the subsequent incidents
involving Chang Sheng and Ch'en Ching-chi, they are merely dictated
by the exigencies of the plot [*ch'ing yin wen sheng* 情因文生] and represent
an expedient tidying up [*sui-shou shou-shih* 隨手收拾] of loose ends.
Otherwise how could Sun Hsüeh-o's life as a prostitute be brought to a
conclusion [*chieh-kuo* 結果]?[70]

---

[67] This idea that adultery will come home to roost in the prostitution of one's own wife
appears in the Hsin-hsin Tzu 欣欣子 (pseud.) preface to the earliest edition of the *Chin
P'ing Mei*, but we do not know if Chang Chu-p'o ever saw that preface. The same idea
forms the ostensible moral of the novel *Jou p'u-t'uan* 肉蒲團 (The Prayer Mat of Flesh),
written, in all probability, by Li Yü 李漁 (1611–1680). It seems that that novel, as well as
works more verifiably by Li Yü, had a great influence on Chang Chu-p'o. Members of
Chang Chu-p'o's immediate family were on good terms with Li Yü, but the fact that
Chang Chu-p'o would have been no more than ten years old at the older man's death
would seem to preclude any meaningful acquaintance between the two. It is interesting to
note that some of the 1695 preface editions of the Chang Chu-p'o *Chin P'ing Mei*
commentary attribute the authorship of the novel to Li Yü.

[68] Chap. 94.

[69] Chaps. 22–26.

[70] *TICS* 99/9a, *TGL* 4.99.352.

19. Li Chiao-erh represents the role of money [*ts'ai* 財] in the realm of sex [*se* 色]. This is apparent from the fact that she takes charge of the household accounts[71] and that she lines her pockets before leaving the household.[72] Wang Liu-erh represents the role of sex in the realm of money. When she meets with Hsi-men Ch'ing she is always talking about business deals,[73] getting maidservants and houses,[74] fixing up things for Miao Ch'ing,[75] and so forth, all of which profitable subjects are broached by way of sex.

20. The author needs Sung Hui-lien in his book in order to bring out as completely as possible the viciousness of P'an Chin-lien. This early trial of her powers against Sung Hui-lien foreshadows what she does later on out of jealousy of Li P'ing-erh. How can we see this? When Sung Hui-lien succeeds in attracting her master's attentions, it is P'an Chin-lien who first becomes aware of it,[76] just as it is she who first catches sight of Ying-ch'un pretending to call the cat as a signal for Hsi-men Ch'ing's assignation with Li P'ing-erh.[77] How does P'an Chin-lien's willingness to send Ch'un-mei with a brazier to warm the grotto for Hsi-men Ch'ing and Sung Hui-lien[78] differ from her urging Hsi-men Ch'ing to take Li P'ing-erh into his household and offering to share her quarters with her for the time being?[79] How do her apparent willingness to forgive Sung Hui-lien when she kneels and throws herself upon her mercy and all the other tricks by which she keeps the upper hand over her[80] differ from her pretending to be drunk when Li P'ing-erh first enters the household and saying to her, "Now we walk together on the same path"?[81] How does her double-tongued troublemaking between Sun Hsüeh-o and Sung Hui-lien[82] differ from her telling tales about Li P'ing-erh to Wu Yüeh-niang?[83] To make a long story short, Lai Wang's narrow escape from death[84] and the needless suicide of Sung Hui-lien[85]

[71] *TICS* 11/3b, *TGL* 1.11.146.
[72] *TICS* 79/24b, 80/7a–9a; *TGL* 4.79.98, 4.80.110–12.
[73] *TICS* 50/6a, 61/5b; *TGL* 2.50.317–18, 3.61.103.
[74] *TICS* 38/4a, *TGL* 2.38.156.
[75] *TICS* 47/6b–7a, 48/4a; *TGL* 2.47.272–73, 2.48.281–82.
[76] *TICS* 22/4a–b, *TGL* 1.22.313–14.
[77] *TICS* 13/7a–10a, *TGL* 1.13.183–86.
[78] *TICS* 23/6b–7a, *TGL* 1.23.324.
[79] *TICS* 16/3b–5b, *TGL* 1.16.222–24.
[80] *TICS* 23/10a–11a, *TGL* 1.23.327–28.
[81] *TICS* 21/17a–b, *TGL* 1.21.309–10.
[82] *TICS* 26/15a–b, *TGL* 1.26.371.
[83] *TICS* 51/1a–3b, *TGL* 2.51.324–26.
[84] *TICS* 26/9a–b, *TGL* 1.26.364–65.
[85] *TICS* 26/16b–17a, *TGL* 1.26.372.

are both P'an Chin-lien's doing. The author times this subplot to coincide with Li P'ing-erh's entry into the household for the express purpose of providing her with a warning, but she does not realize her danger and actually befriends P'an Chin-lien. How fitting that disaster should not be long in overtaking her and that she should suffer the fate of which she has been so clearly forewarned [*hou-ch'e chung fu* 後車終覆]. This episode, which I interpret as an early trial of her powers, greatly accentuates P'an Chin-lien's viciousness, but the author has also created here a cautionary example [*yang-tzu* 樣子] for those who do not know how to keep danger at a distance. If you read this episode inattentively you may think that it describes nothing more than Hsi-men Ch'ing's having another affair with the wife of one of his servants. But Hsi-men Ch'ing is a man who kills husbands in order to take their wives and money,[86] protects servants who have killed their master,[87] and puts the law of the land up for sale, so the author scarcely needs to create [*chuan* 撰] this episode merely to add another item to the roster of his crimes. The reader, however, is often deceived by the author.

21. Why does the author in the later part of his narrative depict the relationship between the wet nurse Ju-i and Hsi-men Ch'ing? This is also clearly directed against P'an Chin-lien, for it demonstrates that her successful elimination of Sung Hui-lien and Li P'ing-erh has been an exercise in futility. How can we see this? When Sung Hui-lien dies,[88] P'an Chin-lien is delighted, but then Kuan-ko is born and Li P'ing-erh wins Hsi-men Ch'ing's favor.[89] When Kuan-ko dies[90] and Li P'ing-erh follows him to the grave,[91] P'an Chin-lien is again delighted; but before she knows it, the fragrance of Ju-i's cosmetics attracts Hsi-men Ch'ing's attention by the very side of his dead favorite's spirit tablet.[92] Every time P'an Chin-lien eliminates a rival another comes to take her place. No matter how good she may be at maintaining her lover's favor and gaining the upper hand, what can she do in the face of a situation like this but acknowledge the futility of her efforts and retire from the field? Thus the author's portrayal of Ju-i is really a means of getting at P'an Chin-lien and of expressing the indignation he feels on behalf of Sung Hui-lien and Li P'ing-erh.

[86] Chaps. 5 and 14.

[87] Chap. 47.

[88] *TICS* 26/16b–17a, *TGL* 1.26.372.

[89] Chaps. 30ff.

[90] Chap. 59.

[91] Chap. 62.

[92] *TICS* 65/10a, *TGL* 3.65.185–86. The description of this incident in the novel varies somewhat from Chang Chu-p'o's summary here, which seems to be based more on the language of the last half of the chapter couplet.

22. But why does the author devote space to the various singing girls such as Li Kuei-chieh, Wu Yin-erh, and Cheng Ai-yüeh? They serve the purpose of demonstrating the insatiability, frivolity, and vulgarity of Hsi-men Ch'ing. Li Kuei-chieh and Wu Yin-erh are purposeful duplications [*t'e-fan* 特犯] of P'an Chin-lien and Li P'ing-erh, respectively, demonstrating that by taste and affinity the latter pair are indistinguishable from prostitutes and that though they may never have actually engaged in that trade, their wantonness and depravity are such that they not only show the same proclivities as prostitutes, but will go even further than they do. The author portrays Cheng Ai-yüeh in yet another way—as fragrant, smooth, and soft—in order to bring out the unrelieved boorishness of Hsi-men Ch'ing, who is depicted by contrast [*fan-ch'en* 反襯] as being incapable of fully appreciating even the refinements of a high-class whore.[93]

23. Why has the author created Wang Liu-erh, Pen the Fourth's wife, and Lady Lin? These three characters are depicted in different ways and serve different purposes. The depiction of Wang Liu-erh is solely intended to illustrate the theme that money [*ts'ai* 財] commands sex [*se* 色]. If you observe the lengths to which she goes to ingratiate herself with Hsi-men Ch'ing when he is alive and the alacrity with which she absconds with his property as soon as he is dead,[94] you will see that in the relationship between them, Hsi-men Ch'ing is using money to seek sex and Wang Liu-erh is using sex to seek money. Hsi-men Ch'ing's death follows upon a visit to Wang Liu-erh,[95] so that in the end he finds both sex and money to be empty [*k'ung* 空]. When Wang Liu-erh subsequently meets Ho Kuan-jen, she ends up using sex to seek money just as before.[96] Indeed, though sex can move people, it is no match for money which can be used anywhere for any purpose and is loved by everyone. Thus the author does not conclude [*chieh* 結] the story of Wang Liu-erh, who symbolizes the lust for money, until his last chapter.

The author has created Pen the Fourth's wife as a means of revealing Tai-an's character. He shows that Hsi-men Ch'ing, who seeks only to indulge his own insatiable desires, is unaware of the fact that the example he sets will be followed by his subordinates, who have already learned from him how underlings can take advantage of their masters. Thus, Tai-an's seduction of Hsiao-yü, which eventuates in his marriage to her,[97] is foreshadowed [*fu-hsien* 伏線] in his relations with Pen the

[93] *TICS* 65/10a, *TGL* 3.65.185–86.
[94] *TICS* 81/4b–6a, *TGL* 4.81.119–21.
[95] Chap. 79.
[96] *TICS* 98/11a–b; 100/1a–b, 9a–b; *TGL* 4.98.341; 4.100.357, 365.
[97] *TICS* 95/1b–2b, *TGL* 4.95.292–93.

Fourth's wife.[98] You may say that Pen the Fourth's wife is used as a foil to depict [*p'ei-hsieh* 陪寫] Wang Liu-erh, but this is a subsidiary function.

As for Lady Lin, she serves as a vehicle for expressing the incalculable resentment the author feels in his heart for P'an Chin-lien. Not only does he have her murdered and mutilated,[99] but he is not satisfied until he has damned even the household in which she got her start in life and the persons who taught her to be what she is. How can we see this? P'an Chin-lien is sold as a child into the household of Imperial Commissioner Wang where she is taught to sing and dance.[100] To argue that she is utterly devious and shameless from birth is not consonant with the doctrines that conscience is innate and that human nature is basically good. I am sure that she was not necessarily as dissolute as this at the age of three or four. During the time when she was a member of Imperial Commissioner Wang's establishment, if the male members of the household had shown respect for propriety and righteousness and the female members of the household had honored chastity and integrity so that obscene words and deeds were neither to be heard nor seen, then, even if she had been dissolute to begin with, she would have been transformed into a chaste girl. How is it that this imposing imperial commissioner neither pacifies distant peoples in the name of the Son of Heaven nor proclaims the imperial majesty and virtue but, instead, when the ten-year-old daughter of a tailor enters his household, devotes his leisure time to teaching her how to paint her face with cosmetics and encourages her to put on airs. If he carries on like this with a lowly serving maid, the way he conducts himself with his legitimate wife can be imagined. How fitting that his son, Wang San-kuan, should be a good-for-nothing profligate and his own wife, Lady Lin, a dissolute adulteress. Who is there to blame but himself? But what the imperial commissioner teaches P'an Chin-lien results in incalculable harm to many people, from Wu Ta in the beginning to Hsi-men Ch'ing at the end. It is certainly fitting that the imperial commissioner's retribution [*huan-pao* 還報] should come in the form of Lady Lin's adultery with Hsi-men Ch'ing.[101] This is why I say the author has a profound hatred for P'an Chin-lien, a hatred that extends even to the household in which she got her start in life, and this is why he devotes attention to Lady Lin.

But Chang Ta-hu also contributes to P'an Chin-lien's corruption,[102]

---

[98] Chap. 87.
[99] *TICS* 87/10a–11b, *TGL* 4.87.193–94.
[100] *TICS* 1/22b, *TGL* 1.1.25.
[101] Chap. 69.
[102] *TICS* 1/22a–23b, *TGL* 1.1.24–27.

so why does the author neglect him? The answer is that it is his nephew, Chang Erh-kuan, who takes over Hsi-men Ch'ing's official post after the latter's death, and it is he whom Ying Po-chüeh persuades to take Li Chiao-erh into his household.[103] Clearly, he is another Hsi-men Ch'ing who will suffer a similar indescribable retribution for his own sins. In this novel, undescribed but implied incidents ("pu cho pi-mo ch'u" 不着筆墨處] occur without number. In the case of Chang Erh-kuan, the author has hidden another large book between the lines of his text [*wu-pi ch'u* 無筆處]. This is an example of material implied but not directly written out on the page ["pi pu tao erh i tao" 筆不到而意到].

24. As for the depiction of Wu Yüeh-niang in the *Chin P'ing Mei*, people all say that Hsi-men Ch'ing is lucky to have such a wife. They do not understand that the author describes Wu Yüeh-niang's crimes in such a subtle way [*yin-pi* 隱筆] that people do not realize what he is up to. How can we see this? A husband is the person whom a wife looks up to and depends upon for the remainder of her life. If her husband spent large sums of money on concubines in order to secure a male heir and Wu Yüeh-niang raised no objections, this would truly be an ideal marriage and she would be an exemplary wife. But Hsi-men Ch'ing murders husbands in order to steal their wives, which is the conduct of a gangster. Now, when a husband engages in the conduct of a gangster and his wife does not tearfully remonstrate with him but instead neither expresses approval nor disapproval, treats him as a stranger whose welfare is no concern of hers, and regards her compliance as a virtue, can such an attitude withstand scrutiny? As for her relationship with Ch'en Ching-chi, the author goes out of his way to emphasize Wu Yüeh-niang's responsibility for bringing the fox into the chicken coop,[104] an act of indescribable folly. When she finally gets wind of her son-in-law's adultery with P'an Chin-lien, she can think of nothing better to do than to keep the doors locked in the daytime.[105] Afterward, when she drives Ch'en Ching-chi out of the household,[106] sends his wife back to him,[107] and agrees to sell Ch'un-mei to Chou Hsiu,[108] she is merely adjusting her rudder to the wind without any convictions of her own. Moreover, her fondness for hearing Buddhist nuns recite pious texts and her indiscriminate burning of incense are not proper activities for a wife to engage in. It follows from all this that the words "did not pay much

[103] *TICS* 80/10b–11a, *TGL* 4.80.114.
[104] *TICS* 18/7b–13b, *TGL* 1.18.254–59.
[105] *TICS* 85/3a–5a, *TGL* 4.85.157–59.
[106] *TICS* 86/8b–9a, *TGL* 4.86.174–75.
[107] *TICS* 91/1a–b, *TGL* 4.91.235.
[108] *TICS* 86/4a–b, *TGL* 4.86.169–70.

attention to his studies"[109] are the source of the complete ruination of both Hsi-men Ch'ing and Wu Yüeh-niang. How can we see this? If Hsi-men Ch'ing had adhered to the rules of propriety himself, he would have been able to mold his wife accordingly. But instead, merely because he pays no attention to his studies, Wu Yüeh-niang, who has the capacity for goodness, also ends up lacking any understanding of the dictates of propriety. Her everyday activities show no evidence of the protocol a wife should observe in her relations with her husband, but only a lot of superficial gestures in that direction. Wu Yüeh-niang is described as a woman with good intentions who is ignorant of propriety. But good intentions alone are not enough, for ignorance of propriety can lead to incalculable harm. If Wu Yüeh-niang is ultimately responsible for Ch'en Ching-chi's evil deeds, how much worse might things have been if she were not even well intentioned? However, although it is Wu Yüeh-niang who makes Ch'en Ching-chi's crimes possible, it is Hsi-men Ch'ing who must bear responsibility for having failed to set a proper example for his wife.

25. In the art of writing there is a mode of description characterized by the incremental repetition ["chia i-pei hsieh-fa" 加一倍寫法] [of a motif]. This book excels at this type of incremental description [*chia-pei hsieh* 加倍寫]. For example, after describing Hsi-men Ch'ing's "heat" [*je* 熱] the author goes on to describe that of the two censors, Ts'ai and Sung,[110] then that of Grand Marshal Huang,[111] then that of Grand Preceptor Ts'ai,[112] and finally the "heat" of the imperial court itself.[113] This is the incremental repetition [*chia i-pei* 加一倍] of [the motif of] "heat." After describing Hsi-men Ch'ing's "cold" [*leng* 冷] the author goes on to describe Ch'en Ching-chi in the Beggars' Rest,[114] Grand Preceptor Ts'ai's exile,[115] and finally the captivity of the emperors Hui-tsung and Ch'in-tsung.[116] This is incremental repetition of [the motif of] "cold." In brief, the incremental repetition of [the motif of] "heat" is used especially to show the way that "heat" of the sort Hsi-men Ch'ing attains is no rare thing, but Hsi-men Ch'ing knows nothing but to rely on his wealth to commit crimes. The incremental repetition of [the

---

[109] *TICS* 1/4b, *TGL* 1.1.6.
[110] Chap. 49.
[111] *TICS* 65/13a–15b, *TGL* 3.65.188–91.
[112] *TICS* 55/5a–9b, *TGL* 3.55.17–22.
[113] *TICS* 71/10b–12a, *TGL* 3.71.297–99.
[114] *TICS* 93/2b–6b, *TGL* 4.93.267–71.
[115] *TICS* 98/8b, *TGL* 4.98.337.
[116] *TICS* 100/7a, *TGL* 4.100.363.

motif of] "cold" is used precisely to show that "cold" of the sort Hsi-men Ch'ing experiences knows no limit, but this is a point that Hsi-men Ch'ing himself fails to see.[117]

26. The author insists upon describing Wu Yüeh-niang as a pious Buddhist. Does the reader understand the reason for this? In his opening remarks the author enjoins us to purify our six senses,[118] so we can anticipate that he will certainly conclude [*chieh* 結] his work by showing that the two words money [*ts'ai* 財] and sex [*se* 色] are empty [*k'ung* 空]. But only a monk will do to exemplify the conclusion [*chieh* 結] that everything is empty. Hsi-men Ch'ing is not the sort of person to repent before his dying day, and after his death who is there to play this role? Even if Wu Yüeh-niang, after her husband's death, were to disregard the family property and take the tonsure, what would that have to do with the author's use of Hsi-men Ch'ing to exemplify Buddhist doctrine? Thus the only thing is to have Hsi-men Ch'ing himself take the vows. But how is one to get around the fact that he is already dead? The author, after some hesitation,[119] arranges to have Hsiao-ko born at the very hour of Hsi-men Ch'ing's death,[120] so that in the end he may repent and achieve deliverance.[121] The author's mind is that of a Confucian sage, but he has taken the compassionate vow of a Bodhisattva in the hope that there should be no one in the world who conceals his faults to the end or fails to correct them. He hopes that even those who die unrepentant may be able to correct their faults in the life to come. What magnanimity and compassion the author shows for Hsi-men Ch'ing and how great are his efforts to admonish future generations! The author has this denouement [*ta chieh-shu* 大結束] in mind from the outset, but he does not want baldly to introduce Master P'u-ching all of a sudden at the end to spirit Hsiao-ko away without tying this into the rest of the narrative [*wu-t'ou wu-hsü* 無頭無緒]. First, to do that would be to use a hackneyed narrative cliché [*hsün-ch'ang k'o-chiu* 尋常窠臼].[122] Second, the ending would then seem unconnected [*t'o-lo* 脫落] with the body of the text and would appear contrived [*hen-chi* 痕迹]. Therefore he must depict the motif of Wu Yüeh-niang's Buddhist piety off and on throughout his narrative so that it appears and disappears like a snake in

[117] Read *chi* 機 for *chi* 幾.

[118] *TICS* 1/3b, *TGL* 1.1.4.

[119] Read *ch'ih* 跐 for *ch'ih* 痴.

[120] *TICS* 79/24a–25a, *TGL* 4.79.98–99. In chap. 100, the monk P'u-ching tells Wu Yüeh-niang that Hsiao-ko is a reincarnation of Hsi-men Ch'ing.

[121] *TICS* 100/16b–17b, *TGL* 4.100.373.

[122] Read *k'o* 窠 for *ch'ao* 巢.

the grass or a [discontinuous] chalk line [*ts'ao-she hui-hsien* 草蛇灰線]. He especially describes Wu Yüeh-niang's pilgrimage to the Pi-hsia kung[123] in order to lead up to the scene in the Hsüeh-chien tung [Snow Stream Cave], where he gives the reader a glimpse of P'u-ching.[124] It is not until ten years later in the narrative that he brings them together again in the Yung-fu ssu, where all the major characters in the novel reappear in a phantasmagoria only to fade finally from sight, one after the other.[125] Thus the biography [*chuan* 傳] of each of the characters, all of whom are fated to suffer separation in this life and the next, is brought to a conclusion [*chieh* 結]. This is the grand finale [*ta chieh-shu* 大結束] in which the myriad threads [*ch'ien-chen wan-hsien* 千針萬線] of the author's narrative are all resolved and allowed to recede into the great void from whence they came.

Thus, in depicting Wu Yüeh-niang's Buddhist piety the author is certainly not merely describing in a general way the everyday practices of a lay believer for the benefit of pious village women. The marvelous quality of this book lies in the skill with which the arteries that connect widely separated elements of the plot [*ch'ien-li fu-mai* 千里伏脉] are concealed. The author never resorts to facile writing [*i-an chih pi* 易安之筆] or the use of elements for which connections [*sun* 筍] have not been prepared. That is why the *Ch'in P'ing Mei* surpasses all other books.

27. It is also necessary to keep in mind that the author, in the course of his depiction of Wu Yüeh-niang's Buddhist piety, also unobtrusively [*yin* 隱] describes the numerous secret plots and devious schemes of the three Buddhist nuns, such as inducing Wu Yüeh-niang to burn incense at night [as a means of effecting a reconciliation with Hsi-men Ch'ing],[126] and procuring for her a drug to insure conception.[127] There is nothing they will not stoop to. Thus, the author's description of Wu Yüeh-niang's Buddhist piety is also a means of depicting the darker side of her character. The reader should be aware of this.

28. Meng Yü-lou is the only major character in the book whom the author allows to come to a decent end.[128] Why is this? She functions as a contrastive foil to Li P'ing-erh and P'an Chin-lien. After suffering the misfortune of the early death of her first husband, although she is unable

---

[123] Chap. 84.

[124] *TICS* 84/7a–8a, *TGL* 4.84.153–54.

[125] *TICS* 100/11a–17b, *TGL* 4.100.367–74.

[126] *TICS* 21/1a–4a, *TGL* 1.21.293–96.

[127] *TICS* 40/1a–2b, 50/11a–b, 53/4a–5b, 64/4a; *TGL* 2.40.182–83, 2.50.322–23, 2.53.371–73, 3.64.168.

[128] Chaps. 91–92.

to remain faithful to his memory, at least she lives in quiet seclusion and leaves it to a go-between to find her a match. When she enters Hsi-men Ch'ing's household,[129] although she may be open to criticism for her unseemly haste, this is a common occurrence among widows. She suffers grievously from her husband's neglect, but bears it patiently and is willing to make the best of her fate. This is where her superiority to all the other women in the novel shows up. Ch'un-mei consistently gives herself airs, while Meng Yü-lou is consistently circumspect. Thus, it turns out that Ch'un-mei falls victim to her desires[130] whereas Meng Yü-lou, after undergoing a period of hardship, achieves long-lasting happiness.

29. The episode in which Ch'en Ching-chi goes to Yen-chou [in an abortive attempt to blackmail Meng Yü-lou][131] seems superfluous [*she-tsu* 蛇足] at first glance, but in fact the author uses it for three purposes ["i-pi erh san-yung" 一筆而三用]. First, it provides the cause for Ch'en Ching-chi's sudden descent in the world to the point that he is forced to resort to the Beggars' Rest.[132] Second, it prepares the way [*fu-hsien* 伏線] for the suicide of Ch'en Ching-chi's wife, the daughter of Hsi-men Ch'ing.[133] Third, it demonstrates that Meng Yü-lou in her marriage to Li Kung-pi has really allied herself with an understanding mate whose lifelong companionship will make up for the three or four years of unhappiness she has endured in the household of Hsi-men Ch'ing. How can we see this? The reason why Meng Yü-lou is unmoved by Ch'en Ching-chi's blandishments is that she is in love with her husband, and Li Kung-pi, in turn, would rather die than give up his wife. Can a love that one would rather die than forsake be anything but true love? It is clear that Meng Yü-lou will not have to complain of her husband's infidelities in her old age. If we take a look at Meng Yü-lou's attractive personality, it is clear that she is really a beauty of the first rank, but Hsi-men Ch'ing remains infatuated by his prior conquest, P'an Chin-lien. Thus, the author's description of Meng Yü-lou is clearly intended to emphasize the fact that Hsi-men Ch'ing is a vulgar plebian who is only bent on slaking his lust, but has no appreciation for true beauty.

30. When Meng Yü-lou enters Hsi-men Ch'ing's household she does so with full observance of the proprieties.[134] If we compare this

---

129 Chap. 7.
130 *TICS* 100/1b–6b, *TGL* 4.100.357–62.
131 Chap. 92.
132 *TICS* 93/1b–3a, *TGL* 4.93.266–68.
133 *TICS* 92/12b–14a, *TGL* 4.92.260–62.
134 Chap. 7.

with the furtive way in which Hsi-men Ch'ing carries off P'an Chin-
lien[135] and his adulterous liaison with Li P'ing-erh,[136] the difference is
greater than that between Heaven and earth. These modes of matrimony
also differ in what they portend of good and ill. Meng Yü-lou's marriage
to Li Kung-pi is also arranged for and carried out with full observance of
the proprieties.[137] If we compare this to the way in which Li Chiao-erh
departs the household after the haggling of the old bawd,[138] Sun Hsüeh-
o elopes by night with Lai Wang,[139] and P'an Chin-lien is led away by
Dame Wang without a farewell tear,[140] the difference between the
auspicious and the inauspicious is clear. Thus, the author has made a
point of depicting this true beauty in order to prove how incapable Hsi-
men Ch'ing is of appreciating any refinement.

31. P'an Chin-lien and Li P'ing-erh no sooner enter Hsi-men Ch'ing's
household than they are subjected to humiliation,[141] Meng Yü-lou is the
only person in the household who is never criticized from beginning to
end. Truly, the author had a point in doing this.

32. Hsi-men Ch'ing is an undiscerning scoundrel, Wu Yüeh-niang is
an artful hypocrite, Meng Yü-lou is endearing, P'an Chin-lien is in-
human, Li P'ing-erh is infatuated, Ch'un-mei is unruly, Ch'en Ching-
chi is a frivolous nonentity, Li Chiao-erh is lifeless, Sun Hsüeh-o is
stupid, Sung Hui-lien does not know her place, and Ju-i is a mere
surrogate. As for the rest, Wang Liu-erh, Lady Lin, Li Kuei-chieh, and
the like can scarcely be considered human. Ying Po-chüeh, Hsieh Hsi-ta,
and company are utterly unconscionable, and Grand Preceptor Ts'ai and
the censors, Ts'ai and Sung, might just as well never have been born.

33. Shih-tzu chieh [Lion Street] is the setting in which Wu Sung
finally murders P'an Chin-lien to avenge his brother's death.[142] It is
there that Hsi-men Ch'ing almost loses his life[143] and that Hua Tzu-hsü
also comes to grief not long afterward.[144] Hsi-men Ch'ing frequents it
[in order to carry on his affair with Li P'ing-erh],[145] and later on Wang
Liu-erh moves there on Hsi-men Ch'ing's account.[146] P'an Chin-lien

---

[135] *TICS* 9/1b, *TGL* 1.9.122.

[136] Chap. 13.

[137] Chap. 91.

[138] *TICS* 80/8b–9b, *TGL* 4.80.112.

[139] *TICS* 90/8b–11b, *TGL* 4.90.230–33.

[140] *TICS* 86/8a–12b, *TGL* 4.86.174–78.

[141] *TICS* 12/7a–10b, 19/12a–16b; *TGL* 1.12.161–65, 1.19.271–76.

[142] Chap. 87.

[143] *TICS* 9/9b–11b, *TGL* 1.9.131–33.

[144] *TICS* 14/8a, *TGL* 1.14.97.

[145] *TICS* 16/1a–13b, 17/1a–3a; *TGL* 1.16.217–31, 1.17.232–34.

[146] *TICS* 38/4a–7b, 39/1a–b; *TGL* 2.38.156–60, 2.39.166.

twice visits it to enjoy the Lantern Festival.[147] The author uses this street
to depict to perfection the way in which petty people, in their self-
importance, indulge their evil desires while remaining oblivious to their
ominous surroundings.

34. The *Chin P'ing Mei* is a veritable *Shih-chi* [Records of the Historian; by Ssu-ma Ch'ien, b. 145 B.C.], but the *Shih-chi*, though it contains
both individual biographies [*tu-chuan* 獨傳] and collective biographies
[*ho-chuan* 合傳], treats each biography separately. The hundred chapters
of the *Chin P'ing Mei*, on the other hand, constitute a single biography
[*chuan* 傳] in which hundreds of characters are treated. Though the presentation is discontinuous [*tuan-tuan hsü-hsü* 斷斷續續], each character
has a biography of his own. Thus, it is obvious that the author of the
Chin P'ing Mei could have written a *Shih-chi*. Since he has already accomplished a more difficult task, what difficulty would he have found in
accomplishing an easier one?

35. I have often noticed that those who write commentaries [*p'i* 批]
to any particular book often insist upon criticizing other books as a means
of raising the status of the one they are concerned with. They do not
realize that literature is in the public domain. The fact that one work of
literature is marvelous does not prevent other works from being marvelous too. If I happen to appraise the marvelous qualities of a particular
work, the marvelous qualities of other works do not eclipse the marvels
of the one with which I am primarily concerned. If I were to write a
work myself, I could not claim that once my work appeared, the other
works in the world had ceased to be marvelous. Nor could I claim that
there were not in the world any works more marvelous than mine. Why
should one, then, when writing a commentary on any work, treat it as if
it were one's own and feel the necessity to prove that no work in the
world is its equal? This only reveals a selfish and narrow mind that
would certainly be incapable of producing good writing. If one is incapable of writing well oneself, how can one comment on the good
writing of others? When I say that it would have been easier to compose
the *Shih-chi* than the *Chin P'ing Mei*, I refer to the fact that its component
parts are presented separately [*fen-tso* 分做] whereas those of the *Chin
P'ing Mei* are integrated [*ho-tso* 合做]. If Ssu-ma Ch'ien himself were to
be reborn, I am sure that he would not say that I was being partial to the
Chin P'ing Mei. I am not claiming that the *Shih-chi* is any less marvelous
than the *Chin P'ing Mei*; yet the *Chin P'ing Mei* has succeeded in capturing the marvelous qualities of the *Shih-chi*. The successes and failures of
works of art can only be understood by the discerning. I confine myself

147 Chaps. 15 and 24.

to appreciating the marvelous qualities of the works with which I am particularly concerned. Why should I worry about whether the authors are ancient or modern, engage in debates on their behalf, or apologize for them?

36. The writers of novels never divulge their names, either because they have some axe to grind [*yü-i* 寓意] in their works or because they contain covert references to real people. Since the authors have decided to abide by the principle of only speaking well of others without dwelling on their faults ["yin-e yang-shan chih pi" 隱惡揚善之筆] and conceal the real names of the people on whom their characters are modeled and since they choose not to divulge their own real names, why are men of later times so anxious to search for clues to the underlying reality and call every person by his right name? How petty such desires are! Moreover, hearsay in such matters is generally apocryphal and not to be taken seriously. To sum the matter up in a word: if the author had not had intense feelings he would never have written the book. If the persons whom he wished to describe duly make their appearance in his book, but the author, who had such intense feelings about them, could not bring himself to name them explicitly, it would be the height of inanity for us, who have no such intense feelings ourselves, to insist on identifying them. Therefore I shall ignore the theory that Hsi-men Ch'ing was intended to represent Yen Shih-fan 嚴世蕃 [1513–1565], whose style 別號 was Tung-lou (Eastern Tower] and whose childhood name was Ch'ing-erh.[148] As for the person who wrote this book, I shall simply refer to him as the author. Since he did not choose to attach his name to the book, why should I try to second-guess him?

Recently I saw a work called *Ti-ch'i ts'ai-tzu shu* 第七才子書 [The Seventh Work by and for Geniuses: an edition of the *P'i-p'a chi* 琵琶記 with commentary by Mao Lun 毛綸 and his son, Mao Tsung-kang 毛宗崗] which is full of speculation about Wang the Fourth 王四.[149]

---

[148] The similarity of his style, 東樓, and the main character's surname, Hsi-men 西門 (West Gate), and the identity of the other set of names 慶 was cited to prove a connection between the two. On this theory see Wu Han 吳晗, "*Chin P'ing Mei* ti chu-tso shih-tai chi ch'i she-hui pei-ching" 金瓶梅的著作時代及其社會背景 (The Date of the Composition of the *Chin P'ing Mei* and Its Social Background), in his *Tu shih cha-chi* 讀史劄記 (Notes on Reading the Histories; Peking: San-lien shu-tien, 1956), pp. 1–38 passim, and André Lévy, "Introduction to the French Translation of the *Jin Ping Mei cihua*," Marc Martinez, trans., *Renditions* 24: 109–29 (1985), pp. 116–19. Contemporary material treating rumors that Hsi-men Ch'ing was modeled on Yen Shih-fan or T'ang Shun-chih 唐順之 (1507–1560) and that the author was Wang Shih-chen 王世貞 (1526–1590) has been translated by Yang Qinghua as a supplement to Lévy's introduction, pp. 118–19, 121–22.

[149] The commentary was dictated by the blind Mao Lun to his son, Mao Tsung-kang. It contains two prefaces, dated 1665 and 1666, by personal acquaintances. Throughout the

Although every commentator is entitled to his own views, I wonder if the time spent on these inconclusive speculations might not be better devoted to appreciation of the literary techniques embodied in the work. I merely record this here in order to make my position clear to my contemporaries.

37. The *Shih-chi* contains chronological tables and the *Chin P'ing Mei* is also full of specific dates. At the very outset it is stated that Hsi-men Ch'ing is twenty-seven *sui*.[150] When Wu Shen-hsien physiognomizes him he is said to be twenty-nine *sui*.[151] On his deathbed he is said to be thirty-three *sui*.[152] But Kuan-ko is stated to have been born in the fourth year of the Cheng-ho reign period [1114], during the cyclical year *ping-shen* [1116],[153] and to have died in the fifth year of the Cheng-ho reign period [1115], during the cyclical year *ting-yu* [1117].[154] Now if Hsi-men Ch'ing's son was born when he was twenty-nine *sui* during the cyclical year *ping-shen* [1116], he should have been thirty-three *sui* during the cyclical year *keng-tzu* [1120]. But Hsi-men Ch'ing is said to have died during the cyclical year *wu-hsü* [1118].[155] The death of Li P'ing-erh should also have taken place in the fifth year of the Cheng-ho reign period [1115], but is stated to have occurred in the seventh year of that period [1117].[156] These are all places where the author has deliberately introduced incongruities [*ts'en-tz'u chih ch'u* 參差之處] into the chronology. Why has he done so? Because this book is different from other novels. The events of these three or four years appear to be accounted for day by day, hour by hour. We are told whether it is spring or autumn, cold or hot, that such-and-such a day is someone's birthday, that such-and-such a person is invited for a visit on such-and-such a day of such-and-such a month, that such-and-such a day is the day of a particular

---

commentary the Maos champion the theory that the play is a satirical work aimed at a man called Wang the Fourth. See *Ti-ch'i ts'ai-tzu shu* (Suchou: Ta-wen t'ang, 1735 preface), "Tsung-lun" 總論 (General Comments), p. 1/4a. One of the proofs given that this is so is the fact that there are four *wang* 王 elements in the original title of the play.

[150] *TICS* 1/4a, *TGL* 1.1.6. *Sui* 歲 here is the unit of measure in the Chinese system of counting a person's age and is generally one "year" more than one's age according to the Western system.

[151] *TICS* 29/5b, *TGL* 2.29.16.

[152] *TICS* 79/21a, *TGL* 4.79.96.

[153] *TICS* 30/9b, *TGL* 2.30.39. Both the *TICS* and other editions of the novel ("Ch'ung-chen" 崇禎 edition, 30/49b; and "Tz'u-hua" 詞話 edition, Daian reprint, 30/248.6) give the cyclical year as *wu-shen* 戊申, for which the nearest possible years are 1068 and 1128. At a later point, Chang Chu-p'o notices the discrepancy and ascribes it to the author's use of allegory (*TICS* 39/5b, interlineal comment).

[154] *TICS* 59/16a, *TGL* 3.59.85.

[155] *TICS* 79/21a, *TGL* 4.79.96.

[156] *TICS* 63/8b, *TGL* 3.63.159.

festival. All elapsed time seems to be scrupulously accounted for. But if
the author had arranged the chronology of these three to five years so
that there would be no discrepancies whatever, his work would really
have constituted no more than a daily record of the events in Hsi-men
Ch'ing's household, as some benighted critics have alleged.[157] Thus the
author has deliberately introduced discrepancies into the chronology.
The multitudinous events of these three to five years of prosperity are
brought vividly to life, day by day and festival by festival. They are
not mechanically [*ssu-pan* 死板] strung together. Although they are arranged in order and you can tick them off one by one, they still have the
power to dazzle the reader into feeling as though he has lived through
each and every day. This is marvelous writing. When skill reaches this
level the miraculous plane [*hua* 化] is reached. I dare not treat such a
timeless literary masterpiece as just a work of ordinary fiction.

38. The hundred chapters of this work constitute a single chapter.
Only if you expand your view until you can read it as a single chapter
will you be able to appreciate its overall structure [*ch'i-chin ch'u* 起盡處].

39. These hundred chapters were not written in a day, but they were
conceived on particular days at particular times. If you try to imagine
how the author conceived of this wealth of individually structured
episodes you will come to realize how much planning, interweaving
[*ch'uan-ch'a* 穿插], and tailoring [*ts'ai-chien* 裁剪] was required.

40. If you read the *Chin P'ing Mei* as a description of actual events
you will be deceived by it. You must read it as a work of literature in
order not to be deceived by it.

41. If you read the *Chin P'ing Mei* as a work of literature by the
author you will still be deceived by it. You must read it as though it were
your own work in order not to be deceived by it.

42. Though you should certainly read it as though it were your own
work it is even better to read it as a work that is still in its early planning
stages. Only if you start out with the assumption that you will have to
work out every detail for yourself in order to avoid being deceived will
you avoid being deceived.

43. The prerequisites for a successful literary creation can be summed
up in the two words emotion and reason [*ch'ing-li* 情理]. The key to this
long work of a hundred chapters is also only these two words, emotion
and reason. If you can determine the particular mixture of emotion and
reason in a character's heart you have captured the character. Though this
character's speech may be mixed in with those of many others, whenever

---

[157] Yüan Chung-tao 袁中道 (1570–1624), for example. See Patrick D. Hanan, "The
Text of the *Chin P'ing Mei*," *Asia Major*, n.s. 9.1:44 (1962).

he opens his mouth, what he says will express his particular balance of emotion and reason. It is not that his emotion and reason are revealed only when he opens his mouth, but that only after the author has determined his balance of emotion and reason is he able to open his mouth. Thus the process involved in depicting any number of characters is the same as that involved in depicting any one, and it is possible in this way to produce a work with the plenitude of this great hundred-chapter novel.

44. In the *Chin P'ing Mei* the description of seemingly unrelated events is often inserted [*chia-hsü* 夾叙] at points of high tension in the development of the plot. Thus, the episode in which Hsi-men Ch'ing marries Meng Yü-lou[158] is introduced [*ch'a* 插] into the narrative just before P'an Chin-lien is taken into his household.[159] The marriage of Hsi-men Ch'ing's daughter, Hsi-men Ta-chieh, is inserted into the episode about his marriage to Meng Yü-lou.[160] Wu Tien-en's loan from Hsi-men Ch'ing is inserted right after the birth of Kuan-ko.[161] Ch'ang Shih-chieh comes to request a loan just at the point when Kuan-ko is about to die.[162] The episode in which Yü-hsiao accepts P'an Chin-lien's three conditions comes at the time of Li P'ing-erh's death.[163] The invitation to Grand Marshal Huang occurs in the middle of the arrangements for Li P'ing-erh's funeral.[164] All of these are examples of deliberate retardation at points of high tension in the narrative ["pai-mang-chung ku tso hsiao-hsien chih pi" 百忙中故作消閒之筆]. How could anyone but an author richly endowed with talent be capable of such effects?

There are also cases like that in which Wu Sung demands to know Hsi-men Ch'ing's whereabouts from Manager Fu. During this point of such high tension, the information that the manager receives a salary of two taels of silver a month is slipped in.[165] These are examples of the incidental use of a light touch [*ch'ing-pi* 輕筆] to bring out an essential truth [*shen-li* 神理] and do not belong under the heading of the technique [*chang-fa* 章法] discussed above.

45. One of the marvelous things about the *Chin P'ing Mei* is the expert use of the device of duplication [*fan-pi* 犯筆] without being repetitive [*fan* 犯]. For example, the author depicts an Ying Po-chüeh and then

---

[158] Chap. 7.

[159] *TICS* 9/1b, *TGL* 1.9.122.

[160] *TICS* 8/1a, *TGL* 1.8.109.

[161] *TICS* 31/1a–4a, *TGL* 2.31.42–45.

[162] *TICS* 59/14a, *TGL* 3.59.83–84. Chang Chu-p'o has Hsieh Hsi-ta's name here by mistake.

[163] *TICS* 64/2b–4a, *TGL* 3.64.167–68.

[164] Chap. 65.

[165] *TICS* 9/9b, *TGL* 1.9.131.

goes on to depict a Hsieh Hsi-ta, but throughout the work Ying Po-chüeh remains Ying Po-chüeh and Hsieh Hsi-ta remains Hsieh Hsi-ta. Each of them retains a distinct identity and mode of conversation so that there is never the slightest confusion between them. He depicts a P'an Chin-lien and then goes on to depict a Li P'ing-erh. This could be described as repetitive, yet from first to last, whether they are together or apart, there is never the slightest confusion between them in their words or acts. He depicts a Wang Liu-erh and then insists upon going on to depict the wife of Pen the Fourth. He depicts a Li Kuei-chieh and then insists upon going on to depict a Wu Yin-erh and a Cheng Ai-yüeh. He depicts a Dame Wang and then insists upon going on to depict an Auntie Hsüeh, a Dame Feng, an Auntie Wen, and a Dame T'ao. He depicts a Nun Hsüeh and then insists upon going on to depict a Nun Wang and a Nun Liu. All of these are examples of the marvelous way in which the author purposely duplicates characters [*t'e-t'e fan-shou* 特特犯手] and yet succeeds in individualizing each character so that they all remain distinct.

46. In the *Chin P'ing Mei* Hsi-men Ch'ing is never drawn with cultivated strokes [*wen-pi* 文筆], Wu Yüeh-niang is never drawn with obvious strokes [*hsien-pi* 顯筆], Meng Yü-lou is always drawn with attractive strokes [*ch'iao-pi* 俏筆], P'an Chin-lien is never drawn with dull strokes [*tun-pi* 鈍筆], Li P'ing-erh is never drawn with profound strokes [*shen-pi* 深筆], Ch'un-mei is always drawn with disdainful strokes [*ao-pi* 傲筆], Ch'en Ching-chi is never drawn with appealing strokes [*yün-pi* 韻筆], Hsi-men Ta-chieh is never drawn with refined strokes [*hsiu-pi* 秀筆], Ying Po-chüeh is never drawn with dull-witted strokes [*tai-pi* 呆筆], and Tai-an is never drawn with stupid strokes [*ch'un-pi* 蠢筆]. Thus, each of the characters is successfully individualized.

47. At the beginning [*ch'i-t'ou* 起頭] of the *Chin P'ing Mei* the author introduces a man and a woman into his narrative only to let them go and then proceeds to do the same thing with another man and woman at the end [*chieh-mo* 結末]. Pu Chih-tao and Cho Tiu-erh are the characters he lets go at the beginning and Ch'u-yün[166] and Li An are the characters he lets go at the end.

Pu Chih-tao is let go at the beginning in order to create a vacancy in the brotherhood and thus leave room for his place to be filled by Hua Tzu-hsü. The author is unwilling simply to introduce Hua Tzu-hsü into his narrative directly [*chih-ch'u* 直出], nor does he wish to give his game away by describing only nine of the ten sworn brothers, thus leaving a vacancy which he will have to bring in Hua Tzu-hsü to fill. Therefore he

---

[166] The text gives her name here as Chin-yün 錦雲 by mistake.

introduces Pu Chih-tao only so that he can remove him at his convenience and thereby create a vacancy in the brotherhood that will provide an opening for the introduction of Hua Tzu-hsü.[167] Moreover, the introduction of Hua Tzu-hsü into the narrative provides a convenient occasion for the introduction of Li P'ing-erh at the same time.[168] Otherwise, if he had initially introduced Hua Tzu-hsü as one of the sworn brothers, it would have necessitated additional explanation when the time came to introduce Li P'ing-erh. Thus, although Pu Chih-tao is created for the purpose of providing a vacancy for Hua Tzu-hsü to fill, he also serves to provide an opening [*hsieh-tzu* 楔子] for the introduction of Li P'ing-erh. Since his only function is to provide an opening of this kind, what point would there be in making up a significant name for him? But since a name of some kind is required, why not simply call him Pu Chih-tao [puns with "do not know" 不知道]? Thus his name becomes Pu Chih-tao.

As for Cho Tiu-erh, she too is let go in order to create a vacancy in Hsi-men Ch'ing's household for Meng Yü-lou to fill. Before marrying Meng Yü-lou, Hsi-men Ch'ing had taken Cho Tiu-erh into his household, but after she has been replaced by Meng Yü-lou, Hsi-men Ch'ing forgets about her completely.[169] How different this is from Hsi-men Ch'ing's response to the death of Li P'ing-erh. Day after day he keeps vigil by her coffin or has paper money burnt on her behalf. Her servant girls and the wet nurse keep vigil in her empty chambers[170] and she twice appears to Hsi-men Ch'ing in his dreams.[171] Cho Tiu-erh, by contrast, is allowed to drop completely out[172] of Hsi-men Ch'ing's mind. This is why she is called Tiu-erh [puns with "one who gets dropped" 丟兒]. Thus the author lets these two characters go at the beginning of his work in order to make room for the introduction of other characters.

What of the other characters the author introduces at the end of his work only to let go? Ch'u-yün [Clouds of Ch'u] is introduced as a device to convey indirectly [*ying-tzu* 影子] the idea that the household of Hsi-men Ch'ing will disperse as readily as luminescent clouds at sunset.[173] Though beauty may be inexhaustible, man's life is finite; when death comes to your door, though you should possess beauties such as

---

[167] *TICS* 1/5b–9b, *TGL* 1.1.7–11.

[168] *TICS* 1/9b–11a, *TGL* 1.1.10–12.

[169] *TICS* 1/6b–18b, 2/12a, 7/1b; *TGL* 1.1.8–21, 1.2.44, 1.7.95.

[170] Chaps. 62–67.

[171] *TICS* 67/17b–18a, 71/6b–7b; *TGL* 3.67.221–22, 3.71.293–94.

[172] Read *k'ai* 開 for *hsien* 閒.

[173] *TICS* 77/16b–17b, 81/3a; *TGL* 4.77.44–45, 4.81.117.

Hsi Shih and Wang Ch'iang,[174] what will they avail you? Thus the author introduces Ch'u-yün only in order to reinforce the truths expressed in the prologue of his book.[175]

Li An is introduced for the same reason as Han Ai-chieh and like her is accorded the author's most favorable treatment [*man-hsü chih pi* 滿許之筆]. He introduces this filial son, a man of rectitude and honor, to serve as a rock in midstream that is unmoved by the torrent [*chung-liu ti-chu* 中流砥柱]. Why is this? Of the hundreds of characters in this book, from the Grand Preceptor Ts'ai Ching at the top of the social scale to Hou Lin-erh and his ilk at the bottom, there is hardly a decent person to be found. Those who are not the sort who welcome their own defilement or voluntarily prostitute themselves are the kind who attach themselves to the powerful or toady to the rich. If there were no Li An, the sole example of a filial son, would this not be tantamount to the extinction of men of conscience? Observe how the author tells the tale of the mutual reliance of Li An and his mother to show him as a filial son who maintains his chastity as though it were jade and will let no injury befall the body that he has inherited from his parents,[176] in contrast to the likes of Hsi-men Ch'ing and Ch'en Ching-chi who are really inferior to pigs and dogs.

Thus, in the last part [*mo-chieh* 末節] of his narrative the author lets these two characters go, but cannot do the same for the rest of his cast. In fact, he makes a special point of letting these [aforementioned] characters go in order to stimulate critical self-examination on the part of his readers.

48. If the author had chosen to describe Hua Tzu-hsü as one of the brotherhood of ten at the beginning of the book, why could he not have simply introduced Li P'ing-erh at the same time? Before the author took up his brush, his conception of Li P'ing-erh had already taken shape. Since his conception of Li P'ing-erh had already taken shape, her secret assignation and willing adultery with Hsi-men Ch'ing,[177] her marriage to Chiang Chu-shan,[178] and her subsequent marriage to Hsi-men Ch'ing[179] had all been worked out in the author's mind before he

---

[174] Hsi Shih was a beauty found by a minister of the state of Yüeh and sent by him to distract Yüeh's enemy, King Fu-ch'ai (r. 495–473 B.C.) of Wu. Wang Ch'iang is better known as Wang Chao-chün 王昭君, the title she acquired as consort to Emperor Yüan (r. 49–33 B.C.) of the Han dynasty. In an attempt to keep peace with China's northern neighbors she was sent north to marry into the royal family there.

[175] *TICS* 1/1a–4a, *TGL* 1.1.1–5.

[176] *TICS* 100/2a–b, *TGL* 4.100.358–59.

[177] Chap. 13.

[178] Chap. 17.

[179] Chap. 19.

thought about the problem of what name to give her husband. Since her husband is not required to do anything more than supply the function implied by that term, though his presence may be necessary, he scarcely seems to have any real existence; and so the author gives him the name Tzu-hsü [empty or unreal].[180] A vase [*p'ing* 瓶] exists to hold flowers [*hua* 花], so the author gives him the surname Hua.

It occurred to the author, as he was beginning his task, that he should provide a formal biographical sketch [*cheng-chuan* 正傳] of Hsi-men Ch'ing. If he did not introduce Li P'ing-erh in the course of his biography [*chuan* 傳] of Hsi-men Ch'ing, how was he to work her case [*kung-an* 公案] into the story? If he had chosen to deal with her separately, he could not have had Hsi-men Ch'ing say in the opening scene that his next-door neighbor is named Hua So-and-so and his wife's name is such and such.[181] Her separate introduction at a different point would have been an intrusion for which there would have been no connecting threads to what went before ["wu t'ou-hsü chih pi" 無頭緒之筆] and thus would have been unacceptable. Suppose he had waited until after P'an Chin-lien had been taken into Hsi-men Ch'ing's household[182] to introduce Li P'ing-erh into his narrative? Other novels tend to narrate one incident after another, providing the necessary connecting threads [*t'ou-hsü* 頭緒] for each incident at the time, but the *Chin P'ing Mei* relies purely on the technique of Ssu-ma Ch'ien ["T'ai-shih-kung pi-fa" 太史公筆法]. Now, among the writings of Ssu-ma Ch'ien that were designed to focus on a particular person how could any piece be considered worthy of him if it did not prefigure at the very beginning the pivot [*shu-niu* 樞紐] on which events would turn, so that it would function like the collar of a coat or the calyx of a flower? Nowadays when people write a play they always introduce the roster of major characters in the first few scenes. How much the more might one expect this to be true of the *Chin P'ing Mei*, which is one of the most extraordinary books in the world? Thus, the author could not begin a new section from scratch [*ling-ch'u t'ou-hsü* 另出頭緒] to introduce Li P'ing-erh, but instead took advantage of the introduction of Hua Tzu-hsü into the brotherhood of ten to touch on Li P'ing-erh.[183] Now, if Ying Po-chüeh and the other mem-

---

[180] Dating back at least to Ssu-ma Hsiang-ju's 司馬相如 (179–117 B.C.) "Tzu-hsü fu" 子虛賦 (The Rhyme Prose of Mister Fantasy), the words *tzu-hsü* in a name have been used to indicate to the reader that a character is a made-up person and fulfills allegorical functions.

[181] This is how Li P'ing-erh is actually introduced into the narrative. See *TICS* 1/9b–11a, *TGL* 1.1.11–13.

[182] Chap. 9.

[183] *TICS* 1/9a–18a, *TGL* 1.1.8–20.

bers of the group had not already been introduced as the boon compan-
ions of Hsi-men Ch'ing, what reason would there have been for an oath
of brotherhood? If the author had introduced Hua Tzu-hsü as one of the
original ten members of the brotherhood, then they would have been in
constant contact with each other. In that case, in chapter 1, when Hsi-
men Ch'ing and Ying Po-chüeh meet, Hua Tzu-hsü would be familiar
to both of them, and there would be no reason for Hsi-men Ch'ing to
mention his wife, let alone the fact that they are next-door neighbors or
that his wife is a fine person.[184] Thus the author has chosen not to make
Hua Tzu-hsü a member of the original brotherhood so that he can use
this occasion to bring him into it and give Hsi-men Ch'ing a reason for
mentioning the fact that they are next-door neighbors. By these means
Li P'ing-erh is introduced, the fact of their being next-door neighbors is
made clear, and the whole situation of Hua Tzu-hsü's household is
vividly implied without being explicitly described in words [*pu-yen chih
piao* 不言之表]. This in turn has led the author to think of the death of Pu
Chih-tao[185] as providing a reason for Hsi-men Ch'ing to think of asking
Hua Tzu-hsü to join the brotherhood.

The author achieves his effects with such supernatural skill ["shen-
kung kuei-fu chih pi" 神工鬼斧之筆] that the twists and turns [*ch'ü-che*
曲折] of the plot beguile the reader without permitting him to see where
the golden needle has done its work ["chin-chen chih i tu" 金針之一度].
That is why I say that his mode of composition is purely that of Ssu-ma
Ch'ien [*Lung-men wen-tzu* 龍門文字]. Whenever I concentrate my attention on this kind of writing, following its every twist and turn and
exploring its structure [*ch'i-chin* 起盡], I feel just as though I were dis-
covering the extraordinary sights of the five sacred mountains and the
three islands of the immortals. I can never tire of pleasures such as these.

49. In the *Chin P'ing Mei* even the jokes and songs are all pertinent to
the occasion and contribute to the desired effect. They may reveal something of the meaning of the chapter in which they occur, fill in [*tsu* 足]
something from a previous chapter, or divulge [*t'ou* 透] something about
the chapters to come. I will devote a separate comment [*chu* 注] to each
of them as they occur.

50. There is no feature of the art of writing that is not illustrated in
the *Chin P'ing Mei*. It would be impossible to describe them all adequately at one time, so I will point them out in my comments at the
beginning of the chapters in which they occur.

51. In the *Chin P'ing Mei* lewd language is used more often by P'an

---

[184] *TICS* 1/9b–11a, *TGL* 1.1.11–12.
[185] *TICS* 1/9a–10a, *TGL* 1.1.10–11.

Chin-lien and Wang Liu-erh than by anyone else, with Li P'ing-erh running a poor third. Among the others, Wu Yüeh-niang and Meng Yü-lou are each shown using it only once, and Ch'un-mei's practice in this respect is only hinted [*tien-jan* 點染] at. Why is this? The only time Wu Yüeh-niang is shown using lewd language is on the night before she sweeps snow to make tea.[186] This scene is intended to show both Wu Yüeh-niang and Hsi-men Ch'ing in an unfavorable light. The only time Meng Yü-lou is shown using lewd language is on the night when her bitterness culminates in an upset stomach.[187] This scene is intended to indicate the injustice that Meng Yü-lou has to suffer and to show Hsi-men Ch'ing in an unfavorable light. It is not really the author's intent in these scenes to depict Wu Yüeh-niang or Meng Yü-lou as lascivious. As for Ch'un-mei, the author wishes to save her for the task of illustrating the reversal of fortunes [*yen-liang fan-an* 炎涼翻案], so he has to preserve her dignity and can only hint [*ying-hsieh* 影寫] at her sexual behavior. The author has put into the mouths of P'an Chin-lien and Wang Liu-erh totally shameless and utterly unspeakable things, so intolerable that even Li Kuei-chieh and Cheng Ai-yüeh could never have brought themselves to say them. By so doing the author expresses his profound condemnation of Hsi-men Ch'ing, who is really less than human, for when he is exposed to such bestiality he actually expresses a preference for it. It follows that when Wang Liu-erh and P'an Chin-lien both get a crack at him on the same day, it is the death of Hsi-men Ch'ing.[188] This is the real point that the author wishes to make.

As for Li P'ing-erh, she is capable of forbearance, yet she brings troubles on herself; she doesn't meddle in other peoples' affairs, yet she causes Hua Tzu-hsü to die of chagrin, invites her own seduction, and remarries without a qualm. Thus she is not really very different from P'an Chin-lien, and there is no reason why the author should not also exhibit her in an unfavorable light. But Li P'ing-erh is weak whereas P'an Chin-lien is ruthless, so the author has depicted her lewdness somewhat more favorably than P'an Chin-lien's. Moreover, Li P'ing-erh signs her own death warrant when she permits Hsi-men Ch'ing to try out his aphrodisiac on her while she is in her menstrual period.[189] Thus the author emphasizes the point that when women are given to concupiscence, if they do not hurt others they will hurt themselves. Alas! It is a fearful thing indeed.

As for the likes of Sung Hui-lien and Ju-i, they do not possess

---

[186] *TICS* 21/3b–4a, 9b–10a; *TGL* 1.21.295–96, 302.
[187] *TICS* 75/15b–20a, *TGL* 3.75.370–73.
[188] *TICS* 79/3a–23b, *TGL* 4.79.80–98.
[189] *TICS* 50/9a–11a, *TGL* 2.50.321–22.

anything in the way of moral character that might inhibit the author from portraying them in an offensive light. As I have already pointed out [see item twenty-three above], the author is motivated to create Lady Lin of the household of Imperial Commissioner Wang by his desire to visit retribution [*pao-ying* 報應] upon the household in which P'an Chin-lien got her start in life, so there is no reason for him not to depict her in an offensive light.

52. The *Chin P'ing Mei* should not be read in a desultory fashion. If you read it that way you will only read the obscene passages. Only if you take several days and read it all the way through will you perceive the connecting nerves and arteries [*kuan-t'ung ch'i-mai* 貫通氣脉] that act like a single thread upon which the author has strung together his succession of rising and falling actions [*ch'i-fu* 起伏].

53. Anyone who says the *Chin P'ing Mei* is an obscene book has only taken the trouble to read the obscene passages. I read this book exactly as though it were a work by Ssu-ma Ch'ien [*Shih-kung wen-tzu* 史公文字].

54. If the author of the *Chin P'ing Mei* were to have written another book about loyal ministers and filial sons, he would have been certain to produce an original work on these subjects that depicted its characters with uncanny fidelity to life [*mo-shen hsiao-ying* 摹神肖影], capturing their very spirit [*chui-hun ch'ü-p'o* 追魂取魄]. How do I know this? I know it from his success in representing [*mo-hsieh* 摹寫] adulterous men and lascivious women.

55. Nowadays, if a Buddhist monk reads the *Chin P'ing Mei* openly he is sure to be criticized, so he can only read it on the sly. People do not understand that only a true monk is fit to read the *Chin P'ing Mei*.

56. Nowadays, if a scholar reads the *Chin P'ing Mei* his parents and teachers are sure to forbid it, and they themselves do not dare to read it openly. People do not understand that only a true scholar is able to read the *Chin P'ing Mei* properly. Anyone who reads it on the sly is really reading an obscene book.

57. The author of the *Chin P'ing Mei* must have been an avatar of Sudhana[190] in order to be able to escape so dexterously from all his narrative problems and always find a happy solution. Otherwise, it is hard to imagine how he could have done it.

58. The author of the *Chin P'ing Mei* must have had the capacity to become a Bodhisattva in order to be able to achieve such extraordinary literary effects ["lin-chiao feng-tsui wen-tzu" 麟角鳳嘴文字].

59. The author of the *Chin P'ing Mei* must have experienced danger, difficulty, poverty, and sorrow and must have been thoroughly ac-

---

[190] Read *ts'ai* 財 for *ts'ai* 才. Sudhana was one of the Buddha's disciples.

quainted with the ways of the world in order to be able to depict the inner spirit of his characters with such verisimilitude [*mo-shen* 摹神].

60. However, if the author had felt it necessary to have personally experienced everything he describes in order to produce this book, the *Chin P'ing Mei* could never have been written. Why is this? The various licentious women in the book engage in illicit relations with men in a variety of different ways. If the author had to have personally experienced all of these things in order to understand them, how could he have done it? Thus, it is apparent that there is nothing a genius [*ts'ai-tzu* 才子] cannot apprehend if he concentrates his mind upon it.

61. Once his concentration has enabled him to apprehend what he needs to know about a character, the author must be able to become that character himself [*hsien-shen* 現身] before he can speak for him. Thus, he has actually become the various licentious women whom he describes, and he is able to expound his lesson through them.

62. The author succeeds in portraying each of the characters in his book with utter fidelity to human nature [*jen-ch'ing* 人情]. He transforms himself [*hua-shen* 化身] into a multitude of guises, representing all sorts of people in order to expound his lesson through them.

63. While portraying each of his characters with utter fidelity to human nature [*jen-ch'ing* 人情], the author is also faithful in his portrayal of the way of Heaven [*t'ien-tao* 天道]. From ancient times it is in ways such as these that Heaven has punished the wicked, rewarded the good, and overthrown the powerful and unscrupulous. When we read this book, it seems as though there must have been a person with brush in hand inside the household of Hsi-men Ch'ing, across from the district yamen in Ch'ing-ho hsien, recording everything that happened, great and small, first and last, down to the very plates and bowls. It seems so real that we can hardly believe that the author took brush in hand, spread out a sheet of paper before him, and made it all up. That is why I say that the author's portrayal is faithful to the way of Heaven.

64. In reading the *Chin P'ing Mei* one should pay attention to the points that are only sketched in outline [*pai-miao* 白描]. The novice who can appreciate the points that are only sketched in outline will learn to write with unusual economy and skill.

65. In reading the *Chin P'ing Mei* one should pay attention to the points where a particular narrative line is sloughed off [*t'o-hsieh ch'u* 脫卸處]. The novice who appreciates the points where a particular narrative line is sloughed off will learn to be original in his handling of transitions [*kuo-chieh wen-tzu* 過節文字].

66. In reading the *Chin P'ing Mei* one should pay attention to the points where the author gets out of his difficulties [*pi-nan ch'u* 避難處].

The novice who appreciates the way in which he finds easy ways to get out of his difficulties ["pi-nan chiu-i ch'u" 避難就易處] will learn to prefer the light touch [*ch'ing-pi* 輕筆] to the heavy [*chung-pi* 重筆] and will learn how to make his writing deft and ingenious.

67. In reading the *Chin P'ing Mei* one should pay attention to the points where the author handles a proliferation of events with apparent ease ["shou-hsien shih-mang ch'u" 手閒事忙處]. The novice who learns how to do this will be able to handle complicated passages [*fan-yen wen-tzu* 繁衍文字].

68. In reading the *Chin P'ing Mei* one should pay attention to the points where plot elements are intertwined [*ch'uan-ch'a ch'u* 穿插處]. The novice who learns how to do this will be able to write ornate and dazzling passages.

69. In reading the *Chin P'ing Mei* one should pay attention to the points in the text where narrative sections come together [*chieh-hsüeh* 結穴], where new sections begin [*fa-mai* 發脉], and where the episodes are linked or correlated [*chao-ying* 照應] with each other. The novice who learns how to do this will be able to appreciate the *Tso-chuan* 左傳 [The Tso Commentary], the *Kuo-yü* 國語 [Conversations of the States], the *Chuang Tzu* 莊子, the *Li-sao* 離騷 [Encountering Sorrow], the histories, and the philosophers.

70. In reading the *Chin P'ing Mei* one should pay attention to the points where the author takes special pains. Only if one understands why the author takes special pains at the points where he does, is one fit to read the *Chin P'ing Mei* or to say that he knows how to read literature.

71. When I was a child learning to read and write in school I once saw the teacher punish one of my fellow students while saying to him, "I've told you to study the text word by word, not swallow it whole." I was still very young at the time and on overhearing these words took them very much to heart. Thereafter, when reading a text I would linger over each character as though it were a syllable from an aria in a *K'un-ch'ü* 崑曲 opera, drawing out its pronunciation and repeating it over and over again. I would not stop until I had made each word my own. I particularly remember doing this with the phrase "to love antiquity and be diligent in investigating it."[191] No more than three days after I had begun to do this the teacher set us, as a topic for an examination essay, the line "the superior man maintains his dignity and does not wrangle."[192] I felt

[191] *Confucian Analects*, VII.19. See James Legge, trans., *The Chinese Classics*, 5 vols. (Hong Kong: Hong Kong University Press, 1960), vol. 1, p. 201.

[192] *Confucian Analects*, XV.21. See James Legge, trans., *The Chinese Classics*, vol. 1, p. 300.

as I wrote that the task did not seem too hard. When my essay was completed the teacher was greatly surprised and thought I must have copied from someone else, for he had no other way to account for my rapid progress. I was unable to explain it myself. After this the teacher made a point of keeping an eye on me. When he saw that I sat with my head bent over the table, following the text with one hand as I read it out loud, one character at a time, he exclaimed in delight, "So you weren't deceiving me after all," and turning to the rest of the class admonished them to follow my example.

Although I do not claim to have mastered anything yet, I am convinced that in reading a book one should not try to digest it in large chunks at a time. This is true not only of works in the literary language, but even of novels like the *Chin P'ing Mei*. If one tries to take in large chunks of it at a time it will seem as tasteless as chewing wax. The only thing one will be aware of is page after page of women's talk, and one will be unable to see it for the marvelous work of literature that it is. If one is not concerned with it as a marvelous work of literature, but only anxious to read about the marvelous things it contains, one deserves only contempt.

72. Before reading the *Chin P'ing Mei*, one should sit in contemplation for three months. Otherwise his vision may be so clouded that he will miss the point.

73. Lack of talent is due to carelessness, and carelessness is due to inattention. These two traits tend to reinforce each other. Not only will such a person be unable to write well himself, but he will not even be able to recognize good writing when he sees it. Such a person should never be permitted to read the *Chin P'ing Mei*.

74. If a person who writes indifferently to begin with does not write better after reading the *Chin P'ing Mei*, he should burn his writing implements and take up the plow for his enjoyment. There is no longer any need for him to trouble himself with trying to write.

75. The author of the *Chin P'ing Mei* is certainly a genius [*ts'ai-tzu* 才子], but his learning is that of a Bodhisattva, not that of a Confucian sage, for his message is that everything is empty [*k'ung* 空]. If he had taken the further step to nonemptiness he would have written a different book.

76. The *Chin P'ing Mei* concludes [*chieh* 結] with emptiness [*k'ung* 空], but if we look carefully we will see that it is not complete emptiness. This is apparent from the fact that the author brings his work to a conclusion [*chieh* 結] with the transfiguration of Hsiao-ko 孝哥 [filial son], which signifies the fact that filiality [*hsiao* 孝] has the power to transform all evils.

77. The *Chin P'ing Mei* is characterized by an air of resentful indignation, but then its author is certainly a reincarnation of Ssu-ma Ch'ien [who was wrongfully castrated].[193]

78. The *Chin P'ing Mei* is a book that is intended to correct people's faults, as can be seen from the fact that it concludes [*chieh* 結] with the example of Han Ai-chieh. The pun in her name expresses the idea of "seeking *ai* 艾 [moxa] that is three years old in order to cure an illness that has lasted seven years."[194] [That is to say, though there may be a cure for your illness, you won't be able to find it when you need it unless you have prepared it in advance.]

79. The *Chin P'ing Mei* is the work of a person who has achieved great enlightenment. That is why he describes all the failings of Buddhist monks and nuns. Only by so doing could he reveal himself to be a real Bodhisattva or truly enlightened.

80. If the author of the *Chin P'ing Mei* had not chosen to write about the mundane affairs of the vulgar world he could certainly have written works as elegant and romantic as the *Hsi-hsiang chi* 西廂記 [Romance of the Western Chamber] and its like.

81. People who are unable to write themselves ought never to be permitted to read the *Chin P'ing Mei* or it may affect them just the way vulgar people say it will. For people who are writers themselves, reading the *Chin P'ing Mei* is just like reading the *Shih-chi*.

82. The *Chin P'ing Mei* is a work that women should never be permitted to see. Nowadays there are many men who read passages out loud to their wives or concubines while taking their pleasure with them inside the bed curtains. They do not realize that, even among men, there are few who recognize the force of exhortation and admonition or respond appropriately to what they read. How many women are there who are capable of responding appropriately to what they read? What would be the consequences if they were to imitate, however slightly, the things they read about? Its literary style and technique [*wen-fa* 文法, *pi-fa* 筆法] are not such as could or should be studied by women. If they are well educated enough to do so they should be encouraged to read the *Tso-chuan*, the *Kuo-yü*, the *Shih-ching* 詩經 [Classic of Poetry], and other classics and histories.

But if the *Chin P'ing Mei* is a book that ought not to be read, why should I write a commentary [*p'i* 批] on it and thus do an injury to the world? Such a question does not take into account the fact that I really

---

[193] See chap. II above, translation and notes for item 1 of the *Shui-hu chuan tu-fa* essay, for more on Ssu-ma Ch'ien and the idea that literature is produced from resentment.

[194] *Mencius*, IVA.9. See James Legge, trans., *The Chinese Classics*, vol. 2, p. 301.

believe the *Chin P'ing Mei* to be a literary masterpiece that cannot be allowed to go unread, but that, at the same time, it is a book that is unfit for the eyes of women. It is the fear that some may fail to heed this admonition and then hold the *Chin P'ing Mei* to blame for the consequences that has led me to raise this issue here, for I am unwilling to acknowledge that it is the book itself that is at fault.

Now among those men who have some knowledge of how to read a book, who does not read the *Chin P'ing Mei*? Those who read it and find it enjoyable are a source of anxiety to the *Chin P'ing Mei*; anxiety lest they not know why it should be enjoyed and only enjoy it for its licentiousness. Where this is the case, the *Chin P'ing Mei* may do the reader an injury. But, in fact, it is not the *Chin P'ing Mei* that injures him, but he who injures himself. Those who read it and find it objectionable are a source of sorrow to the *Chin P'ing Mei*, sorrow over the fact that although it actually contains nothing objectionable, they insist on objecting to its descriptions of licentiousness. Where this is the case, the reader is doing the *Chin P'ing Mei* an injury. But, in fact, it is not the reader who does the injury nor the *Chin P'ing Mei* itself, but Hsi-men Ch'ing who does it.

What does it mean to say that the *Chin P'ing Mei* does the reader an injury? People who are not good readers are careless and superficial. If you give them the classics and histories to read, they will not be able to get all the way through them. By contrast, they may enjoy reading the *Chin P'ing Mei*, but will dislike reading the second half [*hsia-pan* 下半] of the book. In such a case, the *Chin P'ing Mei* may be thought to do the reader an injury.

What does it mean to say that the reader injures himself? Now, if one person explains the meaning of theft to another, so that he will know what to guard himself against, but the other person takes advantage of the information to acquire the art of thievery, it is not the fault of the original informant. The one who heard the explanation of theft was already a thief by nature. In like manner, the *Chin P'ing Mei* ought not to be held responsible for the responses of its superficial readers.

What does it mean to say that the reader does the *Chin P'ing Mei* an injury? The author of the *Chin P'ing Mei* employed all the power, wisdom, and intelligence at his disposal to depict his adulterous men and lascivious women, corrupt officials and wicked servants, pimps and whores. He drained himself mentally and physically in order to create this literary masterpiece. Now, if benighted readers should succeed in convincing the rest of society that this literary masterpiece should be regarded as an obscene book and kept out of sight, then the labors of the author who drained himself mentally and physically to create this masterpiece not only for his own benefit, but also for that of the gifted writers of all time, would be undone by vulgar men and would prove to have been expended in vain. This is what is meant by saying that the reader does the *Chin P'ing Mei* an injury.

What does it mean to say that it is Hsi-men Ch'ing who does the *Chin P'ing Mei* an injury? If the reader would not read the book as an account of Hsi-men Ch'ing's affairs, but employ his own literary imagination in the attempt to discover retroactively the secrets of the author's marvelous effects, it would be more valuable to him than reading the *Shih-chi* in its entirety. But, unfortunately, no sooner does he begin to read than he becomes absorbed in what Hsi-men Ch'ing is doing and becomes oblivious to the pains expended on the composition by the author. That is why I say that Hsi-men Ch'ing does the *Chin P'ing Mei* an injury. Nevertheless, readers continue, as before, to misread it as the *Chin P'ing Mei* of Hsi-men Ch'ing, rather than appreciating it as the work of its author. I have seen someone's comment on the *Chin P'ing Mei* which states that it is a voluminous daily record of the events in Hsi-men Ch'ing's household.[195] This is so benighted as to be laughable. On what day of what month in what year did he see the author employed in the household of Hsi-men Ch'ing, engaged in writing a daily record of the events there? But there is even someone who, when he reaches the point where Ch'en Ching-chi seduces P'an Chin-lien and gets Ch'un-mei into the bargain,[196] waxes indignant on Hsi-men Ch'ing's behalf over the fact that Ch'en Ching-chi should have been able to steal these two pearls. This pedant does not realize that he has misread the situation again. P'an Chin-lien did not originally belong to Hsi-men Ch'ing, neither did the author create Ch'un-mei so that she might be a permanent possession of his. This episode is deftly drawn with the author's subtle brush as part of his marvelous design. What need is there for this pedant to vent his blind indignation from the sidelines?

Thus, the readers of the *Chin P'ing Mei* are many, but those who do not read it well are also many. Although I would not be so presumptuous as to say that I have succeeded in getting to the bottom of the author's mind, I have felt compelled to write this commentary [*p'i* 批], despite my own inadequacies, by the desire to defend him against all the undeserved calumnies that have been heaped upon him. I would also like to be able to open the drowsy eyes of aspiring writers to the author's achievement while at the same time making some small contribution to the rules of literary composition ["wen-chia chih fa-lü" 文家之法律]. Who can say that this is not worthwhile?

[195] See n. 157 on Yüan Chung-tao above.
[196] *TICS* 82/3a–5a, *TGL* 4.82.130–31.

83. The *Chin P'ing Mei* consists of two halves [*pan-chieh* 半截]. The first half [*shang pan-chieh* 上半截] is "hot" [*je* 熱] and the second half [*hsia pan-chieh* 下半截] is "cold" [*leng* 冷], but in the first half there is "cold" in the "heat" and in the second half there is "heat" in the "cold."

84. The author of the *Chin P'ing Mei*, in the course of describing the household of Hsi-men Ch'ing, also describes quite a few other households, such as those of Wu Ta, Hua Tzu-hsü, Ch'iao Hung, Ch'en Hung, Wu K'ai [Wu Yüeh-niang's elder brother], Chang Ta-hu, Imperial Commissioner Wang, Ying Po-chüeh, Chou Hsiu, and Hsia Yen-ling. This list does not include the household of Chai Ch'ien in the Eastern Capital, or those of Hsi-men Ch'ing's employees, or the relatives by marriage with whom Hsi-men Ch'ing is not on intimate terms. These households alone would account for most of the important officials and prominent families in Ch'ing-ho hsien. Thus, through the description of one man the author has described an entire district. Alas! "Such a chief criminal is greatly to be abhorred."[197] I have not even taken into account the households that suffer complete ruination or gross abuse at Hsi-men Ch'ing's hands. How detestable! How detestable!

85. The author of the *Chin P'ing Mei* depicts Hsi-men Ch'ing as being without a single relative. He has no parents alive in the generation above his, no children or grandchildren in the generation below his, and no siblings in his own generation. Luckily for him, Wu Yüeh-niang does not insist upon her prerogatives as his legitimate second wife. If she had persisted in giving him the silent treatment on P'an Chin-lien's account,[198] what pleasure could Hsi-men Ch'ing have found in life? Yet even with this reprieve he does not correct his faults or engage in self-cultivation, but abandons himself to evil without compunction. It is no wonder that he should go to his death unrepentant.

86. All the relatives of Hsi-men Ch'ing described in the book are false relatives. Kinsman Ch'iao [Ch'iao Hung] is a false kinsman. Kinsman Chai [Chai Ch'ien] is an even falser kinsman. Whose paternal aunt is Aunt Yang? She is a false paternal aunt. Ying Po-chüeh is a false brother. Hsieh Hsi-ta is a false friend. As for the Hua brothers [siblings of Hua Tzu-hsü], they are even more laughable. This is really carrying falseness to the point where it becomes hard to comprehend. Ch'en Ching-chi twice wears mourning,[199] but he is a false filial son. As for the brothers-in-law Shen [husband of Wu Yüeh-niang's eldest sister] and Han [husband of Meng Yü-lou's eldest sister], we hear nothing of their wives,[200]

[197] *Book of Documents*, v.9.16. See James Legge, trans., *The Chinese Classics*, vol. 3, p. 392.
[198] Chaps. 18–20.
[199] *TICS* 63/6b, 79/26b; *TGL* 3.63.156, 4.79.101.
[200] Chang Chu-p'o is in error here.

so they are also false brothers-in-law. The only relatives Hsi-men Ch'ing has are Wu the First [Wu K'ai] and Wu the Second [Wu Yüeh-niang's second brother], and the latter is a very shadowy figure. Wu the First is not a bad sort, and that is why in the end he helps Wu Yüeh-niang out on a number of occasions.[201] Hsi-men Ch'ing does not have a single relative from his own family. The retribution [*pao-ying* 報應] meted out by Heaven is cruel enough, but the author's hatred for him is also virulent. How is it that the people of this day who have a full complement of relatives treat them so coldly and only wish they could find a way of getting rid of them? What sort of attitude is that?

87. Why does the author of the *Chin P'ing Mei* feel it necessary to describe Hsi-men Ch'ing as being alone in the world without a single relative? Only by so doing can be bring out the laughableness of his "heat" [*je* 熱] at the beginning and the completeness of his "cold" [*leng* 冷] at the end, a cold that can never become warm again.

88. Although the author's allegorical purpose [*yü-yen* 寓言] is served by making the fate of Hsi-men Ch'ing's family in Ch'ing-ho hsien so utterly "cold" [*leng* 冷] that not a single person is left to perpetuate it, it is also his hatred for such people that causes him to make sure that there can never be so much as the hope of a rekindled ember. Indeed, a writer, too, can be ruthless!

89. In the *Chin P'ing Mei* there is a Li An who is a filial son,[202] a Wang Hsüan who is a charitable man,[203] an An-t'ung who is a faithful servant,[204] a Huang Mei who is a generous friend,[205] a Tseng Hsiao-hsü who is a loyal official,[206] and a Wu Sung who is both a hero and a devoted brother.[207] Who can say that in this novel's world of lust and desire the will of Heaven and the virtue of the people have been completely obliterated?

90. Although there are numerous good characters in the *Chin P'ing Mei*, all of them are men. There is not a single good woman. If we count them off, the only one who remains faithful to a single mate is Wu Yüeh-niang. But she does not understand that the role of a wife is to govern her household with propriety and that she herself is responsible

---

[201] See Chap. 84 and *TICS* 92/14b–15a, 95/5a–6a; *TGL* 4.92.262, 4.95.296–97.

[202] *TICS* 100/2a–b, *TGL* 4.100.358–59.

[203] *TICS* 93/3a–9a, *TGL* 4.93.268–74.

[204] *TICS* 47/2b–11a, 48/1a–3b; *TGL* 2.47–48.267–81.

[205] *TICS* 47/2a, 11a; 48/1a–2b; *TGL* 2.47.267, 276; 2.48.278–279. On p. 276 Egerton has left out a section that mentions Huang Mei's name and on p. 278 his name is mistakenly romanized as Huang Tuan.

[206] *TICS* 48/1a–3b, 9b–12a; 49/1b; *TGL* 2.48.278–81, 286–90; 2.49.293–94.

[207] Chaps. 1–10, 87.

for much of the trouble that occurs. Han Ai-chieh's final fidelity to the memory of Ch'en Ching-chi is certainly commendable, but the relationship to which she shows such fidelity is not itself a proper one, and her earlier life is anything but blameless.[208] As for Ko Ts'ui-p'ing, her mother takes her away,[209] and since the author does not tell us what becomes of her, we cannot be sure how she turns out. Egregious, indeed, is the *yin* 陰 nature of women. Although it can scarcely be said that there are no examples of chastity among them, yet they find it all too easy to abandon it. Everything depends on the sort of family instruction each woman receives. Only one who recognizes this can take on the fearful responsibility of setting a proper example for his womenfolk. This is a matter in which the head of a family cannot be too careful.

91. In the *Chin P'ing Mei* there are two Taoist masters [Wu Shen-hsien[210] and Huang Chen-jen[211]] and a living Buddha [P'u-ching],[212] and yet they are unable to undo the damage done by a single profane monk. Who is this profane monk? The one who gives Hsi-men Ch'ing the aphrodisiac.[213]

92. Since it is Hsi-men Ch'ing who provides the poison that kills Wu Ta,[214] someone is bound to appear with the poison that proves to be Hsi-men Ch'ing's undoing.[215] How can an immortal [Wu Shen-hsien], a Taoist master [Huang Chen-jen], or a living Buddha [P'u-ching] be of any avail against the will of Heaven?

93. The *Chin P'ing Mei* should not be read inattentively. If the reader allows his attention to wander he will go astray.

94. The reader of the *Chin P'ing Mei* should keep a spittoon handy in order to have something to bang on.

95. The reader of the *Chin P'ing Mei* should keep a sword ready to hand so that he can hack about him to relieve his indignation.

96. The reader of the *Chin P'ing Mei* should hang a bright mirror [*ching* 鏡] in front of himself so that he can see himself fully revealed.

97. The reader of the *Chin P'ing Mei* should keep a good wine by his side so that he can drink lustily in order to dispel the reek of worldliness.

98. The reader of the *Chin P'ing Mei* should burn fine incense on his desk in order to express his gratitude to the author for creating this

---

[208] Chaps. 98–100.
[209] *TICS* 100/7a, *TGL* 4.100.363.
[210] Chap. 29 and *TICS* 79/20b–21b, *TGL* 4.79.95–96.
[211] *TICS* 65/11b–12b, *TGL* 3.65.186–87, and chap. 66.
[212] *TICS* 84/7a–8a, 100/10a–17b; *TGL* 4.84.153–54, 4.100.366–74.
[213] *TICS* 49/11b–16b, *TGL* 2.49.305–11.
[214] *TICS* 5/7a–9a, *TGL* 1.5.81–84.
[215] Chaps. 49 and 79.

literary masterpiece, in all its intricacy [*ch'ü-ch'ü che-che* 曲曲折折], for his enjoyment.

99. The reader of the *Chin P'ing Mei* should keep fragrant tea on his table as an offering of thanks to the author for his pains.

100. The *Chin P'ing Mei* is a clear example of what the Zen school calls exercising one's powers after having attained perfect mastery. In my commentary [*p'i* 批] on the *Chin P'ing Mei* I call attention to the places where the author's perfect mastery is evident.

101. The author of the *Chin P'ing Mei* did not know that he had achieved any such thing as perfect mastery. In my commentary [*p'i* 批] I also call attention to the places where he did not know what perfect mastery he had achieved.

102. The *Chin P'ing Mei* begins [*ch'i* 起] and concludes [*chieh* 結] with "emptiness" [*k'ung* 空].[216] In my commentary [*p'i* 批] I do no more than call attention to this fact. I would certainly not presume to use the word "emptiness" to denigrate the Confucian sages.

103. The author of the *Chin P'ing Mei* is faithful in every particular to human nature [*jen-ch'ing* 人情] and the principles of Heaven [*t'ien-li* 天理]. This shows that he has truly attained complete enlightenment, and in this he is not empty [*k'ung* 空].

104. The *Chin P'ing Mei* is a work of enormous scale and yet it required the most meticulous thought to produce.

105. The *Chin P'ing Mei* is a cautionary work [*ch'eng-jen ti shu* 懲人的書] that may be said to be admonitory in intent. Nevertheless, it has also been described as a book that immerses its reader in the ways of the world [*ju-shih* 入世]. But one could also say that it is a book that enables its reader to escape from the ways of the world [*ch'u-shih* 出世].

106. The three characters of the title *Chin P'ing Mei* [literally, "plum blossoms in a golden vase"] constitute a metaphor for the author's accomplishment. Although this book embodies so many of the beauties of spring, every blossom and every petal of which cost the author the creative powers of spring [*ch'un-kung* 春工] itself to evoke, these beauties should be placed in a golden vase where they can diffuse their fragrance in a cultivated environment and adorn the desks of men of literary talent for all time. They must never be allowed to become the playthings of the rustic or the vulgar. Indeed, plum blossoms in a golden vase depend for their effect on the ability of human effort to enhance the handiwork of Heaven [*t'ien-kung* 天工]. In like manner, the literary quality of this book is such that it seems, in passage after passage, to have stolen the creative powers of nature [*hua-kung* 化工] itself.

[216] *TICS* 1/1a, 100/10a–17b; *TGL* 1.1.4, 4.100.366–74.

107. This book was written as a continuation [*chi* 繼] of the *Sha-kou chi* [The Slaying of the Dog; a famous play on the theme of brotherly love].[217] In place after place it alludes [*ying-hsieh* 影寫] to the relationship between brothers. Even Ho the Ninth has a younger brother, Ho the Tenth;[218] Yang the First has a younger brother, Yang the Second;[219] Chou Hsiu has a younger brother, Chou Hsüan;[220] and Han Tao-kuo has a younger brother, Han the Second.[221] As might be expected, it is only Hsi-men Ch'ing and Ch'en Ching-chi who do not have any brothers.

108. The story begins [*ch'i* 起] with Meng Yü-lou playing the guitar [*t'an-yüan* 彈阮; puns with *t'an-yüan* 歎冤, to sigh with resentment] and concludes [*chieh* 結] with Han Ai-chieh carrying her guitar [*pao-yüan* 抱阮; puns with *pao-yüan* 抱冤, to harbor resentment].[222] This is because the author had a bellyful of outraged tears but no place to shed them. Therefore, he created the *Chin P'ing Mei* as an outlet for his tears.

[217] This play is performed by puppets as part of the funeral ceremonies for Hsi-men Ch'ing (*TICS* 80/5a, *TGL* 4.80.107). At that point in the text, and in item 7 of the chapter comments for that chapter, Chang Chu-p'o mentions again his ideas concerning a special connection between this play and the novel. For a discussion of the use of this play in the novel, see Katherine Carlitz, *The Rhetoric of Chin p'ing mei* (Bloomington, Indiana: Indiana University Press, 1986), p. 99.

[218] *TICS* 76/16b–21a, *TGL* 4.76.16–20.

[219] *TICS* 93/1b–2a, *TGL* 4.93.266–67.

[220] *TICS* 100/3a–7a, *TGL* 4.100.359–65.

[221] Chaps. 33–34, 38, and 100.

[222] *TICS* 27/6b–7a, 100/7b; *TGL* 1.27.381, 4.100.363. The first description of Meng Yü-lou and her guitar does not come until chap. 27, but we are first told that she can play the instrument in chap. 7, and it is perhaps this that Chang Chu-p'o has in mind, as he also discusses this pun in the last item of his chapter comments for chap. 7. The name of this instrument is pronounced *juan* in Standard Chinese, but in Chang Chu-p'o's dialect it could be read as *yüan*. In the text, Han Ai-chieh holds a *yüeh-ch'in* 月琴 (balloon guitar) and not a *juan*, but the two instruments are somewhat similar, and in the chapter comment for chap. 7 Chang Chu-p'o claims that the two instruments are the same.

CHAPTER V

The Wo-hsien ts'ao-t'ang Commentary on the *Ju-lin wai-shih* (The Scholars)

INTRODUCTION:
The Wo-hsien ts'ao-t'ang Commentary on *The Scholars*

Of the six novels that are the focus of this volume, the *Ju-lin wai-shih* 儒林外史 (The Scholars; or The Informal History of the Literati) is the only one that lacks a *tu-fa* essay. However, a fairly high-quality preface and set of anonymous chapter comments from the Wo-hsien ts'ao-t'ang 卧閑草堂 edition can serve as a substitute. The preface and the chapter comments, of course, represent quite a different sort of genre from the *tu-fa* essay, and they in turn are representatives of two quite different genres themselves. The preface tries to establish an overall view of the novel and its place in the novelistic tradition in China, while the chapter comments tend to concentrate on local issues that arise in each particular chapter.

The Wo-hsien ts'ao-t'ang edition of the *Ju-lin wai-shih* is dated 1803 on the title page and is the earliest extant edition of the novel.[1] Unlike the *Hung-lou meng* 紅樓夢 (Dream of the Red Chamber), the only extant manuscript copy of the novel postdates this published version and in fact represents a corrected copy of it.[2] The preface to the edition is dated 1736 and is signed by someone calling himself Hsien-chai lao-jen 閑齋老人 (Old Man of Leisure Studio). There are fifty-six chapters in this version of the novel and all but six[3] of them are followed by unsigned chapter comments varying in length from a sentence or two to several paragraphs.

---

[1] There is a photo-reprint of this edition, *JLWS*.

[2] See Ch'en Hsin 陳新, "*Ju-lin wai-shih* Ch'ing-tai ch'ao-pen ch'u-t'an" 儒林外史清代抄本初探 (A Preliminary Investigation of the Ch'ing Dynasty Manuscript Copy of the *Ju-lin wai-shih*), in *Wen-hsien* 12:83–87 (1982) for a description of this manuscript copy of the novel.

[3] Chaps. 42–44, 53–55.

The edition is unpunctuated, a function often undertaken by the commentator, as in the expression *p'i-tien* 批點 (to add comments and punctuation). The only interlineal comments consist of the rare insertion of one-character indications (*chü* 句) to the reader to treat a certain section as a complete sentence where the context is ambiguous.[4]

The 1736 date of the Hsien-chai lao-jen preface is a problem. Although there is very little positive evidence on the matter, it is generally thought that in 1736 the novel was at best only at an early stage of development. The earliest notice of the novel as a separate, substantially complete work does not come until 1749.[5] Seventeen thirty-six was a watershed year for Wu Ching-tzu 吳敬梓 (1701–1754), the novel's author. The year before, he was recommended for participation in a special examination where the regular "eight-legged essay" form was not used. This examination was designed to promote to the attention of the emperor talented men who were unable to succeed in the regular examinations. However, in 1736, when it came time to travel to the capital to take part in the examination, Wu Ching-tzu was unable to go because of illness.[6] From that time on he seems to have given up all interest in civil service degrees and an official career. Many scholars argue that the bulk of the novel could not have been written until after this time because of the need for growth and change in the author's personal philosophy and because many of the incidents used by him as models for his fictional re-creations had not yet occurred in 1736.

The preface is a fairly perceptive piece of work that in a brief space outlines both the general structure and theme of the novel and lays out its place in the tradition of full-length fiction in the vernacular. It is tempting to speculate that the preface is by Wu Ching-tzu himself. There are cases where an author purposely backdated his text so as to

---

[4] For example, *JLWS* 1/9b.

[5] The novel is mentioned in a poem, "Huai-jen shih" 懷人詩 (Poem of Remembrance), about the author of the novel, Wu Ching-tzu 吳敬梓 (1701–1754), by his friend, Ch'eng Chin-fang 程晉芳 (1718–1784). The poem is quoted in the convenient collection of research materials on the novel, *JLWSYCTL*, p. 9.

[6] Whether Wu Ching-tzu was actually ill or only faked illness has been a matter of debate. However, the facts as we have them seem to indicate that the former is true and that the portrayal of Tu Shao-ch'ing (usually taken as an autobiographical character) faking illness to avoid taking the imperial examination is not based on the author's actual experience. See Ch'en Mei-lin 陳美林, "Kuan-yü Wu Ching-tzu ying cheng-pi wen-t'i" 關於吳敬梓應徵辟問題 (Concerning Wu Ching-tzu and the Special Imperial Examination), collected in his *Wu Ching-tzu yen-chiu* 吳敬梓研究 (Studies on Wu Ching-tzu; Shanghai: Shang-hai ku-chi, 1984), pp. 330–34 for a review of the problem.

avoid political repercussions.[7] However, in this instance, there seems to be a lack of hard evidence to back up such a conjecture.

As for the postchapter comments, the fact that the last item for chapter 30[8] refers to a work first published in 1785 that mentions events that took place in 1782 definitely precludes the idea that the comments are by Wu Ching-tzu or that he even got to see them in a fairly complete state. Critics have pointed out similarities in viewpoint, language, and style between the preface and the chapter comments and have speculated that they are perhaps from the same hand.[9] Some also hold that the authors of the preface and of the chapter comments were probably close friends of Wu Ching-tzu.[10] The lack of balance in the lengths of the different chapter comments and the complete lack of them for some chapters was upsetting to the editor of the Ch'i-hsing t'ang 齊省堂 edition (1874) of the novel, who took it upon himself not only to supply chapter comments for the six chapters missing them, but also to fill out the chapter comments that he considered too brief.[11] None of these added comments will be translated below.

Early notices of the *Ju-lin wai-shih* speak of it as being composed of fifty *chüan* 卷 (chapters). The most influential of these is in the biography of Wu Ching-tzu by Ch'eng Chin-fang 程晉芳 (1718–1784).[12] It has

---

[7] This, for example, was the case with Ch'en Ch'en 陳忱 (b. 1614) and his *Shui-hu houchuan* 水滸後傳 (Continuation of the *Shui-hu chuan*), earliest edition, 1664. Ch'en Ch'en was a Ming dynasty (1368–1644) loyalist. To throw his readers off the track, he attributed his novel to a Sung dynasty (960–1279) loyalist and backdated the commentary (written by himself using a pen name) to 1608, before the fall of the Ming.

[8] *JLWS* 30/16b.

[9] For instance, see *LCH*, vol. 1, p. 463, n. 1, also *JLWSYCTL*, preface by Li Han-ch'iu, p. 7.

[10] See *JLWS*, p. 3a of the 1974 preface and Ch'en Hsin and Tu Wei-mo 杜維沫, "*Ju-lin wai-shih* ti wu-shih-liu hui chen-wei pien" 儒林外史的五十六回真偽辨 (The Authenticity of Chapter Fifty-six of the *Ju-lin wai-shih*), in *Ju-lin wai-shih yen-chiu lun-wen chi* 儒林外史研究論文集 (Collected Articles on the *Ju-lin wai-shih*; Hofei: An-hui jen-min, 1982), p. 160.

[11] The "Li-yen" 例言 (Statement of Editorial Principles) for this edition is quoted in *JLWSYCTL*, p. 132. See especially item number two. These added comments as well as those of other editions by Chang Wen-hu 張文虎 (style T'ien-mu shan-ch'iao 天目山樵, 1808–1885) and others, plus collation notes on the various editions, are conveniently available in the recently published *JLWSHCHPP*.

[12] Quoted in *JLWSYCTL*, pp. 11–13. For other notices of a fifty-chapter version, see Cheng Ming-li 鄭明娳, *Ju-lin wai-shih yen-chiu* 儒林外史研究 (A Study of the *Ju-lin wai-shih*; Taipei: Commercial Press, 1982), p. 31. The most detailed and well-argued proposal for what a fifty-chapter version of the novel should have been like is put forward by Chang P'ei-heng 章培恒, "*Ju-lin wai-shih* yüan-mao ch'u-t'an" 儒林外史原貌初探 (A Preliminary Investigation into the Original State of the *Ju-lin wai-shih*), *Hsüeh-shu yüeh-k'an*, 1982.7:32–39.

been argued that fifty is just a round number used by Ch'eng Chin-fang and copied from him by other writers.[13] In any case, all known premodern editions of the novel (except the sixty-chapter augmented version by the Ch'i-hsing t'ang) have fifty-six chapters.[14]

Chin Ho 金和 (1818–1885) was distantly related by marriage to Wu Ching-tzu and several generations below him. He was also a relative of Chin Chao-yen 金兆燕 (1718–1789+), a personal friend of Wu Ching-tzu's. Chin Ho's assertion that the first edition of the novel was published in Yangchou by Chin Chao-yen when he was an official there (1772–1779) and consisted of only fifty-five chapters[15] has been taken very seriously until recent times. Although there are several factual errors in the short postface in which he set out these ideas and there is a complete lack of corroborating evidence for them (they are based almost entirely on his mother's testimony and first written down more than fifty years after the earliest extant edition of the novel and a century after Wu Ching-tzu's death), editors in the present century have followed his advice by excising chapter 56 and moving the lyric poem that ends that chapter to the end of chapter 55. It is ironic that the credence given to Chin Ho's testimony in modern times far surpasses that given to him by the publishers who printed his postface without making any of the changes that he called for. It would seem that more evidence must be produced before such a drastic step as the deletion of a whole chapter is justified, and this type of thinking is surely behind the recent decision to retain chapter 56 as an appendix in one of the latest reprintings of the novel in China.[16] For our present purposes, it suffices to say that the commentator in the Wo-hsien ts'ao-t'ang edition regarded chapter 56 as genuine.[17]

References to the Chinese text of the *Ju-lin wai-shih* in the translation

[13] Ch'en Hsin and Tu Wei-mo, "*Ju-lin wai-shih* ti wu-shih-liu hui chen-wei pien," p. 160.

[14] The manuscript copy of the novel held in Shanghai contains a copy of Ch'eng Chin-fang's biography of Wu Ching-tzu in which the mention of the novel having fifty chapters is left out. See Ch'en Hsin, "*Ju-lin wai-shih* Ch'ing-tai ch'ao-pen ch'u-t'an," p. 87.

[15] See his 1869 postface to the Suchou Ch'ün-yü chai 群玉齋 edition of the novel, quoted *JLWSYCTL*, pp. 128–30.

[16] See Ch'en Mei-lin, *Wu Ching-tzu yen-chiu*, p. 287.

[17] For further discussion of the problem of chap. 56, see the article by Ch'en Hsin and Tu Wei-mo cited above. Although Chang P'ei-heng thinks the original version of the novel only had fifty chapters, his attack on the reliability of Chin Ho's evidence is even more compelling than that in Ch'en Hsin and Tu Wei-mo's article. See Chang P'ei-heng, "*Ju-lin wai-shih* yüan-shu ying wei wu-shih chüan" 儒林外史原書應為五十卷 (The Original Text of the *Ju-lin wai-shih* Was Fifty Chapters Long), *Fu-tan hsüeh-pao*, 1982.4: 54–61.

below are to a photo-reprint of the Wo-hsien ts'ao-t'ang edition.[18] For English versions of the passages alluded to, the reader is referred to the translation of the novel by Gladys and Hsien-yi Yang, entitled *The Scholars*.[19] Chapter 56 was not translated by the Yangs, who followed the "standard" published version that does not include that chapter. It has not been translated elsewhere into English, to the best of our knowledge, but a summary of its contents is given below as a note to the translation of the chapter comments for that chapter. Since the bulk of the various chapter comments is about events and details that occur in the chapter to which they were appended, many of those types of references have not been annotated. The reader who wishes to know the details is invited to look at the text of the particular chapter commented on. As a general rule, the various comments for each chapter reflect the order in which their related subject matter is presented in the chapter itself.

[18] *JLWS*.
[19] Peking: Foreign Languages Press, 1957.

The Hsien-chai lao-jen (Old Man of Leisure Studio) Preface to the Wo-hsien ts'ao-t'ang Edition of *The Scholars*

Translated by DAVID L. ROLSTON

The total number of ancient and modern works of fiction [*pai-kuan* 稗官] and informal history [*yeh-shih* 野史] must number in the hundreds or thousands, but the ones that everyone loves to read are the *San-kuo chih* 三國志 [Romance of the Three Kingdoms], *Hsi-yu chi* 西遊記 [The Journey to the West], *Shui-hu chuan* 水滸傳 [The Water Margin], and the *Chin P'ing Mei* 金瓶梅, known to the world as the four great marvelous books [*ssu ta ch'i-shu* 四大奇書]. I, however, have my doubts about this.

Fiction [*pai-kuan* 稗官] is one of the [minor] branches of historiography. If one is good at reading such fiction, one can advance to reading real histories. Because of this, works of fiction also [along with regular works of history] have to delineate clearly good and evil [*shan-shan wu-e* 善善惡惡][1] so as to cause the readers to be moved to emulate the good examples given and take the evil ones as a warning. In this way it is perhaps possible to keep social customs and the hearts of men from corruption.

The *Hsi-yu chi* is fantastic and absurd. Critics say that it is a book with a message about the *Tao* 道, that the underlying meaning of its use of phrases such as "the monkey of the mind and the horse of the will" [*hsin-yüan i-ma* 心猿意馬] and "Metal Lord and Wood Mother" [*chin-kung mu-mu* 金公木母][2] is that the heart-mind is none other than the Buddha. This is something I cannot pretend to know anything about. As for the *San-kuo yen-i*, it is not completely in accord with the official historical works. However, the way that the usurpation of the Han by the Wei dynasty [A.D. 220] is followed by the usurpation of the Wei by the Chin dynasty [265] shows clearly how the one was patterned on the other [*i-yang hu-lu* 依樣葫蘆] and was an instance of divine retribution [*t'ien-tao hsün-huan* 天道循環], and this is a fit warning for all those who harbor disloyal hearts. Moreover, there is also the presentation of the reasons for the rise and fall of the states of Shu [221–263] and Wu

[1] This phrase is used in Ssu-ma Ch'ien's 司馬遷 (b. 145 B.C.) discussion of the writing of the *Ch'un-ch'iu* 春秋 (The Spring and Autumn Annals) by Confucius. See the *Shih-chi* (Records of the Historian; Peking: Chung-hua shu-chü, 1975), p. 130.3297.

[2] For a discussion of the use of allegory and these terms in the *Hsi-yu chi*, see Andrew H. Plaks, "Allegory in *Hsi-yu chi* and *Hung-lou meng*," in *Chinese Narrative: Critical and Theoretical Essays*, pp. 175–87. See also Robert E. Hegel, *The Novel in Seventeenth-Century China* (New York: Columbia University Press, 1981), pp. 156–57.

[222–280]—food for deep reflection [*chien* 鑒] on the part of the reader. Considering all this, how can I have anything harsh to say about this novel?

As for the *Shui-hu chuan* and the *Chin P'ing Mei*, the one incites the reader to brigandage and the other incites him to lewdness. Both have been on the proscribed list for a long time.[3] People speak with great interest of their marvelous structure [*chang-fa* 章法] and style. They add that, as for the representation [*mo-hsieh* 摹寫] of characters and incidents —even the description of the most petty details of everyday life—these two novels succeed in capturing both their spirit and appearance [*ch'iung-shen chin-hsiang* 窮神盡像] on paper. They say that this is the successful combination of the attainments of the artisan [*hua-kung* 畫工] and the divinely inspired artist [*hua-kung* 化工] in one author, unsurpassed by other works of fiction [*pai-kuan* 稗官] before or after. Alas! It must be that they have not yet read the *Ju-lin wai-shih!*

Now the term *wai-shih* 外史 [informal history] indicates that this novel does not consider itself a work of official history. The words *ju-lin* 儒林 [forest of literati] in the title indicate that the subject is vastly different from empty and fantastic talk. The novel uses the words "success, fame, riches, and rank" [*kung ming fu kuei* 功名富貴] as the skeleton [*ku* 骨] that holds it together. There are characters who are infatuated by success, fame, riches, and rank and who flatter others and fawn on them; there are characters who rely on their success, fame, riches, and rank to puff themselves up and bully others; there are those who feign disinterest in success, fame, riches, and rank, considering themselves to be miles above the vulgar crowd, but who are seen through and ridiculed by others; finally there are those who refuse the temptations of success, fame, riches, and rank and who are of the highest moral fiber and stand steadfast like pillars in the midst of the strong current [*chung-liu ti-chu* 中流砥柱][4] of debased culture flowing around them. The number of characters who appear in the novel is beyond counting, but their temperament [*hsing-ch'ing* 性情] and the inner springs of their hearts and minds [*hsin-shu* 心術] are all revealed and brought to

---

[3] The *Shui-hu chuan* was first banned in 1642 and was the only novel banned under the Ming dynasty (1368–1644). Both novels were placed on lists of proscribed books in the Ch'ing dynasty (1644–1911). For material on censorship of novels in China, see Wang Li-ch'i 王利器, ed., *Yüan Ming Ch'ing san-tai chin-hui hsiao-shuo hsi-ch'ü shih-liao* 元明清三代禁毀小說戲曲史料 (Historical Materials on the Censorship and Prohibition of Fiction and Drama in the Yüan, Ming, and Ch'ing Dynasties; Shanghai: Shang-hai ku-chi, revised edition, 1981), and Ma T'ai-loi, "Censorship of Fiction in Ming-Ch'ing China," Master's thesis, University of Chicago, Chicago, 1972.

[4] There is a rocky mountain named Ti-chu in the middle of the Yellow River in Shansi Province.

life, one by one, on the pages of the novel. No matter what sort of person the reader may be, he can be sure of coming across characters who will mirror [*ching* 鏡] to him the very depths of his own soul.

The commentary [by Chu Hsi on the *Confucian Analects*] says, "Good examples call forth good from the hearts of men, while bad examples serve to punish and chastise waywardness in men's hearts."[5] This novel contains both, in full measure. The novel has the brilliance of style of the *Shui-hu chuan* and the *Chin P'ing Mei*, but it is not harmful to social customs or the minds and morality of the readers such as they are. Therefore, instead of reading the *Shui-hu chuan* and the *Chin P'ing Mei*, why not read the *Ju-lin wai-shih?* I think that those who are good at reading [*shan-tu* 善讀] fiction [*pai-kuan* 稗官] will not take my words to be an exaggeration.

[5] Chu Hsi 朱熹 (1130–1200) makes this comment in reference to the poems of the *Shih-ching* 詩經 (Classic of Poetry) in his *Ssu-shu chi-chu* 四書集注 (Collected Commentary on the Four Books), *Ssu-pu pei-yao* 四部備要 edition (Taipei: Chung-hua shu-chü, 1965), *Lun-yü* 論語, II.2, p. 1/6b. There is some variation in the exact wording as quoted here. This comment is also quoted in an essay defending the *Chin P'ing Mei* against charges of obscenity ("*Ti-i ch'i-shu* fei yin-shu lun" 第一奇書非淫書論) that appears in some of the Chang Chu-p'o 張竹坡 (1670–1698) commentary editions of that novel.

The Chapter Comments from the Wo-hsien ts'ao-t'ang Edition of *The Scholars*

Translated by SHUEN-FU LIN
Annotation by DAVID L. ROLSTON

Chapter 1   1. Yüan dynasty [1279–1368] *tsa-chü* 雜劇 plays usually begin with a prologue [*hsieh-tzu* 楔子].[1] The prologue introduces the incident to be related by way of something else. However, if it does not have anything to do with the main incident, this is but the random piling up of words by a hack with no refinement. How can one see in that any subtlety of brush and ink? The author of this book uses the talent of a Ssu-ma Ch'ien 司馬遷 [b. 145 B.C., author of the *Shih-chi* 史記 (Records of the Historian)] or a Pan Ku 班固 [32–92, author of the *Han-shu* 漢書 (History of the Han Dynasty)] to write fiction [*pai-kuan* 稗官]. From the prologue in the first chapter one can see how the arteries and veins [*hsieh-mai ching-lo* 血脉經絡] of the entire book are finely interconnected [*kuan-ch'uan ling-lung* 貫穿玲瓏]. The author truly is not willing to waste brush and ink.

2. The four words "success, fame, riches, and rank" [*kung ming fu kuei* 功名富貴] are the number one focal point [*cho-yen ch'u* 着眼處] of the whole book. Therefore this theme is broached [*tien-tou* 點逗] right at the beginning, though only casually and tersely. All the multifarious variations of the rest of the book are nothing but hellish transformations [*ti-yü pien-hsiang* 地獄變相][2] of these four words made manifest. It can be said that this is similar to a blade of grass turning into a sixteen-foot golden Buddha.

3. The incidents of Wang Mien wearing a loose robe and tall hat and sighing over the northward flooding of the Yellow River are taken

---

[1] In Yüan drama the *hsieh-tzu* could be placed before any of the four mandatory acts and did not necessarily have an introductory function. The use of the term here is influenced by Chin Sheng-t'an's comments on the *hsieh-tzu* that he devised for his edition of the *Shui-hu chuan*. See *SHCHPP*, "Hsieh-tzu" prechapter comments, p. 39.

[2] In the Chinese Hades, devices (such as magic mirrors) were used to reveal inner corruption masked by outward appearances. It appears that the commentator seems to understand *ti-yü pien-hsiang* in this more dynamic sense rather than in the more static tradition of Buddhist paintings of hell. For more background on that tradition, see Victor Mair, "Records of Transformation Tableaux (*Pien-hsiang*)," *T'oung Pao*, 72.1–3:2–43 (1986). Mirrors were long considered to have the ability to force demons and genies to reveal their true forms. For examples of this, see the early T'ang dynasty literary language tale, *Ku-ching chi* 古鏡記 (The Ancient Mirror), translated in Chi-chen Wang, *Traditional Chinese Tales* (New York: Columbia University Press, 1944), pp. 3–11.

from the standard biography of Wang Mien [1287–1359].[3] The original
material is incorporated without any trace of stiffness.

4. Success, fame, riches, and rank [*kung ming fu kuei* 功名富貴] are
what all men strive for, but Wang Mien not only does not pursue them,
he avoids them. Not only does Wang Mien himself avoid them, his
mother is afraid of nothing more than them. Alas! Is it really true that
their nature is different from other people? Heaven and Earth are vast,
what do they not contain between them? There has always been a kind
of man who does not eat the food of the mundane world. It is difficult
for him to find those who share the same tastes among the men of the
world.

5. Bailiff Chai does things for Magistrate Shih and Magistrate Shih
does things for his teacher, Mr. Wei. Since each is doing his job on behalf
of his superior, Wang Mien is not the man whom they really have on
their minds. There are poor pedants who, having been befriended by a
magistrate, brag to themselves that once a man has found someone who
really understands him, one can die without regret. How can they be
sure that the magistrate does not come to see them only because of his
superior?

6. The three anonymous characters[4] are the shadows [*ying-tzu* 影子]
of the rest of the characters in the book. Their conversation is the pattern
[*ch'eng-shih* 程式] for the conversations in the rest of the book. Although
just a brief passage, it is very relevant [to the structure of the novel].

7. Before the section about Wang Mien's learning to paint lotus blossoms, there is a passage about the scenery of the lake after the rain clears.[5]
When the stars are about to be banished from Heaven, there is a passage
describing the cold dew and the tranquility of the night.[6] This is a special
way of highlighting [*hung-jan* 烘染] what follows after.

8. Old Ch'in is an extremely kind person. That he neither studies
nor becomes an official does not get in the way of his being an upright
person and a superior man. Through his example the author expresses no
small amount of strong emotion.

Chapter 2 1. The four words "success, fame, riches, and rank" [*kung
ming fu kuei* 功名富貴] are the heart [*chu-nao* 主腦] of the book. The

---

[3] *JLWS* 1/6a, 14a–b. The corresponding passages in the English translation, *Scholars*,
occur on pp. 1.5 and 1.10. The description in the novel borrows most heavily from Chu
I-tsun's 朱彝尊 (1629–1709) biography of Wang Mien, quoted in *JLWSYCTL*, pp.
166–67.

[4] *JLWS* 1/4a–5a, *Scholars* 1.3–4.

[5] *JLWS* 1/3a–b, *Scholars* 1.3.

[6] *JLWS* 1/17b–18a, *Scholars* 1.13.

author does not begrudge using thousands of variations to treat them fully. In the beginning, he does not portray kings, dukes, generals, or ministers, but first he takes up Village Head Hsia. What success, fame, riches, or rank does Village Head Hsia command? Yet he is haughty and full of himself, very much the same as if he were an official promoted to president of one of the Six Boards or a clerk promoted to chief secretary. This is just what Buddha said about the differences among the various chilocosms or what Chuang Tzu [369?–286? B.C.] said about the morning mushroom knowing nothing of the first and last day of the month or the striped cicada knowing nothing about spring and autumn.[7] The subtlety of the writing can reach such heights!

2. Mei Chiu is conceited and is exceedingly pleased with himself, unaware that there is a Provincial Graduate Wang Hui [who far surpasses him in this]. Alas! Can there be levels of obsession with success, fame, riches, and rank [*kung ming fu kuei* 功名富貴]?

3. The story of a spirit jumping into the examination cell [to help Wang Hui][8] is a fabricated dream, but to appear on the same list of successful candidates with Hsün Mei[9] is a genuine dream. Yet Wang Hui, on the contrary, talks about the fabricated dream as if there were indisputable proof for it, but regards the genuine dream as unbelievable. This incident vividly portrays the character and inner workings [*hsin-shu* 心術] of the amoral man of mediocre talent.

4. Chou Chin is an old, ridiculous pedant. If you look into his mind, apart from keeping the vow to maintain a fast that he made in the shrine to Kuan-yin [on behalf of his sick mother] and reading Provincial Graduate Wang Hui's examination essays, there is nothing else up there.

5. The topic of fasting leads to that of dreams. Mei Chiu's dream is used to set off [*yen-ying* 掩映] Wang Hui's dream. The interconnection [*kou-lien* 勾聯] between the fibers [*lo-lo* 羅絡] that make up the text produces a pattern with a myriad of colors and shapes [*wu-hua pa-men* 五花八門].

6. In the novel, neither Bailiff Huang, Constable Li, nor Chief Accountant Ku put in an appearance. The various characters talk about them[10] with such intense interest that it is as if these three people were really present before us. If the author did not have a profound under-

---

[7] *Chuang Tzu* 莊子, *Ssu-pu ts'ung-k'an* 四部叢刊, first series, vol. 31 (Taipei: Commercial Press, 1965), p. 1/5a. See also Burton Watson, trans., *The Complete Works of Chuang Tzu* (New York: Columbia University Press, 1968), p. 30.

[8] *JLWS* 2/12a–b, *Scholars* 2.22–23.

[9] *JLWS* 2/12b–14a, *Scholars* 2.23. The dream comes true *JLWS* 7/9a, *Scholars* 7.80–81.

[10] For Bailiff Huang and Constable Li, see *JLWS* 2/2b–3b, 8b–9a; *Scholars* 2.16, 20. For Chief Accountant Ku, see *JLWS* 2/4b–5a, 7b, 11b; *Scholars* 2.17–18, 22.

standing of the literary techniques of the *Shih-chi* [*Shih-chi pi-fa* 史記筆 法], he would not have been able to achieve this.

7. Chin Yu-yü says, "In this world, the really difficult thing to obtain is a bowl of ready-cooked rice."[11] This remark is enough to cause all the heroes and men of outstanding talent of the myriad generations to shed tears in unison. It is not solely scholar-officials forced to play the flute and beg in the marketplace[12] and princes who have to become fishermen[13] who are the only miserable people.

8. To go to the provincial capital to buy goods is an extremely ordinary thing. Unexpectedly, they [Chin Yu-yü, Chou Chin, etc.] come upon the repairing of the examination school. How true to life [*pi-chen* 逼真] is all this!

Chapter 3 1. On seeing the examination desk, Chou Chin bursts out into loud crying until he vomits blood. The miseries of a lifetime suffered by this old, poverty-stricken pedant—he must have met with countless people like Mei Chiu and Wang Hui—come gushing into his heart all at once. His understanding cannot reach beyond this level. He is not like Juan Chi [210–263] or Shen Ch'u-ming 沈初明 who had something more profound afflicting their hearts.[14]

2. How admirable are Chin Yu-yü and the other merchants! A most heroic and generous act is done by none other than people who neither study nor are officials. This is the author's subtle satire [*wei-tz'u* 微刺], but it is also true to life.

3. Chou Chin has nothing worthy of emulation about him. Apart from examination essays, there is probably nothing else in his head. If he is so obtuse in his grading of examination essays, you can see how obtuse his own essays must have been. The reason for the lateness of his success [in the examinations] is obliquely indicated here. The delicacy of the author's pen in his composition is as fine as hair.

4. When Chou Chin is reading Fan Chin's essay, the passage about

[11]*JLWS* 2/15b. Not translated, *Scholars* 2.24.

[12] In popular accounts, Wu Tzu-hsü 伍子胥, dressed in rags, plays the flute in the marketplace of the Wu capital to get the attention of a patron to help him take revenge against King P'ing (r. 528–514 B.C.) of Ch'u for the murder of his father.

[13] According to popular legend, Chiang Tzu-ya 姜子牙, after an unsuccessful career climaxed by the disgrace of his wife divorcing him, took to fishing to earn his living. He used a straight hook, which he explained by saying that he was fishing for men and not for fish. He finally caught the right man in King Wu of Chou, whom he helped to found the Chou dynasty (1122–256 B.C.), for which he was rewarded with a kingdom.

[14] I have been unable to identify Shen Ch'u-ming. According to Donald Holzman, *Poetry and Politics: The Life and Works of Juan Chi* (Cambridge: Cambridge University Press, 1976), the crucial blow to Juan Chi was the usurpation of power by the Ssu-ma clan at the court of the Wei dynasty (220–265).

Wei Hao-ku is effortlessly inserted [*chia-ch'u* 夾出]. Thus, contour and flex [*po-che* 波折] are introduced into the writing. When the ancient masters wrote, they wanted every brushstroke to have verve and were determined not to let the results come out looking like the tips of a garlic plant [i.e., straight and ordered].

5. The terms "civil service examinations" and "miscellaneous learning," which receive great elaboration later, are casually set out [*fu-an* 伏案] here [in this chapter]. The writing is like a dragon vein stretching thousands of miles [*ch'ien-li lai-lung* 千里來龍], turning and twisting.

6. Butcher Hu is only sketched in lightly, but the way that his person and actions are so marvelous and yet true to life really causes the reader to sigh in appreciation and yell bravo. A friend of mine once said, "One must be careful not to read the *Ju-lin wai-shih* because once having read it, one will feel that in daily social intercourse one runs into nothing but [the kind of people and events portrayed in] the *Ju-lin wai-shih*." In this respect the book is like the nine tripods cast by Emperor Yü [trad. dates, r. 2207–2198 B.C.] decorated with images of all the objects in nature [*chu-ting hsiang-wu* 鑄鼎象物], on which even the hair of the demons and sprites was mercilessly portrayed.[15]

7. When Fan Chin passes the prefectural examination, Butcher Hu brings pork sausages and a bottle of wine himself [to congratulate him]. When he leaves, Butcher Hu throws his jacket over his shoulders and puffs out his stomach.[16] When Fan Chin passes the provincial examination, Butcher Hu has an assistant bring seven or eight catties of meat and four or five thousand cash. The butcher leaves with his head down, smiling.[17] The way that the former and latter passages illuminate each other [*ch'ien-hou ying-tai* 前後映帶] shows how carefully the writing is done.

8. Butcher Hu's words should not be harshly repudiated. When he yells at Fan Chin,[18] this is where he shows that he really loves him. It is only because his temperament is as it is that his words come out like that. When one reviews his words carefully, there is nothing really detestable about them.

9. The subtlety of the introduction of the Chou and Chang families into the narration lies in the fact that it [the description of them] all

---

[15] The description of the tripods that the author of the comments is borrowing from is found in the *Tso-chuan* 左傳 (The Tso Commentary), third year of Duke Hsüan (605 B.C.). See James Legge, trans., *The Chinese Classics*, 5 vols. (Hong Kong: Hong Kong University Press, 1960), vol. 5, pp. 292–93 for Chinese and English text.

[16] *JLWS* 3/8a–9b, *Scholars* 3.31–32.

[17] *JLWS* 3/14a, 20a; *Scholars* 3.35, 39.

[18] *JLWS* 3/9b–10b, *Scholars* 3.32.

comes from Butcher Hu's mouth [*k'ou-chung tai-ch'u* 口中帶出].[19] This really is as subtle as spiders' webs and horses' tracks [*chu-ssu ma-chi* 蛛絲馬迹].

10. At their first meeting, Chang Ching-chai gives silver and a house to Fan Chin. It appears that he is a generous person who loves to make friends, but in reality he is an extremely vulgar and crude person. The writing from the author's pen is like snow that takes the shape of a jade tablet [*kuei* 珪] when it encounters a square shape and takes the shape of a piece of round jade [*pi* 璧] when it encounters a round shape. It is also like water that is round when the basin is round and square when the basin is square.

Chapter 4   1. This text is like water passing through a gorge [*kuo-hsia* 過峽, i.e., transitional], so most of it is composed of the narration of events [*hsü-shih* 敘事]. In reading the narration, one can discern countless literary techniques such as "modulating the rise and fall of narrative segments" [*ch'i-fu* 起伏], "forward and backward reflection between narrative elements" [*chao-ying* 照應], "causing mutual illumination between early and later passages" [*ch'ien-hou ying-tai* 前後映帶], etc. A sloppy writer could never dream of such literary techniques.

2. A monk drinking wine in a family compound is something that ought not to happen.[20] When the tenant farmers break in on the party, this truly catches the drinkers off guard.[21] When Ho Mei-chih pours out wine and his wife comes and sits at the table, the scene really borders on debauchery. But when one reads on to see that what his wife talks about is nothing but her jealousy of Fan Chin's wife, how refined the writing reveals itself to be. This takes the four words, "success, fame, riches, and rank" [*kung ming fu kuei* 功名富貴] right into the mind of a common woman. How can one evaluate the author's elegant thoughts and expressions [*chin-hsin hsiu-k'ou* 錦心繡口]?

3. In the sacrificial hall, when Wei Hao-ku is entertaining guests and the monks are playing tricks, the marriage of Mr. Chou's second daughter is casually mentioned [*tai-ch'u* 帶出].[22] The subtlety of the stitching [*chen-hsien* 針線] [of the text] is difficult to exhaust through explanation.

4. The conversations at the small drinking party in Kuan Yü Temple are beyond the talent of an artisan's brush [*hua-kung* 畫工]. It would take a divinely inspired brush [*hua-kung* 化工] to bring it off. The beginning remarks of this section are especially marvelous. The reader should try

[19] *JLWS* 3/10a, 17a, 19a–20a; *Scholars* 3.32, 37, 39. In the last instance, Butcher Hu says that the Chang family has more gold than the emperor.

[20] *JLWS* 4/4a–b, *Scholars* 4.42.

[21] *JLWS* 4/4b, *Scholars* 4.43.

[22] *JLWS* 4/6b–7a, *Scholars* 4.44.

closing the book [*shih yen-chüan* 試掩卷] and ponder this: if you were to write this section, would you be able to come out with such a beginning? Reading a poem by Tu Fu [712–770], an ancient read the line, "By Yangtze and Han, a stranger who thinks of home," and did not know what could follow in the next line, but when he read on to "One withered pedant, between the *ch'ien* and the *k'un*," he then broke out in praise.[23]

5. Senior Licentiate Yen [Yen Chih-chung] has no sooner said, "I have never cheated anybody out of even an inch of silk or a grain of rice," than we find out that he is keeping someone else's pig as his own.[24] This incident makes the reader understand [Senior Licentiate Yen's character] without wasting too many words. If a clumsy hand had done it, he would surely have said, "Gentle reader pay heed: in reality Senior Licentiate Yen was such-and-such a person." The writing then would be completely without flavor.

6. The author has devoted much effort to the passage about Fan Chin's refusal to use the cups and chopsticks inlaid with silver.[25] There is nothing more detestable on earth than to neglect the fundamental aspects of the pinciples of loyalty, filial piety, integrity, and chastity while keeping severe standards with respect to trivial proprieties. The whole world does this and no one objects and imitators of this kind of debased conduct are everywhere. Therefore, the author does not use serious language to attack it but instead uses jeering words to annihilate it.

7. In the section in which Chang Ching-chai advises the magistrate to pile the beef on the cangue of the imam, the author purposely has him bring up the story about Liu Chi [1311–1375].[26] The host and the two guests at the table speak straightforwardly without any sense of shame. The reader immediately knows that the three of them are benighted to an extreme degree. This is the author's skill that can capture the very wind and water on paper. It is a case of directly narrating the incident itself without expressing one's own judgment ["chih shu ch'i-shih, pu-chia tuan-yü" 直書其事, 不加斷語] so as to let the truth of the matter reveal itself.

Chapter 5   1. This chapter takes up at random the word "riches"

[23] The title of the poem is "The Yangtze and the Han" ("Chiang Han" 江漢). For the Chinese text of the entire poem, see *A Concordance to the Poems of Tu Fu*, 3 vols. (Peiping: Harvard-Yenching Institute, 1940), vol. 2, p. 463. The translation of the two lines follows that of A. C. Graham, *Poems of the Late T'ang* (Harmondsworth: Penguin Books, 1965), p. 45. The *ch'ien* 乾 and *k'un* 坤 are the first two hexagrams of the *I Ching* 易經 (Book of Changes) and stand for Heaven and Earth, respectively.

[24] *JLWS* 4/11a–b, *Scholars* 4.47–48.

[25] *JLWS* 4/12b–13a, *Scholars* 4.48–49.

[26] *JLWS* 4/14a–b, *Scholars* 4.49–50.

from the four words "success, fame, riches, and rank" [*kung ming fu kuei* 功名富貴] and depicts the ways of vulgar and petty people. The stinginess of the miser [Yen Chih-ho] and the cunning of the freeloading licentiates Wang Te and Wang Jen are so minutely portrayed that their hair seems to move. Even if Ssu-ma Ch'ien himself were to wield the pen, he probably could not surpass this to any degree.

2. Yen Chih-chung's character is completely revealed from the mouth of [*k'ou-chung hsieh-ch'u* 口中寫出] his younger brother, Yen Chih-ho.[27] Detail by detail his family's love for food, extreme lack of moral education, and lack of planning are described, forming a sharp contrast to the character of the younger brother. The older brother cheats everyone and lies all his life, but he knows how to pass the time and one does not see him have a single day's difficulty. The younger brother has more than one hundred thousand taels of silver at home, but he constantly worries about becoming poor and every day fears getting into trouble, so one does not see him enjoy his wealth even for a single day. Here is the subtle influence of the Creator. I do not know how the author has penetrated this subtle truth so that he is able to reveal Heaven's secrets.

3. Concubine Chao must have schemed her promotion to chief wife with Yen Chih-ho for a long time. Even people with hearts of iron or stone cannot help being moved by Concubine Chao's words when she is weeping at the foot of Mrs. Yen's bed,[28] but like Yen Chih-chung, in mind and speech Mrs. Yen seems not to be convinced. The author's pen is like the ant that can go through a "nine-crooked pearl" [*chiu-ch'ü chu* 九曲珠, i.e., the hole bends nine times].

4. The two Wang brothers share the same temperament [*hsing-ch'ing* 性情] and pattern of thought [*hsin-shu* 心術]. Examining them carefully, Wang Jen's talent is superior to that of Wang Te. As the saying goes, "One who has a sense of timeliness is an outstanding person." Before the Wang brothers see the mementos [silver and jewelry left behind by their sister for them], they pull long faces and say nothing. Once they see the mementos, they burst into tears until their eyes turn red.[29] They can do what is suitable to the occasion without the least sign of a faux pas. I imagine that people like them must think that with their talent and sensitivity they can control every situation. This has become habitual for them, so they do not feel the least shame.

At the family banquet on New Year's Eve, a frightened cat unexpectedly knocks down a wicker basket containing some silver [that

[27] *JLWS* 5/6a, 8a–b; *Scholars* 5.56–57.
[28] *JLWS* 5/9a–b, *Scholars* 5.57.
[29] *JLWS* 5/10b–11a, *Scholars* 5.58–59.

Mrs. Yen saved up over the years].[30] This incident makes Yen Chih-ho
think of his deceased wife until he becomes ill. This shows the true love
of an ordinary couple who shared the sweet and the bitter alike. One
feels that [Hsün Ts'an's] "cooling his body in the courtyard" [in order to
use it to cool his wife's fever] or [P'an Yüeh's grief at seeing] "her things
left forgotten, still hung on the walls"[31] is not as moving. The marvelousness of the writing really is beyond words to express.

   Chapter 6   1. This chapter presents an unrestrained portrait [*fang-pi
hsieh* 放筆寫] of the wickedness of Yen Chih-chung. However, the
writing has its proper order [*yu tz'u-ti* 有次第] and sequence [*yu hsien-hou*
有先後], just like a fountain spring which fills every hole before it flows
on into the four seas[32] and which, though it divides into branches,
maintains the integrity of its arteries [*mai-lo* 脉絡]. This is unlike fiction
[*pai-kuan* 稗官] written by hacks who, whenever they depict a wicked
person, want him beaten, scolded, slain, or hacked, fearing only that
people will not hate him. The incidents they relate are preposterous and
not to be found in the real world. This is a case of what the ancients
meant when they said, "It is easy to paint ghosts and demons but difficult
to paint human beings" ["hua kuei-kuai i, hua jen-wu nan" 畫鬼怪易, 畫
人物難].[33] Most difficult of all is to capture the spirit [*shen-ssu* 神似] of
ordinary subjects who can be observed by all eyes.

   2. Returning from the provincial capital after the provincial examinations, Yen Chih-chung is overjoyed to see two sets of silk clothes and

---

[30] *JLWS* 5/15a–16a, *Scholars* 5.61–62.

[31] One winter, when his beloved wife had a fever, Hsün Ts'an 荀粲 (courtesy name
Feng-ch'ien 奉倩, fl. 3d century) went out into the courtyard to cool his body, then came
back in to lie with her and cool her down. His wife died anyway, and he followed shortly
after. This story is included in the chapter on "infatuation" (*huo-ni* 惑溺) in Liu I-ch'ing
劉義慶 (403–444), *Shih-shuo hsin-yü* 世說新語 (A New Account of Tales of the World),
Kuo-hsüeh chi-pen ts'ung-shu 國學基本叢書 (Basic Sinological Collection; Taipei: Commercial Press, 1968 reprint, vol. 244) edition, p. 35.228; translated in Richard Mather, *A
New Account of Tales of the World* (Minneapolis: University of Minnesota Press, 1976), pp.
485–86. In that work and in others such as the *Meng-ch'iu* 蒙求, a primer on historical
figures, Hsün Ts'an is treated as an example of reckless infatuation, but in this comment, as well as in a poem by Wu Ching-tzu himself lamenting the death of his wife (see
his collected writings, *Wen-mu shan-fang chi* 文木山房集 [Shanghai: Ku-tien wen-hsüeh,
1957 reprint], p. 4/3a), Hsün Ts'an is treated more sympathetically. The phrase concerning
P'an Yüeh (247–300) comes from the first of three of his poems lamenting his dead wife
("Tao-wang shih" 悼亡詩), quoted in the *Wen-hsüan* 文選 (The Anthology of Refined
Literature; Shanghai: Shang-hai ku-chi, 1986), p. 23.1091. The poem is translated in
Burton Watson, *Chinese Lyricism* (New York: Columbia University Press, 1971), p. 97.

[32] This passage is modeled on *Mencius* IVB.18. See James Legge, trans., *The Chinese
Classics*, vol. 2, p. 324.

[33] The earliest statement of this common conceit is in the *Han Fei Tzu* 韓非子, *Ssu-pu
ts'ung-k'an*, first series, vol. 20, 11/4b (p. 57). See also W. K. Liao, trans., *The Complete
Works of Han Fei Tzu*, 2 vols. (London: Arthur Probsthain, 1939), vol. 2, p. 40.

two hundred taels of silver [gifts from Concubine Chao][34] and repeatedly calls Concubine Chao "sister-in-law." At this moment, Yen Chih-chung desires nothing more than this. Since he is already satisfied, what else could he desire? The author's use of this incident to portray the nature of men in recent days shows his remarkable skill in crafting his characters [*k'o-chi k'o-ch'u* 刻棘刻楮]. If one were to say that, at this point, Yen Chih-chung is already planning to appropriate the property of his brother's widow, this would not only be something that has never existed, but also something that is against all reason. One should know that Yen Chih-chung is nothing but a scoundrel and not necessarily a poisonous snake or a fierce beast.

3. Yen Chih-chung's style of writing must be dry and withered, while that of the Wang brothers is most certainly mixed-up and confused. When the three of them meet and talk at the same table, verbal sparks fly out and no sentence is let go unchallenged.[35] Such a delight to read!

4. Everything Yen Chih-chung has said all his life is probably just a load of lies, but in the lot there are probably a couple of things that are true. For instance, the story about Chang Ching-chai's serving as a go-between is not believable,[36] but the marriage with the Chou family is true.[37] His falling ill on the boat,[38] however, is such that even today no one is able to tell whether it was genuine or faked. As for whether the walnut wafers are medicine or not, not only the steersman knows the truth, but also the dockers, Ssu-tou the servant, and even the reader knows the truth. Why is this? Because it is impossible that there could have been ginseng and gentian in the wafers.[39]

5. Concubine Chao [now the newly widowed Mrs. Yen Chih-ho] thinks that she has the support of the two Wang brothers and that they will be as solid as Mt. T'ai for her. Who would expect that, when she really needs help, they are not the least to be relied on. Abroad in the world, it is this kind of person who is most numerous. They also believe that they can get along by means of their cunning and fraudulence. Therefore, I hate the Wang brothers even more than Yen Chih-chung.

6. Yen Chih-chung's whole life is abnormal and unusual, but he also has some of the style of an unconventional man of letters [*ming-shih* 名士]. He always calls himself one of the gentry, but what status does a senior licentiate have? He constantly refers to Magistrate T'ang as his

[34] *JLWS* 6/2a–b, *Scholars* 6.65.
[35] *JLWS* 6/3a–5a, *Scholars* 6.65–67.
[36] *JLWS* 6/4a, *Scholars* 6.66.
[37] *JLWS* 6/8b–9a, *Scholars* 6.69.
[38] *JLWS* 6/9b, *Scholars* 6.70.
[39] *JLWS* 6/9b–12a, *Scholars* 6.70–71.

friend, yet in reality Magistrate T'ang does not even know him personally. Such brazenness is not easily come by!

7. Many laughable and detestable things, such as the fuss over hiring the musicians,[40] having the attendants wear red and black caps,[41] and putting up the placard with the words "Expectant Magistrate,"[42] are all summarized in Ssu-tou's remark, "empty show."[43] The writing really has tendons and sinews that articulate its entire body [*t'ung-shen chin-chieh* 通身筋節].

Chapter 7   1. This chapter is divided into three sections [*tuan* 段]. The first section is about Mei Chiu's only obtaining the fourth rank in the provincial examination.[44] It is enough to make the reader gladly drink a big cup of wine in homage. After Mei Chiu has been consigned to the fourth rank, he still talks and chatters like a waterfall, acting as if he is really a senior student of the same teacher [as Hsün Mei], completely without any sense of shame.[45] The world is never at a loss for brazen people like him. I think that Mei Chiu and Yen Chih-chung belong to the same category of people. Suppose Mei Chiu were in the other's [Yen Chih-chung's] place and had only a licentiate's degree. He would also refer to himself incessantly as a member of the gentry and an intimate friend of the local magistrate. And if Yen Chih-chung had obtained the fourth rank in the provincial examination, he would brag about being a senior classmate of Hsün Mei's and claim that the examiner had intentionally done him a favor [by upbraiding him].[46]

2. Ch'en Ho-fu's calling up of a spirit is the second section [*tuan* 段].[47] The author has vividly portrayed the manner of talking of an itinerant fortune-teller—absurd, mixing the true and the false, giving out eccentric titles to himself and others, and a mouth full of sophistry. The most laughable thing is that Kuan Yü [160–219] is able to write a lyric song to the tune of "Moonlight on the West River."[48] Anybody with any judgment would never fall for it. Yet Wang Hui and Hsün Mei are so overwhelmed with awe that their hair stands on end.[49] The author can bring out on paper the very marrow of the bones of such ignorant characters.

---

[40] *JLWS* 6/8a–9a, *Scholars* 6.68–69.

[41] *JLWS* 6/7a, *Scholars* 6.68.

[42] *JLWS* 6/7b, *Scholars* 6.68.

[43] *JLWS* 6/8b, *Scholars* 6.69.

[44] *JLWS* 7/4b, *Scholars* 7.78.

[45] *JLWS* 7/5a, *Scholars* 7.78.

[46] As Mei Chiu claims happens to him when Fan Chin scolds him, *JLWS* 7/6a–b, *Scholars* 7.79.

[47] *JLWS* 7/10b–14a, *Scholars* 7.82–84.

[48] *JLWS* 7/13a–b, *Scholars* 7.84. The practice of writing lyric poems to this tune title became popular only centuries after the death of Kuan Yü.

[49] *JLWS* 7/13a, *Scholars* 7.83.

3. Hsün Mei's decision to announce the death of his mother is the third section [*tuan* 段]. Alas! How on earth can the announcement of mourning be hesitated over? The fantastic thing is that when Hsün Mei and Wang Hui seek help from a friend [Chin Tung-ya] in the Board of Rites, he recommends a possible method.[50] When they seek help from Hsün Mei's teachers [Chou Chin and Fan Chin], they are told that the suspension of mourning might be arranged.[51] Only after all methods have been exhausted does Hsün Mei announce his mourning.[52] At the time, nobody regards this as improper. The titular couplet [for the chapter] even attributes the words "showing kindness to a friend" to Wang Hui [who first mentions the idea of suppressing the announcement of mourning]. Is the author really so dim in the head that he does not even know that such people would not be tolerated in a sage king's world? How could he not know this? This is just another example of what the ancients called "directly narrating the incident itself without expressing one's own judgment ["chih shu ch'i-shih, pu chia lun-tuan" 直書其事, 不加論斷], so as to let the truth of the mattr reveal itself."

4. After reading the passage set in Hsüeh Market,[53] I cannot help putting the book aside and sighing. Alas! There are so many people who tease and jeer at the poverty-stricken scholar who buries his head in teaching, struggling all year round, whose name never gets onto the roster of successful provincial examination candidates and whose fame never goes beyond the alleys in his village. However, if one day he should spread his wings and ascend into the blue clouds, winning a place among the most prominent, then even if people in his hometown worship and respect him, he knows nothing of it. One exhausts all one's energy in the pursuit of success, fame, riches, and rank [*kung ming fu kuei* 功名富貴], but once having obtained them, one will not have a moment's peace because the ways of the world are treacherous and official life is full of wind and waves. Po Chü-i [772–846] has the following couplet: "Only on seeing the guests joyous and the manservants well fed, / Does one realize that official position only brings benefit to people other than oneself."[54] In the end, what is it all for?

Chapter 8 1. This chapter concludes [*chieh-kuo* 結過] the story of

[50] *JLWS* 7/15a, *Scholars* 7.85.
[51] *JLWS* 7/15a–b, *Scholars* 7.85.
[52] *JLWS* 7/15b, *Scholars* 7.85.
[53] *JLWS* 7/7a–8b, *Scholars* 7.79–80.
[54] The first two lines of this quatrain read: "Banquets, travel, sleep, and food have gradually lost their appeal; / Wine and music have become nothing but an encumbrance" 宴遊寢食漸無味, 杯酒管絃徒繞身. This poem, titled "Tzu-t'an" 自歎 (Lament for Myself), is included in Po Chü-i's collected poems, *Pai-hsiang shan shih-chi* 白香山詩集, *Ssu-pu pei-yao* 四部備要 (Taipei: Chung-hua shu-chü, 1966 reprint, vols. 148–49) edition, p. 25/9b.

Wang Hui and moves into that of the two Lou brothers. The language gradually becomes more elegant. This is like travelling in the mountains when, after having passed unusual peaks, exotic rocks, and steep hills and cliffs, one suddenly encounters a verdant green stretch which opens up like an entirely new world before one, a world so full of wonders that it is hard to take it all in.

2. Frustration in their official careers while they are young has embittered the two Lou brothers.[55] This is what Su Shih [1037–1101] called "a bellyful of dissatisfaction with the temper of the times."[56] Although they have the manner of unconventional men of letters [*ming-shih* 名士], they are different from the common variety of superficial literary men [*tou-fang ming-shih* 斗方名士].

Chapter 9 1. Because the Lou brothers were not able to acquire the *chin-shih* degree and win a post in the Han-lin Academy in their youth, they have accumulated a lot of bitterness. This is the source of their problems. When they spoke their wild nonsense in front of Prefect Ch'ü, the Prefect sternly reprimanded them.[57] Who would have expected that there is an illiterate villager [Tsou Chi-fu] in a remote place who shares their opinion?[58] How can they not regard this villager as a man of discernment? Upon carefully inquiring into the matter, they realize that there is somebody else from whom he got these ideas.[59] At this point, even if there were a hundred people claiming that Yang Chih-chung is an old loony who does not understand anything, this still could not dampen the Lou brothers' enthusiasm for meeting him. Therefore, the more Yang Chih-chung does not come to see them, the more the Lou brothers become set in their desire to meet him. The author uses the episodes of the old crone answering the door[60] and the boy selling water chestnuts[61] to bring this out lightly, teasing the reader's expectations at the same time. A lofty aftertaste rises up here and there from between the lines of the text.

2. Only after carefully examining the section about Ex-Commander Liu's boatmen using the Lou family name to intimidate other boatmen[62] and the section about the Lou brothers ordering Chin Chüeh to ransom

[55] *JLWS* 8/14a, *Scholars* 8.96.

[56] I have been unable to identify the source of this quotation.

[57] *JLWS* 8/13b, *Scholars* 8.96. The brothers compared the taking of the throne by Emperor Ch'eng-tsu (r. 1402–1424) with Prince Ning's (1478–1521) failed attempt to do the same, related earlier in the chapter.

[58] *JLWS* 9/4a–b, *Scholars* 9.101.

[59] *JLWS* 9/4b–5a, *Scholars* 9.101–2. They learn that Yang Chih-chung is the source.

[60] *JLWS* 9/13b–15b, *Scholars* 9.107–9.

[61] *JLWS* 9/15b–16a, *Scholars* 9.109.

[62] *JLWS* 9/10b–12b, *Scholars* 9.105–7.

Yang Chih-chung[63] does one get a good idea of the true status of members of the gentry class. The Lou brothers are not like Yen Chih-chung, who constantly says he is going to send his calling card to Magistrate T'ang [to get Magistrate T'ang to punish someone on his behalf] even though he has never really met him. In any case, the thing that one should avoid most when writing is bluntness and directness [*chih-shuai* 直率]. If the Lou brothers simply took a boat to New Market and easily met up with Yang Chih-chung, then all of their adventures on the road back and forth would never have happened. Would that not be no different from the abominable style of writing found in vulgar contemporary fiction? What flavor could be found in such writing?

Chapter 10   1. One should compare [*tui-k'an* 對看] this chapter with the passage concerning the wedding of Yen Chih-chung's son.[64] One will find that in the later section the descriptions dazzle like laid-out brocade, while in the earlier section there is an acrid taste that oppresses one.

2. Compiler Lu's pouring a bucket of cold water on the Lou brothers' desire to seek out worthies and visit the virtuous[65] is as bracing as a pair of scissors from Ping-chou or as delicious as the pears of the Ai family.[66] It also vividly shows that Compiler Lu judges people only according to their status and that whenever he speaks he talks of nothing but the usual gossip from the various yamens.[67] Thus, the thrust of this section cuts both ways [*shuang-kuan ch'i-hsia* 雙管齊下]. When Lou Feng calls Compiler Lu "the most vulgar person one can imagine,"[68] this captures in a word the essence of Compiler Lu.

3. On the auspicious day, two strange things happen all of a sudden at the wedding banquet.[69] This plants the seed [*mai-fu* 埋伏] for Compiler Lu falling ill and dying in a later section.[70] The author points out at the time that Compiler Lu feels that these two incidents are not auspicious,[71] but at this point the reader will probably only feel that the incidents are like hills suddenly appearing as if coming from beyond the skies. The

---

[63] *JLWS* 9/8a, *Scholars* 9.103–4.

[64] *JLWS* 7/7a–9a, *Scholars* 7.68–69.

[65] *JLWS* 10/2b–3a, *Scholars* 10. 112.

[66] The metaphor of the scissors comes from a poem by Tu Fu, *A Concordance to the Poems of Tu Fu*, vol. 2, p. 107. The pears of the Ai family are mentioned in the text and notes of the *Shih-shuo hsin-yü*, translated in Richard Mather, *A New Account of Tales of the World*, p. 440 (xxvi.33).

[67] *JLWS* 10/2b, *Scholars* 10.112.

[68] *JLWS* 10/4a, *Scholars* 10.113.

[69] A rat drops from the rafters (*JLWS* 10/13b–14a, *Scholars* 10.128) and a boot goes flying (*JLWS* 10/14a–15b, *Scholars* 10.120–21).

[70] *JLWS* 11/14b–15b, 12/14b–15a; *Scholars* 11.131–32, 12.142.

[71] *JLWS* 10/15a–b, *Scholars* 10.121.

reader will be busy admiring the writing and will not have time to seek out the subtlety in the way that the narrative threads [*hsien-so* 線索] are strung together.

Chapter 11   1. Historically there have been talented women who were skilled in writing poetry, but there has never been a talented woman expert in the civil service examinations. When a woman becomes expert in the civil service examinations, you can be sure that she is a vulgar person. The author wants to exhaust all means possible in his description of Compiler Lu's vulgarity, but he is not willing to use direct description [*cheng-pi* 正筆]. Everywhere he uses only contrastive [*fan-pi* 反筆] and oblique [*ts'e-pi* 側筆] techniques simultaneously to portray and criticize him [*hsing-chi* 形擊]. Writing about the vulgarity of Compiler Lu's daughter is his means of describing the Compiler's vulgarity.

Those who talk about the civil service examinations in the book are many in number. For instance, there are K'uang Ch'ao-jen and Ma Ch'un-shang's editing of examination essays,[72] Wei T'i-shan and Sui Ts'en-an's talk of rectifying the style of the examination essays,[73] and Han-lin Academician Kao's discussion of the secret of how to win first place in the civil service examinations.[74] Every one of them thinks that he has got hold of an all-powerful charm that gives him the edge, not knowing that Compiler Lu's daughter is the only one who is really a professional when it comes to the civil service examinations. One of Lu Chiu-yüan's [1139–1193] disciples once said, "Heroic talent and stature are not embodied in men but in women."[75] The author's implied meaning [*yü-i* 喻意] in this chapter is truly profound and far-reaching.

2. Yang Chih-chung is a loony. Where would an ordinary writer begin if he were to describe his foolish behavior and words? This chapter only uses incidents such as Yang Chih-chung's fondling of the incense burner,[76] his explanation of the mistaking of the surname Lou for Liu,[77] and the bursting in of his drunken second son[78] to depict vividly the sound and demeanor of an old loony. This is like Ku K'ai-chih's [ca. 344–406] adding three hairs to the cheek to make his portrait of P'ei K'ai [237–291] come alive [*chia-shang san-hao* 頰上三毫].[79] Without an outstanding literary mind, it would be very hard to achieve this.

---

[72] Ma Ch'un-shang gives his famous talk on examination essays to Ch'ü Hsien-fu, *JLWS* 13/7a–10a, *Scholars* 13.148–50.

[73] *JLWS* 18/7b–8b, *Scholars* 18.203–5.

[74] *JLWS* 49/5a–7b, *Scholars* 49.539–40.

[75] I have not been able to identify the source of this quotation.

[76] *JLWS* 11/8a–9a, *Scholars* 11.127–28.

[77] *JLWS* 11/10a–b, *Scholars* 11.128.

[78] *JLWS* 11/11a–12a, *Scholars* 11.129.

[79] See Ku K'ai-chih's biography in the *Chin-shu* 晋書 (History of the Chin Dynasty; Peking: Chung-hua shu-chü, 1974), p. 92.2405.

3. All of a sudden there is someone knocking on the door.[80] One would think that it must be the Lou brothers arriving. Who would have expected that it is a stinking drunk [Yang Chih-chung's son] who bursts in? This incident can cause the reader to blink his eyes in surprise. It is totally unexpected. Here the flattest language turns out to contain the most unusual and unexpected peaks and hills. From this one can see that the places where [characters'] introductions are made [*ch'u-lo ch'u* 出落 處] are very important. One can never be slipshod about such places.

4. The old loony no sooner enters the Lou's residence than he re-commends to them another scholar-recluse.[81] The reader is already well aware of the nature of the old loony's personality, so one can imagine that a person recommended by him ought to be really quite ordinary. What the reader doesn't know is that this new person is even more ridiculous than Yang Chih-chung himself. This is just like Wu Tao-tzu's [early 8th century] painting of demons. His portrait of Ox-Head [along with Horse-Face below, he was assistant to the King of Hell] seemed to have already exhaustively captured the horrific fierceness of his subject but, when he went on to paint Horse-Face, he also captured the [dif-ferent and even more awesome] horrific fierceness of Horse-Face.[82] The number of demons that the author could create in his mind is far beyond ordinary conception.

Chapter 12 1. The Lou brothers regard friendship as if it were as important as their very lives. They treat friends with respect and pro-priety. Aren't they elegant and worthy young gentlemen living in a corrupt world? However, they are too gullible and are not selective in their choice of friends. They do not investigate whether someone is genuinely worthy or not, but when they hear of his name they imme-diately go to make friends with him. This is like Duke Tzu-kao of She who did not know that what he actually loved were not dragons but only scaly carps.[83] When Yang Chih-chung comes to stay [at the Lou brothers' residence], he is worried that his position will be too pre-carious, so he is anxious to invite Ch'üan Wu-yung to come help him. Yet only a few days after Ch'üan Wu-yung arrives, they butt heads over

[80] *JLWS* 11/11a, *Scholars* 11.129.

[81] *JLWS* 11/16a–17/1a, *Scholars* 11.132–12.133.

[82] Wu Tao-tzu was especially known for his murals of scenes of hell. Those who saw his work said that all the hellish figures were individually realized. See Chung-kuo shu-hua yen-chiu hui 中國書畫研究會 (Society for the Study of Chinese Calligraphy and Painting), *Chung-kuo ming hua-chia ts'ung-shu* 中國名畫家叢書 (Collectanea on Famous Chinese Painters; Hong Kong: T'ai-p'ing yang t'u-shu, 1970), vol. 1, pp. 207, 210.

[83] The story of Tzu-kao and the dragons comes from Liu Hsiang's 劉向 (77–6 B.C.) *Hsin-hsü* 新序, *Ssu-pu ts'ung-k'an*, first series, vol. 19 (Taipei: Commercial Press, 1965), p. 5/14a. Tzu-kao decorated his house with dragon motifs but was scared to death when a real dragon came to see him.

a mere five hundred coppers.[84] This shows how and why a demon is a demon.

Chapter 13   1. When the leather bag [which is supposed to contain a man's head] is opened,[85] the reader will certainly burst out laughing. But the novel is full of people like Iron-armed Chang [who brought the leather bag]. Those who talk about influence and prominence or rely on power and rank all are doing nothing but using masks to scare ghosts. The author uses one Iron-armed Chang to call up [*yin-ch'i* 引起] countless other Iron-armed Changs.

2. All of Iron-armed Chang's affected manners have the dignity of a supreme counterfeiter. What is the difference between him and those who only cultivate the manner and style of the famous literati [*ming-shih* 名士] without having anything to back it up? Here the author's acupuncture [*chen* 針] is aimed at curing just such people.

Chapter 14   1. When Ma Ch'un-shang is exclaiming over the scenery [at West Lake], he can only think to recite some lines from the *Chung-yung* [The Doctrine of the Mean].[86] It is evident that there is only room enough in his head for exegeses of the classics prepared for examination takers.

Chapter 15   1. Though but a poor pedant, Ma Ch'un-shang is capable of the deed of a very generous man.[87] He ends up being repaid for this by Hung Han-hsien.[88] The author enlightens the reader to no small degree through this incident.

Chapter 16   1. K'uang Ch'ao-jen's filial piety is described as coming out of the sincerity of his basic nature, but once he starts on the path to officialdom, he quickly abandons his wife and remarries another.[89] Is it circumstances that make him behave this way? Or is it because the path of prominent officials and that of beasts share the same spoke on the wheel of transmigration?

Chapter 17   1. The writing of this book involves a myriad variations in style and technique. One cannot simply restrict oneself to one aspect and discuss its marvelousness. For instance, when the book describes women, petty men, and the different lower classes in society, there are

---

[84] *JLWS* 12/12a–13a, *Scholars* 12.140–41.

[85] *JLWS* 13/2a, *Scholars* 13.145.

[86] *JLWS* 14/14b, *Scholars* 14.165. "The earth, which carries Mt. Hua and Mt. Yüeh without feeling their burden, and safely contains the rivers and seas without letting them leak away, supports the myriad things." (*Chung-yung* 中庸 26.9). See James Legge, trans., *The Chinese Classics*, vol. 1, pp. 420–21.

[87] In chap. 14 he gives all his money to help his friend, Ch'ü Hsien-fu.

[88] Ma Ch'un-shang is given some silver by this phony immortal (*JLWS* 15/4a–b, *Scholars* 15.169–70).

[89] *JLWS* 20/3b–4a, *Scholars* 20.222–23.

none but are completely and perfectly captured on paper. Those scholars with their pretenses to refinement and elegance [*tou-fang ming-shih* 斗方名士] and those "masters" of poetry are the real core of the novel's concern, so how can they not be described in detail [*hsieh-chao* 寫照]? In the chapters prior to this, the sights and sounds of such characters as Yang Chih-chung and Ch'üan Wu-yung are so well portrayed as to cause the reader to strike the table and yell "bravo!" [*p'ai-an chiao-chüeh* 拍案叫絕]. One feels that the novel already rivals the nine tripods [of Emperor Yü][90] which bore pictures of all the objects in nature [*chu-ting hsiang-wu* 鑄鼎象物]. There is nothing else that could be added to it. Who could have known that when the book comes to describe characters like Chao Hsüeh-chai and Ching Lan-chiang, it shifts to a new style completely different from the one used to describe Yang Chih-chung and Ch'üan Wu-yung. Chien-yang Palace [built by Emperor Wu of the Han dynasty] had a multitude of doors and rooms.[91] How could wonderful and crafty writing be any way but this?

2. Ssu-ma Kuang [1019–1086] once said, "A simple and honest servant doing just fine all by himself was ruined by Su Shih."[92] As for K'uang Ch'ao-jen, he possesses neither profound learning nor a stable character. If all he met up with were people like Ma Ch'un-shang, he probably would not turn so quickly into a man only concerned with power and status. Unfortunately, once he leaves home again, he runs into people like Ching Lan-chiang and Chao Hsüeh-chai. Even if he desired to resist becoming obsessed with power and status [*shih-li* 勢利], how could he succeed? Fleabane growing amid hemp grows straight without need of support, but raw silk fibers almost always end up getting stained.[93] Whenever I see some bright young people who, once they know how to compose a few lines of pentasyllabic

[90] See n. 15 above.

[91] The building of this palace is described in the *Shih-chi* 史記 (Peking: Chung-hua shu-chü, 1972), p. 28.1402. See also Burton Watson, trans., *Records of the Grand Historian of China*, 2 vols. (New York: Columbia University Press, 1963), vol. 2, p. 66.

[92] The same incident alluded to here is mentioned twice in Chin Sheng-t'an's 金聖歎 (1608–1661) commentary on the *Shui-hu chuan* 水滸傳. See *SHCHPP*, pp. 37.697 and 37.709 (both are interlineal comments). For the original anecdote, see K'ung P'ing-chung 孔平仲 (c. 1040–1105), *K'ung-shih t'an-yüan* 孔氏談苑 (Mr. K'ung's Garden of Anecdotes), quoted in Yen Chung-ch'i 顏中其, ed., *Su Tung-p'o i-shih hui-pian* 蘇東坡軼事彙編 (Collected Anecdotes About Su Tung-p'o; Ch'ang-sha: Yüeh-lu shu-she, 1984), p. 109.

[93] That is to say, environment can influence personal morality and behavior. This saying seems to refer to a similar discussion by Hsün Tzu 荀子 (fl. 3d century B.C.). See *A Concordance to Hsün Tzu*, Harvard-Yenching Sinological Index Supplement 22 (Taipei: Ch'eng-wen, 1966 reprint), "Ch'üan-hsüeh" 勸學 (Encouraging Study) chapter, p. 1.1.11.

regulated verse, want to make friends with those pretenders to scholarly refinement and elegance [*tou-fang ming-shih* 斗方名士] in order to make a name for themselves, I know that they will never accomplish anything in their whole lives. Why? The pretenders to scholarly refinement and elegance cannot become wealthy and prominent [*fu kuei* 富貴] themselves, so they envy the wealth and prominence of others. They themselves have neither success nor fame [*kung ming* 功名], but they envy the success and fame of other people. At best they join the ranks of those who imitate fowls' crowing and dogs' barking [i.e., retainers of prominent families].[94] At worst they suffer the misery of relying on leftover wine and cold victuals.[95] There is a hell on earth for those yet alive, and it is these people who inhabit it. Yet they still joyfully call themselves famous men of letters [*ming-shih* 名士]. How deplorable!

Chapter 18 1. Ching Lan-chiang is concerned with nothing but worshipping Chao Hsüeh-chai, just like Confucius's seventy disciples who totally submitted themselves to the Sage. His sense of judgment is as debased as this.

2. The author inconspicuously brings Chin Tung-ya and Yen Chih-chung back into the narrative [*tai-ch'u* 帶出],[96] bringing to a conclusion [*chieh* 結] the stories [of Wang Hui and Yen Chih-chung] left unresolved in previous sections.[97] How forceful is such writing!

3. When Wei T'i-shan and Sui Ts'en-an shamelessly talk about the examination essays,[98] it is clear from the beginning that they do not know what they are talking about. Yet they regard themselves as veritable incarnations of the Buddha. How laughable! Ma Ch'un-shang hates "miscellaneous learning" more than anything else, but surprisingly enough, Wei and Sui accuse him of promoting it. The interlinking and interweaving [*chiao-hu hui-huan* 交互廻環] of incidents and themes in the text have successfully captured the secret of creating a seamless web [*lo-lo kou-lien* 羅絡鈎連].

---

[94] Lord Meng-ch'ang had two such retainers who were scorned at first but later proved their worth. See *Shih-chi*, p. 75.2355, and Gladys and Hsien-yi Yang, trans., *Records of the Historian* (Hong Kong: Commercial Press, 1974), pp. 79–80.

[95] This refers to the fate of hangers-on at the courts of the rich who have to put up with what they can get. This phrase is found in the "Tsa-i" 雜藝 (Miscellaneous Arts) chapter of Yen Chih-t'ui's 顏之推 (b. A.D. 531) *Yen-shih chia-hsün* 顏氏家訓 (Yen Family Instructions; Shanghai: Shang-hai ku-chi, 1980), p. 526.

[96] *JLWS* 18/5a–7a, *Scholars* 18.202–3. These two characters last appeared in chap. 7.

[97] The Wang Hui affair is talked about (*JLWS* 18/7a and *Scholars* 18.203) and the outcome of Yen Chih-chung's family dispute is revealed (*JLWS* 18/11a and *Scholars* 18.206).

[98] *JLWS* 18/7b–8b, *Scholars* 18.203–5.

4. Hu the Third has enough money, and he is fortunate enough not to be cheated of it by Hung Han-hsien. However, he enjoys making friends with pretenders to refinement and elegance [*tou-fang ming-shih* 斗方名士]. The meeting on West Lake is dominated by an oppressive, fetid atmosphere.[99] Reading that passage has the power to make one feel like vomiting sour food.

Chapter 19   1. This chapter is devoted to the portrayal of P'an the Third. P'an the Third is an ordinary townsman, so his conduct need not be judged too harshly, but what I especially appreciate is his straight-forwardness, glibness, and enterprise. Compared with those vulgar and contentious people in the business of selling their learning, the difference is like night and day. After reading through this chapter, I found myself sighing over and over again. Alas! The author's meaning is extremely profound and far-reaching.

When the Maker of Things gave birth to men, he gave each of them ears, eyes, hands, and feet. Unless he be obtuse or stupid, who wants to wither away in bondage, who would be content with cold, starvation, and in the end death in a gutter or ditch? When the former kings employed people, from the high ministers down to prefects, clerks, and runners, each person, no matter what kind of talent he possessed, had a chance to contribute to society and no one was just discarded. After the civil service examinations were established, those who had not made it through the three examination sessions and had their names appear on the roster of successful metropolitan candidates were called "unclean" or "irregular." Even they do not dare to rank themselves together with the "pure" or the "regular" [who got official degrees]. Some of the cunning ones among them, proud of their brilliance and talent but aware that they will never be prominent, cannot but end up breaking the examination laws in order to obtain prosperity in this world. The laws become more and more numerous, but this does not bring an end to lawbreaking.[100] Is it all because the people have lost their native good-ness? Or is it because they have been driven into that state by those who rule over them? Alas! I cannot sigh enough!

Chapter 20   1. This chapter shows that immediately after K'uang Ch'ao-jen is recommended to be a tutor in the Imperial College,[101] he completely changes his original character. He is a man of small capacity

---

[99] *JLWS* 18/10b–14b, *Scholars* 18.206–8.

[100] This last line is a variation on one in the *Tao te ching* 道德經. See D. C. Lau, trans., *Lao Tzu: Tao Te Ching* (Hong Kong: Chinese University Press, 1982), pp. 82–83 for Chinese text and translation.

[101] *JLWS* 20/1a, *Scholars* 20.221.

and easily overflows with self-conceit. All his evil deeds are in direct contrast to his father's deathbed advice.[102]

2. Whether P'an the Third is to be executed or given corporal punishment is something only the throne and the magistrates can decide. K'uang Ch'ao-jen has no say in the matter. Not only does he have no say, a real superman [*ch'ao-jen* 超人] would send tea and food to P'an the Third [in prison], seek out help for him, and pay the ransom money to free him in order to repay all the favors and assistance received from him. But K'uang Ch'ao-jen throws his conscience to the winds, making the excuse that he is implementing the punishment decreed by the throne. What's more, he even says, "If I had been in office here I would have had him arrested myself."[103] Neither the black heart of the wolf nor the venom of snake or insect could be worse than this man. In the past, Ts'ai Yung [132–192] wept over Tung Cho's [d. 192] corpse.[104] The reason that the superior man does not regard him as wrong in so doing is because the bonds between friends also have their due. If everybody in the world were like K'uang Ch'ao-jen, friendship would suffer horribly.

Chapter 21 1. Niu P'u's studying poetry solely for the purpose of making the acquaintance of people with status shows that he is the number one debased person in the world. He is someone who does not command success, fame, riches, or rank [*kung ming fu kuei* 功名富貴] but envies those who have got them. This is what Confucianists have in mind when they say that flattering people with fine words and fawning looks is "harder than weeding in the summertime"[105] or, [to describe him] in the words of the Buddhists, "one who eats human feces—not a very good dog."[106]

Niu P'u's grandfather and Old Pu are poor, illiterate men. Yet they are earnest in character, true to friends, and far superior in virtue to many rich and literate men. The author's message behind his special effort in depicting such people is really profound.

2. One who steals money or possessions is a thief. One who steals

---

[102] *JLWS* 17/5a–b, *Scholars* 17.191.

[103] *JLWS* 20/8b, *Scholars* 20.226.

[104] See Ssu-ma Kuang 司馬光, *Tzu-chih t'ung-chien* 資治通鑑 (Comprehensive Mirror for Aid in Government; Peking: Chung-hua shu-chü, 1976), pp. 60.1934–35, This incident is treated in chap. 9 of *The Romance of the Three Kingdoms*. Tung Cho was a usurper and a tyrant. The commentator in the 120-chapter "Li Chih" commentary edition of *The Romance of the Three Kingdoms* approved of Ts'ai Yung's crying for Tung Cho using the same general argument given here. See marginal comment, p. 9/8b; and chapter comment, pp. 9/13b–14a.

[105] *Mencius* IIIB.7. See James Legge, trans., *The Chinese Classics*, vol. 2, p. 277.

[106] This phrase is also used by Chin Sheng-t'an in his *tu-fa* essay on the *Shui-hu chuan*, item 28. See chap. II above.

somebody else's reputation is also a thief. Niu P'u has not only stolen Niu Pu-i's poetry, but also stolen the old monk's cymbals and chimes.[107] He is without doubt a thief. Therefore from his mouth comes nothing but thief's talk, and whatever he does is nothing but thief's deeds. In the novel, he is a person of the very lowest and debased category, deeply hated by the author.

Chapter 22   1. Although the Pu brothers are dull-witted small-time shopkeepers, they have treated Niu P'u well. Why should Niu P'u go out of his way to insult them?[108] It is the first time that Niu P'u has managed to get Magistrate Tung to visit him and he cannot think of any way to show off except by making the Pu brothers act as his servants. Indeed, there are evil creatures like him in this world. If he is allowed to enter the door, he will do many terrible things, and there is nothing one can do with him!

2. The word "Mr." [*lao-yeh* 老爺] is a really plain and ordinary word. Yet when it is used numerous times in the quarrel between Niu P'u and the Pu brothers after Pu Hsin served tea to Mr. Tung,[109] it appears like a flame or a blooming flower, growing more extraordinary as the passage moves along. This passage is just like the story of Mao Sui in "The Biography of Lord P'ing-yüan" [in the *Shih-chi*] in which "sir" [*hsien-sheng* 先生] is used countless times.[110] If one eliminates a "sir" or two, the story would not hold together [*pu-ch'eng wen-fa* 不成文法] and it would lose a lot of its flavor.

3. Niu P'u is an intolerably vulgar person whose mind is obsessed with power and status [*shih-li* 勢利]. Soon after he leaves his house he encounters Niu Yü-p'u with his crowd of attendants, abundance of food, and his flush style of living. Niu P'u covets this in him and, like a dog trying to steal some hot gravy, he is at once both attracted and in awe of him. He is more than willing to call Niu Yü-p'u "great-uncle." When he is peeping into the cabin through the crack between the planks,[111] he is already totally infatuated [with Niu Yü-p'u's power and status].

4. Although Niu Yü-p'u is a debased, no-account type of person, how could he bring himself to swear brotherhood with a pimp [Wang I-an]? There must be reasons for this. Time has passed and the present can no longer be compared to the past. Since it is said that Niu Yü-p'u and Wang I-an became sworn brothers twenty years ago, apparently

[107] *JLWS* 21/2b–3b, 22/7a; *Scholars* 21.232–33, 22.245.

[108] *JLWS* 22/2a–4b, *Scholars* 22.242–43.

[109] *JLWS* 22/3a–6a, *Scholars* 22.243–44.

[110] *Shih-chi*, pp. 76.2366–68. See also Gladys and Hsien-yi Yang, trans., *Records of the Historian*, pp. 129–31.

[111] *JLWS* 22/9a, *Scholars* 22.246–47.

Wang I-an was not a pimp then. Or perhaps Wang I-an was not a steady type and chose to knock about the countryside. Back then, he made friends with Niu Yü-p'u and they called each other "brother." A long time has passed and now they meet again all of a sudden. It is only natural that, before they get to talk in depth, they first greet each other and talk of the old days. When Niu Yü-p'u says that he remembers when they were together in Mr. Ch'i's yamen, Wang I-an is quite taken aback.[112] It is evident that all Niu Yü-p'u wants to do is talk big in order to impress Niu P'u. It's not that he really remembers how it was when they parted.

5. The two passages in which Niu Yü-p'u talks about himself[113] reveal his favorite technique for entrapping other people. He is not aware that Niu P'u has seen through his secret. I am sure that even if Niu P'u did not have a chat with the Taoist monk later,[114] he would still eventually get the better of Niu Yü-p'u. Why? In this world only the most yielding can conquer the most hard. The distinction between the elder Niu and the younger Niu is that between the hard and the soft.

6. Some reader might ask, why does Wang I-an wear a scholar's cap to a restaurant for no reason?[115] There is nothing strange about this. According to the customs of Yangchou, the manager of a brothel does not use his own wife and concubines to do business, but he is simply in charge of the operation. He often lives in a luxurious house, has extensive social connections, and often mixes with the gentry. Those who do not know his background would have no cause to reprimand him. The two licentiates must be villainous literati who live off of prostitutes. It is evident that Wang I-an has been intimidated by them before, so he does not dare to argue when they beat him up.

Chapter 23   1. It is true that Niu P'u has met Mr. Tung of An-tung before. It is also true that Mr. Tung welcomes him with respect and propriety later when Niu P'u arrives in An-tung.[116] But at the time when Niu P'u is talking to the Taoist monk of Tzu-wu Temple,[117] he has not been to An-tung nor has he been welcomed by Mr. Tung there yet. He makes up a story and spins it out voluminously. The Taoist in the book does not know that Niu P'u is lying, but the reader outside the

---

[112] *JLWS* 22/11b–12a, *Scholars* 22.248.
[113] *JLWS* 22/10b–11a, 15a–b; *Scholars* 22.247, 250.
[114] *JLWS* 23/1b–4a, *Scholars* 23.252–54.
[115] *JLWS* 22/11b–13a, *Scholars* 22.248–49.
[116] *JLWS* 23/12b–13a, *Scholars* 23.259–60.
[117] *JLWS* 23/1b–4a, *Scholars* 23.252–54.

book clearly knows that he is lying. The excellence of the writing is like Li Kung-lin's [1040?–1106] skill in sketching outlines [*pai-miao* 白描].[118]

2. It is likely that Wan Hsüeh-chai has never given much in the way of charity to the Taoist monk. Therefore, the Taoist monk long ago became sick of listening to Niu Yü-p'u's constant flattery of Wan Hsüeh-chai. In his conversation [with Niu P'u] in the teahouse,[119] he says more than it is his business to say, but this is because of his dissatisfation with Wan Hsüeh-chai.

3. Niu P'u is ten times as talented as Niu Yü-p'u. For instance, his story about meeting the assistant magistrate shows great thought and discretion.[120] If he had said that he met the magistrate, Niu Yü-p'u knows that Niu P'u does not have the reputation to do so and would surely not believe him. To mention only the assistant magistrate is just right. The writing is as eloquent as a tongue with lotuses blooming on it [*she-shang sheng lien* 舌上生蓮].

4. When Niu Yü-p'u is beating Niu P'u, he says nothing but "What a dirty trick you have played on me!"[121] This shows Niu Yü-p'u's great skill and experience in handling such a matter. If he had made a detailed accusation, Niu P'u would have been able to excuse himself. He could have said, "Great-uncle, you told me yourself that you have been a sworn brother to Mr. Ch'eng Ming-ch'ing for twenty years." In that case, Niu Yü-p'u would have been left with nothing to say.

Chapter 24 1. This chapter concludes [*chieh-kuo* 結過] the story of Niu P'u in the first half and then moves into the story of Pao Wen-ch'ing. The three murder cases are almost equally absurd. The real [*shih* 實] case [Niu Pu-i's wife accuses Niu P'u of murdering her husband] is set off [*ch'en-t'o* 襯托] so skillfully by the use of the two made-up [*hsü* 虛] cases[122] that no trace of this artifice [*hen-chi* 痕迹] can be seen. No ink is wasted in the delineation of Magistrate Hsiang as a well-rounded talent. This is achieved through a couple of general hints [*tien-tou* 點逗] and Pao Wen-ch'ing's remarks.[123] The subtlety of the writing here lies in the avoidance of direct description in favor of indirect description ["*pi-shih chi-hsü chih miao*" 避實擊虛之妙].

2. Pao Wen-ch'ing became an actor because the stage was the pro-

---

[118] See Susan Bush and Hsio-yen Shih, *Early Chinese Texts on Painting* (Cambridge, Mass.: Harvard-Yenching Institute, 1985), pp. 317–18.

[119] *JLWS* 23/2a–b, *Scholars* 23.253.

[120] *JLWS* 23/4b–5a, *Scholars* 23.254.

[121] *JLWS* 23/10a, *Scholars* 23.258.

[122] *JLWS* 24/5a–8b, *Scholars* 24.265–68.

[123] *JLWS* 24/9a–b, *Scholars* 24.268.

fession that was handed down to him from his grandfather. Mixing in
the ranks of theater people, he is self-rectifying and self-respecting and is
someone who lives up to the name of an upright person and a gentle-
man. Although he is but an actor, what harm is there in that? There are
people in the upper classes who behave like actors. In name they are
scholars, but in reality they are actors. Now Pao Wen-ch'ing is but an
actor, but he can be ranked among the upper classes. In name an actor, he
is in reality a scholar. Chuang Tzu said: "Shall I go for the name? The
name is nothing but a guest for the reality. Shall I go for the guest of the
reality?"[124]

3. Places in the book like Yangchou, West Lake, and Nanking are the
most scenic of all the famous sites. Special techniques should be used to
highlight their depiction in the book. The author's method was to syn-
thesize the various descriptive techniques used in the *Ching-Ch'u sui-shih
chi* 荆楚歲時記 [A Record of the Annual Festivals of the Ching and Ch'u
Regions][125] and the *Tung-ching meng-hua lu* 東京夢華錄 [A Record of
the Lost Splendor of the Eastern Capital].[126] Therefore, when the reader
reads his descriptions, they can make him go on a flight of imagination
to those very places without knowing how this has been brought
about.

4. It is appropriate that actors and people of humble occupations do
not dare to see themselves as equal with the upper classes. In recent times,
people from the upper classes often invite such people to sit together
with them when drinking or listening to singing. They regard this as
refined and beyond vulgar distinctions. The actors gradually become
used to it and consider it as their right. Whenever they see those who
don't do it, they regard them as unprofessional. Yet, if there are a couple
of poor scholars at the table, they will go out of their way to mock them.
The rich among their patrons even enjoy the sight of this and laugh
without shame. Alas! Their discernment falls far below that of Pao Wen-
ch'ing.[127]

Chapter 25   1. Since the civil service examinations were instituted,
there has been no man in the world without a sharp desire to strive for

---

[124] *Chuang Tzu, Ssu-pu ts'ung-k'an* edition, p. 1/10a–b. See also *The Complete Works of
Chuang Tzu*, p. 32.

[125] This book is by Tsung Huai 宗懷, an official at the court of Emperor Yüan (r.
552–554) of the Liang dynasty, and it describes the celebration of the yearly festivals in
the capital.

[126] In this book Meng Yüan-lao 孟元老 (fl. 1126–1147) recorded the sights of the
fallen Northern Sung capital, Pien-ching.

[127] He scolds the other actors for putting on airs, *JLWS* 24/14a–16a and *Scholars*
24.271–73.

fame through the examinations, but in fact only one or two out of every thousand or so who seek it this way are able to obtain it. Those who fail fall between the cracks. Since they are not able to farm or to do business, they will have to sit at home eating away their resources. There are few of them who do not end up selling their own children. Ni Shuang-feng says, "I deeply regret that back then I wrongfully studied a few 'dead books.'"[128] The two words "dead books" are really unique and unprecedented. They can serve not only as the medicine to cure the ills of the day, but also as a morning gong to waken the world.

2. Prefect Hsiang is humble and retiring, while Pao Wen-ch'ing is humble and lowly—they can be called a worthy host and a fine guest. That the Prefect's affection for Pao Wen-ch'ing and his son comes sincerely from his heart and that Pao Wen-ch'ing and his son are grateful to him for his favors and do not expect any reward from him is in each instance vividly portrayed before the reader's eyes. A poem in the *Shih-ching* 詩經 [Classic of Poetry] says, "I cherish the favor in my heart, / When dare I forget it?"[129] The Prefect has this sentiment. The *I Ching* 易經 [Book of Changes] says, "A superior man modest about his modesty is lowly in order to guard himself well."[130] Pao Wen-ch'ing has this attitude.

Chapter 26 1. The first half of this chapter describes Intendant Hsiang's mourning for his friend Pao Wen-ch'ing.[131] His mourning is dignified, solemn, and deeply moving. The description is like the calligraphy of Yen Chen-ch'ing [709–785], the strength of whose brushstrokes would almost penetrate right through the paper.

2. When Chin Tz'u-fu first comes to propose a match,[132] he only knows a little bit about Mrs. Wang, so he can only talk about her large dowry and her many chests and cases. She has been looking for a new husband for seven or eight years by now, but Chin Tz'u-fu has only learned about her not long ago. He intends only to hurry up and make the match so that he can receive some wine and food in reward—he has nothing else in mind. Shen T'ien-fu actually knows about her background, so he can talk about her in great detail, but what he says is still but the outer image of Mrs. Wang.[133] Only when we come to Big-Foot

[128] *JLWS* 25/3b, *Scholars* 25.276.

[129] See James Legge, trans., *The Chinese Classics*, vol. 4, p. 415.

[130] *A Concordance to Yi Ching* (Peiping: Harvard-Yenching Institute, 1935), p. 11. The translation follows Richard Wilhelm, *The I Ching or Book of Changes*, Cary F. Baynes, trans. (Princeton: Princeton University Press, 1967), p. 463.

[131] *JLWS* 26/6b–8a, *Scholars* 26.288–89.

[132] *JLWS* 26/8a–9b, *Scholars* 26.289–90.

[133] *JLWS* 26/9a–12a, *Scholars* 26.290–92.

Shen [Shen T'ien-fu's wife], who knows Mrs. Wang's nature and behavior, do we see Mrs. Wang's whole character revealed.[134] Thus the
depiction of Mrs. Wang is divided into three stages [*tuan* 段] with differences in temporal sequence [*yu ch'ien yu hou* 有前有後] and depth of
detail [*yu hsiang yu lüeh* 有詳有略]. The author's intent here is new and
fresh and his language is vigorous and skillful. The marvelousness of his
writing can neither be found in fictional works [*pai-kuan* 稗官] nor in the
writings of famous ancients.

3. Big-Foot Shen's talk is so persuasive that Mrs. Wang cannot help
falling into her trap.[135] In a later section in which Tu Shen-ch'ing takes a
concubine in Nanking, Big-Foot Shen adopts an entirely new way of
talking and Tu Shen-ch'ing cannot help falling into her trap either.[136] It
is like reading the persuasions in the *Chan-kuo ts'e* [Intrigues of the
Warring States]. How can we not strike the table and yell "bravo!"
[*p'ai-an chiao-chüeh* 拍案叫絕].

4. Before Mrs. Wang appears, the author has already depicted her
nature [*hsing-ch'ing* 性情] and behavior in great detail. How is Pao T'ing-
hsi going to manage such a woman, once he marries her and brings her
home? Let the reader close the book and think [*yen-chüan hsi-ssu* 掩卷
細思] on how he could write the rest of the story. It will not be long
before one's imagination dries up. When he reads about all the troubles
that arise after Mrs. Wang enters the Pao family in the next chapter, the
reader will realize that only an elegant and rich mind could lay out [*pu-
chih* 布置] such a narrative. Seeing this, the reader will be forced to
admire the greatness of the author's talents.

Chapter 27   1. It is inconceivable that after Mrs. Wang has moved
into the Pao family that all will be peaceful and uneventful. But where
should one begin? That is the really difficult thing. The author actually
begins with the quarrels arising from the bride's failure to act as a new
bride should.[137] Such an opening makes one feel that this is entirely
understandable and reasonable [*chin-ch'ing cho-li* 近情着理], and that it is
a neat and trim solution to the problem. Just when the bride is making a
great disturbance in the house, Big-Foot Shen comes in with a gift. The
bride smears Big-Foot Shen's face with stinking human feces.[138] This
incident is enough to make the reader die with laughter. A clumsy pen
could not be so vivid. Li Po [701–762] once said, "The scene is right in

---

[134] *JLWS* 26/12b–13a, *Scholars* 26.292.
[135] *JLWS* 26/13a–15b, *Scholars* 26.292–94.
[136] *JLWS* 30/2a–3a, *Scholars* 30.326.
[137] *JLWS* 27/3a–4a, *Scholars* 27.296–97.
[138] *JLWS* 27/5a–b. This section is not fully translated, *Scholars* 27.297–98.

front of me, but I am unable to put it into words."[139] This expresses precisely how I feel about this incident.

2. When Mrs. Wang was poor, she felt quite healthy and rarely got sick. But as soon as she meets her flush brother-in-law [Ni T'ing-chu], who gives the couple seventy taels of silver, she begins to feel unwell and every day she has to take eight cents' worth of medicine.[140] In general, most women are like this.

3. That Pao T'ing-hsi's foster mother and her son-in-law Kuei do not care a hoot about Pao T'ing-hsi is penetratingly depicted.

4. Ni T'ing-chu suddenly appears out of the blue. He talks without end about the pain of separation felt by him and his brothers and their father.[141] His natural disposition toward love for his relatives is really moving, and this feeling can penetrate into the very mind and viscera of the reader. This passage has much merit for its promotion of morality in the world [*yu kung shih-tao* 有功世道]. The author is about to abandon Pao T'ing-hsi below and adopt another style of writing to portray the Tu cousins. The narrative thread [*hsien-so* 線索] is passed on entirely through Chi Wei-hsiao, whom Pao T'ing-hsi meets by chance on the riverbank.[142] The switch takes place as suddenly as a hare starting to run or a falcon beginning his dive. Truly, the author had the complete pattern in his mind ["*yu ch'eng-chou tsai hsiung*" 有成軸在胸] before he began to write.

Chapter 28 1. [It is said that] the rich officials from the Salt Gabelle only sip a mouthful of soup from an eight-cent bowl of noodles and give the rest to their sedan-chair bearers. In actual fact, they have already filled themselves up at home on rice-crust soup.[143] These thickheaded

---

[139] According to the anecdote from which this line comes, Li Po once climbed the Yellow Crane Tower (Huang-ho lou 黃鶴樓) in Wu-ch'ang. He was unable to write a poem on the view because Ts'ui Hao's 崔顥 (704?–754) famous poem "On Climbing Yellow Crane Tower" ("Teng Huang-ho lou" 登黃鶴樓) was inscribed there and left him nothing to say. He later wrote a poem in imitation of Ts'ui Hao's poem describing the view from the Phoenix Tower (Feng-huang t'ai 鳳凰台) in Nanking. According to a work written in 1206, the *Chu-chuang shih-hua* 竹莊詩話 (Chu-chuang Talks on Poetry), the anecdote was recorded in an earlier work, Li T'ien's 李畋 *Kai-wen lu* 該聞錄 (Record of Things to Be Known), but the extant portions of that work do not seem to contain this anecdote. In any case, a fuller version is to be found under Ts'ui Hao's name in Hsin Wen-fang 辛文房, *T'ang ts'ai-tzu chuan* 唐才子傳 (Geniuses of the T'ang; Shanghai: Ku-tien wen-hsüeh, 1957 reprint), pp. 17–18.

[140] *JLWS* 27/11b–13a, *Scholars* 27.301–2.

[141] *JLWS* 27/9a–10b, *Scholars* 27.300.

[142] *JLWS* 27/13a–14b, *Scholars* 27.302–3.

[143] *JLWS* 28/5a–b, *Scholars* 28.306. This information is presented by one of the characters in the novel.

salt merchants are thus captured down to the most minute detail. A Yangchou ballad says: "In the Second Month, the east wind stirs the yellow dust. Sedan chairs fly along Minister's Street." A later section continues: "An old man by the roadside cries in praise, 'You old man, you old man, what strong shoulders you have! You carry water from the Eastern Gate all the way to the Western Gate to sell!'"[144] The song expresses the same idea as this passage.

2. The repulsiveness of the nasty old monk portrayed in this chapter can make the reader angry enough for his hair to stand on end. His scolding of the little monk is an attempt to raise his own status.[145] His talk about manservants is intended to insult the three scholars.[146] Following on this passage, the author portrays an enlightened and accommodating prior as a contrast [*ch'en-tieh* 襯跌] to the old monk.[147] The description really brings the characters to life!

Chapter 29   1. The author uses Tu Shen-ch'ing's unconventional elegance to show [*hsing* 形] the distastefulness [by contrast] of Chi T'ien-i, Hsiao Chin-hsüan, and Chu-ko T'ien-shen. When they meet again in the tavern,[148] Tu Shen-ch'ing's self-esteem is easy to see; yet Chi T'ien-i still introduces him to Chi Wei-hsiao by saying, "This is the grandson of Minister Tu." This shows that in both speech and thought Chi T'ien-i cares for nothing but social status. It can be said that for Tu Shen-ch'ing to spend several days with Chi T'ien-i and his two friends must make him feel quite low in spirits, so he cannot help being overjoyed when he hears a few words of compliment from Chi Wei-hsiao.[149]

2. The purpose of the description of Rain Flower Mount[150] is to describe Tu Shen-ch'ing. Such description of brilliant scenery as this could not come from the mind of a rotten pedant.

3. Some of the edges of Tu Shen-ch'ing's eccentric nature are revealed in his discussion of Fang Hsiao-ju [1357–1402].[151]

Chapter 30   1. The author should have had Tu Shen-ch'ing say, "If men could bear children from their anuses, there would be no need of

---

[144] A comment on this passage by Chang Wen-hu 張文虎 (style T'ien-mu shan-ch'iao 天目山樵) in the 1881 Shen-pao kuan edition of the novel refers the reader to Shen Ch'i-feng's 沈起鳳 *Hsieh-to* 諧鐸 (Cautionary Anecdotes) for this song. See *Hsieh-to* (Peking: Jen-min wen-hsüeh, 1985), pp. 32–33.

[145] *JLWS* 28/13a, *Scholars* 28.311.

[146] *JLWS* 28/13a, *Scholars* 28.311. The monk's implication is that the three men cannot afford to hire the necessary menservants to live in the monastery.

[147] *JLWS* 28/13b–14a, *Scholars* 28.312.

[148] *JLWS* 29/12b–13a, *Scholars* 29.322.

[149] *JLWS* 29/15b, *Scholars* 29.324.

[150] *JLWS* 29/13a–14a, *Scholars* 29.322–23.

[151] *JLWS* 29/14a, *Scholars* 29. 322–23.

women in this world." It is not fitting for him to quote the Hung-wu emperor [Chu Yüan-chang, r. 1368–1398].[152]

2. The previous chapter talks about Hsiao Chin-hsüan and his two friends and this chapter goes on to write about Tsung Tzu-hsiang[153] and Kuo T'ieh-pi.[154] By nature Tu Shen-ch'ing hates meeting prominent people, but here he is even more unfortunate in having to confront a woman.[155] The world speaks of failing to please, and that is what happens here. He must have felt wretched at heart.

3. The *Ming-chi hua an* [Beauties of the Ming][156] is like a *Pan-ch'iao tsa-chi* [Miscellaneous Notes on the Pan-ch'iao Section of Nanking].[157] The acting contest on Mo-ch'ou Lake[158] is like a *Yen lan hsiao-p'u* 燕蘭小譜 [A Little Roster of Actors in Peking].[159]

Chapter 31 1. Tu Shen-ch'ing and Tu Shao-ch'ing are both young dandies, but they are quite different from each other. Tu Shen-ch'ing is liberal and brisk while Tu Shao-ch'ing is "foolish" from top to bottom. With one pen the author describes both of them without the least overlap [*fan* 犯].

2. Mr. Lou secretly schemes to get money from Tu Shao-ch'ing while Mr. Wei openly takes advantage of him. Even the tailor and Whiskers Wang each have their own schemes to get the better of Tu Shao-ch'ing. The debasement and unfeeling nature of worldly morality is completely revealed.

Chapter 32 1. The description of Tu Shao-ch'ing not giving a hoot about how he spends his money can make one weep for those who have painfully to calculate everything.

Chapter 33 1. Tu Shao-ch'ing is extravagant and self-indulgent, and his disposition seems quite different from that of Ch'ih Heng-shan.

[152] *JLWS* 30/3a–b, *Scholars* 30.326–27. The emperor is quoted as having said, "If not for the fact that I was born of a woman, I would kill all of the women in the world."

[153] *JLWS* 30/1b–2a, *Scholars* 30.325–26. One of Tsung Tzu-hsiang's relatives claims descent from him in front of Tu Shen-ch'ing and angers him by this name-dropping.

[154] *JLWS* 30/3b–4a, *Scholars* 30.327. Kuo T'ieh-pi upsets Tu Shen-ch'ing with his flattery.

[155] *JLWS* 30/2a–3b, *Scholars* 30.326–27. The woman he meets is Big-Foot Shen.

[156] This is a made-up title that seems to refer to comments by Tu Shen-ch'ing and the others in this chapter about the various actors playing female roles.

[157] This work is by Yü Huai 余懷 (1616–1696) and describes the pleasure quarters in Nanking. It has been translated by Howard S. Levy under the title, *A Feast of Mist and Flowers: The Gay Quarters of Nanking at the End of the Ming* (Yokohama: Hakuensha, 1966).

[158] *JLWS* 30/13b–15b, *Scholars* 30.333–35.

[159] This work by Wu Ch'ang-yüan 吳長元 describes the famous actors of his day, has a preface dated 1785, and records items up to 1782. The mention of it by the commentator here sets the upper limit for the composition of the Wo-hsien ts'ao-t'ang commentary.

Yet once they meet, they immediately become infatuated with each other. From this we can see that genuine people do not have to share the same disposition to become friends. Ch'ih Heng-shan's pedantry and Tu Shao-ch'ing's eccentricity are like small flaws in a jade. Beautiful jades are prized for lack of flaws, but it is from their flaws that we know that they are genuine. Confucius said, "In antiquity the people had three defects."[160] He also used "foolish," "obtuse," "rustic," and "coarse" to describe four of his favorite disciples.[161] Therefore people need not be scorned for having flaws—it all depends on what kind of flaws they have.

2. The incident where Tu Shao-ch'ing meets Lai Hsia-shih and Wei Ssu-yüan at Boat Watchers' Pavilion [and receives financial help from them] is really delightful to read.[162] Tu Fu once said [in a poem], "Career at an end, I have to rely on friends for a living."[163] If you have never personally been in such a situation before, you will not be able to understand how trying and moving [when finally rescued by your friend] the experience can be. I suppose the author imitated Ssu-ma Ch'ien in studying many books and travelling to all the famous mountains and rivers in the empire[164] so that he acquired such broad experience that he could write about this kind of situation.

3. The dedication of T'ai-po Temple [in chapter 37] is the number one grand unifying episode [*ta chieh-shu* 大結束] in the book. Writing a big book is like an artisan's constructing a mansion. The artisan has to have the whole structure [*chieh-kou* 結構] in his mind before starting in. He must know where to put the main hall, the sleeping chambers, the study, the kitchen, and the stables. Only after everything has been plotted out can he begin the actual construction work.[165] The dedication

---

[160] *Confucian Analects* XVI.16. See James Legge, trans., *The Chinese Classics*, vol. 1, p. 325. The three defects are wildness, conceit, and foolishness.

[161] *Confucian Analects* XI.11. See James Legge, trans., *The Chinese Classics*, vol. 1, p. 243.

[162] *JLWS* 33/12a–14a, *Scholars* 33.368–69.

[163] *A Concordance to the Poems of Tu Fu*, vol. 2, p. 23. The poem is entitled "K'o-yeh" 客夜 (A Night as a Guest), and is translated in Florence Ayscough, *Travels of a Chinese Poet*, 2 vols. (London: Jonathan Cape, 1934), vol. 1, p. 127.

[164] Ssu-ma Ch'ien describes his education and travels in the last chapter of his *Shih-chi*, p. 130.3293. See also Burton Watson, *Ssu-ma Ch'ien: Grand Historian of China* (New York: Columbia University Press, 1958), p. 48. As a matter of fact, the description in a *tz'u* poem, "Chien-tzu mu-lan hua" 減字木蘭花, by Wu Ching-tzu in his collected poetry (*Wen-mu shan-fang chi*, p. 4/9a), proves that the author once had an experience very similar to Tu Shao-ch'ing's in this chapter.

[165] The use of architectural metaphors to talk about literary structure here follows in the footsteps of similar usage by Wang Chi-te 王驥德 (d. 1623) in his *Ch'ü-lü* 曲律 (Rules of Dramatic Prosody) and Li Yü 李漁 (1611–1680) in his *Hsien-ch'ing ou-chi*

of T'ai-po Temple in this book is comparable to the main hall of the mansion. From the beginning of the book the author has been portraying various types of scholars [*ming-shih* 名士]. Dr. Yü Yü-te is their culmination and summation [*chieh-hsüeh ch'u* 結穴處]. Therefore, the dedication of the T'ai-po Temple is also a culmination and a summation [*chieh-hsüeh ch'u* 結穴處]. This can be compared to the way that the Min River flows out through the Min Mountains [in Szechwan] into the Yangtze and down to Fu-ch'ien yüan [at the juncture of the Yangtze and Lake P'o-yang], where the tributaries join together, and then [together with them] flows along into the ocean. The position of the T'ai-po Temple in the book can be compared to the importance of Fu-ch'ien yüan to the Yangtze and the Han rivers.[166]

Chapter 34 1. Reader Kao of the Han-lin Academy and Compiler Lu are of the same ilk. Therefore, just as Compiler Lu criticized the Lou brothers,[167] Reader Kao finds fault with Tu Shao-ch'ing.[168] Why do they do this? Different types of people cannot tolerate each other. Compiler Lu's criticism of the Lou brothers is rather mild, but Reader Kao's criticism of Tu Shao-ch'ing is quite fierce. The reason that Tu Shao-ch'ing is attacked more than the Lou brothers is that the former is more threatening than the latter. Han Yü [768–824] wrote: "If I feel slightly satisfied with a piece of writing, others will find some fault with it. If I feel greatly satisfied with a piece of writing, they will find great fault with it."[169] This is not only the case with writing. The section in which Tu Shao-ch'ing discusses the *Shih-ching* is concerned with true scholar-

---

閒情偶記 (Random Repository of Idle Thoughts). See *Wang Chi-te Ch'ü-lü*, Ch'en To 陳多 and Yeh Ch'ang-hai 葉長海, eds. (Ch'ang-sha: Hu-nan jen-min, 1983), "Lun chang-fa" 論章法 (On Structure), p. 121 and *Li Li-weng ch'ü-hua* 李笠翁曲話 (Li Yü on Drama), Ch'en To, ed. (Ch'ang-sha: Hu-nan jen-min, 1981), "Chieh-kou" 結構 (Structure), p. 7.

[166] Fu-ch'ien yüan 敷淺原 is an old place name. There are three candidates for its modern-day location, two mountains (Lu-shan 廬山, Po-yang shan 博陽山) and a plain (southeast of Lu-shan), but all three are rather far from the confluence of the Han and Yangtze Rivers at Wuhan. The commentator seems to be combining the language of two sections of the "Yü-kung" 禹貢 (Tribute of Yü) chapter of the *Shu-ching* 書經 (Classic of History). For Chinese text and translation, see James Legge, trans., *The Chinese Classics*, vol. 3, pp. 136–37 (sec. 9, dealing with the Min Mountains) and vol. 3, p. 130 (sec. 4, on Fu-ch'ien yüan), but this still does not explain why he seems to take Fu-ch'ien yüan as the point of confluence of the Yangtze and the Han.

[167] *JLWS* 10/2b–3a, *Scholars* 10.112.

[168] *JLWS* 34/5b–6b, *Scholars* 34.375–76.

[169] See his letter to Feng Su 馮宿 discussing literature ("Yü Feng Su lun wen shu" 與馮宿論文書), included in his collected works, *Ssu-pu ts'ung-k'an* edition, first series, vol. 39, p. 17/9a (p. 140). There are textual variants between the original and the version quoted here.

ship.[170] One must not skim over it as if it were merely fiction [*pai-kuan* 稗官].

The description of Chuang Shao-kuang as a scholar of elegance and cultivation, superior to other people, is done in a very elevated tone. You cannot expect the uninitiated to understand this. The section about the encounter with the mounted bandits comes and goes unexpectedly and is a marvel to read. It has been said that the *Tso-chuan* 左傳 [The Tso Commentary] is the best at describing battles. This book unabashedly holds its own with the *Tso-chuan* in this respect. The best part of this section is that no sooner has Chuang Shao-kuang said that the authorities have taken no steps to eliminate bandits and bring peace to the people than he is almost scared to death and left with no place to hide when he personally encounters the bandits.[171] From this we can tell that scholars like to talk big but do not necessarily have the capacity to solve the problem. This is an example of the author's discreet use of the critical method of the *Ch'un-ch'iu* [The Spring and Autumn Annals (*p'i-li yang-ch'iu* 皮裏陽秋)].[172] Truly, you cannot expect the uninitiated to understand this.

Chapter 35 1. Chuang Shao-kuang is extremely learned, but at the same time he is somewhat affected [*tso-tso* 做作]. How do we know that he is learned? From the couple of remarks that he makes to Lu Hsin-hou[173] we can see that, if he had not studied and nourished his spirit for tens of years, he would not have been able to arrive at such understanding. In the novel, as for this kind of learning, probably only Dr. Yü Yü-te is capable of reaching it. As for Tu Shao-ch'ing, he is not there yet. Therefore, this is why Chuang Shao-kuang has to be put forward as the number two scholar in the book. How do we know that he is somewhat affected? When he meets Vice-Minister Hsü, he does not greet him as a former student.[174] His reply to the Prime Minister, although really quite respectful, sounds haughty.[175] This incident is like that at the Hung-men banquet, where Fan K'uai abused Hsiang Yü [232–202 B.C.], but Hsiang Yü did not show any anger because he was being respected as the leader of the alliance.[176] Again, when Lu Hsin-hou is arrested, Chuang Shao-

[170] *JLWS* 34/8a–10a, *Scholars* 34.377–79.

[171] *JLWS* 34/14a–b, 16a; *Scholars* 34.382, 383.

[172] Subtle criticism of the historical characters mentioned in the *Ch'un-ch'iu* 春秋 (The Spring and Autumn Annals) was supposed to have been imbedded in the text by the use of precise terminology.

[173] *JLWS* 35/2a–b, *Scholars* 35.386.

[174] *JLWS* 35/6a, *Scholars* 35.389.

[175] *JLWS* 35/6a, *Scholars* 35.389.

[176] See the biography of Hsiang Yü in the *Shih-chi*, p. 7.313, and Burton Watson, *Records of the Grand Historian of China*, vol. 1, pp. 53–54.

kuang writes letters to the prominent officials that he knows in the capital to fix Lu Hsin-hou's case.[177] Are these the sort of things that a scholar-recluse residing on an island in a lake should do? Therefore, I say that he is somewhat affected. The author uses Ssu-ma Ch'ien's miraculous technique [*Lung-men miao-pi* 龍門妙筆] of indirect portrayal [*p'ang-chien ts'e-ch'u* 旁見側出] to bring out this side of Chuang Shao-kuang's character. The author is like the white clouds on top of the mountains which only seek self-gratification. He is not interested in whether later generations will understand or not.

Chapter 36   1. This chapter is written entirely in a direct [*cheng-pi* 正筆] and straightforward style [*chih-pi* 直筆]. Nowhere is the oblique [*p'ang-pi* 旁筆] or indirect style [*ch'ü-pi* 曲筆] used. Because of this there are no peaks or high points. But, if we think about it carefully, we will realize that this chapter is really the most difficult to write. Dr. Yü Yü-te is the number one person in the book. He is pure, upright, and without flaw. [Portraying him] is like the preparation of meat juice and sacrificial water. Even I Ya [who gained the attention of Duke Huan of Ch'i (r. 685–643 B.C.) with his culinary skill] would be left with no place to show off his expertise in cooking. As an ancient scholar said, it is easier to paint ghosts and demons than human beings ["hua-kuei i, hua jen-wu nan" 畫鬼易,畫人物難].

2. This is because, unlike ghosts and demons, human beings are something seen by everybody all the time, so you cannot let the least bit of falseness enter into their composition. This is unlike ghosts and demons where you can add or subtract at will. Ssu-ma Ch'ien had a love for the unusual all his life. For instance, I do not know from what sources he obtained stories like that of Ch'eng Ying saving the orphan of the Chao family,[178] but he energetically fills out [*tien-chui* 點綴] those stories, wanting every phrase of his narration to come alive. When he came to write his "Hsia pen-chi" 夏本紀 [Annals of the Hsia Dynasty; a chapter in the *Shih-chi*], he could not help but quote respectfully from the *Shu-ching* 書經 [Classic of History].[179] It wasn't that he was better at writing about the Ch'in [221–207 B.C.] and the Han [206 B.C.–8 A.D.] dynasties than about the three most ancient dynasties [the Hsia, Shang, and Chou]. He was just tailoring the clothes to fit the body [*liang-t'i ts'ai-i* 量體裁衣] and setting the style to fit the subject [*hsiang-t'i li-ko* 相題立格].

[177] *JLWS* 35/13a, *Scholars* 35.394.

[178] *Shih-chi*, pp. 43.1783–85. Translated by Edouard Chavannes into French, *Les mémoires historique de Se-ma Ts'ien*, 6 vols. (Paris: Adrien-Maisonneuve, 1967), vol. 5, pp. 18–22.

[179] Until very recently the very historicity of the Hsia dynasty was in doubt. By the time Ssu-ma Ch'ien wrote his history, the only material on the Hsia was contained in canonical works such as the *Shu-ching*.

Chapter 37   1. This chapter is broadly permeated with an archaic style and feel, just as if it had come from the hand of Shu-sun T'ung[180] or Ts'ao Pao.[181] One feels that even if Academician Hsiao Sung[182] of the Academy of Scholarly Worthies and his like had exhausted their strength [trying to duplicate the ceremony at the T'ai-po Temple], the result would not surpass it. How austere and impressive! How beautiful it is!

2. All the people participating in the dedication are very familiar to the reader. The marvelousness of the book's layout [*pu-chü* 布局] has no equal.

3. This chapter is the grand unifying episode [*ta chieh-shu* 大結束] in the book. Part of the title of the book, "The Forest of Scholars" [*ju-lin* 儒林], refers to the literati and scholars. Numerous scholars are gathered in this chapter. Before this chapter, the literary gathering at Oriole Throat Lake[183] and the poetry gathering at West Lake[184] are two small unifying episodes [*hsiao chieh-shu* 小結束]. The progression is like ascending Mt. T'ai—only after one has climbed past Cloud Pavilion and Mt. Liang-fu does one come to Mt. T'ai itself. Musically, it is like the climax where all the instruments sound at once [*pa-yin fan-hui* 八音繁會]. What follows after this is nothing but reprise and variation [*man-sheng pien-tiao* 慢聲變調].

Chapter 38   1. The language of this book reaches a height of suspense and the unusual in this chapter. If read when one's head gets heavy in the middle of a long summer's day it will wake one to clarity or even cure an illness.

2. Filial Son Kuo is a desiccated and lonely man, so he gets along well with the old monk.[185]

3. Filial Son Kuo suffers cold wind and snow, fierce tigers and strange beasts. "Hardship" is probably not strong enough a word to

---

[180] Shu-sun T'ung established the court ritual used by the court of the Western Han dynasty (206 B.C.–8 A.D.). See his biography in the *Shih-chi*, pp. 99.2722–23, and *The Records of the Grand Historian of China*, vol. I, pp. 293–95.

[181] Ts'ao Pao was an admirer of Shu-sun T'ung and compiled books on official rites. See his biography in the *Hou Han-shu* 後漢書 (History of the Later Han Dynasty; Shanghai: Chung-hua shu-chü, 1963), pp. 35.1201–5.

[182] Read *sung* 嵩 for *hao* 蒿. Hsiao Sung (d. 749) came from a prominent family and had a very successful military and civil career. He was the chief compiler of a book on official ceremony. We can speculate that part of his appeal for the commentator might also be a function of his official title as cited in the comment, *Chi-hsien [yüan] hsüeh-shih* 集賢[院]學士. The standard translation of the academy's name does not do justice to the verbal quality of the first character, which conveys the image of a gathering together of worthies, an image that goes well with the description of the ritual at the T'ai-po Temple.

[183] *JLWS* 12/13a–14a, *Scholars* 12.141–42.

[184] *JLWS* 18/10b–14b, *Scholars* 18.206–8.

[185] *JLWS* 38/4a–5b, *Scholars* 38.420.

describe all of his sufferings. All of a sudden the old monk falls into the hands of a veritable demon and his life is in great danger.[186] Where on earth can one find a more startling and strange thing than this? I never expected that my eyes and ears would encounter such a fantastic story.

Chapter 39   1. In the episode of the evil monk, the author uses suspense-building language, which gets more and more intense as the story goes along. It gets so intense that the reader can hardly bear to read it through closely. While the old monk's life hangs by a thread, the author is deliberately unhurried in his narration, fully explaining peripheral details. It is like reading the story about Ching K'o's attempt to assassinate the first emperor of the Ch'in dynasty [r. 221–210 B.C.] in which a map is slowly unrolled, revealing Ching K'o's dagger.[187]

2. Hsiao Yün-hsien comes from a family famed for pellet archery. Yet the way he shoots his pellets is different from that of his father, Hsiao Hao-hsüan. The author's writing is so fluent and compelling that he can do almost anything he wants.

3. I once told a friend that, whenever a scholar writes something, he should have a reason for writing. Foremost, he should regard benefiting the morality of the world and its people ["yu kung yü shih-tao jen-hsin" 有功于世道人心] as primary. This is why Confucius said, "By working on his words, he establishes his sincerity [and makes his works endure]."[188] If Confucius were to come back to life today, he would not alter anything in Filial Son Kuo's advice to Hsiao Yün-hsien.[189] The fictional works [*pai-kuan* 稗官] that are being transmitted in the world now are often concerned with officials appointed by the central court who are forced to become bandits living in the marshlands.[190] In contrast, this book is able to encourage those brave and selfless people to go fight on the battlefields for the state. It is true, then, when a superior man writes a book, he will surely acquire immortality through it.[191]

4. The crushing of the enemy forces on Chair Mountain and the

---

[186] *JLWS* 38/14b–16a, *Scholars* 38.427.

[187] See the account in the *Shih-chi*, p. 86.2534 and the translation in Burton Watson, *Records of the Historian: Chapters from the Shih-chi of Ssu-ma Ch'ien* (New York: Columbia University Press, 1969), p. 63.

[188] *A Concordance to Yi Ching*, p. 2. See also Richard Wilhelm, *The I Ching*, pp. 380–81.

[189] *JLWS* 39/6b–7a, *Scholars* 39.432–33.

[190] This is a reference to the interpretation of the *Shui-hu chuan* as expressed in Li Chih's 李贄 (1527–1602) preface to the novel. For the Chinese text of the appropriate section of the preface, see *SHCTLHP*, p. 192.

[191] This is one of the three paths to eternal fame mentioned in the *Tso-chuan*, twenty-fourth year of Duke Hsiang (548 B.C.). See James Legge, trans., *The Chinese Classics*, vol. 5, pp. 505–7.

capture of Green Maple City[192] is known by everyone for all time as
Hsiao Yün-hsien's achievement. The two commanders had no part in it
at all. Yet in the end, Hsiao Yün-hsien is only confirmed in his appointment as lieutenant, while the two commanders return to their posts to
await imminent promotion. Li Ts'ai was not even of mediocre talent,
but ended up being given the title of marquis.[193] This is also something
that will be lamented over a thousand generations. Alas! What can one
say about things like this?

Chapter 40 1. In Green Maple City, Hsiao Yün-hsien is able to
nourish and educate the people, to extend downward the imperial grace,
and to report upward the people's genuine feelings. He is a man of talent
in both idealistic and concrete terms, but because he is limited by his lack
of official prerequisites, he ends up like a frustrated dragon unable to take
to the skies. The author channeled his anger into his writing of this book
[*fa-fen chu-shu* 發憤著書][194] in order to give outlet to his sympathy for
victims of injustice [*pu-p'ing chih ming* 不平之鳴] such as Hsiao Yün-
hsien.[195]

2. In the past, Juan Chi once ascended Kuang-wu Mountain and
sighed: "There are no heroes today. That is why idiots have become
celebrities!"[196] The passage in which Hsiao Yün-hsien watches the snow
[on Kuang-wu Mountain][197] alludes [*yin-k'uo* 隱括] to this. The brief
conversation between Hsiao Yün-hsien and Mu Nai is really a match for
Li Ling's [d. 74 B.C.] letter to Su Wu [d. 60 B.C.], which can still move
the reader to tears after all these centuries.[198]

3. As soon as the author finishes the story of Hsiao Yün-hsien, he
goes on to write about Shen Ch'iung-chih. Both Hsiao Yün-hsien and
Shen Ch'iung-chih are of heroic character. Although Hsiao Yün-hsien's
unjust failure to rise from low position and Shen Ch'iung-chih's sinking

---

[192] *JLWS* 39/11a–13b, *Scholars* 39.435–37.

[193] Li Ts'ai was a cousin of Li Kuang 李廣 (d. 119 B.C.), a famous general who never
managed to gain a marquisate. See Li Kuang's biography, *Shih-chi*, p. 109.2873, and
Burton Watson, *Records of the Grand Historian of China*, vol. 2, pp. 148–49.

[194] For more on this concept, see the text and notes to item 1 of the *Shui-hu chuan tu-fa*
essay, chap. II above.

[195] This language refers to an extension of the concept of *fa-fen chu-shu* advanced by
Han Yü 韓愈 (768–824) in a preface written for Meng Chiao 孟郊 (751–814), "Sung
Meng Tung-yeh hsü" 送孟東野序. See Kuo Shao-yü 郭紹虞, ed., *Chung-kuo li-tai wen-
lun hsüan* 中國歷代文論選 (Selections in Traditional Chinese Literary Theory), 4 vols.
(Shanghai: Shang-hai ku-chi, 1980), vol. 2, p. 125.

[196] This is recorded in his biography in the *Chin-shu*, p. 49.1361. For a translation of the
poem that Juan Chi wrote after climbing the mountain, see Donald Holzman, *Poetry and
Politics*, pp. 219–20.

[197] *JLWS* 40/7a–8b, *Scholars* 40.443.

[198] For the text of this letter, see *Wen-hsüan*, pp. 41.1847–53.

into the hands of a vulgar salt merchant are two different types of situations, their sadness and tears flow as if from the same breast. The author wants to combine these two sets of crying eyes and let them cry out in chorus.

Chapter 41   1. [In this chapter the image of] the unconventional scholar suddenly turns romantic, bringing a feminine air into the narrative. Yet the author does not portray in detail her [Shen Ch'iung-chih's] delicate skin and frail body clothed in fine gauze. The author must be a heroic and debonair figure, so here he transforms himself [*hua-tso* 化作] into a woman [Shen Ch'iung-chih] in order to expound his message to the world.

Chapter 45[199]   1. There is a saying, "Having eaten one's own white rice cooked in pure water [i.e., with a clean conscience], one goes to meddle in somebody else's business." People like T'ang San-t'an go to gossip about this and that in front of the county yamen every day, but what good does this bring them in daily life? They continue on this way unflaggingly until their hair turns completely white and still they aren't tired of it. They are like the maggots in the privy that wriggle up and down, appearing to be quite busy and in a hurry, just as if they had many things to attend to. However, though they spend their entire lives like this, is there one among them who is able to wriggle himself out of the privy?

2. It is understandable that T'ang San-t'an would want to meddle in Yü Yu-chung's court case, since he is only a stranger to him. Yet Chao Lin-shu is a close relative of Yü Yu-chung, so why should he want to meddle in this business? In order to describe debased and degenerate customs, the author starts from the relationships between close relatives. There is deep meaning in this.

3. The way that every conversation always brings in Squire P'eng and Salt Merchant Fang is the focus [*e-yao ch'u* 扼要處] of this chapter.

4. From the way that Yü Fu and Yü Yin talk, one knows that the two brothers are completely ignorant, so the idiocy of their geomancy[200] need not be pointed out. The marvelous thing is that they are portrayed so vividly [*huo-se sheng-hsiang* 活色生香] that you could almost call them up off the page. Their idiotic figures and manner seem to be really present before one's eyes.

Chapter 46   1. After Dr. Yü Yü-te leaves Nanking, the scholarly circles become dormant. Dr. Yü is the foremost scholar in the book, and the dedication of the T'ai-po Temple is the foremost event in the book.

---

[199] Chaps. 42–44 have no postchapter comments in the original edition.
[200] *JLWS* 45/9b–12b, *Scholars* 45.500–501.

After Dr. Yü leaves, all the remaining episodes are nothing but lingering traces and echoes [of what went before]. Therefore when Dr. Yü departs, only Tu Shao-ch'ing goes to see him off and the few words said at their parting are infinitely sad.[201] A thousand years later the reader will still hear their voices in his ears.

2. The few people who maintain their self-respect in a world of degenerate and debased customs cannot be tolerated by the others. Right in Yü Hua-hsüan's study there are [such vulgar people as] Batty T'ang the Second and Yao the Fifth. This description of the customs of a small provincial town has moved beyond even the realm of divine artistry [*ch'u-shen ju-hua* 出神入化]. You cannot find its peer in all of previous fiction [*pai-kuan* 稗官].

3. Batty T'ang the Second and Yao the Fifth are already enough to turn the reader's stomach, but the author insists on adding an Old Mr. Ch'eng. The author's literary genius is like the flowers of late spring in full bloom without any reserve—even nature's secrets [*t'ien-kung* 天工] are not held back.

Chapter 47   1. This chapter picks up Yü Hua-hsüan and portrays him once more. It is a variation [*pien-t'i* 變體] of what has gone before. The various evils of degenerate customs are completely revealed. People find it hard not to be covetous when they see money, but Yü Hua-hsüan can be proud of himself for not being that way. This sets up [*fu* 伏] his not buying the piece of land toward the end of the chapter.[202] The author is like a premier chess player whose every move fits in with and strengthens the other moves ["kuo-shou pu tzu, pu-pu chao-ying" 國手布子, 步步照應].

2. The reader cannot help but die of laughter when he comes to the section about Old Ch'eng going to the Fang's house for lunch.[203]

3. The author's portrayal of Batty T'ang the Second cuts far below the surface. Having fulfilled his wish to meet the prefect, he still regrets that he has not been able to drink and joke with the prefect's son.[204] It is truly difficult to cure this man's greed. I cannot conceive of how he could ever be satisfied in his pursuit of the powerful and rich.

4. Although the section about the enshrining of virtuous women[205] is written in a mocking tone, it everywhere bears marks of the author's tears. It grieves one's heart to observe the debasement and degeneration of social customs, to see how people's attitudes vary according to the

[201] *JLWS* 46/5b–6a, *Scholars* 46.508–9.

[202] *JLWS* 47/16a, *Scholars* 47.525.

[203] *JLWS* 47/5b–7a, *Scholars* 47.519–20.

[204] *JLWS* 47/8b–9b, *Scholars* 47.521.

[205] *JLWS* 47/11a–14a, *Scholars* 47.522–24.

other person's status, and to watch the behavior of the spoiled children. Everywhere the text harks back nostalgically to Dr. Yü Yü-te. This is the skeleton that holds the whole thing together [*t'ung-shen chin-chieh* 通身筋節].

Chapter 48 1. Wang Yü-hui is what the ancients would call a "foolish bookworm." His foolishness is precisely where he surpasses other people. In observing him, we can see that he is the kind of person whose determination cannot be broken when he is faced with a crisis. Those who can accomplish great things by making a brave and irrevocable choice in matters concerning the five human relationships[206] are, of necessity, not what the world regards simply as "nice and obedient" people.

2. His wife regards Wang Yü-hui as a fool while Wang Yü-hui thinks the same of her. The mutual reflection [*chao-ying* 照應] between this pair of fools is most interesting.

3. The enshrining of the chaste woman [Wang Yü-hui's daughter][207] is used to make a sharp contrast [*tui-chao* 對照] to [the enshrining of the virtuous women in] Wu-ho County.[208]

4. The passage about the visit to T'ai-po Temple[209] is infinitely poignant and discreet, incorporating boundless lamentation and mourning over what is past and gone. This is not only the climax [*chieh-shu* 結束] of this chapter, but also of the entire book. The style and content alike possess great beauty.

Chapter 49 1. The chapters that come after Dr. Yü leaves Nanking are "leftovers" [*yü-wen* 餘文] from the main story. The author is afraid that the reader might think that he has exhausted all of his talents and is unable to produce anything as startling and unusual, colorful and extraordinary, that has as much bite and vigor as the previous sections. Therefore, the author uses Academician Kao, who is already very familiar to the reader, to introduce [*yin-ch'u* 引出] the story of Mr. Wan, Secretary of the Imperial Patent Office. The story of Mr. Wan is a complement [*p'ei-pi* 陪筆] to the story of Feng the Fourth. As a character, Feng the Fourth has his own unique temperament [*hsing-ch'ing* 性情] and style, quite unlike any of the others. How can the author produce such fantastic things without end?

2. The banquet in Secretary Ch'in's home could be called a hell complete with food and drink. Since it is a hell, there must also be a

---

206 The five relationships are those between ruler and subject, father and son, older and younger brother, husband and wife, and friend and friend.

207 *JLWS* 48/7b–8b, *Scholars* 48.531.

208 *JLWS* 47/11a–14a, *Scholars* 47.522–24.

209 *JLWS* 48/14a–b, *Scholars* 48.535.

revelation of inner corruption [*ti-yü pien-hsiang* 地獄變相].[210] In the midst of the feasting, without any warning, an official rushes in, arrests, and drags off one of the guests [Secretary Wan].[211] If you called the [arresting] officials Ox-Heads or Rakshas,[212] who could object?

Chapter 50   1. Secretary Ch'in is a person who is timid and afraid of stirring up trouble. When Feng the Fourth uses his "persuader's" eloquence to frighten Secretary Ch'in with the seriousness of Mr. Wan's case,[213] he cannot help falling for it. This incident is like a marvelous piece of "persuasion" in the *Chan-kuo ts'e*.

2. In the Ming dynasty, one could become a secretary of the Imperial Patent Office either by first acquiring the *chin-shih* degree or by possessing only the status of a student at the Imperial College. There were in fact these two paths to that office. The author has not made this up.[214]

Chapter 51   1. The first half of the chapter describes the swindle perpetrated by the young woman on the small boat.[215] Her seductive charms almost cause the morally loose young man to fall into her trap without the least regret. If it were not for Feng the Fourth, he would have lost his two hundred taels of silver as surely as if he had cast them into the water.

2. Feng the Fourth is described as someone who enjoys himself no matter where he goes. His getting back the two hundred taels of silver for the silk merchant[216] is like his getting back a thousand taels of silver for Ch'en Cheng-kung later on.[217] In this world there are people like him who enjoy helping others, but there are not very many of them.

3. Mr. Wan keeps saying that he wants to repay Feng the Fourth for his help to him. Yet it is evident from what he says that this is all only empty talk and he has no real intention of repaying Feng the Fourth. On the other hand, since Feng the Fourth has no use for money, he would not accept anything from Mr. Wan even if the other sincerely wanted to thank him. He especially reveals this when he says: "It is not because I like you, sir, that I got you out of trouble. It was only because I felt like

---

[210] Special mirrors were used in hell to reveal the concealed sins of the wicked.

[211] *JLWS* 49/13b–14a, *Scholars* 49.544. It turns out that Secretary Wan is no secretary at all.

[212] These demons, particularly Ox-Head, are often involved in the carrying away of souls to hell.

[213] *JLWS* 50/9b–11b, *Scholars* 50.551–52.

[214] These two paths are described in the novel, *JLWS* 49/3a and *Scholars* 49.537.

[215] *JLWS* 51/2a–3b, *Scholars* 51.555–56.

[216] *JLWS* 51/3b–7a, *Scholars* 51.556–58.

[217] *JLWS* 52/14a–15b, *Scholars* 52.570–71.

doing it."[218] His heroic stature soars taller than a one-hundred-foot tower.

4. If a hack writer were to do the section in which Feng the Fourth undergoes torture,[219] he would surely add explanatory details such as "he has so much strength" and "he has so much martial skill," but the vitality of the section would be lost. In the previous chapter it was already mentioned that Feng the Fourth would not feel it even if a stone weighing over a thousand catties were to fall on his head.[220] From this comment, the reader will naturally understand that he is able to withstand the torture. This section is used to set off [*ch'en-t'o* 襯托] the next chapter so that the later section's vitality is increased one hundredfold.

Chapter 52   1. The author has saved up "Yankee" Ch'in the Second [Secretary Ch'in's younger brother] in order to use him here in this chapter. The author is like a blacksmith who can hammer out many new, interesting things.

2. "Messed-up" Hu the Eighth and "Yankee" Ch'in the Second are the same type of person. Their dislike for their older brothers is vividly depicted.

3. The section in which Feng the Fourth breaks the square bricks and lets Hu the Eighth kick his groin[221] portrays in a lively manner the very aspect of the love of bravery and taste for dirty fighting of a young rascal [Hu the Eighth]. Marvelous!

4. Whiskers Mao is an old, devious schemer. He wants to deceive Ch'en Cheng-kung in such a way that the latter cannot take him to court or sue him, but his secret is revealed by Ch'in the Second in one phrase.[222] However, when Feng the Fourth tears down Whiskers Mao's house [in order to make him repay Ch'en Cheng-kung],[223] this is also something that Whiskers Mao cannot take Feng the Fourth to court for. It is evident from this incident that cunning and trickery are of no use in this world because whatever tricks I play on others, others will play them right back on me! This book has a lot to teach people about how to conduct themselves in the world.

5. The two little instances of Whiskers Mao earning interest for Ch'en Cheng-kung[224] reflect forward [*tao-she* 倒攝] to later incidents. Truly, the author never wastes words.

---

[218] *JLWS* 51/11b, *Scholars* 51.561.
[219] *JLWS* 51/10b–11a, *Scholars* 51.560.
[220] *JLWS* 49/12a and *Scholars* 49.543. This is said by Secretary Ch'in.
[221] *JLWS* 52/5b–7a, *Scholars* 52.565.
[222] *JLWS* 52/15a, *Scholars* 52.570.
[223] *JLWS* 52/14b, *Scholars* 52.570.
[224] *JLWS* 52/9a–10a, *Scholars* 52.567.

Chapter 56[225] 1. An imperial edict, a memorial to the throne, and a sacrificial proclamation:[226] these three compositions form a tripartite structure that concludes [*chieh* 結] the novel. The lyric poem[227] is added [*chui* 綴] to give a personal touch, similar to the last chapter of Ssu-ma Ch'ien's *Shih-chi*.[228]

[225] Chaps. 53–55 have no postchapter comments in the original edition.

[226] This chapter is untranslated in *The Scholars* and is often left out of modern editions of the novel in Chinese. The chapter is composed mainly of an example each of the three types of writing pointed out by the commentator here. The edict (*JLWS* 56/1a–b) sets up the *problematique* (what is wrong with the empire) and is responded to by a memorial (*JLWS* 56/1b–3b) suggesting that those scholars that fell through the cracks of the examination system should be awarded posthumous degrees to show the state's recognition of talent. This is approved by the emperor and a list of those eligible is drawn up (*JLWS* 56/3b–9a). Finally, a proclamation (*JLWS* 56/9a–10a) is read at a sacrificial ceremony where the posthumous degrees are awarded. As a coda to the entire novel, a lyric poem in the voice of the implied author is appended (*JLWS* 56/10a–b).

[227] Following the suggestion of a distant relation of Wu Ching-tzu, Chin Ho 金和 (1818–1885), the edition of the novel translated by the Yangs places this poem at the end of chap. 55 (*Scholars* 55.601–2).

[228] This chapter of the *Shih-chi* contains a variety of material held together by the common objective of introducing to the reader the authors of the book (Ssu-ma Ch'ien and his father, Ssu-ma T'an) as well as the nature of the work itself. Some of the material is autobiographical, which also seems to be the case with the lyric poem at the end of chap. 56.

CHAPTER VI

Liu I-ming on How to Read the *Hsi-yu chi* (The Journey to the West)

INTRODUCTION:
Liu I-ming and His "*Hsi-yu yüan-chih* tu-fa" (How to Read *The Original Intent of the Journey to the West*)

Liu I-ming 劉一明 (style Wu-yüan-tzu 悟元子 or Wu-yüan lao-jen 悟元老人, 1734–1820+), was a Taoist priest who resided for the majority of his life in the Chin-t'ien Monastery in Lan-chou, Kansu Province. He completed a commentary on *The Journey to the West* entitled *Hsi-yu yüan-chih* 西遊原旨 (The Original Intent of the *Hsi-yu chi*) by 1778, but it was not published until after 1808. An undated postface indicates that it was because of the expense of the endeavor that the commentary, although one of the earliest of Liu I-ming's writings to be completed, was the last to be published in complete form.[1] The printed commentary contains numerous prefaces, two of which are by Liu I-ming himself

---

[1] A microfilm of an 1819–20 reprint (Ch'ang-te 常德, Hunan: Hu-kuo 護國 Monastery) is available, but for convenience citation of the prefatory matter to the commentary will be to the recently published *HYCTLHP*. The postface referred to is signed Fan Yü-li 樊于禮 and the section of the postface under consideration is reprinted in *HYCTLHP*, p. 258. Most of Liu I-ming's other writings consist of commentaries on or essays about the *I Ching* 易經 (Book of Changes) and important Taoist texts. This material (including the *tu-fa* essay, the concluding poems or *chieh-shih* 結詩 from the chapter comments, the "*Hsi-yu yüan-chih* ko" [Song of the *Hsi-yu yüan-chih*], and some of the prefaces from the commentary) was first gathered together and published in a collection entitled *Chih-nan chen* 指南針 (The Compass) prior to 1810. Later reprints of this material include *Tao-shu erh-shih-ssu chung* 道書二十四種 (Twenty-four Texts on Taoism; Shanghai, 1880), and *Tao-shu shih-erh chung* 道書十二種 (Twelve Texts on Taoism; 1913), reprinted under the title *Ching-yin Tao-shu shih-erh chung* 精印道書十二種 (Twelve Texts on Taoism, Finely Printed; Taipei, Hsin-wen-feng, 1975). A commentary by Liu I-ming on the *I Ching* has been translated by Thomas Cleary, *The Taoist I Ching* (Boston: Shambala, 1986).

(dated 1758[2] and 1810). There is a biography of the reputed author of the novel, Ch'iu Ch'u-chi 丘處機 (also known as Ch'iu Ch'ang-ch'un 長春, 1148–1227). Attribution of the authorship of the novel to this Taoist figure became standard after the appearance of Huang T'ai-hung 黃太鴻 (personal name Chou-hsing 周星, 1611–1680) and Wang Hsiang-hsü's 汪象旭 edition of the novel with commentary, *Hsi-yu cheng-tao shu* 西遊證道書 (The Way to Enlightenment through the *Hsi-yu chi*), which also contains a biography of Ch'iu Ch'u-chi. One of Ch'iu Ch'u-chi's disciples wrote an account of his master's travels with the same title as the novel, and this might be the source of the confusion over authorship, if outright deceit was not involved. The attribution to Ch'iu Ch'u-chi was not seriously challenged until late in the nineteenth century.[3] The *Hsi-yu yüan-chih* also contains the forty-five-item *tu-fa* essay translated below and two long poems, "Shan-chü ko" 山居歌 (Song of Life in the Mountains) and "*Hsi-yu yüan-chih* ko" 西遊原旨歌 (Song of the *Hsi-yu yüan-chih*), the last of which is unsigned but most likely was also written by Liu I-ming.[4] The commentary itself consists of Liu I-ming's chapter comments after each chapter, invariably concluded by a four-line poem, called by him "chieh-shih" 結詩 (concluding poem). Several postfaces by some of Liu I-ming's disciples and friends are appended to the end of the commentary.

The allegorical interpretation of *The Journey to the West* has a long

[2] Wang Shou-ch'üan 王守泉, "*Hsi-yu yüan-chih* ch'eng-shu nien-tai chi pan-pen yüan-liu k'ao" 西遊原旨成書年代及版本源流考 (On the Date of Composition and the Filiation of the Editions of the *Hsi-yu yüan-chih*), *Lan-chou ta-hsüeh hsüeh-pao* 蘭州大學學報 (Academic Journal of Lan-chou University), 1986.1:76–81, pp. 77–78 has shown that the 1758 date in this preface is almost certainly a mistake for 1778.

[3] Some scholars, however, doubted the attribution long before then. Chi Yün 紀昀 (1724–1805) tells of a divination session in which the spirit of Ch'iu Ch'u-chi claimed authorship for the novel but was unable to reply when asked why the novel contains Ming dynasty official titles not used in the Yüan dynasty, when Ch'iu Ch'u-chi lived. Quoted in K'ung Ling-ching 孔另境, *Chung-kuo hsiao-shuo shih-liao* 中國小說史料 (Historical Material on Chinese Fiction; Shanghai: Shang-hai ku-chi, 1982 reprint), p. 69. For a detailed investigation of the case for a connection between the sect of Taoism associated with Ch'iu Ch'u-chi and the *Hsi-yu chi*, see Liu Ts'un-jen 柳存仁, "Ch'üan-chen chiao ho hsiao-shuo *Hsi-yu chi*" 全真教和小說西遊記 (The Ch'üan-chen Sect and the *Hsi-yu chi*), *Ming-pao yüeh-k'an*, 1985.5:55–62 (pt. 1); 1985.6:59–64 (pt. 2); 1985.7:85–90 (pt. 3); 1985.8:85–90 (pt. 4); and 1985.9:70–74 (pt. 5).

[4] The 1819–20 reprint lacks the "Shan-chü ko" and adds a preface and a postface. The material in *HYCTLHP* is all based on the reprint edition. According to Wang Shou-ch'üan, "*Hsi-yu yüan-chih* ch'eng-shu nien-tai chi pan-pen yüan-liu k'ao," p. 79, the woodblocks for the original edition (repaired earlier in this century for reprinting) were still extant in Lan-chou until the Cultural Revolution. All references to the original edition of the commentary in this introduction are based on information in Wang Shou-ch'üan's article.

history that dates back to the earliest extant dated edition of the novel.[5] This trend is also evident in the rather sparse commentary on the novel attributed to Li Chih 李贄 (1527–1602)[6] and reached a new plateau in the commentary of Wang Hsiang-hsü, which appeared in the latter half of the seventeenth century. Wang Hsiang-hsü's commentary is also important in that it is the first in a line of abridged versions of the novel that do not contain all of the poetry and circumstantial detail of the earlier editions.[7] Liu I-ming accepted both Wang Hsiang-hsü's attribution of the novel to Ch'iu Ch'u-chi and his abridged version of the text, but he was critical of Wang Hsiang-hsü's commentary, which he considered too frivolous. He also thought that Wang Hsiang-hsü had missed the true import of the novel.[8]

Liu I-ming considered his own work on the novel to be a continuation of the Ch'en Shih-pin 陳士斌 (style Wu-i-tzu 悟一子) commentary on *The Journey to the West* published under the title *Hsi-yu chen-ch'üan* 西遊真詮 (The True Explication of the *Hsi-yu chi*).[9] One of the shortcomings that Liu I-ming saw in the work of Ch'en Shih-pin that he hoped to correct in his own commentary was what he considered to be an overemphasis on literary technique instead of the underlying meaning of the novel.[10] Liu I-ming told his readers that in order to save space and time, features of the text already adequately explained by Ch'en Shih-pin would not be further discussed by him.[11]

Like Ch'en Shih-pin, Liu I-ming saw *The Journey to the West* as containing the essential truths of all three of the major Chinese religions: Confucianism, Taoism, and Buddhism.[12] Liu I-ming might be said to surpass even Ch'en Shih-pin in his desire to turn the reader's attention

[5] See Ch'en Yüan-chih's 陳元之 preface, dated 1592, in the Shih-te t'ang 世德堂 edition of the novel, which discusses the book using allegorical terminology borrowed from the *Chuang Tzu* 莊子, quoted in *HYCTLHP*, pp. 212–13.

[6] This edition has a preface by Yüan Yü-ling 袁于令 (1599–1674).

[7] For information on these abridgments and a description of the major filiations of the novel, see Glen Dudbridge, "The Hundred-Chapter *Hsi-yu chi* and Its Early Versions," *Asia Major*, n.s. 14.2:141–91 (1969).

[8] See Liu I-ming's first preface to the novel, quoted in *HYCTLHP*, p. 245.

[9] This commentary has a preface by Yu T'ung 尤侗 (1618–1704), dated 1696.

[10] See Liu I-ming's first preface to the novel (*HYCTLHP*, p. 245) and the quotation of his ideas on the subject by Fan Yü-li in his postface to the commentary (*HYCTLHP*, p. 259).

[11] See his first preface to the novel, *HYCTLHP*, p. 245. For an example of a slight difference of opinion between the two men on a specific issue, see the chapter comments by both men for the opening chapter, where they discuss the interpretation of the phrase "slanting moon and three stars" (*hsieh-yüeh san-hsing* 斜月三星).

[12] Both men, however, were personally far more interested in Taoism than either of the other two religions.

away from the surface of the text toward a concentration on the deeper meaning of the novel as seen by him. The writer of one of the prefaces to the commentary exhorts the reader to treat Liu I-ming's commentary in the same way. Using metaphors from the *Chuang Tzu* 莊子, he likened the work to a fish trap that should be forgotten once the fish has been caught.[13] Of all the commentators translated in this volume, Liu I-ming pays the least attention to the writer's craft and literary technique and is most preoccupied with allegorical meanings embedded in the text. In these qualities he is fairly representative of most of the commentators on *The Journey to the West*.

In the notes to the translation of Liu I-ming's essay below, references to the Chinese text will be to the standard version published in 1954, which is for the most part based on the earliest extant full version of the novel.[14] References to the English translation of the novel will be to the recently completed translation of the 1954 edition by Anthony C. Yu, entitled *The Journey to the West*.[15] The text of the *tu-fa* essay is based on the 1819–20 reprint of the commentary.

[13] See the Yang Ch'un-ho 楊春和 preface, dated 1799, quoted in *HYCTLHP*, pp. 255–56.

[14] *HYC*.

[15] *JW*.

How to Read *The Original Intent of the Journey to the West*

Translated and Annotated by ANTHONY C. YU*
Additional Annotation by DAVID L. ROLSTON

1. The book, *The Journey to the West*, is the great way transmitted from mouth to mouth and from mind to mind by the sages, generation by generation. What the ancients dared not speak of was spoken of by Patriarch Ch'iu [Ch'iu Ch'u-chi 丘處機, 1148–1227]; what the ancients dared not relate was related by Patriarch Ch'iu [in this book].[1] When the heavenly mysteries are revealed so abundantly, this is a matter of the utmost consequence. Wherever this book resides, there are heavenly deities standing guard over it. The reader should purify his hands and burn incense before reading it, and it should be read with the utmost reverence. If he becomes bored or tired, the reader should close the book and return it to its place on high so that it will not meet with disrespect. Only he who knows this can read *The Journey to the West*.

2. The rhetoric of *The Journey to the West* is quite similar to the mysteries of Zen. The real message completely transcends the actual words of the text. Sometimes it is hidden in vulgar or ordinary language, sometimes it is conveyed through [the description] of the terrain and the characters. Sometimes truth and perversity are distinguished from each other through a joke or jest; sometimes the real is set off from the false in the space of a word or a phrase. Sometimes the real is made manifest through the false; sometimes truth is upheld in order to vanquish perversity. There are countless variations, appearing and then vanishing like gods or demons, and it is most difficult to divine their depths. The student must undertake a regimen of profound reflection and research; to be satisfied with but the surface meaning of the text is like scratching an itch with your boots on. Only he who knows this can read *The Journey to the West*.

3. *The Journey to the West* is a book of gods and immortals, quite different from those "books by and for geniuses" [*ts'ai-tzu chih shu* 才子之書].[2] "Books by and for geniuses" talk about the way of the world, and although they may seem true, they are actually false; the books of gods and immortals speak of the way of Heaven, and though

---

* The translator would like to acknowledge gratefully the kind and learned assistance of Professor Nathan Sivin.

[1] See the discussion of the attribution of authorship of *The Journey to the West* to this figure in the introduction to this chapter above.

[2] See chap. I above, essay d, n. 14, and the introduction to chap. II for more on the concept of *ts'ai-tzu shu*.

they may seem false they are actually true. Since literary technique is what is valued in those "books by and for geniuses," the language is ornate but the meaning shallow. Since the meaning is what is valued in those books of gods and immortals, the style is plain but the ideas are profound. Only he who knows this can read *The Journey to the West*.

4. *The Journey to the West* is a book that is permeated through and through with the truth of the unity of the Three Teachings [Buddhism, Taoism, and Confucianism]. This truth is found in the *Diamond Sūtra* and the *Lotus Sūtra* in Buddhism; in Confucianism it is found in the *Ho t'u* 河圖 [The Diagram of the Yellow River], the *Lo shu* 洛書 [The Book of the Lo River],[3] and the *I Ching* 易經 [Book of Changes]; and in Taoism it is found in the *Ts'an t'ung ch'i* 參同契 [The Kinship of the Three][4] and the *Wu-chen p'ien* 悟真篇 [Poetical Essay on the Primary Vitalities].[5] Therefore the story of the acquiring of the scriptures in the Western Heaven is used to expound the mysteries of the *Diamond* and *Lotus Sūtras*; the principle of Nine Times Nine to Return to the Real[6] is used to explain the secret of the *Ts'an t'ung ch'i* and the *Wu-chen p'ien*;

[3] These two documents of combinatorial analysis are said to date back to early in the Chou dynasty (1122–256 B.C.) according to the literature of the Warring States period (475–221 B.C.). For description and discussion of these texts, see Needham, vol. 3, pp. 55–62, and John S. Major, "The Five Phases, Magic Squares, and Schematic Cosmography," in *Explorations in Early Chinese Cosmology* (published as vol. 50.2 of *The Journal of the American Academy of Religion and Thematic Studies*), Henry Rosemont, ed. (Chico, California: Scholars Press, 1984), pp. 146–51.

[4] The *Ts'an t'ung ch'i* by Wei Po-yang 魏伯陽 of the Later Han (2d century A.D.) is the earliest extant Chinese text on alchemical theory. See Needham, vol. 5, pt. 3, pp. 50–75. A different work on alchemy in four hundred characters attributed to Wei Po-yang and Liu I-ming's commentary on that work have been translated by Thomas Cleary, *The Inner Teachings of Taoism* (Boston: Shambala, 1986).

[5] The *Wu-chen p'ien* is a treatise by Chang Po-tuan 張伯端 (d. 1082), a famous disciple of the founder of the Southern school of Taoism. See Needham, vol. 5, pt. 3, pp. 200–203. The *Wu-chen p'ien* and Liu I-ming's commentary to it have been translated by Thomas Cleary, *Understanding Reality: A Taoist Alchemical Classic* (Honolulu: University of Hawaii Press, 1987). For the novel's use of this treatise and some of its ideas, see *HYC*, 36.410–20 and the translation in *JW*, 2.36.163–78 (i.e., chap. 36, pp. 163–78 in vol. 2). The *Ts'an t'ung ch'i*, *Wu-chen p'ien*, *Lo shu*, and *Ho t'u* are all quoted from and referred to in Ch'en Shih-pin's commentary on the novel.

[6] In reference to the novel, Nine Times Nine to Return to the Real might be an allusion to the titular couplet of chap. 99 or to the fact that the pilgrims must pass through eighty-one (nine times nine) trials before they attain their goal. A list of the first eighty trials is given in the novel (*HYC* 99.1115–16, *JW* 4.99.398–402). The list in *HYC* is based on the eighteenth-century *Hsin-shuo Hsi-yu chi* 新說西遊記 (A New Explication of the *Hsi-yu chi*) and not on the earliest texts (see *HYC*, "Publisher's Preface," p. 5). For the use of terminology such as "nine nines" and "nine times nine" in the *I Ching* and the *Lo shu*, see Andrew H. Plaks, "Allegory in *Hsi-yu chi* and *Hung-lou meng*," in *Chinese Narrative: Critical and Theoretical Essays*, p. 179.

and the T'ang Monk and his disciples are used to expound the meaning of the *I Ching*, the *Ho t'u*, and the *Lo shu*. Only he who knows this can read *The Journey to the West*.

5. In *The Journey to the West* each episode [*an* 案] has its own meaning, each chapter has its own meaning, and each word has its own meaning. The Adept [Ch'iu Ch'u-chi] never spoke without purpose or used a superfluous word. The reader must pay attention to every line and every phrase, not even a single word should be permitted to slip by. Only he who knows this can read *The Journey to the West*.

6. In *The Journey to the West* is to be found an exhaustive treatment of the principles of the mundane world and of the Tao, of the seasons of Heaven and the affairs of men. As for such as the method of learning the Tao, the art of self-cultivation, and the proper way to conduct oneself in the world, there is not one of these that is not dealt with completely. Among the various alchemical classics past and present, this is the number one extraordinary book. Only he who knows this can read *The Journey to the West*.

7. *The Journey to the West* possesses the power to alter [the processes of] birth and death and appropriate the secrets of Creation. [Like the Great Man], when it precedes Heaven [*hsien-t'ien* 先天], Heaven does not contradict it; when it follows after Heaven [*hou-t'ien* 後天], it never contradicts Heaven's timing.[7] It is against complete immersion in one's own mind and thoughts and the mere playing with the concepts of vacuity [*k'ung* 空] and nirvana. The student must not become too preoccupied with the "monkey of the mind" [*hsin-yüan* 心猿], the "horse of the will" [*i-ma* 意馬], "the transformed body" [*hua-shen* 化身], or the "bag of flesh" [*jou-nang* 肉囊].[8] He ought rather to begin without any conception of form or image and from there work toward the apprehension of the real nature and pattern [of the cosmos]; only then will he not labor in vain. Only he who knows this can read *The Journey to the West*.

8. The great way of *The Journey to the West* deals with the methods of prefiguring Heaven [*hsien-t'ien* 先天] before it reveals itself in form; it has nothing to do with the various perverse manipulations of form and appearance after Heaven has revealed itself [*hou-t'ien* 後天]. One must

---

[7] These two phrases are quoted from the *I Ching*. See *A Concordance to Yi Ching* (Peiping: Harvard-Yenching Institute, 1935), p. 3 and Richard Wilhelm, *The I Ching or Book of Changes*, Cary Baynes, trans. (Princeton: Princeton University Press, 1967), pp. 382–83.

[8] These terms are part of the most immediate allegorical level of the novel. For instance, Sun Wu-k'ung is frequently referred to by the phrase "monkey of the mind." See Andrew H. Plaks, "Allegory in *Hsi-yu chi* and *Hung-lou meng*," pp. 176–77.

first discard such things as the making of internal elixirs of immortality through refinement by brazier and fire. Only then can one go on to investigate thoroughly the correct doctrines and obtain success. Only he who knows this can read *The Journey to the West.*

9. As for the episodes [*kung-an* 公案] of *The Journey to the West*, some of them take up the space of one or two chapters, some take up three or four chapters, and some take up five or six chapters; the number of chapters is not equal. The central idea of each, however, is always to be found at the very beginning of each episode, where it is plainly and clearly pointed out.[9] If one passes carelessly over these parts, the rest of the episode may seem completely without focus. Not only will the subtle meaning of the episode then be difficult [for the reader] to realize, but even the literal meaning of the sentences and phrases will be hard to construe. The reader will obtain results only by first distinguishing clearly the important points of connection [*lai-mai* 來脉] to the rest of the novel and then going on to read carefully what follows in the episode. Only he who knows this can read *The Journey to the West.*

10. The subtle meaning of each chapter of *The Journey to the West* is to be found in the titular couplet [*t'i-kang* 提綱], and the crucial words of the titular couplet are never more than one or two. Take for example the titular couplet for the first chapter: "When the spiritual root is nourished and brought to term, the origin emerges; / Once the moral nature is cultivated and maintained, the great Tao is born."[10] The crucial words of the first line are "spiritual root" [*ling-ken* 靈根]; in the second line the crucial words are "moral nature" [*hsin-hsing* 心性]. We can see that the spiritual root is the spiritual root and the moral nature is the moral nature, but the spiritual root is used to cultivate the moral nature—it is not the case that the cultivation of the moral nature is [the same as] the cultivation of the spiritual root. How clear, how plain is the meaning! Again, take the couplet for the second chapter: "Thoroughly comprehend the true and wondrous doctrine of the Boddhi; / Destroy *māra*, return to the root and unify the soul."[11] "Thoroughly comprehend" [*wu-ch'e* 悟徹] would be the crucial words of the first line, "destroy *māra*" [*tuan-mo* 斷魔] would be the crucial words of the second line. One must comprehend a principle thoroughly before one can act, for it is comprehension that unifies action, while it is action that verifies com-

---

[9] Read *t'i* 題 as *t'i* 提.

[10] The couplet is translated in accordance with Liu I-ming's understanding of it, therefore the translation here varies from *JW* 1.2.83.

[11] Again, this translation follows Liu I-ming's conception of the couplet's meaning and differs from *JW* 1.2.83.

prehension. When knowledge and action are seen to be mutually reliant, then one can return to the origin and unify the soul. Within the chapter, there may be thousands of words and countless transformations, but they are always contained within the central idea of the titular couplet. It is the same with all of the chapters, and the reader should pay strict attention [*cho-yen* 着眼] [to the titular couplets]. Only he who knows this can read *The Journey to the West*.

11. The acquisition of the true scriptures by means of the journey to the West actually means the acquisition of the true scripture of *The Journey to the West*. Apart from *The Journey to the West* there are no other true scriptures to be acquired. *The Journey to the West* is transmitted through the story of the transmission of the scriptures by the Tathāgata Buddha, that is all. If one can truly understand *The Journey to the West*, then the three baskets of the true scripture will be found within it. Only he who knows this can read *The Journey to the West*.

12. At the conclusion [*shou-shu ch'u* 收束處] of every episode [*kung-an* 公案] in *The Journey to the West*, there are two lines of summary [*tsung-chieh* 總結] which provide, as it were, the skeletal structure [*ku-tzu* 骨子] of the entire episode. Countless subtle meanings are to be found in these pairs of lines. They must not be lightly skimmed over. Only he who knows this can read *The Journey to the West*.

13. *The Journey to the West* treats the truth of the union of [the] Three and [the] Five[12] and that of "after firmness arises origination" [*chen-hsia ch'i yüan* 貞下起元].[13] This is why the T'ang Monk begins

---

[12] There are too many phrases that deal with sets of three and five items to allow a definitive translation in the present instance, especially as the context gives few clues as to which pair the author has in mind. It is also possible (judging from what continuity can be found in this item of the *tu-fa* essay) that the concept is purely numerological. For an instance of numerology that also mentions the *Wu-chen p'ien* by the author of the "*Hung-lou meng* tu-fa" 紅樓夢讀法, Chang Hsin-chih 張新之, see *CYY*, interlineal comment, p. 1.80. Ch'en Shih-pin also indulges in numerology stressing these two numbers. See his chapter comments to chap. 3, *Kuo-hsüeh chi-pen ts'ung-shu* 國學基本叢書 (Basic Sinological Collection) edition (Taipei: Commercial Press, 1968), p. 3.35–36.

[13] This phrase appears in the novel, *HYC* 1.1 and *JW* 1.1.65, as part of the numerological and cyclical speculation that precedes the birth of Sun Wu-k'ung. Ch'en Shih-pin uses a similar phrase, *chen-hsia huan-yüan* 貞下還元, in his commentary on the novel (see, for instance, his chapter comments to chap. 49, *Kuo-hsüeh chi-pen ts'ung-shu* edition, v.27, p. 49.499). *Chen* and *yüan* are the last and first of a four-character cycle that appears at the very beginning of the *I Ching*. These four characters are often used as a substitute for ordinal numbers and are conceived of as a regenerative cycle. See *Shih-san ching ching-wen* 十三經經文 (Text of the Thirteen Classics; Taipei: T'ai-wan K'ai-ming shu-tien, 1955), *I Ching*, p. 1 and Richard Wilhelm, *The I Ching*, p. 4, where the generative properties of this cycle are discussed. The phrase also occurs in item 17 below.

his journey in the thirteenth year of the Chen-kuan reign period [A.D. 639],[14] why he takes on three disciples during the journey,[15] and why he returns to the East after fourteen years.[16] One must scrutinize [*cho-yen* 着眼] such passages carefully. Only he who knows this can read *The Journey to the West*.

14. The official rescript that serves as a passport [for Tripitaka] in *The Journey to the West* is in effect the certificate or license of one who practices the Tao. It is a key item [*kuan-mu* 關目] in the entire book. This is why it has stamped on it precious seals of the various nations and why it was obtained [from the emperor] at the beginning of the journey to the West and returned [to the emperor] when the pilgrims returned to the East. From beginning to end, it has been handled with care and reverence, never leaving [its owner] for a single moment. One must think carefully and discriminate clearly before one can apprehend the truth behind this. Only he who knows this can read *The Journey to the West*.

15. There are many inconsistencies [*p'o-chan ch'u* 破綻處] in *The Journey to the West*, but those are the very places where secret formulas are likely to be found. For it is only by means of inconsistencies that the suspicion of later readers may be aroused. Without such suspicion, the reader will not ponder [the meaning hidden in the text]. These are places on which the Adept [Ch'iu Ch'u-chi] expended a lot of thought and where he employed his most subtle brushstrokes. Take, for example, the fact that Sun Wu-k'ung, the Great Sage Equal to Heaven, is refined in the Brazier of the Eight Trigrams and attains an indestructible, diamond-hard body.[17] How then could he be imprisoned beneath the Mountain of the Five Phases [by the Tathāgata Buddha]?[18] Hsüan-tsang was born in the thirteenth year of the Chen-kuan reign period.[19] By the time he

[14] *HYC* 13.143 and *JW* 1.13.282. Note the occurrence of the numerals three and five in the day of departure, "the third day before the fifteenth of the ninth month." The numeral three also occurs in the "thirteenth" year and the "thirteenth" chapter (in which this event takes place). The *chen* 貞 in Chen-kuan is the same *chen* that appears in the sentence immediately preceding in the text of the essay.

[15] The taking on of these three brings the total number of scripture seekers to five (the other two being Tripitaka and the dragon horse).

[16] *HYC* 100.1123–25 and *JW* 4.100.412–17. Is the point that the integers one and four in fourteen add up to five?

[17] *HYC* 6.69–70, *JW* 1.6.166–68.

[18] *HYC* 7.74, *JW* 1.7.174.

[19] The assertion that Tripitaka was born in the thirteenth year of the Chen-kuan reign period is made only in the later versions of chap. 9, the first of which appeared in the edition of the novel by Huang T'ai-hung 黃太鴻 and Wang Hsiang-hsü 汪象旭 entitled *Hsi-yu cheng-tao shu* 西遊證道書 (The Way to Enlightenment through the *Hsi-yu chi*), first published in the latter half of the seventeenth century. Liu I-ming's edition of the

avenges his father's murder eighteen years later,[20] it would already be the thirty-first year of the Chen-kuan reign period. How could it be that it is still the thirteenth year of the Chen-kuan reign period when he begins his journey to acquire the scriptures? In the Lotus Flower Cave [episode], the fact that Sun Wu-k'ung has already killed Mountain-climbing Tiger and Sea-reclining Dragon was already known to the old fiends [the Gold-Horn and Silver-Horn Demons]. Why then does Sun Wu-k'ung change into [the form] of Sea-reclining Dragon when he tries to steal the magic gourd later?[21] One must pay special attention to such places in the text. Only he who knows this can read *The Journey to the West*.

16. That the official rescript in *The Journey to the West* has been stamped with the precious seals of the various nations is the subtle message of the book. It makes the book a place where a person who practices self-cultivation may bring peace to his life and establish himself. It is, in effect, a formula for immortality when abroad. Concerning such places [in the text] one must tenaciously seek out the true reason for them. Only he who knows this can read *The Journey to the West*.

[margin note: Passport and seals]

17. Every time the pilgrims pass through an ordeal in *The Journey to the West*, the author invariably records the year and the month first before continuing the narration. The hidden allegorical meaning found in the compression of years into months, months into days, and days into hours is similar to the device of relating how the official rescript issued in the thirteenth year of the Chen-kuan reign period is returned after the pilgrims return to the East with the scriptures.[22] This is the so-called "after firmness arises origination" [*chen-hsia ch'i yüan* 貞下起元]. Within a single hour, the elixir of immortality is complete. Only he who knows this can read *The Journey to the West*.

18. Among the crucial and climactic episodes ["cho-chin ho-chien ch'u" 着緊合尖處] in *The Journey to the West*, there are none that surpass the episodes of the Plantain Cave,[23] the Heaven-reaching River,[24] and

---

novel uses this later version of this chapter, and it is one of these later versions that is used as the base text for this chapter in *HYC* (see "Publisher's Preface," p. 4). The year of Tripitaka's birth is mentioned in *HYC* 9.89 and *JW* 1.9.198.

[20] *HYC* 9.96–98, *JW* 1.9.209–11.

[21] In point of fact, it is not altogether clear that the demons know of the death of the tiger and dragon (which takes place in *HYC* 34.390 and *JW* 2.34.140). They are only told that their mother has been killed (*HYC* 34.393 and *JW* 2.34.140). Sun Wu-k'ung changes into the dragon at the end of the chapter (*HYC* 34.397 and *JW* 2.34.146–47).

[22] The author is probably referring here to the fact that the return journey covers the same distance as the journey out in only a few days.

[23] Chaps. 59–61.

[24] Chaps. 47–49.

the Scarlet-Purple Kingdom.[25] The way in which the "temperature, timing, and sequences" [*huo-hou tz'u-hsü* 火候次序] of alchemical refinement are treated in [the episode of] the Plantain Cave, the way that the "weighing out of medicinal substances" [*yao-wu chin-liang* 藥物斤兩] is treated [in the episode of] the Heaven-reaching River,[26] the way that the process of "summoning and integrating the soul" [*chao-she tso-yung* 招攝作用][27] is treated in [the episode of] the Scarlet-Purple Kingdom may be said to be profound and exhaustive indeed. If the student will delve deeply into such places, he may be assured that he will come to understand a large part of the Great Way of the Golden Elixir. Only he who knows this can read *The Journey to the West*.

19. There is both unified narration [*ho-shuo* 合說] and separate narration [*fen-shuo* 分說] in *The Journey to the West*. The first seven chapters are [an example of] unified narration. They move from activity [*yu-wei* 有為] to nonactivity [*wu-wei* 無為]; and from the cultivation of life-store [*ming* 命] they proceed to the cultivation of nature [*hsing* 性].[28] The sequence of elixir formation and the labor of refinement by heat—none of this is not completely covered there. The rest of the ninety-three chapters treat either the orthodox or the heterodox, nature or life-store; or they speak of nature along with life-store or life-store along with nature; or they relate the true fire-times [*huo-hou* 火候] or point out the errors in the fire-times [of the alchemical refinement of the elixir of

[25] Chaps. 68–71.

[26] This may be an oversight on the part of Liu I-ming, since it is the episode of the Scarlet-Purple Kingdom that treats the "weighing out of medicinal substances."

[27] The exact meaning of the phrase *chao-she* 招攝 is unclear.

[28] Nature and life-store are two key concepts used by the physiological alchemists who advocate the doctrine of "dual-cultivation" (*shuang-hsiu* 雙修). According to Judith A. Berling, *The Syncretic Religion of Lin Chao-en* (New York: Columbia University Press, 1980, pp. 95–96), they held that "humans were composed of two elements, *hsing* (human nature) and *ming* (life store). Nature is the source of human spiritual faculties (*shen*, spirit), while life store is the font of vitality (*ching*, vital essence)....Over time the spiritual faculties are clouded over by desires, things, sensory stimuli (activities of the mind), and the vital forces are wasted in sex, violent emotions, and desires, which cause the vital fluids (sexual fluids, sweat, saliva, moist breath) to drain away. When the spiritual faculties are dimmed and the life store exhausted, the result is death. Only by recovering the original *hsing* and *ming* can the process be reversed. The restoration of original *hsing* and *ming* in the microcosm of the self was parallel to the nondifferentiated state at the beginning of creation—that which antedated Heaven [i.e., *hsien-t'ien*]. In the human microcosm this state represented the original self prior to impure thoughts; it was called the uncarved block or the infant in *Lao Tzu*, and the sage or immortal embryo in Inner Alchemy. Through this recreation, the Taoist became physically and spiritually identified with the underlying unity of the Tao." For the specifically sexual implications of such "cultivation," see Needham, vol. 5, pt. 5, pp. 239–40. In the translation of the *tu-fa* essay, "life store" is written with a hyphen to remind the reader that this is a special usage.

immortality]. They amount to nothing more than making analyses by means of single incidents and do not depart from the subtle truths [embodied] in the first seven chapters. Only he who knows this can read *The Journey to the West*.

20. [The heart of] *The Journey to the West* is the same as the teachings of Confucius on the exhaustive investigation of truth [*ch'iung-li* 窮理], the perfection of nature [*chin-hsing* 盡性], and the fulfillment of one's life-store [*chih-ming* 至命].[29] When the Monkey King learns the Tao at the West Aparagodānīya Continent, this is illustrative of the exhaustive investigation of truth; when he thoroughly comprehends the wondrous doctrine of Boddhi, this also illustrates the exhaustive investigation of truth; when he destroys *māra* and returns to the origin, this is illustrative of the perfection of nature.[30] His acquisition of the gold-hooped rod and full battle dress and his erasure of his name from the Register of Life and Death,[31] his becoming Great Sage Equal to Heaven[32] and his entering the Brazier of the Eight Trigrams[33] to be refined are illustrative of the fulfillment of life-store. Kuan-yin's redemption of the three disciples and her search for the scripture pilgrim are illustrative of the exhaustive investigation of the truth.[34] Again, the T'ang Monk's passing the Double-Fork Ridge and arriving at the Mountain of the Two Frontiers[35] are illustrative of the perfection of nature, while the taking of the three disciples[36] and the crossing of the Flowing-Sand River[37] exemplify the fulfillment of life-store. Similarly, the episodes that relate the pilgrims' passing through countless foreign regions, traversing a thousand mountains and ten thousand waters, their arrival at Cloud-transcending Stream, and [their sailing in] the bottomless boat[38] are all illustrative of such teachings. Only he who knows this can read *The Journey to the West*.

[29] These phrases appear in a sentence in the "Shuo-kua" 說卦 (Discussion of the Trigrams) section of the *I Ching*. The sentence is translated in Richard Wilhelm, *The I Ching*, p. 262 as: "By thinking through the order of the outer world to the end [*ch'iung-li*], and by the exploring the law of their nature to the deepest core [*chin-hsing*], they arrived at an understanding of fate [*i chih yü ming* 以至於命]." For Chinese text and context, see *Shih-san ching ching-wen, I Ching*, "Shuo-kua," sec. 1, p. 28. This sentence has been interpreted differently by the various schools of philosophy.

[30] Chaps. 1–2.

[31] *HYC* 3.25–33, *JW* 1.3.100–112.

[32] *HYC* 4.40–43, *JW* 1.4.123–26.

[33] *HYC* 6.69–70, *JW* 1.6.166–68.

[34] *HYC* 8.78–88, *JW* 1.8.190–97.

[35] *HYC* 13.143–53, *JW* 1.13.282–98.

[36] Chaps. 14–22.

[37] *HYC* 22.245–55, *JW* 1.22.429–43.

[38] *HYC* 98.1102–6, *JW* 4.98.379–85.

21. *The Journey to the West* has passages that have the power to strike a blow at perverse doctrine in order to bring the reader back to sound doctrine and there are passages that have the power to verify sound doctrine in order to strike a blow at perverse doctrine. For example, in the episodes of the marriage in the Land of Women[39] and of becoming an imperial son-in-law in India,[40] you have the attacking of perversity in the midst of the verification of sound doctrine. In the episodes of subduing the three fiends at Lion-Camel Kingdom,[41] the submission of Yellow Brows at the Little Western Heaven,[42] and the elimination of the leopard at Mist-concealing Mountain,[43] you have attacking perverse doctrine in order to bring the reader back to sound doctrine. The reason why the Adept [Ch'iu Ch'u-chi] used such a double-edged [*shuang-kuan* 雙關] style and expended an immeasurable amount of compassionate care on this was surely his desire that every person might become an immortal or a Buddha. Only he who knows this can read *The Journey to the West*.

22. In *The Journey to the West* there are passages that expound orthodoxy, and there are those that attack heterodoxy. The passages that portray the various monsters in different mountain caves are attacks on heterodoxy, whereas those treating the kings and rulers of various lands expound orthodoxy. This is the fundamental significance of the entire book. Only he who knows this can read *The Journey to the West*.

23. The so-called monsters in *The Journey to the West* are of two kinds: they are either monsters of the orthodox tradition or monsters of the heterodox tradition. Monsters like those of Little Western Heaven and Lion-Camel Cave belong to the heretical or heterodox tradition. Monsters like the Bull Monster King and the Rakṣa Woman,[44] the Great King of Miraculous Power,[45] Jupiter's Rival,[46] and the Jade Hare[47] are unenlightened monsters who nonetheless belong to the orthodox tradition and are thus different from the other monsters. Only he who knows this can read *The Journey to the West*.

24. Among the hexagrams and their images from the *I Ching* expounded in *The Journey to the West*, some are used more than once but,

[39] HYC 54.620–30, JW 3.54.52–68.
[40] Chaps. 93–95.
[41] Chaps. 74–78.
[42] Chaps. 65–66.
[43] Chaps. 85–86.
[44] Chaps. 59–61.
[45] Chaps. 47–49.
[46] Chaps. 69–71.
[47] Chaps. 95–96.

since each is used because of a particular incident, although the hexagram might be the same, the meaning is not the same. Therefore it does not matter that some are used more than once. Only he who knows this can read *The Journey to the West*.

25. In *The Journey to the West*, there is the method of first striking down the false when one wants to show forth the true ["yü shih-chen erh hsien p'i-chia chih fa" 欲示真而先劈假之法]. For example, when the author wishes to describe the true tiger [nature] of Pilgrim at the Mountain of the Two Frontiers, he first uses the ordinary tiger of Double-Fork Ridge to lead into [yin 引] the topic.[48] When he wishes to describe the true dragon [nature] of the Dragon King of the Eastern Ocean,[49] he first uses the serpents and snakes of Double-Fork Ridge[50] to lead into the topic. When he wishes to describe the true yin 陰 and yang 陽 of Pilgrim and Pa-chieh, he first uses the false yin and yang of Kuan-yin Hall[51] to lead into the topic. When he wishes to describe the dragon horse of the Serpent-coiled Mountain, he first uses the ordinary horse given by the T'ang emperor to lead into the topic.[52] When he wishes to describe the true earth [nature] of Sha Monk, he first uses the false earth [nature] of the Yellow Wind Monster.[53] Such a device is used extensively throughout the work. Only he who knows this can read *The Journey to the West*.

26. In *The Journey to the West*, there are some passages that are very difficult to understand, but are nevertheless really very easy to understand. Take, for example, the fact that Tripitaka's three disciples have attained immortality. How, then, could Sun Wu-k'ung end up pressed beneath the Mountain of the Five Phases? How could Chu Wu-neng [Pa-chieh] get reincarnated into the wrong womb and Sha Wu-ching [Sha Monk] be banished to the Flowing-Sand River? Why did they have to embrace Buddhism before they could truly attain ultimate fruition? That the three disciples must still embrace Buddhism points to the fact that they have perfected their life-stores but not their natures. Moreover, the episodes of the Mountain of the Five Phases, the Cloudy Paths Cave,[54] and the Flowing-Sand River point to the fact that the T'ang

---

[48] Guardian Liu kills the ordinary tiger in chap. 13 (*HYC* 13.289–90 and *JW* 1.13.148–49) while in the following chapter (*HYC* 14.301–2 and *JW* 1.14.156) Pilgrim kills a tiger and then wears its skin.

[49] *HYC* 14.310–11, *JW* 1.14.162–63.

[50] *HYC* 13.288, *JW* 1.13.147.

[51] Chaps. 16–18.

[52] *HYC* 15.168–76, *JW* 1.15.315–29. The horse given Tripitaka is eaten by the dragon horse. The latter, once subdued, takes the place of the ordinary horse as Tripitaka's mount.

[53] Chaps. 20–22.

[54] It is here that Sun Wu-k'ung subdues Pa-chieh in chap. 19.

Monk has not perfected his life-store though he has perfected his nature. This use of the same pen to treat two sides of a problem at once [*i-pi shuang-hsieh* 一筆雙寫] shows the truth that there can be no cultivation of nature without the cultivation of life-store and no cultivation of life-store without the cultivation of nature. Only he who knows this can read *The Journey to the West*.

27. There are many passages in *The Journey to the West* that seem to deal with different incidents, but ultimately refer to the same thing ["pu t'ung erh ta-t'ung-che" 不同而大同者]. *The Journey to the West*, for example, takes its name from the story of the T'ang Monk's journey to acquire scriptures in the Western Heaven. Why, then, does the story of Sun Wu-k'ung appear in the beginning?[55] What the reader overlooks is the fact that Sun Wu-k'ung's birth in the Pūrvavideha Continent is analogous to the T'ang Monk's birth in Great T'ang of the Land of the East; that Sun Wu-k'ung's learning the Way in the West Aparagodānīya Continent is analogous to the T'ang Monk's acquisition of the scriptures in the Thunderclap Temple of the Western Heaven; that Sun Wu-k'ung's return to his mountain after attaining enlightenment is analogous to the T'ang Monk's return to his country after the acquisition of the true scriptures; and that Sun Wu-k'ung's being caught in Buddha's palm after getting out of the Brazier is analogous to the T'ang Monk's return to the Western Heaven after the transmission of the scriptures.[56] Though the incidents are different, the meaning is the same, for they are all summed up and unified in the [idea of a] journey to the West. Only he who knows this can read *The Journey to the West*.

28. Whenever a most difficult or perilous situation occurs during the journey to the West, Pilgrim seeks assistance from Kuan-yin. This is a most important feature [*kuan-mu* 關目] of *The Journey to the West*, for it embodies the most crucial lesson for the person practicing self-cultivation. Success in the cultivation of life-store and nature is entirely dependent on the assistance of the superintending gods and spirits.[57] Only he who knows this can read *The Journey to the West*.

29. The first seven chapters of *The Journey to the West* proceed from life-store to nature, from activity to nonactivity. The remaining ninety-three chapters proceed from nature to life-store and return from non-activity to activity. The profound truth of the entire work is nothing

[55] Chaps. 1–7.

[56] Tripitaka's birth is related in chap. 9, he reaches the Thunderclap Temple in chap. 98, returns to China and then retires to the Western Heaven in chap. 100. The incidents concerning Sun Wu-k'ung alone take place in chaps. 1–7.

[57] Both Ch'en Shih-pin and Liu I-ming insist on the importance of the teacher in self-cultivation and the impossibility of the project without external help.

more than this. Only he who knows this can read *The Journey to the West*.

30. In *The Journey to the West*, Tripitaka represents the substance [*t'i* 體] of the Supreme Ultimate, while the three disciples represent the energies of the five phases. Tripitaka's acceptance of the three disciples thus refers to the control of the five phases by the Supreme Ultimate, while the fact that the three disciples make their submission to Tripitaka means that the five phases are what constitutes the Supreme Ultimate. Only he who knows this can read *The Journey to the West*.

31. When *The Journey to the West* speaks of the T'ang Monk and each of his disciples, two different sets of names are used, and they ought not to be thought of in the same breath. For example, [the names] Hsüan-tsang, Wu-k'ung, Wu-neng, and Wu-ching refer to the substance [*t'i* 體] of the Tao, whereas [the names] Tripitaka, Pilgrim, Pa-chieh, and Monk refer to the function [*yung* 用] of the Tao. Since function does not exist apart from substance nor does substance exist apart from function, therefore there are two names for each of them. Only he who knows this can read *The Journey to the West*.

32. The references in *The Journey to the West* to the T'ang Monk and his disciples have both primary and auxiliary functions [*yung* 用]. Take, for example, the names Ch'en Hsüan-tsang, Tripitaka T'ang, Sun Wu-k'ung, Pilgrim Sun, Chu Pa-chieh, Chu Wu-neng, Sha Wu-ching, and Sha Monk—these are made to serve the primary function. The names T'ang Monk, Pilgrim, Idiot, and Monk are made to serve the auxiliary function. The primary function serves solely to explicate the substantive truths of life-store and nature, whereas the auxiliary function serves simultaneously to give form to the meanings of the ordinary world. People should not regard them as if they were all the same. Only he who knows this can read *The Journey to the West*.

33. *The Journey to the West* uses the three disciples to represent the great medicine outside of the five phases. This belongs to the category of prenatal endowment [*hsien-t'ien* 先天] and is not to be compared with the perverse five phases that belong to the postnatal condition [*hou-t'ien* 後天], where they possess shape and form. One must clearly distinguish the true source of things and not try to locate it on the bag of flesh or skin [i.e., the body]. Only he who knows this can read *The Journey to the West*.

34. *The Journey to the West* describes all three disciples as having hideous features. Hideous features are, in fact, distinguished features, and distinguished features are marvelous features. They may be said to be hideous, but what they do is marvelous. Moreover, they possess neither "egotistical" features nor "popular" features, neither the features of the

moral multitudes nor those of the long-lived ones. That is why, wherever the three disciples go, people fail to recognize them [for what they really are] and become afraid or amazed at the sight of them. In such places [in the text], one must take careful note of this feature. Only he who knows this can read *The Journey to the West*.

35. *The Journey to the West* describes all three disciples as having different abilities. Sha Monk is not capable of transformations at all, Pa-chieh knows thirty-six transformations, while Pilgrim knows seventy-two transformations. Though his number of transformations is said to be seventy-two, Pilgrim is actually capable of countless transformations. Why is this? He is the Metal within Water, the true *yang* principle external to one's self. Belonging to the category of life-store, lord of hardness and motion, he signifies the primal breath of all living creatures and unites the strategic nodes of the seventy-two time periods [*hou* 候] of the year.[58] There is nothing that is not included in him, nothing that is not perfected by him. A perfect substance [*t'i* 體] having a great function [*yung* 用], he is an all-pervading principle of unity. That is why he is capable of boundless transformations, unimaginably wonderful and mysterious. Pa-chieh happens to be the Wood within the Fire, the true *yin* principle internal to one's self. Belonging to the category of nature, lord of pliancy and quiescence, he holds the handle by which the illusory body is controlled, but he can only change into substance that is posterior to Heaven [*hou-t'ien* 後天] and not the true treasure that is anterior to Heaven [*hsien-t'ien* 先天]. His transformations are incomplete, and that is why, of the seventy-two transformations, he is capable of only thirty-six. As for Sha Monk, he is the true Earth, and he lives to guard the Central Quarter and to harmonize the *yin* and *yang*. He is incapable of any transformations. Only he who knows this can read *The Journey to the West*.

36. There is great significance in *The Journey to the West*'s description of the divine weapons belonging to the three disciples. Both Pa-chieh and Sha Monk carry their divine weapons along with them in their hands. The gold-hooped rod of Pilgrim, however, can be transformed into the size of an embroidery needle; it is then stored in his ear and taken out only when needed. Why is this so? The rake and the priestly staff, you see, though treasures in themselves, represent the practice of the perfection of form by means of the Tao. Once the matter has been pointed out by the teacher, the person himself can attain its realization. The gold-hooped rod, on the other hand, is actually the secret truth that has been transmitted from mouth to mouth by sages through succeeding

[58] These time periods were made up of five days each. There may be a pun involved here, as the name of the time period and the word monkey (*hou* 猴) are homonyms.

generations, a secret that was whispered from ear to ear. It is the technique of prolonging one's life through magic, fabricated out of nothingness. It is so huge that it has no circumference, so small that it has no interior. It roams at will between Heaven and Earth, with nothing to withstand it, and that is why it must be stored in the ear. These mysterious and marvelous functions [of the gold-hooped rod] are as different as night and day from those of the rake and priestly staff. Only he who knows this can read *The Journey to the West*.

37. In *The Journey to the West*, the three disciples represent the substance [*t'i* 體] of the five phases, while the three weapons represent the function [*yung* 用] of the five phases. When the five phases are compressed together,[59] then both substance and function are perfectly present. This is why they can successfully escort the T'ang Monk to fetch the true scriptures and meet the real Buddha. Only he who knows this can read *The Journey to the West*.

38. There are many accounts in *The Journey to the West* of how Sun Wu-k'ung triumphs over the most difficult of obstacles by pulling off pieces of hair from his body and transforming them. The pieces of hair, however, are not all the same nor are the transformations. Sometimes he pulls off pieces of hair from behind his head or from either his left or right arm, sometimes he pulls off pieces of hair from both arms or from his tail. There are great differences here, and one must not be careless in distinguishing between them. Only he who knows this can read *The Journey to the West*.

39. When *The Journey to the West* describes Sun Wu-k'ung's changing into someone else, the accounts vary: sometimes he himself is tranformed, sometimes he uses his rod, and sometimes he uses pieces of hair. The transformations of himself and his rod are true transformations, whereas the transformations of the pieces of hair are false transformations. Only he who knows this can read *The Journey to the West*.

40. In *The Journey to the West*, Sun Wu-k'ung is called the Great Sage and Pilgrim. These two names are vastly different from each other and they ought not to be thought of in the same breath. One must look to the source. If the source is real, then everything is real; but if the source is false, then everything is false. Never confuse the real with the false, or the false with the real. Only he who knows this can read *The Journey to the West*.

41. Sun Wu-k'ung calls himself Sun Wai-kung 孫外公 [Maternal Grandfather Sun] everywhere he goes and always mentions "that bit of

---

[59] The term "compress together the five phases" (*ts'uan-ts'u wu-hsing* 攢簇五行) occurs in the novel, HYC 2.20, JW 1.2.88. See also Andrew H. Plaks, "Allegory in *Hsi-yu chi* and *Hung-lou meng*," p. 185, where it is translated as "fully integrate the five elements."

business five hundred years ago."[60] Now, Sun Wai-kung actually refers to the emptiness within, while "five hundred years ago" actually refers to that which is anterior to Heaven [*hsien-t'ien* 先天]. One must realize that the vital force anterior to Heaven originates from nothingness. It is the formula for immortality external to oneself and not something that one can produce within oneself. Only he who knows this can read *The Journey to the West*.

42. After Sun Wu-k'ung attains the Tao on his journey to the West,[61] he can neither be drowned in water nor burned by fire. When he caused a great uproar in Heaven,[62] even the divine warriors of the various Heavens could not prevail against him. Why, then, is he repeatedly overcome by monsters when he is accompanying the T'ang Monk to acquire scriptures in the Western Heaven? The reader must take such problems and carefully distinguish the issues involved; only then can he discover their true meaning. If he just muddles through his reading, he will never gain any insight. Remember that the name Pilgrim is a nickname given by the T'ang Monk to Sun Wu-k'ung. Now this nickname may be explained as referring to someone who has understood the truth but who must still engage in action or as a name for any person practicing self-cultivation. The Pilgrim who is overcome by monsters refers, in fact, to any pilgrim practicing self-cultivation. Do not confuse one with the other. Only he who knows this can read *The Journey to the West*.

43. Whenever the T'ang Monk and his disciples pass through a country in *The Journey to the West*, the official rescript must first be examined and stamped with the precious seals [of the country] before they are permitted to proceed. This is a matter of primary importance in the whole enterprise of acquiring scriptures. One must seek out the true meaning of this matter. Only he who knows this can read *The Journey to the West*.

44. *The Journey to the West* has been annotated [*chu-chieh* 注解] countless times. As for quality explanations, there is not one per hundred. The *Chen-ch'üan* 真詮 [True Explication] of Wu-i-tzu[63] may be con-

[60] This refers to his making an uproar in Heaven. See chaps. 5–7 of the novel.

[61] Chaps. 1–2.

[62] Chaps. 5–7.

[63] Wu-i-tzu 悟一子 is the style of Ch'en Shih-pin, the editor and commentator of an edition of the novel titled *Hsi-yu chen-ch'üan* 西遊真詮 (The True Explication of the *Hsi-yu chi*), with a preface by Yu T'ung 尤侗 (1618–1704) dated 1696. His edition only contained chapter comments, but reprints sometimes have additional interlineal and marginal comments by a later writer. Ch'en Shih-pin interpreted the novel primarily according to "golden elixir" (*chin-tan* 金丹) alchemical theory. On the debt of Liu I-ming to Ch'en Shih-pin, see the introduction to this chapter.

monkey-
overcome
by monsters

行者

sidered the foremost set of annotations for this book, but it is unavoidable that even it overlooks certain things. The reader should not read only the annotations and neglect the text itself. He should rather read the annotations only from the perspective of the text. In this way he may avoid the mistake of compounding the errors of others. Only he who knows this can read *The Journey to the West*.

45. The reader of *The Journey to the West* should first exert great effort on the text itself. He should again and again strive to comprehend its meaning, and he should not rest until he has savored its true flavor and truly gained insight [into its real meaning]. If he has indeed gained some insight, he can then read annotations [*chu-chieh* 注解] done by others in order to enlarge his understanding. This will enable him to distinguish between that which should be accepted or rejected in the other interpretations, and he can also find out the validity or speciousness of his own perceptions. If he persists in such efforts for a long time, he will certainly arrive at an advanced state of understanding. But even then he must not consider himself always in the right. He should seek out teachers for further illumination. Only then will he be able to see the bright flame of real knowledge and avoid the mistake of regarding the semblance of truth as truth itself. The foregoing forty-five items constitute the essentials of how to read *The Journey to the West*. I have carefully recorded them at the beginning of this volume as an act of friendship extended to the appreciative reader.

CHAPTER VII

Chang Hsin-chih on How to Read the
Hung-lou meng (Dream of the Red Chamber)

INTRODUCTION:
Chang Hsin-chih and His "*Hung-lou meng* tu-fa"
(How to Read the *Dream of the Red Chamber*)

Chang Hsin-chih 張新之 (studio name Miao-fu hsüan 妙復軒; fl. 1828–1850) completed an extended commentary on the *Hung-lou meng* 紅樓夢 (Dream of the Red Chamber; also known as the *Shih-t'ou chi* 石頭記 [Story of the Stone]) in 1850. The earliest extant version of his commentary, *Miao-fu hsüan p'ing Shih-t'ou chi* 妙復軒評石頭記 (Commentary on the *Story of the Stone* from Miao-fu Studio), is a manuscript copy held in the Peking Library. The first section of that copy consists of various prefaces as well as the *tu-fa* essay translated below.[1] According to his 1850 preface and the notes to three poems appended to the commentary and dated to the same year, Chang Hsin-chih had been reading the *Hung-lou meng* since he was quite young, but did not begin his commentary on it until 1828.[2] For over twenty years he worked on it as his career and travels took him from the capital to Manchuria in the north, through South China, and twice to Taiwan. It was during the second stay in Taiwan that the commentary was completed. The little that we know about Chang Hsin-chih comes solely from the prefatory material to his commentary and from scattered remarks in the commentary itself. He seems to have been an itinerant scholar who supported

---

[1] These prefaces, the *tu-fa* essay, and three poems written by Chang Hsin-shih to commemorate the completion of his commentary are available in typeset form in *HLMC*, pp. 34–38, 153–59, and 506–7 and *HLMSL*, pp. 48–53.

[2] For the preface, see *HLMC*, p. 34 and *HLMSL*, pp. 50–52. For the poems and the notes to them, see *HLMC*, pp. 506–7 and *HLMSL*, p. 52. Most of the details are corroborated in the other prefatory pieces, particularly the one by Wu-kuei shan-jen 五桂山人, *HLMC*, pp. 35–36 and *HLMSL*, pp. 49–50.

himself by doing secretarial work on the staffs of local government officials. One of the reasons that it took so long to finish the project was surely the fact that a friend who borrowed his only copy managed to lose it, forcing him to start all over again.

Perhaps Chang Hsin-chih originally planned to publish a printed edition of his commentary. At one point he remarks that his commentary would surely justify the cutting of woodblocks for its publication,[3] and the last item of the *tu-fa* essay says that the illustrations and accompanying colophons in his edition are based on that of the twenty-four woodblock illustrations in the original text of the novel that he used for his commentary.[4] The Peking Library copy, however, contains no illustrations. The earliest notice of the commentary found outside the work itself is by Liu Ch'üan-fu 劉銓福 (ca. 1818–1880). He was a book collector of wide fame who was one of the owners of the so-called "Chia-hsü" 甲戌 (1754) copy of the *Shih-t'ou chi* with commentary by the group of commentators collectively known by the name of their most famous member, Chih-yen chai 脂硯齋 (Red Inkstone Studio). In two notes written by him on the end pages of the "Chia-hsü" edition, Liu Ch'üan-fu mentioned that he obtained a copy of the Miao-fu hsüan commentary ("bound in twelve oversize volumes") in 1863 and lent it to Sun T'ung-sheng 孫桐生 in 1867.[5] Sun T'ung-sheng (1852 *chin-shih*) published the first printed edition of the commentary in 1881.[6] According to him, Liu Ch'üan-fu's copy did not contain the text of the novel and he had to spend about ten years matching the comments to the text

---

[3] See his preface, *HLMC*, p. 34 and *HLMSL*, p. 50.

[4] The description of the twenty-four illustrations matches those of the 1791–92 printed editions of the novel published by Ch'eng Wei-yüan 程偉元. In this item, Chang Hsin-chih also mentions what he considers to be an inferior edition with only fifteen illustrations. The earliest edition described in *HLMSL* that fits his description dates to about 1818 (see *HLMSL*, p. 39, T'eng-hua hsieh edition), and was followed by numerous reprints.

[5] A facsimile edition is available, *Ch'ien-lung chia-hsü pen Chih-yen chai ch'ung-p'ing Shih-t'ou chi* 乾隆甲戌本脂硯齋重評石頭記 (1754 Copy of the Repeated Commentary on the *Story of the Stone* from Red Inkstone Studio), 2 vols. (Taipei: Commercial Press, 1961). There is a discussion of Liu Ch'üan-fu and Sun T'ung-sheng in the last section of the postface by Hu Shih appended to the second volume (pp. 8a–9a). Chang Hsin-chih seems to indicate that his commentary used oversized woodblocks (see item 30 of the *tu-fa* essay below). In both the *tu-fa* essay item and the note by Liu Ch'üan-fu, the wording is very vague.

[6] Entitled *Miao-fu hsüan p'ing-pen hsiu-hsiang Shih-t'ou chi Hung-lou meng* 妙復軒評本繡像石頭記紅樓夢. There is a microfilm copy of this edition, courtesy of Professor Itō Sōhei of Tokyo University, in the Gest Oriental Library of Princeton University. For description and text of prefatory matter, see *HLMSL*, pp. 53–56 and *HLMC*, pp. 39–41, 534–35.

and doing general editing work on them prior to the publication of his edition.[7] Of the material in the manuscript copy of *Miao-fu hsüan p'ing Shih-t'ou chi* besides the chapter and interlineal comments, Sun T'ung-sheng's edition contains only Chang Hsin-chih's poems commemorating the completion of the commentary and a reduced version (missing the last three items) of the "*Hung-lou meng* tu-fa."[8]

It seems unlikely that Sun T'ung-sheng omitted the prefaces by Chang Hsin-chih and his friends in order to present his own candidate for authorship of the commentary, T'ung Pu-nien 仝卜年 (1811 *chin-shih*, Prefect of Taiwan from 1847 till his death). Instead of slandering him with the charge of being deceitful or incompetent, it seems better to assume that Liu Ch'üan-fu's copy of the commentary did not contain those prefaces.[9] As for the three items of the *tu-fa* essay that were left out, all of them seem to be linked to either a planned or finished edition of the commentary not available to Sun T'ung-sheng. Whether they were omitted by him or by someone before him cannot be ascertained at present. Sun T'ung-sheng was forced to guess the identity of the commentator on the basis of the rather skimpy material to be found in Chang Hsin-chih's poems and his notes to them.[10] The only positive information contained there is the style (*hao*) of the commentator, "T'ai-p'ing hsien-jen" 太平閑人 (Man of Leisure of the Great Peace), and the fact that the poems were composed in the yamen of the Prefect of Taiwan in 1850. Sun T'ung-sheng appears to have come to the conclusion that this last bit of information must indicate that the commentator was none other than the Prefect of Taiwan during that year, T'ung Pu-nien.

Sun T'ung-sheng's edition is the only printed one that consists primarily of nothing but Chang Hsin-chih's commentary and the text of the novel. All other editions of the novel with his commentary contain comments and essays by other writers as well, notably Wang Hsi-lien 王希廉 (courtesy name Hsüeh-hsiang 雪香, style Hu-hua chu-jen 護花主人; his commentary edition first appeared in 1832) and Yao Hsieh 姚燮

---

[7] See his postface and the notes to his poems in response to those of Chang Hsin-chih, *HLMC*, p. 41 and *HLMSL*, p. 55. Comparison of the interlineal comments in the Peking Library copy and Sun T'ung-sheng's 1881 edition shows that some of the longer, esoteric passages are not to be found in the latter. Also, the order of the items in the postchapter comments is often different.

[8] The poems are placed after the last chapter of the novel and the *tu-fa* essay appears before chap. 1 in the 1881 edition.

[9] In any case, the discrepancy between the actual small format of the Peking Library copy and Liu Ch'üan-fu's "oversized fascicles" (*chü-ts'e* 巨冊) would seem to establish that they are not one and the same.

[10] *HLMSL*, p. 52 and *HLMC*, pp. 507–8.

(1805–1864, courtesy name Mei-po 梅伯, style Ta-mei shan-min 大某
山民). The first such edition dates from 1884.[11]

An important problem that remains to be discussed is the relationship
between the versions of the *tu-fa* essay already treated above and a
shorter one found in editions without Chang Hsin-chih's chapter and
interlineal comments but with chapter comments by Wang Hsi-lien and
Yao Hsieh, as well as interlineal and marginal comments attributed to
Yao Hsieh.[12] The first edition of this type appeared in the Kuang-hsü
reign period (1875–1908), long after the death of Yao Hsieh.[13] Yao
Hsieh left behind a manuscript of a separate work on the novel called *Tu
Hung-lou meng kang-ling* 讀紅樓夢綱領 (An Outline for Reading the
Hung-lou meng; preface dated 1860). In its preface he mentions a section-
by-section commentary that he had written for the novel.[14] In the Che-
kiang Provincial Library there is a copy of a Wang Hsi-lien edition of
the *Hung-lou meng* onto which Yao Hsieh's comments and notes have

[11] See *HLMSL*, pp. 60–66 for descriptions of several of these editions, the first of
which dates from 1884 and was published by the T'ung-wen shu-chü of Shanghai.
Citations made from Chang Hsin-chih's commentary on the novel itself (aside from the
text of the *tu-fa* essay), as well as the Chinese text of the novel made in this chapter, will
be from a reprint from this series of editions, *Tseng-p'ing pu-hsiang ch'üan-t'u Chin-yü yüan*
增評補像全圖金玉緣 (The Affinity of Gold and Jade [a late alternate title for the novel
probably used to avoid Ch'ing dynasty suppression of the publication of the *Hung-lou
meng*], Fully Illustrated, with Additional Comments and Illustrations), dated 1908. It was
republished under the title *P'ing-chu Chin-yü yüan* 評註金玉緣 (Annotated and Commentated Affinity of Gold and Jade [*CYY*]). This edition has inadvertently left out the
text of the *tu-fa* essay (promised in the table of contents). Examination of actual late
Ch'ing editions from this filiation held in the University of Chicago Far Eastern Library
and the Gest Oriental Library of Princeton University reveals the same basic version of
the essay as first published by Sun T'ung-sheng.

[12] The *tu-fa* essay in these texts is divided into twenty-seven items, which would be the
same number of items in the Peking Library copy version of the *tu-fa* essay once the last
three items left out in the 1881 edition are subtracted. The 1881 version, however,
actually has thirty-one items, the four extra ones having been produced by dividing four
of the original items in two. That practice is followed in the Wang-Yao editions, but the
elimination of old items and the addition of some new ones brings the total down to
twenty-seven.

[13] The first edition, brought out by the Kuang-pai-sung chai of Shanghai (see *HLMSL*,
p. 57) is undated, but a rival publisher brought out a reprint of the edition in 1886, so the
original edition must date from that year or earlier.

[14] "Tu *Hung-lou meng* kang-ling" is the original title of this work, which consists
mainly of lists of characters, material objects, and events that appear in the novel. Two of
the sections from the third *chüan* are reproduced in *HLMC*, pp. 164–75. The work was
published under the title *Hung-lou meng lei-so* 紅樓夢類索 (An Index to Categories of
Things in the *Hung-lou meng*), Wei Yu-fei 魏友棐 and Hung Ching-shan 洪荆山, eds.
(Shanghai: Chu-lin shu-tien, 1940).

been transcribed. Yao Hsieh's notes contain extracts from the work of other writers on the novel, and the transcriber has also added his and other people's comments to this conglomeration.[15] It is fairly clear that this copy or one like it was the base text for the commentary in the "Wang-Yao" edition,[16] but whereas the complex provenance of the various comments is kept clear in the original by the use of different colored inks and the location of the comments, this material has been indiscriminately copied into the later printed edition and all loosely attributed to Yao Hsieh.[17]

Starting with the decade of the 1880s, new editions of the *Hung-lou meng* with commentary appeared at a stupendous pace. This decade saw the large-scale introduction and use of modern printing techniques like lithography and metallic movable type, with Shanghai as the center of activity. That there was money to be made printing new editions can be seen from the sheer number of editions produced, and from the fact that in 1892 a printing of 2,500 copies was sold off in a month.[18] In this kind of climate it is understandable that publishers used somewhat unorthodox methods to try to gain a share of this market. In the 1880s two main kinds of editions vied for supremacy. On the one hand there were the lithographic editions titled *Chin-yü yüan* 金玉緣 (Affinity of Gold and Jade) put out by the T'ung-wen shu-chü with textual commentary by Wang Hsi-lien, Yao Hsieh, and Chang Hsin-chih. The first edition of this type dates from 1884, only three years after the first printed edition of the Chang Hsin-chih commentary by Sun T'ung-sheng. On the other

[15] Some of the sections of Yao Hsieh's commentary are dated to 1849. Some of the other material from other sources dates from after his death.

[16] Two sources that attest to the independent existence of a manuscript copy of Yao Hsieh's textual commentary on the novel are quoted in *HLMSL*, pp. 57–58. One asserts that a copy belonging to Hsü Yü-chih 徐雨之 was used by him when he brought out the first printed edition in which it appeared. It should be added that the Yao Hsieh chapter comments and the "Tsung-p'ing" 總評 (General Comments) attributed to him appear in both the Wang-Yao-Chang and the Wang-Yao editions and are based on the same source. The "Tsung-p'ing" is particularly interesting. In the transcribed version of Yao Hsieh's comments, these short, elliptic comments are correctly described as notes to Chiang Ch'i's 姜祺 "*Hung-lou meng* shih" 紅樓夢詩 (Poems on the *Hung-lou meng*; for the text of the poems and notes, see *HLMC*, pp. 475–90), but in the printed editions they are presented (after minimal editing) as summary comments on the novel by Yao Hsieh.

[17] The most easily available reprint of the Wang-Yao commentary editions of the *Hung-lou meng* is probably that reproduced in the *Kuo-hsüeh chi-pen ts'ung-shu* 國學基本叢書 (Basic Sinological Collection; Taipei: Commercial Press, 1968), vols. 257–58. This is a reprint of the first publication of this series in 1933 by the same publisher. The title page reads *Tseng-p'ing pu-t'u Shih-t'ou chi* 增評補圖石頭記 (*Story of the Stone* with Added Commentary and Illustrations).

[18] See *HLMSL*, p. 63.

hand there were the editions entitled *Shih-t'ou chi* put out first by the Kuang-pai-sung chai in or slightly before 1886. The founder of the latter publishing house, Hsü Yü-chih 徐雨之, was one of the cofounders of the T'ung-wen shu-chü. An 1889 edition of the *Chin-yü yüan* has a notice stating that the edition was printed by the T'ung-wen shu-chü, but that the blocks are the property of the Kuang-pai-sung chai.[19] Instead of antagonistic competition between the two publishers, it seems more like a case of splitting the market, with two different titles used to sell very similar material. The fact that in the "Shih-t'ou chi" editions spoken of here the name *Hung-lou meng* was changed to *Shih-t'ou chi* wherever it occurs in the "*Hung-lou meng* tu-fa" and in the Ch'eng Wei-yüan 程偉元 preface to the novel reprinted in both filiations seems to indicate an attempt by the publisher to differentiate this new edition from the earlier one. Thus Hsü Yü-chih could avoid competition between the two publishing houses for the sale of a novel with the same name.[20]

The shorter version of the *tu-fa* essay in the "Shih-t'ou chi" editions, does not, however, have anything to do with Yao Hsieh. There is no evidence that Yao Hsieh, an avid reader and critic of any kind of material dealing with his favorite novel, even knew of the Chang Hsin-chih commentary. The transcribed version of Yao Hsieh's commentary does not contain the *tu-fa* essay. We can only assume that Hsü Yü-chih or others involved in publishing the Wang-Yao commentary editions concocted it themselves. The editing work was done very roughly, but one trend is very clear. The most tendentious (and in the end most representative of Chang Hsin-chih) of the original items in the *tu-fa* essay have been omitted or shortened. All personalizing elements have been removed, such as Chang Hsin-chih's habit of referring to himself in the third person by a shortened form of his nom de plume or his narrative in item twenty-six about how he arrived at his "breakthrough" in understanding the *Hung-lou meng*.

Chang Hsin-chih's reputation as a critic of fiction does not stand very high either in China or abroad. Part of that might simply be due to unfamiliarity with his work or prejudice against some of the basic ideas

---

[19] See *HLMSL*, p. 62. These two publishing houses also collaborated on an edition of the *Liao-chai chih-i* 聊齋誌異 (Strange Stories from Desultory Studio) and a Mao Tsung-kang commentary edition of the *San-kuo yen-i* in 1886.

[20] To avoid a ban on the publication of the *Hung-lou meng* in Shanghai, publishers used a variety of names on the title pages to avoid confiscation. Two more names used at this time were *Ta-kuan yüan so-lu* 大觀園瑣錄 (Rambling Record of Grand Prospect Garden) and *Ching-huan hsien chi* 警幻仙記 (Story of the Goddess of Disillusionment). In the latter work, the editing was not done very carefully—the earlier titles for the novel appear in several places in the body of the work.

that he manipulates in his commentary, but it cannot be denied that many of his ideas are quite strange at first sight, a fact that he mentions himself in his interlineal and chapter comments. One of his less forgiving detractors once said, "This kind of person cannot even read himself, yet he goes and composes a 'how to read' [*tu-fa* 讀法] essay."[21] Whatever quarrel we might have with Chang Hsin-chih's often reductionist arguments that the multitextured and subversive narrative of the *Hung-lou meng* is nothing but a restatement in a slightly unorthodox style of the basic teachings of the Confucian classics, we should not allow our distance from or impatience with such a notion to prevent us from taking him seriously either as a critic or as a representative and influential reader of the novel.

In the translation of the "*Hung-lou meng* tu-fa" below, the text of the essay follows that of the manuscript version. References to the Chinese text of the novel are to the reprint of a late Ch'ing edition with interlineal and chapter comments by Chang Hsin-chih.[22] References to English translations of the novel are to *The Story of the Stone* by David Hawkes and John Minford.[23]

---

[21] Yeh-ho 野鶴 (pseud.), "Tu *Hung-lou meng* cha-chi" 讀紅樓夢札記 (Notes on Reading the *Hung-lou meng*), reproduced in *HLMC*, pp. 285–92. The quotation occurs on p. 286. This is a late Ch'ing work.

[22] See n. 11 above for details.

[23] Abbreviated as *Stone*.

How to Read the *Dream of the Red Chamber*

Translated and Annotated by ANDREW H. PLAKS
Additional Annotation by DAVID L. ROLSTON

1. The *Hung-lou meng* is a literary work that is not only very appealing [*k'uai-chih jen-k'ou* 膾炙人口] but, more important, it also carves a deep impression on the mind, moving and transforming one's nature and emotions [*hsing-ch'ing* 性情].[1] It goes even further than the *Chin P'ing Mei* in producing potentially dangerous effects, in that readers are prone to recognize only its immediate surface [*cheng-mien* 正面], failing to perceive what lies on the other side [*fan-mien* 反面].[2] Occasionally someone with great vision may perceive and fathom [its true meaning], but still, due to its elusive and confusing quality, no sooner has he grasped it than it slips away again, so that it is still very hard to avoid becoming entangled. My[3] commentary [*p'i-p'ing* 批評] makes the central meaning

---

[1] This translation is based on the text of the thirty-item manuscript copy of the essay transcribed in *HLMC*, pp. 153–159 and checked against the manuscript copy held in the Peking Library upon which it was based. Where relevant, reference will be made to textual variants in two other filiations of the text: (1) the 1881 version published by Sun T'ung-sheng without the last three items, also reprinted in late Ch'ing editions generally using the title "Chin-yü yüan" 金玉緣 (Affinity of Gold and Jade), and (2) a shorter version found in late Ch'ing editions with commentary by Wang Hsi-lien 王希廉 and Yao Hsieh 姚燮 but without that of Chang Hsin-chih 張新之, usually with "Shih-t'ou chi" 石頭記 (Story of the Stone) in the title. "Shih-t'ou chi" is the preferred title of the novel found in the early manuscript copies with commentary by Chih-yen chai, but from the time of the first printed edition at the end of the eighteenth century on into the middle of the following century, the alternate title of *Hung-lou meng* 紅樓夢 (Dream of the Red Chamber) was the most popular designation for the novel. As stated in the introduction above, there is a fairly concerted effort in the late Ch'ing "Shih-t'ou chi" editions to change the title of the novel from "Hung-lou meng" to "Shih-t'ou chi" in preexisting pieces republished in those editions. In the "Shih-t'ou chi" version of this essay, the title "Hung-lou meng" is never used as the general title of the novel and is not even to be found in the list of alternate titles in the last item of that version (not found in the manuscript or "Chin-yü yüan" versions). Not only is "Hung-lou meng" changed to "Shih-t'ou chi," often the latter title is inserted into the text where the other version merely says "this book" or uses similar indirect phrases.

[2] Many of the traditional critics of the *Hung-lou meng* dwell at length on the discrepancy between the mimetic surface and the hidden meaning of the text, particularly as allegorized in the two-sided mirror that proves to be the undoing of Chia Jui in chap. 12. Chih-yen chai draws an explicit analogy between the fateful mirror and the text of the novel in a comment on that passage of the novel, in *Chih-yen chai ch'ung-p'ing Shih-t'ou chi* 脂硯齋重評石頭記 (Repeated Commentary on the *Story of the Stone* by Red Inkstone Studio; Peking: Wen-hsüeh ku-chi k'an-hsing she, 1955), p. 12.268.

[3] Throughout this essay and in his interlineal and chapter comments on the novel, Chang Hsin-chih refers to himself from time to time as "Hsien-jen" 閑人 (The Man of Leisure), a shortened form of his style, "T'ai-p'ing hsien-jen" 太平閑人 (Man of Leisure of the Great Peace).

—the other side of the book—come welling up into full view, making it possible for those who read the book to derive the proper warning and those who discourse on it to be free of guilt.[4] Is this not a marvelous achievement?

2. The *Story of the Stone* is a book that sets forth latent patterns of nature and reason [*hsing-li* 性理]. In this it traces its ancestry to the *Ta-hsüeh* 大學 [The Great Learning] and derives its lineage from the *Chung-yung* 中庸 [The Doctrine of the Mean]. That is why it states, through Pao-yü, "There are no real books other than that which teaches the 'restoration of the original brightness of one's inherent virtue' "[5] or "Nothing but the *Ta-hsüeh* and the *Chung-yung*."[6] The main purpose of this book is to elucidate the teachings of the *Ta-hsüeh* and the *Chung-yung*. It uses the example of the *I Ching* 易經 [Book of Changes] to portray the waxing and waning of fortunes; it uses the example of the "Kuo-feng" 國風 [Airs of the States; a section of the *Shih-ching* 詩經 (Classic of Poetry)] to set apart the chaste from the lewd; it uses the

[4] The last part of this sentence recalls the language of a section of the so-called "Great Preface" (*Ta-hsü* 大序) to the *Shih-ching* 詩經 (Classic of Poetry) on the admonitory meaning of the important term *feng* 風, which reads, in James J.Y. Liu's translation, "Then the one who speaks does not commit any offense, while it is enough for the one who listens to take warning." See his *Chinese Theories of Literature* (Chicago: University of Chicago Press, 1975), p. 112. The personal tone of the first part of the sentence is avoided in the "Shih-t'ou chi" versions, where the entire sentence reads, "Once having been commented on, this causes the author's central meaning—the other side of the book—to be as readily accessible to one's perception as the whorl patterns on one's own fingertips, so that one can finally decide whether or not the *Story of the Stone* produces dangerous effects."

[5] Hsi-jen (Aroma) attributes this saying to Pao-yü in chap. 19, *CYY* 19/5a (283) and *Stone* 1.19.391. References to *CYY* indicate chapter and original page number, with modern pagination in parentheses. References to *Stone* indicate volume, chapter, and page number. The quote in the essay is from the opening section of the *Ta-hsüeh*, referred to by David Hawkes as *Illumination of Clear Virtue*. For Chinese text and translation, see James Legge, trans., *The Chinese Classics*, 5 vols. (Hong Kong: Hong Kong University Press, 1960), vol. 1, p. 356. The passage in the novel in question is crucial to the meaning of the larger work, in that the orthodox interpretation of the expression *ming ming-te* 明明德 as the proper ordering of self and world in the Confucian sense was also subject to a quite opposite exegesis in terms of the cultivation of the individual self in isolation. The occurrence in the novel is particularly ironic, since it is the maid Hsi-jen who warns Pao-yü to refrain from voicing this sort of exaggerated emphasis on the *ming-te* concept to the exclusion of all other learning, while at the same time exhorting him to serious study of the Four Books, which include this very passage.

[6] *CYY* 23/27a (327) and *Stone* 1.23.463–64. Pao-yü makes this remark when Tai-yü catches him reading the romantic play *Hsi-hsiang chi* 西廂記 (Romance of the Western Chamber) and asks him what he is reading. In an interlineal comment on the text at this point, Chang Hsin-chih paraphrases Pao-yü's remark, "The entire *Hung-lou meng* is nothing but the *Chung-yung* and the *Ta-hsüeh*" 一部紅樓不過是中庸大學.

example of the *Ch'un-ch'iu* 春秋 [The Spring and Autumn Annals] to convey praise and blame [*yü-to* 予奪] and borrows also from the examples of the *Li-ching* 禮經 [Classic of Rites] and the *Yüeh-chi* 樂記 [Record of Music].[7]

3. The *I Ching*, the *Ta-hsüeh*, and the *Chung-yung* are all standard texts.[8] The *Hung-lou meng*, which borrows from and expands upon their teachings, is an extraordinary text.[9] That is why it says, "Whom can I ask to pass on this extraordinary tale?"[10]

4. Master Hu said, "When Confucius composed the *Ch'un-ch'iu* he did not set down everyday events, but only recorded on bamboo slips instances of the breakdown of standards and the violation of principles, with the purpose of edifying later generations so that they might rectify their ways of thinking, restore moral order and the adherence to principle, and bring social interaction into a state of harmony,"[11] This book [the *Hung-lou meng*] definitely borrows this idea [from the *Ch'un-ch'iu*].

5. "True learning is based on clear insight into human activities, / Genuine culture lies in the skillful manipulation of human relationships."[12] It is to this point that our attention is called throughout the book. For this reason, in its representation [*p'u-hsü* 鋪叙] of "human nature" and "mundane affairs," these [qualities] emerge with brilliant

---

[7] *Li-ching* is another name for the *I-li* 儀禮 (Book of Etiquette and Ceremonial), and the *Yüeh-chi* is the name of one of the chapters in the *Li-chi* 禮記 (Book of Rites). To this list of classical works that allegedly influenced the author, the "Shih-t'ou chi" versions add two literary works: the *Chuang Tzu* 莊子 by Chuang Chou and the *Li-sao* 離騷 (Encountering Sorrow) by Ch'ü Yüan.

[8] The list of orthodox texts in the "Shih-t'ou chi" versions also includes the *Chuang Tzu*, the *Li-sao*, the "Kuo-feng," and the *Ch'un-ch'iu*.

[9] Chang Hsin-chih uses this same type of opposition in his chapter comment to chap. 3, *CYY*, p. 3/7b (110). The "Shih-t'ou chi" versions give the title here as *Story of the Stone*.

[10] See *CYY*, 1/2a (73) and *Stone*, 1.1.49. This is the last line in a *gāthā* (a Buddhist verse form) on the reverse side of the stone upon which the original "story of the stone" is recorded.

[11] The 1881 Sun T'ung-sheng edition and the "Shih-t'ou chi" and some of the "Chin-yü yüan" versions as well have the additional words "Chih-t'ang" 致堂 before Master Hu's name which, if there is anything behind it, would identify the Master Hu in question as Hu Yin 胡寅 (1098–1156). Another candidate is Hu Yin's uncle, Hu An-kuo 胡安國 (1073–1138). Both men were classicists and Hu An-kuo in particular wrote a standard commentary on the *Ch'un-ch'iu*, *Ch'un-ch'iu Hu-shih chuan* 春秋胡氏傳 (Master Hu's Commentary on The Spring and Autumn Annals). As this quote has not yet been identified as coming from either man, the attribution must remain open for the present.

[12] *CYY*, 5/14a (123) and *Stone*, 1.5.126. The sight of this couplet hanging in Ch'in K'o-ch'ing's room makes Pao-yü ill at ease.

clarity as if a phosphorescent "rhinoceros-horn" candle [*hsi-chu* 犀燭] had been turned on them.[13] In comparison with other works of fiction, this book is ahead of its predecessors.[14]

6. The entire text of the *Hung-lou meng* can be summed up in one phrase from the *Tso-chuan* 左傳 [The Tso Commentary], "condemnation for failure to instruct" [*shih-chiao* 失教].[15]

7. The *I Ching* has the following passage: "When a minister murders his lord or a son murders his father, this is not due to the events of a single morning and evening. The ultimate causes lie in the gradual development of circumstances."[16] Therefore one must assiduously guard against the frost developing into ice underfoot.[17] The entire text of the

---

[13] By lighting a rhinoceros-horn torch, Wen Ch'iao 溫嶠 (288–329) was able to see the demons inhabiting deep water, who were usually hidden from sight. See Wen Ch'iao's biography in the *Chin-shu* 晉書 (History of the Chin Dynasty; Peking: Chung-hua shu-chü, 1974), p. 67.1795. This allusion is also used in the "Hsieh I" preface to the Chang Chu-p'o commentary on the *Chin P'ing Mei* to describe the effect of that commentary on the reader's perception of what he reads in that novel, "Like the fox spirit revealed in the Ch'in mirror and the water demons exposed by Wen Ch'iao's rhinoceros torch, the real appearance [of the characters in the novel] is completely revealed" 皆如狐窮秦鏡, 怪窘溫犀, 無不洞鑒原形.

[14] The "Shih-t'ou chi" versions omit the first half of the set phrase *hou-lai chü-shang* 後來居上 "a case of the latecomer surpassing those who came before."

[15] This phrase is used in the *Tso-chuan*, first year of Duke Yin (721 B.C.), to explain the reason why the *Ch'un-ch'iu* refers to the ruler of Cheng only as an earl (*po* 伯). See James Legge, trans., *The Chinese Classics*, vol. 5, pp. 1–7. According to a standard interpretation of this famous narrative, the ruler of Cheng, Duke Chuang (r. 743–701 B.C.), preferred to give his brother enough rope to hang himself rather than try to instruct him in the proper way of conducting himself. Chang Hsin-chih uses this phrase in his textual commentary on the novel, see chapter comments *CYY*, 9/5a (181), 11/13b (198), 23/28a (329), 34/4b (450). This section of the *Tso-chuan* is also referred to by him in an interlineal comment, *CYY*, 17/41b (254).

[16] See *Shih-san ching ching-wen* 十三經經文 (Text of the Thirteen Classics; Taipei: T'ai-wan K'ai-ming shu-tien, 1955), *Wen-yen* 文言 (Commentary on the Words of the Text) appendix to the *k'un* 坤 hexagram of the *I Ching*, p. 2 and Richard Wilhelm, *The I Ching or Book of Changes*, Cary F. Baynes, trans. (Princeton: Princeton University Press, 1967), p. 393.

[17] This conceit has its source in a comment on one of the lines of the *k'un* hexagram (*Shih-san ching ching-wen*, p. 2 and Richard Wilhelm, *The I Ching*, p. 389), "When there is hoarfrost underfoot, solid ice is not far off" ("lü shuang chien ping chih" 履霜漸冰至) but the author might have in mind a line from the concluding remarks in the biography of Emperor Kao-tsung of the T'ang (r. 649–683) in the *Hsin T'ang-shu* 新唐書 (New History of the T'ang Dynasty; Peking: Chung-hua shu-chü, 1975), p. 3.79, in reference to the failure of the emperor's father to take steps to avert disruption to the dynasty later caused by Wu Tse-t'ien (624–705), "Not taking warning from the gradual development of frost underfoot, the poison was allowed to spread throughout the land, bringing great misfortune to the nation" 不戒履霜之漸, 而毒流天下, 貽禍家邦.

Hung-lou meng is an elaboration of just this concept of "gradual development" [*chien* 漸].[18]

8. According to the *Ho-lin yü-lu*,[19] "the writing of Chuang Tzu brings being out of nothingness; the writing of the *Chan-kuo ts'e* 戰國策 [Intrigues of the Warring States] turns indirectness into directness. All his life, Su Tung-p'o [1037–1101] was well versed in these two books, so in his prose the meaning reaches beyond what the actual text says, the argument is refined and to the point, without the least bit of hesitation."[20] I would like to use these same words to describe the *Story of the Stone*.

9. The narration [*hsü-shih* 敘事] in this book is mostly modeled after passages in the *Chan-kuo ts'e*, the *Shih-chi* 史記 [Records of the Historian], and the prose writings of the "three masters of the Su family."[21]

10. The *Hung-lou meng* grows out of [*t'o-t'ai* 脫胎] the *Hsi-yu-chi* 西遊記 [The Journey to the West],[22] takes a trail [*chieh-ching* 借逕] blazed by the *Chin P'ing Mei*, and takes its spirit [*she-shen* 攝神] from the *Shui-hu chuan* 水滸傳 [The Water Margin].

11. The *Hung-lou meng* conceals within itself a *Chin P'ing Mei*. That is why [Pao-yü is said to indulge in] "excess of the mind" [*i-yin* 意淫].[23]

[18] Chang Hsin-chih uses this concept frequently in his commentary. See *CYY*, 3/5b (108), 10/8b (188), and 28/7a (379), all interlineal comments.

[19] A collection of scholarly notes and random jottings by the Sung scholar Lo Ta-ching 羅大經 (1226 *chin-shih*). See *Ho-lin yü-lu* 鶴林玉露 (Peking: Chung-hua shu-chü, 1983), p. 167 for the passage quoted by Chang Hsin-chih below.

[20] The citation has omitted here four characters found in the original text (*heng-shuo shu-shuo* 橫說豎說 "discoursing at will backwards and forwards"). The wording of the "Shih-t'ou chi" versions is slightly different.

[21] Su Hsün 蘇洵 (1009–1066) and his two sons, Su Shih 蘇軾 (1037–1101) and Su Ch'e 蘇轍 (1039–1112).

[22] Some critics hold rather that it is Chang Hsin-chih's style of criticism that grows out of the work of commentators on the *Hsi-yu chi* such as Wang Hsiang-hsü 汪象旭, Ch'en Shih-pin 陳士斌, Chang Shu-shen 張書紳, and Liu I-ming 劉一明. See Ts'ai Yüan-p'ei 蔡元培 (1867–1940), *Shih-t'ou chi so-yin* 石頭記索隱 (The Key to the *Story of the Stone*), quoted in *HLMC*, p. 319 and Han Chin-lien 韓進廉, *Hung-hsüeh shih-kao* 紅學史稿 (A Draft History of Redology [The Study of the *Hung-lou meng*]; Shih-chia-chuang: Ho-pei jen-min, 1981), p. 132. For other premodern discussions of the relationship between these two novels, see Chou Ch'un 周春, *Yüeh Hung-lou meng sui-pi* 閱紅樓夢隨筆 (Random Notes on Reading the *Hung-lou meng*), quoted in *HLMC*, p. 77 and Meng-ch'ih hsüeh-jen 夢痴學人 (pseud.), *Meng-ch'ih shuo-meng* 夢痴說夢 (Dream Talk from Dream-Crazy), quoted in *HLMC*, pp. 220, 224. The phrase *t'o-t'ai* 脫胎 is similar to the Ch'an slogan used by Huang T'ing-chien 黃庭堅 (1045–1105), *to-t'ai huan-ku* 脫胎換骨, through which he advocated the production of new poetry by starting out with and transforming the works of the famous poets.

[23] The *Chin P'ing Mei* is renowned for its depiction of sexual indulgence on the part of its main character, Hsi-men Ch'ing. In the passage in chap. 5 where Pao-yü is told that he is characterized by "excess of the mind," a distinction is made between carnal and mental excess. See *CYY* 5/19b (134) and *Stone* 1.5.146.

For the *Chin P'ing Mei* we have the theory of frustrated filiality [*k'u-hsiao shuo* 苦孝說];[24] accordingly that book concludes [*chieh* 結] explicitly with the concept of filial piety.[25] This book, on the other hand, concludes with a vague implication of filiality.[26] As for the hidden suffering contained in this work, it is far deeper than that of the author of the *Chin P'ing Mei*. The *Chin P'ing Mei* works out the concepts of "cold" [*leng* 冷] and "heat" [*je* 熱].[27] This book also works out the concepts of "cold" and "heat." The *Chin P'ing Mei* works out the concepts of

[24] See the essay of that title included among the introductory essays prefacing Chang Chu-p'o's commentary to the *Chin P'ing Mei*. Chang Chu-p'o's argument seems to be an extension of the popular idea that Wang Shih-chen 王世貞 (1526–1590) wrote the novel as part of a plot to avenge the death of his father at the hands of Yen Sung 嚴嵩 (1481–1568) and his son, Yen Shih-fan 嚴世蕃 (1513–1565), but in the essay only the idea of frustrated filiality is kept, without any of the details of the Wang Shih-chen story. In his *tu-fa* essay on the novel, Chang Chu-p'o seems to deny the notion that Wang Shih-chen is the author as claimed in the traditional story (see chap. IV above, item 36), and one of his interlineal comments on the novel says that the work was probably completed after the fall from power of Yen Sung and his son. See p. 98/8b of the 1695, large-character Tsai-tzu t'ang 在茲堂 edition.

[25] The *Chin P'ing Mei* ends with Hsi-men Ch'ing's posthumous son, Hsiao-ko 孝哥 ("Filial Brother"), becoming the disciple of a Buddhist monk. Chang Chu-p'o interprets this event positively, taking Hsiao-ko as the reincarnation of Hsi-men Ch'ing and his joining the Buddhist faith as an act of atonement for the sins of his previous life. See chap. IV above, item 26 of the *Chin P'ing Mei tu-fa* essay.

[26] As proof of the contention that the novel ends with the concept of filiality, Chang Hsin-chih points to the fact that the title of chap. 116 contains the words *ch'üan hsiao-tao* 全孝道 ([Chia Cheng] completes the way of filial piety), although the author of that chapter probably only had in mind the rather prosaic idea of Chia Cheng escorting his mother's corpse home for burial. See *CYY* 116/23a (1487), chapter comment, for Chang Hsin-chih's remarks. He uses the concept of "frustrated filiality" to explain the novel in chapter comments, *CYY* 3/7a (109), 120/54a (1549), and interlineal comments such as 5/13b (122). Chang Hsin-chih also held that Pao-yü appears in the last chapter wearing a red cape because the author wanted to criticize his failure to fulfill the demands of filial piety. See *CYY* 120/47b (1536), interlineal comment.

[27] For Chang Chu-p'o's discussion of this pair of concepts as metaphors for structural principles in the novel, see chap. IV above, items 10, 25, 83, 87, and 88 of his *Chin P'ing Mei tu-fa* essay. He also has a separate essay on this subject, "Leng-je chin-chen" 冷熱金針 (The Secret of Hot and Cold), included in his prefatory pieces to his commentary on that novel. For further discussion, see Andrew H. Plaks, *The Four Masterworks of the Ming Novel* (Princeton: Princeton University Press, 1987), pp. 81–85. A related usage can be found in Mao Tsung-kang's discussion of "hot" and "cold" passages in the *San-kuo yen-i* 三國演義 (The Romance of the Three Kingdoms), in item 15 of his *tu-fa* essay for that novel (see chap. III above). In *Hung-lou meng* criticism this distinction takes on a particular significance in terms of the alternation between excitement (*je-nao* 熱鬧) and ennui (*wu-liao* 無聊) in the life of the characters in the Grand Prospect Garden. See Andrew H. Plaks, *Archetype and Allegory in the Dream of the Red Chamber* (Princeton: Princeton University Press, 1976), chap. 4, pp. 54–83, for further discussion of this aspect of the text.

money [*ts'ai* 財] and sex [*se* 色]. This book also works out the concepts of money and sex.[28] Among the works of fiction now current, there are only two that I consider superior:[29] the *Liao-chai chih-i* 聊齋誌異 [Strange Stories from Desultory Studio],[30] and the *Hung-lou meng*. The superiority of the *Liao-chai chih-i* is manifest in the conciseness [*chien* 簡] of its prose; that of the *Hung-lou meng* is seen in its fullness [*fan* 煩]. The *Liao-chai chih-i* is composed of unlinked sections [*san-tuan* 散段], such that one who tries repeatedly to imitate them might eventually come up with something. The *Hung-lou meng* is all of a piece [*cheng-chang* 整章],[31] so there is no place to begin imitating it from. Perhaps many thousands of years hence there may be someone who is able to duplicate it, but then that will be a book for the people of future ages, it will no longer be the *Hung-lou meng* of our own day. Who knows, perhaps the two will exist side by side without either eclipsing the other. At any rate, in this book we have a work complete unto itself for all time. That is why I have made so bold as to add my poor commentary to it.[32] As for the various sequels and sequels to the sequels, as well as the various kinds of sorry imitations, those as a whole are not worthy of the student's attention.

12. *Hung-lou meng* is the official title of this book, but at the very start of the text, in the passage in which Reverend Vanitas [K'ung-k'ung tao-jen] learns that "all manifestations are born of nothingness,"[33] we have various alternate titles— *The Story of the Stone, The Record of the Monk of Passion, The Precious Mirror of Love,* and *The Twelve Beauties of Chin-ling*—but no mention whatsoever of the words "Hung-lou meng." In this regard we have a case of letting go of the outward form of the object in favor of the reflection [*she-hsing ch'ü-ying* 捨形取影], which is the basic intention of the author.[34] Accordingly, whenever he [the author] delineates his characters in the book, he always begins from their reflection [*ying-ch'u* 影處].

13. The words "Hung-lou meng" first appear in chapter 5, where

---

[28] For Chang Chu-p'o on these two concepts, see chap. IV above, items 19, 23, and 26 of the *Chin P'ing Mei tu-fa* essay. For a discussion of the relations between money and sex in the *Chin P'ing Mei* by a more recent critic, see Patrick Hanan's essay, "A Landmark of the Chinese Novel," *University of Toronto Quarterly* 30.3:325–35 (1961).

[29] The last portion of this item is omitted in the "Shih-t'ou chi" versions.

[30] The *Liao-chai chih-i* is a collection of short tales in literary Chinese by P'u Sung-ling 蒲松齡 (1640–1715).

[31] The 1881 Sun T'ung-sheng version and the "Chin-yü yüan" texts read *tuan* 段 for *chang* 章, perhaps for the sake of the parallelism with the previous term, *san-tuan*.

[32] Literally, "to put ordure on the head of the Buddha."

[33] *CYY* 1/2a–b (73–74), *Stone* 1.1.51. This item, as well as items 13 and 14 below, is omitted in the "Shih-t'ou chi" version.

[34] The manuscript version seems to have omitted the word *che* 者 by mistake.

they are the name of the song-suite on the "twelve beauties."[35] That is
to say, "the twelve beauties" is the descriptive outline [*mu* 目] of the
dream, while the term "passion" in "The Record of the Monk of
Passion" is its summation [*kang* 綱]. That is why I have posited three
major structural sections [*tuan* 段] within the first twelve chapters: the
first section wrapping up [*chieh* 結] the "story of the stone," the second
section wrapping up the "dream in the red chamber," and the third
section wrapping up the story of the "precious mirror of love," with the
story of the "Monk of Passion" and the "Twelve Beauties" serving as
the summation and detailed outline of it all.[36]

14. This monumental text in one hundred and twenty chapters is
vast and boundless like an ocean and, yet, it still has its own structural
divisions [*tuan-lo* 段落] which one can seek out. Sometimes four chapters
comprise a section [*tuan* 段]; sometimes three chapters comprise a section; even one or two chapters can comprise a section. The divisions
between them are always clearly demarcated [in my commentary]; it
would never do to try to take it all in in a single gulp. My pointing out
of these [the structural divisions] will save the reader a considerable
amount of mental effort.

15. Pao-yü has a personal name but no courtesy name [*tzu* 字], thus
causing the reader to search for meaning within that very nameless-
ness.[37] This is what is meant by the idea that there is a so-called state of
latency "before the concrete feelings of joy, anger, sorrow, and delight
have arisen [*wei-fa* 未發]"[38] or that "within the original state of the
universe prior to the emergence of concrete manifestations [*hsien-t'ien*
先天] there are no names."[39]

16. In this book Pao-ch'ai and Tai-yü are presented in tandem with

---

[35] See *CYY* 5/17b–19a (130–33), *Stone* 1.5.139–44.

[36] For more on Chang Hsin-chih's division of these twelve chapters, see his chapter
comments to chaps. 1 (*CYY* 1/6b [82]), 4 (4/12b [120]), 5 (5/20a [135]), 9 (9/5a [181]), and
12 (12/17b [206]). The three sections are all four chapters in length (chaps. 1–4, 5–8,
9–12).

[37] The author is here playing with a verbal pun that arises from the fact that the phrase
wu-tzu 無字 can refer both to the absence (*wu* 無) of a courtesy name (*tzu* 字) and also to
the Chinese character (*tzu*) for nothingness (*wu*).

[38] This refers to the fourth section of the opening paragraph of the *Chung-yung*. See
James Legge, trans., *The Chinese Classics*, vol. 1, p. 384. In both this and the following
allusion, it is not so much a prior state in temporal sequence as an omnipresent latent
dimension that is stressed in classical exegesis and is at issue here.

[39] For the concept of *hsien-t'ien* (variously: anterior to Heaven, prenatal state, etc.), see
chap. VI above, text and notes to items 7, 8, 33, 35, and 41 of the *Hsi-yu chi tu-fa* essay. The
usage of this term in the metaphysical sense discussed in the preceding note may be traced
more directly to such treatises as Shao Yung's 邵雍 (1011–1077) *Huang-chi ching-shih shu*
黃極經世書 (The Book for Ordering the World of the Yellow Ultimate).

each other. The maids Hsi-jen [Aroma] and Ch'ing-wen [Skybright] are the "shadows" [*ying-tzu* 影子] of these two characters. At every point where a scene involving Pao-yü and Tai-yü is presented, it is always Pao-ch'ai who is taken up for treatment immediately after. When scenes involving Pao-yü and Pao-ch'ai are depicted, it is always Tai-yü who is taken up for treatment immediately after. Failing that, Hsi-jen may be used as a substitute for Pao-ch'ai, or Ch'ing-wen may be used to substitute for Tai-yü, while occasionally attention is turned to a third party, but such cases are never far removed from the original situation. This is a major compositional principle [*chang-fa* 章法] of the entire text from which the author never strays by even as much as a hair, retaining it firm and unshakable. As for the depiction of Tai-yü, she constantly causes injury to others with her sharp tongue. She is a person who is extremely unadept at getting along with other people, extremely lacking in concern for protecting herself even to the point that she unwittingly treads right upon the trigger of destruction [*sha-chi* 殺機].[40] As for the depiction of Pao-ch'ai, she constantly uses material possessions to ingratiate herself with other people. She is a person who keeps her own counsel and is extremely practiced in the ways of the world. Ultimately, however, this too is all for naught. One should not try to be like either of these two types of characters.

17. One might ask why the marriage plot of this novel must invoke an inner bond between wood and stone, and an outer one between gold and jade.[41] I would answer that the stone of jade represents the human soul. The mind should strive toward the good, rather than toward evil. Thus, in the philosophy of the *I Ching*, the principle of yang 陽 is regarded as superior and the principle of yin 陰 as inferior; hence the sage suppresses yin and elevates yang.[42] The element wood is assigned to the eastern quarter, where it holds sway over springtime and growth; the

[40] Chang Hsin-chih describes Tai-yü's partial responsibility for her tragic fate in similar terms in a chapter comment (*CYY* 14/26b [224]) and interlineal comments (7/29b [154], 28/9a [383]).

[41] The wood-stone, gold-jade links, of course, describe the predestined love and marriage relations among Pao-yü, Tai-yü, and Pao-ch'ai, as made abundantly clear at various points in the text. What is of significance in this formulation is not its facile use of five phases mumbo jumbo, but rather the manner in which the five phases conceptual model is used as the central structural framework around which innumerable details of the fabric of the narrative are woven. For a fuller elaboration of these structural relations in the novel, see Andrew H. Plaks, *Archetype and Allegory in the Dream of the Red Chamber*, chap. 4, pp. 54–83.

[42] This is of course but one interpretation of the yin-yang relationship in the *I Ching*, which actually would seem to stress more the mutual complementarity of yin and yang lines rather than their antagonism. See below, item 26.

element gold is assigned to the western quarter, where it holds sway over autumn and death. The trees of the "forest" ["Lin," Tai-yü's surname] are engendered by the waters of the sea. The ocean is located in the Southeast, the domain of *yang*. Gold is engendered by the Hsüeh family [Pao-ch'ai is surnamed Hsüeh], that is to say, by snow [*hsüeh* 雪].[43] This congealed and accumulated cold comes under the sign of *yin*. It is in this sense that the names of Lin and Hsüeh, referring to the elements wood and gold, take on their full significance.

18. Whenever this book narrates patterns of union and separation [*li-ho* 離合] bound by marriage affinity—as in the cases of Yu Erh-chieh, Yu San-chieh, Hsia Chin-kuei,[44] and others too numerous to mention—it is always talking about nothing other than the relations among Pao-yü, Tai-yü, and Pao-ch'ai. Whenever it presents cases in which the opposition between predetermined destiny and individual effort is at issue—such as those of the Taoist priest Wang, the physician Wang, Pao Yung, Sha Ta-chieh,[45] and others too numerous to mention—it is always talking about the role of Liu Lao-lao [Granny Liu]. It is simply a case of changing the water in the brew without changing the prescription. When one knows how to view it in this way, then it will be as simple as splitting bamboo [to understand this book].

19. Every one of the poems in the text has a hidden meaning, much like riddles. The words go in one direction, but the eye is drawn elsewhere. The degree of poetic skill is always in accordance with the specific character in question, like a hat that is tailor-made to fit the size of the head. Therefore no attempt is made to reach for the lofty lyricism of the great masters. In this it differs from other works of fiction where the author first comes up with a few poems and then arbitrarily forces them onto a given character.

[43] Some of these associations are summed up by the author of the novel in the second half of the four-line poem that is part of the dossier on them found by Pao-yü in his dream in chap. 5. See *CYY* 5/16a (127) and *Stone* 1.5.133. Lin Tai-yü is associated with the ocean through her father's courtesy name, Ju-hai 如海 (Like, or Goes to, the Ocean).

[44] For the subplot involving Yu Erh-chieh and Yu San-chieh, see chaps. 64–69. For the bitter fate of Hsia Chin-kuei, see chap. 103.

[45] The expression *t'ien jen ting sheng* 天人定勝 is most likely a variation on the set phrase *jen ting sheng t'ien* (a determined man can overcome fate). Wang the Taoist appears in chap. 80, where he warns Pao-yü against the scourge of jealousy. Wang the physician appears in chap. 83, where his diagnosis of Tai-yü's illness sets the seal on her fate, both metaphorically and in terms of plot causality. Pao Yung arrives at the gates of the Chia compound bearing the news of the fall of the Chen clan in Nanking and is later appointed guardian of the garden gates, where he figures in the abduction of Miao-yü in chap. 112. Sha Ta-chieh's discovery of the incense bag embroidered with an erotic picture in chap. 73 sets the stage for the miniature "raid" on the garden in chap. 74 and hence for the confiscation of the family's wealth shortly thereafter. She is also responsible for telling Tai-yü about the fact that Pao-ch'ai is to wed Pao-yü in chap. 96.

20. The names of the various characters in the book, from the most important to the most insignificant, all have allegorical meaning [*yü-i* 寓意]. In the case of Chen Shih-yin and Chia Yü-ts'un, the book itself gives the proper exegesis.[46] The others are left to the reader to grasp on his own. Some of the names are used straightforwardly, some are ironic. Some are offered in solemn earnest, others in jest. Some provide a pattern of projection and reflection [*chao-ying* 照應] which extends over the entire text, some subtly wrap up [*yin-k'uo* 隱括] a given chapter, others only have reference to a specific incident and are just made up casually, but there are none that are just patched together for no purpose. These can be called examples of the author's miraculous skill and penetrating insight, his ability to manipulate the text at will.

21. Throughout the book, at every point where there is a pause in the action, the author consistently uses an eating scene. Some people may consider this to be a somewhat ludicrous idea, not knowing that the great Tao is manifest therein. For Pao-yü represents the human mind and, according to the *Ta-hsüeh*, one must first bring the thoughts into a state of calm seriousness before one can rectify the mind.[47] Now the thoughts correspond to the element earth, associated with the organ the spleen. Once having fortified the element earth in the spleen, one can bring one's thoughts into the requisite state of calm seriousness. I wonder whether there are any people in the world who really understand the significance of eating.[48]

22. In this book we find frequent use of popular sayings and clever expressions, always in authentic northern dialect and the speech of the capital region, with little mixing in of other regional dialects. Whenever there is an overly unfamiliar usage, I will insert an explanatory note at the proper point.[49]

23. This book, moreover, is divided into three major segments [*chih* 支]. From Pao-yü's first taste of the experience of "clouds and rain" in chapter 6 to the prophetic dream in the Chiang-yün Pavilion in chapter 36 comprises the first segment. Liu Lao-lao is the dominant figure,

[46] See the opening passage of the traditional text of the novel, *CYY* 1/1a (71) (not translated in *Stone*), and the closing section of the novel, *CYY* 120/53a–b (1547–48) and *Stone* 5.120.375.

[47] See section four of the first paragraph of the *Ta-hsüeh*, James Legge, trans., *The Chinese Classics*, vol. 1, p. 358. The translation is based on various Neo-Confucian commentaries that interpret the expression more in terms of a state of calm, almost reverent equanimity—a state often nearly indistinguishable from the quietude of Taoist and Buddhist enlightenment—than in the literal sense of "sincerity."

[48] Chang Hsin-chih discusses the use of scenes of eating in the novel in the following interlineal comments: *CYY* 21/13b (300), 25/39b (352), 28/8b (382), and 120/52b (1546). The comment in chap. 28 refers the reader to this item of the *tu-fa* essay for details.

[49] This item is omitted in the "Shih-t'ou chi" versions.

Yüan-ch'un takes the secondary role, Ch'in Chung suffers the onus, and the Prince of Pei-ching is the witness.[50] From Yüan-yang's three turns as master of ceremonies in the dominoes and drinking game in chapter 40 to the suicide of Yu Erh-chieh by swallowing unalloyed gold in chapter 69 comprises the second segment. Yüan-yang is the dominant figure, Hsüeh Pao-ch'in takes the secondary role, Yu Erh-chieh suffers the onus, and Yu San-chieh is the witness.[51] From Yüan-yang's unwitting encounter with the "sporting mandarin ducks" in chapter 71 to Wang Hsi-feng's final charge to the old peasant woman [Liu Lao-lao] in chapter 113 comprises the third segment. Liu Lao-lao and Yüan-yang share the central position, Sha Ta-chieh takes the secondary role, Hsia Chin-kuei suffers the onus, and Pao Yung is the witness.[52] This is another dimension of the overall structure [*chieh-kou* 結構] of the entire work.

24. The entire text of the *Story of the Stone*, one hundred and twenty chapters in all, vast and expansive, may be said to be prolix [*fan* 繁], but there is actually not a single line of idle verbiage in it. This commentary on the *Story of the Stone*, more than three hundred thousand words in all, is quite detailed and fragmentary, one might also call it prolix.[53] There still remain thousands upon thousands of additional points not touched upon, but it is hoped that the adept reader will be able to extrapolate by analogy [*ch'u-lei p'ang-t'ung* 觸類旁通] in order to perceive what has not been touched upon [in the commentary].[54]

25. Some say this book has only eighty chapters and that the addi-

---

[50] "Clouds and rain" is a euphemism for sexual intercourse. In chap. 36, Pao-yü cries out in his sleep his defiance of the predestined union of gold and jade, while Pao-ch'ai sits beside his bed embroidering a "mandarin-duck" coverlet (a topos of conjugal bliss), and Tai-yü eavesdrops from outside the window. Chang Hsin-chih borrows the phrasing of the chapter title couplet to refer to this incident, as is the case below as well. The use of the name "Chiang-yün hsüan" to refer to Pao-yü's apartment, the I-hung yüan, makes allusion to both the mythical parable at the beginning of the novel describing Tai-yü's "debt of tears" to Pao-yü and Pao-yü's dream vision in chap. 5.

[51] The manuscript version mistakenly reads chapter 60 instead of chapter 69. The correct figure appears in the other versions.

[52] The text gives chapter 71 as chapter 70. The correct figure appears in the other versions. In Chang Hsin-chih's chapter comment to chap. 70 (*CYY* 70/34a–b [927–28]) he uses the same terminology and concepts to discuss the structure of the novel.

[53] The "Shih-t'ou chi" versions substitute *chih* 至 (perfect) for the first occurrence of *fan* in this item. Other changes include the omission of the length of the commentary.

[54] At this point, the "Shih-t'ou chi" versions add the following item: "It is already a long time that this book has had currency in the world. It is regrettable that there has been a dearth of people who can truly read and understand it, and there have even been some who let their ears do their tasting for them, who have even regarded it as an obscene book. This is just one more example of 'a humane man sees it and finds humanity in it, while a wise man sees it and finds wisdom in it.'"

tional forty chapters come from another hand. I have no way of determining this.[55] But one need only observe its overall structure [*chieh-kou* 結構], interconnected from start to finish [*shou-wei hsiang-ying* 首尾相應] like the Ch'ang-shan snake formation [*Ch'ang-shan she* 常山蛇][56] with its roots planted firmly [*an-ken* 安根] and its narrative threads laid out in advance [*fu-hsien* 伏線], so marvelously responsive that one could make the entire body move by pulling a single hair. In addition, its style and diction show scarcely any disparity from first to last. Can we say, then, that the allegedly added forty chapters have been grafted on toward the end?[57] Or that they have been patched into the text haphazardly? One eventually realizes that the difficulty thus involved would be many times greater than that of writing the book itself. Even if the task were entrusted to me with as much weight as a command from my father or an elder or a reward of ten thousand in gold were offered, if I were made to add half a chapter I would be unable to do so. Why, then, are there so many people who substitute their ears for their eyes and "follow the tune and join in the chorus."[58]

26. When I first read the *Story of the Stone* and came to the [first] part depicting Liu Lao-lao, I took it to be an interlude of comic relief [*ch'a-k'o ta-hun* 插科打諢], like the appearance of a clown figure [*ch'ou* 丑] in a dramatic work, designed to keep the book as a whole from becoming too somber [*chi-mo* 寂寞]. Afterward, I went on to consider whether or not the author had indeed designed this to be comic relief [*k'o-hun* 科諢], for then he should have been expected to insert comic scenes at periodic intervals. But, in fact, in the entire 120-chapter text I have only noted six visits [by Liu Lao-lao] to the Jung-kuo fu compound, with three toward the end of the book to balance out the three earlier visits, still people only speak of "three visits." This gives the impression of narrative frugality [*sheng* 省] and raises their importance. Moreover, the third visit takes place during a chaotic period of mourning observance, in which there

---

[55] Instead of "I have no way of determining this," the "Shih-t'ou chi" versions exclaim, "What sort of talk is this?"

[56] This type of battle formation, first described in the Chou dynasty military treatise the *Sun Tzu* 孫子, was supposed to be so supple that when the head or tail was attacked its opposite number would come to the rescue, and when the belly of the formation was attacked, both ends would respond. This conceit is used as a metaphor for well-articulated structural linkages in the writings of many Ming-Ch'ing fiction critics (see essay d in chap. 1 above).

[57] The words "scarcely" (*lüeh* 略) and "allegedly" (*so-wei* 所謂) do not appear in the "Shih-t'ou chi" versions.

[58] The expression "substitute their ears for their eyes" is omitted in the "Shih-t'ou chi" versions. Chang Hsin-chih also treats this problem in *CYY* 11/45a–b (1531–32), chapter comment.

is no point in using comic relief, so I began to have my doubts about this. When later on I read carefully through the song entitled "The Survivor,"[59] I saw that the rescue of Ch'iao-chieh is in reward for Wang Hsi-feng's kindness to her in her poverty, and this seemed to me to be the answer. But at that point in the novel [Liu Lao-lao's first visit], it is only the sixth chapter, and a lot of the principal characters have not yet been introduced; also, immediately after the scene of Pao-yü's first taste of "clouds and rain," precisely where one would expect an extended treatment of the problem of emotional experience, the narrative comes to a conspicuous halt and she [Liu Lao-lao] is singled out for special attention. Pointing up her importance, special attention is given to tracing her origins and roots and to laying out her genealogical connections over a number of generations. Considering all this greatly increased my doubts. From this point on I tried reading the sections separately [*fen-k'an* 分看] and together with each other [*ho-k'an* 合看], line by line and word by word, carefully savoring the flavor within. Yet it was not until three years later that I finally hit upon it: it was the Way of the *I Ching*, the whole book was nothing more or less than the Way of the *I Ching*! In fact, the commentary [*p'i-p'ing* 批評] on the *Story of the Stone* by the "Man of Leisure of the Great Peace"[60] really began from this point.

Let us take Liu Lao-lao as an example. She corresponds to a pure *k'un* 坤 hexagram, in which the "old *yin*" generates a "young *yang*," which explains why she saves Ch'iao-chieh.[61] Now, Ch'iao-chieh's birthday is on the seventh day of the seventh lunar month, and the number seven is the numerical equivalent of the "young *yang*." But *yin* does not suddenly become *yin*; it must begin from a single *yin* line.[62] When a single *yin* line appears in the initial position at the bottom of the hexagram, it forms the new hexagram *kou* ☰.[63] If we take Pao-yü to be the embodiment of pure *yang*, then the "first taste of clouds and rain" represents the entry of a *yin* line into the first position, thus forming the hexagram *kou*. That explains why this scene is immediately followed up by the scene of "Liu Lao-lao's first entry into the Jung-kuo fu." After the *yin* line has moved into place, the process continues in orderly sequence, bringing us to the

[59] This song is part of the song cycle heard by Pao-yü in his dream of chap. 5 and pertains particularly to the rescue of Wang Hsi-feng's daughter Ch'iao-chieh by Liu Lao-lao. See *CYY* 5/19a (133) and *Stone* 1.5.143.

[60] Here Chang Hsin-chih refers to himself formally by the use of the full form of his style or *nom de plume*.

[61] For the terms "young *yin*" and "old *yang*," see Richard Wilhelm, *The I Ching*, p. 722.

[62] As the author goes on to explain, this means that the *k'un* hexagram of pure *yin* lines can only be obtained through the gradual buildup of *yin* line by *yin* line.

[63] For the *kou* hexagram, see Richard Wilhelm, *The I Ching*, pp. 170–73, 608–13.

hexagram *po* ䷖,[64] at which point Liu Lao-lao's true image finally takes shape, with a single *yang* line significantly left over at the top of the hexagram. Now, *po* is the hexagram of the ninth month, which at the juncture with the tenth month is replaced by *k'un* ䷁.[65] That is why her arrival takes place at the end of the season of autumn and the beginning of winter, the very height of the season of "greater goings and lesser comings."[66] For this reason, when the narrator is searching for a narrative thread [*t'ou-hsü* 頭緒] to follow, he describes a "small, humble family" and says that this "small, humble family was surnamed Wang" and descended from a "small, humble official in the capital."[67] Here the words "small, humble" appear three times in all, comprising six occurrences of the character *hsiao* 小 ["small"], all of which has an ineffable meaning. The three horizontal lines in the *ch'ien* trigram [☰] correspond to the three horizontal strokes in the character *wang* 王 which, when we add a straight line intersecting them, splits them vertically, forming the *k'un* trigram.[68] This splitting proceeds from bottom to top. When the first line is split it forms the trigram *hsün* ☴, representing the eldest daughter, which is why we have a mother living in the daughter's house. When the second line is split, it forms the trigram *ken* ☶, corresponding to a dog, which is why her son-in-law is called Kou-erh ["Little Dog"]. When the third line is split, it forms the *k'un* trigram ☷, which represents the minister as opposed to the ruler. This is why she has a family member serving in an official capacity, with clan links to the Wang family.[69] On this basis, this is doubled to form the entire *k'un* hexagram composed of six lines. The successive moves from *kou* ䷫, to *tun* ䷠,[70] to *p'i* ䷋,[71] to *kuan* ䷓,[72] to *po* ䷖, and then to *k'un* ䷁ᅠall derive from the idea of advancement from smallness. The force of this is extremely advantageous, one that cannot be suppressed. The linking of the families was in order to gain power and advantage, and the Jung-kuo fu is at this point in a phase of prosperity whose apex is still far off, which is why

---

[64] For the *po* hexagram, see Richard Wilhelm, *The I Ching*, pp. 93–96, 500–504.

[65] For the *k'un* hexagram, see Richard Wilhelm, *The I Ching*, pp. 10–15, 385–97.

[66] For this line, see *Shih-san ching ching-wen*, *I Ching*, *p'i* hexagram, p. 5, and Richard Wilhelm, *The I Ching*, pp. 52, 447.

[67] "Small, humble" (*hsiao-hsiao* 小小) might be more literally translated as "small, small." For the text of the novel, see *CYY* 6/21b–22a (138–39) and *Stone* 1.6.150.

[68] Chang Hsin-chih is comparing the written form of the surname of Liu Lao-lao's son-in-law, Wang, with the form of the *k'un* trigram.

[69] For a review of the trigrams and their associations, see Richard Wilhelm, *The I Ching*, pp. 266–79.

[70] For the *tun* hexagram, see Richard Wilhelm, *The I Ching*, pp. 129–32, 550–54.

[71] For the hexagram *p'i*, see Richard Wilhelm, *The I Ching*, pp. 52–55, 446–50.

[72] For the *kuan* hexagram, see Richard Wilhelm, *The I Ching*, pp. 82–85, 485–89.

these people are accepted as distant relatives. Of Kou-erh's grandfather we are only told that he was surnamed Wang and a native of the place [literally, the local soil], but no given name is supplied. With respect to the expression "local soil," we note that *k'un* represents the earth, but in this case the "way of the earth" is not successful, and the generations are about to come to an end. That is why he has no given name, but his son is named "Ch'eng" [success], because he will carry on his physical descent. If Kou-erh is equivalent to the *ken* trigram, Wang Ch'eng also corresponds to a *ken* trigram. *Ken* is the trigram of the northeast, where the myriad things of creation reach both the end and the beginning of the process of completion. That is why he is called "Ch'eng." Also, the northeast is marked by the intersection of winter and spring phases. That is why he has a son named Pan-erh, since the character *pan* 板 is composed of the graph for wood [*mu* 木] and the phonetic element *fan* 反 [to return], thus expressing the idea that the season of water recedes, giving way to the return of the season of wood.[73] He also has a daughter named Ch'ing-erh, "ch'ing" 青 being the archetypal color of the element "wood," which grows from north to east, which is equivalent to the birth of the "young *yang*" out of the "old *yin*." In the five phases scheme the trigram *ken* signifies earth, which is why he is engaged in agriculture as an occupation. As long as the old widow has no offspring, her *yin* cannot engender life. After a long period over several generations, the cycle of ending and beginning makes a complete revolution [*chen yüan yün-hui* 貞元運會].[74] It has been thus since time immemorial. And so, the sage composed the *I Ching*, in which *yang* is elevated and *yin* is suppressed, to the point at which no outside influence on the system is possible. This is the true seed of continuous creation, which must be painstakingly nurtured. That is why this character is called Liu Lao-lao, "Liu" is homophonous with *liu* 留 [to preserve]. It is too bad that most people are bounded by the limitations of their mortal existence and consciousness and fail to understand the significance of just this one character Liu Lao-lao, so that she [Liu Lao-lao] is subject to ridicule by the likes of Wang Hsi-feng. What a shame![75]

[73] Here Chang Hsin-chih uses the technique of splitting Chinese characters (*ch'ai-tzu* 拆字) to make his point. The manuscript version mistakenly reads *ling* 令 for *leng* 冷.

[74] For the terms *chen* 貞 and *yüan* 元 as the ending and beginning of a cycle, see Richard Wilhelm, *The I Ching*, pp. 4–6, 373. See also chap. VI above, items 13 and 17 of the *Hsi-yu chi tu-fa* essay.

[75] This section is repeated almost exactly in Chang Hsin-chih's interlineal comments at the point in chap. 6 where Liu Lao-lao appears in the narrative, but does not appear in the interlineal comments of the 1881 or the "Chin-yü yüan" editions. This and the following four items are not found in the "Shih-t'ou chi" versions. Instead there appear the two following items, which bring that version to an end:

27. The manner in which images from the *I Ching* are taken over and worked out in this book is most evident, and yet most obscure, in the case of Pao-yü's four "sisters": Yüan-ch'un, Ying-ch'un, T'an-ch'un, and Hsi-ch'un. Yüan-ch'un corresponds to the hexagram *t'ai* ䷊,[76] the hexagram of the first month, so she is the eldest sibling. Ying-ch'un corresponds to the hexagram *ta-chuang* ䷡,[77] the hexagram of the second month, so she is the second oldest daughter. T'an-ch'un corresponds to the hexagram *kuai* ䷪,[78] the hexagram of the third month, so she is the third oldest daughter. Hsi-ch'un corresponds to the hexagram *ch'ien* ䷀,[79] which is the hexagram of the fourth month, so she is the fourth oldest daughter. But since all of them are female, their *yang* lines are transformed into *yin* lines. Thus Yüan-ch'un's *t'ai* is transformed into *p'i* ䷋, Ying-ch'un's *ta-chuang* is transformed into *kuan* ䷓, T'an-ch'un's *kuai* is transformed into *po* ䷖, and Hsi-ch'un's *ch'ien* is transformed into *k'un* ䷁.[80] This is one of the most important messages in the book, and I make comment [*p'ing* 評] on this in turn during the biographies [*pen-chuan* 本傳] of each of them.

28. As a rule, in editions of fiction, the symbols ○, ◗, △, and — are used to elucidate points in the text, but this can be dispensed with as unnecessary. The reason for this is that once the essential meanings, examples of fine prose, and profound messages have been brought out by means of commentary [*p'ing* 評], there is no need to go to further effort to point them out. Therefore, all I do is simply put in

---

At the conclusion of the book we have the granting of the title "Taoist Master of Literary Brilliance" to Pao-yü [in chap. 120], whereby the outstanding accounts of the entire text are settled in full. This means, in effect, that this is the most truly brilliant literary work in the world. There seems to be little we can do about the fact that most readers fail to see this.

The *Story of the Stone* has the various alternate titles *Record of the Monk of Passion*, *Precious Mirror of Love*, and *The Twelves Beauties of Chin-ling*. Now, a name is something that is self-determined. The form of the character "name" [*ming* 名] is derived from the graph for "evening" [*hsi* 夕] and the graph for "mouth" [*k'ou* 口]. Evening means darkness. In darkness we cannot see one another, therefore we use the voice to identify ourselves—that is what is called a "name." This book explicitly purports to narrate the events recorded on the stone. That is why it was originally entitled the *Story of the Stone*.

[76] For the hexagram *t'ai*, see Richard Wilhelm, *The I Ching*, pp. 48–52, 440–45.

[77] For the hexagram *ta-chuang*, see Richard Wilhelm, *The I Ching*, pp. 133–36, 555–59.

[78] For the hexagram *kuai*, see Richard Wilhelm, *The I Ching*, pp. 166–70, 602–7.

[79] For the hexagram *ch'ien*, see Richard Wilhelm, *The I Ching*, pp. 3–10, 369–85.

[80] The second set of "transformation hexagrams" (*pien-kua* 變卦) are here derived by the simple process of changing every *yin* and *yang* line to its opposite. Further information on why Chang Hsin-chih linked the four girls with their particular hexagrams can be found in his textual commentary, particularly in an interlineal comment upon the first appearance of the younger three girls, *CYY* 3/2a–b (99–100). The reasons presented tend to dwell on linguistic clues that he claims to find in the text, such as the word *kuan* 觀 (same as the hexagram) in the description of Ying-ch'un.

single circles [*tan-ch'üan* 單圈] in the text itself and single dots [*tan-tien* 單點] in the commentary and notes [*p'ing-chu* 評注] in order to punctuate sentences and clauses.[81]

29. In this book there is a causal link between the western compound and the eastern compound, which is occupied by Chia Chen. This is actually talking about Ch'in K'o-ch'ing, who is the originator of the discord in the family. Here I revise "eastern compound" to "Ying-kuo fu" 嬴國府, which conforms precisely to the position of Ch'in K'o-ch'ing, "Ying" being the surname of the royal house of Ch'in. The name of the "second master" Chia [Chia Lien] is also revised here to the character *lien* 楝, which is a homophone of the original and is explained in the same way.[82]

30. In the original printing there are twenty-four engraved illustrations, all matched to the ideas in the novel. Only the dedicatory poems provided for the first illustration, that of the preincarnate stone, and the last, that of the Buddhist monk and the Taoist priest, implicitly correspond to the basic message of the book, according to which the stone represents the undifferentiated mind, while the Buddhist monk and the Taoist priest represent the workings of the way of the *I Ching*. The remainder are all drawn up in accordance with the surface of the story, with an ambiguous range of meaning somewhere between presence and absence or between meaningfulness and meaninglessness, all of which derive from the author's own hand. In revising the original edition and adding comments in an enlarged format, the engraved illustrations and dedicatory verses have been copied according to those of the original edition in order to preserve their former appearance. There are also other editions put out by local commercial printers, in which the illustrations are reduced to fifteen in number and contain portraits with no backgrounds. They are missing the illustration of the scene at the Chia clan temple and the portraits of Grandmother Chia; Chia Cheng's wife, Madame Wang; Pao-ch'in; Li Wen and Li Ch'i; Hsiu-yen, Yu San-chieh, Hsiang-ling and Hsi-jen; Ch'ing-wen, and the female singers. These deficiencies are a great mistake in respect to the plot of the novel.[83]

---

[81] For a discussion of the use of diacritical marks as a mode of criticism, see essays c and d in chap. 1 above. On the question of whether the manuscript copy of the commentary contained the full text of the novel, see the introduction to this chapter.

[82] The exact reason why Chang Hsin-chih would want to change *lien* 璉 to *lien* 楝 is not immediately apparent. The second character is much rarer and does not have as many associational meanings as the former one. It is also unclear whether Chang Hsin-chih did any of the revisions mentioned in this item in the text of the novel or not. These changes are not evident in the Peking Library manuscript copy of the commentary.

[83] For the identification of these two types of editions and the problem of what physical form Chang Hsin-chih's commentary actually circulated in before being printed by Sun T'ung-sheng, see the introduction to this chapter.

APPENDIX I

Finding List of Terminology Used by Chinese Fiction Critics

Translations of the terms cited below only refer to the particular patterns of usage by the individual critics in the contexts identified immediately following the translations. They do not represent any attempt at universally applicable definitions. The chapters in this volume are referred to by the use of roman numerals, with the four introductory essays labeled as Ia, Ib, Ic, and Id. Citations to the translated *tu-fa* essays are indicated by the chapter number (in roman numerals) followed by the number of the item in that essay. In the case of chapter V, "P" is used to refer to the translation of the Hsien-chai lao-jen preface, while the two middle numbers of the other chapter V citations indicate which chapter comment and which item of that chapter comment are involved. The last number in all citations refers to the page number in this volume. The number of occurrences of the term with the same meaning in a single item of a *tu-fa* essay or chapter comment follows in parentheses whenever that number exceeds one. Please note that as a general rule, in the translation of the essays, romanization and Chinese characters are only inserted for the first occurrence of the term in each item and for any other occurrence where necessary to avoid ambiguity. The reader can identify the exact location of multiple occurrences not marked by insertion of romanization and characters by the identification of the phrases used to translate the terms or by reference to the Chinese text. The terms are arranged below in alphabetical order according to their romanized forms; in cases where the romanized spelling is the same, Chinese words with fewer character strokes precede homonyms with more strokes and all phrases beginning with the same character are cited together before listing phrases beginning with a homonym of the first character. Characters romanized with apostrophes appear after those without (*ch'ang* after *chang*), as is also the case for characters romanized with umlauts (*ch'ü* after *ch'u*).

an-ken 安根, "to plant the roots [of the narrative] firmly," VII.25.335.
an 案, "episode," VI.5.301; "its," VI.5.301.
an-chieh 暗結, "conclude unobstrusively," IV.18.210.

ao-pi 傲筆, "disdainful strokes," IV.46.226.

ch'a 插, "introduced," IV.44.225.

ch'a-ch'u 插出, "brought out," IV.13.206.

ch'a-ju 插入, "insertion of passages," Id.105; "is introduced," IV.13.206 (ten).

ch'a-k'o ta-hun 插科打諢, "interlude of comic relief," VII.26.335.

chang-fa 章法, "compositional principle or technique," Ia.13, Id.85, 86n,
       II.18.135, III.6.165, III.21.192, IV.7.204, IV.44.225, V.P.250, VII.16.331.

chang-fa lao-ch'u 章法老處, "seasoned stylistic technique," IV.7.203.

Ch'ang-shan she 常山蛇, "Ch'ang-shan snake formation," Id.90, 90n, 96,
       VII.25.335.

chao-ying 照應, "pattern of projection and reflection," Ic.48, Id.95, 98,
       III.21.192, IV.3.202, IV.69.234, V.4.1.257, V.47.1.290, V.48.2.291, VII.20.333.

chen 針, "acupuncture," V.13.2.268. Related to *chen-pien* 針砭 rather than to
       chen-hsien 針線.

chen-hsien 針線, "needle and thread," Id.88n, 93; "stitching," V.4.3.257.

chen-pien 針砭, "acupuncture," IV.17.209.

ch'en 襯, "offset," Id.98, 108, 112, 120, III.9.168.

ch'en-tieh 襯跌, "portray as a contrast," V.28.2.280.

ch'en-t'o 襯托, "set off," V.24.1.275, V.51.4.293.

cheng-ching hsieh 正經寫, "pay serious attention to the description," IV.16.208.

cheng-chuan 正傳, "formal biographical sketch," IV.48.229.

cheng-fan 正犯, "direct repetition of topic," Id.101, II.59.143.

cheng-hsieh 正寫, "give the full treatment," IV.16.208.

cheng-mien 正面, "immediate surface," VII.1.323.

cheng-pi 正筆, "direct description," V.11.1.266; "direct style," V.36.1.285.

cheng-tui 正對, "analogous parallels," III.20.189, 191 (two); "parallels juxtaposed
       to bring out similarities," III.20.188.

cheng-wen 正文, "significant passage," III.13.179.

cheng-chang 整章, "all of a piece," VII.11.329.

ch'eng 承, "continue," II.8.133.

ch'eng-shih 程式, "pattern," V.1.6.253.

ch'eng-jen ti shu 懲人的書, "cautionary work," IV.105.242.

chi-mo 寂寞, "insufficiency," III.18.186; "too somber," VII.26.335.

chi pu-sheng fa 極不省法, "extreme avoidance of narrative frugality," Id.110,
       114, II.61.144.

chi sheng fa 極省法, "extreme narrative frugality," Id.110, 114, II.62.144.

chi 繼, "continuation/continued," III.14.180, IV.107.243.

"*ch'i-feng tui-ch'a, chin-p'ing tui-chih chih miao*" 奇峯對插, 錦屏對峙之妙,
       "the technique of balancing one striking peak against another and placing
       brocade screens face-to-face," III.20.188.

ch'i 起, "begin," Id.97, II.8.133, III.6.164–65 (eight), IV.102.242 (two),
       IV.108.243; "beginning," III.6.164; "introduced," III.21.191 (two).

ch'i ch'eng chuan ho 起承轉合, "begin, continue, change direction then sum up,"
       Id.95, II.8.133.

ch'i-chin 起盡, "structure," IV.48.230.

ch'i-chin ch'u 起盡處, "overall structure," IV.38.224.

ch'i-fu 起伏, "modulated rise and fall of narrative segments," Id.105, 105n,
    IV.52.232, V.4.1.257.
ch'i-t'ou 起頭, "beginning," IV.47.226–28 (four).
chia i pei 加一倍, "incremental repetition," IV.25.216 (three).
"*chia i pei hsieh-fa*" 加一倍寫法, "incremental repetition," Id.99, IV.25.216.
chia-pei hsieh 加倍寫, "incremental description," IV.25.216.
chia-ch'u 夾出, "inserted," V.3.4.256.
chia-hsieh 夾寫, "weave in," IV.5.203.
chia-hsü 夾叙, "inserted," IV.44.225.
chia-hsü fa 夾叙法, "simultaneous narration," II.52.140.
chia-shang san-hao 頰上三毫, "adding three hairs to the cheek," V.11.2.266.
"*chiang hsüeh chien hsien, chiang yü wen lei chih miao*" 將雪見霰, 將雨聞雷
    之妙, "the technique of making sleet appear when it is about to snow and
    thunder reverberate when it is about to rain," Id.93, III.13.179.
chiao-hu hui-huan 交互廻環, "interlinking and interweaving," V.18.3.270.
chiao-liang erh pi-kuan 較量而比觀, "compare and evaluate," III.20.191.
"*ch'iao-shou huan-chieh chih miao*" 巧收幻結之妙, "the technique of artful
    disposition and mysterious consummation," III.8.166.
ch'iao-pi 俏筆, "attractive strokes," IV.46.226.
chieh-ching 借逕, "takes a shortcut," VII.10.327.
chieh 結, "conclusion," III.6.164, IV.26.217–18 (two), IV.76.235, V.18.2.270;
    "concludes," III.6.164–65 (eight), IV.11.205, IV.23.213, IV.26.217, IV.76.235,
    IV.78.236, IV.108.243, V.56.1.294, VII.11.328 (two); "concluded," III.21.191–
    92 (four); "ends," IV.102.242; "wrapping up," VII.13.330 (three).
chieh-chuan 結撰, "concocted," II.4.132.
chieh-hsüeh ch'u 結穴處, "places of summation," Ic.48; "where narrative sections
    come together," IV.69.234; "culmination and summation," V.33.3.283.
chieh-kou 結構, "structure," Ia.32, Id.85, 121, III.21.192, V.33.3.282, VII.23.334,
    VII.25.335.
chieh-kuo 結果, "brought to a conclusion," IV.18.210.
chieh-kuo 結過, "concludes," V.8.1.263, V.24.1.275.
chieh-mo 結末, "the end," IV.47.226–28 (three).
chieh-shu 結束, "climax," V.48.4.291; "summation," IV.4.202.
chien-hsiung 奸雄, "unscrupulous hero," Id.80, 118, III.2.158, III.20.190.
chien 漸, "gradual development," VII.7.327, 327n.
chien 簡, "conciseness," VII.11.329.
chien 鑒, "reflection," V.P.250.
ch'ien-chen wan-hsien 千針萬綫, "myriad threads," IV.26.218.
ch'ien-li fu-mai 千里伏脉, "arteries that connect widely separated elements of
    the plot," IV.26.218.
ch'ien-li lai-lung 千里來龍, "dragon vein stretching thousands of miles,"
    V.3.5.256.
ch'ien-hou ying-tai 前後映帶, "former and latter passages mutually illuminate
    each other," V.3.7.256, V.4.1.257.
ch'ien-pan 前半, "first half," IV.10.204.
ch'ien pan-pu 前半部, "first half," IV.1.202 (two).

chih 支, "suprachapter sequences," Id.89; "segment," VII.23.333–34 (four).

chih-ch'u 直出, "directly introduce into the narrative," IV.47.226.

chih-pi 直筆, "direct narration," Id.110; "direct technique," IV.13.206; "straight-forward style," V.36.1.285.

"*chih shu ch'i-shih, pu chia lun-tuan [yü]*" 直書其事, 不加論斷[語], "directly narrating the incident itself without expressing one's own judgment," V.4.7.258, V.7.3.263.

chih-shuai 直率, "bluntness and directness," V.9.2.265.

chin-ch'ing cho-li 近情着理, "understandable and reasonable," V.27.1.278.

"*chin-shan nung-mo, yüan-shu ch'ing-miao chih miao*" 近山濃墨, 遠樹輕描, "the technique of meticulously rendering the hills in the foreground and lightly sketching the trees in the distance," III.19.186–87.

"*chin-chen chih i tu*" 金針之一度, "where the golden needle has done its work," IV.48.230.

chin-hsin hsiu-k'ou 錦心繡口, "fine thoughts and polished phrases," II.1.131; "elegant thoughts and expressions," V.4.2.257.

ching 鏡, "mirror," IV.96.241, V.P.251.

ch'ing-li 情理, "emotion and reason," IV.43.224–25 (six).

ch'ing yin wen sheng 情因文生, "incidents dictated by the exigencies of the plot," IV.18.210.

ch'ing-pi 輕筆, "light touch," IV.44.225, IV.66.234.

chiu-ch'ü chu 九曲珠, "nine-crooked pearl," V.5.3.259.

ch'iung-shen chin-hsiang 窮神盡像, "capture both spirit and appearance," V.P.250.

"*cho-chin ho-chien ch'u*" 着緊合尖處, "crucial and climactic episodes," VI.18.305.

cho-yen 着眼, "pay attention," Id.81, VI.10.303, VI.13.304.

cho-yen ch'u 着眼處, "focal point," V.1.2.252.

ch'ou 丑, "clown," VII.26.335.

chu-nao 主腦, "main brain," Ia.30; "central conception or character," Id.88, 88n; "heart," V.2.1.253.

chu 注, "note, comment," IV.49.230.

chu-chieh 注解, "annotation," VI.44.314 (four), VI.45.315.

chu-ssu ma-chi 蛛絲馬迹, "spiders' webs and horses' tracks," V.3.9.257.

chu-ting hsiang-wu 鑄鼎象物, "tripods of Emperor Yü with images of all the objects of nature," V.3.6.256, V.17.1.269.

ch'u-lo ch'u 出落處, "place where [characters'] introduction is made," V.11.3.267.

ch'u-shen ju-hua 出神入化, "move beyond even the realm of divine artistry," V.46.2.290.

ch'u-shih 出世, "escape the ways of the world," IV.105.242.

ch'u-lei p'ang-t'ung 觸類旁通, "extrapolate by analogy," VII.24.334.

chü-fa 句法, "pattern of organization of the sentence," II.18.135.

ch'ü 曲, "indirect," IV.13.206.

ch'ü-ch'ü che-che 曲曲折折, "twists and turns," IV.48.230; "intricacy," IV.98.242.

ch'ü-pi 曲筆, "circuitous, indirect style or technique," Id.76n, 110, IV.13.206, V.36.1.285.

chuan 傳, "biography," IV.26.218, IV.34.221 (two), IV.48.229.

chuan 撰, "create," IV.20.212.

chuan 轉, "change direction," Id.92, II.8.133.

ch'uan-ch'a 穿插, "insertion of material, dovetailing," Id.95, 110, IV.5.203, IV.39.224.

ch'uan-ch'a ch'u 穿插處, "place where material is interwined," IV.68.234.

chui-hun ch'ü-p'o 追魂取魄, "capturing their very spirit," IV.54.232.

"*chui-pen chiu-yüan chih miao*" 追本究源之妙, "the technique of tracing things to their roots and divulging their sources," III.7.165.

chui 綴, "to add to," V.56.1.294.

ch'un-kung 春工, "creative powers of spring," IV.106.242.

ch'un-pi 蠢筆, "stupid strokes," IV.46.226.

chung-liu ti-chu 中流砥柱, "resisting pillar in the midst of the current," IV.47.228, V.P.250.

chung-pi 重筆, "heavy touches," IV.66.234.

e-yao ch'u 扼要處, "focus," V.45.3.289.

erh-chung t'ing-lai 耳中聽來, "heard through the ears of," III.19.187.

fa-fen chu-shu 發憤著書, "write a book to express one's resentment," Ib.38, II.1.132, V.40.1.288.

fa-mai 發脈, "place where a new section begins," IV.69.234.

fan-ch'en 反襯, "depict by contrast," Id.100, IV.22.213.

fan-mien 反面, "other side," VII.1.323.

fan-pi 反筆, "contrastive techniques," V.11.266.

fan-tui 反對, "contrastive parallelism," Id.107; "contrastive parallels," III.20.189, 191 (two); "juxtapose to bring out differences," II.20.188.

fan 犯, "violation of redundancy," Id.101, 106; "repeat the topic," II.59.143; "duplication," III.10.170, IV.45.225; "duplicating," III.10.170–73 (six); "repetitive," IV.45.225–26 (two); "overlap," V.31.1.281.

fan-pi 犯筆, "device of duplication," IV.45.225.

fan-shou 犯手, see *t'e-t'e fan-shou*.

fan 煩, "fullness," VII.11.329.

fan 繁, "prolix," Id.109, VII.24.334 (two).

fan-yen wen-tzu 繁衍文字, "complicated passages," IV.67.234.

fan-an 翻案, "reversal of fortunes," IV.17.209.

fang-pi hsieh 放筆寫, "unrestrained portrait," V.6.1.260.

fen-k'an 分看, "read separately," VII.26.336.

fen-shuo 分說, "separate narration," VI.19.306.

fen-tso 分做, "presented separately," IV.35.221.

fu 伏, "set up," Id.97, V.47.1.290.

fu-an 伏案, "set out," V.3.5.256.

fu-hsia i-pi 伏下一筆, "foreshadow," III.17.183–86 (twelve).

fu-hsien 伏線, "prepare the way," Id.97n, IV.23.213, IV.29.219; "narrative threads laid out in advance," VII.25.335.

fu-pi 伏筆, "device of foreshadowing," III.17.185.

"*han-ping p'o-je, liang-feng sao-ch'en chih miao*" 寒冰破熱, 涼風掃塵之妙, "the technique of introducing cold ice to break the heat and cool breezes to sweep away the dust," Id.102, III.15.180.

hen-chi 痕迹, "contrived," IV.26.217; "trace of artifice," V.24.1.285.

"*heng-yün tuan shan fa*" 橫雲斷山法, "clouds cutting the mountains in half,"
    II.64.144.

"*heng-yün tuan shan, heng-ch'iao so hsi chih miao*" 橫雲斷山, 橫橋鎖溪之妙,
    "the technique of intersecting mountain ranges with clouds and inter-
    lacing streams with bridges," III.12.178.

ho 合, "sum up," II.8.133.

ho-chang 合掌, "similarity," 1d.100n, III.5.164.

ho-chuan 合傳, "collective biography," IV.34.221.

ho-k'an 合看, "read together," VII.26.336.

ho-shuo 合說, "unified narration," VI.19.306 (two).

ho-tso 合做, "integrated," IV.35.221.

hou-ch'e chung fu 後車終覆, "suffer the fate clearly forewarned," IV.20.212.

hou-pan 後半, "second half," IV.10.204.

hou pan-pu 後半部, "second half," IV.1.202 (two).

hou-t'ien 後天, "follow after Heaven," VI.7.301; "after Heaven revealed itself,"
    VI.8.301; "postnatal condition," VI.33.311; "posterior to Heaven,"
    VI.35.312.

hsi-chu 犀燭, "rhinoceros-horn candle," VII.5.326.

hsia-pan 下半, "second half," IV.82.237.

hsia pan-chieh 下半截, "second half," IV.83.239.

hsia pan-pu 下半部, "second half," IV.6.203.

hsiang-t'i li-ko 相題立格, "set the style to fit the subject," V.36.2.285.

hsiao chieh-shu 小結束, "small unifying episode," V.37.3.286.

hsiao-wen 小文, "minor passage," III.13.179.

hsiao-wu 肖物, "lifelike," II.29.137.

hsiao 孝, "filial," IV.76.235.

hsieh-mai ching-lo 血脉經絡, "arteries and veins," V.1.1.252.

hsieh-tzu 楔子, "prologue," 1d.90, V.1.1.252; "opening," IV.47.227 (two).

hsieh-chao 寫照, "describe in detail," V.17.1.269.

hsieh-ch'u 寫處, "focus," IV.16.209.

hsien-sheng 先聲, "prelude," III.14.180.

hsien-t'ien 先天, "precede Heaven," VI.7.301; "prefigure Heaven,"
    VI.8.301; "prenatal endowment," VI.33.311; "anterior to Heaven,"
    VI.35.312, VI.41.314 (two); "state of the universe prior to the emergence
    of concrete manifestations," VII.15.330.

hsien-wen 閒文, "inconsequential passage," 1d.110, III.13.179 (three).

hsien-shen 現身, "become that character," IV.61.233.

hsien-so 線索, "connecting thread," II.53.141; "narrative thread," V.10.3.266,
    V.27.4.279.

hsien-pi 顯筆, "risky techniques," IV.14.207.

hsien-pi 險筆, "obvious strokes," IV.46.226.

hsin-shu 心術, "inner springs of the hearts and minds," V.P.250; "pattern of
    thought," V.5.4.259; "character and inner workings," V.2.3.254.

hsing 形, "show by contrast," V.29.1.280.

hsing-chi 形擊, "unflattering contrast," II.27.137; "simultaneously portray and criticize," V.11.1.266.

hsing-ch'ing 性情, "nature and emotions," VIII.1.323; "temperament," V.P.250, V.5.4.259, V.26.4.278, V.49.1.291.

hsing-ko 性格, "personality," II.4.132, II.16.135.

hsing-li 性理, "nature and reason," VII.2.324.

"*hsing-i tou-chuan, yü-fu feng-fan chih miao*" 星移斗轉, 雨覆風翻之妙, "the technique of making the stars move and the dipper revolve and causing rain to inundate things and wind to overturn them," Id.93, III.11.173–74.

hsiu-pi 秀筆, "refined strokes," IV.46.226.

hsü-shih 叙事, "narration," III.18.185, III.22.192, 193 (two), V.4.1.257, VII.9.327.

hsü 虛, "made-up, fabricated," Id.104, V.24.1.275.

hsü-hsieh 虛寫, "described indirectly," III.19.187 (two); "describe by implication," IV.18.209.

hsüan-jan 緒染, "adumbration," Id.111; "enhance," III.18.186.

hsün-ch'ang k'o-chiu 尋常窠臼, "hackneyed narrative cliché," IV.26.217.

hu-ying 呼應, "interrelated," III.11.178.

hua 化, "the miraculous plane," IV.37.224.

hua-kung 化工, "divine achievement," Ib.37; "most natural," II.29.137; "powers of nature," IV.106.242; "attainments of the divinely inspired artist," V.P.250; "divinely inspired brush," V.4.4.257.

hua-pi 化筆, "miraculous technique," IV.14.207.

hua-shen 化身, "author transforms self into," IV.62.233.

hua-tso 化作, "transform into," V.41.1.289.

"*hua kuei [-kuai] i, hua jen-wu nan*" 畫鬼[怪]易, 畫人物難, "it is easy to paint ghosts and demons but difficult to paint human beings," V.6.1.260, V.36.1.285.

hua-kung 畫工, "artisanly achievement," Ib.37; "attainments of the artisan," V.P.250; "talent of an artisan's brush," V.4.4.257.

hung-jan 烘染, "adumbration," Id.111; "highlighting," V.1.7.253.

huo-se sheng-hsiang 活色生香, "portrayed vividly," V.45.4.289.

i-pi erh san-yung 一筆而三用, "use for three purposes," Id.109, IV.29.219.

i-pi shuang-hsieh 一筆雙寫, "treat two sides of a problem at once," VI.26.310.

"*i-p'ien ju i-chü*" 一篇如一句, "the work is as closely interrelated as a sentence," Id.87, III.18.186.

"*i pin ch'en chu chih miao*" 以賓襯主之妙, " the technique of using the guest as a foil for the host," III.9.166.

i-wen yün-shih 以文運事, "use words to carry events," II.10.133.

i-yang hu-lu 依樣葫蘆, "one patterned on the other," V.P.249.

i-an chih pi 易安之筆, "facile writing," IV.26.218.

jen-ch'ing 人情, "human nature," IV.62.233, IV.63.233, IV.103.242.

ju-shih 入世, "immerse [oneself] in the ways of the world," IV.105.242.

ju-sun ch'u 入筍處, "place at which the tenon is inserted," Id.94; "place where one element is used to lead into another," IV.13.205–206.

kang 綱, "summation," VII.13.330 (two).

"ko-nien hsia-chung, hsien-shih fu-cho chih miao" 隔年下種, 先時伏着之妙, "sowing seeds a year in advance and making preliminary moves to set up later strategies," 1d.97, III.17.183.

k'o-chi k'o-ch'u 刻棘刻楮, "remarkable skill in crafting characters," V.6.2.261.

k'o-hun 科諢, "comic interlude," VII.26.335; "comic relief," VII.26.336.

kou-lien 勾聯, "interconnection," V.2.5.254.

k'ou-chung hsieh-ch'u 口中寫出, "revealed from the mouth of," V.5.2.259.

k'ou-chung hsü-lai 口中敘來, "learn from his own mouth," III.19.187; "learn from his remark," III.19.187.

k'ou-chung tai-ch'u 口中帶出, "comes from his mouth," V.3.9.257.

ku 骨, "skeleton," V.P.250.

k'u-hsiao shuo 苦孝說, "theory of frustrated filiality," VII.11.328.

k'uai-chih jen-k'ou 膾炙人口, "appealing," VII.1.323.

kuan-ch'uan 貫串, "connecting link," 1d.87, II.6.133, III.23.193.

kuan-ch'uan ling-lung 貫穿玲瓏, "finely interconnected," V.1.1.252.

kuan-t'ung ch'i-mai 貫通氣脉, "connecting nerves and arteries," IV.52.232.

kuan-chien ch'u 關鍵處, "place of pivotal importance," 1d.88, IV.2.202.

kuan-ho 關合, "link together," 1d.87, III.21.192.

kuan-mu 關目, "key item," 1d.88, VI.14.304; "important feature," VI.28.310.

kung-an 公案, "case," IV.48.229; "episode," 1d.89, VI.9.302 (two), VI.12.303.

kung ming fu kuei 功名富貴, "success, fame, riches, and rank," V.P.250 (five), V.1.2.252, V.1.3.253, V.2.1.253−54 (two), V.2.2.254, V.4.2.257, V.5.1.259, V.7.4.263, V.17.2.270 (two), V.21.1.272 (two); "them," V.1.4.253 (four).

k'ung 空, "empty," IV.23.213, IV.26.217−18 (two), IV.75.235, IV.76.235, IV.102.242 (three), IV.103.242; "emptiness," 1d.90, IV.76.235; "vacuity," VI.7.301.

"kuo-shou pu-tzu, pu pu chao-ying" 國手布子, 步步照應, "a premier chess player whose every move fits in with and strengthens the other moves," V.47.1.290.

kuo-chieh 過節, "transition," IV.8.204.

kuo-chieh wen-tzu 過節文字, "transitions," IV.65.233.

kuo-hsia 過下, "mortised," IV.8.204.

kuo-hsia 過峽, "like water passing through a gorge," V.4.1.257.

lai-mai 來脉, "points of connection," VI.9.302.

"lang-hou po-wen, yü-hou mo-mu chih miao" 浪後波文, 雨後霢霖之妙, "the technique of making ripples follow in the wake of waves and drizzle continue after rain," III.14.180.

lei-t'ung 雷同, "exactly alike," 1d.100n, III.5.164.

leng-je 冷熱, "heat and cold," 1d.101, 105, IV.10.204, IV.25.216−17 (three), IV.83.239, IV.87.240, IV.88.240, VII.11.328 (two).

li chu-nao 立主腦, "set up the central conception or character," 1d.88.

li-ho 離合, "separation and union," 1d.103−4, VII.18.332.

liang-tui chang-fa 兩對章法, "structural device of juxtaposing two episodes," IV.8.204.

liang-t'i ts'ai-i 量體裁衣, "tailor the clothes to fit the body," V.36.2.285.

lieh-chuan 列傳, "biography," II.15.135, IV.22.193.

lien-hsü 連叙, "treated consecutively," III.11.178 (two).

lien-tuan 連斷, "consecutive and nonconsecutive, respectively," Id.105, III.12.178 (two of each).

"*lin-chiao feng-tsui wen-tzu*" 麟角鳳嘴文字, "extraordinary literary effects," IV.58.232.

ling-ch'u t'ou-hsü 另出頭緒, "begin a new section from scratch," IV.48.229.

lo-lo 羅絡, "fibers," V.2.5.254.

lo-lo kou-lien 羅絡鈎連, "create a seamless web," V.18.3.270.

"*luan-chiao hsü-hsien fa*" 鸞膠續絃法, "joining a broken zither string with glue," II.65.145.

lüeh-fan fa 略犯法, "incomplete repetition," Id.101, II.60.143.

Lung-men miao-pi 龍門妙筆, "Ssu-ma Ch'ien's miraculous technique," V.35.1.285.

Lung-men wen-tzu 龍門文字, "composition like that of Ssu-ma Ch'ien," IV.48.230.

mai-lo 脉絡, "arteries," Id.93, 95, V.6.1.260.

mai-fu 埋伏, "forward projection," Ic.48; "plant a seed," Id.97n, V.10.3.265.

man-sheng pien-tiao 慢聲變調, "reprise and variation," V.37.3.286.

man-hsü chih pi 滿許之筆, "favorable treatment," IV.47.228.

men-mien 門面, "frontispiece," II.11.133.

"*mien-chen ni-tz'u fa*" 綿針泥刺法, "needles wrapped in cotton and thorns hidden in mud," II.55.141.

ming-shih 名士, "unconventional man of letters," V.6.6.261, V.8.2.264; "famous literati," V.13.2.268; "famous men of letters," V.17.2.270; "scholars," V.33.3.283.

mo-chieh 末節, "last part," IV.47.228.

mo-hsieh 摹寫, "representing," IV.54.232; "representation," V.P.250.

mo-shen 摹神, "depict the inner spirit," IV.59.233.

mo-shen hsiao-ying 摹神肖影, "depict with uncanny fidelity," IV.54.232.

mu 目, "detailed outline," VII.13.330.

ni 逆, "unexpected," IV.13.206.

ni-pi 逆筆, "unexpected techniques," IV.13.206.

nung-yin fa 弄引法, "displaying the bait," II.57.142.

pa-yin fan-hui 八音繁會, "climax where all the instruments sound at once," V.37.3.286.

pai-miao 白描, "sketch in outline," IV.64.233 (two), V.23.1.275.

"*pai-mang chung ku tso hsiao-hsien chih pi*" 百忙中故作消閒之筆, "deliberate retardation at points of high tension," IV.44.225.

pai-kuan 稗官, "fiction [writer]," Id.82, III.4.162 (two), V.P.249–51 (four), V.1.1.252, V.6.1.260, V.26.2.278, V.34.1.284, V.39.3.287, V.45.2.290.

pai-kuan chia 稗官家, "novelists," III.12.178, III.17.185.

p'ai-an chiao-chüeh 拍案叫絕, "strike the table and yell 'bravo,'" V.17.1.269, V.26.3.278.

pan-chieh 半截, "half," IV.83.239.

"*pan-ting ta chang-fa*" 板定大章法, "regular structural device," IV.7.203.

p'ang-chien ts'e-ch'u 旁見側出, "indirect portrayal," v.35.1.285.

p'ang-hsieh 旁寫, "devote peripheral attention to," III.10.171.

p'ang-pi 旁筆, "oblique style," v.36.1.285.

pao 報, "retribution," III.8.166, IV.18.210 (four), IV.23.214–15 (two).

pao-ch'ou 報仇, "retribution," III.8.166.

pao-ying 報應, "retribution," IV.51.232, IV.86.240.

"*pei-mien p'u [fu] fen fa*" 背面鋪[傅]粉法, "whitening the background to bring out the foreground," id.107, II.56.142.

p'ei 陪, "to act as a foil," III.4.162 (three).

p'ei-hsieh 陪寫, "use as a foil," IV.23.214.

p'ei-pi 陪筆, "a complement," v.49.1.291.

pen-chuan 本傳, "biography," VII.27.339.

pi-fa 筆法, "technique," IV.82.236.

"*pi pu tao erh i tao*" 筆不到而意到, "implied but not written on the page," IV.23.215.

pi-chen 逼真, "true to life," id.112, v.2.8.255.

pi 避, "avoid," III.10.170 (two); "avoiding," III.10.170, 173 (four).

"*pi-nan chiu-i ch'u*" 避難就易處, "easy way to get out of difficulties," IV.66.234.

pi-nan ch'u 避難處, "place where he gets out of difficulties," id.109, IV.66.233.

"*pi-shih chi-hsü chih miao*" 避實擊虛之妙, "avoid direct description in favor of indirect description," v.24.1.275.

p'i-li yang-ch'iu 皮裏陽秋, "discreet use of the critical method of the *Ch'un-ch'iu* [The Spring and Autumn Annals]," id.76n, v.34.1.284.

p'i 批, "commentary," III.5.164, IV.35.221 (two), IV.82.236, 238 (two), IV.100.242, IV.101.242, IV.102.242.

p'i-p'ing 批評, "commentary," VII.1.323, VII.26.336.

p'i-k'ung chuan-ch'u 劈空撰出, "invent," IV.1.202.

pien 變, "reversal," III.11.174–78 (forty-one).

pien-t'i 變體, "variation," v. 47.1.290.

pin-chu 賓主, "subordination of elements," Ia.13; "guest and host, respectively," id.108, III.9.167–170 (twenty-four of each).

p'ing 評, "comment," VII.27.339; "commentary," VII.28.339.

p'ing-chu 評注, "commentary and notes," VII.28.340.

p'ing-k'ung tsao-huang 憑空造謊, "made up out of thin air," II.21.136.

po-che 波折, "contour and flex," v.3.4.256.

po-lan 波瀾, "natural periodic variations," III.4.162.

p'o-chan 破綻, "flaws in the stitching," id.92; "clandestine activities are disclosed," IV.14.207; "inconsistencies," VI.15.304 (two).

pu-ch'eng wen-fa 不成文法, "does not hold together," v.22.2.273.

"*pu-cho pi-mo ch'u*" 不着筆墨處, "undescribed but implied incident," IV.23.215.

"*pu-t'ung erh ta-t'ung-che*" 不同而大同者, "seem different but are ultimately the same," VI.27.310.

pu-p'ing chih ming 不平之鳴, "sympathy for victims of injustice," v.40.1.288.

pu-yen chih piao 不言之表, "implied without being described in words,"
    IV.48.230.

pu-chih 布置, "narrative layout," V.26.4.278.

pu-chü 布局, "layout," V.37.2.286.

p'u-hsü 鋪叙, "representation," VII.5.325.

san-wu ts'o-tsung 參伍錯綜, "completely intermingled," IV.8.204.

san-tuan 散段, "unlinked sections," VII.11.329.

se 色, "sex," IV.19.211 (three), IV.23.213 (six), IV.26.217, VII.11.329 (two).

sha-chi 殺機, "trigger of destruction," VII.16.331.

shan-shan wu-e 善善惡惡, "clearly delineate good and evil," V.P.249.

shang pan-chieh 上半截, "first half," IV.83.239.

shang pan-pu 上半部, "first half," IV.6.203.

she-shang sheng-lien 舌上生蓮, "eloquent as a tongue sprouting lotuses,"
    V.23.3.275.

she-hsing ch'ü-ying 捨形取影, "let go the outward form in favor of the reflec-
    tion," VII.12.329.

she-tsu 蛇足, "superfluous," IV.29.219.

she-shen 攝神, "takes its spirit from," VII.10.327.

"*shen-kung kuei-fu chih pi*" 神工鬼斧之筆, "effects produced by supernatural
    skill," IV.48.230.

shen-li 神理, "essential truth," IV.44.225.

shen-ssu 神似, "capture the spirit of," V.6.1.260.

shen-pi 深筆, "profound strokes," IV.46.226.

sheng 省, "narrative frugality," VII.26.335.

sheng-ch'üeh 省却, "to save," III.19.188.

"*sheng-hsiao chia ku, ch'in-se chien chung chih miao*" 笙簫夾鼓, 琴瑟間鐘
    之妙, "the technique of interrupting drums with woodwinds and inter-
    spersing strings among the bells," id.93, 110, III.16.181.

Shih-chi pi-fa 史記筆法, "literary technique of the *Shih-chi*," V.2.6.255.

Shih-kung wen-tzu 史公文字, "a work by the Grand Historian [Ssu-ma
    Ch'ien]," IV.53.232.

shih-chiao 失教, "failure to instruct," VII.6.326.

shih-li 勢利, "power and status," V.17.2.269, V.22.3.273.

shih yen-chüan 試掩卷, "try closing the book," id.81, V.4.4.258.

shih 實, "real," id.104, V.24.1.275.

shih-hsieh 實寫, "describe directly," III.19.187; "describe in full," IV.18.209.

shih-hsü 實叙, "faithfully relate," III.24.194.

"*shou-hsien shih-mang ch'u*" 手閑事忙處, "handle proliferation of events with
    ease," IV.67.234.

shou-shu ch'u 收束處, "conclusion," VI.12.303.

shou-wei 首尾, "head and tail," id.96; "beginning and end," III.21.191, 192
    (two).

shou-wei hsiang-ying 首尾相應, "interconnected from start to finish,"
    VII.25.335.

shu-niu 樞紐, "pivot," IV.48.229.

shuang-kuan 雙關, "double-edged," VI.21.308.

shuang-kuan ch'i-hsia 雙管齊下, "cuts both ways," V.10.2.265.

shun-pi 順筆, "straightforward techniques," IV.13.206.

ssu ta ch'i-shu 四大奇書, "four great marvelous books," Id.84n, V.P.249.

ssu-pan 死板, "mechanically," IV.37.224.

sun 榫, 筍, or 笋, "dovetail, mortise and tenon," Id.94, IV.8.204; "connections," IV.26.218.

ta chao-ying 大照應, "significant correlation," III.21.191, 192 (three).

ta chieh-shu 大結束, "denouement," IV.26.217; "grand finale," IV.26.218; "grand unifying episode," V.33.3.282, V.37.3.286.

ta chien-chia ch'u 大間架處, "significant features of the spatial setting," IV.12.205.

ta-kang 大綱, "the plot," IV.16.208.

ta kuan-so ch'u 大關鎖處, "passages that serve to link them significantly together," III.21.191.

ta lo-mo fa 大落墨法, "detailed and extended narration," II.54.141.

ta-wen 大文, "major passage," III.13.179.

t'a-t'o 沓拖, "diffuseness," III.18.186.

t'a-wei fa 獺尾法, " the otter's tail," Id.92, II.58.142.

tai-pi 呆筆, "dull-witted strokes," IV.46.226.

tai-ch'u 帶出, "bring out," V.4.3.257, V.18.2.270.

"T'ai-shih kung pi-fa" 太史公筆法, "technique of Ssu-ma Ch'ien," IV.48.229.

tan-ch'üan 單圈, "single circle," VII.28.340.

tan-hsieh 單寫, "concentrate on," IV.16.209.

tan-tien 單點, "single dots," VII.28.340.

tang-yang 蕩漾, "reecho," III.14.180.

tao-ch'a fa 倒插法, "advance insertion," Id.91, 98, II.51.140.

tao-she 倒攝, "reflect forward," V.52.5.293.

t'e-fan 特犯, "purposeful duplication," IV.22.213.

t'e-t'e fan-shou 特特犯手, "purposefully duplicates," IV.45.226.

ti-yü pien-hsiang 地獄變相, "hellish transformations," V.1.2.252, V.49.2.292.

t'i-kang 題綱, "titular couplet," VI.10.302–3 (three).

t'i-mu 題目, "topic," II.1.131, II.4.132 (two), II.5.132 (two), II.6.132, II.20.135, II.59.143.

t'i 體, "substance," VI.31.311 (three), VI.35.312, VI.37.313 (two).

t'iao-kan 條幹, "framework," IV.8.204.

tien-chui 點綴, "fill out," Id.112, V.36.2.285.

tien-jan 點染, "only hinted at," IV.51.231.

tien-tou 點逗, "broach," V.1.2.252; "hint," V.24.1.275.

tien-yüeh 點閱, "punctuation and commentary," II.66.145.

t'ien-kung 天工, "creative powers of Heaven," IV.5.203; "handiwork of Heaven," IV.106.242; "nature's secrets," V.46.3.290.

t'ien-li 天理, "principles of Heaven," IV.103.242.

t'ien-tao 天道, "way of Heaven," IV.63.233.

t'ien-tao hsün-huan 天道循環, "divine retribution," V.P.249.

"t'ien-ssu pu-chin, i-chen yün-hsiu chih miao" 添絲補錦, 移針勻綉之妙, "the technique of inserting additional threads to fill out the figure and adjusting the needlework to balance the pattern," 1d.93, 99, III.18.185.

t'o-hsieh ch'u 脫卸處, "where a particular narrative line is sloughed off," 1d.92, IV.65.233 (two).

t'o-lo 脫落, "unconnected," IV.26.217.

t'o-t'ai 脫胎, "grows out of," VII.10.327, 327n.

tou-fang ming-shih 斗方名士, "superficial literary men," V.8.2.264; "pretenders to scholarly refinement and elegance," V.17.1.269, V.17.2.270 (two), V.18.4.271.

t'ou 透, "divulge," IV.49.230.

t'ou-hsü 頭緒, "narrative thread," IV.13.206 (two), VII.26.337; "connecting threads," IV.48.229.

ts'ai-tzu 才子, "genius," IV.60.233, IV.75.235.

ts'ai-tzu [chih] shu 才子[之]書, "works of genius," 1d.83, 84n–85n, III.25.195, VI.3.299.

ts'ai 財, "money," IV.19.211 (two), IV.23.213 (seven), IV.26.217, VII.11.329 (two).

ts'ai-chien 裁剪, "tailoring," IV.39.224.

ts'ao-she hui-hsien 草蛇灰線, "snake in the grass or discontinuous chalk line," 1d.95, 99n, II.53.140–41, IV.26.218.

ts'e-pi 側筆, "oblique techniques," V.11.1.266.

ts'en-tz'u chih ch'u 參差之處, "incongruities," IV.37.223.

ts'eng-che 層折, "periodic configurations," III.4.162.

tso-tui 作對, "juxtaposed as parallels," IV.9.204.

tso-tso 做作, "affected," V.35.1.284–85 (three).

ts'o-tsung 錯綜, "rich narrative texture," 1d.105, III.12.178.

tsu 足, "fill in previous material," IV.49.230.

tsung-ch'i 總起, "initial beginning," III.6.164.

tsung-chieh 總結, "final conclusion," III.6.164; "summary," VI.12.303.

tu-chuan 獨傳, "individual biography," IV.34.221.

tuan 段, "section," V.7.1.262 (two), V.7.2.262, V.7.3.263, VII.13.330 (four), VII.14.330 (three); "stages," V.26.2.278.

tuan-lo 段落, "structural division," VII.14.330.

tuan-hsü 斷續, "interrupted or resumed," III.6.165.

tuan-tuan hsü-hsü 斷斷續續, "discontinuous," IV.34.221.

tui 對, "parallel or paired episodes," IV.9.204 (two).

tui-chao 對照, "sharp contrast," 1d.100, V.48.3.291.

tui-k'an 對看, "compare," V.10.1.265.

tun-pi 鈍筆, "dull strokes," IV.46.226.

"*t'ung-shu i-chih, t'ung-chih i-yeh, t'ung-yeh i-hua, t'ung-hua i-kuo chih miao*" 同樹異枝, 同枝異葉, 同葉異花, 同花異果之妙, "the technique of portraying different branches growing on the same tree, different leaves stemming from the same branch, different flowers blooming on the same leaf, and different fruits developing from the same flower," III.10.170.

t'ung-shen chin-chieh 通身筋節, "tendons and sinews that articulate the entire
    body," v.6.7.262, v.47.4.291.
tzu-fa 字法, "organization of each word," II.18.135.
tzu wei tui 自為對, "parallel each other," III.20.188, 189 (two).
wei-fa 未發, "not yet arisen," VII.15.330.
wei-tz'u 微辭, "subtle satire," v.3.2.255.
"*wen-chia chih fa-lü*" 文家之法律, "rules of literary composition," IV.82.238.
wen-fa 文法, "literary style," IV.82.236.
wen-pi 文筆, "cultured strokes," IV.46.226.
wu-pi ch'u 無筆處, "between the lines of the text," IV.23.215.
"*wu t'ou-hsü chih pi*" 無頭緒之筆, "no connecting threads to what went
    before," IV.48.229.
wu-t'ou wu-hsü 無頭無緒, "without tying into," IV.26.217.
wu-wei 無謂, "irrelevant," IV.15.207, 208 (two).
yang-tzu 樣子, "cautionary example," IV.20.212.
yao-tui 遙對, "parallel each other at a distance," IV.9.204.
yao [hsiang] wei tui 遙[相]為對, "parallel each other at a distance," III.20.188,
    191 (two).
yao-yao hsieh-lai 遙遙寫來, "go to such pains [to depict over a long distance],"
    IV.15.208.
yeh-shih 野史, "informal history," v.P.249.
yen-liang 炎涼, "theme of 'hot and cold,'" IV.17.209; "social status," IV.17.209.
yen-liang fan-an 炎涼翻案, "reversal of fortunes," IV.51.231.
yen 衍, "supplemented," III.14.180.
yen-chüan hsi-ssu 掩卷細思, "close the book and [carefully] think," v.26.4.278.
yen-ying 掩映, "set off," v.2.5.254.
"*yen-chung erh-chung t'ing-lai*" 眼中耳中聽來, "through the ears and eyes
    of," III.19.187.
yen-i 演義, "novel," III.21.192.
yen-yang 演漾, "gradual tapering off," II.58.143.
yin 引, "lead into," VI.24.309 (five).
yin-ch'i 引起, "call up," v.13.1.268.
yin-ch'u 引出, "introduce," v.49.1.291.
yin-wen sheng-shih 因文生事, "events are produced from the words," II.10.133.
yin 隱, "unobtrusively," IV.27.218.
"*yin-e yang-shan chih pi*" 隱惡揚善之筆, "principle of only speaking well of
    others without dwelling on their faults," IV.36.222.
yin-k'uo 隱括, "allude," v.40.2.288; "subtly wrap up," VII.20.333.
yin-pi 隱筆, "describe in a subtle way," IV.24.215.
ying-tai 映帶, "enhance," III.14.180.
ying-ch'u 影處, "the reflected side," VII.12.329.
ying-hsieh 影寫, "only hint at," IV.51.231; "alludes," IV.107.243.
ying-tzu 影子, "shadows," id.98, 108, v.1.6.253, VII.16.331; "device to
    convey indirectly," IV.47.227.
"*yu ch'eng-chou tsai hsiung*" 有成軸在胸, "had the complete pattern in his
    mind," v.27.4.279.

yu ch'ien yu hou 有前有後, "differences in temporal sequence," v.26.2.278.

yu hsiang yu lüeh 有詳有略, "differences in depth of detail," v.26.2.278.

yu hsien-hou 有先後, "has proper sequence," v.6.1.260.

yu kung shih-tao 有功世道, "has merit for the promotion of morality in the world," v.27.4.279.

"yu kung yü shih-tao jen-hsin" 有功于世道人心, "benefiting the morality of the world and its people," v.39.3.287.

yu tz'u-ti 有次第, "has proper order," v.6.1.260.

yü to 予奪, "accord and deny [legitimacy]," III.1.153; "praise and blame," VII.2.325.

yü-i 寓意, "axe to grind," IV.36.222; "allegorical meaning," VII.20.333.

yü-yen 寓言, "allegorical purpose," IV.88.240.

"yü-ho ku-tsung fa" 欲合故縱法, "introducing new twists into the narrative just as you are about to bring it to a close," II.63.144.

"yü shih-chen erh hsien p'i-chia chih fa" 欲示真而先劈假之法, "the method of first striking down the false when one wants to show the true," VI.25.309.

yü-i 喻意, "implied meaning," v.11.1.266.

yü-po 餘波, "after-ripples," 1d.98, II.58.142.

yü-shih 餘勢, "postlude," III.14.180.

yü-wen 餘文, "leftovers," v.49.1.291.

yüan-ku 緣故, "reason," II.26.137 (three).

yün-pi 韻筆, "appealing strokes," IV.46.226.

yung 用, "function," VI.31.311 (three), VI.32.311 (five), VI.35.312, VI.37.313 (two).

APPENDIX 2

The Authenticity of the Li Chih Commentaries on the *Shui-hu chuan* and Other Novels Treated in This Volume

That Li Chih 李贄 (1527–1602) wrote a commentary on a printed edition of the *Shui-hu chuan* 水滸傳 (The Water Margin) and that he had a manuscript copy made of the text and commentary seem beyond question. Li Chih requested a copy of the novel around 1589 and, in all likelihood, received it not long after, and it was this text that he used for his commentary.[1] According to his preface to the novel published in the collection of his writings, *Fen-shu* 焚書 (Book for Burning; first printing, 1590), it would seem certain that he was working with a hundred-chapter version such as the T'ien-tu wai-ch'en 天都外臣 preface edition (preface dated 1589), or earlier editions commonly associated with Kuo Hsün 郭勛 (1475–1542). When the 120-chapter Yüan Wu-yai 袁無涯 edition appeared in 1612 or slightly earlier, the editors changed one section of the Li Chih preface so that it would accord with the new, longer version of the novel. In a note written in 1614 Yüan Chung-tao 袁中道 (1570–1624), in his *Yu-chü Fei lu* 游居杮錄 (Travels in the Fei Region), recorded that in 1592 he saw one of Li Chih's disciples engaged in making a fair copy of the novel and Li Chih's commentary at the latter's request.[2] In a letter published posthumously in *Hsü Fen-shu* 續焚書 (Book for Burning, Continued; first published 1618), Li Chih specifically mentions that he enjoyed doing the commentary on the *Shui-hu chuan*.[3]

The first datable commentary on the *Shui-hu chuan* claiming to be by Li Chih is the reprint of the Jung-yü t'ang edition published in 1610 in Hangchou. In Ch'ien Hsi-yen's 錢希言 (fl. 1596–1622) *Hsi-hsia* 戲瑕 (preface 1613), the author claims that the "Li Chih" commentaries on the *Shui-hu chuan*, *San-kuo yen-i* 三國演義 (The Romance of the Three Kingdoms), *Hsi-yu chi* 西遊記 (The Journey to the West), and various dramatic works are not by Li Chih but are the work of Yeh Chou 葉畫

---

[1] See "Fu Chiao Jo-hou" 復焦弱侯 (Reply to Chiao Hung 焦竑, 1541–1620), *Fen-shu* 焚書 (Book for Burning; Peking: Chung-hua shu-chü, 1961), "Tseng-pu erh" 增補二 (Supplement 2), p. 275. This letter is copied from an edition of Li Chih's collected works, *Li Wen-ling chi* 李溫陵集, *chüan* 4.

[2] Although some of the material offered up by Yüan Chung-tao on the Li Chih commentary requires interpretation and should be used with care, that he saw the disciple making this copy seems beyond doubt. See the quotation of this material in *SHCTLHP*, p. 223.

[3] "Yü Chiao Jo-hou" 與焦弱侯 (Letter to Chiao Hung), *Hsü Fen-shu* (Peking: Chung-hua shu-chü, 1959), pp. 34–35, also quoted in *SHCTLHP*, p. 191.

(courtesy name Wen-t'ung 文通, fl. 1595–1624), a native of Wu-hsi in what is now Kiangsu Province.[4] Besides the *Shui-hu chuan* commentary, the Jung-yü t'ang also produced five plays with "Li Chih" commentaries, all in similar format. These five plays, plus a sixth, are discussed briefly by Li Chih in essays published in the *Fen-shu*,[5] but aside from two of them, the *Hsi-hsiang chi* 西廂記 (Romance of the Western Chamber) and the *P'i-p'a chi* 琵琶記 (Story of the Lute), there exists no evidence that Li Chih ever wrote anything more than these short remarks for them. In his comments to his collated edition of the *Hsi-hsiang chi*, Wang Chi-te 王驥德 (d. 1623) labels these dramatic commentaries as forgeries and suggests that the publisher merely took advantage of the existence of these short pieces to link Li Chih's name to the commentaries.[6] The Jung-yü t'ang "Li Chih" commentaries, whether for the *Shui-hu chuan* or the dramatic works, are all written in a similar style (characterized by frequent acerbic remarks directed at the text, a lighthearted attitude in general, and a preference for marking sections of the texts for excision) and would seem to be from the same hand.

As for the commentaries attributed to Li Chih for the other five novels treated in this volume, those for the *Hsi-yu chi* and the 120-chapter version of the *San-kuo yen-i* have some similarities with the Jung-yü t'ang commentaries as described above. Furthermore, in the 120-chapter *San-kuo yen-i* commentary, Yeh Chou's name is mentioned prominently in three of the postchapter comments (chapters 96, 105, and 112), and in the last instance his name is put at the head of the comments in the same way that Li Chih's name or nickname is used to preface the chapter comments in the other commentaries. A similar joke at the expense of the text is used in both the Jung-yü t'ang *Shui-hu chuan* commentary (chapter comment for chapter 88) and in the 120-chapter *San-kuo yen-i* "Li Chih" commentary (chapter comment for chapter 112). The exact dates for the publication of the *San-kuo yen-i* and *Hsi-yu chi* "Li Chih" commentaries are unknown but, in the case of the one for the *Hsi-yu chi*, a reprint of the commentary appeared in 1631. This reprint edition described the commentary as being "after the fashion"

---

[4] Quoted in *SHCTLHP*, pp. 150–51.

[5] *Fen-shu*, "Tsa-shuo" 雜說 (Miscellaneous Remarks), *chüan* 3, pp. 96–97 (*Hsi-hsiang chi*, *P'i-p'a chi*); and *chüan* 4, pp. 194–96 (*Yü-ho* 玉合, *K'un-lun nu* 崑崙奴, *Pai-yüeh* 拜月, and *Hung-fu* 紅拂).

[6] Quoted in *Wang Chi-te Ch'ü-lü* 王驥德曲律 (Wang Chi-te's Rules of Dramatic Prosody), Ch'en To 陳多 and Yeh Ch'ang-hai 葉長海, eds. (Ch'ang-sha: Hu-nan jen-min, 1983), p. 350. Only the edition of the *Pai-yüeh t'ing* 拜月亭 (Pavilion for Praying to the Moon) reprints the appropriate section in the *Fen-shu* and labels it a preface.

(*fang* 仿) of the Li Chih commentaries. As is the case with the three plays mentioned above, there is no evidence in Li Chih's writings or in those of his personal acquaintances that he ever wrote any commentary for either of these two novels.

There are other reasons to be suspicious of the Jung-yü t'ang edition of the *Shui-hu chuan*. The "Shu-yü" 述語 of that edition signed Huai-lin 懷林 (the name of a monk friend of Li Chih who died in 1598 or 1599) is written in a tone that suggests that Li Chih was already dead at the time, but it was actually Li Chih who outlived Huai-lin. Also, "Huai-lin" claims that Li Chih read and commented on the novel for thirty years after he first moved to Lung-hu 龍湖 (near Ma-ch'eng, Hupei Province). That figure is entirely too long, and some scholars have suggested that the two integers must have been accidentally inverted (*san-shih* 三十 "thirty," instead of *shih-san* 十三 "thirteen"), but for a writer to use such a concrete number instead of something like "ten-plus" years seems to contradict general practice. The "Shu-yü" also mentions two works (neither now extant) that were supposedly compiled by Li Chih. One is *Ch'ing-feng shih* 青風史 (History of Ch'ing-feng), centered on a character in the novel named Hua Jung, and the other is *Hei-hsüan-feng chi* 黑旋風集 (The Collected Works of Li K'uei). The latter is specifically mentioned by Ch'ien Hsi-yen in his *Hsi-hsia* as having been compiled by Yeh Chou.[7] Small print at the end of the "Shu-yü" says that both works are available through the publisher of the commentary.

So far we have been concerned primarily with the Jung-yü t'ang commentary on the *Shui-hu chuan*. As for the Yüan Wu-yai edition, we have already mentioned that it seems certain that Li Chih did his commentary on a 100-chapter version of the novel. Some scholars hold that the Yüan Wu-yai edition appeared too late for Ch'ien Hsi-yen to have had it in mind when he said that the Li Chih commentaries were by Yeh Chou, but *Hsi-hsia* mentions a 1612 work, the *Shu-chai man-lu* 樗齋漫錄 (Leisurely Notes from Useless Wood Studio), that describes the production of the Yüan Wu-yai edition. Thus, not only was the Yüan Wu-yai edition available before the completion of the *Hsi-hsia*, but Ch'ien Hsi-yen was also probably familiar with some of the details of its production.

The *Shu-chai man-lu* bears the name of the late Ming playwright, Hsü Tzu-ch'ang 許自昌 (fl. 1596–1623), as its author, but the *Hsi-hsia* claims that the work is actually by Yeh Chou. There are several modern scholars who allege that Yeh Chou wrote this work and then sold the right of

---

[7] *SHCTLHP*, p. 151. The "Collected Works of Li K'uei" is also mentioned in the last item of the "Fa-fan" 發凡 (General Remarks) of the Yüan Wu-yai edition, without attribution to Li Chih and without any discussion of its authenticity. The section of the "Fa-fan" is quoted in *SHCTLHP*, p. 149.

authorship to Hsü Tzu-ch'ang for financial gain,[8] which does fit in with
the picture given by his contemporaries of his reliance on his pen to earn
money to support his drinking habit, among other things. The exact
nature of the relationship between Yeh Chou and Hsü Tzu-ch'ang is not
very clear. One of Hsü Tzu-ch'ang's plays, *Chü-p'u chi* 橘浦記 (Tale of
the Orange Marsh), bears a prefatory piece (*t'i* 題) signed with the name
of Yeh Chou, and this, in fact, is the only signed piece of Yeh Chou's
writing extant today. In the *Shu-chai man-lu*, the author relates that he
took part, along with Yüan Wu-yai, Feng Meng-lung 馮夢龍 (1574–
1646), and some other Suchou literati, in the preparation and editing of
the Yüan-wu yai edition. The prefatory piece entitled "Fa-fan" 發凡 in
that edition claims that its rearrangement of the Yen P'o-hsi story follows that in an old edition, but it seems that in terms of fictional treatment, this innovation originates in the Yüan Wu-yai edition itself. The
first literary work to use this rearrangement is a play by Hsü Tzu-ch'ang
called *Shui-hu chi* 水滸記 (Tale of the Water Margin). The author of the
Shu-chai man-lu, whether Hsü Tzu-ch'ang or Yeh Chou, says that although he offered the use of some of his books for this new edition of the
Shui-hu chuan, he fell into disagreement with the editors and the section
in the *Shu-chai man-lu* that deals with this episode ends with harsh words
for both Li Chih and the editors.

The Yüan Wu-yai edition clearly postdates the Jung-yü t'ang edition. Both in the text and commentary there are indications that the
compilers of the later edition had the earlier one before them. Where the
Jung-yü t'ang edition marked passages for excision, the Yüan Wu-yai
edition often excises or changes the same passages. As for the commentary, there are several places where the Yüan Wu-yai edition comments
borrow from or constitute a reply to Jung-yü t'ang comments.

The fact that some of the Yüan Wu-yai edition comments refute

[8] Yeh Chou's name is mentioned five times (1/6b, 1/13a, 1/13a–b, 9/2a, and 10/1b) in
the *Shu-chai man-lu* and each time he is quoted making quips similar to those attributed to
him in the chapter comments of the 120-chapter "Li Chih" commentary on the *San-kuo
yen-i*. There are also a variety of figures only referred to by pseudonyms who are cut
from the same mold as Yeh Chou and may be indirect references to him. Interesting
enough in this context, there is also an expression of disgust over the growing trend of
publishing collections of examination essays with falsely attributed commentary and
made-up prefaces (*wei-p'ing yen-hsü* 偽評贗序), p. 1/1b. In the first passage in which Yeh
Chou's name appears, he makes a remark about Confucius also to be found in the
commentary in *Ssu-shu p'ing* 四書評 (Comments on the Four Books; Shanghai: Jen-min
wen-hsüeh, 1975), *Lun-yü* 論語 (The Confucian Analects), XVII.1, p. 145. The commentary in that work is attributed by the publisher to Li Chih, but it is among those
singled out by Sheng Yü-ssu 盛于斯 (1598–1639) as really from Yeh Chou's hand. See
SHCTLHP, p. 351.

comments in the Jung-yü t'ang edition has been used to argue that Yeh
Chou could not have been involved in the publication of both of the
major "Li Chih" commentaries. On the other hand, the Yüan Wu-yai
commentary does not appear to be the work of any one hand, as it
includes a variety of writing styles and attitudes. If the account in the
Shu-chai man-lu is correct and if that work is by Yeh Chou, then it would
appear that Yeh Chou did not necessarily take a major part in the
writing of the commentary itself. In the *Hsiu-an ying-yü* 休庵影語
(Shadowy Words from Hsiu-an), Sheng Yü-ssu 盛于斯 (1598–1639)
quotes Yeh Chou on the *Shui-hu chuan*. In that passage Yeh Chou clearly
has in mind an expanded version of the novel including the Wang
Ch'ing and T'ien Hu campaigns.[9] In the same work, Sheng Yü-ssu
attributes the "Li Chih" commentaries on the Four Books, the *Hsi-yu
chi*, and the *Shui-hu chuan* to Yeh Chou.[10] Sheng Yü-ssu was a contemporary of Yeh Chou and a native of the same part of China. Another
famous literatus of that age, Ch'en Chi-ju 陳繼儒 (1558–1639), asserted
that the Li Chih commentaries *from Suchou* (Yüan Wu-yai's center of
operation) were forgeries.[11]

The Yüan Wu-yai edition has a preface (*hsiao-yin* 小引) signed Yang
Ting-chien 楊定見 (the name of a disciple of Li Chih's). The author of
this preface mentions that, when he offered Li Chih's commentary to the
Shui-hu chuan to Yüan Wu-yai, at the same time he handed over a
commentary by Li Chih on the works of Yang Shen 楊慎 (1488–1559)
entitled *Yang Sheng-an chi* 楊升庵集 (Collected Works of Yang Shen). In
a letter to Fang Jen-an 方訒菴 written around 1596 and preserved in the
Hsü Fen-shu, Li Chih said that he had already completed five hundred
pages of a work called *Tu Sheng-an chi* 讀升庵集 (Reading the Collected
Works of Yang Shen).[12] The exact nature of the work is hard to figure
out from its brief mention there, and it is not now extant. There exists a
short essay entitled "Yang Sheng-an" in the *Fen-shu*,[13] known as "Yang
Sheng-an chi" in an alternate collection of Li Chih's literary works, *Li*

---

[9] Quoted in *SHCTLHP*, pp. 350–51. Some of the comments in the Yüan Wu-yai
edition seem to fit in fairly well with Yeh Chou's interpretation of the novel as presented
by Sheng Yü-ssu. See a comment in chap. 89 on the tribute arrangement between the
Chinese and the foreign Liao dynasty and a comment in chap. 95 on the battle of 1274,
SHCHPP, pp. 89.1375 and 95.1383.

[10] Quoted, *SHCTLHP*, pp. 350–51.

[11] Quoted, *SHCTLHP*, p. 225. Another reason for suspecting the legitimacy of the
Yüan Wu-yai commentary is the fact that the chapter comment for chap. 3 quotes a
remark made by Ch'en Chi-ju after Li Chih's death.

[12] *Hsü Fen-shu*, chüan 1, pp. 7–9.

[13] *Fen-shu*, chüan 5, pp. 208–9.

Wen-ling chi 李溫陵集,[14] that has been thought to be the preface for this work. Since in both collections it is included in the section devoted to comments on history (*tu-shih* 讀史), and not with the other prefaces, this does not seem very likely. Is the title given in the Yang Ting-chien preface a mistake for *Tu Sheng-an chi*, or did he get his title from the *Li Wen-ling chi*? The comments on *Tu Sheng-an chi* in the *Ssu-k'u ch'üan-shu tsung-mu t'i-yao* 四庫全書總目提要 (Annotated Catalogue of the Imperial Library; Chi Yün 紀昀 [1724–1805] et al., eds.), are adamant in regarding that book as a forgery produced for profit.[15]

On the whole question of Yüan Wu-yai's ethical and professional standards as a book publisher, scholarly opinion is divided. Those who support him point to Yüan Chung-tao's testimony that the commentary in the Yüan Wu-yai edition of the *Shui-hu chuan* was substantially the same, with some additions, to what he had seen earlier at Li Chih's residence in 1592,[16] and a section of a letter from him to Yüan Wu-yai reads:

> Recently there are many falsely attributed books on the market, such as *K'uang-yen* 狂言 [Wild Words] and the like. This is a great evil and I deeply regret that I have not been able to do anything to rectify it. Books have also been falsely attributed to Li Chih, and this also is a crime. I should come to Suchou and together with you put a stop to this.
>
> 近日書坊贗刻如狂言等, 大是惡道, 恨未能訂正之. 李老龍湖書亦被人假托攙入, 可恨可恨. 比當至吳中與兄一料理之.[17]

[14] Taipei: Kuang-wen shu-chü, 1971 reprint of Wan-li period (1573–1620) edition, p. 16/17b–19a.

[15] See *chüan* 131, p. 69 of the Commercial Press edition (Shanghai, 1933). Part of the reasoning given there, that Li Chih and Yang Shen were unlikely bedfellows because of their different philosophical orientations, could not be more misguided. Part of the comment reads: "Their paths were different, and it does not necessarily stand to reason that he [Li Chih] would make such a compilation. The writing in the preface is very crude and very unlike Li Chih's work. The Wan-li period was the time when Li Chih's fame was at its peak, so this book was probably produced by commercial printers who borrowed his name in hopes of making a profit." 道不相同, 亦未必為之編輯. 序文淺陋, 尤不類贅筆, 殆萬曆間贅名正盛之時, 坊人假以射利者耳. I have been unable to find any bibliographic reference to the holding by any library of a copy of Yang Shen's works with commentary by Li Chih, although one scholar has made reference to such an edition with commentary by Chiao Hung as well. There is a work, *Sheng-an wai-chi* 升庵外集 (Supplement to the Collected Works of Yang Shen; Taipei: Hsüeh-sheng shu-chü, 1971 reprint) that was edited by Chiao Hung.

[16] See his *Yu-chü Fei lu*, quoted in *SHCTLHP*, pp. 223–24.

[17] "Ta Yüan Wu-yai" 答袁無涯 (Reply to Yüan Wu-yai), in *K'o-hsüeh chai ch'ien-chi* 珂雪齋前集 (First Collection of Yüan Chung-tao's Works; Taipei: Wei-wen t'u-shu, 1976 reprint, author's preface 1618), pp. 23/35a–b. The first part of this letter complains about a misprint made by Yüan Wu-yai in a printing of one of Yüan Hung-tao's poems and requests that it be corrected.

This is all very well until one finds out that one of the publishers of *K'uang-yen* (a short work attributed to Yüan Hung-tao [1568–1610], elder brother of Yüan Chung-tao), around 1610, was Yüan Wu-yai himself.[18] *K'uang-yen* is also singled out as a forgery by Ch'ien Hsi-yen.[19]

To summarize what we have discussed so far, there are serious problems with the provenance of both the Jung-yü t'ang and Yüan Wu-yai "Li Chih" commentaries to the *Shui-hu chuan*. That does not preclude the idea that some of the material was originally written by Li Chih; however, it is extremely unlikely that either is a faithful representation of his commentary on that novel.

Besides the two editions of the *Shui-hu chuan* discussed above, there also exists a third type of "Li Chih" commentary on the novel that has perhaps as good a case for authenticity but which is much less well known. The only extant complete copy of this edition is held in the Mukyūkai 無窮會 Library in Japan, and there is a Japanese reprint of the first twenty chapters of the novel whose text and "Li Chih" commentary are supposed to be derived from that edition. Information available on the nature of the commentary in the Mukyūkai copy is very inadequate, but examination of the Japanese reprint reveals a sparse and sketchy style of commentary similar to Li Chih's commentary to the *Shih-shuo hsin-yü pu* 世說新語補 (Supplement to a New Account of Tales of the World). This material has been neglected in the past, and it is to be hoped that future research will turn up evidence for or against its claim to authenticity.[20]

---

[18] See Tu Hsin-fu 杜信孚, *Ming-tai pan-k'o tsung-lu* 明代版刻總錄 (Complete Record of Ming Dynasty Printed Books; Yangchou: Chiang-su Kuang-ling ku-chi k'o-yin she, 1983), pp. 4/25b–26a (item number 10/399 in the code used in this work). It should also be pointed out, however, that according to the general principles ("Fan-li" 凡例) to a modern collation of the collected works of Yüan Hung-tao, *Yüan Hung-tao chi chien-chiao* 袁宏道集箋校, Ch'ien Po-ch'eng 錢伯城, ed. (Shanghai: Shang-hai ku-chi, 1981), p. 1, the Yüan Wu-yai edition does not contain *K'uang-yen*. On the other hand, the Yüan Wu-yai edition was brought out in installments over several years, and the total number of fascicles cited by Ch'ien Po-ch'eng is much less than that given by Tu Hsin-fu. In other writings Yüan Chung-tao never accused the Yüan Wu-yai edition of containing forgeries. In the 1619 preface to an edition of his brother's literary works, he described the Yüan Wu-yai edition as well done but incomplete (*ching erh pu pei* 精而不備) and complains that recent printings are numerous and contain the *K'uang-yen* and other forged works (quoted in *Yüan Hung-tao chi chien-chiao*, p. 1711). Also, the name of one of the collections of his brother's works containing *K'uang-yen* is mentioned in a letter by Yüan Chung-tao, and it is not the Yüan Wu-yai edition (quoted in *Yüan Hung-tao chi chien-chiao*, pp. 1670–71).

[19] See *SHCTLHP*, p. 151.

[20] For a summary of recent scholarly opinion on the problem of the "Li Chih"

An enormous number of editions of various novels advertise Li Chih's name as commentator on the title page. Some of these editions, such as a San-yü t'ang 三餘堂 edition of the *San-kuo yen-i*, contain no commentary of any kind. In this appendix, we have turned our attention only toward those attributions that have been championed in the past as authentic. The case for the various *Shui-hu chuan* editions is very complex and is further complicated by our imperfect knowledge of the chronology and filiation of the texts of the various extant editions of that novel. A truly complete variorum edition of the texts of and commentaries on the *Shui-hu chuan* would facilitate our research greatly.

---

commentaries, see Andrew H. Plaks, *The Four Masterworks of the Ming Novel* (Princeton: Princeton University Press, 1987), "Appendix: The 'Li Cho-wu' Commentary Editions," pp. 513–17.

APPENDIX 3

Conversion Table from Wade–Giles to *Pinyin* Romanizaton of Chinese

INITIALS

Wade-Giles	Pinyin	Wade-Giles	Pinyin
ch- (-i, -ü)	j-	p-	b-
ch- (all other)	zh-	p'-	p-
ch'- (-i, ü)	q-	ss-	s-
ch'- (all other)	ch-	t-	d-
hs-	x-	t'-	t-
i	yi	ts-	z-
j-	r-	ts'-	c-
k-	g-	tz-	z-
k'-	k-	tz'-	c-

MEDIALS AND FINALS

Wade-Giles	Pinyin	Wade-Giles	Pinyin
-eh (with y-)	-e (*ye*)	-u (ss-, tz-, tz'-	-i
-en (with y-)	-an (*yan*)	-u (with y-)	-ou (*you*)
erh	er	-uei	-ui
-ieh	-ie	-ung	-ong
-ien	-ian	-ü (n-, l-)	-ü
-ih	-i	-ü (all other)	-u
-iung	-iong	-üan	-uan
-o (l-, k-, k'-, h-)	-e	-üeh	-ue
-o (all other)	-uo	-ün	-un

BIBLIOGRAPHICAL
MATERIAL

Contents of Bibliographical Material

List of Journals and Anthologies Cited More than Once in the Bibliographies

Below is a list of journals and anthologies cited more than once in the bibliographies. In the case of Chinese and Japanese publications the list provides Chinese and Japanese characters to supplement the romanized titles used in the entries. Publication information for anthologies of articles is also given, provided that the collection is cited more than once. Publication information for periodicals published on a regular, fixed basis is not given.

Ch'ang-liu 暢流.
Che-chiang hsüeh-k'an 浙江學刊.
Cheng-chou ta-hsüeh hsüeh-pao 鄭州大學學報.
Cheng-ming 爭鳴.
Chi-lin ta-hsüeh hsüeh-pao 吉林大學學報.
Chi-lin ta-hsüeh she-hui k'o-hsüeh hsüeh-pao 吉林大學社會科學學報.
Chi-nan hsüeh-pao 暨南學報.
Chi-ning shih-chuan hsüeh-pao 濟寧師專學報.
Ch'i-ch'i ha-erh shih-fan hsüeh-yüan hsüeh-pao 齊齊哈爾師範學院學報.
Ch'i Lu hsüeh-k'an 齊魯學刊.
Chiang Hai hsüeh-k'an 江海學刊.
Chiang Han lun-t'an 江漢論壇.
Chiang-hsi ta-hsüeh hsüeh-pao 江西大學學報.
Chin-hsi t'an 今昔談.
Chin P'ing Mei ch'eng-shu yü pan-pen yen-chiu 金瓶梅成書與版本研究, by Liu Hui 劉輝 (Shenyang: Liao-ning jen-ming, 1986).
Chin P'ing Mei lun-chi 金瓶梅論集, Hsü Shuo-fang 徐朔方 and Liu Hui 劉輝, eds. (Peking: Jen-min wen-hsüeh, 1986).
Chin Sheng-t'an tzu-liao chi 金聖歎資料集 (Hong Kong: The Sinological Bibliocenter, 1983).
Chinese Narrative: Critical and Theoretical Essays, Andrew H. Plaks, ed. (Princeton: Princeton University Press, 1977).
Ch'iu-shih hsüeh-k'an 求是學刊.
Ch'iu-so 求索.
Ch'ung-ch'ing shih-yüan hsüeh-pao 重慶師院學報.
Chung-chou hsüeh-k'an 中州學刊.
Chung-hua wen-shih lun-ts'ung 中華文史論叢 (Shanghai: Shang-hai ku-chi).
Chung-kuo hsi-ch'ü shih t'an-wei 中國戲曲史探微, by Chiang Hsing-yü 蔣星煜 (Tsinan: Ch'i Lu shu-she, 1985).
Chung-kuo ku-tai hsiao-shuo li-lun yen-chiu 中國古代小說理論研究 (Wuhan: Hua-chung kung-hsüeh yüan, 1985).

Chung-kuo ku-tien hsiao-shuo i-shu ti ssu-k'ao 中國古典小說藝術的思考, by Hu
    Pang-wei 胡邦煒 and Wu Hung 吳紅 (Ch'ung-ch'ing: Ch'ung-ch'ing
    ch'u-pan she, 1986).

Chung-kuo ku-tien hsiao-shuo yen-chiu chuan-chi 中國古典小說研究專集 (Taipei:
    Lien-ching ch'u-pan she).

Chung-kuo ku-tien wen-hsüeh lun-ts'ung 中國古典文學論叢 (Peking: Jen-min
    wen-hsüeh).

Chung-kuo wen-hsüeh lun-chi 中國文學論集, by Cheng Chen-to 鄭振鐸 (Shang-
    hai: K'ai-ming shu-tien, 1934).

Chung-kuo wen-i ssu-hsiang shih lun-ts'ung 中國文藝思想史論叢 (Peking: Pei-
    ching ta-hsüeh).

Chung-nan min-tsu hsüeh-yüan hsüeh-pao 中南民族學院學報.

Chung-wai wen-hsüeh 中外文學.

Chung-yang jih-pao 中央日報.

Fu-chien shih-ta hsüeh-pao 福建師大學報.

Fu-tan hsüeh-pao 復旦學報.

Fu-yang shih-fan hsüeh-yüan hsüeh-pao 阜陽師範學院學報.

Ha-erh-pin shih-yüan hsüeh-pao 哈爾濱師院學報.

Hai-nan shih-chuan hsüeh-pao 海南師專學報.

Hai-wai Hung-hsüeh lun-chi 海外紅學論集, Hu Wen-pin 胡文彬 and Chou Lei
    周雷, eds. (Shanghai: Shang-hai ku-chi, 1982).

Hang-chou shih-yüan hsüeh-pao 杭州師院學報.

Hang-chou ta-hsüeh hsüeh-pao 杭州大學學報.

Hiroshima daigaku bungakubu kiyō 広島大学文学部紀要.

Hsi-chü i-shu 戲劇藝術.

Hsi-ch'ü yen-chiu 戲曲研究, reprint series (Peking: Chinese People's University).

Hsi-ch'ü yen-chiu 戲曲研究 (Peking: Wen-hua i-shu).

Hsi-nan shih-fan hsüeh-yüan hsüeh-pao 西南師範學院學報.

Hsiao-kan shih-chuan hsüeh-pao 孝感師專學報.

Hsiao-shuo hsien-t'an ssu-chung 小說閑談四種, by A-ying 阿英 (Shanghai: Shang-
    hai ku-chi, 1985).

Hsieh-tso 寫作.

Hsin-chiang ta-hsüeh hsüeh-pao 新疆大學學報.

Hsin chien-she 新建設.

Hsin-min pao wan-k'an 新民報晚刊.

Hsin-min wan-pao 新民晚報.

Hsü-chou shih-fan hsüeh-yüan hsüeh-pao 徐州師範學院學報.

Hsüeh-lin man-lu 學林漫錄 (Peking: Chung-hua shu-chü).

Hsüeh-shu yen-chiu 學術研究.

Hsüeh-shu yüeh-k'an 學術月刊.

Hu-nan chiao-yü hsüeh-yüan hsüeh-pao 湖南教育學院學報.

Hu-nan chiao-yü hsüeh-yüan yüan-k'an 湖南教育學院院刊.

Hua-chung shih-fan hsüeh-yüan hsüeh-pao 華中師範學院學報.

Hua-chung shih-fan hsüeh-yüan yen-chiu sheng hsüeh-pao 華中師範學院研究
    生學報.

Hua-chung shih-yüan hsüeh-pao 華中師院學報.

Hua-nan shih-fan ta-hsüeh hsüeh-pao 華南師範大學學報.

Hua-tung shih-fan ta-hsüeh hsüeh-pao 華東師範大學學報.

Huai-pei mei-shih-yüan hsüeh-pao 淮北煤師院學報.

Hung-hsüeh san-shih nien lun-wen hsüan-pien 紅學三十年論文選編, 3 vols. (Tientsin: Pai-hua wen-i, 1983-84).

Hung-hsüeh shih-chieh 紅學世界, Hu Wen-pin 胡文彬 and Chou Lei 周雷, eds. (Peking: Pei-ching ch'u-pan she, 1984).

Hung-hsüeh ts'ung-t'an 紅學叢譚, Hu Wen-pin 胡文彬 and Chou Lei 周雷, eds. (T'ai-yüan: Shan-hsi jen-min, 1983).

Hung-hsüeh wen-ts'ung 紅學文叢, see *Wo tu Hung-lou meng.*

Hung-lou meng hsin-cheng 紅樓夢新證, by Chou Ju-ch'ang 周汝昌 (Peking: Jen-min wen-hsüeh, revised edition, 1976).

Hung-lou meng hsin-lun 紅樓夢新論, by Liu Meng-hsi 劉夢溪 (Peking: Chung-kuo she-hui k'o-hsüeh, 1982).

Hung-lou meng hsüeh-k'an 紅樓夢學刊.

Hung-lou meng k'ao-lun chi 紅樓夢考論集, by P'i Shu-min 皮述民 (Taipei: Lien-ching ch'u-pan she, 1984).

Hung-lou meng pan-pen hsiao-k'ao 紅樓夢版本小考, by Wei Shao-ch'ang 魏紹昌 (Peking: Chung-kuo she-hui k'o-hsüeh, 1982).

Hung-lou meng pan-pen lun-ts'ung 紅樓夢版本論叢 (Nanking: Nan-ching shih-yüan, 1976).

Hung-lou meng t'an-so 紅樓夢探索, by Na Tsung-hsün 那宗訓 (Taipei: Hsin wen-feng, 1982).

Hung-lou meng t'an-yüan wai-pien 紅樓夢探源外編, by Wu Shih-ch'ang 吳世昌 (Shanghai: Shang-hai ku-chi, 1980).

Hung-lou meng ti hsiu-tz'u i-shu 紅樓夢的修辭藝術, by Lin Hsing-jen 林興仁 (Fu-chou: Fu-chien chiao-yü, 1984).

Hung-lou meng tzu-liao chi 紅樓夢資料集, 5 vols. (Hong Kong: The Sinological Bibliocenter, 1983).

Hung-lou meng yen-chiu 紅樓夢研究, reprint series (Peking: Chinese People's University).

Hung-lou meng yen-chiu chi-k'an 紅樓夢研究集刊 (Shanghai: Shang-hai ku-chi).

Hung-lou meng yen-chiu chuan-k'an 紅樓夢研究專刊 (Hong Kong: Chinese University of Hong Kong).

Hung-lou meng yen-chiu lun-ts'ung 紅樓夢研究論叢 (Ch'ang-ch'un: Chi-lin jen-min, 1981).

Hung-lou meng yen-chiu ts'an-k'ao tzu-liao hsüan-chi 紅樓夢研究參考資料選輯 (Peking: Jen-min wen-hsüeh, 1973-78).

Hung-lou meng yen-chiu tzu-liao 紅樓夢研究資料 (Peking: Pei-ching shih-ta, 1975).

Hung-lou meng yü Chin P'ing Mei 紅樓夢與金瓶梅, by Sun Hsün 孫遜 and Ch'en Chao 陳詔 (Yin-ch'uan: Ning-hsia jen-min, 1982).

I-t'an 藝譚.

Jen-chien shih 人間世.

Jen-wen tsa-chih 人文雜志.

Ju-lin wai-shih tzu-liao chi 儒林外史資料集, 2 vols. (Hong Kong: The Sinological Bibliocenter, 1983).

Kan-su shih-ta hsüeh-pao 甘肅師大學報.

Ku-tai wen-hsüeh li-lun yen-chiu 古代文學理論研究 (Shanghai: Shang-hai ku-chi).

Ku-tai wen-hsüeh li-lun yen-chiu lun-wen chi 古代文學理論研究論文集, by Wang Ta-chin 王達津 (Tientsin: Nan-k'ai ta-hsüeh, 1985).

Ku-tien hsiao-shuo hsi-ch'ü t'an-i lu 古典小說戲曲探藝錄 (Tientsin: T'ien-chin jen-min, 1982).

Ku-tien wen-hsüeh lun-ts'ung 古典文學論叢 (Tsinan: Ch'i Lu shu-she).

Kuang-ming jih-pao 光明日報.

Kuei-chou she-hui k'o-hsüeh 貴州社會科學.

Li-shih yen-chiu 歷史研究.

Lien-ho pao 聯合報.

Lun Chin P'ing Mei 論金瓶梅, Hu Wen-pin 胡文彬 and Chang Ch'ing-shan 張慶善, eds. (Peking: Wen-hua i-shu, 1984).

Mei-hsüeh wen-hsüeh lun-wen chi 美學文學論文集 (Peking: Pei-ching shih-yüan, 1986).

Meng-pien chi 夢邊集, by Feng Ch'i-yung 馮其庸 (Hsi-an: Shan-hsi jen-min, 1982).

Ming-Ch'ing hsiao-shuo lun-kao 明清小說論稿, by Sun Hsün 孫遜 (Shanghai: Shang-hai ku-chi, 1986).

Ming-Ch'ing hsiao-shuo lun-ts'ung 明清小說論叢 (Shenyang: Ch'un-feng wen-i).

Ming-Ch'ing hsiao-shuo t'an-yu 明清小說探幽, by Ts'ai Kuo-liang 蔡國梁 (Hang-chou: Che-chiang wen-i, 1985).

Ming-Ch'ing hsiao-shuo yen-chiu 明清小說研究 (Peking: Chung-kuo wen-lien).

Ming-k'an-pen Hsi-hsiang chi yen-chiu 明刊本西廂記研究, by Chiang Hsing-yü 蔣星煜 (Peking: Chung-kuo hsi-chü, 1982).

Ming-pao yüeh-k'an 明報月刊.

Nan-ching shih-yüan hsüeh-pao 南京師院學報.

Nan-ching ta-hsüeh hsüeh-pao 南京大學學報.

Nan-k'ai hsüeh-pao 南開學報.

Nan-k'ai ta-hsüeh hsüeh-pao 南開大學學報.

Nan-t'ung shih-chuan hsüeh-pao 南通師專學報.

Nan-yang ta-hsüeh hsüeh-pao 南洋大學學報.

Nei-meng-ku ta-hsüeh hsüeh-pao 內蒙古大學學報.

Nihon Chūgoku gakkai hō 日本中国学会報.

Pei-ching shih-fan ta-hsüeh hsüeh-pao 北京師範大學學報.

Pei-ching ta-hsüeh hsüeh-pao 北京大學學報.

Pei-fang lun-ts'ung 北方論叢.

P'u Sung-ling yen-chiu chi-k'an 蒲松齡研究集刊 (Tsinan: Ch'i Lu shu-she).

San-kuo yen-i hsüeh-k'an 三國演義學刊 (Ch'eng-tu: Ssu-ch'uan sheng she-hui k'o-hsüeh yüan).

San-kuo yen-i lun-wen chi 三國演義論文集 (Cheng-chou: Chung-chou ku-chi, 1985).

San-kuo yen-i tsung-heng t'an 三國演義縱橫談, by Ch'iu Chen-sheng 丘振聲 (Nan-ning: Li-chiang ch'u-pan she, 1983).

Shan-tung shih-ta hsüeh-pao 山東師大學報.

Shang-hai hsi-chü 上海戲劇.

Shang-hai shih-fan hsüeh-yüan hsüeh-pao 上海師範學院學報.

Shang-hai shih-yüan hsüeh-pao 上海師院學報.

She-hui k'o-hsüeh 社會科學.

She-hui k'o-hsüeh chan-hsien 社會科學戰綫.

She-hui k'o-hsüeh chi-k'an 社會科學輯刊.

She-hui k'o-hsüeh yen-chiu 社會科學研究.

Shinagaku kenkyū 支那学研究.

Shoshigaku 書誌学.

Shu-lin 書林.

Shu-mu chi-k'an 書目季刊.

Shu-p'ing shu-mu 書評書目.

Shui-hu cheng-ming 水滸爭鳴 (Wuhan: Ch'ang-chiang wen-i).

Shui-hu chuan lun-wen chi 水滸傳論文集, by Cheng Kung-tun 鄭公盾 (Yin-ch'uan: Ning-hsia jen-min, 1983).

Shui-hu hsin-i 水滸新議, by Ou-yang Chien 歐陽健 and Hsiao Hsiang-k'ai 蕭相愷 (Ch'ung-ch'ing: Ch'ung-ch'ing ch'u-pan she, 1983).

Shui-hu yen-chiu lun-wen chi 水滸研究論文集 (Peking: Tso-chia ch'u-pan she, 1957).

Shui-hu yü Chin Sheng-t'an yen-chiu 水滸與金聖歎研究, by Chang Kuo-kuang 張國光 (Cheng-chou: Chung-chou shu-hua she, 1981).

Su-chou ta-hsüeh hsüeh-pao 蘇州大學學報.

Ta-ch'eng 大成.

Ta-lien shih-chuan hsüeh-pao 大連師專學報.

Ta-lu tsa-chih 大陸雜志.

T'ai-wan Hung-hsüeh lun-wen hsüan 台灣紅學論文選, Hu Wen-pin 胡文彬 and Chou Lei 周雷, eds. (Tientsin: Pai-hua wen-i, 1981).

Tenri daigaku gakuhō 天理大学学報.

Theories of the Arts in China, Susan Bush and Christian Murck, eds. (Princeton: Princeton University Press, 1983).

T'ien-chin she-hui k'o-hsüeh 天津社會科學.

T'ien-chin shih-ta hsüeh-pao 天津師大學報.

Ts'ao Hsüeh-ch'in ts'ung-k'ao 曹雪芹叢考, by Wu En-yü 吳恩裕 (Shanghai: Shang-hai ku-chi, 1980).

Tso-p'in 作品.

Tu-shu 讀書.

Wen-chiao tzu-liao chien-pao 文教資料簡報.

Wen-hsien 文獻.

Wen-hsüeh chih-shih 文學知識.

Wen-hsüeh i-ch'an 文學遺產.

Wen-hsüeh i-ch'an tseng-k'an 文學遺產增刊 (Peking: Chung-hua shu-chü).

Wen-hsüeh li-lun ts'ung-k'an 文學理論叢刊.

Wen-hsüeh p'ing-lun 文學評論 (Peking: Chung-kuo she-hui k'o-hsüeh).

Wen-hsüeh p'ing-lun ts'ung-k'an 文學評論叢刊 (Peking: Chung-kuo she-hui k'o-hsüeh).

Wen-hui pao 文匯報.

Wen-i li-lun yen-chiu 文藝理論研究.

Wen-i lun-ts'ung 文藝論叢 (Shanghai: Shang-hai wen-i).

Wen-i pao 文藝報.

Wen-i yen-chiu 文藝研究.

Wen shih chih-shih 文史知識.

Wen-wu 文物.

Wo tu Hung-lou meng 我讀紅樓夢 (Tientsin: T'ien-chin jen-min, 1982).

Wu-han shih-fan hsüeh-yüan hsüeh-pao 武漢師範學院學報.

Wu-han shih-yüan Han-k'ou fen-pu hsiao-k'an 武漢師院漢口分部校刊.

Wu-han shih-yüan hsüeh-pao 武漢師院學報.

Yang-ch'eng wan-pao 羊城晚報.

Yang-chou shih-yüan hsüeh-pao 揚州師院學報.

General Bibliography

Western-language materials are placed at the head of each section for the convenience of the general reader.

It should be noted that, in the bibliographical entries below, information on the reprinting of articles by the Chinese People's University Book and Periodical Materials Center (*Chung-kuo jen-min ta-hsüeh shu-pao tzu-liao chung-hsin* 中國人民大學書報資料中心) of Peking in their "Selections of Material from Periodicals" (*Pao-k'an tzu-liao hsüan-hui* 報刊資料選匯) series is indicated in parentheses immediately after the version of the article reprinted. There are almost one hundred separate subject titles in this reprint series, but the type of material that concerns us only appears under three: *Chung-kuo ku-tai chin-tai wen-hsüeh yen-chiu* 中國古代近代文學研究 (Studies in Ancient and Modern Chinese Literature; abbreviated as *Ku-chin* in the bibliographies), *Hung-lou meng yen-chiu* 紅樓夢研究 (Studies on the *Hung-lou meng*), and *Hsi-ch'ü yen-chiu* 戲曲研究 (Studies in Traditional Chinese Drama). It should also be noted that universities and colleges in China that publish academic journals usually publish two, both under the same title. The difference between them is that one is devoted to the social sciences (*she-hui k'o-hsüeh* 社會科學) and the other to the hard sciences. In those cases where two academic journals under the same name are published by a single institution, it is to be understood that in the bibliographies below it is the social sciences edition that is meant.

Traditional Chinese Literary Criticism in General

Liu, James J.Y. *Chinese Theories of Literature*. Chicago: University of Chicago Press, 1975.

Nienhauser, William, Jr., ed. *Indiana Companion to Traditional Chinese Literature* Bloomington: Indiana University Press, 1986.

Sun Chang, K'ang-i. "Chinese 'Lyric Criticism' in the Six Dynasties." In *Theories of the Arts in China*, pp. 215–24.

Wong, Siu-kit. "*Ch'ing* in Chinese Literary Criticism." Ph.D. thesis, Oxford University, Oxford, 1969.

Aoki Masaru 青木正兒. *Ch'ing-tai wen-hsüeh p'ing-lun shih* 清代文學評論史. Translated by Ch'en Shu-nü 陳淑女. Taipei: K'ai-ming shu-tien, 1969.

Chang Lien-ti 張連第 et al. *Chung-kuo ku-tai wen-lun chia shou-ts'e* 中國古代文論家手冊. Ch'ang-ch'un: Chi-lin jen-min, 1985.

Chang Pi-po 張碧波. "Shih-lun p'ing-tien p'ai tsai Chung-kuo wen-hsüeh shih shang ti li-shih ti-wei" 試論評點派在中國文學史上的歷史地位. In *Chung-kuo ku-tai hsiao-shuo li-lun yen-chiu*, pp. 79–84.

Chang Ping 張兵. "Chien-kuo hou ku-tai wen-lun yen-chiu shu-p'ing" 建國後古代文論研究述評. *Ch'i Lu hsüeh-k'an*, 1985. 1:111–16 (*Ku-chin* reprint, 1985. 4:134–39).

Chang Shao-k'ang 張少康. *Chung-kuo ku-tai wen-hsüeh ch'uang-tso lun* 中國古代文學創作論. Peking: Pei-ching ta-hsüeh, 1983.

Chang Sheng-i 張聲怡, and Liu Chiu-chou 劉九州. *Chung-kuo ku-tai hsieh-tso li-lun* 中國古代寫作理論. Wu-ch'ang: Hua-chung kung-hsüeh yüan, 1985.

Chang Shou-k'ang 張壽康 et al. *Ku-tai wen-chang-hsüeh kai-lun* 古代文章學概論. Wu-ch'ang: Wu-han ta-hsüeh, 1983.

Chao Tse-ch'eng 趙則誠 et al. *Chung-kuo ku-tai wen-hsüeh li-lun tz'u-tien* 中國古代文學理論辭典. Ch'ang-ch'un: Chi-lin wen-shih, 1985.

Ch'en Shao-sung 陳少松. "Ku-tai wen-lun chung 'ch'i cheng' shuo ch'u-t'an" 古代文論中奇正說初探. *Hsüeh-shu yüeh-k'an*, 1981. 6:23–29.

Cheng Tien 鄭奠, and T'an Ch'üan-chi 譚全基, eds. *Ku Han-yü hsiu-tz'u hsüeh tzu-liao hui-pien* 古漢語修辭學資料匯編. Peking: Commercial Press, 1980.

Chiang Fan 蔣凡. "'Chen-shih,' 'hsü-wu' yü ku-tien wen-i li-lun ti li-shih fa-chan" 真實虛無與古典文藝理論的歷史發展. *Hsüeh-shu yüeh-k'an*, 1980. 10:70–73.

Ch'ien Chung-shu 錢鍾書. *Kuan-chui pien* 管錐編. 4 vols. Peking: Chung-hua shu-chü, 1979.

——. *T'an-i lu* 談藝錄. Peking: Chung-hua shu-chü, revised edition, 1984.

Ch'iu Chen-sheng 丘振聲. *Chung-kuo ku-tien wen-i li-lun li-shih* 中國古典文藝理論例釋. Nan-ning: Kuang-hsi jen-min, 1981.

Chou Chih-wen 周志文. "T'ai-chou hsüeh-p'ai tui wan-Ming wen-hsüeh feng-ch'i ti ying-hsiang" 泰州學派對晚明文學風氣的影響. Master's thesis, National Taiwan University, 1977.

Furukawa Sueki 古川末喜. "Jih-pen yu-kuan Chung-kuo ku-tai wen-lun yen-chiu ti wen-hsien mu-lu (1945–1982)" 日本有關中國古代文論研究的文献目錄. *Chung-kuo wen-i ssu-hsiang shih lun-ts'ung* 2:388–438 (1985).

Hsia Yin 夏寅. "Shuo ch'ü-pi" 說曲筆. *Nan-ching ta-hsüeh hsüeh-pao*, 1981. 2:43.

Hsü K'o-wen 徐克文. "Shih-t'an Chung-kuo ch'uan-t'ung ti wen-hsüeh p'i-p'ing hsing-shih: p'ing-tien" 試談中國傳統的文學批評形式:評點. *Liao-ning ta-hsüeh hsüeh-pao* 遼寧大學學報, 1983. 3:77–80 (*Ku-chin* reprint, 1983. 6:211–14).

Hu Hsi-chi 胡熙績. "Ming niu an k'ou, ch'ing hu man ying: ch'ien-t'an ku-tai wen-chang hsieh-tso chung yu-kuan chao-ying ti lun-shu" 明鈕暗扣輕呼慢應:淺談古代文章寫作中有關照應的論述. *Hsieh-tso*, 1985. 5:14–17.

Idema, W.L. "Chung-kuo ku-tai wen-hsüeh li-lun Hsi-wen lun-chu ch'u-pien" 中國古代文學理論西文論著初編. Translated by Ch'en Hsi-chung 陳西中. *Chung-kuo wen-i ssu-hsiang shih lun-ts'ung* 2:356–87 (1985).

Kazemura Shigeru 風村繁. "Jih-pen yen-chiu Chung-kuo ku-tai wen-lun ti kai-k'uang" 日本研究中國古代文論的概況. Translated by Hsi-chung 曦鍾 (Ch'en Hsi-chung 陳曦鍾). In *Jih-pen yen-chiu Wen-hsin tiao-lung lun-wen chi* 日本研究文心雕龍論文集. Tsinan, 1983, pp. 297–308.

Kuo Shao-yü 郭紹虞, ed. *Chung-kuo li-tai wen-lun hsüan* 中國歷代文論選. 4 vols. Shanghai: Shang-hai ku-chi, 1980.

———. *Chung-kuo wen-hsüeh p'i-p'ing shih* 中國文學批評史. Shanghai: Hsin wen-i, 1955.

Lai Li-hsing 賴力行. "Lüeh-t'an Chung-kuo ku-tien wen-i li-lun chung ti 'hsü' 'shih' shuo" 略談中國古典文藝理論中的虛實說. *Hu-nan chiao-yü hsüeh-yüan yüan-k'an*, 1983. 3:58–61 (*Ku-chin* reprint, 1984. 8:127–30).

Lin T'ung-hua 林同華. *Chung-kuo mei-hsüeh shih lun-chi* 中國美學史論集. Nanking: Chiang-su jen-min, 1984.

Liu Hsi-tsai 劉熙載. *I-kai* 藝概. Shanghai: Shang-hai ku-chi, 1978.

Liu Yen-wen 劉衍文. "Lun pin-chu—wen-hsüeh ti mei-hsüeh kuan chih i" 論賓主—文學的美學觀之一. *Shang-hai shih-fan ta-hsüeh hsüeh-pao*, 1985. 2:49–53.

Lo Ken-tse 羅根澤. *Chung-kuo wen-hsüeh p'i-ping shih* 中國文學批評史. Shanghai: Shang-hai ku-chi, 1984.

Lo Ta-t'ung 羅大同. "Wo-kuo ch'uan-t'ung ti chiao-hsüeh fang-fa—p'ing-tien" 我國傳統的教學方法—評點. *Wu-han shih-fan hsüeh-yuan hsüeh-pao*, 1983. 1:81–83.

Maeno Naoaki 前野直彬 et al. *Chung-kuo wen-hsüeh kai-lun* 中國文學概論. Translated by Hung Shun-lung 洪順隆. Taipei: Ch'eng-wen ch'u-pan she, 1971.

Min Tse 敏澤. *Chung-kuo wen-hsüeh li-lun p'i-p'ing shih* 中國文學理論批評史. Peking: Jen-min wen-hsüeh, 1981.

———. "Ku-tai wen-lun ti 'chen' yü 'i-shu hsü-kou'" 古代文論的真與藝術虛構. *Kuang-ming jih-pao*, 5/24/1983 (*Ku-chin* reprint, 1983. 6:209–10).

———. "Shih-lun 'Ch'un-ch'iu pi-fa' tui yü hou-shih wen-hsüeh li-lun ti ying-hsiang" 試論春秋筆法對於後世文學理論的影響. *She-hui k'o-hsüeh chan-hsien*, 1985. 3:254–62.

Nanking University. *Ku-jen lun hsieh-tso* 古人論寫作. Ch'ang-ch'un: Chi-lin jen-min, 1981.

Peking University Department of Philosophy, ed. *Chung-kuo mei-hsüeh shih tzu-liao hsüan-pien* 中國美學史資料選編. Peking: Chung-hua shu-chü, 1980–81.

Shantung University Department of Chinese. *Chung-kuo ku-tai wen-i li-lun tzu-liao mu-lu hui-pien* 中國古代文藝理論資料目錄匯編. Tsinan: Ch'i Lu shu-she, 1983.

Sun Te-ch'ien 孫德謙. *Ku-shu tu-fa lüeh-li* 古書讀法略例. Shanghai: Commercial Press, 1936; Shanghai: Shang-hai shu-tien, 1983 reprint.

T'an Fan 譚帆. "Lun Chung-kuo ku-tai wen-hsüeh p'i-p'ing ti chi chung chu-yao mo-shih" 論中國古代文學批評的幾種主要模式. *Hua-tung shih-fan ta-hsüeh hsüeh-pao*, 1985. 4:46–51.

———. "Shih-hsi ku-tai wen-lun li-lun shu-yü ti kou-hsüan t'e-cheng" 試析古代文論理論術語的構選特徵. *Chung-chou hsüeh-k'an*, 1985. 6:75–80 (*Ku-chin* reprint, 1986. 2:281–86).

Ts'ai Fang-ting 蔡芳定. "Chung-kuo wen-hsüeh p'i-p'ing shih shang chih mei-hsüeh p'i-p'ing fa" 中國文學批評史上之美學批評法. *Kuo-li T'ai-wan shih-fan ta-hsüeh kuo-wen yen-chiu chi-k'an* 國立台灣師大學國文研究集刊

30:487–620 (1986).

Tseng Yung-i 曾永義, ed. *Yüan-tai wen-hsueh p'i-p'ing tzu-liao hui-pien* 元代文學批評資料彙編. Taipei: Ch'eng-wen ch'u-pan she, 1978.

Wang Kou 王構. *Hsiu-tz'u heng-chien* 修辭衡鑒. Shanghai: Chung-hua shu-chü, 1958.

Wang Li-ch'i 王利器, ed. *Yüan-Ming-Ch'ing san-tai chin-hui hsiao-shuo hsi-ch'ü shih-liao* 元明清三代禁毀小說戲曲史料. Shanghai: Shang-hai ku-chi, revised edition, 1981.

Wang Te-yung 王德勇. "Wo-kuo ku-tai wen-hsüeh p'ing-tien chung ti jen-wu su-tsao li-lun" 我國古代文學評點中的人物塑造理論. *Ch'eng-te shih-chuan hsüeh-pao* 承德師專學報, 1984. 1:27–31, 10.

Wang Yen-ts'ai 王延才. "Wo-kuo ku-tai mei-hsüeh chung ti i-shu chieh-kou kuan" 我國古代美學中的藝術結構觀. *She-hui k'o-hsüeh chi-k'an*, 1984. 4:146–53 (*Ku-chin* reprint, 1984. 16:145–52).

Wang Ying-chih 王英志. "'Fa-fen chu-shu' shuo shu-p'ing" 發憤著書說述評. *Ku-tai wen-hsüeh li-lun yen-chiu* 11:125–56 (1986).

Wang Yün-hsi 王運熙 et al. *Chung-kuo wen-hsüeh p'i-p'ing shih* 中國文學批評史. Shanghai: Shang-hai ku-chi, vol. 2, 1981; vol. 3, 1985.

Wu Hung-i 吳宏一, ed. *Ch'ing-tai wen-hsüeh p'i-p'ing tzu-liao hui-pien* 清代文學批評資料彙編. Taipei: Ch'eng-wen ch'u-pan she, 1979.

Yeh Ch'ing-ping 葉慶炳, ed. *Ming-tai wen-hsüeh p'i-p'ing tzu-liao hui-pien* 明代文學批評資料彙編. Taipei: Ch'eng-wen ch'u-pan she, 1979.

Yü Chung-shan 于忠善, ed. *Li-tai wen-jen lun wen-hsüeh* 歷代文人論文學. Peking: Wen-hua i-shu, 1985.

Traditional Chinese Poetry Criticism

Bodman, Richard Wainright. "Poetics and Prosody in Early Medieval China: A Study and Translation of Kūkai's *Bunkyō Hifuron*." Ph.D. thesis, Cornell University, Ithaca, 1978.

Owen, Stephen. *Traditional Chinese Poetry and Poetics: Omen of the World*. Madison: University of Wisconsin Press, 1985.

Wong, Wai-leung. "Chinese Impressionistic Criticism: A Study of the Poetry Talk." Ph.D. thesis, Ohio State University, Columbus, 1976.

Yu, Pauline. *The Reading of Imagery in the Chinese Poetic Tradition*. Princeton: Princeton University Press, 1987.

Chang Hsieh 章燮. *T'ang-shih san-pai shou chu-shu* 唐詩三百首注疏. Hofei: An-hui jen-min, 1983, based on 1884 edition.

Chang Pao-ch'üan 張葆全. *Shih-hua yü tz'u-hua* 詩話與詞話. Shanghai: Shang-hai ku-chi, 1983.

Chang Pao-ch'üan, and Chou Man-chiang 周滿江, eds. *Li-tai shih-hua hsüan-chu* 歷代詩話選注. Hsi-an: Shan-hsi jen-min, 1984.

Chou Chen-fu 周振甫. *Shih tz'u li-hua* 詩詞例話. Peking: Chung-kuo ch'ing-nien, 1979.

Fang Hui 方回 et al. *Ying-k'uei lü-sui hui-p'ing* 瀛奎律髓彙評. Edited by Li Ch'ing-chia 李慶甲. Shanghai: Shang-hai ku-chi, 1986.

Huang Wei-liang 黃維樑. "Shih-hua tz'u-hua ho yin-hsiang shih p'i-p'ing" 詩話詞話和印像式批評. In *Chung-kuo shih-hsüeh tsung-heng t'an* 中國詩學縱橫談. Taipei: Hung-fan ch'u-pan she, 1977, pp. 1–26.

Lu Shan-ch'ing 盧善慶. "Chung-kuo ch'uan-t'ung shih-hsüeh shu-yü ho p'i-p'ing fang-fa hsin t'an-so" 中國傳統詩學術語和批評方法新探索. *Ho-pei ta-hsüeh hsüeh-pao* 河北大學學報, 1984. 1:67–74.

Wuhan University Department of Chinese. *Li-tai shih-hua tz'u-hua hsüan* 歷代詩話詞話選. Wuhan: Wu-han ta-hsüeh, 1984.

Yeh Chia-ying 葉嘉瑩. *Tu Fu "Ch'iu-hsing pa-shou" chi-shuo* 杜甫秋興八首集說. Taipei: Chung-hua shu-chü, 1966.

Yen Yü 嚴羽. *Ts'ang-lang shih-hua chiao-shih* 滄浪詩話校釋. Edited by Kuo Shao-yü 郭紹虞. Peking: Jen-min wen-hsüeh, 1961.

Traditional Chinese Prose and Historiographical Criticism

Beasley, W.G., and Pulleyblank, E.G., eds. *Historians of China and Japan.* New York: Oxford University Press, 1961.

Gardner, Charles S. *Chinese Traditional Historiography.* Cambridge, Mass.: Harvard University Press, 1961.

Han Yu-shan. *Elements of Chinese Historiography.* Hollywood, Calif.: W.M. Hawley, 1955.

Kroll, Jurij. "Ssu-ma Ch'ien's Literary Theory and Literary Practice." *Altorientalische Forschungen* 4:313–25 (1976).

Nivison, David. *The Life and Thought of Chang Hsüeh-ch'eng (1738–1801).* Stanford: Stanford University Press, 1966.

Pollard, David E. *A Chinese Look at Literature: The Literary Values of Chou Tso-jen in Relation to the Tradition.* Berkeley: University of California Press, 1973.

Sargent, Stuart H., trans. "Liu Chih-chi: *Understanding History*: 'The Narration of Events.'" In *The Translation of Things Past.* Edited by George Kao. Hong Kong: Chinese University of Hong Kong, 1982, pp. 27–33.

Twitchett, D.C. "Chinese Biographical Writing." In *Historians of China and Japan.* Edited by W.G. Beasley and E.G. Pulleyblank. New York: Oxford University Press, 1961, pp. 95–114.

Watson, Burton. *Ssu-ma Ch'ien: Grand Historian of China.* New York: Columbia University Press, 1958.

Arii Hampei 有井範平, ed. *Hohyō Shiki hyōrin* 補標史記評林. Taipei: Lan-t'ai shu-chü, 1968 reprint. Selections published as *P'ing-chu Shih-chi hsüan-tu* 評注史記選讀 (Taipei: Lan-t'ai shu-chü, 1969).

Chang Hsüeh-ch'eng 章學誠. *Wen-shih t'ung-i chiao-chu* 文史通義校注. Edited by Yeh Ying 葉瑛. Peking: Chung-hua shu-chü, 1985.

Chang Ta-k'o 張大可, and Hsiao Li 蕭黎. "Lun *Shih-chi* hu-chien fa" 論史記

互見法. *She-hui k'o-hsüeh chi-k'an*, 1983. 3:91–97. Reprinted in Chang Ta-k'o 張大可, *Shih-chi yen-chiu* 史記研究 (Lan-chou: Kan-su jen-min, 1985), pp. 290–307.

Ch'en Ch'ien-chin 陳前進. "Shih-lun *San-kuo chih* ti ch'ü-pi yü chih-pi" 試論三國志的曲筆與直筆. *Ch'ung-ch'ing shih-yüan hsüeh-pao*, 1986. 3:65–68, 53.

Ch'en Chuang 陳莊. "Liu Hsi-tsai *I-kai* 'Wen-kai' ch'u-t'an" 劉熙載藝概文概初探. *Ssu-ch'uan ta-hsüeh hsüeh-pao* 四川大學學報, 1981. 1:63–67.

Ch'en K'uei 陳騤. *Wen-tse* 文則. Hong Kong: Chung-hua shu-chü, 1977.

Chen Te-hsiu 真德秀. *Wen-chang cheng-tsung* 文章正宗. *Ssu-pu pei-yao* edition.

Ch'en Tzu-ch'ien 陳子謙. "Ssu-ma Ch'ien ti 'fa-fen chu-shu shuo' chi ch'i li-shih fa-chan" 司馬遷的發憤著書說及其歷史發展. *Hsia-men ta-hsüeh hsüeh-pao* 廈門大學學報, 1981. 1:122–30 (*Ku-chin* reprint, 1981. 9:81–90).

Ch'ien Chung-lien 錢仲聯. "T'ung-ch'eng p'ai ku-wen yü shih-wen ti kuan-hsi wen-t'i" 桐城派古文與時文的關係問題. In *T'ung-ch'eng p'ai yen-chiu lun-wen chi* 桐城派研究論文集. Ho-fei: An-hui jen-min, 1963, pp. 151–58.

Chou Chen-fu 周振甫. *Wen-chang li-hua* 文章例話. Peking: Chung-kuo ch'ing-nien, 1983.

Chung Hsing 鍾惺. *Chin-wen kuei* 晋文歸. Taipei: Commercial Press, 1973 reprint.

Fang Pao 方苞. *Ku-wen yüeh-hsüan* 古文約選. Taipei: Chung-hua shu-chü, 1969 reprint.

Han Chao-ch'i 韓兆琦. *Shih-chi hsüan-chu chi-shuo* 史記選注集說. Nan-ch'ang: Chiang-hsi jen-min, 1982.

———. "*Shih-chi* shu-fa shih-li" 史記書法釋例. *Pei-ching shih-fan ta-hsüeh hsüeh-pao*, 1984. 3:9–17. Reprinted in his *Shih-chi p'ing-i shang-hsi* 史記評議賞析. Huhehot: Nei-meng-ku jen-min, 1985, pp. 144–60.

Han Hu-ch'u 韓湖初. "Ssu-ma Ch'ien shih-chuan wen-hsüeh li-lun ch'u-t'an" 司馬遷史傳文學理論初探. *Ku-tai wen-hsüeh li-lun yen-chiu* 10:258–71 (1985).

Ho Ming-hsin 何明新. "Ts'ung *P'ing Shih-chi* k'an Chung Hsing ti yung-jen kuan-tien" 從評史記看鍾惺的用人觀點. *Ch'ung-ch'ing shih-yüan hsüeh-pao*, 1986. 1:79–83.

Hsiao Li 蕭黎. "Hu-chien fa ti yün-yung" 互見法的運用. In his *Ssu-ma Ch'ien p'ing-chuan* 司馬遷評傳. Ch'ang-ch'un: Chi-lin wen-shih, 1986, pp. 86–98.

Hsieh Fang-te 謝枋得. *Wen-chang kuei-fan* 文章軌範. Taipei: Kuang-wen shu-chü, 1970 reprint.

Kuei Yu-kuang 歸有光. *Wen-chang chih-nan* 文章指南. Taipei: Kuang-wen shu-chü, 1972 reprint.

Kuei Yu-kuang, and Fang Pao 方苞. *Kuei Fang p'ing-tien Shih-chi ho-pi* 歸方評點史記合筆. Edited by Chang Yü-chao 張裕釗. N.p., 1876.

Kuo Kung 過珙. *Ku-wen p'ing-chu ch'üan-chi* 古文評註全集. Hong Kong: Ch'ung-ming ch'u-pan she, 1963 reprint.

Li Ch'i-ch'ing 李耆卿. *Wen-chang ching-i* 文章精義. Hong Kong: Chung-hua shu-chü, 1977.

Li Fu-chiu 李扶九, and Huang Jen-fu 黃仁黼. *Ku-wen pi-fa pai-p'ien* 古文筆法

百篇. Ch'ang-sha: Hu-nan jen-min, 1983.

Li Shao-yung 李少雍. "*Shih-chi* chi-chuan t'i tui wo-kuo hsiao-shuo fa-chan ti ying-hsiang" 史記紀傳體對我國小說發展的影響. In *Chung-kuo wen-hsüeh shih yen-chiu chi* 中國文學史研究集. Shanghai: Shang-hai ku-chi, 1985, pp. 188–219.

Liang Chang-chü 梁章鉅. *Chih-i ts'ung-hua* 制義叢話. Taipei: Kuang-wen shu-chü, 1976 reprint, 1859 preface.

Lin Ching-liang 林景亮. *P'ing-chu ku-wen tu-pen* 評注古文讀本. Taipei: Chung-hua shu-chü, 1969.

Lin Yün-ming 林雲銘, ed. *Ku-wen hsi-i ho-pien* 古文析義合編. Shanghai: Chin-chang t'u-shu, 1922 reprint of 1716 edition.

———. "Tu *Chuang Tzu* fa" 讀莊子法. In *Chao-tai ts'ung-shu* 昭代叢書. Edited by Chang Ch'ao 張潮. Wu-chiang: Shih-k'ai t'ang, 1833, *chia* 甲 collection, *chüan* 19.

Ling Chih-lung 凌稚隆, ed. *Han-shu p'ing-lin* 漢書評林. Tokyo: Kyuko shoin, 1973 reprint as *Wakokuhon seishi Kansho* 和刻本正史漢書, 1581 preface.

———, ed. *Shih-chi p'ing-lin* 史記評林, 1547 preface. Reprinted as part of Arii Hampei, *Hohyō Shiki hyōrin*.

Liu Chih-chi 劉知幾. *Shih-t'ung* 史通. Peking: Chung-hua shu-chü, 1961.

Lo Chün-ch'ou 羅君籌. *Wen-chang pi-fa pien-hsi* 文章筆法辨析. Hong Kong: Shang-hai yin-shu kuan, 1971.

Lü Tsu-ch'ien 呂祖謙. *Ku-wen kuan-chien* 古文關鍵. Taipei: Kuang-wen shu-chü, 1970 reprint.

Shen Te-ch'ien 沈德潛. *P'ing-chu T'ang-Sung pa chia ku-wen* 評注唐宋八家古文. Shanghai: Sao-yeh shan-fang, 1920; original preface 1750.

Sun Ch'iu-k'o 孫秋克. "*Shih-chi* 'hu-chien fa' ch'ien-i" 史記互見法淺議. *Chiang Huai lun-t'an*, 1983. 1:109–11.

T'ang Yüeh 唐躍. "*Shih-chi* chung ti chao-ying shou-fa" 史記中的照應手法. *I-t'an*, 1980. 2:142–44.

T'ien Lin 田林. "Lüeh-lun 'T'ai-shih kung pi-fa'" 略論太史公筆法. *Ta-lien shih-chuan hsüeh-pao*, 1986. 1:44–46, 67.

Tzu Chung-yün 資中筠. "T'ai-shih kung pi-fa hsiao-i" 太史公筆法小議. *Kuang-ming jih-pao*, 4/16/1980.

Wang Chih-chien 王志堅, and Chang Shih-ch'üan 張士銓, *P'ing-hsüan ssu-liu fa-hai* 評選四六法海. Taipei: Te-chih ch'u-pan she, 1963.

Wang K'ai-fu 王開富 et al. *Ku-tai wen-chang hsüeh kai-lun* 古代文章學概論. Shanghai: Chung-hua shu-chü, 1958.

Wang T'ien-shun 王天順. "Lüeh-lun Ch'un-ch'iu Tso-chuan ti pao-pien shu-fa" 略論春秋左傳的褒貶書法. *Nan-k'ai hsüeh-pao*, 1982. 1:67–70.

Wu Chien-ssu 吳見思. *Shih-chi lun-wen* 史記論文. Shanghai: Chung-hua shu-chü, 1936; original preface 1686.

Yang Ch'eng-fu 楊成孚. "Lun Ssu-ma Ch'ien ti ch'ü-pi" 論司馬遷的曲筆. *Nan-k'ai hsüeh-pao*, 1986. 3:24–31.

Yang Yen-ch'i 楊燕起 et al., eds. *Li-tai ming-chia p'ing Shih-chi* 歷代名家評史記. Peking: Pei-ching shih-ta, 1986.

Yao Yü-t'ien 姚宇田. *Shih-chi ching-hua lu* 史記菁華錄. Han-k'ou: Wu-han

ku-chi, 1986 reprint of 1824 edition. Also Taipei: Lien-ching, 1977 typeset
    reprint.
Yü Ch'eng 余誠. Ch'ung-ting ku-wen shih-i hsin-pien 重訂古文釋義新編. Han-
    k'ou: Wu-han ku-chi, 1986 reprint.
Yüan Huang 袁黃, and Wang Shih-chen 王世貞. "Tu Kang-chien yao-fa" 讀綱
    鑑要法. In Kang-chien ho-pien 綱鑑合編. Peking: Chung-kuo shu-tien, 1985
    reprint, pp. 1–4 (separately paginated).
Yüan Po-ch'eng 袁伯誠. "Shih-lun Ssu-ma Ch'ien 'fa-fen chu-shu' ti yin-su ho
    t'iao-chien" 試論司馬遷發憤著書的因素和條件. Shan-hsi shih-ta hsüeh-pao
    陝西師大學報, 1984. 2:43–48.
———. "Shih-lun Ssu-ma Ch'ien ti 'fa-fen chu-shu' shuo tui feng-yü wen-
    hsüeh li-lun ti ying-hsiang" 試論司馬遷的發憤著書說對諷諭文學理論的
    影響. Ku-yüan shih-chuan hsüeh-pao 固原師專學報, 1984. 2:43–63 (Ku-chin
    reprint, 1984. 21:68–79).

Traditional Chinese Criticism of Painting, Calligraphy, and Music

Bush, Susan. The Chinese Literati on Painting: Su Shih (1037–1101) to Tung Ch'i-
    ch'ang (1555–1636). Cambridge, Mass.: Harvard University Press, 1971.
———. "Lung-mo, K'ai-ho, and Ch'i-fu: Some Implications of Wang Yüan-
    ch'i's Compositional Terms." Oriental Art, n.s. 7:120–27 (1962).
Bush, Susan, and Murck, Christian, eds. Theories of the Arts in China. Princeton:
    Princeton University Press, 1983.
Bush, Susan, and Shih, Hsio-yen. Early Chinese Texts on Painting. Cambridge,
    Mass.: Harvard-Yenching Institute, 1985.
DeWoskin, Kenneth. "Early Chinese Music and the Origins of Aesthetic
    Terminology." In Theories of the Arts in China, pp. 187–214.
———. A Song for One or Two: Music and the Concept of Art in Early China. Ann
    Arbor: Center for Chinese Studies, University of Michigan, 1982.
Hay, John. "The Human Body as a Microcosmic Source of Macrocosmic
    Values in Calligraphy." In Theories of the Arts in China, pp. 74–102.
Silbergeld, Jerome. "Chinese Concepts of Old Age and Their Role in Chinese
    Painting, Painting Theory, and Criticism." Art Journal 46:103–14 (1987).
———. Chinese Painting Style: Media, Methods, and Principles of Form. Seattle:
    University of Washington Press, 1980.
Sirén, Osvald. The Chinese on the Art of Painting. New York: Schocken Books,
    1963.

Ch'en Ch'uan-hsi 陳傳席. Liu-ch'ao hua-lun yen-chiu 六朝畫論研究. Nanking:
    Chiang-su mei-shu, 1985.
Chou Chi-yin 周積寅, ed. Chung-kuo hua-lun chi-yao 中國畫論輯要. Nanking:
    Chiang-su mei-shu, 1985.
Kuo Yin 郭因. Chung-kuo hui-hua mei-hsüeh shih kao 中國繪畫美學史稿. Peking:
    Jen-min mei-shu, 1981.
Yang Ta-nien 楊大年, ed. Chung-kuo li-tai hua-lun ts'ai-ying 中國歷代畫論采英.

K'ai-feng: Ho-nan jen-min, 1984.

Yeh Chiu-ju 葉九如, ed. *San-hsi t'ang hua-pao* 三希堂畫寶. Peking: Chung-kuo shu-tien, 1982.

Traditional Chinese Drama Criticism

Lee, Chi-fang. "A Bibliography of the Criticism of Chinese Poetic Drama." *Tamkang Review* 16. 3:311–22 (1986).

Chao Ching-shen 趙景深. *Ch'ü-lun ch'u-t'an* 曲論初探. Shanghai: Shang-hai wen-i, 1980.

Ch'en Yen 陳衍, ed. *Chung-kuo ku-tai pien-chü li-lun ch'u-t'an* 中國古代編劇理論初探. Wuhan: Hu-pei jen-min, 1984.

Ch'en Yung-piao 陳永標. "Chung-kuo chin-tai hsi-chü li-lun shu-p'ing" 中國近代戲劇理論述評. *Hua-nan shih-fan ta-hsüeh hsüeh-pao*, 1983. 2:83–89.

Ch'i Sen-hua 齊森華. *Ch'ü-lun t'an-sheng* 曲論探勝. Shanghai: Hua-tung shih-fan ta-hsüeh, 1985.

Chiang Hsing-yü 蔣星煜. "Ch'en Mei-kung p'ing-pen *Hsi-hsiang chi* ti hsüeh-shu chia-chih" 陳眉公評本西廂記的學術價值. *Shang-hai she-hui k'o-hsüeh yüan hsüeh-shu chi-k'an* 上海社會科學院學術季刊, 1986. 4:197–205 (*Ku-chin* reprint, 1987. 1:209–17).

Ch'in Hsüeh-jen 秦學人, and Hou Tso-ch'ing 侯作卿, eds. *Chung-kuo ku-tien pien-chü li-lun tzu-liao hui-chi* 中國古典編劇理論資料彙輯. Peking: Chung-kuo hsi-chü, 1984.

Ch'in Wen-hsi 秦文兮. "*T'ao-hua shan* 'Ch'üeh-lien' chi ch'i p'i-yü shang-hsi" 桃花扇却奩及其批語賞析. *Hsiang-t'an shih-chuan hsüeh-pao* 湘潭師專學報, 1985, special issue (*tseng-k'an*), pp. 85–89.

Denda Akira 傳田章. *Minkan Genzatsugeki Seishōki mokuroku* 明刊元雜劇西廂記目録. Tokyo: Tokyo University, 1970.

Fan Min-sheng 范民聲. "Ch'ien-lun Chung-kuo hsi-ch'ü li-lun ti min-tsu t'e-tien" 淺論中國戲曲理論的民族特點. *Ku-tai wen-hsüeh li-lun yen-chiu* 10:332–40 (1985).

Hsia Hsieh-shih 夏寫時. *Chung-kuo hsi-chü p'i-p'ing ti ch'an-sheng ho fa-chan* 中國戲劇批評的產生和發展. Peking: Chung-kuo hsi-chü, 1982.

Hsieh Po-liang 謝伯良. "Chung-kuo ku-tai hsi-ch'ü hsü-pa ti p'i-p'ing mo-shih" 中國古代戲曲序跋的批評模式. *Hua-tung shih-fan ta-hsüeh hsüeh-pao*, 1987. 3:61–68 (*Hsi-ch'ü yen-chiu* reprint, 1987. 8:29–36).

Huang Chung-mo 黃中模. "Shih-lun T'an Yüan-ch'un *P'i-tien Hsiang-tang-jan ch'uan-ch'i*" 試論譚元春批點想當然傳奇. *Ch'ung-ch'ing shih-yüan hsüeh-pao*, 1986. 1:72–78.

Li Jo-ch'ih 李若馳. "Shih-t'an 'ch'ü-hua' ti hsi-chü li-lun t'i-hsi" 試談曲話的戲劇理論體系. *Yen-an ta-hsüeh hsüeh-pao* 延安大學學報, 1985. 1:57–65, 39 (pt. 1); 1985. 2:60–67 (pt. 2).

Li K'o-ho 李克和. "Lun ku-tai ch'ü-lun chung ti mo-hu ssu-pien" 論古代曲論中的模糊思辨. *Chung-kuo she-hui k'o-hsüeh*, 1986. 3:171–92.

Nagasawa Kikuya 長澤規矩也. "Mindai gikyoku kankōsha hyō shokō" 明代
    戲曲刊行者表初稿. *Shoshigaku* 7. 1:2–9 (1936).
Shen Yao 沈堯. "Ming-mo ku-tien chü-lun ti hsin p'ien-chang—Meng
    Ch'eng-shun pien-chü li-lun tsung-shu" 明末古典劇論的新篇章—孟稱舜
    編劇理論綜述. *Hsi-ch'ü yen-chiu* 9:167–86 (1983).
T'eng Chen-kuo 滕振國. "Ming-tai chü-t'an pen-se shuo ti liu-pieh chi ch'i
    hsing-ch'eng" 明代劇壇本色說的流別及其形成. *Chiang-hsi ta-hsüeh hsüeh-*
    pao, 1985. 3:70–75.
Wan Yün-chün 萬雲駿. "Shen-mo shih Yüan-ch'ü ti pen-se" 甚麼是元曲的
    本色. *Ku-tai wen-hsüeh li-lun yen-chiu* 3:269–82 (1981).
Wang Cheng 王政. "Ch'ing-tai hsi-ch'ü shen-mei li-lun fa-chan ta-shih" 清代
    戲曲審美理論發展大勢. *Hsi-ch'ü yen-chiu* 8:54–77 (1983).
Wang Yung-chien 王永健. "Lun Wu Wu-shan san-fu ho-p'ing pen *Mu-tan t'ing*
    chi ch'i p'i-yü" 論吳吳山三婦合評本牡丹亭及其批語. *Nan-ching ta-hsüeh*
    hsüeh-pao, 1980. 4:18–26.
Yao Shu-i 么書儀. "Ming-jen p'i-p'ing *Hsi-hsiang chi* shu-p'ing" 明人批評
    西廂記述評. *Chung-kuo ku-tien wen-hsüeh lun-ts'ung* 1:234–50 (1984).
Yu Yu-chi 游友基. "Chung-kuo ku-tien chü-lun ti i ko shen-mei kuan-tien—
    'ch'ü'" 中國古典劇論的一個審美觀點—趣. *Hsüeh-shu yüeh-k'an*, 1985.
    7:77–79.
Yü Ch'iu-yü 余秋雨. *Hsi-chü li-lun shih-kao* 戲劇理論史稿. Shanghai: Shang-hai
    wen-i, 1983.
Yü Wei-min 俞為民. "P'ing Ming-Ch'ing hsi-ch'ü p'i-p'ing chung ti so-yin
    feng-ch'i" 評明清戲曲批評中的索隱風氣. *Nan-ching ta-hsüeh hsüeh-pao*,
    1985. 4:41–46.

Traditional Chinese Fiction Criticism

"Conference on the Theory of Chinese Narrative," papers and transcript of
    discussions from a conference held at Princeton University, January 20–22,
    1974, copy in Gest Oriental Library, Princeton University.
Frankel, Hans H. "The Chinese Novel: Confrontation of Critical Approaches to
    Chinese and Western Novels." *Literature East and West* 8. 1:2–5 (1964).
Hegel, Robert E. *The Novel in Seventeenth-Century China.* New York: Colum-
    bia University Press, 1981.
———. "*Sui-T'ang yen-i* and the Aesthetics of the Seventeenth-Century
    Suchou Elite." In *Chinese Narrative: Critical and Theoretical Essays*, pp.
    124–59.
Hsia, C.T. *The Classic Chinese Novel: A Critical Introduction.* New York:
    Columbia University Press, 1968.
Li, T'ien-i. *Chinese Fiction: A Bibliography of Books and Articles in Chinese and*
    English. New Haven: Far Eastern Publications, Yale University Press, 1968.
Liu, Ts'un-yan (Liu Ts'un-jen 柳存仁). *Chinese Popular Fiction in Two London*
    Libraries. Hong Kong: Lung-men Bookstore, 1967.
Lu Hsün 魯迅 (Chou Shu-jen 周樹人). *A Brief History of Chinese Fiction.* Trans-

lated by Yang Hsien-yi and Gladys Yang. Peking: Foreign Languages Press, 1959.

Plaks, Andrew H. "Chinese Fiction Criticism and Comparative Narrative Theory." Unpublished paper.

———. "Conceptual Models in Chinese Narrative Theory." *Journal of Chinese Philosophy* 4. 1:25–47 (1977).

———. *The Four Masterworks of the Ming Novel.* Princeton: Princeton University Press, 1987.

———. "Full-length *Hsiao-shuo* and the Western Novel: A Generic Appraisal." In *China and the West: Comparative Literary Studies.* Edited by William Tay et al. Hong Kong: Chinese University Press, 1980, pp. 136–76. Also in *New Asia Academic Bulletin* 1:163–76 (1978).

———. "Issues in Chinese Narrative Theory in the Perspective of the Western Traditions." *PTL* 2:339–66 (1977).

———. "The Problem of Structure in Chinese Narrative." *Tamkang Review* 6. 2–7. 1:429–40 (1975–76).

———. "Towards a Critical Theory of Chinese Narrative." In *Chinese Narrative: Critical and Theoretical Essays*, pp. 309–52.

Wang, John C.Y. "M.H. Abrams' Four Artistic Co-ordinates and Fiction Criticism in Traditional China." *Literature East and West* 16:997–1012 (1972).

———. "The Nature of Chinese Narrative: A Preliminary Statement of Methodology." *Tamkang Review* 6.2–7.1:229–46 (1975–76).

Yang, Winston L.Y. et al. *Classical Chinese Fiction: A Guide to Its Study and Appreciation: Essays and Bibliographies.* Boston: G.K. Hall, 1978.

Chang Pao-k'un 張寶坤. "Chih-jen hsiao-shuo mei-hsüeh tao-yüan" 志人小說 美學導源. *She-hui k'o-hsüeh chi-k'an*, 1986. 6:92–97 (*Ku-chin* reprint, 1987. 2:33–38).

Ch'ang Lin-yen 常林炎. "Kuan-yü ku-tai hsiao-shuo li-lun yen-chiu wen-t'i ti ssu-k'ao" 關於古代小說理論研究問題的思考. *Ho-pei shih-yüan hsüeh-pao* 河北師院學報, 1985. 1:96–106.

Chao Jung 趙鎔. "Chien-i Chung-kuo ku-tai hsiao-shuo li-lun ti chia-chih" 簡議中國古代小說理論的價值. *Wu-han shih-fan hsüeh-yüan hsüeh-pao*, 1984. 4:52–58 (*Ku-chin* reprint, 1984. 18:126–32).

Chao Ming-cheng 趙明政. "Ming-Ch'ing yen-i hsiao-shuo li-lun kai-shuo" 明清演義小說理論概說. *Hang-chou ta-hsüeh hsüeh-pao*, 1985. 3:58–65.

Ch'en Ch'ien-yü 陳謙豫. "Ming-tai hsiao-shuo li-lun kuan-k'uei" 明代小說 理論管窺. *Hua-tung shih-fan ta-hsüeh hsüeh-pao*, 1982. 3:57–62 (*Ku-chin* reprint, 1982. 16:15–21).

———. "Wo-kuo ku-tai hsiao-shuo li-lun-chia tui hsiao-shuo ti-wei tso-yung ti jen-shih" 我國古代小說理論家對小說地位作用的認識. *Hua-tung shih-fan ta-hsüeh hsüeh-pao*, 1984. 3:46–53. Reprinted in *Chung-kuo ku-tai hsiao-shuo li-lun yen-chiu*, pp. 17–32.

Ch'en Liao 陳遼. "Chung-kuo ku-tien hsiao-shuo li-lun p'i-p'ing ti t'e-se" 中國古典小說理論批評的特色. *Chiang Han lun-t'an*, 1984. 7:49–53 (*Ku-chin* reprint, 1984. 18:133–37).

Ch'en Nien-hsi 陳年希. "Shih-lun Ming-Ch'ing hsiao-shuo p'ing-tien p'ai tui wo-kuo ku-tien hsiao-shuo mei-hsüeh ti kung-hsien" 試論明清小說評點派對我國古典小說美學的貢獻. *Shang-hai shih-fan hsüeh-yüan hsüeh-pao*, 1983. 3:70–74 (*Ku-chin* reprint, 1983. 10:244–48).

Ch'en T'ieh-pin 陳鐵鑌. "Ts'ai-tzu chia-jen hsiao-shuo li-lun ch'u-t'an" 才子佳人小說理論初探 (pt. 1). In *Ts'ai-tzu chia-jen hsiao-shuo shu-lin* 才子佳人小說述林. Vol. 2 of *Ming-Ch'ing hsiao-shuo lun-ts'ung* (1985), pp. 84–107.

Cheng Chen-to 鄭振鐸. *Hsi-ti shu-hua* 西諦書話. Peking: San-lien shu-tien, 1983 reprint.

Ch'eng Ch'ien-fan 程千帆. "Kuan-yü ku-tai hsiao-shuo li-lun yen-chiu ti i tien i-chien" 關於古代小說理論研究的一點意見. *Wu-han shih-fan hsüeh-yüan hsüeh-pao*, 1984. 5:2–3.

Cheng Ming-li 鄭明娳. "Ku-tien hsiao-shuo p'i-p'ing li-lun ch'u-t'an" 古典小說批評理論初探. *Kuo-wen hsüeh-pao* 國文學報 15:203–16 (1986).

Chia Wen-chao 賈文昭, and Hsü Chao-hsün 徐召勛. *Chung-kuo ku-tien hsiao-shuo i-shu hsin-shang* 中國古典小說藝術欣賞. Hofei: An-hui jen-min, 1982.

Chiang Jui-tsao 蔣瑞藻. *Hui-yin Hsiao-shuo k'ao-cheng* 彙印小說考證. Taipei: Commercial Press, 1975.

Chien Mao-sen 簡茂森. "*Tsui-weng t'an-lu* hsiao-shuo li-lun ch'u-t'an" 醉翁談錄小說理論初探. *Ku-tien wen-hsüeh lun-ts'ung* 1:319–38 (1980).

Chou Chih-p'ing 周質平. "Lun wan-Ming wen-jen tui hsiao-shuo ti t'ai-tu" 論晚明文人對小說的態度. *Chung-wai wen-hsüeh* 11. 12:100–109 (1983).

Chou Lai-hsiang 周來祥. "Lun Ming-Ch'ing shih-ch'i Chung-kuo hsien-shih chu-i ti hsiao-shuo mei-hsüeh" 論明清時期中國現實主義的小說美學. *Nan-t'ung shih-chuan hsüeh-pao*, 1985. 2:63–70. Also in *Mei-hsüeh yü i-shu p'ing-lun* 2:241–54 (1985).

Chou Wei-min 周偉民. "Chung-kuo ku-tai hsiao-shuo li-lun t'ao-lun hui kai-shu" 中國古代小說理論討論會概述. In *Chung-kuo ku-tai hsiao-shuo li-lun yen-chiu*, pp. 354–58.

———. *Ming-Ch'ing hsiao-shuo li-lun fa-chan shih* 明清小說理論發展史. Kuang-chou: Hua-ch'eng ch'u-pan she, forthcoming.

———. "Ming-Ch'ing hsiao-shuo li-lun ti min-tsu t'e-se ch'u-i" 明清小說理論的民族特色芻議. *Ku-tai wen-hsüeh li-lun yen-chiu* 10:288–300 (1985).

———. "Shih-ssu shih-chi i-ch'ien Chung-kuo hsiao-shuo li-lun p'i-p'ing ti meng-ya ho yen-pien" 十四世紀以前中國小說理論批評的萌芽和演變. *Hua-chung shih-yüan hsüeh-pao*, 1985. 4:56–64 (*Ku-chin* reprint, 1985. 18:133–41).

Fang Sheng 方勝. "'Ch'ing' yü hsiao-shuo ch'uang-tso: Ming-Ch'ing hsiao-shuo li-lun yen-chiu chih i" 情與小說創作:明清小說理論研究之一. *Ming-Ch'ing hsiao-shuo yen-chiu* 4:465–81 (1986).

Fang Shih 方士. "T'an chih-kuai hsiao-shuo ti shen-mei hsing-t'ai" 談志怪小說的審美形態. *Nei-meng-ku she-hui k'o-hsüeh* 內蒙古社會科學, 1986. 6:82–85.

Fu Chi-fu 傅繼馥. "Ku-tai hsiao-shuo i-shu tien-hsing chi-pen hsing-t'ai ti yen-pien" 古代小說藝術典型基本形態的演變. In *Ming-Ch'ing hsiao-shuo ti ssu-hsiang yü i-shu* 明清小說的思想與藝術. Hofei: An-hui jen-min, 1984, pp. 224–47.

Fu Lung-chi 傅隆基. "Shih-lun Chung-kuo ku-tien hsiao-shuo ti yu-liang ch'uan-t'ung" 試論中國古典小說的優良傳統. In *Chung-kuo ku-tai hsiao-shuo li-lun yen-chiu*, pp. 33–46.

Han T'ung-wen 韓同文, and Huang Lin 黃霖. "Ming-Ch'ing hsiao-shuo li-lun chung ti hsien-shih chu-i wen-t'i" 明清小說理論中的現實主義問題. *Hsüeh-shu yüeh-k'an*, 1980. 11:59–64.

Hsü Hung-te 許宏德. "'Fan erh hou pi'—Chung-kuo ku-tien hsiao-shuo li-lun t'an-p'ien" 犯而後避—中國古典小說理論談片. *Tang-tai wen-t'an* 當代文壇, 1986. 1:62–65.

Hu Shih 胡適. *Chung-kuo chang-hui hsiao-shuo k'ao-cheng* 中國章回小說考證. Shanghai: Shang-hai shu-tien, 1979.

Hu Ta-lei 胡大雷. "Han Wei Liu-ch'ao shih-tai hsiao-shuo kuan-shang hsing-chih ti jen-shih" 漢魏六朝時代小說觀賞性質的認識. *Wen-hsüeh p'ing-lun*, 1985. 1:109–16 (*Ku-chin* reprint, 1985. 4:146–53).

Huang Ch'ing-ch'üan 黃清泉. "Kuan-yü 'ch'i' wei mei ti hsiao-shuo li-lun ti hsing-ch'eng" 關於奇為美的小說理論的形成. In *Chung-kuo ku-tai hsiao-shuo li-lun yen-chiu*, pp. 105–18.

Huang Lin 黃霖. "Chung-kuo ku-tai hsiao-shuo li-lun yen-chiu ch'u-i" 中國古代小說理論研究芻議. *She-hui k'o-hsüeh yen-chiu*, 1985. 1:72–75 (*Ku-chin* reprint, 1985. 6:157–60).

———. "Chung-kuo ku-tai hsiao-shuo p'i-p'ing chung ti jen-wu tien-hsing lun" 中國古代小說批評中的人物典型論. *Chung-kuo wen-i ssu-hsiang shih lun-ts'ung* 1:300–18 (1984).

———. *Ku hsiao-shuo lun kai-kuan* 古小說論概觀. Shanghai: Shang-hai wen-i, 1986.

———. "Lüeh-t'an Ming-tai hsiao-shuo li-lun" 略談明代小說理論. *Yü-wen hsüeh-hsi* 語文學習, 1984. 11:33–35.

———. "*San-kuo* yü ku-tai li-shih hsiao-shuo lun" 三國與古代歷史小說論. In *San-kuo yen-i lun-wen chi*, pp. 218–38.

Huang Lin, and Han T'ung-wen 韓同文, eds. *Chung-kuo li-tai hsiao-shuo lun-chu hsüan* 中國歷代小說論著選. 2 vols. Nan-ch'ang: Chiang-hsi jen-min, vol. 1. 1982; vol. 2, 1985.

I-min 一民. "Chung-kuo ku-tai hsiao-shuo li-lun hsüeh-shu t'ao-lun hui tsung-shu" 中國古代小說理論學術討論會綜述. *Wen-hsüeh i-ch'an*, 1984. 3:153–56 (*Ku-chin* reprint, 1984. 20:117–20).

Juan Kuo-hua 阮國華. "T'an wo-kuo ku-tai 'huan-ch'i p'ai' hsiao-shuo li-lun ti fa-chan li-ch'eng" 談我國古代幻奇派小說理論的發展歷程. In *Chung-kuo ku-tai hsiao-shuo li-lun yen-chiu*, pp. 119–36. Reprinted in *Nan-k'ai hsüeh-pao*, 1986. 1:47–56.

K'ang Lai-hsin 康來新. *Wan-Ch'ing hsiao-shuo li-lun yen-chiu* 晚清小說理論研究. Taipei: Ta-an ch'u-pan she, 1986.

K'ung Ling-ching 孔另境. *Chung-kuo hsiao-shuo shih-liao* 中國小說史料. Shanghai: Shang-hai ku-chi, 1982.

Li Jan-ch'ing 李燃青. "Ming-Ch'ing hsiao-shuo mei-hsüeh chung ti tien-hsing li-lun" 明清小說美學中的典型理論. *Wen-i li-lun yen-chiu*, 1984. 1:31–38.

Liang Kuei-chih 梁歸智. "Ts'ao-she hui-hsien tsai ch'ien li chih wai" 草蛇灰線

在千里之外. *Ming-tso hsin-shang* 名作欣賞, 1984. 2:106-8.

Lin Ch'en 林辰. "Chung-kuo hsiao-shuo li-lun ti ch'u-hsing—Tu Ming-Ch'ing chih chi hsiao-shuo ti hsü-pa" 中國小說理論的雛形—讀明清之際小說的序跋. *Kuang-ming jih-pao*, 4/26/1983.

———. "Pai-lun chui-i—Chung-kuo ku-tai hsiao-shuo li-lun shu-lu" 稗論綴遺—中國古代小說理論述錄. In *Chung-kuo ku-tai hsiao-shuo li-lun yen-chiu*, pp. 47-61.

Lin Heng-hsün 林衡勛, "Ming-Ch'ing p'ing-tien p'ai ti wen-hsüeh tien-hsing ssu-hsiang ch'u-t'an" 明清評點派的文學典型思想初探. *Lei-chou shih-chuan hsüeh-pao* 雷州師專學報, 1984. 1:58-65.

Lin Wen-shan 林文山. "Cheng-fan fa—*Shui-hu* yü *Hung-lou meng* pi-chiao yen-chiu" 正犯法—水滸與紅樓夢比較研究. *Ch'i Lu hsüeh-k'an*, 1986. 1:56-61.

Liu Chien-fen 劉健芬. "Chung-kuo hsien-shih chu-i hsiao-shuo li-lun ti li-shih fa-chan" 中國現實主義小說理論的歷史發展. *Ku-tien wen-hsüeh lun-ts'ung* 3:184-219 (1982).

———. "Lüeh-t'an Chung-kuo ku-tien hsiao-shuo li-lun ti min-tsu t'e-se" 略談中國古典小說理論的民族特色. *Ku-tai wen-hsüeh li-lun yen-chiu* 10: 272-87 (1985).

———. "Ming-Ch'ing hsiao-shuo mei-hsüeh chung ti chen-shih lun" 明清小說美學中的真實論. *Hsi-nan shih-fan hsüeh-yüan hsüeh-pao*, 1985. 4:81-88 (*Ku-chin* reprint, 1985. 22:153-60).

Liu Hsiu-yeh 劉修業. *Ku-tien hsiao-shuo hsi-ch'ü ts'ung-k'ao* 古典小說戲曲叢考. Peking: Tso-chia ch'u-pan she, 1958.

Liu Liang-ming 劉良明. "Ming-tai chung hou ch'i hsiao-shuo li-lun ti fa-chan chi ch'i yüan-yin" 明代中後期小說理論的發展及其原因. In *Chung-kuo ku-tai hsiao-shuo li-lun yen-chiu*, pp. 137-50.

———. "Shih-lun wan-Ming ti hsien-shih chu-i hsiao-shuo li-lun" 試論晚明的現實主義小說理論. *Wu-han ta-hsüeh hsüeh-pao* 武漢大學學報, 1981. 1:93-97, 84.

Liu Ts'un-jen 柳存仁. "Lun Ming-Ch'ing Chung-kuo t'ung-su hsiao-shuo chih pan-pen yen-chiu" 論明清中國通俗小說之版本研究. *Lien-ho shu-yüan hsüeh-pao* 聯合書院學報, 2:1-36 (1963). Separate printing, Hong Kong: Chung-shan t'u-shu, 1972.

———. *Lun-tun so-chien Chung-kuo hsiao-shuo shu-mu t'i-yao* 倫敦所見中國小說書目提要. Peking: Shu-mu wen-hsien, 1982 (reprint of Chinese portion of his *Chinese Popular Fiction in Two London Libraries*).

Liu Yung-ch'iang 劉勇強. "Ming-mo Ch'ing-ch'u hsiao-shuo li-lun chung ti tao-te kuan" 明末清初小說理論中的道德觀. *Ming-Ch'ing hsiao-shuo lun-ts'ung* 4:24-43 (1986).

Lu Hsün 魯迅 (Chou Shu-jen 周樹人). *Chung-kuo hsiao-shuo shih-lüeh* 中國小說史略. Vol. 9 of *Lu Hsün ch'üan-chi* 魯迅全集. Peking: Jen-min wen-hsüeh, 1982.

———. *Hsiao-shuo chiu-wen ch'ao* 小說舊聞鈔. Hong Kong: Ta-t'ung shu-chü, 1959.

Lu K'an 路侃. "Pei jen kuei chih t'ai, chien chen huan chih ch'ang—T'an Ming-

Ch'ing hsiao-shuo li-lun chung ti 'ch'i' yü 'cheng'" 備人鬼之態, 兼真幻
之長—談明清小說理論中的奇與正. *Wen shih chih-shih*, 1983. 10:106–9.

Lu Lien-hsing 陸聯星. "Chung-kuo ku-tai hsiao-shuo li-lun p'i-p'ing chih kai-
kuan" 中國古代小說理論批評之概觀. *Huai-pei mei-shih-yüan hsüeh-pao*,
1983. 1:65–78 (*Ku-chin* reprint, 1983. 6:215–29).

Lu Te-ts'ai 魯德才. "Lüeh-lun Ming-Ch'ing pai-hua hsiao-shuo i-shu fa-chan
kuei-lü ti chi ko wen-t'i" 略論明清白話小說藝術發展規律的幾個問題. In
Chung-kuo ku-tai hsiao-shuo li-lun yen-chiu, pp. 62–69.

Ma Ch'eng-sheng 馬成生. "Chu wen-chang chih mei, ch'uan yao-miao chih
ch'ing—Lüeh-t'an T'ang-tai hsiao-shuo chia ti hsiao-shuo kuan" 著文章
之美傳要妙之情—略談唐代小說家的小說觀. *Pei-fang lun-ts'ung*, 1986.
1:42–47.

———. "I ching tang-shih chih tao (Shih-shu Ming-Ch'ing tso-chia tui 'fa-fen
shu-ch'ing shuo' ti chi-ch'eng yü fa-chan)" 以警當世之道(試述明清作
家對發憤抒情說的繼承與發展). *Che-chiang hsüeh-k'an*, 1987. 1:110–15
(*Ku-chin* reprint, 1987. 4:179–84).

———. "Lüeh-shuo wo-kuo ku-tien p'ing-lun chia kuan-yü hsiao-shuo chih
hsing yü shen ti lun-shu" 略說我國古典評論家關於小說之形與神的論述.
She-hui k'o-hsüeh, 1986. 3:68–75.

———. "Wo-kuo ku-tien tso-chia lun hsiao-shuo chi-ch'iao" 我國古典作家論
小說技巧. *Wen shih che* 文史哲, 1985. 4:12–16, 19.

Ma Ch'ing-fu 馬清福. "Ch'ing-tai ti Man-tsu hsiao-shuo li-lun" 清代的滿族
小說理論. *She-hui k'o-hsüeh chi-k'an*, 1986. 1:78–83.

Mao Ch'ing-ch'i 毛慶其. "Ming-Ch'ing hsiao-shuo hsü-pa ch'u-t'an" 明清小說
序跋初探. *Hsüeh-shu yüeh-k'an*, 1985. 12:46–52 (*Ku-chin* reprint, 1986.
2:190–96).

Mu-sung 慕松. "Chung-kuo ku-tien hsiao-shuo li-lun t'ao-lun hui shu-p'ing"
中國古典小說理論討論會述評 *Chung-nan min-tsu hsüeh-yüan hsüeh-pao*,
1984. 3:94–95 (*Ku-chin* reprint, 1984. 18:117–18).

Nagasawa Kikuya 長澤規矩也. "Genson Mindai shōsetsu sho kankōsha hyō
shohen" 現存明代小說書刊行者表初編. *Shoshigaku* 3. 3:41–48 (1934).

Ōtsuka Hidetaka 大塚秀高. *Zōho Chūgoku tsūzoku shōsetsu shomoku* 增補中國
通俗小說書目. Tokyo: Kyūko shoin, 1987.

Pai Tun 白盾. "Shuo Chung-kuo hsiao-shuo p'ing-tien yang-shih" 說中國小說
評點樣式. In *Chung-kuo ku-tai hsiao-shuo li-lun yen-chiu*, pp. 95–104. Also in
I-t'an, 1985. 3:53–55.

P'an Chih-ch'ang 潘知常. "Ming-Ch'ing hsiao-shuo p'ing-tien mei-hsüeh erh
t'i" 明清小說評點美學二題. *Yün-nan she-hui k'o-hsüeh* 雲南社會科學, 1986.
3:86–90.

P'an Ming-shen 潘銘燊 (Poon Ming-sun). *Chung-kuo ku-tien hsiao-shuo lun-wen
mu, 1912–1980* 中國古典小說論文目. Hong Kong: Chinese University of
Hong Kong, 1984.

Pi Kuei-fa 畢桂發. "Lüeh-lun hsien-Ch'in liang-Han shih-ch'i ti hsiao-shuo li-
lun" 略論先秦兩漢時期的小說理論. *Hsü-ch'ang shih-chuan hsüeh-pao* 許昌
師專學報, 1986. 2:56–62 (*Ku-chin* reprint, 1986. 5:257–63).

P'ing Lun 平侖. "To-fang t'an-t'ao cho yu chien-shu—Liu T'ing-chi wen-i ssu-hsiang ch'u-t'an" 多方探討卓有建樹—劉廷璣文藝思想初探. *Shen-yang shih-fan hsüeh-yüan hsüeh-pao* 瀋陽師範學院學報, 1986. 1:69–74, 62.

Sun Chü-ling 孫菊玲, ed. *Ming-Ch'ing chang-hui hsiao-shuo yen-chiu tzu-liao* 明清章回小說研究資料. Peking: Chung-yang min-tsu hsüeh-yüan, 1981.

Sun Hsün 孫遜. "Chung-kuo hsiao-shuo p'i-p'ing ti tu-t'e fang-shih—ku-tien hsiao-shuo p'ing-tien lüeh-shu" 中國小說批評的獨特方式—古典小說評點略述. *Wen shih chih-shih*, 1986. 2:90–95.

———. "Ku-tai ti hsiao-shuo li-lun tui i-shu ho sheng-huo kuan-hsi ti lun-shu" 古代小說理論對藝術和生活關係的論述. *Wen-hsüeh i-ch'an*, 1987. 1:99–107.

———. "Ming-Ch'ing hsiao-shuo li-lun ti 'chen' 'chia' kai-nien chi ch'i nei-han" 明清小說理論的真假概念及其內涵. In *Ming-Ch'ing hsiao-shuo lun-kao*, pp. 81–96.

———. *Ming-Ch'ing hsiao-shuo lun-kao* 明清小說論稿. Shanghai: Shang-hai ku-chi, 1986.

———. "Wo-kuo ku-tien hsiao-shuo p'ing-tien p'ai ti ch'uan-t'ung mei-hsüeh kuan" 我國古典小說評點派的傳統美學觀. *Wen-hsüeh i-ch'an*, 1981. 4:66–75. Reprinted in his *Ming-Ch'ing hsiao-shuo lun-kao*, pp. 62–80.

Sun K'ai-ti 孫楷第. *Chung-kuo t'ung-su hsiao-shuo shu-mu* 中國通俗小說書目. Peking: Jen-min wen-hsüeh, 1982.

———. *Jih-pen Tung-ching so-chien hsiao-shuo shu-mu* 日本東京所見小說書目. Peking: Jen-min wen-hsüeh, 1981.

Ta-lien Library Reference Section, ed. *Ming-Ch'ing hsiao-shuo hsü-pa hsüan* 明清小說序跋選. Shenyang: Ch'un-feng wen-i, 1983.

Tai Pu-fan 戴不凡. *Hsiao-shuo chien-wen lu* 小說見聞錄. Hangchou: Che-chiang jen-min, 1980.

T'an Cheng-pi 譚正璧, and T'an Hsün 譚尋. *Ku-pen hsi-chien hsiao-shuo hui-k'ao* 古本希見小說彙考. Hangchou: Che-chiang wen-i, 1984.

T'an Feng-liang 談鳳梁. "Shih-lun Chung-kuo ku-tai hsiao-shuo kai-nien ti yen-pien" 試論中國古代小說概念的演變. *Wen-i lun-ts'ung* 10:63–93 (1980).

Ts'ai Ching-k'ang 蔡景康. "Shih-lun hsiao-shuo p'ing-tien chi ch'i tui wo-kuo ku-tai hsiao-shuo li-lun ti kung-hsien" 試論小說評點及其對我國古代小說理論的貢獻. *Ku-tai wen-hsüeh li-lun yen-chiu* 11:329–48 (1986).

———. "Wo-kuo tu-t'e ti wen-hsüeh p'i-p'ing hsing-shih—hsiao-shuo p'ing-tien" 我國獨特的文學批評形式—小說評點. *Pai-k'o chih-shih* 百科知識, 1983. 9:32–34 (*Ku-chin* reprint, 1983. 10:241–43).

Ts'ai Kuo-liang 蔡國梁. "Ch'ing p'ing-tien p'ai lun jen-wu miao-hsieh" 清評點派論人物描寫. *Wen-i li-lun yen-chiu*, 1984. 3:67–72. Also in his *Ming-Ch'ing hsiao-shuo t'an-yu*, pp. 279–90.

———. "Ming-Ch'ing hsiao-shuo hsü-pa chung ti hsien-shih chu-i lun" 明清小說序跋中的現實主義論. In *Ming-Ch'ing hsiao-shuo t'an-yu*, pp. 291–305.

Tseng Tsu-yin 曾祖蔭 et al., eds. *Chung-kuo li-tai hsiao-shuo hsü-pa hsüan-chu* 中國歷代小說序跋選注. Hsien-ning: Ch'ang-chiang wen-i, 1982.

Tung Kuo-yen 董國炎. "Ming-Ch'ing hsiao-shuo p'i-p'ing yü hsi-chieh miao-hsieh" 明清小說批評與細節描寫. *Wen-hsüeh i-ch'an*, 1986. 6:69–74.

Wang Hsien-p'ei 王先霈. "'Chien-teng erh-chung' yü Ming-ch'u wen-jen i wen wei hsi ti hsiao-shuo kuan" 剪燈二種與明初文人以文為戲的小說觀. *Hua-chung shih-fan hsüeh-yüan hsüeh-pao*, 1986. 2:94–99 (*Ku-chin* reprint, 1986. 6:157–62).

———— et al. "Chung-kuo ku-tai hsiao-shuo li-lun chia tui hsü-kou ti jen-shih ho lun-shu" 中國古代小說理論家對虛構的認識和論述. *Ku-tai wen-hsüeh li-lun yen-chiu* 5:80–91 (1981).

Wang Ju-mei 王汝梅. "Chin-nien lai Ming-mo Ch'ing-ch'u hsiao-shuo chi hsiao-shuo li-lun yen-chiu lun-wen p'ien-mu so-yin (ch'u-kao)" 近年來明末清初小說及小說理論研究論文篇目索引 (初稿). *Ming-Ch'ing hsiao-shuo lun-ts'ung* 3:202–16 (1985).

Wang Jung-wei 王榮偉. "Chung-kuo hsiao-shuo ch'uang-tso chung i-shu hsü-kou li-lun ti fa-chan" 中國小說創作中藝術虛構理論的發展. *Ch'i-ch'i ha-erh shih-fan hsüeh-yüan hsüeh-pao*, 1984. 1:53–57.

Wang K'ai-fu 王開富. "T'ang-Sung hsiao-shuo li-lun shu-lüeh" 唐宋小說理論述略. *Ch'ung-ch'ing shih-yüan hsüeh-pao*, 1986. 3:48–53 (*Ku-chin* reprint, 1986. 11:269–74).

Wang Li-na 王麗娜, and Tu Wei-mo 杜維沫. "Mei-kuo hsüeh-jen tui Chung-kuo hsü-shih t'i wen-hsüeh ti yen-chiu" 美國學人對中國敘事體文學的研究. *I-t'an*, 1983. 3:132–36 (*Ku-chin* reprint, 1983. 10:41–44).

Wang Yung-chien 王永健. "Ming-Ch'ing hsiao-shuo 'tu-fa' ch'u-lun" 明清小說讀法芻論. *Ming-Ch'ing hsiao-shuo yen-chiu* 2:373–83 (1985).

Wu Kung-cheng 吳功正. "Chung-kuo ku-tien hsiao-shuo ti ch'ing-chieh chieh-kou li-lun ch'u-t'an" 中國古典小說的情節結構理論初探. *Chiang Han lun-t'an*, 1984. 7:54–58.

————. *Hsiao-shuo mei-hsüeh* 小說美學. Nanking: Chiang-su jen-min, 1985.

————. "Ku-tai hsiao-shuo kuan-nien ho mei-hsüeh kuan-hsi t'an-so" 古代小說觀念和美學關係探索. *Ming-Ch'ing hsiao-shuo yen-chiu* 2:1–23 (1985).

————. "Ku-tai li-shih hsiao-shuo li-lun ch'u-t'an" 古代歷史小說理論初探. *She-hui k'o-hsüeh yen-chiu*, 1986. 1:97–103 (*Ku-chin* reprint, 1986. 11:275–81).

————. "Ku-tien hsiao-shuo li-lun ti min-tsu t'e-se" 古典小說理論的民族特色. *Wen-hsüeh p'ing-lun*, 1986. 4:78–84 (*Ku-chin* reprint, 1986. 8:283–89).

Wu Shih-yü 吳士余. "Ku-tien hsiao-shuo chung ti wen-hsüeh i-lun" 古典小說中的文學議論. *Ch'i-ch'i ha-erh shih-fan hsüeh-yüan hsüeh-pao*, 1983. 1:88–94.

————. *Ku-tien hsiao-shuo i-shu so-t'an* 古典小說藝術索探. Wu-ch'ang: Ch'ang-chiang wen-i, 1985.

Wu Tsu-hsiang 吳組緗. "Kuan-yü wo-kuo ku-tai hsiao-shuo ti fa-chan ho li-lun" 關於我國古代小說的發展和理論. *Wen-i pao*, 1983. 3:19–23 (*Ku-chin* reprint, 1983. 4:177–81).

Yang Ch'ing-ts'un 楊慶存. "Ku-tai li-shih hsiao-shuo li-lun ch'u-t'an" 古代歷史小說理論初探. *Ch'i Lu hsüeh-k'an*, 1986. 1:71–74.

Yang Hsing-ying 楊星映. "Chung-kuo ku-tien hsiao-shuo p'i-p'ing chung ti jen-wu su-tsao li-lun ch'u-t'an" 中國古典小說批評中的人物塑造理論初探. *Chung-kuo wen-i ssu-hsiang shih lun-ts'ung* 1:319–47 (1984).

Yeh Lang 葉朗. *Chung-kuo hsiao-shuo mei-hsüeh* 中國小說美學. Peking: Pei-ching ta-hsüeh, 1982.

———. "Chung-kuo hsiao-shuo mei-hsüeh yü Ming-Ch'ing hsiao-shuo p'ing-tien" 中國小說美學與明清小說評點. *Hsüeh-shu yüeh-k'an*, 1982. 11:65–70 (*Ku-chin* reprint, 1983. 1:219–24).

———. "Ming-Ch'ing hsiao-shuo mei-hsüeh" 明清小說美學. In his *Chung-kuo mei-hsüeh shih ta-kang* 中國美學史大綱. Shanghai: Shang-hai jen-min, 1985, pp. 357–410.

———. "Ming-Ch'ing hsiao-shuo mei-hsüeh kuan-yü su-tsao tien-hsing jen-wu ti li-lun" 明清小說美學關於塑造典型人物的理論. *Mei-hsüeh wen-hsien* 美學文獻 (Peking: Shu-mu wen-hsien) 1:166–201 (1984).

Yü Chih-yüan 于植元. "Ying-tai pen-wen, tseng ch'i chün-yung—*Lin Lan Hsiang* ti p'ing-tien wen-tzu" 映帶本文增其雋永—林蘭香的評點文字. *Ta-lien shih-chuan hsüeh-pao*, 1984. 1–2:42–48.

Yü Hsing-han 于興漢. "Chung-kuo ku-tai hsiao-shuo hsü-pa tui hsiao-shuo li-lun ti kung-hsien" 中國古代小說序跋對小說理論的貢獻. *Shan-hsi shih-ta hsüeh-pao* 山西師大學報, 1986. 4:77–78 (*Ku-chin* reprint, 1987. 1:18–19).

Late Ch'ing Fiction Criticism (Traditional School)

A-ying 阿英 (Ch'ien Hsing-ts'un 錢杏邨), ed. "Hsiao-shuo hsi-ch'ü yen-chiu chüan" 小說戲曲研究卷. In *Wan-Ch'ing wen-hsüeh ts'ung-ch'ao* 晚清文學叢鈔. Peking: Chung-hua shu-chü, 1960.

———. "Wu Chien-jen ti hsiao-shuo li-lun" 吳趼人的小說理論. In *Hsiao-shuo erh-t'an* 小說二談. Shanghai: Ku-tien wen-hsüeh, 1958, pp. 79–82. Reprinted in *Hsiao-shuo hsien-t'an ssu-chung*.

Ch'ang Cheng 常徵. "Wan-Ch'ing hsiao-shuo li-lun wai-pu kuei-lü hsüeh-shuo ch'u-t'an" 晚清小說理論外部規律學說初探. *Nan-ching shih-yüan hsüeh-pao*, 1982. 1:41–47.

Ch'en Chien-sheng 陳健生. "Lüeh-t'an wan-Ch'ing hsiao-shuo li-lun" 略談晚清小說理論. *Hsü-chou shih-fan hsüeh-yüan hsüeh-pao*, 1983. 2:24–29 (*Ku-chin* reprint, 1983. 8:251–56).

Ch'en Ch'ien-yü 陳謙豫. "Wan-Ch'ing hsiao-shuo li-lun kuan-k'uei" 晚清小說理論管窺. *Hua-tung shih-fan ta-hsüeh hsüeh-pao*, 1982. 3:57–62. Also in *Ku-tai wen-hsüeh li-lun yen-chiu*, 3:316–28 (1981).

Ch'en Yung-piao 陳永標. "Lüeh-lun Wu Chien-jen ti hsiao-shuo li-lun" 略論吳趼人的小說理論. *Kuang-chou yen-chiu* 廣州研究, 1985. 1:84–88.

Chiang Tung-fu 姜東賦. "Chieh tiao-ch'ung chih hsiao-chi, yü tsun-to chih wei-yen—Wan-Ch'ing hsiao-shuo li-lun shu-p'ing" 借雕蟲之小技, 寓遵鐸之微言—晚清小說理論述評. In *Ku-tien hsiao-shuo hsi-ch'ü t'an-i lu*, pp. 288–319.

———. "Lüeh-shuo Chung-kuo chin-tai hsiao-shuo li-lun ti t'e-tien" 略說中國近代小說理論的特點. *T'ien-chin shih-ta hsüeh-pao*, 1985. 2:66–69, 85.

Chou Sung-hsi 周頌喜. "Wan-Ch'ing hsiao-shuo ch'uang-tso li-lun shu-p'ing"

晚清小說創作理論述評. *Ch'iu-so*, 1982. 2:70–75 (*Ku-chin* reprint, 1982. 12:115–21).

Hsü P'eng-hsü 徐鵬緒. "Wan-Ch'ing tui hsiao-shuo i-shu t'e-cheng ti jen-shih" 晚清對小說藝術特徵的認識. *Liao-ch'eng shih-fan hsüeh-yüan hsüeh-pao* 聊城師範學院學報, 1982. 3:38–44.

Hsü Ying-yüan 徐應元. "*Shui-hu chuan* yü wan-Ch'ing hsiao-shuo li-lun p'i-p'ing" 水滸傳與晚清小說理論批評. *Shui-hu cheng-ming* 2:443–50 (1983).

Huang Lin 黃霖. "Wu Chien-jen ti hsiao-shuo li-lun" 吳趼人的小說理論. *Ming-Ch'ing hsiao-shuo yen-chiu* 3:340–56 (1986).

K'ang Lai-hsin 康來新. *Wan-Ch'ing hsiao-shuo li-lun yen-chiu* 晚清小說理論研究. Taipei: Ta-an ch'u-pan she, 1986.

Liang Shu-an 梁淑安. "Chin-tai hsiao-shuo li-lun ch'u-t'an" 近代小說理論初探. *Chiang Hai hsüeh-k'an*, 1963. 7:41–46. Reprinted in *Chung-kuo chin-tai wen-hsüeh lun-wen chi: Hsiao-shuo chüan* 中國近代文學論文集:小說卷. Peking: Chung-kuo she-hui k'o-hsüeh, 1983, pp. 131–47.

P'ei Hsiao-wei 裴效維. "Su Man-shu hsiao-shuo lun" 蘇曼殊小說論. *Wen-hsüeh i-ch'an*, 1983. 1:123–32.

Ts'ai Ching-k'ang 蔡景康. "Lüeh-lun Huang Mo-hsi ti hsiao-shuo li-lun" 略論黃摩西的小說理論. *Ku-tai wen-hsüeh li-lun yen-chiu* 5:113–29 (1981).

———. "Wan-Ch'ing hsiao-shuo li-lun ch'u-t'an" 晚清小說理論初探. *Ku-tai wen-hsüeh li-lun yen-chiu* 1:403–21 (1979).

Tu Ching-hua 杜景華. "Chin-tai hsiao-shuo lun-chia ti ch'eng-chiu yü p'ien-p'o" 近代小說論家的成就與偏頗. *She-hui k'o-hsüeh chi-k'an*, 1986. 6:103–7 (*Ku-chin* reprint, 1987. 2:269–73).

Yüan Chin 袁進. "Huang Mo-hsi, Hsü Nien-tz'u hsiao-shuo li-lun ti mao-tun yü chü-hsien" 黃摩西徐念慈小說理論的矛盾與局限. *Hua-tung shih-fan ta-hsüeh hsüeh-pao*, 1986. 3:15–19 (*Ku-chin* reprint, 1986. 9:316–20).

Individual Traditional Critics of Fiction and Drama

(Takizawa) Bakin (1767–1848)

Widmer, Ellen. "Bakin and Chinese Theories of Fiction." Unpublished paper.

———. "*Chinsetsu Yumiharizuki* in Sino-Japanese Perspective." Unpublished draft, 1987.

Hamada Keisuke 浜田啟介. "Bakin no iwayuru haishi shichi hōsoku ni tsuite" 馬琴の所謂稗史七法則について. In *Bakin* 馬琴. Edited by Nihon bungaku kenkyū shiryō kankōkai 日本文学研究資料刊行会. Tokyo: Yūseitō, 1974, pp. 136–45.

Itasaka Noriko 板坂則子. "Haishi shichi hōsoku no happyō o megutte" 稗史七法則の発表をめぐって. *Kokugo to kokubungaku* 国語と国文学 55. 11:77–93 (1978).

Tokuda Takeshi 德田武. "Bakin no haishi shichi hōsoku to Mō Seizan no 'Doku Sankoku shi hō" 馬琴の稗史七法則と毛声山の読三国史法. *Bungaku* 文学 48. 6:14–29 (pt. 1); 48. 7:64–76 (pt. 2; 1980).

Ch'en Ch'en (1614–1666+)

Widmer, Ellen. *The Margins of Utopia*. Cambridge, Mass.: Harvard University Press, 1987.

———. "*Shui-hu hou-chuan* in the Context of Seventeenth-Century Chinese Fiction Criticism." Ph.D. thesis, Harvard University, 1981.

Chou Wei-min 周偉民. "Ch'en Ch'en hsiao-shuo li-lun ch'ien-shuo" 陳忱小說理論淺說. *Ku-tien wen-hsüeh chih-shih* 古典文學知識, 1986. 5:88–91.

Feng Meng-lung (1574–1646)

Ch'en T'ai-shan 陳太山. "Man-t'an Feng Meng-lung ti hsiao-shuo li-lun" 漫談馮夢龍的小說理論. *Ning-te shih-chuan hsüeh-pao* 寧德師專學報, 1984. 1:48–50.

Chuang Wei 莊葳, and Kuo Ch'ün-i 郭群一. "Feng Meng-lung p'ing-tsuan pen *T'ai-p'ing kuang-chi ch'ao* ch'u-t'an" 馮夢龍評纂本太平廣記鈔初探. *She-hui k'o-hsüeh*, 1980. 5:145–47.

Fang Sheng 方勝. "Lun Feng Meng-lung ti 'ch'ing-chiao' kuan" 論馮夢龍的情教觀. *Wen-hsüeh i-ch'an*, 1985. 4:113–21.

Hsieh Cheng 謝徵. "*San-yen* ti p'ing-chiao-che ho tso-hsü-che tou shih Feng Meng-lung" 三言的評校者和作序者都是馮夢龍. *Kuang-ming jih-pao*, 4/2/1980.

Hu Wan-ch'uan 胡萬川. "Feng Meng-lung sheng-p'ing chi ch'i tui hsiao-shuo chih kung-hsien" 馮夢龍生平及其對小說之貢獻. Master's thesis, Political University, Taipei, 1973.

———. "*San-yen* hsü chi mei-p'i ti tso-che wen-t'i" 三言序及眉批的作者問題. *Chung-kuo ku-tien hsiao-shuo yen-chiu chuan-chi* 2:281–94 (1980).

Kuo Ch'ün-i 郭群一, and Chuang Wei 莊葳. "Feng Meng-lung p'ing-tsuan *T'ai-p'ing kuang-chi ch'ao* p'i-yü hsüan-chi" 馮夢龍評纂太平廣記鈔批語選輯. *Ku-tien wen-hsüeh lun-ts'ung* 2:488–570 (1981).

———. "Feng Meng-lung ti '*T'ai-p'ing kuang-chi ch'ao* hsiao-yin'" 馮夢龍的太平廣記鈔小引. *Hsüeh-lin man-lu* 2:182–83 (1981).

Kuo Hsiao-fei 郭曉飛. "Man-t'an Feng Meng-lung ti wen-hsüeh kuan" 漫談馮夢龍的文學觀. *Chiang-hsi ta-hsüeh hsüeh-pao*, 1982. 3:29–35.

Li Wen 力文. "Lun Feng Meng-lung ti wen-hsüeh kuan" 論馮夢龍的文學觀. *Chung-chou hsüeh-k'an*, 1984. 2:91–94, 41.

Lu Shu-lun 陸樹崙. "Shih-lun Feng Meng-lung ti hsiao-shuo li-lun" 試論馮夢龍的小說理論. *Fu-tan hsüeh-pao*, 1984. 3:55–62 (*Ku-chin* reprint, 1984. 12:82–89). Reprinted in *Chung-kuo ku-tai hsiao-shuo li-lun yen-chiu*, pp. 151–64.

P'an Shih-hsiu 潘世秀. "Lun Feng Meng-lun ti hsiao-shuo li-lun" 論馮夢龍的小說理論. *Wen-hsüeh i-ch'an*, 1986. 6:92–98 (*Ku-chin* reprint, 1987. 3:314–20).

Yüan Hsing-yün 袁行雲. "Feng Meng-lung *San-yen* hsin-cheng" 馮夢龍三言新證. *She-hui k'o-hsüeh chan-hsien*, 1980. 1:337–48.

Hsü Wei (1521–1593)

Leung, K.C. *Hsü Wei as Drama Critic: An Annotated Translation of the Nan-tz'u hsü-lu*. Eugene: Asian Studies Program, University of Oregon, 1988.

Chiang Hsing-yü 蔣星煜. "Liu-chung Hsü Wen-ch'ang pen *Hsi-hsiang chi* ti chen-wei wen-t'i" 六種徐文長本西廂記的真偽問題. In his *Ming k'an-pen Hsi-hsiang chi yen-chiu*, pp. 113–27.

Hu Ying-lin (1551–1602)

Wang Hsien-p'ei 王先霈. "Hu Ying-lin ti hsiao-shuo li-lun" 胡應麟的小說理論. *Hua-chung shih-yüan hsüeh-pao*, 1981. 3:14–19.

K'ung Shang-jen (1648–1718)

Strassberg, Richard E. *The World of K'ung Shang-jen: A Man of Letters in Early Ch'ing China*. New York: Columbia University Press, 1983.

Wang Hsiao-chia 王曉家. "'*T'ao-hua shan* fan-li' shih-i" 桃花扇凡例釋義. *Hsi-chü i-shu*, 1981. 1:107–9.
Wang Yung-chien 王永健. "*T'ao-hua shan* chung ti t'ao-hua shan—*T'ao-hua shan* p'i-yü" 桃花扇中的桃花扇—桃花扇批語. *Chiang-su hsi-chü* 江蘇戲劇, 1981. 3:53–54.

Li Chih (1527–1602)

Chan, Hok-lam. *Li Chih in Contemporary Historiography: New Light on His Life and Work*. White Plains, N.Y.: M. E. Sharpe, 1980.
Cheang, Eng-chew. "Li Chih as a Critic: A Chapter of the Ming Intellectual History." Ph.D. thesis, University of Washington, Seattle, 1973.

Ch'en Ch'ien-yü 陳謙豫. "Li Cho-wu p'ing-tien hsiao-shuo ti kung-hsien" 李卓吾評點小說的貢獻. *Shang-hai shih-fan ta-hsüeh hsüeh-pao*, 1979. 3:59–63.
Ch'en Chin-chao 陳錦釗. *Li Chih chih wen-lun* 李贄之文論. Taipei: Chia-hsin shui-ni kung-ssu, 1974.
Ch'en Man-p'ing 陳曼平, and Chang K'o 張克. "Li Chih ti mei-hsüeh ssu-hsiang" 李贄的美學思想. *Yen-pien ta-hsüeh hsüëh-pao* 延邊大學學報, 1983. 4:67–75.
Cheng P'ei-k'ai 鄭培凱. "Ts'ung *Ssu-shu p'ing* k'an Li Chih ssu-hsiang fa-chan yü Ju-hsüeh ch'uan-t'ung ti kuan-hsi" 從四書評看李贄思想發展與儒學傳統的關係, *Tou-sou* 抖擻 28:1–28 (July 1981).
Chiang Hsing-yü 蔣星煜. "Li Cho-wu pen *Hsi-hsiang chi* tui Ming-mo Sun Yüeh-feng pen, Wei Chung-hsüeh pen ti ying-hsiang" 李卓吾本西廂記對明末孫月峰本, 魏仲雪本的影響. *Hsüeh-shu yüeh-k'an*, 1982. 5:51–56.
———. "Li Cho-wu p'i-pen *Hsi-hsiang chi* ti t'e-cheng, chen-wei yü ying-hsiang" 李卓吾批本西廂記的特徵真偽與影響. *Hsi-ch'ü yen-chiu* 4:132–51 (1981). Reprinted in his *Ming k'an-pen Hsi-hsiang chi yen-chiu*, pp. 88–103.

————. "Ming Jung-yü t'ang k'an-pen Li Cho-wu *Hsi-hsiang chi* tui Sun Yüeh-feng, Wei Chung-hsüeh pen chih ying-hsiang" 明容與堂刊本李卓吾西廂記對孫月峰魏仲雪本之影響. In his *Chung-kuo hsi-ch'ü shih kou-ch'en* 中國戲曲史鉤沉. Cheng-chou: Chung-chou shu-hua she, 1982, pp. 134–45.

————. "T'ang Hsien-tsu p'ing-pen *Hsi-hsiang chi* shih wei-chuang ti Li Cho-wu pen" 湯顯祖評本西廂記是偽裝的李卓吾本. In *Ming k'an-pen Hsi-hsiang chi yen-chiu*, pp. 104–12.

————. "Tsai-lun *Hsi-hsiang hui-chen chuan* wei Min-k'an Min-p'ing pen—Ta Chang Jen-ho t'ung-chih" 再論西廂會真傳為閔刊閔評本—答張人和同志. In his *Chung-kuo hsi-ch'ü shih t'an-wei*, pp. 172–79.

————. "*Yüan-pen ch'u-hsiang Pei Hsi-hsiang chi* ti Wang, Li ho-p'ing yü Shen-t'ien Hsi-i-lang [Kanda Kiichirō] ts'ang-pen" 元本出像北西廂記的王李合評與神田喜一郎藏本. *Chung-hua wen-shih lun-ts'ung*, 1984. 1:119–36. Reprinted in his *Chung-kuo hsi-ch'ü shih t'an-wei*, pp. 130–49.

Funatsu Tomihiko 船津富彦. "Ri Takugo no bungaku hyōron ni tsuite" 李卓吾の文学評論について. *Tōyō bungaku kenkyū* 東洋文学研究 (Waseda University) 19:1–21 (1971).

Huang Kao-hsien 黃高憲. "Li Chih lun wen-hsüeh ch'uang-tso" 李贄論文學創作. *Wen-hsüeh p'ing-lun ts'ung-k'an* 18:336–51 (1983).

Hung T'u 洪途. "Li Chih hsi-ch'ü p'i-p'ing chung ti fan-Ju ching-shen" 李贄戲曲批評中的反儒精神. *Wen-hui pao*, 2/18/1975.

Li Chih 李贄. *Ch'u-t'an chi* 初潭集. Peking: Chung-hua shu-chü, 1974.

————. *Fen-shu* 焚書. Peking: Chung-hua shu-chü, 1961.

————. *Hsü fen-shu* 續焚書. Peking: Chung-hua shu-chü, 1959.

———— (attributed). *Ssu-shu p'ing* 四書評. Shanghai: Jen-min ch'u-pan she, 1975.

Lin Ch'i-hsien 林其賢. "Li Cho-wu yen-chiu ch'u-pien" 李卓吾研究初編. Master's thesis, Soochow University, Taipei, 1981.

Liu Chien-kuo 劉建國. "Yeh t'an Li Chih *Ssu-shu p'ing* ti chen-wei wen-t'i" 也談李贄四書評的真偽問題. *Kuei-chou she-hui k'o-hsüeh*, 1983. 3:19–25.

Ma Ch'eng-sheng 馬成生. "Li Chih—Chung-kuo ku-tien hsiao-shuo li-lun ti tien-chi jen" 李贄—中國古典小說理論的奠基人. *Hang-chou shih-yüan hsüeh-pao*, 1985. 4:144–50 (*Ku-chin* reprint, 1986. 2:307–13).

Min Tse 敏澤. *Li Chih* 李贄. Shanghai: Shang-hai ku-chi, 1984.

Pai Chien 白堅. "Ts'ao Hsüeh-ch'in ti hsiao-shuo kuan ho Li Chih ti 't'ung-hsin' wen-hsüeh kuan" 曹雪芹的小說觀和李贄的童心文學觀. In *Chung-kuo ku-tai hsiao-shuo li-lun yen-chiu*, pp. 275–93.

Ssu-t'u Chi 司徒季. "P'ing *Li Cho-wu p'i-tien Huang-Ming t'ung-chi*" 評李卓吾批點皇明通記. *Hsüeh-hsi yü p'i-p'an* 學習與批判, 1974. 12:20–24.

Ts'ui Wen-yin 崔文印. "Li Chih *Ssu-shu p'ing* chen-wei pien" 李贄四書評真偽辨. *Wen-wu*, 1979. 4:31–34.

————. "*Ssu-shu p'ing* pu-shih Li Chih chu-tso ti k'ao-cheng" 四書評不是李贄著作的考證. *Che-hsüeh yen-chiu* 哲學研究, 1980. 4:69–71.

————. "T'an *Shih-kang p'ing-yao* ti chen-wei wen-t'i" 談史綱評要的真偽問題. *Wen-wu*, 1977. 8:29–34.

Tung Kuo-yen 董國炎. "Li Chih ti wen-hsüeh ssu-hsiang yü hsiao-shuo p'i-p'ing" 李贄的文學思想與小說批評. *Shan-hsi ta-hsüeh hsüeh-pao* 山西大學學報, 1985. 2:61–65.

Wang Hsien-p'ei 王先霈. "Li Cho-wu ho hsiao-shuo li-lun chung ti fa-fen chu-shu shuo" 李卓吾和小說理論中的發憤著書說. *Hua-chung shih-yüan hsüeh-pao*, 1983. 1:111–17 (*Ku-chin* reprint, 1983. 4:211–17).

Wang Sung-mei 王頌梅. "Li Cho-wu ti wen-hsüeh li-lun chi ch'i shih-chien" 李卓吾的文學理論及其實踐. Master's thesis, Soochow University, Taipei, 1983.

Wu Hsin-lei 吳新雷. "Kuan-yü Li Cho-wu p'i-p'ing ti ch'ü-pen" 關於李卓吾批評的曲本. *Chiang Hai hsüeh-k'an*, 1963. 4:40–42.

Li Yü (1611–1680)

Hayden, George. "Li Li-weng: A Playwright on Performance." *Chinoperl Papers* 9:80–91 (1979–80).

Henry, Eric P. *Chinese Amusements: The Lively Plays of Li Yü*. Hamden, Conn.: Archon Books, 1980.

Mao, Nathan, and Liu Ts'un-yan. *Li Yü*. Boston: Twayne, 1977.

Martin, Hellmut. *Li Li-weng über das Theater*. Taipei: Chinese Materials Center, 1968.

Ch'en To 陳多, ed. *Li Li-weng ch'ü-hua* 李笠翁曲話. Ch'ang-sha: Hu-nan jen-min, 1980.

———. "Li Yü 'li chu-nao' p'ing-shih" 李漁立主腦評釋. *Shang-hai hsi-chü*, 1980. 2:55–57.

Ch'en Wei-hsiung 陳維雄. "Lüeh-t'an Li Yü hsi-ch'ü li-lun chung ti ch'uang-hsin" 略談李漁戲曲理論中的創新. *Shang-hai shih-yüan hsüeh-pao*, 1983. 3:66–69.

Hsieh Ming 謝明. "'Li chu-nao' ti san ting-lü—Li-weng chü-lun chin chieh chih i" 立主腦的三定律—笠翁劇論今解之一. *Hsin chü-tso* 新劇作, 1980. 6:9–10.

Hsü Shou-k'ai 徐壽凱. *Li Li-weng ch'ü-hua chu-shih* 李笠翁曲話注釋. Hofei: An-hui jen-min, 1981.

Huang Hsien-yu 黃賢友. "Chung-kuo chieh-ch'u ti ku-tien hsi-chü wen-hsüeh li-lun chia—Li Yü" 中國杰出的古典戲劇文學理論家—李漁. In *Mei-hsüeh wen-hsüeh lun-wen chi*, pp. 260–75.

Kuo Kuang-yü 郭光宇. "Li Yü ti pien-chü li-lun yü ch'uang-tso shih-chien" 李漁的編劇理論與創作實踐. In *Chung-kuo i-shu yen-chiu yüan shou-chieh yen-chiu sheng shuo-shih hsüeh-wei lun-wen chi: Hsi-ch'ü chüan* 中國藝術研究院首屆研究生碩士學位論文集:戲曲卷. Peking: Wen-hua i-shu, 1985, pp. 195–237.

Shen Mo 沈默, and Ch'en Lei 陳雷. "Li chu-nao, mi chen-hsien, t'o k'o-chiu—Tu Li Yü *Hsien-ch'ing ou-chi* 'Chieh-kou p'ien'" 立主腦密針綫脫窠臼—讀李漁閑情偶寄結構篇. *Kuang-chou wen-i* 廣州文藝, 1981. 3:62–63.

Tu Shu-ying 杜書瀛. *Lun Li Yü ti hsi-chü mei-hsüeh* 論李漁的戲劇美學. Peking: Chung-kuo she-hui k'o-hsüeh, 1982.

Wang Ju-mei 王汝梅. "Li Yü ti *Wu-sheng hsi* ch'uang-tso chi ch'i hsiao-shuo li-lun" 李漁的無聲戲創作及其小說理論. *Wen-hsüeh p'ing-lun*, 1982. 2:129–34.

Wu Cheng 吳鄭. "Yeh t'an Li Yü ti 'li chu-nao'" 也談李漁的立主腦. *Shang-hai hsi-chü*, 1980. 5:41–42.

Yang Ming-hsin 楊明新. "Li Yü ti hsi-ch'ü li-lun ch'u-t'an" 李漁的戲曲理論初探. *Wen-hsüeh i-ch'an tseng-k'an* 15:39–63 (1983).

Yang Wei-hao 楊位浩. "Kuan-yü Li Yü 'li chu-nao' shuo ti t'an-t'ao" 關於李漁立主腦說的探討. *Chi-ning shih-chuan hsüeh-pao*, 1984. 1:23–30.

Yu Yu-chi 游友基. "Lüeh lun Li Yü hsi-chü mei-hsüeh ssu-hsiang ti t'e-tien" 略論李漁戲劇美學思想的特點. *Ku-tai wen-hsüeh li-lun yen-chiu* 10:301–14 (1983).

Ling Meng-ch'u (1580–1644)

Wang Ta-chin 王達津. "Ling Meng-ch'u ti hsiao-shuo li-lun ho shih-chien" 凌濛初的小說理論和實踐. *Ku-tien wen-hsüeh lun-ts'ung* 3:174–83 (1982). Reprinted in his *Ku-tai wen-hsüeh li-lun yen-chiu lun-wen chi*, pp. 203–12.

Liu Ch'en-weng (1232–1297)

Wu Ch'i-ming 吳企明. "Liu Ch'en-weng sheng-p'ing san-t'i" 劉辰翁生平三題. *Chung-kuo ku-tien wen-hsüeh lun-ts'ung* 2:312–16 (1985).

Lü T'ien-ch'eng (1580–1618)

Wu Shu-yin 吳書蔭. "Ts'ung *Ch'ü-p'in* k'an Lü T'ien-ch'eng ti hsi-ch'ü li-lun" 從曲品看呂天成的戲曲理論. *Chung-kuo wen-i ssu-hsiang lun-ts'ung* 1:281–99 (1984).

P'u Sung-ling (1640–1715) and the Liao-chai chih-i

Chu I-hsüan 朱一玄, ed. *Liao-chai chih-i tzu-liao hui-pien* 聊齋誌異資料匯編. Cheng-chou: Chung-chou ku-chi, 1985.

Ho Chin-wen 何金文, and Hu Pang-wei 胡邦煒. "Feng Chen-luan p'ing-pen *Liao-chai chih-i* ch'u-t'an" 馮鎮鸞評本聊齋誌異初探. *She-hui k'o-hsüeh yen-chiu*, 1984. 4:83–89.

Hu I-hsiao 胡憶肖. "Ch'ung-p'ing *Liao-chai chih-i hui-chiao hui-chu hui-p'ing* ti p'ing" 重評聊齋誌異會校會注會評的評. *Wu-han shih-yüan hsüeh-pao*, 1983. 5:47–51.

Lo Wei 駱偉. "*Liao-chai chih-i* pan-pen lüeh-shu" 聊齋誌異版本略述. *P'u Sung-ling yen-chiu chi-k'an* 3:306–20 (1982). Reprinted in *Pan-pen*, pp. 367–81.

Lü Yang 呂揚. "P'u Sung-ling ti hsiao-shuo li-lun ch'u-t'an" 蒲松齡的小說理論初探. *Shan-tung shih-ta hsüeh pao*, 1984. 6:87–88, 86.

Shen Chi-ch'ang 沈繼常, and Ch'ien Mo-hsiang 錢模祥. "Tan Ming-lun lun tso-wen chih yao tsai yü 'li-t'ai'—*Liao-chai chih-i* Tan-p'ing yen-chiu chih i" 但明倫論作文之要在於立胎—聊齋誌異但評研究之一. *Ming-Ch'ing hsiao-shuo yen-chiu* 2:401–15 (1985).

———. "T'an Tan Ming-lun kuan-yü *Liao-chai* 'shuang-t'i' hsieh-fa ti p'ing-tien" 談但明倫關於聊齋雙提寫法的評點. *Nan-t'ung shih-chuan hsüeh-pao*, 1985. 4:43–48.

Sheng Jui-yü 盛瑞裕. "*Liao-chai* Tan-p'ing t'e-se ti wo-chien" 聊齋但評特色
的我見. In *Chung-kuo ku-tai hsiao-shuo li-lun yen-chiu*, pp. 340–53.

Sun I-chen 孫一珍. "P'ing Tan Ming-lun tui *Liao-chai chih-i* ti p'ing-tien"
評但明倫對聊齋誌異的評點. *P'u Sung-ling yen-chiu chi-k'an* 2:282–310
(1981). Reprinted in her *Liao-chai chih-i ts'ung-lun* 聊齋誌異叢論 (Tsinan:
Ch'i Lu shu-she, 1984), pp. 212–43.

Ts'ai Kuo-liang 蔡國梁. "Shih tse fan-fu li-ch'i, wen tse tsung-heng kuei-pien
—Ch'ing-jen p'ing *Liao-chai* ti mou-p'ien pu-chü" 事則反復離奇, 文則縱橫
詭變—清人評聊齋的謀篇布局. *Wen-i li-lun yen-chiu*, 1982. 4:109–17 (*Ku-
chin* reprint, 1983. 2:148–56).

Yang Chen-fang 楊震方. "Yu-cheng pen *Yüan-pen Liao-chai chih-i* shu-lüeh"
有正本原本聊齋誌異述略. *Chung-hua wen-shih lun-ts'ung*, 1980. 1:306.

T'ang Hsien-tsu (1550–1616)

Chang Jen-ho 張人和. "*Hsi-hsiang hui-chen chuan* 'T'ang Hsien-tsu Shen Ching
p'ing' pien-wei" 西廂會真傳湯顯祖沈璟評辨偽. *She-hui k'o-hsüeh chan-
hsien*, 1981. 2:338–47.

Chiang Hsing-yü 蔣星煜. "*Hsi-hsiang hui-chen chuan* shih Shen Ching, T'ang
Hsien-tsu ti ho-p'ing pen ma?" 西廂會真傳是沈璟湯顯祖的合評本嗎. In
his *Ming k'an-pen Hsi-hsiang chi yen-chiu*, pp. 198–209.

Hsü Shuo-fang 徐朔方. "*Yü-ming t'ang p'i-p'ing Tung Hsi-hsiang* pien-wei"
玉茗堂批評董西廂辨偽. *She-hui k'o-hsüeh chan-hsien*, 1984. 2:328–29.

Lan Fan 藍凡. "T'ang Hsien-tsu ti hsi-ch'ü mei-hsüeh ssu-hsiang" 湯顯祖的戲曲
美學思想. *Chiang-hsi ta-hsüeh hsüeh-pao*, 1982. 2:75–82.

Liu Yen-chün 劉彥君. "Ying-i pu-ch'ün, hsia-ch'ing kao-li: T'ang Hsien-tsu
hsi-chü li-lun p'ing-lüeh" 穎異不群, 遐清高屬:湯顯祖戲劇理論評略. *Hsi-
chü: Chung-yang hsi-chü hsüeh-yüan hsüeh-pao* 戲劇:中央戲劇學院學報,
1987. 2:62–71 (*Ku-chin* reprint, 1987. 7:311–20).

Lung Hua 龍華. "T'ang Hsien-tsu ti hsi-chü li-lun" 湯顯祖的戲劇理論. *Ku-tai
wen-hsüeh li-lun yen-chiu* 6:194–213 (1982).

Mao Hsiao-t'ung 毛效同. *T'ang Hsien-tsu yen-chiu tzu-liao hui-pien* 湯顯祖
研究資料彙編. Shanghai: Shang-hai ku-chi, 1986.

Wang Cheng 王政. "Lun Lin-ch'uan p'ai ti hsi-ch'ü mei-hsüeh li-lun" 論臨川派
的戲曲美學理論. *Ku-tai wen-hsüeh li-lun yen-chiu* 9:266–92 (1984).

Wang Chi-te (d. 1623)

Ch'en Chang-i 陳長義. "Lun Wang Chi-te ti *Ch'ü-lü*" 論王驥德的曲律. *Ku-tai
wen-hsüeh li-lun yen-chiu* 9:292–308 (1984).

Ch'en To 陳多, and Yeh Ch'ang-hai 葉長海, eds. *Wang Chi-te Ch'ü-lü* 王驥德
曲律. Ch'ang-sha: Hu-nan jen-min, 1983.

Yeh Ch'ang-hai 葉長海. *Wang Chi-te Ch'ü-lü yen-chiu* 王驥德曲律研究. Peking:
Chung-kuo hsi-chü, 1983.

Yeh Chou (fl. 1595–1624)

Ts'ui Wen-yin 崔文印. "T'o-ming tso-wei ti chuan-chia Yeh Chou" 托名作偽
的專家葉晝. *Shu-lin*, 1981. 3:23.

Yü Hsiang-tou (ca. 1550–1637)

Hsiao Tung-fa 蕭東發. "Chung-kuo k'o-shu shih—Chien-yang Yü-shih k'o-shu k'ao-lüeh" 中國刻書史—建陽余氏刻書考略. *Wen-hsien*, 1985. 1:236–50 (pt. 2).

―――. "Ming-tai hsiao-shuo chia, k'o-shu chia Yü Hsiang-tou" 明代小說家刻書家余象斗. *Ming-Ch'ing hsiao-shuo lun-ts'ung* 4:195–211 (1986).

Kuan Kuei-ch'üan 官桂銓. "Ming hsiao-shuo chia Yü Hsiang-tou chi Yü-shih k'o hsiao-shuo hsi-ch'ü" 明小說家余象斗及余氏刻小說戲曲. *Wen-hsüeh i-ch'an tseng-k'an* 15:125–30 (1983).

Yüan Mei (1716–1798)

Funatsu Tomihiko 船津富彦. "En Mei no shōsetsu ron" 袁枚の小說論. *Tōyōgaku ronsō* 東洋学論叢 7:63–76 (1982).

Descriptive Bibliography (for Commentary Editions and Traditional Works of Criticism on the Six Novels)

This part of the bibliography describes briefly all commentary editions and premodern works of any influence or intrinsic interest dealing with the six novels, criticism of which is the subject of this volume; these descriptions are followed by a listing of secondary material. Scholarly attention to the various traditional critics has been very uneven, with the bulk of it going originally to Chin Sheng-t'an and Chih-yen chai; more recently, peripheral attention has been given to Chang Chu-p'o and Mao Tsung-kang. In regard to Chin Sheng-t'an and Chih-yen chai, the bibliographies make no pretense to being exhaustive. Much of the material on Chin Sheng-t'an produced during the Cultural Revolution in China, for instance, was written by political hacks or against the will of the authors, and it is no great loss to let it slide into oblivion. Availability has also been a factor in deciding on the inclusion or exclusion of descriptions of commentary editions as well as bibliographic entries. In general, unpublished private commentaries on particular novels have not been included. The editor has made an effort to examine personally and read all sources cited in the bibliographies, but has not been completely successful. Some of the unseen bibliographic items lack page numbers, as it is only in the last several years that bibliographies published in the People's Republic of China have included such information, but these entries have not been excluded in the hope that even in their imperfect state they may be of use or interest.

The six novels are taken up in turn in the order in which the translations of the *tu-fa* essays and chapter comments appear in this volume. Under the heading of each novel, chronological order of publication or composition is followed as well as can be ascertained in our present state of knowledge on these matters, except where certain commentaries are treated in sequence because they are textually related. Information on availability is based on the situation of the scholar residing in the United States who has access to university libraries or is able to borrow or purchase reprints of the original materials. This information is very far from representing a complete listing of such material, especially in regard to individual holdings of copies of editions in university libraries and other collections. The frequent mention of holdings in the University of Chicago and Princeton University Asian collections is explained by the fact that it was these two collections to which the editor had most extensive access while preparing this material. More attention has been given to noting the existence of microfilm copies over individual copies as it is fairly likely that microfilms held by Chicago or Princeton will also be available in other major collections. For the convenience of the general reader, under each heading in the bibliographical entries Western-language works once again precede all entries in Chinese or

Japanese. General bibliographies of material concerning fiction criticism and the six novels (usually works that deal with more than one commentary edition to a novel) are appended after the individual entries on the commentary editions of each novel.

Shui-hu chuan

ABBREVIATED TITLE: Yü Hsiang-tou 余象斗 edition. FULL TITLE: *Ching-pen tseng-pu chiao-cheng ch'üan-hsiang Chung-i Shui-hu chih-chuan p'ing-lin* 京本增補校正全像忠義水滸志傳評林 (Expanded, Collated, Illustrated, Capital Edition of The Water Margin with Forest of Commentary). LENGTH: 104 chapters in 25 *chüan*. In the original, the chapters after chap. 30 are not numbered. PUBLISHER: Shuang-feng t'ang 雙峰堂. DATE: 1594. PREFATORY MATERIAL: "T'i *Shui-hu chuan* hsü" 題水滸傳序 (*Shui-hu chuan* Preface), "*Shui-hu* pien" 水滸辨 (On [This Edition of] the *Shui-hu chuan*). The last piece is printed in the upper register above the preface. It mentions "Mr. Yü of Shuang-feng t'ang" and explains the procedure used in editing the poetry in the novel. COMMENTARY: Marginal comments. DISTINGUISHING FEATURES: The text belongs to the set of editions described as "simple" (*chien* 簡) or abridged and is based on fuller, earlier editions. Almost all of the opening poems at the head of each chapter of the older versions have been moved up to the upper register or deleted. This edition preserves the short prologue (*yin-shou* 引首) of the older versions. REMARKS: The comments are usually prefaced by a short heading indicating their subject. The comments are not all from the same hand, although they are commonly attributed to one man, Yü Hsiang-tou (ca. 1550–1637). There is a radical change in style and subject matter of the comments from the beginning of the T'ien Hu and Wang Ch'ing campaigns until the end of the novel. Each page has three registers. The comments appear in the uppermost register, illustrations in the middle register, and the text of the novel is printed in the bottommost register. AVAILABILITY: There is a photo-reprint of a complete copy held in the Jigendō Library, Nikko, Japan: *Shui-hu chih-chuan p'ing-lin* 水滸志傳評林 (Forest of Comments Edition of the *Shui-hu chuan*; Peking: Wen-hsüeh ku-chi, 1956), and a microfilm of an incomplete copy in the University of Michigan series of rare Chinese fiction held in Japan. Some, but not all, of the comments in this edition are found in *SHCHPP*.

Ōuchida Saburō 大內田三郎. "Eiin *Suiko shiden hyōrin* kanpon o te ni shite" 影印水滸志伝評林完本を手にして. *Shinagaku kenkyū* 24. 5:239–45 (1960).
———. "*Suikoden* hanponkō: *Suiko shiden hyōrin*-bon no seiritsu katei o chūshin ni" 水滸伝版本考:水滸志伝評林本の成立過程を中心に. *Tenri daigaku gakuhō* 64:1–13 (1969).
Wang Ku-lu 王古魯. "T'an *Shui-hu chih-chuan p'ing-lin*" 談水滸志傳評林. *Chiang Hai hsüeh-k'an*, 1958. 2:54–60.

ABBREVIATED TITLE: Jung-yü t'ang 容與堂 edition. FULL TITLE: *Li Cho-wu hsien-sheng p'i-p'ing Chung-i Shui-hu chuan* 李卓吾先生批評忠義水滸傳 (Loyal and Righteous *Shui-hu chuan* with Commentary by Li Chih). Two main versions exist: (A) earlier edition (now?) lacking Li Chih preface, exemplar held in Peking Library, and (B) later edition with Li Chih preface, exemplar held in Naikaku Bunko, Japan. A third version (exemplar also held in Peking Library) has the alternate title *Chu ming-chia hsien-sheng p'i-p'ing Chung-i Shui-hu chuan* 諸名家先生批評忠義水滸傳 (*Chung-i Shui-hu chuan* with Commentary by Famous Literati). LENGTH: 100 chapters in 100 *chüan*. PUBLISHER: Jung-yü t'ang, Hangchou. DATE: A note at the end of the Li Chih preface of version B indicates that the text for the woodblocks for it was written in 1610 by a Sun P'u 孫樸. The A version is estimated by some to be as early as 1602. PREFATORY MATERIAL: Li Chih preface (same text as in his *Fen-shu* 焚書 [Book for Burning], first published 1590), "P'i-p'ing *Shui-hu chuan* shu-yü" 批評水滸傳述語 (Recorded Remarks on Commenting on the *Shui-hu chuan*) signed "Huai-lin" 懷林 (a monk friend of Li Chih's), "Liang-shan po i-pai tan-pa jen yu-lieh" 梁山泊一百單八人優劣 (The Character of the 108 Heroes of Liang-shan Marsh), "*Shui-hu chuan* i-pai hui wen-tzu yu-lieh" 水滸傳一百回文字優劣 (The Writing in the 100 Chapters of the *Shui-hu chuan*), and "Yu lun *Shui-hu chuan* wen-tzu" 又論水滸傳文字 (Again on the Writing in the *Shui-hu chuan*). In version B, the order of the last two items is inexplicably reversed. COMMENTARY: Single-column interlineal, marginal, and postchapter (except chap. 86) comments. Where there is sufficient blank space on the page, such as at the end of indented material (see p. 10/6a for example), single-column interlineal comments are printed in double columns, proof perhaps that the commentary in this edition was more of an afterthought than an integral part of the edition. DISTINGUISHING FEATURES: In the commentary there is liberal use of acerbic comments and marking of sections for excision. The postchapter comments are prefixed by short phrases referring in fourteen different ways to Li Chih. REMARKS: Errors in grammar and orthography in the text of version A are often corrected in version B if the change could be effected without major revision of the woodblocks. On the question of the authenticity of the attribution of the commentary to Li Chih, see appendix 2 in this volume. AVAILABILITY: There is a facsimile reprint of version A (Shanghai: Chung-hua shu-chü, 1966), as well as a reduced photo-reprint (Shanghai: Shang-hai jen-min, 1975). A microfilm of version B (original in Naikaku Bunko, Japan) is available in the University of Michigan series. Most of the prefatory material and comments are included in *SHCHPP*.

Ch'en Chin-chao 陳錦釗. "Li Cho-wu p'i-tien *Shui-hu chuan* chih yen-chiu" 李卓吾批點水滸傳之研究. *Shu-mu chi-k'an* 7. 4:45–65 (1974).

Ch'en Hung 陳洪. "*Shui-hu chuan* Li Cho-wu p'ing pen chen-wei i pien" 水滸傳李卓吾評本真偽一辨. *Nan-k'ai hsüeh-pao*, 1981. 3:50–52.

Ch'en Hung, and Shen Fu-shen 沈福身. "Li Cho-wu hsiao-shuo ch'uang-tso p'ing-shu" 李卓吾小說創作評述. *T'ien-chin she-hui k'o-hsüeh*, 1983. 2:87–93 (*Ku-chin* reprint, 1983. 5:244–50).

Chin Tai-t'ung 靳岱同 (Yü Sung-ch'ing 喻松青). "Li Chih yü *Shui-hu*" 李贄與水滸. *Li-shih yen-chiu*, 1976. 6:72–84.

Chu En-pin 朱恩彬. "Li Chih p'ing-tien ti *Shui-hu chuan* pan-pen pien-hsi" 李贄評點的水滸傳版本辨析. *Shan-tung shih-ta hsüeh-pao*, 1984. 1:57–65.

———. "Li Chih ti ssu-hsiang yü Jung-jü t'ang i-pai hui k'o-pen *Shui-hu chuan* p'ing-pen" 李贄的思想與容與堂一百回刻本水滸傳評本. *Ku-tien wen-hsüeh li-lun yen-chiu* 9:309–22 (1984).

Hsiao Hsiang-k'ai 蕭相愷. "Li Cho-wu *Shui-hu chuan* p'ing-pen ti i-ko hsin t'ui-ts'e" 李卓吾水滸傳評本的一個新推測. *Wen-k'o t'ung-hsün* 文科通訊, 1985. 4:16–18 (*Ku-chin* reprint, 1986. 3:215–17).

Hsiao Wu 蕭伍 (Cheng Kung-tun 鄭公盾). "Shih-lun Li Cho-wu tui *Shui-hu chuan* ti p'ing-tien" 試論李卓吾對水滸傳的評點. *Hsüeh-shu yüeh-k'an*, 1964. 5. Also in his *Shui-hu chuan lun-wen chi*, pp. 391–414.

Hsü Tzu-ch'ang 許自昌. *Shu-chai man-lu* 樗齋漫錄. N.p.: 1612 preface, copy in Peking Library.

Kung Chao-chi 龔兆吉. "Jung-pen Li-p'ing wei Yeh Chou wei-tso shuo chih-i" 容本李評為葉晝偽作說質疑. *Shui-hu cheng-ming* 2:155–67 (1983).

Kuramitsu Urai 倉光印平. "Ri Takugo no bungakukan—*Suikoden* no hihyō o miru" 李卓吾の文学観—水滸伝の批評を見る. *Sainan gakuin daigaku bungaku ronshū* 西南学院大学文学論集 4. 1:1–14 (1957).

Liu Chih-chung 劉致中. "Kuan-yü Li Cho-wu tui *Shui-hu chuan* ti p'ing-tien wen-t'i" 關於李卓吾對水滸傳的評點問題. *Kuang-ming jih-pao*, 3/28/1965.

Ma Ch'eng-sheng 馬成生. "Hsü-lun ts'ung Li Cho-wu tao Chin Sheng-t'an" 續論從李卓吾到金聖歎. *Hang-chou shih-yüan hsüeh-pao*, 1983. 3:60–67.

———. "Jung-yü t'ang pen *Shui-hu chuan* Li Cho-wu p'ing fei Yeh Chou wei-t'o pien" 容與堂本水滸傳李卓吾評非葉晝偽托辨. In *Chung-kuo ku-tai hsiao-shuo li-lun yen-chiu*, pp. 181–96.

———. "Shih-lun Li Cho-wu tui *Shui-hu chuan* ti p'i-p'ing" 試論李卓吾對水滸傳的批評. *Hang-chou shih-yüan hsüeh-pao*, 1979. 1:22–30, 37.

———. "'Tsao-p'o so ch'uan fei ts'ui-mei'—Li Cho-wu shih tsen-yang tui-tai nung-min ch'i-i ti?" 糟粕所傳非粹美—李卓吾是怎樣對待農民起義的. *Hang-chou shih-yüan hsüeh-pao*, 1980. 1:33–39.

———. "Ts'ung Li Cho-wu chih Chin Sheng-t'an—lüeh-t'an Li-p'ing *Shui-hu* yü Chin-p'ing *Shui-hu* tsai ssu-hsiang fang-mien ti chi-ch'eng kuan-hsi" 從李卓吾至金聖歎—略談李評水滸與金評水滸在思想方面的繼承關係. *Hang-chou hsüeh-yüan hsüeh-pao*, 1982. 3:42–49 (*Ku-chin* reprint, 1983. 1:145–52).

Ma Chi-kao 馬積高. "Lun Yeh Chou tui *Shui-hu chuan* ti p'i-p'ing" 論葉晝對水滸傳的批評. *Hu-nan chiao-yü hsüeh-yüan hsüeh-pao* 湖南教育學院學報, 1984. 4:14–21.

Ma T'i-chi 馬蹄疾. "Jung-yü t'ang k'o-pen *Shui-hu chuan*—*Shui-hu* shu-lu chih san" 容與堂刻本水滸傳—水滸書錄之三. *Wen-hui pao*, 11/16/1961.

Nieh Kan-nu 聶紺弩. "*Shui-hu* wu-lun" 水滸五論. In his *Chung-kuo ku-tien hsiao-shuo lun-chi* 中國古典小說論集. Shanghai: Shang-hai ku-chi, 1981, pp. 9–204.

Ou-yang Tai-fa 歐陽代發. "Ho-che wei *Shui-hu chuan* Li Chih p'ing-pen chen-chi?—yü Chu En-pin t'ung-chih shang-ch'üeh" 何者為水滸傳李贄評本真迹?—與朱恩彬同志商榷. *Shan-tung shih-ta hsüeh-pao*, 1984. 5:74–79.

————. "Yüan-k'an pen *Shui-hu* 'Li-p'ing' ch'üeh ch'u Li Chih chih shou—chien p'ing 'Jung-pen' Li-p'ing wei Yeh Chou wei-tso shuo" 袁刊本水滸李評確出李贄之手—兼評容本李評為葉晝偽作說. *Shui-hu cheng-ming* 3. 251–62 (1984).

Ōuchida Saburō 大內田三郎. "*Shui-hu chuan* ti yü-yen—kuan-yü 'Jung-yü t'ang pen' ti tzu-chü yen-chiu" 水滸傳的語言—關於容與堂本的字句研究. Translated by T'ung Chin-ming 佟金銘. *Yang-chou shih-yüan hsüeh-pao*, 1986. 3:131–38 (*Ku-chin* reprint, 1986. 12:221–29). For the original Japanese version see *Biburia* ビブリア 79:8–24 (1982).

Pai Chien 白堅. "Ts'ung Jung-yü t'ang pen *Shui-hu chuan* p'ing k'an Yeh Chou ti 'ch'uan-shen' lun" 從容與堂本水滸傳評看葉晝的傳神論. In *Chung-kuo mei-hsüeh shih hsüeh-shu t'ao-lun hui lun-wen hsüan* 中國美學史學術討論會論文選. Wu-hsi: Chiang-su sheng mei-hsüeh hsüeh-hui, 1984, pp. 109–24.

Wang An-ch'üan 王安全, and Chao Ai-kuo 趙愛國. "P'ing Li Chih p'i-tien *Chung-i Shui-hu chuan*" 評李贄批點忠義水滸傳. *Kan-su shih-ta hsüeh-pao*, 1976. 1:50–55.

Wang Hsien-p'ei 王先霈. "Jung-pen yü Yüan-pen *Shui-hu chuan* p'ing-tien tsai wen-hsüeh p'i-p'ing shih shang ti ti-wei" 容本與袁本水滸傳評點在文學批評史上的地位. In *Chung-kuo ku-tai hsiao-shuo li-lun yen-chiu*, pp. 165–80.

Wang Li-ch'i 王利器. "*Shui-hu* Li Cho-wu p'ing-pen ti chen-wei wen-t'i" 水滸李卓吾評本的真偽問題. *Wen-hsüeh p'ing-lun ts'ung-k'an*, 1979. 2:365–81.

Yeh Lang 葉朗. "Yeh Chou p'ing-tien *Shui-hu chuan* k'ao-cheng" 葉晝評點水滸傳考證. *Ku-tai wen-hsüeh li-lun yen-chiu* 5:91–112 (1981).

ABBREVIATED TITLE: Chung Hsing 鍾惺 edition. FULL TITLE: *Chung Po-ching hsien-sheng p'i-p'ing Shui-hu chung-i chuan* 鍾伯敬先生批評水滸忠義傳 (Tale of the Loyal and Righteous of the Water Margin with Commentary by Chung Hsing). The Ssu-chih kuan 四知館 edition adds to the beginning of the title the words *Hsiang fang ku-chin ming-jen pi-i* 像仿古今名人筆意 (With Illustrations in the Style of Famous Men of the Past and Present). LENGTH: 100 chapters in 100 *chüan*. PUBLISHER: Ssu-chih kuan and Chi-ch'ing t'ang 積慶堂 editions. DATE: Estimated on the basis of the illustrations and general format as 1625–27. PREFATORY MATERIAL: Preface signed Chung Hsing (1574–1625), and "*Shui-hu* jen-p'in p'ing" 水滸人品評 (Evaluations of the Characters in the *Shui-hu chuan*). COMMENTARY: Chi-ch'ing t'ang edition has postchapter comments only, Ssu-chih kuan edition also has marginal and single-column interlineal comments. DISTINGUISHING FEATURES: The prologue (*yin-shou* 引首) of earlier editions, which usually appears before the table of contents, has been left out. REMARKS: The "Chung Hsing" preface, "*Shui-hu* jen-p'in p'ing" and over twenty of the postchapter comments are heavily indebted to similar material in the Jung-yü t'ang edition. A sentence in the preface copied from the earlier edition mentions the benefits of Li Chih's commentary and the heading of the postchapter comment for chap. 66 still retains the original Jung-yü t'ang heading, "Li the Monk says."

AVAILABILITY: A microfilm of the Ssu-chih kuan edition (original in the Bibliothèque nationale, Paris) is held in the Gest Oriental Library, Princeton University. Because of its rareness, this edition was not used in the collation notes for either the variorum edition of the novel edited by Cheng Chen-to 鄭振鐸 et al., *Shui-hu ch'üan-chuan* 水滸全傳 (Peking: Jen-min wen-hsüeh, 1954) or *SHCHPP*. The full text of the prefatory material and some of the postchapter comments of the Ssu-chih kuan edition are reprinted in the Hsi-chung article cited below.

Hsi-chung 曦鐘 (Ch'en Hsi-chung 陳曦鐘). "Kuan-yü *Chung Po-ching hsien-sheng p'i-p'ing Shui-hu chung-i chuan*" 關於鍾伯敬先生批評水滸忠義傳. *Wen-hsien* 15:42–52 (1983).

Shiroki Naoya 白木直也. "Shō Hakkei hihyō Shichikan kanpon no kenkyū" 鍾伯敬批評四知館刊本の研究. Pt. 1 in *Shūkan Tōyō gaku* 集刊東洋学 42:98–113 (1971), pt. 2 in *Nihon Chūgoku gakkai hō* 23:171–85 (1971); pt. 3 in *Hiroshima daigaku bungakubu kiyō* 31. 1:116–48 (1972).

ABBREVIATED TITLE: Yüan Wu-yai 袁無涯 edition. FULL TITLE: *Li Cho-wu p'ing Chung-i Shui-hu ch'üan-chuan* 李卓吾評忠義水滸全傳 (The Full Tale of the Loyal and Righteous Water Margin with Commentary by Li Chih). Alternate titles: *Cho-wu p'ing-yüeh hsiu-hsiang ts'ang-pen Shui-hu ssu-chuan ch'üan-shu* 卓吾評閱繡像藏本水滸四傳全書 (Li Chih Commentary, Illustrated, Complete Book of the Four Narratives of the *Shui-hu chuan*) and *Hsin-chüan Li-shih ts'ang-pen Chung-i Shui-hu ch'üan-shu* 新鐫李氏藏本忠義水滸全書 (Newly Cut Li Chih Private Edition of the Complete Book of the Loyal and Righteous Water Margin). LENGTH: 120 chapters (no *chüan* divisions). PUBLISHER: Yüan Wu-yai, Suchou. DATE: This edition is first mentioned in the 1612 work, *Shu-chai man-lu* 樗齋漫錄, and postdates the Jung-yü t'ang edition. PREFATORY MATERIAL: Li Chih preface (not found in all printings, text slightly different from *Fen-shu* and Jung-yü t'ang versions); "Hsiao-yin" 小引 (Little Preface) signed with the name of one of Li Chih's disciples, Yang Ting-chien 楊定見; "Fa-fan" 發凡 (General Principles); the section of the *Hsüan-ho i-shih* 宣和遺事 (Anecdotes from the Hsüan-ho Reign Period) dealing with Sung Chiang; and "Shui-hu chung-i i-pai pa jen chi-kuan ch'u-shen" 水滸忠義一百八人籍貫出身 (Birthplace and Background of the 108 Loyal and Righteous Heroes of the Water Margin). COMMENTARY: Single-column interlineal, marginal, and postchapter comments. DISTINGUISHING FEATURES: The prologue (*yin-shou* 引首) is separated from the rest of the text by the table of contents and 120 pages of illustrations. There are twenty extra chapters detailing the campaigns against T'ien Hu and Wang Ch'ing. REMARKS: On the authenticity of the attribution of the commentary to Li Chih, see appendix 2 in this volume. AVAILABILITY: Copies held in the Library of Congress and Harvard-Yenching Library, Harvard University. A microfilm of a later printing (original in Academia Sinica, Taiwan) is held in the Gest Oriental Library, Princeton University. The prefatory material and most of the comments are included in *SHCHPP*.

Chao Ming-cheng 趙明政. "'*Shui-hu ch'üan-chuan* Li Chih p'ing yeh shu wei-t'o' pu-cheng" 水滸全傳李贄評也屬偽托補證. *Chiang Han lun-t'an*, 1983. 7:41–43.

Ch'in Wen-hsi 秦文兮. "Yang Ting-chien hsü pen *Shui-hu ch'üan-chuan* tui T'ien-tu wai-ch'en hsü pen ti ts'uan-kai" 楊定見序本水滸全傳對天都外臣序本的篡改. *Shui-hu cheng-ming* 2:168-74 (1983).

Huang Lin 黃霖. "*Shui-hu ch'üan-chuan* Li Chih p'ing yeh shu wei-t'o" 水滸全傳李贄評也屬偽托. *Chiang Han lun-t'an*, 1982. 1:44-51. Reprinted in *Shui-hu chuan tzu-liao chi* 水滸傳資料集. Hong Kong: The Sinological Bibliocenter, 1984, vol. 5, pp. 10-15.

Shiroki Naoya 白木直也. "Ippyaku nijūkai *Suikozenden* no kenkyū: Hatsubon o tsūjite kokoromita" 一百二十回水滸全伝の研究:発凡を通じて試みた. *Nihon Chūgoku gakkai hō* 25:125-39 (1973).

————. "Ippyaku nijūkai *Suikozenden* no kenkyū: Sono Ri Takugo hyō o megutte" 一百二十回水滸全伝の研究:その李卓吾評をめぐって. *Nihon Chūgoku gakkai hō* 26:95-111 (1974).

————. *Suiko zenden hatsubon no kenkyū* 水滸全伝発凡の研究. Hiroshima: Ryūjō sha, 1966.

————. "Yō Teiken hon *Suikoden* 'hatsubon' no kaishaku o megutte" 楊定見本水滸伝発凡の解釈をめぐって. *Hiroshima daigaku bungakubu kiyō* 8:243-72 (1955).

Tai Wang-shu 戴望舒. "Yüan-k'an *Shui-hu chuan* ti chen-wei" 袁刊水滸傳的真偽. In *Hsiao-shuo hsi-ch'ü lun-chi* 小說戲曲論集. Edited by Tai Wang-shu and Wu Hsiao-ling 吳曉鈴. Peking: Tso-chia ch'u-pan she, 1958, pp. 59-66.

Ts'ui Wen-yin 崔文印. "Yüan Wu-yai k'an-pen *Shui-hu* Li Chih p'ing pien-wei" 袁無涯刊本水滸李贄評辨偽. *Chung-hua wen-shih lun-ts'ung*, 1980. 2:311-17.

ABBREVIATED TITLE: Li Hsüan-po 李玄伯 edition. FULL TITLE: *Chung-i Shui-hu chuan* 忠義水滸傳 (Tale of the Loyal and Righteous in the Water Margin). LENGTH: 100 chapters (no *chüan* divisions). PUBLISHERS: No information. DATE: Estimated by some as 1620-30, but also considered a twentieth-century concoction by others. PREFATORY MATERIAL: Ta-ti yü-jen 大滌餘人 (pseud.) preface (same as in Chieh-tzu yüan edition). COMMENTARY: Details unclear, but seems to have at least marginal comments similar to the Chieh-tzu yüan edition commentary. DISTINGUISHING FEATURES: The prologue (*yin-shou* 引首) has been incorporated into chap. 1, according to report. REMARKS: The woodblocks for this edition are said to be related to those used for the Yüan Wu-yai edition. Problems in the linkage between the campaign against the Liao and that against Fang La show that this edition has been cut down from the 120-chapter version. AVAILABILITY: Li Hsüan-po (1895-1974, personal name Tsung-t'ung 宗侗) was the owner of this copy. Its exact whereabouts are not certain, but it is possible that it is still part of Li Hsüan-po's collection of books, presently held by the Academia Sinica but uncatalogued. A typeset reprint, rare in itself, exists: *Ch'ung-k'an Chung-i Shui-hu chuan* 重刊忠義水滸傳 (Peking: Yen-ching yin-shu chü, 1925), copy held in Harvard-Yenching Library, Harvard University, but the commentary seems to have been deleted.

I Ting 一丁. "Li Hsüan-po so ts'ang pai-hui *Chung-i Shui-hu chuan*" 李玄伯所藏百回忠義水滸傳. *Hsin-min pao wan-k'an*, 10/12/1956.

Ma T'i-chi 馬蹄疾. "Li Tsung-t'ung ch'ung-k'an ti *Shui-hu—Shui-hu* shu-lu chih liu" 李宗侗重刊的水滸—水滸書錄之六. *Wen-hui pao*, 1/23/1962.

ABBREVIATED TITLE: Chieh-tzu yüan 芥子園 edition. FULL TITLE: *Li Cho-wu hsien-sheng p'i-tien Chung-i Shui-hu chuan* 李卓吾先生批點忠義水滸傳 (Loyal and Righteous Tale of the Water Margin with Commentary by Li Chih). A later printing by San-to chai 三多齋 using the same woodblocks uses the title: *Shih Nai-an yüan-pen Li Cho-wu hsien-sheng p'ing Shui-hu ch'üan-chuan* 施耐庵原本李卓吾先生評水滸全傳 (Shih Nai-an's Original Edition of the Full Tale of the Water Margin with Commentary by Li Chih). LENGTH: 100 chapters (no *chüan* divisions). PUBLISHER: Chieh-tzu yüan. DATE: Late Ming or early Ch'ing. PREFATORY MATERIAL: Ta-ti yü-jen 大滌餘人 (pseud.) preface titled "K'o *Chung-i Shui-hu chuan* yüan-ch'i" 刻忠義水滸傳緣起 (The Background Behind the Printing of the Loyal and Righteous Tale of the Water Margin). COMMENTARY: Marginal and single-column interlineal comments. DISTINGUISHING FEATURES: A large proportion of the comments are taken from the Yüan Wu-yai edition and the prologue has been omitted. REMARKS: This edition seems to be a reworking of the 120-chapter Yüan Wu-yai edition. The twenty chapters detailing the T'ien Hu and Wang Ch'ing campaigns have been removed, but the clumsy transitions of the Li Hsüan-po edition have also been avoided. Some hold that this edition is very early and actually predates the Yüan Wu-yai edition. The author of the preface seems to be claiming authorship for the commentary. AVAILABILITY: A microfilm of an incomplete copy (Chaps. 1, 71–100), original in the Bibliothèque nationale, Paris, is held in the Gest Oriental Library, Princeton University. A photo-reprint of a copy with lacunae filled in by hand has been published in the series titled *Ming-Ch'ing shan-pen hsiao-shuo ts'ung-k'an* 明清善本小說叢刊 (Collection of Rare Editions of Ming-Ch'ing Fiction; Taipei: T'ien-i ch'u-pan she, 1985).

ABBREVIATED TITLE: Mukyūkai 無窮会 edition. FULL TITLE: *Ch'üan-hsiang Chung-i Shui-hu chuan* 全像忠義水滸傳 (Fully Illustrated Loyal and Righteous Tale of the Water Margin). Alternate title: *Li Cho-wu hsien-sheng p'i-tien Chung-i Shui-hu chuan* (Loyal and Righteous Tale of the Water Margin with Commentary by Li Chih). LENGTH: 100 chapters (no *chüan* divisions). PUBLISHER: No information. DATE: Early Ch'ing reprint of Ming edition. PREFATORY MATERIAL: Li Chih preface with minor changes (disrespectful references to non-Chinese barbarians deleted, as is Li Chih's name). COMMENTARY: Marginal, double- and single-column interlineal comments that differ from the other published "Li Chih" commentaries. DISTINGUISHING FEATURES: The prologue (*yin-shou* 引首) has been omitted. REMARKS: In terms of the handling of chapter opening poems, the omission of the prologue, and the rearrangement of the Yen P'o-hsi episode, this edition is similar to the Chieh-tzu yüan edition. AVAILABILITY: No copies exist in the U.S. to the editor's knowledge. The original is held in the Mukyūkai Library in Japan.

Kutō Takamura 工藤篁. "Ota Kakusai shi kyuzō Shina shōsetsu no nisan" 績田碓齋氏舊藏支那小說の二三. *Kangakukai zashi* 6. 2:118–24 (1938).

Shiroki Naoya 白木直也. "Wakoku hon *Suikoden* no kenkyū—iwayuru Mukyūkai hon to no kankei" 和刻本水滸伝の研究—所謂無窮会本との関係. *Nihon Chūgoku gakkai hō* 20:203–15 (1968).

ABBREVIATED TITLE: Japanese reprint. FULL TITLE: *Li Cho-wu hsien-sheng p'i-tien Chung-i Shui-hu chuan* 李卓吾先生批點忠義水滸傳 (Loyal and Righteous Tale of the Water Margin with Commentary by Li Chih). LENGTH: Only two installments of ten chapters each were completed. PUBLISHER: Hayashi Kyūbei 林九兵衛, the Keishi shobō 京師書房 of Kyoto, Japan. DATE: 1728 (first ten chapters) and 1759 (second ten chapters). PREFATORY MATERIAL: Li Chih preface (same as in *Fen-shu* and Jung-yü t'ang edition). COMMENTARY: Marginal and double- and single-column interlineal comments generally identical with those in the Mukyūkai edition. DISTINGUISHING FEATURES: Pronunciation marks for the Japanese audience have been added by Okajima Kanzan 岡島冠山 (d. 1727). This printing would seem to be based on an original edition that also served as the base text for the Mukyūkai edition, but the Japanese reprint has the prologue lacking in the Mukyūkai edition. REMARKS: For remarks on the authenticity of this commentary, see app. 2 in this volume. AVAILABILITY: Copies held in the Ta-lien Library, Peking Library, and elsewhere in China, but not available in the U.S. to the editor's knowledge.

Shiroki Naoya 白木直也. "Wakoku hon *Suikoden* no kenkyū—shohongen ni shimeru datōna ichi o momete" 和刻本水滸伝の研究—諸本間に占める妥当な位置を求めて. *Hiroshima daigaku bungakubu kiyō* 28. 1:277–304 (pt. 1; 1968); 29. 1:120–44 (pt. 2; 1970).

ABBREVIATED TITLE: Pao-han lou 寶瀚樓 edition. FULL TITLE: *Wen-hsing t'ang p'i-p'ing Shui-hu chuan* 文杏堂批評水滸傳 (Wen-hsing t'ang Commentary Edition of the *Shui-hu chuan*). Alternate title: *Li Cho-wu yüan-p'ing Chung-i Shui-hu ch'üan-chuan* 李卓吾原評忠義水滸全傳 (Full Tale of the Loyal and Righteous Water Margin with the Original Commentary of Li Chih). LENGTH: 30 *chüan* (no chapter divisions in the ordinary sense). PUBLISHER: Pao-han lou. DATE: Late Ming or early Ch'ing. PREFATORY MATERIAL: Wu-hu lao-jen 五湖老人 (pseud.) preface. COMMENTARY: Details unclear. DISTINGUISHING FEATURES: The text is not separated within each *chüan*, but is printed in a solid block with *i* 乙 marks indicating breaks in the text. REMARKS: This text is perhaps the most abbreviated of the "simple" versions of the novel. Although in the title the commentary is attributed to Li Chih, the preface mentions that the commentary was added by the publisher. AVAILABILITY: Copy held in Paris. Not available in any form in the U.S., to the editor's knowledge.

Ōuchida Saburō 大內田三郞. "*Shui-hu chuan* pan-pen k'ao—kuan-yü Wen-hsing t'ang p'i-p'ing *Shui-hu chuan* san-shih chüan pen" 水滸傳版本考—關於文杏堂批評水滸傳三十卷本. Translated by P'eng Hsiu-ken 彭修艮. *Shui-hu cheng-ming* 3:163–82 (1984). For the original Japanese version see *Tenri daigaku gakuhō* 119:50–67 (1979).

ABBREVIATED TITLE: Ying-hsüeh ts'ao-t'ang 映雪草堂 edition. FULL TITLE: *Shih Nai-an yüan-pen Li Cho-wu hsien-sheng p'ing Shui-hu ch'üan-chuan* 施耐庵原本 李卓吾先生評水滸全傳 (Shih Nai-an's Original Edition of the Full Tale of the Water Margin with Commentary by Li Chih). Alternate title (at the head of each *chüan*): *Chin Sheng-t'an p'ing Shui-hu ch'üan-chuan* 金聖歎評水滸全傳 (Complete Edition of the *Shui-hu chuan* with Commentary by Chin Sheng-t'an). LENGTH: 30 *chüan* with titles for 355 *tse* 則 (sections), although the text does not treat all of the incidents mentioned in the *tse* titles listed at the head of each *chüan*. No chapter divisions. PUBLISHER: Ying-hsüeh ts'ao-t'ang, Suchou. DATE: Early Ch'ing? PREFATORY MATERIAL: Wu-hu lao-jen preface (very abbreviated form of same preface as in Pao-han lou edition). COMMENTARY: Marginal (few in number and short in length) and post-*chüan* comments by Wu-hu lao-jen and his publishing associates. DISTINGUISHING FEATURES: The sections treating the campaigns against T'ien Hu and Wang Ch'ing are not from the same source as the rest of the novel and contain passages unlike any other known extant edition. Almost all of the poetry from the older editions has been excised. REMARKS: The commentary in this edition is attributed both to Li Chih and to Chin Sheng-t'an. The truth, however, seems to be revealed in a single attribution of the commentary to the publisher (*t'ang-chu* 堂主) at the head of *chüan* 24. AVAILABILITY: Not available in the U.S. Copy held in Tokyo Imperial University Library. The text of this version of the Wu-hu lao-jen preface is given in Liu Shih-te, *Shui-hu cheng-ming* 3 : 134–62 (1984), pp. 140–41.

Liu Shih-te 劉世德. "*Shui-hu chuan* Ying-hsüeh ts'ao-t'ang k'an-pen—chien-pen ho shan-chieh pen" 水滸傳映雪草堂刊本—簡本和刪節本. *Shui-hu cheng-ming* 4 : 154–76 (1985).
———. "T'an *Shui-hu chuan* Ying-hsüeh ts'ao-t'ang k'an-pen ti kai-k'uang, hsü-wen ho piao-mu" 談水滸傳映雪草堂刊本的概況序文和標目. *Shui-hu cheng-ming* 3 : 134–62 (1984).
———. "T'an *Shui-hu chuan* Ying-hsüeh ts'ao-t'ang k'an-pen ti ti-pen" 談水滸傳映雪草堂刊本的底本. *Ming-Ch'ing hsiao-shuo yen-chiu* 2 : 95–113 (1985).
Lu Shu-lun 陸樹崙. "Ying-hsüeh ts'ao-t'ang pen *Shui-hu ch'üan-chuan* chien-chieh" 映雪草堂本水滸全傳簡介. *Shui-hu cheng-ming* 4 : 142–53 (1985).

ABBREVIATED TITLE: *Ying-hsiung p'u* 英雄譜 edition. FULL TITLE: *Ching-chüan ho-k'o San-kuo Shui-hu ch'üan-chuan* 精鐫合刻三國水滸全傳 (Finely Cut, Combined Printing of The Romance of the Three Kingdoms and the Full Tale of the Water Margin). Alternate titles: *Ying-hsiung p'u* 英雄譜 (The Roster of Heroes), and *Ming-kung p'i-tien ho-k'o San-kuo Shui-hu ch'üan-chuan* 名公批點合刻三國 水滸全傳 (Combined Printing of The Romance of the Three Kingdoms and the Full Tale of The Water Margin with Commentary by Famous Scholars). LENGTH: 110 chapters in 20 *chüan*. PUBLISHER: Hsiung-fei kuan 雄飛館. DATE: Around 1620? PREFATORY MATERIAL: Prefaces by Hsiung Fei 熊飛 and Yang Ming-lang 楊明琅, and "*Shui-hu chuan* ying-hsiung hsing-shih" 水滸傳英雄姓氏 (List of the Names of the Heroes of the *Shui-hu chuan*). COMMENTARY: Marginal and single-column interlineal comments. DISTINGUISHING FEATURES: Printed together with a 240-*tse* version of the *San-kuo yen-i*. REMARKS: The commentary is unattributed. AVAILABILITY: A photo-reprint of a so-called second printing, *Erh-k'o Ying-hsiung p'u* 二刻英雄譜 (Tokyo: Dotomo sha, 1981), is available in the East Asian Library of Columbia University, but the marginal comments are usually illegible or cut off. There is a microfilm copy in the University of Michigan series.

ABBREVIATED TITLE: Chin Sheng-t'an 金聖歎 edition. FULL TITLE: *Ti-wu ts'ai-tzu shu Shih Nai-an Shui-hu chuan* 第五才子書施耐庵水滸傳 (The Fifth Book of Genius, Shih Nai-an's *Shui-hu chuan*). LENGTH: 70 chapters plus prologue, in 71 *chüan* (plus 4 *chüan* of prefatory matter). PUBLISHER: Kuan-hua t'ang 貫華堂 is usually given as the name of the publisher, but according to Chin Sheng-t'an it was the name of the studio of a friend where he found an old edition of the novel. DATE: Chin Sheng-t'an's third preface is dated 1641. According to *Hsin-ch'ou chi-wen* 辛丑紀聞 (A Record of Events Heard in 1661), anonymous, the commentary was published in 1644. The third preface also mentions that Chin Sheng-t'an started the commentary when he was in his teens. PREFATORY MATERIAL: Three prefaces by Chin Sheng-t'an; "Sung-shih kang" 宋史綱 and "Sung-shih mu" 宋史目, which consist of quotations concerning the real Sung Chiang from the *Hsü Tzu-chih t'ung-chien kang-mu* 續資治通鑑綱目 (Continuation of the Outline and Explanation of the Comprehensive Mirror for Aid in Government) or later works based on it; "Tu *Ti-wu ts'ai-tzu shu* fa" 讀第五才子書法 (How to Read The Fifth Book of Genius); and a preface attributed to Shih Nai-an but most certainly by Chin Sheng-t'an himself. COMMENTARY: Double-column interlineal, marginal, and prechapter comments. DISTINGUISHING FEATURES: The "Yin-shou" and chap. 1 of the earlier editions have been combined into a separate prologue, the last part of which contains a modified table of contents. The story ends with the first half of chap. 71 of the older editions, plus an ending added by Chin Sheng-t'an. AVAILABILITY: The personal copy of Liu Fu 劉復 (1891–1934), judged by him to be from the original printing, was photoreproduced by the Chung-hua shu-chü of Shanghai in 1934 and has been reprinted several times since by various publishers in China and Taiwan. There is also a 1975 Chung-hua shu-chü (Peking) photo-reprint of a different printing. A typeset version of both the commentary and text of Chin Sheng-t'an's edition is found in *SHCHPP*.

Wang, John Ching-yu. *Chin Sheng-t'an*. New York: Twayne, 1972.

Chai Chien-po 翟建波. "Lüeh-lun Chin Sheng-t'an tui-yü *Shui-hu chuan* wen-fa ti p'ing-tien" 略論金聖歎對於水滸傳文法的評點. *Jen-wen tsa-chih*, 1986. 5:122–28 (*Ku-chin* reprint, 1986. 12:230–36).

Chang Ch'eng-huan 張澄寰. "Kuan-yü Chin Sheng-t'an ti p'ing-chia wen-t'i" 關於金聖歎的評價問題. *Kuang-ming jih-pao*, 7/11/1962.

Chang Hsiao-hu 張嘯虎. "Lun Chin-pen *Shui-hu* ti lang-man chu-i ching-shen" 論金本水滸的浪漫主義精神. *Shui-hu cheng-ming* 1:242–54 (1983).

———. "Lun Chin-p'i *Shui-hu* ti ssu-hsiang ch'ing-hsiang yü cheng-lun feng-mang" 論金批水滸的思想傾向與政論鋒芒. *Shui-hu cheng-ming* 2:379–91 (1983).

Chang Hsü-jung 張緒榮 (Chang Kuo-kuang). "Chin Sheng-t'an shih feng-chien fan-tung wen-jen ma?" 金聖歎是封建反動文人嗎. *Hsin chien-she*, 1964. 4:96–105. Also in *Shui-hu chuan lun-wen chi*, pp. 465–81; and *Shui-hu yü Chin Sheng-t'an yen-chiu*, pp. 112–32.

Chang Kuo-kuang 張國光. "Chin-pen *Hsi-hsiang chi* p'i-wen hsin-p'ing" 金本西廂記批文新評. *Ku-tai wen-hsüeh li-lun yen-chiu* 3:150–62 (1981). Also in *Shui-hu yü Chin Sheng-t'an yen-chiu*, pp. 290–307.

———. "Chin Sheng-t'an—chieh-ch'u ti wu-shen lun ssu-hsiang chia: *Chin Sheng-t'an p'ing-chuan* chih i chang" 金聖歎—杰出的無神論思想家:金聖歎評傳之一章. *Hu-pei ta-hsüeh hsüeh-pao* 湖北大學學報, 1986. 6:62–70, 83.

———. "Chin Sheng-t'an hsiao-shuo li-lun ti kang-ling—'Tu *Ti-wu ts'ai-tzu shu* fa' p'ing-shu" 金聖歎小說理論的綱領—讀第五才子書法評述. *Wu-han shih-fan hsüeh-yüan hsüeh-pao*, 1983. 1:63–69, 80.

———. "Chin Sheng-t'an kuan-yü i-shu kuei-lü ti li-lun ch'u-t'an" 金聖歎關於藝術規律的理論初探. In *Shui-hu yü Chin Sheng-t'an yen-chiu*, pp. 133–72.

———. "Chin Sheng-t'an p'i-kai *Shui-hu* ti kung-hsien" 金聖歎批改水滸的貢獻. In *Shui-hu yü Chin Sheng-t'an yen-chiu*, pp. 190–207.

———. "Chin Sheng-t'an shih *Shui-hu* tsui hsiung-e ti ti-jen ma?" 金聖歎是水滸最凶惡的敵人嗎. *Shang-hai shih-fan hsüeh-yüan hsüeh-pao*, 1982. 2:19–24. (*Ku-chin* reprint, 1982. 16:37–42). Also reprinted in *Chin Sheng-t'an tzu-liao chi*, pp. 89–94.

———. "Chin Sheng-t'an *Ts'ai-tzu pi-tu ku-wen* p'ing-chieh" 金聖歎才子必讀古文評介. *Chiang Han lun-t'an*, 1985. 5:55–60.

———. "Chin Sheng-t'an wen-hsüeh p'i-p'ing chung fan-tui feng-chien li-hsüeh ti ssu-hsiang" 金聖歎文學批評中反對封建理學的思想. *Shui-hu cheng-ming* 4:323–39 (1985).

———. "Ch'ü-wei ts'un-chen, yu-piao chi-li—kuan-yü Chin Sheng-t'an p'i-kai *Shui-hu* pu-te-i erh yung 'pao-hu-se' ti wen-t'i" 去偽存真由表及裏—關於金聖歎批改水滸不得已而用保護色的問題. In *Shui-hu yü Chin Sheng-t'an yen-chiu*, pp. 219–37.

———. "Hsin-pan *Lu Hsün ch'üan-chi* chu-shih hai ying ching i ch'iu-ching—kuan-yü *Shui-hu* yü Chin Sheng-t'an t'iao-mu chu-wen ti shang-ch'üeh" 新版魯迅全集注釋還應精益求精—關於水滸與金聖歎條目注文的商榷. *Chung-nan min-tsu hsüeh-yüan hsüeh-pao*, 1982. 2:87–97. Reprinted in *Chin Sheng-t'an tzu-liao chi*, pp. 64–74.

———. "'K'ou-chi' ti chu-tso ch'üan ying-kai kuei-kei Chin Sheng-t'an pien" 口技的著作權應該歸給金聖歎辨. In *Shui-hu yü Chin Sheng-t'an yen-chiu*, pp. 308–16.

———. "Liang chung *Shui-hu*, liang ko Sung Chiang" 兩種水滸兩個宋江. *Wu-han shih-yüan hsüeh-pao*, 1979. 1:75–83. Another version in *Hsüeh-shu yüeh-k'an*, 1979. 7:67–74, 55; reprinted in *Shui-hu yü Chin Sheng-t'an yen-chiu*, pp. 173–89 and in *Chin Sheng-t'an tzu-liao chi*, pp. 24–32.

———. "Lun Chin Sheng-t'an ti shih chi ch'i fan-Ch'ing ssu-hsiang" 論金聖歎 的詩及其反清思想. In *Shui-hu yü Chin Sheng-t'an yen-chiu*, pp. 317–34.

———. "Nan-tao hai pu ying wei Chin Sheng-t'an p'ing-fan?—tu Ho Man-tzu t'ung-chih pien Chin Sheng-t'an ti hsin-tso chi ch'i chiu-chu po-lun" 難道還不應為金聖歎平反 — 讀何滿子同志貶金聖歎的新作及其舊著駁論. *Chung-nan min-tsu hsüeh-yüan hsüeh-pao*, 1984. 3:76–88.

———. "Pieh-ch'u hsin-ts'ai ti wen-hsüeh p'i-p'ing—t'an ju-ho li-chieh Chin Sheng-t'an kuan-yü Sung Chiang 'shih pu-k'o' ti p'ing-lun" 別出心裁的 文學批評 — 談如何理解金聖歎關於宋江十不可的評論. In *Shui-hu yü Chin Sheng-t'an yen-chiu*, pp. 238–62.

———. "Shih chih hao-li, ch'a i ch'ien-li—lun *Shui-hu* ch'i-shih i hui-pen yü ch'i-shih hui-pen ti ssu-hsiang fen-ch'i" 失之毫厘差以千里—論水滸 七十一回本與七十回本的思想分歧. In *Shui-hu yü Chin Sheng-t'an yen-chiu*, pp. 263–73.

———. "*Shui-hu* yen-chiu chung ti pien-cheng fa—tui 'P'ing "Liang-chung *Shui-hu*, liang ko Sung Chiang"' i-wen ti ta-pien" 水滸研究中的辨證法— 對評兩種水滸兩個宋江一文的答辨. *Shui-hu cheng-ming* 3:302–20 (1984).

———. *Shui-hu yü Chin Sheng-t'an yen-chiu* 水滸與金聖歎研究. Cheng-chou: Chung-chou shu-hua she, 1981.

———. "Tsao-pai pu fen, shih-fei nan ming—ts'ung Chin Sheng-t'an tui *Shui-hu* san-ta Chu-chia-chuang ku-shih ti p'i-kai, k'an Chin-pen yü chiu-pen ti yu-lieh, Chin-p'i yü Wang Wang-ju tseng-p'i ti hao-huai" 皂白不分是非 難明—從金聖歎對水滸三打祝家莊故事的批改看金本與舊本的優劣金批與 王望如增批的好壞. In *Shui-hu yü Chin Sheng-t'an yen-chiu*, pp. 208–18.

———. "Wo-kuo chieh-ch'u ti ch'i-meng ssu-hsiang chia Chin Sheng-t'an" 我國杰出的啟蒙思想家金聖歎. In *Shui-hu yü Chin Sheng-t'an yen-chiu*, pp. 91–111.

———. "Wo-kuo ku-tai hsiao-shuo li-lun fa-chan hsien-so—chien lun Chin Sheng-t'an tsai wen-hsüeh p'i-p'ing shih shang ti ti-wei" 我國古代小 說理論發展綫索— 兼論金聖歎在文學批評史上的地位. *Wu-han shih-yüan hsüeh-pao*, 1984. 3:24–32, 37. Reprinted in *Chung-kuo ku-tai hsiao-shuo li-lun yen-chiu*, pp. 1–16.

———. "Yao ch'üan-mien jen-shih Chin Sheng-t'an p'ing-kai *Shui-hu* ti chung-ta kung-hsien" 要全面認識金聖歎評改水滸的重大貢獻. *Hang-chou shih-yüan hsüeh-pao*, 1985. 2:13–17 (*Ku-chin* reprint, 1985. 16:70–74).

———. "Yü pao-pien yü pi-mo chih wai—kuan-yü Chin Sheng-t'an *Shui-hu* p'i chung ti pao-hu-se wen-t'i" 寓褒貶於筆墨之外—關於金聖歎水滸批中 的保護色問題. *She-hui k'o-hsüeh*, 1980. 5:141–44.

———. "Yu pi-chiao ts'ai neng chien-pieh—Chin *Hsi-hsiang* yu yü Wang *Hsi-hsiang* chih wo chien" 有比較才能鑒別— 金西廂優於王西廂之我見. *Wen-hsüeh p'ing-lun ts'ung-k'an* 3:328–42 (1979). Reprinted in *Shui-hu yü Chin Sheng-t'an yen-chiu*, pp. 274–89.

Chang Tsai-hsüan 張載軒. "T'an Chin Sheng-t'an ti '*Shui-hu* wen-fa'" 談金聖 歎的水滸文法. *Huai-yin shih-chuan hsüeh-pao* 淮陰師專學報, 1986. 1:53–57.

Chang Yu-luan 張友鸞. "Chin Sheng-t'an tsen-yang wu-mieh Sung Chiang ti" 金聖歎怎樣誣蔑宋江的. In *Shui-hu yen-chiu lun-wen chi*, pp. 324–34.

Chao-chi 兆吉 (Kung Chao-chi 龔兆吉). "Chin Sheng-t'an t'ung-ch'ing nung-min ch'i-i ma?" 金聖歎同情農民起義嗎. *Wen-hui pao*, 1/15/1963.

Chao Ming-cheng 趙明政. "Chin Sheng-t'an ti hsiao-shuo li-lun" 金聖歎的小說理論. *Wen-hsüeh p'ing-lun ts'ung-k'an*, 13:84–122 (1982).

Ch'en Ch'ang-heng 陳昌恒. "Yeh t'an Chin Sheng-t'an ti wen-hsüeh tien-hsing kuan" 也談金聖歎的文學典型觀. *Chung-nan min-tsu hsüeh-yüan hsüeh-pao*, 1984. 3:89–93.

Ch'en Ch'ien-chih 陳潛之. "Chin Sheng-t'an 'san-ching lun' ch'u-t'an" 金聖歎三境論初探. *Hsü-chou shih-fan hsüeh-yüan hsüeh-pao*, 1985. 1:63–66, 20.

———. "Lun Chin Sheng-t'an ti jen-ko" 論金聖歎的人格. *Hsüeh-shu yüeh-k'an*, 1985. 7:57–64.

Ch'en Ch'ien-yü 陳謙豫. "P'ing Chin Sheng-t'an ti hsiao-shuo li-lun" 評金聖歎的小說理論. *Ku-tai wen-hsüeh li-lun yen-chiu* 9:335–47 (1984).

Ch'en Chin-chao 陳錦釗. "T'an Kuan-hua t'ang Chin Sheng-t'an p'i-pen *Shui-hu chuan*" 談貫華堂金聖歎批本水滸傳. *Shu-mu chi-k'an* 7. 2:59–64 (1972).

Ch'en Hsiang 陳香. "Lun Chin Sheng-t'an shih ti p'i-p'ing" 論金聖歎式的批評. *Shu-p'ing shu-mu* 11:30–36 (1974).

———. "Lun Chin Sheng-t'an ti p'i-p'ing fang-fa" 論金聖歎的批評方法. *Shu-p'ing shu-mu* 17:39–48, 18:80–86, 19:59–66, 20:51–61 (1974).

Ch'en Hung 陳洪. "Chin Sheng-t'an 'Chang hsing' shuo pien-i" 金聖歎張姓說辨疑. *Chiang Hai hsüeh-k'an*, 1983. 5:98.

———. "Shih *Shui-hu* Chin-p'i 'yin-yüan sheng-fa' shuo" 釋水滸金批因緣生法說. *Nan-k'ai hsüeh-pao*, 1984. 2:42–47, 75.

———. "Ts'ung *Ch'en-yin lou shih-hsüan* k'an Chin Sheng-t'an" 從忱吟樓詩選看金聖歎. *Nan-k'ai hsüeh-pao*, 1982. 6:15–21. Reprinted in *Chin Sheng-t'an tzu-liao chi*, pp. 110–16.

Ch'en Teng-yüan 陳登原. *Chin Sheng-t'an chuan* 金聖歎傳. Shanghai: Commercial Press, 1935.

Ch'en Wan-i 陳萬益. *Chin Sheng-t'an ti wen-hsüeh p'i-p'ing k'ao-shu* 金聖歎的文學批評考述. Taipei: T'ai-ta wen-hsüeh yüan, 1976.

Ch'en Wei-en 諶偉恩. "Lun Li Yü tui Chin Sheng-t'an hsi-ch'ü li-lun ti p'i-p'an" 論李漁對金聖歎戲曲理論的批判. *Kuang-chou shih-yüan hsüeh-pao* 廣州師院學報, 1984. 1:47–51, 46.

Ch'eng Chin-chieh 程金階 et al. "Shih-p'ing Chin Sheng-t'an p'ing-chia chung liang chung tui-li ti kuan-tien" 試評金聖歎評價中兩種對立的觀點. *Shui-hu cheng-ming* 2:423–29 (1983).

Cheng Kung-tun 鄭公盾. "Chin Sheng-t'an hsin-lun" 金聖歎新論. *Jen-wu* 人物, 1947. 7. Reprinted in his *Shui-hu chuan lun-wen chi*, pp. 711–15.

Ch'i Sen-hua 齊森華. "Chin Sheng-t'an ti hsi-ch'ü chu-chang shu-p'ing" 金聖歎的戲曲主張述評. *Wen-i li-lun yen-chiu*, 1984. 1:82–87.

———. "Ling i piao hsin, pieh k'ai sheng-mien—lüeh-t'an Chin Sheng-t'an hsi-ch'ü li-lun ti kung-hsien" 領異標新別開生面—略談金聖歎戲曲理論的貢獻. *Ku-tai wen-hsüeh li-lun yen-chiu* 10:315–31 (1985).

Chia Wen-chao 賈文昭. "Chin Sheng-t'an tsai *Shui-hu* chien-shang chung ti 'chun hsing-hsiang ssu-wei'" 金聖歎在水滸鑒賞中的準形象思維. *Wen-i li-lun yen-chiu*, 1986. 4:39–46 (*Ku-chin* reprint, 1986. 10:216–23).

Chiang Chü-jung 江巨榮. "Ts'ung *Ti-liu ts'ai-tzu shu* k'an Chin Sheng-t'an ti wen-i kuan" 從第六才子書看金聖歎的文藝觀. *Ku-tai wen-hsüeh li-lun yen-chiu* 2:301–17 (1980).

Chiang Chü-ying 江巨英. "Chin Sheng-t'an ti san-wen ch'uang-tso lun" 金聖歎的散文創作論. *Yü-wen hsüeh-hsi* 語文學習, 1985. 1:40–43.

Chiang Hsing-yü 蔣星煜. "Chin Sheng-t'an tui *Hsi-hsiang chi* ti t'i-li tso-kuo 'ko-hsin' ma?—ching-chih Chang Kuo-kuang t'ung-chih" 金聖歎對西廂記的體例作過革新嗎—敬質張國光同志. In *Chung-kuo hsi-ch'ü shih t'an-wei*, pp. 180–89.

———. "Chou Ang tui *Hsi-hsiang chi* ti yen-chiu chi ch'i tui Chin-p'i ti tsai p'i-p'ing—*Tseng-ting Chin-p'i Hsi-hsiang* mien-mien kuan" 周昂對西廂記的研究及其對金批的再批評—增訂金批西廂面面觀. *Chung-kuo ku-tien wen-hsüeh lun-ts'ung* 2:270–85 (1985).

Chin Chao-tzu 金兆梓. "T'an Chin Sheng-t'an ti p'i-kai *Shui-hu* ho *Hsi-hsiang*" 談金聖歎的批改水滸和西廂. *Hsin chien-she*, 1962. 1.

Chin Chia-hsing 金家興. "Wei Chin Sheng-t'an ma Sung Chiang i-pien" 為金聖歎罵宋江一辨. *Wu-han Hsiao-kan fen-yüan hsüeh-pao* 武漢孝感分院學報, 1981. 1:38–41 (*Ku-chin* reprint, 1982. 7:117–20).

Chin Hsing-yao 金性堯. "Sheng-t'an chih liu shu-chung tsai" 聖歎只留書種在. *Shu-lin*, 1983. 5:54–55.

Chin Sheng-t'an 金聖歎. *Ch'en-yin lou shih-hsüan* 忱吟樓詩選. Edited by Liu Hsien-t'ing 劉獻廷. Shanghai: Shang-hai ku-chi, 1979.

———. *Chin Sheng-t'an ch'üan-chi* 金聖歎全集. 4 vols. Nanking: Chiang-su ku-chi 1985.

———. *Chin Sheng-t'an p'i-pen Hsi-hsiang chi* 金聖歎批本西廂記. Edited by Chang Kuo-kuang 張國光. Shanghai: Shang-hai ku-chi, 1986.

———. *Chin Sheng-t'an p'i Ts'ai-tzu ku-wen* 金聖歎批才子古文. Edited by Chang Kuo-kuang. Wuhan: Hu-pei jen-min, 1986.

———. *Chin Sheng-t'an shih-wen p'ing-hsüan* 金聖歎詩文評選. Edited by Chang Kuo-kuang. Ch'ang-sha: Yüeh-lu shu-she, 1986.

———. *Ti-liu ts'ai-tzu Hsi-hsiang chi* 第六才子西廂記. Taipei: Wen-kuang t'u-shu, 1978 reprint of *Tseng-p'i hui-hsiang Ti-liu ts'ai-tzu shu* 增批繪像第六才子書, 1720.

———. *T'ien-hsia ts'ai-tzu pi-tu shu* 天下才子必讀書. Taipei: Shu-hsiang ch'u-pan she, 1978 reprint.

Chin Sheng-t'an yen-chiu tzu-liao 金聖歎研究資料. Taipei: T'ien-i ch'u-pan she, 1981.

Chin Te-men 金德門 (I-ming). "Chin Sheng-t'an shih pu fan-tung ti feng-chien wen-jen—yeh yü Kung-tun t'ung-chih shang-ch'üeh" 金聖歎是不反動的封建文人—也與公盾同志商榷. *She-hui k'o-hsüeh*, 1980. 5:135–40, 134.

———. "Chin Sheng-t'an shih-liao pien-cheng" 金聖歎史料辨正. *Chung-hua wen-shih lun-ts'ung*, 1986. 3:195–99.

Chin Yü-t'ien 金玉田 et al. "Tui Chin Sheng-t'an yao-chan, p'ing-tien *Shui-hu* ti t'an-t'ao" 對金聖歎腰斬評點水滸的探討. *Cheng-chou ta-hsüeh hsüeh-pao*,

1982. 2:85–90 (*Ku-chin* reprint, 1982. 16:43–48). Also reprinted in *Chin Sheng-t'an tzu-liao chi*, pp. 83–88.

Cho Chih-chung 卓支中. "Shih-p'ing Chin Sheng-t'an ti wen-hsüeh hsing-hsiang yü tien-hsing lun" 試評金聖歎的文學形象與典型論. *Chi-nan hsüeh-pao*, 1983. 4:83–97 (*Ku-chin* reprint, 1983. 11:240–48).

Chou Hsi-shan 周錫山. "Chin Sheng-t'an chu-mu shu-lüeh" 金聖歎著目述略. *Su-chou ta-hsüeh hsüeh-pao*, 1986. 3:59–60 (*Ku-chin* reprint, 1986. 8:237–38).

Chou Hsüeh-yü 周學禹. "Shih-lun Chin Sheng-t'an so-wei 'tu-wu Sung Chiang' shuo" 試論金聖歎所謂獨惡宋江說. *Hsin-yang shih-yüan hsüeh-pao* 信陽師院學報, 1984. 2:70–76.

Chou Shu-wen 周書文. "Chin Sheng-t'an p'ing-tien *Hsi-hsiang chi* ti hsi-chü wen-i kuan" 金聖歎評點西廂記的戲劇文藝觀. *Pei-ching shih-yüan hsüeh-pao* 北京師院學報, 1985. 3:29–37 (*Ku-chin* reprint, 1985. 16:43–51).

Chou Tso-jen 周作人. "T'an Chin Sheng-t'an" 談金聖歎. *Jen-chien shih* 31:3–5 (1935).

———. "T'an Feng Meng-lung yü Chin Sheng-t'an" 談馮夢龍與金聖歎. *Jen-chien shih* 19:16–18 (1935).

Chu Chao-nien 祝肇年. "Tsen-yang p'ing-chia Chin Jen-jui ti wen-hsüeh li-lun" 怎樣評價金人瑞的文學理論. *Wen-hsüeh i-ch'an tseng-k'an* 9:12–24 (1962).

Chuang Lien 莊練. "Chin Sheng-t'an 'Ch'un-kan pa-shou' shih-chieh" 金聖歎春感八首試解. *Chung-yang jih-pao*, 4/21/1981.

Chung Lai-yin 鍾來因. "Ch'u-p'ing Chin Sheng-t'an ti *Tu-shih chieh*" 初評金聖歎的杜詩解. *Ts'ao-t'ang* 草堂, 1982. 1:81–87. Reprinted in *Chin Sheng-t'an tzu-liao chi*, pp. 57–63.

———. "Ts'ung 'Ch'un-kan pa-shou' k'an Chin Sheng-t'an ti wan-nien ssu-hsiang" 從春感八首看金聖歎的晚年思想. *Ming-Ch'ing hsiao-shuo yen-chiu* 1:278–92 (1985).

Fang Fu-jen 方福仁. "Ts'ung *Ch'en-yin lou shih-hsüan* k'an Chin Sheng-t'an" 從忱吟樓詩選看金聖歎. *Kuang-ming jih-pao*, 4/23/1980.

Fu Hsiao-hang 傅曉航. "Chin Sheng-t'an shan-kai *Hsi-hsiang chi* ti te-shih" 金聖歎刪改西廂記的得失. *Chung-yang hsi-chü hsüeh-yüan hsüeh-pao* 中央戲劇學院學報, 1986. 3:91–98 (*Hsi-ch'ü yen-chiu* reprint, 1986. 11:63–70).

Fu Lung-chi 傅隆基. "Chin Sheng-t'an shih chia-wu Sung Chiang hai-shih chen-wu Sung Chiang?" 金聖歎是假惡宋江還是真惡宋江. *Chiang Han lun-t'an*, 1982. 2:54–59. Reprinted in *Chin Sheng-t'an tzu-liao chi*, pp. 51–56.

———. "P'ing 'Liang chung *Shui-hu*, liang ko Sung Chiang' shuo" 評兩種水滸兩個宋江說. *Shui-hu cheng-ming* 3:284–301 (1984).

Fu Mao-mien 傅懋勉. "Kuan-yü p'ing-chia Chin Sheng-t'an ti wen-t'i" 關於評價金聖歎的問題. *Wen-i pao*, 9/28/1962.

Hao Lien-ch'ang 郝連昌. "Chin Sheng-t'an chih ssu" 金聖歎之死. *Pei-fang lun-ts'ung*, 1980. 4:11.

Ho Chin-ts'an 何錦嶸. "Chin Sheng-t'an wei-ho hsiu-kai *Shui-hu chuan*?" 金聖歎為何修改水滸傳. *Ta-ch'eng* 44:36–39 (1977).

Ho Man-tzu 何滿子. "Chin Sheng-t'an" 金聖歎. In *Chung-kuo li-tai chu-ming wen-hsüeh chia p'ing-chuan* 中國歷代著名文學家評傳. 6 vols. Tsinan: Shan-tung chiao-yü, 1985, vol. 5, pp. 17–42.

———. "Chin Sheng-t'an ti sheng-p'ing, jen-sheng t'ai-tu ho wen-hsüeh kuan" 金聖歎的生平人生態度和文學觀. *Chung-hua wen-shih lun-ts'ung*, 1983. 2:273–95.

———. *Lun Chin Sheng-t'an p'ing-kai Shui-hu chuan* 論金聖歎評改水滸傳. Shanghai: Shang-hai ch'u-pan she, 1954.

Hou Min-chih 侯民治. "'Yin-wen sheng-shih' shih wo-kuo ku-tai hsiao-shuo ch'uang-tso li-lun chung ti chu-yü" 因文生事是我國古代小說創作理論中的珠玉. *Hsieh-tso*, 1985. 5:12–13, 7.

Hsiao Hsiang-k'ai 蕭相愷, and Ou-yang Chien 歐陽健. "Chin Sheng-t'an *Shui-hu* p'ing-kai tung-chi t'an" 金聖歎水滸評改動機探. *Kuei-chou she-hui k'o-hsüeh*, 1981. 2:88–96 (*Ku-chin* reprint, 1981. 10:79–87). Also reprinted in *Shui-hu hsin-i*, pp. 340–57.

———. "Ho chih tsou-le i hsiao-pu—p'ing 'Liang chung *Shui-hu*, liang chung Sung Chiang' lun" 何止走了一小步—評兩種水滸兩種宋江論. *Su-chou ta-hsüeh hsüeh-pao*, 1983. 2:124–29 (*Ku-chin* reprint, 1983. 8:159–65). Also reprinted in *Shui-hu hsin-i*, pp. 392–408.

Hsin Wen-chien 新文建. "Kuan-yü Chin Sheng-t'an p'ing-chia wen-t'i ti t'ao-lun" 關於金聖歎評價問題的討論. *Kuang-ming jih-pao*, 8/2/1964.

Hsü Hui-min 胥惠民. "Chin Sheng-t'an ti hsi-chü ssu-hsiang" 金聖歎的戲劇思想. *Hsin-chiang shih-fan ta-hsüeh hsüeh-pao* 新疆師範大學學報, 1986. 2:129–36.

———. "Chin Sheng-t'an tien-hsing kuan ch'ien-i" 金聖歎典型觀淺議. In *Chung-kuo ku-tai hsiao-shuo li-lun yen-chiu*, pp. 197–204.

Hsü Li 徐立. "Chin Sheng-t'an ti p'ing-tien feng-ko" 金聖歎的評點風格. *Hua-nan shih-fan ta-hsüeh hsüeh-pao*, 1985. 4:79–85 (*Ku-chin* reprint, 1986. 1:309–15).

Hsü T'ao 徐濤. "Chin Sheng-t'an hsien-shih chu-i hsiao-shuo li-lun t'an-sheng" 金聖歎現實主義小說理論探勝. *Wu-han shih-fan hsüeh-yüan hsüeh-pao*, 1984. 3:33–36.

———. "Lüeh-lun Lu Hsün hsien-sheng tui Chin Sheng-t'an ti p'i-p'ing chi ch'i t'a" 略論魯迅先生對金聖歎的批評及其他. *Shui-hu cheng-ming* 1:255–66 (1983).

Hsüeh Ch'iang 薛强 (Cheng Kung-tun). "Tu Chin Sheng-t'an chi-p'ien *Shui-hu chuan* hsü-wen hou-chi" 讀金聖歎幾篇水滸傳序文後記. *Kuang-ming jih-pao*, 8/2/1964. Also reprinted in his *Shui-hu chuan lun-wen chi*, pp. 568–84.

Hu Shih 胡適. "Lun Chin Sheng-t'an k'o-pen *Shui-hu chuan* li pi-hui ti chin-yen" 論金聖歎刻本水滸傳裏避諱的謹嚴. *Ta-kung pao* 大公報, 11/14/1947.

Hu Tzu-yüan 胡子元, and Kuei-ts'ui 桂萃. "Wen-yüan i-ts'ai Chin Sheng-t'an" 文苑異才金聖歎. *I-t'an*, 1982. 1:127–28 (*Ku-chin* reprint, 1982. 10:119–20).

Huang Cheng-hsiang 黃正湘. "'Ko-wu' 'chung-shu' 'yin-yuan sheng fa'—Chin Sheng-t'an ti hsiao-shuo li-lun ch'ien-t'an" 格物忠恕因緣生法—金聖歎的小說理論淺談. *Hu-nan chiao-yü hsüeh-yüan hsüeh-pao*, 1985. 1:18–22.

Huang Ch'iu-pao 黃求保. "Ts'ung *Shui-hu* pai-hui pen ch'ien-yu hou-lieh k'an Chin Sheng-t'an yao-chan *Shui-hu* ti kung-kuo" 從水滸百回本前優後劣看金聖歎腰斬水滸的功過. *Shui-hu cheng-ming* 2:225-32 (1983).

Huang Chung-mo 黃中模. "Lun Li Chih yü Chin Sheng-t'an p'ing *Shui-hu* ti chu-yao fen-ch'i" 論李贄與金聖歎評水滸的主要分歧. *Shui-hu cheng-ming* 1:347-59 (1983).

———. "Pu neng kei *Shui-hu* Chin-p'i chia-shang 'hsing-shih chu-i' ti tsui-ming" 不能給水滸金批加上形式主義的罪名. *Shui-hu cheng-ming* 2:411-22 (1983).

———. "Ts'ung 'ching-tzu' lun k'an Ta-fen-ch'i yü Chin Sheng-t'an ti mei-hsüeh ssu-hsiang" 從鏡子論看達芬奇與金聖歎的美學思想. *Shui-hu cheng-ming* 4:372-80 (1985).

Huang Lin 黃霖. "Chin Sheng-t'an 'hsiang-hsing Chang' pien" 金聖歎庠姓張辨. *Chiang Hai hsüeh-k'an*, 1985. 1:52-54.

———. "Tu Chin Sheng-t'an ti *Ch'en-yin lou shih-hsüan*" 讀金聖歎的忱吟樓詩選. In *Ku-tien wen-hsüeh lun-ts'ung* 古典文學論叢. Shanghai: Shang-hai jen-min, 1980, pp. 204-20.

Huang T'ien-chi 黃天驥. "Chin Sheng-t'an lun hsiao-shuo ch'uang-tso" 金聖歎論小說創作. *Tso-p'in*, 1981. 7:53-57 (*Ku-chin* reprint, 1981. 16:107-11).

Hung K'o-i 洪克夷. "Ts'ung *Ch'en-yin lou shih-hsüan* k'an Chin Sheng-t'an" 從忱吟樓詩選看金聖歎. *Hang-chou ta-hsüeh hsüeh-pao*, 1981. 1:91-95.

Huo Sung-lin 霍松林. "Chin Sheng-t'an p'i-kai *Hsi-hsiang chi* ti fan-tung i-t'u" 金聖歎批改西廂記的反動意圖. *Kuang-ming jih-pao*, 5/29/1955. Reprinted in *Yüan Ming Ch'ing hsi-ch'ü yen-chiu lun-wen chi* 元明清戲曲研究論文集 (Peking: Jen-min wen-hsüeh, 1959), vol. 2, pp. 197-206.

I-ming 易名 (Chin Te-men). "'Chiao yang-mu' pien" 嚼楊木辨. *Hsüeh-shu yen-chiu*, 1982. 4:32. Reprinted in *Chin Sheng-t'an tzu-liao chi*, p. 101.

———. "San-chung *Shui-hu* pan-pen, san-ko Sung Chiang hsing-hsiang" 三種水滸版本三個宋江形象. *Chiang Han lun-t'an*, 1982. 2:48-54.

———. "T'an Chin-pen *Shui-hu* yü Wu Chih-ta t'ung-chih shang-ch'üeh" 談金本水滸與吳志達同志商榷. *Chiang Han lun-t'an*, 1979. 4:101-7. Reprinted in *Chin Sheng-t'an tzu-liao chi*, pp. 33-39.

———. "Tsai t'an Chin-pen *Shui-hu*" 再談金本水滸. *Shang-hai shih-yüan hsüeh-pao*, 1981. 3:149-54.

———. "Ts'ung 'K'u-miao an' k'an Chin Sheng-t'an" 從哭廟案看金聖歎. *Kuang-ming jih-pao*, 3/24/1962.

———. "Yeh t'an Chin Sheng-t'an" 也談金聖歎. *Wen-hui pao*, 10/16/1962.

I-ming, and Ho Man-tzu 何滿子. "Kuan-yü Chin Sheng-t'an shih-t'i chung 'Ching-ko' ti t'ao-lun" 關於金聖歎詩題中境哥的討論. *Chung-hua wen-shih lun-ts'ung*, 1984. 2:201-4.

K'ang Pai-shih 康百世. "Chin Sheng-t'an p'ing-kai *Shui-hu chuan* ti yen-chiu" 金聖歎評改水滸傳的研究. Master's thesis, Political University, Taipei, 1971.

Kao Ming-ko 高明閣. "Chin Sheng-t'an tui *Shui-hu chuan* ti p'ing-tien yü ts'uan-kai" 金聖歎對水滸傳的評點與篡改. *She-hui k'o-hsüeh chi-k'an*, 1979. 5:155-60. Reprinted in *Chin Sheng-t'an tzu-liao chi*, pp. 45-50.

Kao Sung-nien 高松年. "Yin jen fei wen i-li" 因人廢文一例. *Che-chiang hsüeh-k'an*, 1981. 1:120–21.

Kao Tan-yün 高淡雲. "Pu ying-kai na 'k'u miao an' lai wei fan-tung wen-jen Chin Sheng-t'an fan-an—p'ing Chang Hsü-jung, I-ming teng hsien-sheng ti kuan-tien" 不應該拿哭廟案來為反動文人金聖歎翻案—評張緒榮易名等先生的觀點. *Kuang-ming jih-pao*, 11/8/1964.

Karashima Takeshi 辛島驍. "Kin Seitan" 金聖歎. In *Uno Tetsujin hakushi beiju kinen ronshū—Chūgoku no shisōka* 宇野哲人博士米壽記念論集—中國の思想家. Tokyo: Keisō shobō, 1963, pp. 642–53.

Ko Ch'u-ying 葛楚英. "Chin Sheng-t'an lun 'no-chan'" 金聖歎論那輾. *Hsiao-kan shih-chuan hsüeh-pao*, 1985. 1:1–8.

——. "Chin Sheng-t'an p'ing *Shui-hu chuan* ti hsi-chieh miao-hsieh" 金聖歎評水滸傳的細節描寫. In *Chung-kuo ku-tai hsiao-shuo li-lun yen-chiu*, pp. 218–31.

——. "Chuai chih t'ung-t'i chü tung—Chin Sheng-t'an ti hsi-chieh miao-hsieh" 拽之通體俱動—金聖歎的細節描寫. *Hsiao-kan shih-chuan hsüeh-pao*, 1984. 2:33–40.

——. "Mu-chu pi-ch'u, shou-hsieh tz'u-ch'u—Chin Sheng-t'an chih i-shu shen-ching lun" 目注彼處手寫此處—金聖歎之藝術神經論. *Hsiao-kan shih-chuan hsüeh-pao*, 1983. 2:13–25 (*Ku-chin* reprint, 1983. 8:238–50).

Ko Ch'u-ying, and Chin Chia-hsing 金家興. "Chin Sheng-t'an yao-chan *Shui-hu* ti i-shu kou-ssu" 金聖歎腰斬水滸的藝術構思. *Chiang Han lun-t'an*, 1983. 4:50–54.

Ku Tai 谷岱. "Kuan-yü Chin Sheng-t'an p'ing-chia wen-t'i ti t'ao-lun" 關於金聖歎評價問題的討論. *Hsin chien-she*, 1963. 4:96–97.

Kuan Hsien-chu 關賢柱. "Chin-pen *Shui-hu chuan* chih chen-ti—po Chin-pen *Shui-hu* hsü-wen wei 'fan-mien chiao-ts'ai' shuo" 金本水滸傳之真諦—駁金本水滸序文為反面教材說. *Shui-hu cheng-ming* 3:470–78 (1984).

Kung Chao-chi 龔兆吉. "Lun Chin Sheng-t'an p'ing *Shui-hu chuan* ti kuan-tien" 論金聖歎評水滸傳的觀點. *Pei-ching shih-fan ta-hsüeh hsüeh-pao*, 1963. 2:55–67.

——. "Ming-mo she-hui yü Chin Sheng-t'an p'ing-tien *Shui-hu chuan* ti li-shih i-i" 明末社會與金聖歎評點水滸傳的歷史意義. *Shih-hsüeh shih yen-chiu* 史學史研究, 1985. 3:40–49.

——. "Shih-lun Li Chih, Chin Sheng-t'an p'ing-tien *Shui-hu chuan* ti chi-ch'eng kuan-hsi" 試論李贄金聖歎評點水滸傳的繼承關係. In *Mei-hsüeh wen-hsüeh lun-wen chi*, pp. 231–59.

——. "Tzu yu hou-jen shuo tuan-ch'ang—lun Chin Sheng-t'an p'ing-tien *Shui-hu chuan* ti li-shih i-i" 自有後人說短長—論金聖歎評點水滸傳的歷史意義. *Shui-hu cheng-ming* 1:281–301 (1983).

Kung Jung 功榮. "Shih 'hsiao chung-i erh jeng *Shui-hu*'—chien lun Kung Chao-chi hsien-sheng ju-ho ch'ü-chieh Chin Sheng-t'an" 釋削忠義而仍水滸—兼論龔兆吉先生如何曲解金聖歎. *Shui-hu cheng-ming* 3:449–63 (1984).

Kung-tun 公盾 (Cheng Kung-tun). "Chin Sheng-t'an tsai *Shui-hu chuan* p'ing-tien chung ti i-shu fen-hsi chih-te sung-yang ma?" 金聖歎在水滸傳評點中

的藝術分析值得頌揚嗎. *Kuang-ming jih-pao*, 11/20/1964. Reprinted in his *Shui-hu chuan lun-wen chi*, pp. 534–54.

———. "Pu-yao mei-hua Chin Sheng-t'an" 不要美化金聖歎. *Hsin chien-she*, 1963. 3. Reprinted in his *Shui-hu chuan lun-wen chi*, pp. 415–40.

———. "Tsai lun pu-yao mei-hua Chin Sheng-t'an" 再論不要美化金聖歎. *Li-shih yen-chiu*, 1966. 1. Reprinted in his *Shui-hu chuan lun-wen chi*, pp. 441–64.

Kuo Jui 郭瑞. "Chin Sheng-t'an hsiao-shuo mei-hsüeh" 金聖歎小說美學. *Tu-shu*, 1982. 1:130–36 (*Ku-chin* reprint, 1982. 4:71–76).

———. "Wo-kuo ku-tien wen-hsüeh ssu-hsiang i-ko t'u-p'o—Chin Sheng-t'an ti jen-wu 'hsing-ko shuo'" 我國古典文學思想一個突破—金聖歎的人物性格說. *Wen-i yen-chiu*, 1982. 2:66–72 (*Ku-chin* reprint, 1983. 1:237–43). Reprinted in *Chin Sheng-t'an tzu-liao chi*, pp. 75–81.

Li Ch'ien 李騫. "Chin Sheng-t'an lun hsiao-shuo ti ch'ing-chieh kou-ch'eng, pien-hua ti t'e-cheng" 金聖歎論小說的情節構成變化的特徵. *Shui-hu cheng-ming* 3:464–69 (1984).

Li Chin-te 李金德. "Chin Sheng-t'an ti tien-hsing kuan shih Chung-kuo tien-hsing li-lun ti ch'eng-shu" 金聖歎的典型觀是中國典型理論的成熟. *Shui-hu cheng-ming* 4:363–71 (1985).

Li Hsing-sheng 李興盛. "Chin Sheng-t'an ti chia-shu chiu-ching shih ch'ien-shu Ning-ku-t'a hai-shih t'a-ch'u" 金聖歎的家屬就境是遣戍寧古塔還是他處. *She-hui k'o-hsüeh chi-k'an*, 1985. 6:62–63.

Li Jan-ch'ing 李燃青. "Chin Sheng-t'an jen-wu hsing-ko lun ch'u-t'an" 金聖歎人物性格論初探. *Ning-po shih-yüan hsüeh-pao* 寧波師院學報, 1984. 2:23–32 (*Ku-chin* reprint, 1984. 20:151–60).

Li Mao-su 李茂肅. "Chin Sheng-t'an p'ing *Shui-hu* chi ch'i yen-chung chü-hsien" 金聖歎評水滸及其嚴重局限. *Liu-ch'üan* 柳泉, 1984. 1:206–10 (*Ku-chin* reprint, 1984. 4:79–83).

———. "Chin Sheng-t'an tui *Shui-hu chuan* ti i-shu p'ing-lun" 金聖歎對水滸傳的藝術評論. In *Chung-kuo ku-tai hsiao-shuo li-lun yen-chiu*, pp. 205–17.

Li Tse-min 李澤民, and Shih Ch'iao-yün 史巧雲. "Chin Sheng-t'an ti shih-wen p'ing-tien" 金聖歎的詩文評點. *Yü-wen yüeh-k'an* 語文月刊, 1985. 11:16–18.

Liao Yen 廖燕. "Chin Sheng-t'an hsien-sheng chuan" 金聖歎先生傳. In *Erh-shih ch'i sung t'ang chi* 二十七松堂集. Tokyo: Hakuetsu dō, 1862, 14/5b–7b.

Lin T'ung-hua 林同華. "Kuan-yü Chin Sheng-t'an ti liang ko wen-t'i yü Chang Kuo-kuang t'ung-chih shang-ch'üeh" 關於金聖歎的兩個問題與張國光同志商榷. *Wu-han shih-fan hsüeh-yüan hsüeh-pao*, 1983. 2:17–21.

———. "Lun Chin Sheng-t'an ti che-hsüeh wen-hsüeh ssu-hsiang" 論金聖歎的哲學文學思想. In *Chung-kuo mei-hsüeh shih lun-chi* 中國美學史論集. Nanking: Chiang-su jen-min, 1984, pp. 285–301.

———. "Tsai lun Chin Sheng-t'an ti che-hsüeh wen-hsüeh ssu-hsiang" 再論金聖歎的哲學文學思想. In *Chung-kuo mei-hsüeh shih lun-chi*, pp. 302–14.

Lin Wen-shan 林文山. "Chin Sheng-t'an yü *Shui-hu*" 金聖歎與水滸. *Chung-hua wen-shih lun-ts'ung*, 1980. 1:241–58.

———. "Lun Chin Sheng-t'an p'ing-kai *Hsi-hsiang*" 論金聖歎評改西廂. *She-*

hui k'o-hsüeh yen-chiu, 1981. 5:80–85, 68.

———. "Lun Chin Sheng-t'an p'ing *Shui-hu* ti chieh-kou" 論金聖歎評水滸的結構. *She-hui k'o-hsüeh yen-chiu*, 1985. 2:74–77, 89.

———. "No-chan—Chung-kuo ku-tai wen-hsüeh ch'uang-tso ti chung-yao i-shu tso-fa" 那輾—中國古代文學創作的重要藝術作法. *Hsüeh-shu yen-chiu*, 1984. 3:97–103.

———. "P'ing Chin *Hsi-hsiang*" 評金西廂. *Hsi-ch'ü i-shu* 戲曲藝術. 1985. 3:60–64 (pt. 1); 1985. 4:11–19, 92 (pt. 2).

Liu Ching-an 劉靖安. "Shih-lun Chin-pen *Shui-hu* chung Sung Chiang ti hsing-hsiang" 試論金本水滸中宋江的形像. *Shui-hu cheng-ming* 2:322–32 (1983).

Liu Hsin-chung 劉欣中. *Chin Sheng-t'an ti hsiao-shuo li-lun* 金聖歎的小說理論. Shih-chia-chuang: Ho-pei jen-min, 1986.

Liu Hung-pin 劉厷彬. "Lun Chin Sheng-t'an p'ing-tien *Shui-hu chuan*—chien p'ing Ho Man-tzu hsien-sheng tui Chin Sheng-t'an ti ch'üan-p'an fou-ting t'ai-tu" 論金聖歎評點水滸傳—兼評何滿子先生對金聖歎的全盤否定態度. *Shui-hu cheng-ming* 3:440–48 (1984).

Liu I-sheng 劉逸生. "Lun Chin Sheng-t'an wei-tsao Shih Nai-an hsü hsien-cheng" 論金聖歎偽造施耐庵序顯證. *Hsüeh-shu yen-chiu*, 1981. 3:87–88 (*Ku-chin* reprint, 1981. 14:87–88).

Liu Shih-hsing 劉士興, and Liu Tao-en 劉道恩. "Kuan-yü Chin Sheng-t'an p'ing-kai *Shui-hu* ti yen-chiu" 關於金聖歎評改水滸的研究. *Wu-han shih-fan hsüeh-yüan hsüeh-pao*, 1979. 1:84–90.

Liu Shih-te 劉世德. "Chin Sheng-t'an ti sheng-nien" 金聖歎的生年. *Wen-hui pao*, 6/20/1962.

———. "Pai-sheng ts'o chi" 稗乘脞記. *Hsüeh-lin man-lu* 2:176–81 (1981).

Liu Ta-chieh 劉大杰, and Chang P'ei-heng 章培恒. "Chin Sheng-t'an ti wen-hsüeh p'i-p'ing" 金聖歎的文學批評. *Chung-hua wen-shih lun-ts'ung*, 3:145–62 (1963). Reprinted in *Shui-hu chuan lun-wen chi*, pp. 555–67.

Lo Mao-lin 羅茂林, "Yeh t'an Chin Sheng-t'an p'i-kai *Shui-hu* ti chen-i—yü Chin Yü-t'ien teng t'ung-chih shang-ch'üeh" 也談金聖歎批改水滸的真意—與金玉田等同志商榷. *Shao-yang shih-chuan hsüeh-pao* 邵陽師專學報, 1985. 1:58–62 (*Ku-chin* reprint, 1985. 14:33–37).

Lo Ssu-ting 羅思鼎. "San-pai nien lai ti i-chuang kung-an—p'ing Chin Sheng-t'an yao-chan *Shui-hu* chi ch'i yin-ch'i ti cheng-lun" 三百年來的一樁公案—評金聖歎腰斬水滸及其引起的爭論. *Hsüeh-hsi yü p'i-p'an* 學習與批判, 1975. 10:24–31. Reprinted in *Chin Sheng-t'an tzu-liao chi*, pp. 7–14.

Lo Te-jung 羅德榮. "Chin Sheng-t'an ti jen-wu hsing-ko lun" 金聖歎的人物性格論. *Nan-k'ai hsüeh-pao*, 1982. 4:46–50, 58. Reprinted in *Chin Sheng-t'an tzu-liao chi*, pp. 95–100.

———. "Wei Chin Sheng-t'an 'ts'ao-she hui-hsien fa' i-pien" 為金聖歎草蛇灰線法一辨. *T'ien-chin shih-ta hsüeh-pao*, 1985. 2:70–74.

Lu Hsin 盧炘. "Chin-p'i *Shui-hu* ti ch'ü-pi yü *Shih-chi*" 金批水滸的曲筆與史記. *Che-chiang hsüeh-k'an*, 1984. 1:49–54 (*Ku-chin* reprint, 1984. 6:33–37).

———. "Chin Sheng-t'an ti 't'o-pi ma-shih' shuo" 金聖歎的托筆罵世說. *Shui-hu cheng-ming* 4:353–62 (1985).

Lu Hsün 魯迅 (Chou Shu-jen 周樹人). "T'an Chin Sheng-t'an" 談金聖歎. In *Nan-ch'iang pei-tiao* 南腔北調. Vol. 4 of *Lu Hsün ch'üan-chi* 魯迅全集. Shanghai: Jen-min wen-hsüeh, 1981, pp. 527–30.

Lu Lien-hsing 陸聯星. "Chin Sheng-t'an ti hsiao-shuo p'i-p'ing—Chung-kuo ku-tai hsiao-shuo li-lun kai-kuan chih erh" 金聖歎的小說批評—中國古代小說理論概觀之二. *Huai-pei mei-shih-yüan hsüeh-pao*, 1983. 3 : 50–62.

Ma Ch'eng-sheng 馬成生. "Lüeh-lun 'tzu ch'eng ming, wei chih hsing'—tu Chin p'ing-pen *Shui-hu chuan* ti ssu-shih erh hui ti p'ing-yü" 略論自誠明謂之性—讀金評本水滸傳的四十二回的評語. *Shui-hu cheng-ming* 4 : 340–52 (1985).

———. "Ying-kai shih-shih ch'iu shih—kuan-yü p'ing-chia Chin Sheng-t'an ti i-hsieh kan-hsiang" 應該實事求是—關於評價金聖歎的一些感想. *Wen-hui pao*, 4/29/1963.

Ma Pi-sheng 馬必勝. "Hsi-ch'ü li-lun fa-chan shih shang ti t'u-p'o hsing kung-hsien—*Ti-liu ts'ai-tzu shu* shu-p'ing chih i" 戲曲理論發展史上的突破性貢獻—第六才子書述評之一. *Su-chou ta-hsüeh hsüeh-pao*, 1985. 4 : 83–87.

Ma T'i-chi 馬蹄疾. "Chin Sheng-t'an chi-ch'eng Li Cho-wu fan-feng tou-cheng ti ch'uan-t'ung ma?—kuan-yü Li Cho-wu yü Chin Sheng-t'an tui *Shui-hu chuan* ti p'i-p'ing kuan-tien" 金聖歎繼承李卓吾反封鬥爭的傳統嗎—關於李卓吾與金聖歎對水滸傳的批評觀點. *Kuang-ming jih-pao*, 7/26/1964.

———. "Kuan-yü Chin Sheng-t'an yao-chan *Shui-hu* wen-t'i" 關於金聖歎腰斬水滸問題. *Hsin chien-she*, 1963. 8 : 93–94.

———. "Lüeh-t'an Chin-p'i *Shui-hu chuan* ti liu-ch'uan chi ch'i yü *Tang-k'ou chih* ti kuan-hsi" 略談金批水滸傳的流傳及其與蕩寇志的關係. *Hsin chien-she*, 1965. 7 : 60–63.

Maeno Naoaki 前野直彬. "Ming-Ch'ing shih-ch'i liang-chung tui-li hsiao-shuo lun—Chin Sheng-t'an yü Chi Yün" 明清時期兩種對立小說論—金聖歎與紀昀. Translated by Ch'en Hsi-chung 陳曦鐘. *Ku-tai wen-hsüeh li-lun yen-chiu* 5 : 44–70 (1981). For the original see *Nihon Chūgoku gakkai hō* 10 : 7–25 (1958) and his *Chūgoku shōsetsu shi kō* 中国小說史考 (Tokyo: Kyosan shoten, 1975), pp. 357–93.

Meng Sen 孟森. "Chin Sheng-t'an k'ao" 金聖歎考. Appendix to Chin Sheng-t'an, *T'ien-hsia ts'ai-tzu pi-tu shu*, Shu-hsiang ch'u-pan she reprint.

Nakahachi Masakazu 中鉢雅量. "Chien p'ing *Shui-hu* yü Chin Sheng-t'an yen-chiu" 簡評水滸與金聖歎研究. Translated by P'eng Hsiu-ken 彭修艮 and Chang San-hsi 張三夕. *Shui-hu cheng-ming* 4 : 398–402 (1985).

———. "Kin Seitan no *Suikoden* kan" 金聖歎の水滸伝観. *Nogusa* 野草 4 : 23–34 (1971).

Nieh Kan-nu 聶紺弩. "Lin Ssu-huan ch'ao-hsi Chin Sheng-t'an ti wen-chang" 林嗣環抄襲金聖歎的文章. *Kuang-ming jih-pao*, 6/24/1962.

———. "Wo ai Chin Sheng-t'an" 我愛金聖歎. *Kuang-ming jih-pao*, 11/2/1982.

Ou-yang Chien 歐陽健. "Shih-lun Chin Sheng-t'an, Yü Wan-ch'un tzu-shen chung ti mao-tun chi hsiang-hu kuan-hsi" 試論金聖歎俞萬春自身中的矛盾及相互關係. *Shui-hu cheng-ming* 4 : 381–97 (1985).

Ōuchida Saburō 大內田三郎. "Kin Seitan to *Suikoden*—Kin Seitan no *Suiko* kan o chūshin ni" 金聖歎と水滸伝―金聖歎の水滸観を中心に. *Tenri daigaku gakuhō* 62:47–59 (1969).

P'an Shih-hsiu 潘世秀. "Chin-p'ing Sung Chiang mao-tun ti yu-lai" 金評宋江矛盾的由來. *Chiang Han lun-t'an*, 1983. 2:37–41.

―――. "Chin Sheng-t'an hsiao-shuo li-lun tsai p'i-p'ing shih shang ti kung-hsien" 金聖歎小說理論在批評史上的貢獻. *Shui-hu cheng-ming* 2:430–42 (1983).

P'an Yün-hao 潘雲浩. "Chin Sheng-t'an yü tsao-ch'i ch'i-meng ssu-hsiang chia chih pi-chiao" 金聖歎與早期啟蒙思想家之比較. *Ch'iu-so*, 1985. 3:116–20.

Po-ch'ing 柏青 (Liang Hsiao 梁效). "P'ing Chin Sheng-t'an yao-chan *Shui-hu*" 評金聖歎腰斬水滸. *Pei-ching ta-hsüeh hsüeh-pao*, 1975. 5:28–32.

Po Lin 伯林. "Lüeh-t'an Chin Sheng-t'an kuan-yü hsiao-shuo ch'ing-chieh chieh-kou ti mei-hsüeh ssu-hsiang" 略談金聖歎關於小說情節結構的美學思想. *Fu-yang shih-fan hsüeh-yüan hsüeh-pao*, 1985. 3:51–55 (*Ku-chin* reprint, 1986. 1:316–20).

Pu Shu 卜束. "Ts'ung Chin Sheng-t'an ti chüeh-ming shih shuo-ch'i" 從金聖歎的絕命詩說起. *Shu-lin*, 1982. 3:50. Reprinted in *Chin Sheng-t'an tzu-liao chi*, p. 82.

Shang T'ao 商韜. "Chin Sheng-t'an p'i-kai *Shui-hu* ti ssu-hsiang li-ch'ang" 金聖歎批改水滸的思想立場. *Shang-hai shih-yüan hsüeh-pao*, 1981. 1:75–82 (*Ku-chin* reprint, 1981. 8:97–104).

―――. "Tsai-lun Chin Sheng-t'an p'i-kai *Shui-hu* ti ssu-hsiang li-ch'ang" 再論金聖歎批改水滸的思想立場. *Shang-hai shih-yüan hsüeh-pao*, 1982. 3:51–58. Reprinted in *Chin Sheng-t'an tzu-liao chi*, pp. 102–9.

Shen Chia-jen 沈家仁. "Chin Sheng-t'an shih feng-chien fan-tung wen-jen ma?" 金聖歎是封建反動文人嗎. *Cheng-ming*, 1986. 1:38–40 (*Ku-chin* reprint, 1986. 3:275–77).

Shih Chung-wen 施鍾文. "Ti-chu chieh-chi ti chao-fu cheng-ts'e yü *Shui-hu* ti chu-t'i―chien po Chin Sheng-t'an kuan-yü *Shui-hu* chu-t'i ti miu-lun" 地主階級的招撫政策與水滸的主題―兼駁金聖歎關於水滸主題的謬論. *Kan-su shih-ta hsüeh-pao*, 1975. 4:30–36.

Shih Wei 式微. "Yu-jen san-mei" 優人三昧. *Ku-tai wen-hsüeh li-lun yen-chiu* 5:112 (1981).

Sun Hsün 孫遜. "Chin Sheng-t'an yao-chan *Shui-hu* ti tsai p'ing-chia" 金聖歎腰斬水滸的再評價. In *Ming-Ch'ing hsiao-shuo lun-kao*, pp. 112–25.

Sung K'o-fu 宋克夫. "Chin-p'i chung ti hsiao-shuo i-shu pien-cheng fa" 金批中的小說藝術辨證法. *Wu-han shih-fan hsüeh-yüan hsüeh-pao*, 1983. 6:116–20.

Sung Mou-yang 宋謀瑒. "Huan Chin Sheng-t'an i pen-lai mien-mu" 還金聖歎以本來面目. *Shui-hu cheng-ming* 2:392–401 (1983).

Sung Yün-pin 宋雲彬. "T'an Chin Sheng-t'an" 談金聖歎. *Wen-i yüeh-pao* 文藝月報, 1954. 1:61–63. Reprinted in *Shui-hu yen-chiu lun-wen chi*, pp. 332–35.

Tai Pu-fan 戴不凡. "*Ti-liu ts'ai-tzu shu* fa-fu" 第六才子書發復. In *Lun Ts'ui Ying-ying* 論崔鶯鶯. Shanghai: Shang-hai wen-i, 1963, pp. 154–86.

T'an Fan 譚帆. "Chin Sheng-t'an hsi-ch'ü jen-wu li-lun ch'u-i" 金聖歎戲曲

人物理論芻議. *Wen-hsüeh i-ch'an*, 1987. 2:105–12.

———. "Chin Sheng-t'an hsi-ch'ü wen-hsüeh ch'uang-tso lun ti lo-chi chieh-kou" 金聖歎戲曲文學創作論的邏輯結構. *Hsüeh-shu yüeh-k'an*, 1986. 6:17–23 (*Hsi-ch'ü yen-chiu* reprint, 1986. 8:48–54).

T'ang Chia-tso 唐家祚. "Chin Sheng-t'an kuan-yü *Shui-hu chuan* ch'i-chieh ti san-p'i" 金聖歎關於水滸傳起結的三批. *Ch'i-ch'i ha-erh shih-fan hsüeh-yüan hsüeh-pao*, 1984. 1:70–75, 78.

———. "Chin Sheng-t'an tui Sung Chiang tsan yü ma ti pien-cheng fa" 金聖歎對宋江贊與罵的辨證法. *Ch'i-ch'i ha-erh shih-fan hsüeh-yüan hsüeh-pao*, 1986. 2:19ff.

———. "Chin Sheng-t'an yü *Ti-ssu ts'ai-tzu shu*" 金聖歎與第四才子書. *Ch'i-ch'i ha-erh shih-fan hsüeh-yüan hsüeh-pao*, 1983. 3:99–105.

———. "Lun Chin Sheng-t'an chih-yü *Ti-wu ts'ai-tzu Shui-hu chuan* chüan-shou ti liu p'ien wen-tzu" 論金聖歎置於第五才子水滸傳卷首的六篇文字. *Ch'i-ch'i ha-erh shih-fan hsüeh-yüan hsüeh-pao*, 1985. 4:72–79.

T'ang Kuo-liang 湯國梁. "Lun Chin-pen *Shui-hu* chung ti Sung Chiang—chien p'ing so-wei Chin Sheng-t'an 'tu-wu Sung Chiang' lun" 論金本水滸中的宋江—兼評所謂金聖歎獨惡宋江論. *Shui-hu cheng-ming* 4:177–88 (1985). For an earlier version see *Chi-ning shih-chuan hsüeh-pao*, 1983. 1:40–45 (*Ku-chin* reprint, 1983. 7:177–83).

———. "Ying-tang ch'ung-hsin p'ing-chia Chin Sheng-t'an—tu 'Wo ai Chin Sheng-t'an'" 應當重新評價金聖歎—讀我愛金聖歎. *Chi-ning shih-chuan hsüeh-pao*, 1983. 4:57–59 (*Ku-chin* reprint, 1984. 2:45–48).

Teng Ch'iao-pin 鄧喬彬. "Ch'u chih huo-jan, ju i pi-jan—ts'ung Chin *Hsi-hsiang* k'an Chin Sheng-t'an hsi-chü kuan ti i-ko mao-tun hsien-hsiang" 出之或然入以必然—從金西廂看金聖歎戲劇觀的一個矛盾現象. *I-t'an*, 1983. 4:99–101.

Teng Hsin-hua 鄧新華. "Shih-lun Chin Sheng-t'an kuan-yü i-shu hsü-kou mei-hsüeh ssu-hsiang" 試論金聖歎關於藝術虛構美學思想. *I-ch'ang shih-chuan hsüeh-pao* 宜昌師專學報, 1983. 1:59–66 (*Ku-chin* reprint, 1983. 4:240–46).

T'eng Yün 滕雲. "Lun p'i-p'ing chia Chin Sheng-t'an" 論批評家金聖歎. In *Ku-tien hsiao-shuo hsi-ch'ü t'an-i lu*, pp. 1–27.

———. "*Shui-hu chuan* ti liang ta p'i-p'ing chia—Li Cho-wu ho Chin Sheng-t'an" 水滸傳的兩大批評家—李卓吾和金聖歎. *Wen shih chih-shih*, 1981. 3:84–88 (*Ku-chin* reprint, 1981. 18:67–70).

Tu Jo 杜若. "Chin Sheng-t'an ti wen-hsüeh p'i-p'ing" 金聖歎的文學批評. *Tzu-yu t'an* 自由談 31. 5:22–24 (1980).

Tuan Mao-nan 段茂南. "Tui Chin-p'i *Hsi-hsiang chi* ti wo-chien" 對金批西廂記的我見. *Kuang-ming jih-pao*, 3/6/1966.

Tung-kuo hsien-sheng 東郭先生 (pseud.). *Chin Sheng-t'an wai-chuan* 金聖歎外傳. Taipei: Shih-shih ch'u-pan she, 1978.

Wan Pao-ch'üan 萬寶全. "Chin Sheng-t'an yü liu ts'ai-tzu shu" 金聖歎與六才子書. *Ta-ch'eng* 44:43–46 (1977).

Wang Ch'ang-hsin 王常新. "Chin Jen-jui ti hsien-shih chu-i shih-tso" 金人瑞的現實主義詩作. *Hua-chung shih-yüan hsüeh-pao*, 1984. 6:99–107.

Wang Ch'i-chou 王齊洲. "Chin Sheng-t'an hsiao-shuo li-lun ch'u-t'an" 金聖歎

小說理論初探. *Ching-chou shih-chuan hsüeh-pao* 荊州師專學報, 1981. 1:89–98. Also in *She-hui k'o-hsüeh yen-chiu*, 1981. 5:86–92 (*Ku-chin* reprint, 1982. 12:87–96).

———. "Lun 'tung-hsin shuo'—Chin Sheng-t'an hsiao-shuo li-lun tsai-t'an" 論動心說—金聖歎小說理論再探. *Cheng-ming*, 1983. 2:95–100 (*Ku-chin* reprint, 1983. 5:251–56).

Wang Ch'i-ho 王啟和. "Ts'ung hsing-hsiang ssu-wei ti chiao-tu k'an 'Liang chung *Shui-hu*, liang ko Sung Chiang'" 從形象思維的角度看兩種水滸兩個宋江. *Shui-hu cheng-ming* 4:189–90 (1985).

Wang Chün-nien 王俊年. "Ying-kai shih-shih ch'iu shih ti p'ing-chia Chin Sheng-t'an" 應該實事求是的評價金聖歎. *Hsin chien-she*, 1964. 7:70–75.

Wang Hsiao-chia 王曉家. "Jung-yü t'ang k'o-pen yü Kuan-hua t'ang k'o-pen—chien lun Chin Sheng-t'an wei shen-mo pu man-i Li Cho-wu" 容與堂刻本與貫華堂刻本—兼論金聖歎為甚麼不滿意李卓吾. *She-hui k'o-hsüeh*, 1985. 3:40–45.

Wang Hsien-p'ei 王先霈. "Chin Sheng-t'an lun jen-wu su-tsao chung ti i-shu ssu-wei" 金聖歎論人物塑造中的藝術思維. *Shui-hu cheng-ming* 3:426–439 (1984).

Wang Yeh-sen 汪葉森. "Chin-pen *Shui-hu* ti 'pao-hu-se' shuo pu-cheng" 金本水滸的保護色說補證. *Shui-hu cheng-ming* 1:375–81 (1983).

———. "I-ssu chih chi, pu k'o pu ch'a chih—shih-lun Chin-p'i *Shui-hu* ti ch'ü-pi" 疑似之迹不可不察之—試論金批水滸的曲筆. *Chiang Han lun-t'an*, 1979. 4:108–12. Reprinted in *Chin Sheng-t'an tzu-liao chi*, pp. 40–44.

Wen Chung 聞鍾. "P'ing Chin Sheng-t'an yao-chan *Shui-hu*—chien po Hu Shih ch'ui-p'eng Chin-pen *Shui-hu* ti miu-lun" 評金聖歎腰斬水滸—兼駁胡適吹捧金本水滸的謬論. *Jen-min jih-pao*, 10/17/1975. Reprinted in *Chin Sheng-t'an tzu-liao chi*, pp. 1–6.

Weng Po-nien 翁柏年. "'Ching-e meng' hsin-hsi" 驚惡夢新析. *Shui-hu cheng-ming* 2:402–10 (1983).

———. "Tui 'shuang-liang shuo' chih wo chien" 對雙兩說之我見. *Shui-hu cheng-ming* 3:336–44 (1984).

Wu Chih-ta 吳志達. "P'ing Chin Sheng-t'an p'i-kai *Shui-hu* ti wen-t'i—chien yü Chang Kuo-kuang t'ung-chih shang-ch'üeh" 評金聖歎批改水滸的問題—兼與張國光同志商榷. *Chiang Han lun-t'an*, 1979. 2:38–44. Reprinted in *Chin Sheng-t'an tzu-liao chi*, pp. 17–23.

Wu-han shih-fan hsüeh-yüan hsüeh-pao pien-chi pu 武漢師範學院學報編輯部. *Chin Sheng-t'an yü ch'i-shih hui Shui-hu yen-chiu* 金聖歎與七十回水滸研究. Wuhan: Wu-han shih-fan hsüeh-yüan ts'ung-shu, 1980.

Wu-han shih-yüan *Shui-hu* yen-chiu shih 武漢師院水滸研究室. *Chin Sheng-t'an chi ch'i Shui-hu p'ing-lun yen-chiu lun-chu so-yin* 金聖歎及其水滸評論研究論著索引.

Wu Hung 吳洪. "Che ts'ai shih i-ko chen-shih ti Chin Sheng-t'an" 這才是一個真實的金聖歎. *Yang-ch'eng wan-pao*, 4/3/1983 (*Ku-chin* reprint, 1983. 4:125–26). Reprinted in *Chung-kuo ku-tien hsiao-shuo i-shu ti ssu-k'ao*, pp. 253–61.

———. "Chieh ch'uan ku-fen mo yu hsin—Chin Sheng-t'an ti i-p'ien i-wen"

借傳孤憤墨猶新—金聖歎的一篇遺文. In *Chung-kuo ku-tien hsiao-shuo i-shu ti ssu-k'ao*, pp. 262–68.

Yeh Ch'ang-hai 葉長海. "Chin Sheng-t'an ti *Hsi-hsiang chi* p'i-p'ing" 金聖歎的 西廂記批評. In *Hsi-ch'ü lun-ts'ung* 戲曲論叢. Lan-chou: Kan-su jen-min, 1986, vol. I, pp. 248–64.

Yeh Lang 葉朗. "Chin Sheng-t'an ti hsiao-shuo mei-hsüeh" 金聖歎的小說美學. *Wen-i lun-ts'ung* 15:248–82 (1982).

Yeh-ma 野馬. "Lüeh-t'an Chin Sheng-t'an *Shui-hu* ti chien-chieh" 略談金聖歎 水滸的簡介. *Wen-i pao*, 1961. 11:27–29.

Yeh-ma et al. "Kuan-yü Chin Sheng-t'an ti p'ing-chia" 關於金聖歎的評價. *Wen-hui pao*, 7/28/1962.

Yin Chieh 殷杰. "'Liang chung *Shui-hu*, liang ko Sung Chiang' shuo chih-i" 兩種水滸兩個宋江說質疑. *Shui-hu cheng-ming* 3:321–29 (1984).

Yü Ch'ang-ku 俞昌谷. "Tien-hsing li-lun ti li-shih hsing t'u-p'o—ch'ien-lun Chin Sheng-t'an ti jen-wu 'hsing-ko' shuo" 典型理論的歷史性突破— 淺論金聖歎的人物性格說. *Fu-yang shih-fan hsüeh-yüan hsüeh-pao*, 1984. 1–2:99–104 (*Ku-chin* reprint, 1984. 18:148–53).

Yü Hsüeh-ts'ai 喻學才. "Lun pao-hu-se—t'an ju-ho cheng-ch'üeh li-chieh Chin Sheng-t'an p'ing chung ti ssu-hsiang mao-tun wen-t'i" 論保護色—談如何 正確理解金聖歎評中的思想矛盾問題. In *Chung-kuo ku-tai hsiao-shuo li-lun yen-chiu*, pp. 231–39.

Yü San-ting 余三定. "Chin Sheng-t'an *Shui-hu chuan* p'ing-tien chung ti pien-cheng ssu-hsiang ch'ien-t'an" 金聖歎水滸傳評點中的辨證思想淺探. *Hsiang-t'an ta-hsüeh she-hui k'o-hsüeh hsüeh-pao* 湘潭大學社會科學學報, 1983. 3:84–89, 110.

Yü Yüan 郁沅. "Chin Sheng-t'an Kuan-hua t'ang pen *Shui-hu chuan* k'ao-p'ing" 金聖歎貫華堂本水滸傳考評. *Wu-han shih-fan hsüeh-yüan hsüeh-pao*, 1979. 1:91–101. Reprinted in *Ku-tai wen-hsüeh li-lun yen-chiu* 1:387–402 (1979) and summarized in *Chin Sheng-t'an tzu-liao chi*, pp. 15–16.

ABBREVIATED TITLE: Wang Wang-ju 王望如 edition. FULL TITLE: *Wang Wang-ju hsien-sheng P'ing-lun ch'u-hsiang Shui-hu chuan* 王望如先生評論出像水滸傳 (Commentated and Illustrated *Shui-hu chuan* of Wang Wang-ju). ALTERNATE TITLE: *Ti-wu ts'ai-tzu shu* 第五才子書 (The Fifth Book of Genius). LENGTH: 70 chapters plus prologue in 71 *chüan*, plus 4 *chüan* of prefatory material. Later editions in 20 *chüan*. PUBLISHER: Tsui-keng t'ang 醉耕堂. DATE: 1657 (preface date). PREFATORY MATERIAL: Same as Chin Sheng-t'an edition with addition of T'ung-an lao-jen 桐庵老人 (Wang Wang-ju) preface (1657); "Tsung-lun" 總論 (General Remarks), signed by Wang Wang-ju (personal name Shih-yün 仕云, style T'ung-an 桐庵); and *P'ing-lun ch'u-hsiang Shui-hu chuan* hsing-shih" 評論出 像水滸傳姓氏 (Names of [the Characters of] *P'ing-lun ch'u-hsiang Shui-hu chuan*). COMMENTARY: Contains the original Chin Sheng-t'an comments plus new post-chapter comments by Wang Wang-ju as well as what appear to be new marginal comments concerned mainly with the marking off of textual units. AVAILABILITY: Copy in Harvard-Yenching Library, Harvard University. Microfilm copies available in the Far Eastern Library of the University of Chicago and Gest

Oriental Library, Princeton University. Wang Wang-ju's postchapter comments are included in *SHCHPP*.

Cheng Kung-tun 鄭公盾. "Tu Wang Wang-ju ti *Shui-hu chuan* p'ing-tien" 讀王望如的水滸傳評點. In *Shui-hu chuan lun-wen chi*, pp. 585–93.

T'an T'o 譚拓. "Pu-yao hu-shih wo-kuo ku-tien wen-hsüeh p'ing-lun chung ti chieh-chi tou-cheng—tu Wang Wang-ju *Shui-hu chuan* p'ing-tien cha-chi" 不要忽視我國古典文學評論中的階級鬥爭—讀王望如評點札記. *Kuang-ming jih-pao*, 6/20/1965.

ABBREVIATED TITLE: Ch'eng Mu-heng 程穆衡 annotations. FULL TITLE: *Shui-hu chuan chu-lüeh* 水滸傳注略 (Concise Annotations to the *Shui-hu chuan*). LENGTH: 2 *chüan* (no text of the novel). PUBLISHER: Wang-shih T'ing-hsiang ko (Wang K'ai-wo?). DATE: Wang K'ai-wo 王開沃 expanded edition, 1845. PREFATORY MATERIAL: "Hsiao-yin" 小引 preface by Ch'eng Mu-heng, 1779; and Yün-hsiang chü-shih 蘊香居士 (pseud.) preface, 1845. DISTINGUISHING FEATURES: The annotations are keyed to the 70-chapter Chin Sheng-t'an edition, although the author is familiar with the longer versions. The text of the novel itself is not quoted. AVAILABILITY: The complete text of the 1845 edition is reproduced in *SHCTLHP*, pp. 429–93 and Ma T'i-chi, ed., *Shui-hu tzu-liao hui-pien*, pp. 270–344 (see general bibliography on *Shui-hu chuan* below for publication information).

Ma T'i-chi 馬蹄疾. "Erh-pai nien ch'ien ti *Shui-hu* chu-pen" 二百年前的水滸注本. *Yang-ch'eng wan-pao*, 1/30/1964.

TITLE: *Hsin-p'ing Shui-hu chuan* 新評水滸傳 (New Commentary on the *Shui-hu chuan*). LENGTH: 70 chapters. PUBLISHER: Pao-ting Chih-li kuan shu-chü 保定直隸館書局. DATE: 1908. PREFATORY MATERIAL: Preface (dated 1908), "Fan-li" 凡例 (General Principles; also dated 1908), "Hsin huo-wen" 新或問 (New Questions and Answers), and "Ming-ming shih-i" 命名釋義 (Explanation of Names), all by Yen-nan Shang-sheng 燕南尚生 (pseud.). COMMENTARY: Retains some of the Chin Sheng-t'an and Wang Wang-ju commentary (comments on literary technique have mostly been cut out), plus additional comments by Yen-nan Shang-sheng added as marginal or postchapter comments. Some glosses dealing with dialect and difficult vocabulary have been added. REMARKS: The new commentary stresses a political interpretation of the novel. AVAILABILITY: Not available in the U.S., to the editor's knowledge.

General Bibliography on Fiction Criticism and the Shui-hu chuan

Irwin, Richard G. *The Evolution of a Chinese Novel*. Cambridge, Mass.: Harvard University Press, 1953.
———. "*Water Margin* Revisited." *T'oung Pao* 48. 4–5:393–415 (1960).

Ch'en Hsi-chung 陳曦鐘 et al., eds. *Shui-hu chuan hui-p'ing pen* 水滸傳會評本. Peking: Pei-ching ta-hsüeh, 1981.

Cheng Chen-to 鄭振鐸. "*Shui-hu chuan* ti yen-hua" 水滸傳的演化. In *Chung-kuo wen-hsüeh lun-chi*, pp. 176–251.

Cheng Chen-to et al., eds. *Shui-hu ch'üan-chuan* 水滸全傳. Peking: Jen-min wen-hsüeh, 1954.

Chinese Department of Nanking University. *Shui-hu yen-chiu tzu-liao* 水滸研究資料. Nanking: Nan-ching ta-hsüeh, 1980.

Chu I-hsüan 朱一玄, and Liu Yü-ch'en 劉毓忱, eds. *Shui-hu chuan tzu-liao hui-pien* 水滸傳資料彙編. Tientsin: Pai-hua wen-i, 1981.

Fan Ning 范寧. "*Shui-hu* pan-pen yüan-liu k'ao" 水滸版本源流考. *Chung-hua wen-shih lun-ts'ung*, 1982. 4:65–77. Reprinted in *Pan-pen*, pp. 99–113.

Hsü Chung-yüan 徐仲元. "Man-hua wan-Ch'ing shih-ch'i ti *Shui-hu chuan* p'ing-lun" 漫話晚清時期的水滸傳評論. *Nei-meng-ku ta-hsüeh hsüeh-pao*, 1983. 1:51–58.

Hsü Shuo-fang 徐朔方. "Kuan-yü Chang Feng-i ho T'ien-tu wai-ch'en ti *Shui-hu chuan* hsü" 關於張鳳翼和天都外臣的水滸傳序. *Kuang-ming jih-pao*, 5/10/1983.

Ma T'i-chi 馬蹄疾, ed. *Shui-hu shu-lu* 水滸書錄. Shanghai: Shang-hai ku-chi, 1986.

———, ed. *Shui-hu tzu-liao hui-pien* 水滸資料彙編. Peking: Chung-hua shu-chü, 1980.

Seida Tanso 清田儋叟 (1719–1785). "*Suikoden* hihyō kai" 水滸伝批評解. In *Tōwa jisho ruishū* 唐話辞書類集. Tokyo: Kyūko shoin, 1969–71, vol. 3, pp. 345–635.

Shih Ta-ch'ing 施達青. "Ming-Ch'ing shih-tai *Shui-hu* ti p'ing-lun (tzu-liao)" 明清時代水滸的評論(資料). *Pei-ching shih-fan ta-hsüeh hsüeh-pao*, 1975. 5:29–36.

Shih-te 試得 (pseud.). "Tu Chang Feng-i '*Shui-hu chuan* hsü'" 讀張鳳翼水滸傳序. *Kuang-ming jih-pao*, 5/9/1965 and 1/4/1983.

Sun K'ai-ti 孫楷第. "*Shui-hu chuan* chiu-pen k'ao" 水滸傳舊本考. *T'u-shu chi-k'an* 圖書集刊, n.s. 3–4:193–207 (1941). Reprinted in *Ts'ang-chou chi* 滄州集. Peking: Chung-hua shu-chü, 1965, vol. 1, pp. 149–208.

Teng K'uang-yen 鄧狂言. *Shui-hu so-yin* 水滸索隱. Shanghai: Ta-tung shu-chü, 1929.

Wang Hsiao-i 汪效倚. "Kuan-yü T'ien-tu wai-ch'en Wang Tao-k'un" 關於天都外臣汪道崑. *Kuang-ming jih-pao*, 12/20/1983.

Yen Tun-i 嚴敦易. *Shui-hu chuan* ti yen-pien 水滸傳的演變. Shanghai: Ku-tien wen-hsüeh, 1957.

San-kuo yen-i

ABBREVIATED TITLE: 1522 edition. FULL TITLE: *San-kuo chih t'ung-su yen-i* 三國志通俗演義 (A Popularization of the Chronicle of the Three Kingdoms). LENGTH: 240 *tse* in 24 *chüan*. PUBLISHER: It has been suggested that this edition was published by Kuo Hsün 郭勛 (1475–1542) and is the one mentioned in the *Pao-wen t'ang shu-mu* 寶文堂書目 (List of Books in Pao-wen t'ang). DATE: 1522.

PREFATORY MATERIAL: Chiang Ta-ch'i 蔣大器 (Yung-yü tzu 庸愚子) preface, 1494; Chang Shang-te 張尙德 (Hsiu-jan tzu 修髯子) preface, 1522; "San-kuo chih tsung-liao" 三國志宗僚 (Comprehensive List of People in the San-kuo chih). COMMENTARY: Double-column interlineal comments. REMARKS: Most of the comments are informational or supplemental. Their provenance and date are a matter of debate. Some scholars argue that they are quite early or written by the author of the novel, while others see them as the work of later writers. AVAILABILITY: Copy held in the Library of Congress, Washington, D.C. Photo-reprint edition (Peking: Jen-min wen-hsüeh, 1975; Taipei: Hsin wen-feng, 1979) and typeset edition (Shanghai: Shang-hai ku-chi, 1980) available.

Chang Kuo-kuang 張國光. "San-kuo chih t'ung-su yen-i ch'eng-shu yü Ming chung-yeh pien—yü Wang Li-ch'i, Chou Ts'un, Chang P'ei-heng t'ung-chih shang-ch'üeh—chien lun tz'u shu hsiao-tzu chu ti wen-t'i" 三國志通俗演義成書於明中葉辨 — 與王利器周邨章培恒同志商榷 — 兼論此書小字注的問題. She-hui k'o-hsüeh yen-chiu, 1983. 4:32–40.

Chang P'ei-heng 章培恒. "Kuan-yü Chia-ching pen San-kuo chih t'ung-su yen-i hsiao-chu ti tso-che" 關於嘉靖本三國志通俗演義小注的作者. Fu-tan hsüeh-pao, 1985. 3:173–83.

Wang Ch'ang-yu 王長友. "Chia-ching pen San-kuo chih t'ung-su yen-i hsiao-tzu chu shih tso-che shou-pi ma?" 嘉靖本三國志通俗演義小字注是作者手筆嗎. Wu-han shih-fan hsüeh-yüan hsüeh-pao, 1983. 2:48–53, 38.

ABBREVIATED TITLE: Chou Yüeh-chiao 周曰校 (fl. 1583–1628) edition. FULL TITLE: Hsin-k'an chiao-cheng ku-pen ta-tzu yin-shih San-kuo chih-chuan t'ung-su yen-i 新刊校正古本大字音釋三國志通俗演義 (Newly Cut, Collated, Large-Character, Ancient Edition of the Popularization of the Chronicle of the Three Kingdoms with Phonetic Glosses and Explanations). LENGTH: 240 tse in 12 chüan. PUBLISHER: Jen-shou t'ang 仁壽堂, Chou Yüeh-chiao, Nanking. DATE: 1591. PREFATORY MATERIAL: Chou Yüeh-chiao prefatory remarks ("Chih-yü" 識語). Rest same as 1522 edition. COMMENTARY: Phonetic glosses and explanations printed in double-column interlineal form, mostly prefixed with headings such as "Shih-i" 釋義 (Explanations) or "Pu-i" 補遺 (Supplementary Material). AVAILABILITY: Microfilm of Peking University Library copy held in Far Eastern Library, University of Chicago and Gest Oriental Library, Princeton University.

ABBREVIATED TITLE: Yü Hsiang-tou 余象斗 Chih-chuan 志傳 edition. FULL TITLE: Hsin-k'o an-chien ch'üan-hsiang p'i-p'ing San-kuo chih-chuan 新刻按鑑全像批評三國志傳 (Newly Cut, Fully Illustrated, Commentated Edition of the Chronicle of the Three Kingdoms Based on the Comprehensive Mirror for Aid in Government). LENGTH: 240 tse in 20 chüan. PUBLISHER: Shuang-feng t'ang 雙峰堂 of Yü Hsiang-tou. DATE: 1592. PREFATORY MATERIAL: Details unclear. COMMENTARY: Marginal and interlineal (rare) comments, attributed to Yü Hsiang-wu 余象烏 and Yü Shih-t'eng 余世騰, both of which names are thought to refer to none other than Yü Hsiang-tou. DISTINGUISHING FEATURES: Same three-register layout as the Yü Hsiang-tou Shui-hu chuan edition. REMARKS: The comments are supposed to be mostly informational. AVAILABILITY: Not available in the U.S. Fragmentary copies held in different locations in England.

ABBREVIATED EDITION: Yü Hsiang-tou *P'ing-lin* 評林 edition. FULL TITLE: *Hsin-k'an chiao-cheng yen-i ch'üan-hsiang San-kuo chih-chuan p'ing-lin* 新刊校正演義全像三國志傳評林 (Newly Cut, Collated, Fully Illustrated, Popular Edition of the Chronicle of the Three Kingdoms with Forest of Comments). LENGTH: 240 *tse* in 20 *chüan*. PUBLISHER: Yü Hsiang-tou. DATE: Wan-li reign period (1573–1620). PREFATORY MATERIAL: Details unclear. COMMENTARY: Marginal comments. DISTINGUISHING FEATURES: Division into three registers per page as in other Yü Hsiang-tou editions. COMMENTARY: The comments are prefaced by short headings such as "explanations" (*shih-i* 釋義), "supplementary material" (*pu-i* 補遺), "evaluation" (*tuan-lun* 斷論), or "comment" (*p'ing* 評). AVAILABILITY: Microfilm of incomplete copy (104 of the total 240 *tse*) is available in the University of Michigan series.

ABBREVIATED TITLE: *Yüan-pen* 原本 "Li Chih" edition. FULL TITLE: *Li Cho-wu hsien-sheng p'i-tien Yüan-pen San-kuo chih-chuan* 李卓吾先生批點原本三國志傳 (Original Edition of the Chronicle of the Three Kingdoms with Commentary by Li Chih). Title at head of *chüan* 1: *Hsin-k'o yin-shih p'ang-hsün p'ing-lin yen-i San-kuo chih shih-chuan* 新刻音釋旁訓評林演義三國志史傳 (Newly Cut, Popularized Chronicle of the Three Kingdoms Forest of Comments Edition with Phonetic Glosses and Interlineal Notes). Title appears with great variation throughout the work. LENGTH: 235 *tse* (according to the table of contents) in 20 *chüan*. PUBLISHER: Wang Ssu-yüan 王泗源. DATE: Early 17th century? PREFATORY MATERIAL: Preface signed Yü-p'ing shan-jen Ju-chien-tzu 玉屏山人如見子 (pseud.). COMMENTARY: Interlineal glosses, plus occasional short notes on the sides of the illustrations. REMARKS: Although the comments are attributed to Li Chih on the title page, there is no connection between him and this edition. AVAILABILITY: Copy held in British Library, London; microfilm copy in Harvard–Yenching Library, Harvard University.

ABBREVIATED TITLE: Cheng I-chen 鄭以楨 edition. FULL TITLE: *Hsin-chüan chiao-cheng ching-pen ta-tzu yin-shih ch'üan-tien San-kuo chih yen-i* 新鐫校正京本大字音釋圈點三國志演義 (Newly Cut, Collated, Large-Character Capital Edition of the *San-kuo yen-i* with Punctuation, Annotations, and Phonetic Glosses). Alternate title: *Li Cho-wu hsien-sheng p'ing-shih ch'üan-tien San-kuo chih* 李卓吾先生評釋圈點三國志 (Edition of the *San-kuo yen-i* with Commentary, Notes, and Punctuation by Li Chih). LENGTH: 240 *tse* in 12 *chüan*. PUBLISHER: Pao-shan t'ang 寶善堂, Nanking. Edited by Cheng I-chen. DATE: Later than 1592 Yü Hsiang-tou edition, from which it borrows. PREFATORY MATERIAL: Details unknown. COMMENTARY: Marginal comments, plus occasional notes in the text. AVAILABILITY: Recorded by Cheng Chen-to, present location unknown.

ABBREVIATED TITLE: 120-chapter "Li Chih" edition. FULL TITLE: *Li Cho-wu p'i-tien San-kuo chih ch'üan-hsiang pai erh-shih hui* 李卓吾批點三國志全像百二十回

(Fully Illustrated, 120-Chapter *San-kuo chih* with Commentary by Li Chih). Alternate Titles: *San-kuo chih yen-i p'ing* 三國志演義評 (*San-kuo yen-i* with Commentary) and *Li Cho-wu hsien-sheng p'i-p'ing San-kuo yen-i* 李卓吾先生批評 三國演義 (Li Chih Commentary Edition of the *San-kuo yen-i*). LENGTH: 120 chapters. There are no *chüan* divisions, but the remains of a former division into 24 *chüan* can be seen from the fact that each 10 chapters is taken as a group and the time period covered in each decade of chapters is mentioned at the end of every tenth chapter. PUBLISHER: Wu Kuan-ming 吳觀明 of Chien-yang 建陽. The "Li Chih" preface has a note saying that it was copied for carving on the woodblocks by Wen Pao-kuang 文葆光 of Suchou. DATE: Earliest editions are not dated but are estimated to be from the 1620s. PREFATORY MATERIAL: Preface attributed to Li Chih, Miao Tsun-su 繆尊素 preface, the Yung-yü tzu preface from the 1522 edition, "Tu San-kuo shih ta-wen" 讀三國史答問 (Questions and Answers on Reading the History of the Three Kingdoms), and "*San-kuo chih* tsung-liao hsing-shih" 三國志宗僚姓氏 (Names of the Persons in the *San-kuo chih*). Later editions add a piece by Tai I-nan 戴易南 on Kuan Yü's temple, dated 1687. COMMENTARY: Marginal, double-column interlineal, and postchapter comments. DISTINGUISHING FEATURES: This is the first 120-chapter version of the novel, but the transition is not yet complete. Many relics of the older 240 *tse* arrangement remain. REMARKS: The double-column interlineal comments are mostly informational or supplemental. Many of them have been carried over from the 1522 edition. The rest of the commentary (marginal and postchapter comments) is now thought by many scholars to be by Yeh Chou. On this problem, see appendix 2 in this volume. AVAILABILITY: There is a microfilm of the 1687 edition in Gest Oriental Library, Princeton University. A photo-reprint is available in *Taiyaku Chūgoku rekishi shōsetsu* 対訳中国歴史小說 (Chinese Historical Fiction with Parallel Translations [into Japanese]; Tokyo: Yumani shobō, 1983). The woodblocks used for the printing of these two original copies are similar but not exactly the same. The comments are included in the variorum commentary edition of the novel edited by Ch'en Hsi-chung 陳曦鐘 et al., *San-kuo yen-i hui-p'ing pen* 三國演義會評本 (Peking: Pei-ching ta-hsüeh, 1986).

Ch'iu Chen-sheng 丘振聲. "Li Cho-wu p'ing-tien *San-kuo*" 李卓吾評點三國. In *San-kuo yen-i tsung-heng t'an*, pp. 360–62.
Li Wan-chün 李萬鈞. "I fan ch'ien-nien ma Ts'ao ni-liu—Li Chih shih tsen-yang p'ing-tien *San-kuo yen-i* ti" 一反千年罵曹逆流—李贄是怎樣評點 三國演義的. *Fu-chien shih-ta hsüeh-pao*, 1975. 1.
Lu Lien-hsing 陸聯星. "Li Chih p'ing *San-kuo yen-i* pien-wei" 李贄評三國演義 辨偽. *Kuang-ming jih-pao*, 4/7/1963.

ABBREVIATED TITLE: Chung Hsing 鍾惺 edition. FULL TITLE: *Chung Po-ching hsien-sheng p'i-p'ing San-kuo chih* 鍾伯敬先生批評三國志 (The Romance of the Three Kingdoms with Commentary by Chung Hsing). LENGTH: 240 *tse* in 20 *chüan*. Every second *tse* has a note indicating the chapter number according to the 120-chapter system. PUBLISHER: Suchou? DATE: Late Ming? PREFATORY

MATERIAL: Extant copy lacks even table of contents. COMMENTARY: Marginal and postchapter comments attributed to Chung Hsing. Some of the double-column interlineal notes from earlier editions have been preserved. REMARKS: Several of the chapter comments make reference to comments in the "Li Chih" 120-chapter edition (chaps. 4, 13, 14, etc.). AVAILABILITY: Comments from this edition are included as an appendix to *San-kuo yen-i hui-p'ing pen*. A photocopy of the original (held in Tokyo Imperial University Library) was seen by the editor courtesy of Professor Ch'en Hsi-chung, Peking University.

ABBREVIATED TITLE: *Ying-hsiung p'u* 英雄譜 (The Roster of Heroes) edition. FULL TITLE: Same as *Ying-hsiung p'u* edition of the *Shui-hu chuan* cited above. LENGTH: 240 *tse* in 20 *chüan*. PUBLISHER, DATE, AND PREFATORY MATERIAL: Same as *Shui-hu chuan* entry except for the addition of "An Chin-yang hou Ch'en Shou shih-chuan tsung-ko" 按晉陽侯陳壽史傳總歌 (Comprehensive Song Based on the History [of the Three Kingdoms] Written by the Marquis of Chin-yang, Ch'en Shou), and "San-kuo ying-hsiung ti-hou ch'en-liao hsing-shih" 三國英雄帝后臣僚姓氏 (Names of the Heroes, Emperors and Empresses, and Officials of the Three Kingdoms). COMMENTARY: Marginal and single- and double-column interlineal comments attributed to Li Chih. DISTINGUISHING FEATURES: The text of the novel is printed on the bottom half of the page while that of the *Shui-hu chuan* is printed on the upper half of the page. REMARKS: the comments are mostly informational or supplementary and appear to have nothing to do with either Li Chih or Yeh Chou. AVAILABILITY: Same as *Shui-hu chuan* edition.

ABBREVIATED TITLE: Mao Tsung-kang 毛宗崗 edition. FULL TITLE: *Sheng-shan pieh-chi, Ku-pen San-kuo chih, Ssu ta ch'i-shu ti-i chung* 聲山別集古本三國志四大奇書第一種 (Mao Lun's Number One of the Four Great Marvelous Books, Ancient Edition of The Romance of the Three Kingdoms). Later editions titled: *Ti-i ts'ai-tzu shu* 第一才子書 (Number One Work of Genius). LENGTH: 120 chapters in 60 *chüan*. Some later editions are divided into 19 *chüan* of text and one of prefatory material. PUBLISHER: Tsui-keng t'ang 醉耕堂. DATE: Preface dated 1679. PREFATORY MATERIAL: 1679 Li Yü preface (later reworked, attributed to Chin Sheng-t'an, and dated 1644), "Fan-li" 凡例 (General Principles), and "Tu *San-kuo chih* fa" 讀三國志法 (How to Read *The Romance of the Three Kingdoms*). COMMENTARY: Prechapter and double-column interlineal comments by Mao Lun and his son, Mao Tsung-kang. In some editons, the comments are wholly or partly attributed to Chin Sheng-t'an. DISTINGUISHING FEATURES: The text of the novel has been edited and rearranged by the Maos. Many of the changes are mentioned in the "Fan-li," although their provenance there is given as an "ancient edition" of the novel available to the Maos. REMARKS: The commentary seems to have been a collective endeavor by Mao Tsung-kang and his father similar to their work on the *P'i-p'a chi* 琵琶記 (Story of the Lute), although the entire credit is commonly given to Mao Tsung-kang. AVAILability: A copy of the 1679 edition is the personal possession of Professor Ogawa Tamaki, formerly of Kyoto University. There are numerous later editions and reprints available. A typeset reprint of an 1853 edition was published in 1983 (*SKYI*) and a photo-reprint of a late Ch'ing edition (*Tseng-hsiang ch'üan-t'u San-kuo yen-i* 增像全圖三國演義 [Peking: Chung-kuo shu-tien, 1985]) also exists.

Campbell, Duncan M. "The Techniques of Narrative: Mao Tsung-kang (fl. 1661) and *The Romance of the Three Kingdoms*." *Tamkang Review* 16. 2:139–61 (1985).

Scott, Mary E. "How to Read Mao Tsung-kang's Commentary to *San-kuo yen-i*." Unpublished paper.

Arai Mizuo 荒井瑞雄. "Mō Seizan ni tsuite" 毛声山について. *Kangakukai zashi* 漢学会雑志 8. 1:79–91 (1940).

Chang Hung 張虹. "Ts'ung *San-kuo yen-i* ti p'ing-tien k'an Mao Tsung-kang hsiao-shuo chieh-kou mei-hsüeh ssu-hsiang" 從三國演義的評點看毛宗崗小說結構美學思想. *Wu-han shih-fan hsüeh-yüan hsüeh-pao*, 1983. 4:45–51.

Chang Kuo-kuang 張國光. "Mao Tsung-kang chi-ch'eng Chin Sheng-t'an hsiao-shuo li-lun p'ing-kai *San-kuo yen-i* ti kung-hsien" 毛宗崗繼承金聖歎小說理論評改三國演義的貢獻. In *San-kuo yen-i lun-wen chi*, pp. 445–57.

Ch'ang Lin-yen 常林炎. "P'ing Mao Tsung-kang hsiu-ting *San-kuo yen-i*" 評毛宗崗修訂三國演義. *Hsüeh-shu yüeh-k'an*, 1985. 9:55–61.

———. "Ts'ung Chin Sheng-t'an ti 'p'ing-fan' hsiang tao tui Mao Tsung-kang ti p'ing-chia" 從金聖歎的平反想到對毛宗崗的評價. In *Chung-kuo ku-tai hsiao-shuo li-lun yen-chiu*, pp. 240–46.

Chao Ch'ing-yung 趙清永. "Lo Kuan-chung ti cheng-chih kuan chi *San-kuo yen-i* ch'uang-tso ssu-hsiang kuan-k'uei" 羅貫中的政治觀及三國演義創作思想管窺. In *San-kuo yen-i lun-wen chi*, pp. 358–68.

Ch'en Chou-ch'ang 陳周昌. "Mao Tsung-kang p'ing-kai *San-kuo yen-i* ti te-shih" 毛宗崗評改三國演義的得失. *She-hui k'o-hsüeh yen-chiu*, 1982. 4:24–29.

Ch'en Hung 陳洪. "*San-kuo* Mao-p'i k'ao-pien erh-tse" 三國毛批考辨二則. In *Ming-Ch'ing hsiao-shuo yen-chiu* 3:300–306 (1986).

Cheng Ming-li 鄭明娳. "Mao-p'i *San-kuo yen-i* chang-fa lun" 毛批三國演義章法論. *Ku-tien wen-hsüeh* 古典文學 7:809–54 (Taipei: Hsüeh-sheng shu-chü, 1985).

Chiang Sung-yuan 蔣松源. "Ch'ien-i Mao Tsung-kang ti hsiao-shuo ch'uang-tso kuan" 淺議毛宗崗的小說創作觀. In *Chung-kuo ku-tai hsiao-shuo li-lun yen-chiu*, pp. 247–56.

Chien To 劍鐸. "P'ing Mao Lun, Mao Tsung-kang hsiu-ting ti *San-kuo yen-i*" 評毛綸毛宗崗修訂的三國演義. *Hai-nan shih-chuan hsüeh-pao* 海南師專學報, 1981. 2:33–40.

Ch'in K'ang-tsung 秦亢宗. "T'an Mao Tsung-kang hsiu-ting *San-kuo chih t'ung-su yen-i*" 談毛宗崗修訂三國志通俗演義. *Che-chiang hsüeh-k'an*, 1981. 3:64–68.

———. "Tu Mao-p'i *San-kuo yen-i* cha-chi" 讀毛批三國演義札記. *Chieh-fang chün wen-i* 解放軍文藝, 1963. 6:75–80.

Ch'iu Chen-sheng 丘振聲. "Mao Tsung-kang t'an *San-kuo yen-i* jen-wu ti su-tsao" 毛宗崗談三國演義人物的塑造. In *San-kuo yen-i tsung-heng t'an*, pp. 366–69.

Chou Ch'ang-tsung 周嘗棕. "Shuo-shuo Mao-p'i pen *San-kuo*" 說說毛批本三國. *Tu-shu*, 1983. 4:89–95.

Chou Shu-wen 周書文. "Mao Tsung-kang lun *San-kuo yen-i* jen-wu hsing-ko su-tsao ti pien-cheng ching-shen" 毛宗崗論三國演義人物性格塑造的辨證精神. *San-kuo yen-i hsüeh-k'an*, 1:256–66 (1985).

———. "Mao Tsung-kang lun shen-mei ch'ing-ch'ü ti i-shu ch'u-li" 毛宗崗論審美情趣的藝術處理. *Kan-nan shih-fan hsüeh-yüan hsüeh-pao* 贛南師範學院學報, 1986. 1:25–31.

Chou Wei-min 周偉民. "Mao Tsung-kang lun *San-kuo yen-i* ti chieh-kou ho ch'ing-chieh" 毛宗崗論三國演義的結構和情節. *Hua-tung shih-fan ta-hsüeh hsüeh-pao*, 1987. 2:76–83 (*Ku-chin* reprint, 1987. 5:189–96).

Ho Man-tzu 何滿子. "Lun Mao Tsung-kang tui *San-kuo yen-i* ti p'ing-kai" 論毛宗崗對三國演義的評改. *Wen-hsüeh i-ch'an*, 1986. 4:59–63.

Hsiao Hsiang-k'ai 蕭相愷. "*San-kuo yen-i* Mao-p'ing ti ch'u-fa tien ho chi-pen ch'ing-hsiang" 三國演義毛評的出發點和基本傾向. *San-kuo yen-i hsüeh-k'an* 1:267–78 (1985).

Hsiung Tu 熊篤. "Kuan-yü Mao Tsung-kang tui *San-kuo yen-i* ti p'ing-kai" 關於毛宗崗對三國演義的評改. *Ch'ung-ch'ing shih-yüan hsüeh-pao*, 1983. 1:40–45 (*Ku-chin* reprint, 1983. 2:135–40).

Hsü Chung-wei 徐中偉. "Pu-k'o teng-liang ch'i-kuan ti liang-pu *San-kuo*— Chia-ching pen yü Mao-pen 'yung-Liu fan-Ts'ao' chih pu t'ung" 不可等量齊觀的兩部三國—嘉靖本與毛本擁劉反曹之不同. *Wen-hsüeh i-ch'an*, 1983. 2:88–100.

Huang Chung-mo 黃中模. "Lun Mao Tsung-kang p'ing-kai *San-kuo yen-i* ti chu-yao ssu-hsiang i-i—Mao-pen *San-kuo* shih 'wei-hu Ch'ing wang-ch'ao ti cheng-t'ung ti-wei' pien" 論毛宗崗評改三國演義的主要思想意義—毛本三國是維護清王朝的正統地位辨. *Ming-Ch'ing hsiao-shuo yen-chiu* 3:283–96 (1986).

———. "Wei pien Mao Tsung-kang ti wen-i ssu-hsiang ming pu-p'ing—*San-kuo yen-i* Mao-p'i 'pao-shou' yü 'tao-t'ui' pien" 為貶毛宗崗的文藝思想鳴不平—三國演義毛批保守與倒退辨. *Chung-chou hsüeh-k'an*, 1985. 3:73–78.

Huang Lin 黃霖. "Yu kuan Mao-p'ing *San-kuo yen-i* ti jo-kan wen-t'i" 有關毛評三國演義的若干問題. In *San-kuo yen-i lun-wen chi*, pp. 326–43.

Huo Yü-chia 霍雨佳. "Lun Mao Tsung-kang ti jen-ts'ai mei-hsüeh ssu-hsiang" 論毛宗崗的人才美學思想. *Hai-nan ta-hsüeh hsüeh-pao* 海南大學學報, 1986. 1:39–46 (*Ku-chin* reprint, 1986. 8:313–20).

Li Ch'ing-hsi 李慶西. "Kuan-yü Ts'ao Ts'ao hsing-hsiang ti yen-chiu fang-fa, chien t'an ju-ho k'an-tai Mao-shih hsiu-ting *San-kuo yen-i*" 關於曹操形像的研究方法兼談如何看待毛氏修訂三國演義. *Wen-hsüeh p'ing-lun*, 1982. 4:3–17.

Li P'ei-k'un 李培坤. "P'u-su ti i-shu pien-cheng ssu-hsiang" 樸素的藝術辨證思想. *Jen-wen tsa-chih*, 1987. 3:109–16 (*Ku-chin* reprint, 1987. 7:211–18).

Li Yü-ming 李玉銘. "Lun Mao Tsung-kang ti hsiao-shuo kuan" 論毛宗崗的小說觀. *Wen-i lun-kao* 文藝論稿. Ch'ang-ch'un: Chi-lin jen-min, 1983.

———. "Mao Tsung-kang *San-kuo yen-i* p'ing-lun ti chi-ko t'e-tien" 毛宗崗
三國演義評論的幾個特點. *Chi-lin ta-hsüeh she-hui k'o-hsüeh hsüeh-pao*, 1985.
1:44–50 (*Ku-chin* reprint, 1985. 4:52–58).

———. "Mao Tsung-kang ti tien-hsing kuan" 毛宗崗的典型觀. *Hsi-nan shih-
fan hsüeh-yüan hsüeh-pao*, 1986. 4:56–64.

Liu Ching-ch'i 劉敬圻. "Kuan-yü *San-kuo yen-i* ti yen-chiu fang-fa—tu 'Kuan-
yü Ts'ao Ts'ao hsing-hsiang yen-chiu fang-fa' so hsiang tao ti" 關於三國
演義的研究方法—讀關於曹操形像研究方法所想到的. In *San-kuo yen-i
lun-wen chi*, pp. 419–44.

———. "*San-kuo yen-i* Chia-ching pen ho Mao-pen chiao-tu cha-chi" 三國
演義嘉靖本和毛本校讀札記. *Ch'iu-shih hsüeh-k'an*, 1981. 1:22–32 (pt. 1);
1981. 2:71–80 (pt. 2).

Liu Shao-chih 劉紹智. "Mao Tsung-kang lun li-shih hsiao-shuo ti t'e-tien"
毛宗崗論歷史小說的特點. *Ning-hsia chiao-yü hsüeh-yüan hsüeh-pao* 寧夏
教育學院學報, 1986. 1:18–25.

Mao Lun 毛綸, and Mao Tsung-kang 毛宗崗. *Ti-ch'i ts'ai-tzu shu* 第七才子書.
Ta-wen t'ang 1735 reprint.

Ning Hsi-yuan 寧希元. "Mao-pen *San-kuo yen-i* chih-miu" 毛本三國演義指謬.
She-hui k'o-hsüeh yen-chiu, 1983. 4:41–46, 40.

Ogawa Tamaki 小川環樹. "*Sankoku engi* no Mō Seizan hihyōbon to Ri Ryūō
bon" 三国演義の毛声山批評本と李笠翁本. In *Chūgoku shōsetsu shi no
kenkyū* 中国小説史の研究. Tokyo: Iwanami shoten, 1968, pp. 153–62.

P'eng Fei 彭飛. "Mao-pen *San-kuo yen-i* tui *San-kuo* hsi ti ying-hsiang" 毛本
三國演義對三國戲的影響. In *San-kuo yen-i lun-wen chi*, pp. 379–91.

Shang T'ao 商韜, and Ch'en Nien-hsi 陳年希. "*San-kuo yen-i* Mao-p'ing kai-
shu" 三國演義毛評概述. *Chiang Huai hsüeh-k'an* 江淮學刊, 1986. 4.

Shen Kuo-fang 沈國芳. "Mao Tsung-kang hsiao-shuo chieh-kou i-shu li-lun
p'ing-shu—tu Mao-p'ing *Ch'üan-t'u hsiu-hsiang San-kuo yen-i*" 毛宗崗小說
結構藝術理論評述—讀毛評全圖綉像三國演義. *Ku-tai wen-hsüeh li-lun
yen-chiu* 9:323–34 (1984).

Shih Chen 石珍. "*San-kuo yen-i* yü Mao Tsung-kang" 三國演義與毛宗崗. *Hsin-
min wan-pao*, 12/13/1953.

Sun Hsün 孫遜. "Mao-shih fu-tzu p'ing *San-kuo*" 毛氏父子評三國. *Shu-lin*,
1983. 4:43–44.

T'eng Yün 滕雲. "Lun Mao Tsung-kang tui *San-kuo yen-i* ti p'i-p'ing" 論毛
宗崗對三國演義的批評. *San-kuo yen-i hsüeh-k'an* 1:241–55 (1985).

Tokuda Takeshi 德田武. "Bakin no haishi shichi hōsoku to Mō Seizan no 'Doku
Sankoku shi hō'" 馬琴の稗史七法則と毛声山の読三国史法. *Bungaku* 文学
48. 6:14–29 (pt. 1); 48. 7:64–76 (pt. 2; 1980).

Tu Kuei-ch'en 杜貴晨. "Mao Tsung-kang p'ing-kai *San-kuo yen-i* chih wo-
chien" 毛宗崗評改三國演義之我見. *Ch'i Lu hsüeh-k'an*, 1984. 3:124–28.

———. "Mao Tsung-kang tui Chung-kuo ku-tai hsiao-shuo li-lun ti kung-
hsien—chien lun Chung-kuo ku-tai hsiao-shuo li-lun ti chen-cheng hsing-
ch'eng" 毛宗崗對中國古代小說理論的貢獻—兼論中國古代小說理論的
真正形成. *She-hui k'o-hsüeh yen-chiu*, 1986. 3:115–18, 125 (*Ku-chin* reprint,
1986. 7:303–7).

———. "Mao Tsung-kang yung-Liu fan-Ts'ao i tsai fan-Ch'ing fu-Ming" 毛宗崗擁劉反曹意在反清復明. *San-kuo yen-i hsüeh-k'an*, 1:279–84 (1985).

Wen Erh-wei 聞而畏 (Ch'en Hsi-chung 陳曦鐘). "Lüeh-t'an Mao Tsung-kang ti hsiao-shuo li-lun chi ch'i p'ing-chia wen-t'i" 略談毛宗崗的小說理論及其評價問題. *Chung-kuo wen-i ssu-hsiang shih lun-ts'ung* 2:317–29 (1985).

Yeh Wei-ssu 葉維四, and Mao Hsin 冒炘. "San-kuo yen-i ti liang-chung chung-yao pan-pen" 三國演義的兩種重要版本. In *San-kuo yen-i ch'uang-tso lun* 三國演義創作論. Nan-t'ung: Chiang-su jen-min, 1984, pp. 327–59.

Yü P'ing-po 俞平伯. "San-kuo chih yen-i yü Mao-shih fu-tzu" 三國志演義與毛氏父子. In *Tsa-pan-erh* 雜拌兒. Nan-ch'ang: Chiang-hsi jen-min, 1983 reprint, vol. 2, pp. 123–26.

Yüan 淵. "Mao-p'ing *San-kuo yen-i* shih wei Mao-shih fu-tzu ho-tso" 毛評三國演義實為毛氏父子合作. *Shang-hai shih-yüan hsüeh-pao*, 1979. 2:41.

ABBREVIATED TITLE: Li Yü 李漁 edition. FULL TITLE: *Li Li-weng p'ing-yüeh hsiu-hsiang San-kuo chih Ti-i ts'ai-tzu shu* 李笠翁評閱綉像三國志第一才子書 (Illustrated Romance of the Three Kingdoms Number One Work of Genius, with Commentary by Li Yü). LENGTH: 120 chapters in 24 *chüan*. PUBLISHER: Liang-heng t'ang 兩衡堂. DATE: 1679 or 1680 (if attribution to Li Yü is bona fide). PREFATORY MATERIAL: Li Yü preface, "San-kuo chih tsung-liao" 三國志宗僚 (Comprehensive List of People in the *San-kuo chih*). COMMENTARY: Marginal and double-column interlineal comments. DISTINGUISHING FEATURES: Uses some of the innovations of the Mao version of the text, but not extensively. Mainly based on the 120-chapter "Li Chih" version. REMARKS: Although generally based on the 120-chapter "Li Chih" edition, both the text and marginal commentary of this edition borrow from the Mao version. The double-column interlineal comments are mostly informational or supplementary and based on those in the 120-chapter "Li Chih" edition. AVAILABILITY: There is a microfilm of this edition (original held in the Bibliothèque nationale, Paris) in the Gest Oriental Library, Princeton University. The comments from this edition are included in the variorum commentary edition of the novel, *San-kuo yen-i hui-p'ing pen*.

Ogawa Tamaki 小川環樹, "Sankoku engi no Mō Seizan hihyōbon to Ri Ryūō bon" 三国演義の毛声山批評本と李笠翁本. In *Chūgoku shōsetsu shi no kenkyū* 中国小説史の研究. Tokyo: Iwanami shoten, 1968, pp. 153–62.

ABBREVIATED TITLE: Mao Tsung-kang, Li Yü combined edition. FULL TITLE: *Ti-i ts'ai-tzu San-kuo chih* 第一才子三國志 (Number One Work of Genius, Romance of the Three Kingdoms). The title at the beginning of each *chüan* is: *Kuan-pen ta-tzu ch'üan-hsiang p'i-p'ing San-kuo chih* 官本大字全像批評三國志 (Fully Illustrated, Official, Large-Character, Commentary Edition of The Romance of the Three Kingdoms). The title page also says in black ink that there is commentary by Chin Sheng-t'an and Mao Sheng-shan 毛聲山 (Mao Lun) and in a lighter-colored ink that there is "added full commentary by Li Yü" (*Li Li-weng hsi-chia p'i-yüeh* 李笠翁細加批閱). LENGTH: 120 chapters in 24 *chüan*. DATE: 1734. PUBLISHER: Combined printing by Yü-yü t'ang 郁郁堂 and

Yü-wen t'ang 郁文堂. PREFATORY MATERIAL: Preface dated 1734 by Huang Shu-ying 黃叔英, Mao Tsung-kang *tu-fa* essay and "Fan-li." The "Tsung-liao hsing-shih" 宗寮姓氏 (Names of Characters) encountered in other editions is reprinted in the upper register above the *tu-fa*, "Fan-li," and the table of contents (the fact that this piece has been added to the edition is especially noted on the title page). COMMENTARY: Double-column interlineal and prechapter comments from the Mao Tsung-kang edition, plus marginal comments from the "Li Yü" edition of the novel. REMARKS: Not all of the "Li Yü" comments found in the Li Yü edition are reprinted here, but the editors of this edition do not seem to have been overly disturbed by the fact that many of the "Li Yü" comments repeat or are based on comments in the Mao edition. AVAILABILITY: There is a copy held in the Ma Lien Collection in the Peking University Library.

General Bibliography on Fiction Criticism and the San-kuo yen-i

Cheng Chen-to 鄭振鐸. "*San-kuo yen-i* ti yen-hua" 三國演義的演化. In his *Chung-kuo wen-hsüeh lun-chi*, pp. 252–349.

Chou Ts'un 周邨. "*San-kuo yen-i* k'an-chiao cha-chi" 三國演義看校札記. *Chung-hua wen-shih lun-ts'ung*, 1979. 3:255–70.

Chu I-hsüan 朱一玄, and Liu Yü-ch'en 劉毓忱, eds. *San-kuo yen-i tzu-liao hui-pien* 三國演義資料彙編. Tientsin: Pai-hua wen-i, 1983.

Ma Lien 馬廉. "Chiu-pen *San-kuo yen-i* pan-pen ti tiao-ch'a" 舊本三國演義版本的調察. *Pei-p'ing Pei-hai t'u-shu kuan yüeh-k'an* 北平北海圖書館月刊. 2. 5:397–401 (1929).

Wu Chien-li 吳堅立. "*San-kuo yen-i* k'ao-shu" 三國演義考述. Master's thesis, Soochow University, Taipei, 1976.

Chin P'ing Mei

ABBREVIATED TITLE: "Ch'ung-chen" 崇禎 editions. FULL TITLE: *Hsin-k'o hsiu-hsiang p'i-p'ing Chin P'ing Mei* 新刻繡像批評金瓶梅 (Newly Cut, Illustrated, and Commented *Chin P'ing Mei*). Alternate titles add the words *yüan-pen* 原本 (original edition) and/or substitute *p'ing-tien* 評點 or *p'i-tien* 批點 for *p'i-p'ing* 批評 (these terms are basically interchangeable). This edition actually exists in two main types with slightly different content, especially with regard to commentary. They will be referred to as the A and B editions. See REMARKS below for details. LENGTH: 100 chapters in 20 *chüan*. PUBLISHER: Possibilities are Lu Chung-min 魯重民 of Hangchou or Li Yü 李漁 (1611–1680). DATE: Commonly dated to the Ch'ung-chen reign period (1628–1644) on the basis of the illustrations in the B editions. PREFATORY MATERIAL: Nung-chu k'o 弄珠客 (pseud., thought by some to be Feng Meng-lung 馮夢龍, 1574–1646) preface, and Nien-kung 廿公 (pseud.) preface. The Capital Library (Peking) copy of the A edition has a poem at the end of the illustrations signed Hui-tao jen 回道人 (pseud., identified by some as Li Yü). COMMENTARY: Both A and B editions have single-column interlineal comments, the content of which is mostly identical except for some comments in the A editions not found in the B editions. The B editions have additional marginal comments. DISTINGUISHING FEATURES: The text of the novel differs from that of the earliest extant version, the *Chin P'ing Mei tz'u-hua* 金瓶梅詞話, particularly in chap. 1. REMARKS: The A editions have more characters per page (11 rows of 28 per row) than the B editions (10 rows of 22), while the B editions have more illustrations (200 versus 101). The comments in both are rather sparse and generally lighthearted. AVAILABILITY: There are microfilms of B edition copies (originals held in the Tokyo Imperial University and Naikaku Bunko, Japan) available in the Far Eastern Library, University of Chicago and Gest Oriental Library, Princeton University. The comments from a B edition held in the Peking University Library are reprinted in *CPMTLHP*, pp. 224–457. The comments from these editions are to be included in a variorum commentary edition of the novel under the editorship of Liu Hui 劉輝.

Plaks, Andrew H. "The Chongzhen Commentary on the *Jin Ping Mei*: Gems amidst the Dross." CLEAR 8.1–2: 19–30 (1986).

Araki Takeo 荒本猛. "*Hsin-k'o hsiu-hsiang p'i-p'ing Chin P'ing Mei* ch'u-pan shu-ssu chih yen-t'an" 新刻繡像批評金瓶梅出版書肆之研探. Translated by Jen Shih-yung 任世雍. *Chung-wai wen-hsüeh* 13. 2:106–13 (1984).

Huang Lin 黃霖. "*Hsin-k'o hsiu-hsiang p'i-p'ing Chin P'ing Mei* p'ing-tien ch'u-t'an" 新刻繡像批評金瓶梅評點初探. *Ch'eng-tu ta-hsüeh hsüeh-pao* 成都大學學報, 1983. 1:67ff. Reprinted in *Chin P'ing Mei yen-chiu* 金瓶梅研究. Shanghai: Fu-tan ta-hsüeh, 1984, pp. 67–78.

Liu Hui 劉輝. "Lun *Hsin-k'o hsiu-hsiang p'i-p'ing Chin P'ing Mei*" 論新刻繡像批評金瓶梅. *Wen-hsüeh i-ch'an*, 1987. 3:113–19.

ABBREVIATED TITLE: Chang Chu-p'o 張竹坡 editions. FULL TITLE: *Kao-ho t'ang p'i-p'ing Ti-i ch'i-shu Chin P'ing Mei* 皋鶴堂批評第一奇書金瓶梅 (Number One Marvelous Book *Chin P'ing Mei*, With Commentary from Kao-ho Studio). Alternate titles include such information as "P'eng-ch'eng Chang Chu-p'o p'i-p'ing" 彭城張竹坡批評 (Commentary by Chang Chu-p'o of Hsü-chou) or "Li Li-weng hsien-sheng chu" 李笠翁先生著 (Authored by Mr. Li Yü). A 1747 edition is titled: *Ssu ta ch'i-shu ti-ssu chung* 四大奇書第四種 (Number Four of the Four Great Marvelous Works). LENGTH: 100 chapters, no *chüan* divisions. PUBLISHER: The biography of Chang Chu-p'o by his brother implies that the woodblocks for the edition were cut in Hsü-chou, but some have proposed that it is perhaps more likely that this was done in Nanking. DATE: 1695. PREFATORY MATERIAL: All printings have a preface signed Hsieh I 謝頤 in Kao-ho t'ang. In most cases the preface is dated 1695 (as is the title page of many editions), but changed to 1747 in the *Ssu ta ch'i-shu ti-ssu chung* and 1816 in a T'ai-su hsüan 太素軒 edition. Hsieh I is clearly a pseudonym that puns with the words *chieh-i* 解頤 (to crack a smile), an expression that occurs toward the end of the preface. It is widely held that Chang Ch'ao 張潮 (1650–ca. 1703) of Yangchou wrote the preface because there is extant a letter from Chang Chu-p'o to him expressing thanks for a preface to a commentary. The problem with this interpretation is that the two men do not seem to have been in direct contact with each other until after the *Chin P'ing Mei* commentary was printed; in addition, two earlier letters to Chang Ch'ao (written after his arrival in Yangchou, as was the other letter), make no mention of the preface. The studio name mentioned in the preface is the same as that used in many of the editions to refer to the entire commentary and thus to Chang Chu-p'o himself. This might be a clue that the preface was written by Chang Chu-p'o, perhaps in partial imitation of Chin Sheng-t'an's forged "Shih Nai-an" preface to the *Shui-hu chuan*. However, the preface does not seem to agree with Chang Chu-p'o's ideas on the authorship of the novel and the question of its supposed obscenity. Not counting this preface, some editions have as many as fifteen prefatory items, while others have only twelve. Taking the fifteen-item Tsai-tzu t'ang 在茲堂 1695 large-character edition (reprint, Taipei, 1981) as an example, the items are as follows: (1) "Hsi-men Ch'ing chia-jen ming-shu" 西門慶家人名數 (The Names of the Manservants of the Hsi-men Ch'ing Household), (2) "Hsi-men Ch'ing chia-jen hsi-fu" 西門慶家人媳婦 (The Wives of Hsi-men Ch'ing's Manservants), (3) "Hsi-men Ch'ing yin-kuo fu-nü" 西門慶淫過婦女 (Hsi-men Ch'ing's Amatory Conquests), (4) "P'an Chin-lien yin-kuo jen mu" 潘金蓮淫過人目 (List of P'an Chin-lien's Amatory Conquests), (5) "Hsi-men Ch'ing fang-wu" 西門慶房屋 (The Buildings and Apartments of Hsi-men Ch'ing's Household), (6) "*Chin P'ing Mei* yü-i shuo" 金瓶梅寓意說 (Allegorical Meaning in the *Chin P'ing Mei*), (7) "Fan-li" 凡例 (General Principles), (8) "Tsa-lu hsiao-yin" 雜錄小引 (Brief Introduction to the Miscellaneous Lists), (9) "*Chin P'ing Mei* ch'ü-t'an" 金瓶梅趣談 (Spicy Sayings in the *Chin P'ing Mei*), (10) "Mu-lu" 目錄 (Table of Contents), (11) "Leng-je chin-chen" 冷熱金針 (The Secret of Hot and Cold), (12) "*Ti-i ch'i-shu fei yin-shu lun*" 第一奇書非淫書論 (The Number One Marvelous Book Is Not an Obscene Book), (13) "K'u-hsiao shuo" 苦孝說 (Frustrated Filiality), (14) "Chu-p'o hsien-hua" 竹坡閑話 (Idle Talk from [Chang] Chu-p'o), and (15) "P'i-p'ing *Ti-i ch'i-shu Chin P'ing Mei* tu-fa" 批評第一奇書金瓶梅讀法 (How to Read the Number One Marvelous Book *Chin P'ing Mei* with Commentary). Each of these items are paginated separately and several exemplars of editions of the commentary have bound them into entirely different orders. The sequence in the above list is far from ideal and most likely does not reflect the original order. For instance, items 1–4 are marked "Tsa-lu" 雜錄 (Miscellaneous Lists) on the outside fold of each page, but item 8, which is supposed to be an introduction to them, is bound several items behind them. The authenticity of the three items most often left out of printings of the novel (numbers 7, 11, and 12) has been questioned by Huang Lin (see the article listed in the bibliography below). These three items do contain ideas and language that seem to render them suspect, but they also contain information about Chang Chu-p'o and his work on the commentary that would be difficult for a later publisher to fabricate. COMMENTARY: Most editions have marginal comments, but their contents are not identical. All editions have single- and double-column interlineal comments, but only about half of the editions of the commentary have prechapter comments. Judging from item fifty of Chang Chu-p'o's *tu-fa* essay, prechapter comments must have been part of the original edition. The existence of a "1695" edition that prints only the chapter comments for chap. I (see the Huang Lin article listed below, pp. 280–81) leads one to think that the editions without the bulky chapter comments are later, commercial productions. DISTINGUISHING FEATURES: The text of the novel is basically the same as in the "Ch'ung-chen" editions. REMARKS: Some of Chang Chu-p'o's comments are based on or reflect comments in the "Ch'ung-chen" B editions. AVAILABILITY: A large-character, Tsai-tzu t'ang edition dated 1695 without chapter comments was photo-reprinted in Taiwan (*TICS*). A related edition with publisher's name erased and different order of prefatory items was photo-reprinted along with an incomplete copy from the Ch'ung-ching t'ang 崇經堂 edition (*Liang-chung Chu-p'o p'ing-tien pen ho-k'an T'ien-hsia ti-i ch'i-shu* 兩種竹坡評點本合刊天下第一奇書 [Hong Kong: Hui-wen ko, 1975]). Another "1695" edition without chapter comments is available as part of the Van Gulik collection on microfiche. Individual original copies of various editions are held in the Gest Oriental Library, Princeton University (*pen-ya ts'ang-pan* 本衙藏版 edition, xerox of 1747 edition minus prefatory matter, etc.), Far Eastern Library, University of Chicago (Yüan-hua shu-wu 沅花書屋 edition), and Harvard-Yenching Library, Harvard University (Ch'ung-ching t'ang edition, 1816 preface edition). Some of the prefatory essays and comments from various editions are available in the collections of material on the novel published under the title *Chin P'ing Mei tzu-liao hui-pien* listed in the general bibliography on the *Chin P'ing Mei* below and in Ch'en Ch'ang-heng 陳昌恒, ed., *Chang Chu-p'o Chin P'ing Mei p'ing-yü chi-lu* 張竹坡金瓶梅 評語輯錄 (Collected Comments by Chang Chu-p'o on the *Chin P'ing Mei*; Wuhan: Hua-chung shih-yüan, n.d.). A typeset and collated version of Chang Chu-p'o's commentary based on a copy held in Ch'ang-ch'un, Chi-lin Province, and considered by some to represent a copy from the original edition is available: Wang Ju-mei 王汝梅, ed., *Chang Chu-p'o p'i-p'ing Ti-i ch'i-shu Chin P'ing Mei* 張竹坡批評第一奇書金瓶梅 (Tsinan: Ch'i Lu shu-she, 1987). There are also plans to include the Chang Chu-p'o comments as part of a variorum commentary edition of the novel under the editorship of Liu Hui. A photo-reprint of the *tu-fa* essay has been published separately (*Kao-ho t'ang p'i-p'ing Ming-tai Ti-i ch'i-shu Chin P'ing Mei tu-fa* 皋鶴堂批評明代第一奇書金瓶梅讀法 [Taipei: Kuang-wen shu-chü, 1981]).

Roy, David T. "Chang Chu-p'o's Commentary on the *Chin P'ing Mei*." In *Chinese Narrative: Critical and Theoretical Essays*, pp. 115–23. Translated by Wang Ju-mei 王汝梅 and Chang Hsiao-yang 張曉洋 as "Chang Chu-p'o tui *Chin P'ing Mei* ti p'ing-lun" 張竹坡對金瓶梅的評論, *Ku-tai wen-hsüeh li-lun yen-chiu* 6:263–69 (1982).

———. "Chang Chu-p'o's Critical Approach to the *Chin P'ing Mei*." Unpublished paper.

Ch'en Ch'ang-heng 陳昌恒. "Chang Chu-p'o p'ing *Chin P'ing Mei* li-lun shih-hui" 張竹坡評金瓶梅理論拾慧. *Chung-nan min-tsu hsüeh-yüan hsüeh-pao*, 1986. 2:129–32, 55 (*Ku-chin* reprint, 1986. 6:216–20).

———. "Chang Chu-p'o ti wen-hsüeh tien-hsing lun hsü-shu" 張竹坡的文學

典型論續述. *Hua-chung shih-fan hsüeh-yüan yen-chiu sheng hsüeh-pao*, 1982. 4:19ff.

———. "Hsi-men tien-hsing hai tsai—Chang Chu-p'o ti wen-hsüeh tien-hsing lun kai-shu" 西門典型還在—張竹坡的文學典型論概述. "*Hua-chung shih-fan hsüeh-yüan yen-chiu sheng hsüeh-pao*, 1982.3.

———. "Lun Chang Chu-p'o kuan-yü wen-hsüeh tien-hsing ti mo-shen shuo" 論張竹坡關於文學典型的摹神說. *Hua-chung shih-fan hsüeh-yüan hsüeh-pao*, 1983. 1:118–25.

Ch'en Kuei-sheng 陳桂聲. "Chang Chu-p'o *Chin P'ing Mei* p'i-p'ing erh tse ch'ien-i" 張竹坡金瓶梅批評二則淺議. Paper presented at the 1986 *Chin P'ing Mei* conference, Hsü-chou, China.

Cheng Yün-po 鄭雲波. "Chi-shih t'u-p'o, yu shih ch'i-tien—chien-chieh Wu Kan t'ung-chih kuan-yü Chang Chu-p'o yü *Chin P'ing Mei* ti yen-chiu" 既是突破又是起點—簡介吳敢同志關於張竹坡與金瓶梅的研究. *Hsü-chou shih-fan hsüeh-yüan hsüeh-pao*, 1984. 3:80–81.

"*Chin P'ing Mei* p'ing-tien che Chang Chu-p'o chih mi chieh-hsiao" 金瓶梅評點者張竹坡之謎揭曉. *Chi-lin jih-pao* 吉林日報, 2/17/1986 (*Ku-chin* reprint, 1986. 3:218).

Huang Lin 黃霖. "Chang Chu-p'o chi ch'i *Chin P'ing Mei* p'ing-pen" 張竹坡及其金瓶梅評本. In *Chung-kuo ku-tien wen-hsüeh ts'ung-k'ao* 中國古典文學叢考. Shanghai: Fu-tan ta-hsüeh, 1985, pp. 263–83.

I Ting 一丁 (pseud.). "P'ing *Chin P'ing Mei* chih Chang Chu-p'o" 評金瓶梅之張竹坡. *Hsin-min wan-pao*, 12/5/1956.

Ku Kuo-jui 顧國瑞, and Liu Hui 劉輝. "Chang Chu-p'o chi ch'i *Chin P'ing Mei* p'ing-pen" 張竹坡及其金瓶梅評本. In *Chung-kuo ku-tien hsiao-shuo hsi-ch'ü lun-chi* 中國古典小說戲曲論集. Shanghai: Shang-hai ku-chi, 1985, pp. 344–69. Reprinted in *Chin P'ing Mei ch'eng-shu yü pan-pen yen-chiu*, pp. 114–38.

———. "Ch'ih-tu ou-ts'un, *Yu-sheng* chi ch'i chung ti hsi-ch'ü shih-liao" 尺牘偶存友聲及其中的戲曲史料. *Wen-shih* 15:263–74 (1982).

Li Shih-jen 李時人. "Chang Chu-p'o shih-wen chi-ts'un" 張竹坡詩文輯存. Unpublished paper, 1984.

———. "I-p'i yu-kuan Chang Chu-p'o ti chung-yao tzu-liao chien-chieh" 一批有關張竹坡的重要資料簡介. Unpublished paper.

Liu Hui 劉輝. "Chang Chu-p'o tsung-p'u shih-hsi piao" 張竹坡宗譜世系表. Unpublished paper.

———. "*Chin P'ing Mei* p'ing-pen 'Hsieh I hsü' ti tso-che chi ch'i ying-hsiang" 金瓶梅評本謝頤序的作者及其影響. *I-t'an*, 1985. 2:8–11 (*Ku-chin* reprint, 1985. 16:87–90). Reprinted in *Chin P'ing Mei ch'eng-shu yü pan-pen yen-chiu*, pp. 156–63.

———. "Tsai-t'an Chang Chu-p'o ti chia-shih, sheng-p'ing chi ch'i p'ing *Chin P'ing Mei* ti nien-tai" 再談張竹坡的家世生平及其評金瓶梅的年代. In *Chin P'ing Mei ch'eng-shu yü pan-pen yen-chiu*, pp. 139–55.

Lu Ta-wei 陸大偉 (David Rolston). "Chang Chu-p'o ta-ma Wu Yüeh-niang ti lai-lung ch'ü-mo ch'u-t'an" 張竹坡大罵吳月娘的來龍去脉初探. Paper presented at the 1986 *Chin P'ing Mei* conference, Hsü-chou, China.

P'an Shou-k'ang 潘壽康. "Chang Chu-p'o p'ing *Chin P'ing Mei*" 張竹坡評金瓶梅. In his *Hua-pen yü hsiao-shuo* 話本與小說. Taipei: Li-ming wen-hua, 1973, pp. 76–80.

P'ei Hsin 沛信. "Mei-kuo Han-hsüeh chia P'u An-ti chiao-shou lai-Hsü k'ao-ch'a Chang Chu-p'o sheng-p'ing" 美國漢學家浦安迪教授來徐考察張竹坡生平. *Hsü-chou shih-fan hsüeh-yüan hsüeh-pao*, 1984. 4:53.

Sawada Mizuho 沢田瑞穗. "Chō Takeha no 'dokuhō'" 張竹坡の読法. In *Sō Min Shin shōsetsu sōkō* 宋明清小說叢考. Tokyo: Kenbun shuppan, 1982, pp. 208–12.

Tai Pu-fan 戴不凡. "Chang Chu-p'o p'ing-pen" 張竹坡評本. In *Hsiao-shuo chien-wen lu* 小說見聞錄. Hangchou: Che-chiang jen-min, 1980, pp. 139–41. Reprinted in *Lun Chin P'ing Mei*, pp. 327–28.

Wang Ju-mei 王汝梅. "Chang Chu-p'o tsai hsiao-shuo li-lun shang ti kung-hsien" 張竹坡在小說理論上的貢獻. *Ming-Ch'ing hsiao-shuo lun-ts'ung* 3:134–45 (1985).

———. "Chang Chu-p'o yü *Chin P'ing Mei* p'ing-tien k'ao-lun" 張竹坡與金瓶梅評點考論. *Chi-lin ta-hsüeh she-hui k'o-hsüeh hsüeh-pao*, 1985. 1:36–43 (*Ku-chin* reprint, 1985. 6:99–106).

———. "Lun Chang Chu-p'o p'i-p'ing *Chin P'ing Mei* K'ang-hsi pen" 論張竹坡批評金瓶梅康熙本. *Chi-lin ta-hsüeh she-hui k'o-hsüeh hsüeh-pao*, 1987. 1:68–72 (*Ku-chin* reprint, 1987. 5:206–10).

———. "P'ing Chang Chu-p'o ti *Chin P'ing Mei* p'ing-lun" 評張竹坡的金瓶梅評論. *Wen-i li-lun yen-chiu*, 1981. 2:85–94. Reprinted in *Lun Chin P'ing Mei*, pp. 307–26.

———. "Tsai-t'an Chang Chu-p'o ti *Chin P'ing Mei* p'ing-tien" 再談張竹坡的金瓶梅評點. In *Chung-kuo ku-tai hsiao-shuo li-lun yen-chiu*, pp. 257–74.

Wu Kan 吳敢. "Chang Ch'iao yü Chang Chu-p'o" 張翹與張竹坡. *Ming-Ch'ing hsiao-shuo yen-chiu* 4:188–201 (1986).

———. "Chang Chu-p'o chi ch'i *Chin P'ing Mei* p'ing-tien" 張竹坡及其金瓶梅評點. *Ta-feng* 大風, 1985.2.

———. "Chang Chu-p'o chia-shih kai-shu" 張竹坡家世概述. *Ming-Ch'ing hsiao-shuo yen-chiu* 2:243–53 (1985).

———. "Chang Chu-p'o nien-p'u chien-pien" 張竹坡年譜簡編. *Hsü-chou shih-fan hsüeh-yüan hsüeh-pao*, 1985. 1:68–77 (*Ku-chin* reprint, 1985. 14:47–56).

———. "Chang Chu-p'o sheng-p'ing shu-lüeh" 張竹坡生平述略. *Hsü-chou shih-fan hsüeh-yüan hsüeh-pao*, 1984. 3:74–79.

———. "Chang Chu-p'o *Shih i ts'ao* k'ao-cheng" 張竹坡十一草考證. *Hsü-chou shih-fan hsüeh-yüan hsüeh-pao*, 1985. 3:64–67.

———. "Chang Chu-p'o *Shih i ts'ao* k'ao-p'ing" 張竹坡十一草考評. *Ming-Ch'ing hsiao-shuo yen-chiu* 2:259–70.

———. "Chang Chu-p'o Yang-chou hsing-i hsiao-k'ao" 張竹坡楊州行誼小考. *Yang-chou shih-yüan hsüeh-pao*, 1985. 2:110–12.

———. *Chang Chu-p'o yü Chin P'ing Mei* 張竹坡與金瓶梅. Tientsin: Pai-hua wen-i, 1987.

———. "Chang Tao-yüan yü t'a ti liang-p'ien 'Chung-hsiung Chu-p'o chuan'" 張道淵與他的兩篇仲兄竹坡傳. In *Chin P'ing Mei lun-chi*, pp. 193–203.

―――. *Chin P'ing Mei p'ing-tien chia Chang Chu-p'o nien-p'u* 金瓶梅評點家
張竹坡年譜. Shenyang: Liao-ning jen-min, 1987.

―――. "Hsin fa-hsien ti *Chin P'ing Mei* p'ing-che Chang Chu-p'o tsu-p'u shu-
k'ao (fu Chang Chu-p'o chuan yü ch'i shih-wen)" 新發現的金瓶梅評者
張竹坡族譜述考(附張竹坡傳與其詩文). *Wen-hsien*, 1985. 3:18–33.

Yü Sheng-t'ing 于盛庭, and Wu Yao-chung 吳耀忠. "Ch'ing-i hsien-sheng p'u-kao
yu-kuan Chang Chu-p'o ti chung-yao tzu-liao" 清毅先生譜稿有關張竹坡
的重要資料. *Hsü-chou shih-fan hsüeh-yüan hsüeh-pao*, 1984. 4:49–53.

TITLE: Wen-lung 文龍 commentary. LENGTH: 100 chapters. PUBLISHER: Manuscript comments on a Tsai-tzu t'ang edition of Chang Chu-p'o's commentary on
the novel. DATE: Wen-lung received this copy of the novel from a friend in 1879
and finished his comments in 1882. PREFATORY MATERIAL: Nothing new beyond
that of the original edition. COMMENTARY: Marginal, single-column interlineal,
and postchapter comments by Wen-lung (fl. 1830–1886, courtesy name Yü-men
禹門), original surname Chao 趙. REMARKS: Wen-lung takes frequent and lengthy
exception to comments by Chang Chu-p'o, particularly those concerning the
characters Wu Yüeh-niang, Meng Yü-lou, and P'ang Ch'un-mei. AVAILABILITY:
Only extant copy held in Peking Library. The bulk of the chapter comments have
been edited and published by Liu Hui 劉輝, "Pei-ching t'u-shu kuan ts'ang *Chin
P'ing Mei* Wen-lung p'i-pen hui-p'ing chi-lu" 北京圖書館藏金瓶梅文龍批本
回評輯錄 (Collected Chapter Comments from the Wen-lung Commentary on
the *Chin P'ing Mei* Held in the Peking Library), *Wen-hsien* 文獻 (Literary Arti-
facts), 1985. 4:37–53 (pt. 1), 1986. 1:38–71 (pt. 2), and 1986. 2:33–66 (pt. 3).
Those comments, along with some additional interlineal comments, are reprinted
as an appendix in his *Chin P'ing Mei ch'eng-shu yü pan-pen yen-chiu*, pp. 184–276.

Liu Hui 劉輝. "Lüeh-t'an Wen-lung p'i-p'ing *Chin P'ing Mei*" 略談文龍批評
金瓶梅. *Kuang-ming jih-pao*, 5/21/1985 (*Ku-chin* reprint, 1985. 12:39–40).
Also reprinted in his *Chin P'ing Mei ch'eng-shu yü pan-pen yen-chiu*, pp.
164–68.

―――. "T'an Wen-lung tui *Chin P'ing Mei* ti p'i-p'ing" 談文龍對金瓶梅的
批評. *Wen-hsien*, 1985. 4:54–66 (*Ku-chin* reprint, 1985. 22:47–56).

―――. "Wen-lung chi ch'i p'i-p'ing *Chin P'ing Mei*" 文龍及其批評金瓶梅. In
his *Chin P'ing Mei ch'eng-shu yü pan-pen yen-chiu*, pp. 169–83 (basically the
same as "T'an Wen-lung tui *Chin P'ing Mei* ti p'i-p'ing").

General Bibliography on Fiction Criticism and the Chin P'ing Mei

Hanan, Patrick. "The Text of the *Chin P'ing Mei*." *Asia Major*, n.s. 9:1–57
(1962). Summarized in Chinese in Pao Chen-nan 包振南, "Mei-kuo hsüeh-
che Han-nan ti *Chin P'ing Mei* pan-pen yen-chiu shu-lüeh" 美國學者韓南
的金瓶梅版本研究述略. *Chiang Hai hsüeh-k'an*, 1986. 3:56–60.

Chu I-hsüan 朱一玄, and Liu Yü-ch'en 劉毓忱, eds. *Chin P'ing Mei tzu-liao hui-
pien* 金瓶梅資料彙編. Tientsin: Nan-k'ai ta-hsüeh, 1985.

Hou Chung-i 侯忠義, and Wang Ju-mei 王汝梅, eds. *Chin P'ing Mei tzu-liao hui-pien* 金瓶梅資料滙編. Peking: Pei-ching ta-hsüeh, 1985 (expanded edition forthcoming).

Hu Wen-pin 胡文彬. *Chin P'ing Mei shu-lu* 金瓶梅書錄. Shenyang: Liao-ning jen-min, 1986.

Huang Lin 黃霖, ed. *Chin P'ing Mei tzu-liao hui-pien* 金瓶梅資料彙編. Peking: Chung-hua shu-chü, 1987.

Liu Hui 劉輝. "*Chin P'ing Mei* chu-yao pan-pen so-chien lu" 金瓶梅主要版本所見錄. *Fu-tan hsüeh-pao*, 1986. 2:106–10 (*Ku-chin* reprint, 1986. 7:183–87). Also in his *Chin P'ing Mei ch'eng-shu yü pan-pen yen-chiu*, pp. 86–113.

————. "*Chin P'ing Mei* pan-pen k'ao" 金瓶梅版本考. In his *Chin P'ing Mei ch'eng-shu yü pan-pen yen-chiu*, pp. 59–85. Also in *Chin P'ing Mei lun-chi*, pp. 224–48.

————, ed. *Chin P'ing Mei hui-p'ing pen* 金瓶梅會評本. Cheng-chou: Chung-chou ku-chi, forthcoming.

Lu Ta-wei 陸大偉 (David Rolston). "*Chin P'ing Mei* p'ing-tien chi hsiao-shuo li-lun lun-wen mu-lu ch'u-kao" 金瓶梅評點及小說理論論文目錄初稿. Paper presented at the 1986 *Chin P'ing Mei* conference, Hsü-chou, China.

Torii Hisayasu 鳥居久靖. "*Kin Pei Bai* hanponkō" 金瓶梅版本考. *Tenri daigaku gakuhō* 18:335–66 (1955).

Ts'ai Kuo-liang 蔡國梁. "Ming-jen Ch'ing-jen p'ing *Chin P'ing Mei*" 明人清人評金瓶梅. *She-hui k'o-hsüeh chan-hsien*, 1983. 4:306–13 (*Ku-chin* reprint, 1983. 12:169–74). Reprinted in his *Ming-Ch'ing hsiao-shuo t'an-yu*, pp. 244–62.

Tzu Yang 滋陽. "*Chin P'ing Mei* ti chung-yao pan-pen" 金瓶梅的重要版本. *Chi-lin ta-hsüeh she-hui k'o-hsüeh hsüeh-pao*, 1985. 2:94–95 (*Ku-chin* reprint, 1985. 8:53–54).

Wang Ju-mei 王汝梅. "Chih-yen chai chih ch'ien *Chin P'ing Mei* p'i-p'ing" 脂硯齋之前金瓶梅批評. *Chi-lin ta-hsüeh hsüeh-pao*, 1985. 5:28–33.

Wang Ju-mei et al. *Chin P'ing Mei tz'u-tien* 金瓶梅詞典. Ch'ang-ch'un: Chi-lin wen-shih, forthcoming.

Ju-lin wai-shih

ABBREVIATED TITLE: Wo-hsien ts'ao-t'ang 臥閑草堂 edition. FULL TITLE: *Ju-lin wai-shih*. Title at the head of the table of contents: *Ju-lin wai-shih ch'üan-chuan* 儒林外史全傳 (Complete Tale of The Informal History of the Literati). LENGTH: 56 chapters (no *chüan* divisions). PUBLISHER: Wo-hsien ts'ao-t'ang. DATE: 1803. PREFATORY MATERIAL: Hsien-chai lao-jen 閑齋老人 (pseud.) preface, dated 1736. COMMENTARY: Postchapter comments (except chaps. 42–44, 53–55). REMARKS: Huang Hsiao-t'ien (see the description of his commentary edition below) identified the author of the preface of this edition as a Manchu writer of satirical literary language short fiction, Ho-pang-e 和邦額 (1774 *chü-jen*), but the only evidence he brings forward is a similarity in their pen names and the identification is not generally accepted. Some scholars think that the preface was written by the author of the novel, Wu Ching-tzu (1701–1754). AVAILABILITY: Photo-reprint: *JLWS*. The comments are included in *JLWSHCHPP*.

Lin, Shuen-fu. "Ritual and Narrative Structure in *Ju-lin wai-shih*." In *Chinese Narrative: Critical and Theoretical Essays*, pp. 244–65. Translated in *Wen-hsien*, 12:67–82 (1982) and *Chung-wai wen-hsüeh* 13. 6:116–37 (1984).

Ch'en Mei-lin 陳美林. "Shih chiu 'Wo-pen' p'ing-yü lüeh-lun *Ju-lin wai-shih* ti min-tsu t'e-se" 試就臥本評語略論儒林外史的民族特色. *She-hui k'o-hsüeh yen-chiu*, 1984. 4:90–95 (*Ku-chin* reprint, 1984. 20:66–71). Reprinted, with slight changes, in *Chung-kuo ku-tai hsiao-shuo li-lun yen-chiu*, pp. 324–39.

Chiang Tung-fu 姜東賦. "Yeh shuo Ho-pang-e" 也說和邦額. *Kuang-ming jih-pao*, 9/10/1985.

Fang Jih-hsi 方日晞. "Wo-hsien ts'ao-t'ang pen *Ju-lin wai-shih* hui-p'ing so-t'an" 臥閑草堂本儒林外史回評瑣談. *Hsi-pei ta-hsüeh hsüeh-pao* 西北大學學報, 1982. 3:54–60. Reprinted in *Ju-lin wai-shih tzu-liao chi*, vol. 1, pp. 127–33.

Hsüeh Hung 薛洪. "'Hsien-chai' yü Ni-chai" 閑齋與閟齋. *Kuang-ming jih-pao*, 9/10/1985.

Hsüeh Hung-chi 薛洪績. "Shih-lun Ho-pang-e ho t'a ti *Yeh-t'an sui-lu*" 試論和邦額和他的夜談隨錄. *Man-tsu wen-hsüeh yen-chiu* 滿族文學研究, 1984.1.

Kung Hsiu-sen 龔修森. "Kuo-shou pu tzu, pu-pu chao-ying—hsi *Ju-lin wai-shih* Wo-pen hui-p'ing ti chieh-kou i-shu lun" 國手布子步步照應—析儒林外史臥本回評的結構藝術論. *Nan-ching shih-yüan hsüeh-pao*, 1983. 3:59–62. Reprinted in *Ju-lin wai-shih tzu-liao chi*, vol. 2.

Mai Jo-p'eng 麥若鵬. "Ch'u-chieh 'Hsien-chai lao-jen' chih mi" 初揭閑齋老人之謎. *Kuang-ming jih-pao*, 7/2/1985.

Shen Chi-ch'ang 沈繼常. "*Ju-lin wai-shih* 'Wo-p'ing' man-i" 儒林外史臥評漫議. *Nan-t'ung shih-chuan hsüeh-pao*, 1987. 1:16–21.

Sutō Yōichi 須藤洋一. "Gakan sōdō hon *Jurin gaishi* hyō o yomu—Jigokuzu no yukikata" 臥閑草堂本儒林外史評を讀む—地獄図の行方. In *Itō Sōhei kyōju taikan kinen—Chūgokugaku ronshū* 伊藤漱平教授退官紀念—中国学論集. Tokyo: Kyūko shoin, 1986, pp. 707–34.

Wang Yüeh-tsun 汪岳尊. "Wo-hsien ts'ao-t'ang pen *Ju-lin wai-shih* hsü ti tso-che Hsien-chai lao-jen shih Wu Ching-tzu" 臥閑草堂本儒林外史序的作者閑齋老人是吳敬梓. *Fu-yang shih-fan hsüeh-yüan hsüeh-pao*, 1985. 4:57ff.

Yang I 楊翼, and Ch'iu Ts'ai-mei 邱才妹. "Shih-lun *Ju-lin wai-shih* 'Wo-p'ing' kuan-yü ch'ing-chieh chieh-kou ti lun-shu" 試論儒林外史臥評關於情節結構的論述. *Hang-chou shih-yüan hsüeh-pao*, 1985. 4:97–101.

TITLE: Huang Hsiao-t'ien 黃小田 commentary. LENGTH: 56 chapters. PUBLISHER: This is a transcription of Huang Hsiao-t'ien's comments onto a copy of the 1869 Suchou Ch'ün-yü chai 群玉齋 movable-type edition of the novel. DATE: The original comments were made from 1853 to 1862? PREFATORY MATERIAL: Two separate prefatory remarks (*t'i-chih* 題識), one recorded at the end of the Hsien-chai lao-jen preface of the original edition, one recorded at the end of the table of contents. COMMENTARY: Marginal and chapter comments (chaps. 9, 15–16, 23, 26, 32, 38, 43, 47–49, 54–55 only) by Huang Hsiao-t'ien (1795–1867, personal name Fu-min 富民, style P'ing-sou 萍叟) in black ink. The marginal comments include the three signed with his style in the 1881 and 1885 Chang Wen-hu commentaries on the novel (see below for the description). The chapter comments are attributed. This copy also includes Chang Wen-hu's 1881 comments copied onto the text in red ink. AVAILABILITY: This copy was formerly the property of Hsü Shih-chang 徐世章 (d. 1941) who had it rebound in 1923. The comments are not included in *JLWSHCHPP* but they have been published recently under the title *Ju-lin wai-shih Huang Hsiao-t'ien p'ing-pen* 儒林外史黃小田評本, Li Han-ch'iu 李漢秋, ed. (Hofei: Huang-shan shu-she, 1986).

Li Han-ch'iu 李漢秋. "*Ju-lin wai-shih* Huang Hsiao-t'ien p'ing-tien ti fa-hsien ho i-i" 儒林外史黃小田評點的發現和意義. Paper presented at the 1986 *Ju-lin wai-shih* conference, Ch'üan-chiao, Anhui Province.

————. "Yen erh fu-hsien ti *Ju-lin wai-shih* Huang Hsiao-t'ien p'ing" 湮而復現的儒林外史黃小田評. *Kuang-ming jih-pao*, 10/8/1985.

ABBREVIATED TITLE: 1874 Ch'i-hsing t'ang 齊省堂 edition. FULL TITLE: *Tseng-ting Ju-lin wai-shih* 增訂儒林外史 (Expanded and Edited *Ju-lin wai-shih*). LENGTH: 56 chapters. PUBLISHER: Ch'i-hsing t'ang. DATE: 1874. PREFATORY MATERIAL: Hsing-yüan t'ui-shih 惺園退士 (pseud.) preface, 1874; "Li-yen" 例言 (General Principles); and Hsien-chai lao-jen preface (slightly changed from the original version). COMMENTARY: Includes Wo-hsien ts'ao-t'ang postchapter comments plus additions to them, new chapter comments, and new marginal comments. DISTINGUISHING FEATURES: The text has been slightly edited (see the "Li-yen" for details). AVAILABILITY: The comments and prefatory material from this edition are included in *JLWSHCHPP*.

ABBREVIATED TITLE: Hsü Yün-lin 徐允臨 collated copy. FULL TITLE: *Ju-lin wai-shih*. LENGTH: 56 chapters. PUBLISHER: This is the private copy of an 1869 Ch'ün-yü chai edition of the novel owned by Hsü Yün-lin (style Shih-shih 石史, studio name Ts'ung-hao chai 叢好齋), with his collation notes and comments by himself and friends. DATE: 1879–85. PREFATORY MATERIAL: Various notes and prefaces by Hsü Yün-lin, Hua Yüeh-yü 華約漁, and Wang Ch'eng-chi 王承基. COMMENTARY: Added marginal comments by Hsü Yün-lin and Hua Yüeh-yü. DISTINGUISHING FEATURES: This is basically a collated private edition of the novel and of Chang Wen-hu's comments to it. A version of it may have served as the base text for the 1881 Shen-pao kuan printing of Chang Wen-hu's commentary. AVAILABILITY: The new material by Hsü Yün-lin, Hua Yüeh-yü, and Wang Ch'eng-chi is included in *JLWSHCHPP*. The original copy is held in the library of Shanghai Normal University.

ABBREVIATED TITLE: 1881 Chang Wen-hu 張文虎 edition. FULL TITLE: *Ju-lin wai-shih*. LENGTH: 56 chapters. PUBLISHER: Shen-pao kuan 申報館, Shanghai.

DATE: 1881. PREFATORY MATERIAL: Hsien-chai lao-jen preface, prefatory comments (*Chih* 識) by Chang Wen-hu (1808–1885, style T'ien-mu shan-ch'iao 天目山樵). COMMENTARY: Original Wo-hsien ts'ao-t'ang edition postchapter comments plus double-column interlineal and occasional postchapter comments (signed) by Chang Wen-hu, plus three comments by Huang Hsiao-t'ien (signed P'ing-sou). REMARKS: Chang Wen-hu's comments are heavily influenced by those of Huang Hsiao-t'ien (an estimated 10 percent of his comments are based on those of the other man's). AVAILABILITY: There is a typeset reprint: *Ju-lin wai-shih* (Taipei: Commercial Press, 1970). The comments are included in *JLWSHCHPP*.

ABBREVIATED TITLE: 1885 Chang Wen-hu edition. FULL TITLE: *Ju-lin wai-shih hsin-p'ing* 儒林外史新評 (New Commentary on the *Ju-lin wai-shih*). The word *hsin* (new) was dropped from the title after 1885. LENGTH: Two *chüan* (this work is based on the 56-chapter version but does not contain the complete text of the novel). PUBLISHER: Pao-wen ko 寶文閣, Shanghai. DATE: 1885. This edition was later reprinted as *Ju-lin wai-shih p'ing*, with corrections by Hsü Yün-lin made in 1886, but the date of 1885 was retained on the title page. PREFATORY MATERIAL: Huang An-chin 黃安謹 (son of Huang Hsiao-t'ien) preface, 1885; and prefatory remarks (*Chih* 識) by Chang Wen-hu. COMMENTARY: Printed as double-column interlineal comments after short quotations from the novel. There are also comments on the Wo-hsien ts'ao-t'ang preface and chapter comments. Three of the comments (the same three as in the 1881 version of the commentary) are attributed to Huang Hsiao-t'ien (P'ing-sou). REMARKS: Chang Wen-hu's commentary on the novel circulated among friends in various manuscript versions. In his preface, Huang An-chin discusses his father's commentary and describes the *Ju-lin wai-shih p'ing* as a combined printing of Huang Hsiao-t'ien's and Chang Wen-hu's comments, which does not really accord with the actual nature of this edition. AVAILABILITY: There is a recent undated photo-reprint of the Hsü Yün-lin corrected version: *Ju-lin wai-shih p'ing* (Shanghai: Shang-hai ku-chi, n.d.), copy held in Gest Oriental Library, Princeton University. The comments and prefatory material are included in *JLWSHCHPP*. A manuscript copy of Hsü Yün-lin's corrected version is held in the Shanghai Library and an 1885 uncorrected copy is held in the Peking Library.

ABBREVIATED TITLE: 60-Chapter Ch'i-hsing t'ang edition. FULL TITLE: *Tseng-pu Ch'i-hsing t'ang Ju-lin wai-shih* 增補齊省堂儒林外史 (Augmented Ch'i-hsing t'ang Edition of the *Ju-lin wai-shih*). LENGTH: 60 chapters (the four additional chapters are inserted into the middle of chap. 43 of the 56-chapter version). PUBLISHER: Hung-pao chai 鴻寶齋, Shanghai. DATE: 1888. PREFATORY MATERIAL: Hsing-yüan t'ui-shih 1874 preface of previous edition; Tung-wu Hsi-hung sheng 東武惜紅生 (Chü Shih-shen 居世紳) preface, 1888; and "Li-yen" of the 1874 edition with minor changes. COMMENTARY: Same as the 1874 edition. No comments have been added for the interpolated chapters. DISTINGUISHING FEATURES: Four new chapters, almost universally judged to be far inferior in quality to the original sections of the novel. REMARKS: The Hsi-hung sheng preface borrows freely from the Hsien-chai lao-jen preface without attribution. AVAILABILITY: Of the new commentarial and prefatory material, only the 1888 preface is included in the *JLWSHCHPP*. The four added chapters are also reprinted in that work as an appendix. There is a photo-reprint: *Ju-lin wai-shih* (Peking: Chung-kuo shu-tien, 1988).

TITLE: *Hsia-wai chün-hsieh* 霞外攟屑 (Collected Gleanings). AUTHOR: P'ing Pu-ch'ing 平步青 (1832–1896). REMARKS: *Chüan* 9 of this work contains comments on the *Ju-lin wai-shih* and Chang Wen-hu's commentary on it. AVAILABILITY: This material is reprinted in Li Han-ch'iu, ed., *Ju-lin wai-shih yen-chiu tzu-liao* 儒林外史研究資料 (Research Material on the *Ju-lin wai-shih*), pp. 249–54. Selected comments appear in *JLWSHCHPP*. The entire work was reprinted in 1959 by Chung-hua shu-chü (Peking).

TITLE: Wang Hsieh 王瀣 commentary. LENGTH: 60 chapters. PUBLISHER: Manuscript comments copied onto an 1888 Hung-pao chai edition of the novel. DATE: The comments are estimated to have been written around 1914. PREFATORY MATERIAL: Nothing new. COMMENTARY: Aside from the printed comments belonging to the original edition, there are added marginal comments in red and black (only six) ink. REMARKS: The owner of this copy was Wang Hsieh (1884–1944, courtesy name Po-hang 伯沆). The vast bulk of the added comments have been transcribed from the 1885 Chang Wen-hu commentary. Only around thirty of the comments on sections belonging to the 56-chapter version of the novel are not copied from that commentary. The comments to the added four chapters seem to be original. AVAILABILITY: The comments have been published with a short introduction as "Wang Po-hang *Ju-lin wai-shih* p'i-yü" 王伯沆儒林外史批語 (The Comments of Wang Hsieh on the *Ju-lin wai-shih*), *Wen-chiao tzu-liao chien-pao* 文教資料簡報 (Concise Journal of Material for Teaching in the Humanities), 1985. 5:99–160.

General Bibliography on Fiction Criticism and the Ju-lin wai-shih

Ch'en Hsin 陳新. "*Ju-lin wai-shih* Ch'ing-tai ch'ao-pen ch'u-t'an" 儒林外史清代抄本初探. *Wen-hsien*, 12:83–87. Reprinted in *Pan-pen*, pp. 434–39.

Cheng Ming-li 鄭明娳. "*Ju-lin wai-shih* chih pan-pen chi ch'i liu-ch'uan" 儒林外史之版本及其流傳. *Hsüeh-ts'ui* 學粹 18. 4–5:21–30 (1976).

Chu I-hsüan 朱一玄, and Liu Yü-ch'en 劉毓忱, eds. *Ju-lin wai-shih tzu-liao hui-pien* 儒林外史資料彙編. Tientsin: Pai-hua wen-i, forthcoming.

Ho Tse-han 何澤翰. *Ju-lin wai-shih jen-wu pen-shih k'ao-lüeh* 儒林外史人物本事考略. Shanghai: Shang-hai ku-chi, revised edition, 1985.

Li Han-ch'iu 李漢秋. "*Ju-lin wai-shih* pan-pen yüan-liu k'ao" 儒林外史版本源流考. *Wen-hsüeh i-ch'an*, 1982. 4:117–23. Reprinted in *Ju-lin wai-shih tzu-liao chi*, vol. 1, pp. 166–72.

———. "Li-shih shang ti *Ju-lin wai-shih* p'ing-lun" 歷史上的儒林外史評論. *She-hui k'o-hsüeh chi-k'an*, 1984. 2:141–48. Reprinted in *Ju-lin wai-shih tzu-liao chi*, vol. 2, pp. 27–34.

————, ed. *Ju-lin wai-shih hui-chiao hui-p'ing pen* 儒林外史會校會評本. Shanghai: Shang-hai ku-chi, 1984.

————, ed. *Ju-lin wai-shih yen-chiu tzu-liao* 儒林外史研究資料. Shanghai: Shang-hai ku-chi, 1984.

Sun Hsün 孫遜. "Kuan-yü *Ju-lin wai-shih* ti p'ing-pen ho p'ing-yü" 關於儒林外史的評本和評語. *Ming-Ch'ing hsiao-shuo yen-chiu* 3 : 238–57 (1986). Also in *Ming-Ch'ing hsiao-shuo lun-kao*, pp. 230–51.

Ts'ai Ching-k'ang 蔡景康. "Wan-Ch'ing hsiao-shuo li-lun chia lun *Ju-lin wai-shih*" 晚清小說理論家論儒林外史. In *Ju-lin wai-shih yen-chiu lun-wen chi* 儒林外史研究論文集. Hofei: An-hui jen-min, 1982, pp. 197–208.

Ts'ai Kuo-liang 蔡國梁. "Ts'ung Ch'ing-jen ti p'ing-tien k'an *Ju-lin wai-shih* ti yung-pi" 從清人的評點看儒林外史的用筆. *Shang-hai shih-fan hsüeh-yüan hsüeh-pao*, 1984. 1 : 41–47 (*Ku-chin* reprint, 1984. 10 : 107–13). Reprinted in *Ju-lin wai-shih tzu-liao chi*, vol. 2, pp. 20–26 and in his *Ming-Ch'ing hsiao-shuo t'an-yu*, pp. 263–78.

Hsi-yu chi

ABBREVIATED TITLE: "Li Chih" 李贄 edition. FULL TITLE: *Li Cho-wu hsien-sheng p'i-p'ing Hsi-yu chi* 李卓吾先生批評西遊記 (Commentary Edition of the *Hsi-yu chi* by Li Chih). One copy reads *yüan-p'ing* 原評 (original commentary) for *p'i-p'ing*. LENGTH: 100 chapters (no *chüan* divisions). PUBLISHER: A publisher in Su-chou? DATE: Judged to be 1620–27 on the basis of the illustrations. There seems to be a reference to this work in the 1629 preface to *Yu-kuai shih-t'an* 幽怪詩譚 (Mysterious Tales with Poetic Comments), and a reprint of the commentary by the Min-chai 閔齋 appeared in 1631. PREFATORY MATERIAL: Yüan Yü-ling 袁于令 (1599–1674) preface, and "Fan-li" 凡例 (General Principles). The 1631 Min-chai edition collated by Yang Chü-ch'ien 楊居謙 and one extant exemplar of the earlier edition had a preface entitled "P'i-tien *Hsi-yu chi* hsü" 批點西遊記序 (Preface to the Commentary Edition *Hsi-yu chi*). There is an additional piece, "I k'uan yen" 一窾言 (Words on the One Emptiness), in the Min-chai edition. COMMENTARY: Marginal, double-column interlineal, and postchapter comments. REMARKS: At the head of the first *chüan* of the Min-chai edition are the words: "Fang Li T'u-lao p'i-p'ing" 仿李禿老批評 (Commentary after the Manner of Li Chih). AVAILABILITY: There is a microfilm of the copy held in the Naikaku Bunko, Japan, in the University of Michigan series. There is also a fascimile edition based on two copies found recently in China (Cheng-chou: Chung-chou shu-hua she, 1983) and a typeset version is forthcoming from the same press. These two copies lack title page and "Fan-li," and the Yüan Yü-ling preface is incomplete.

Ku Ting 古丁. "Ming-k'o Li Cho-wu p'ing-pen *Hsi-yu chi* chien-chieh" 明刻李卓吾評本西遊記簡介. *Chin-hsi t'an*, 1981.2.

Liao Nan 蓼南. "Kuo-nei fa-hsien Ming-k'an Li Cho-wu p'ing *Hsi-yu chi*"

國內發現明刊李卓吾評西遊記. *Wen-hsüeh i-ch'an*, 1980. 2:34. Reprinted in
    Pan-pen, pp. 158–59.

———. "T'an-t'an Li Cho-wu p'ing-pen *Hsi-yu chi* chien-chieh" 談談李卓吾
    評本西遊記簡介. *Chin-hsi t'an*, 1982. 2:50–51 (*Ku-chin* reprint, 1982. 11:
    59–60).

"Sheng t'u-shu kuan fa-hsien i-pu Ming-k'o Li Cho-wu p'ing-pen *Hsi-yu chi*"
    省圖書館發現一部明刻李卓吾評本西遊記. *Ho-nan jih-pao* 河南日報,
    12/8/1964.

Su Hsing 蘇興. "T'an *Li Cho-wu hsien-sheng p'i-p'ing Hsi-yu chi* ti pan-k'o"
    談李卓吾先生批評西遊記的版刻. *Wen-hsien*, 1986. 1:35–37.

Teng P'ing 鄧平, and Shih Ning 式寧. "Shih erh fu-te pei chüeh hsin—Li Cho-
    wu p'ing-pen *Hsi-yu chi* chien-chieh" 失而復得倍覺新—李卓吾評本
    西遊記簡介. *Chiang Han hsüeh-k'an*, 1983. 1:67–68. Reprinted in *Pan-pen*,
    pp. 160–62.

ABBREVIATED TITLE: Wang Hsiang-hsü 汪象旭 edition. FULL TITLE: *Chüan-
hsiang ku-pen Hsi-yu cheng-tao shu* 鐫像古本西遊證道書 (Illustrated, Ancient Edition of the Way to Enlightenment through the *Hsi-yu chi*). In an alternate title,
the first two characters are replaced by "Hsin-chüan ch'u-hsiang" 新鐫出像
(Newly Cut, Illustrated . . .). LENGTH: 100 chapters in 20 *chüan*. PUBLISHER: Huang
Chou-hsing 黃周星 (1611–1680, courtesy name T'ai-hung 太鴻, style Chiu-yen
九烟) and Wang Hsiang-hsü (personal name Ch'i 淇, style Tan-i-tzu 憺漪子), in
Hangchou. DATE: 1663. PREFATORY MATERIAL: "Yü Chi" 虞集 (1272–1348) preface dated 1329, biographies of Ch'iu Ch'u-chi 丘處機 (1148–1227) and Hsüan-
tsang 玄奘 (600–661), postface by Huang T'ai-hung. COMMENTARY: Prechapter
and double-column interlineal comments by Wang Hsiang-hsü. DISTINGUISHING
FEATURES: This is the first of one line of abridged editions (different from the
Chu Ting-ch'en 朱鼎臣 or Yang Chih-ho 楊致和 abridged editions) and the
first edition to have a detailed account of Tripitaka's birth and early years in
chap. 9 which appears in all later editions. The publishers claim that their edition
is based on an "ancient edition" (*ku-pen* 古本) published by a Ta-lüeh t'ang
大略堂. REMARKS: The commentary, in a lighthearted manner, puts forth a
syncretic but basically Taoist interpretation of the novel. See the article by Liu
Ts'un-jen listed below for the problem of the "Yü Chi" preface and the influence of Taoism in the novel. AVAILABILITY: There is a microfilm copy (of an
original held in the Naikaku Bunko, Japan) available in the Far Eastern Library,
University of Chicago and the Gest Oriental Library, Princeton University.

Huang Chou-hsing 黃周星. *Chih-ch'ü chih-yü* 制曲枝語. In *Chung-kuo ku-tien
    hsi-ch'ü lun-chu chi-ch'eng* 中國古典戲曲論著集成. 10 vols. Peking: Chung-
    hua shu-chü, 1959, vol. 7, pp. 115–22.

Isobe Akira 磯部彰. "Genpon *Saiyūki* o meguru mondai" 元本西遊記をめぐる
    問題. *Bunka* 文化 42. 3–4:60–75 (1979).

Kuan Kuei-ch'üan 官桂銓. "Huang Chou-hsing yü *Hsi-yu cheng-tao shu*" 黃周星
    與西遊證道書. *Chung-hua wen-shih lun-ts'ung*, 1982. 2:200.

Liu Ts'un-jen 柳存仁. "Ch'üan-chen chiao ho hsiao-shuo *Hsi-yu chi*" 全真教

和小說西遊記. *Ming-pao yüeh-k'an*, 1985. 5:55–62 (pt. 1); 1985. 6:59–64
(pt. 2); 1985. 7:85–90 (pt. 3); 1985. 8:85–90 (pt. 4); and 1985. 9:70–74
(pt. 5).

Ōta Tatsuo 太辰田夫. "*Saiyū shōdōsho kō*" 西遊證道書考. *Kobe gaidai ronshū*
神戶外大論集 21. 5:1–17 (1970).

ABBREVIATED TITLE: Ts'ai Yüan-fang 蔡元放 edition. FULL TITLE: *Sheng-t'an
wai-shu, Mo-ling Ts'ai Yüan-fang tseng-p'ing Hsi-yu cheng-tao ch'i-shu* 聖歎外書
秣陵蔡元放增評西遊證道奇書 (Chin Sheng-t'an Uncollected Work: The Extraordinary Book of the Way to Enlightenment through the *Hsi-yu chi* with
Additional Commentary by Ts'ai Yüan-fang of Nanking). Alternate title: *Hsi-
yu cheng-tao ta ch'i shu* 西遊證道大奇書 (Great Marvelous Book of the Way to
Enlightenment through the *Hsi-yu chi*). LENGTH: 100 chapters in 20 *chüan*. PUB-
LISHER: Woodblocks held by Huai-te t'ang 懷德堂, printed by Chiu-ju t'ang
九如堂. DATE: 1750 (preface). PREFATORY MATERIAL: Ts'ai Yüan-fang (personal
name Ao 鼇, style Yeh-yün chu-jen 野雲主人) preface, 1750; biography of
Tripitaka; and 56-item *tu-fa* essay by Ts'ai Yüan-fang. COMMENTARY: Same as
Wang Hsiang-hsü edition. REMARKS: The only added commentary in this edition
seems to be Ts'ai Yüan-fang's *tu-fa* essay. In his preface Ts'ai Yüan-fang is
appreciative of Wang Hsiang-hsü's commentary, but he adds that since his ideas
are not entirely the same as the other man's, he added his *tu-fa* essay and the
preface. AVAILABILITY: There is a microfilm of the preface and *tu-fa* essay from an
original copy in the Bibliothèque nationale, Paris, held in Gest Oriental Library,
Princeton University.

ABBREVIATED TITLE: Ch'en Shih-pin 陳士斌 edition. FULL TITLE: *Hsiu-hsiang
Hsi-yu chen-ch'üan* 綉像西遊真詮 (Illustrated, True Explication of the *Hsi-yu
chi*). LENGTH: 100 chapters in 8 *chüan*. PUBLISHER: Chiao-ching shan-fang 校經
山房. DATE: This edition has a preface dated 1696, but no edition seen by the
editor seems to predate 1780. PREFATORY MATERIAL: Yu T'ung 尤侗 (1618–1704)
preface. COMMENTARY: Postchapter comments by Ch'en Shih-pin (style Wu-i-
tzu 悟一子). Late Ch'ing editions have marginal comments by an unknown
author and have the words *chia-p'i* 加批 (added commentary) in their titles.
REMARKS: The commentary relies heavily on alchemical and Taoist theory in its
analysis of the novel. AVAILABILITY: A copy of a 1780 edition is held in the East
Asian Library, Columbia University. There is a typeset version (with added
marginal comments) in the *Kuo-hsüeh chi-pen ts'ung-shu* 國學基本叢書 (Basic
Sinological Collection; Taipei: Commercial Press, 1968 reprint), vol. 256, and
the chapter comments appear in the recent reprint *Hsi-yu chi* (Taipei: Ku-lao
wen-hua, 1983).

Ts'ai Kuo-liang 蔡國梁. "Ch'en-p'i *Hsi-yu chi* ling-shih" 陳批西遊記零拾. In
his *Ming-Ch'ing hsiao-shuo t'an-yu*, pp. 230–43 (substantially the same as the
article below).
———. "Ch'en Shih-pin tui *Hsi-yu chi* jen-wu ho ch'ing-chieh chieh-kou ti p'i-
p'ing" 陳士斌對西遊記人物和情節結構的批評. *Wen-hsien*, 1985. 1:12–24
(*Ku-chin* reprint, 1985. 4:73–82).

ABBREVIATED TITLE: Chang Shu-shen 張書紳 edition. FULL TITLE: *Ti-i ch'i-shu Hsin-shuo Hsi-yu chi* 第一奇書新說西遊記 (Number One Marvelous Book, A New Explication of the *Hsi-yu chi*). LENGTH: 100 chapters (no *chüan* divisions). PUBLISHER: Ch'i-yu t'ang 其有堂, woodblocks held by Shu-ku t'ang 述古堂. DATE: 1749. PREFATORY MATERIAL: Preface, "Tsung-lun" 總論 (General Remarks; dated 1748), "Tsung-p'i" 總批 (General Comments), "Ching-shu t'i mu-lu" 經書題目錄 (List of Topics from the Classics), "Mu-lu fu" 目錄賦 (Table of Contents Rhyme Prose), and "Tsung-chieh" 總結 (Final Remarks) at the end of the novel, all by Chang Shu-shen. COMMENTARY: Prechapter, double-column interlineal, and postchapter comments by Chang Shu-shen. REMARKS: The commentary tries to explicate the novel as a parable expounding the truths of the Confucian classics. Item 30 of the "Tsung-p'i" claims that there are three different levels in the novel: (1) the surface narration of events, (2) the hidden allegorical messages, and (3) the literary techniques. AVAILABILITY: A microfilm of an early edition (courtesy of Professor Itō Sōhei of Tokyo University) is held in Gest Oriental Library, Princeton University. There is a photo-reprint of an 1888 edition: *Hsin-shuo Hsi-yu chi t'u-hsiang* 新說西遊記圖像 (Illustrated New Explication of the *Hsi-yu chi*; Peking: Chung-kuo shu-tien, 1985).

ABBREVIATED TITLE: Liu I-ming 劉一明 edition. FULL TITLE: *Chih-nan chen: Hsi-yu yüan-chih* 指南針：西遊原旨 (The Compass: The Original Intent of the *Hsi-yu chi*). LENGTH: 100 chapters in 24 *chüan*. PUBLISHER: The original edition indicates that the woodblocks were held at Ch'i-yün shan, near Lan-chou, Kansu Province. DATE: Original edition, 1810. First reprint, 1819–20 (Hu-kuo an 護國庵, Ch'ang-te, Hunan Province). PREFATORY MATERIAL: The original edition has prefaces by Su Ning-e 蘇寧阿 (dated 1801), Liang Lien-ti 梁聯第 (1798), Yang Ch'un-ho 楊春和 (1799), and Liu I-ming (two, 1778 and 1810); biography of Ch'iu Ch'u-chi; *tu-fa* essay; "Shan-chü ko" 山居歌 (Song of Life in the Mountains); and "*Hsi-yu yüan-chih* ko" 西遊原旨歌 (Song of the *Hsi-yu yüan-chih*). After the text appear postfaces by Fan Yü-li 樊于禮, Wang Yang-chien 王陽健, Chang Yang-chin 張陽金, and Feng Yang-kuei 馮陽貴. The first reprint lacks "Shan-chü ko," but adds a preface and postface by Ch'ü Chia-ao 瞿家鰲 (1819) and Hsia Fu-heng 夏復恒, plus a portrait of Liu I-ming. COMMENTARY: Postchapter comments, each ending with a concluding quatrain (*chieh-shih* 結詩), by Liu I-ming (style Wu-yüan-tzu 悟元子). REMARKS: Liu I-ming saw his commentary as supplemental to that of Ch'en Shih-pin. AVAILABILITY: A copy of the 1810 edition is reported to be held in the Harvard-Yenching Library, Harvard University, but is not available for examination and does not appear in the published catalogue of their holdings. There is a microfilm of the 1819–20 edition in the Far Eastern Library, University of Chicago. The prefatory material from that edition is reprinted in *HYCTLHP*, pp. 244–63. Some of the prefatory material was also reprinted in Wu-i-tzu 悟一子, *Hsi-yu chi* (Taipei: Ku-lao wen-hua, 1983).

Liu I-ming 劉一明. *Ching-yin Tao-shu shih-erh chung* 精印道書十二種. Taipei: Hsin wen-feng, 1975 reprint of 1913 edition.

Wang Shou-ch'üan 王守泉. "*Hsi-yu yüan-chih* ch'eng-shu nien-tai chi pan-pen yüan-liu k'ao" 西遊原旨成書年代及版本源流考. *Lan-chou ta-hsüeh hsüeh-pao* 蘭州大學學報, 1986. 1:76–81 (*Ku-chin* reprint, 1986. 3:219–24).

Wei Hang 韋航. "*Hsi-yu yüan-chih* ping fei hsin fa-hsien" 西遊原旨并非新發現. *Shu-lin*, 1986. 3:27 (*Ku-chin* reprint, 1986. 5:196).

ABBREVIATED TITLE: Chang Han-chang 張含章 edition. FULL TITLE: *T'ung-I Hsi-yu cheng-chih* 通易西遊正旨 (The True Intent of the *Hsi-yu chi* Explained by Way of the *I Ching*). LENGTH: 100 chapters in 10 *chüan*. PUBLISHER: Te-hsin t'ang 德馨堂, woodblocks held by a Mr. Ho (Ho-shih 何氏), probably Ho Yen-ch'un 何延春. DATE: 1839. PREFATORY MATERIAL: Ho Yen-ch'un preface (dated 1839), preface and postface by Chang Han-chang, and a biography of Ch'iu Ch'u-chi. COMMENTARY: Double-column interlineal and postchapter comments. REMARKS: The author is a syncretist who, besides relying on the *I Ching*, also draws on Taoist alchemy and Buddhism. AVAILABILITY: An incomplete microfilm is held in Gest Oriental Library, Princeton University. The two prefaces and the postface are included in *HYCTLHP*, pp. 236–42.

ABBREVIATED TITLE: Han-ching-tzu 含晶子 edition. FULL TITLE: *P'ing-chu Hsi-yu chi* 評注西遊記 (*Hsi-yu chi* with Commentary and Annotations). LENGTH: 100 chapters. PUBLISHER: Details unclear. DATE: 1892. REMARKS: Unseen by editor, details unclear.

ABBREVIATED TITLE: Ch'en Tun-fu 陳敦甫 edition. FULL TITLE: *Hsi-yu chi shih-i—Lung-men hsin-ch'uan* 西遊記釋義一龍門心傳 (Explication of the *Hsi-yu chi* —the Secret Teaching of Patriarch Ch'iu). LENGTH: 100 chapters. PUBLISHER: Ch'üan-chen chiao ch'u-pan she, Taipei. DATE: 1976. PREFATORY MATERIAL: "*Hsi-yu chi shih-i* tsai-pan tzu-hsü" 西遊記釋義再版自序 (Author's Preface to the Second Printing), several essays treating the problem of the authorship of the novel, "Meng chan Ching-ho lung" 夢斬涇河龍 (Execution in a Dream of the Ching River Dragon; quoted from the *Yung-lo ta-tien*), preface to the original edition, and "*Hsi-yu chi* chu-yao jen-wu" 西遊記主要人物 (Important Characters in the *Hsi-yu chi*). Except for quoted material, all of these pieces seem to be by Ch'en Tun-fu. COMMENTARY: The comments from the original edition (which were printed without the text of the novel) are printed after the appropriate chapter as postchapter comments. REMARKS: Ch'en Tun-fu interprets the novel as written to exemplify the teachings of Ch'iu Ch'u-chi. AVAILABILITY: The first edition (same publisher and title, 1965) was published without the text of the novel. According to the preface for the new edition, the first edition was not very well received. It was from a desire to improve reader receptivity that the text of the novel was included in the reprint. The first edition does not mention Ch'en Tun-fu's name, only his pen name, Cho-tsai 拙哉. A copy of the first edition is held in the Far Eastern Library, University of Chicago. A copy of the second edition is held in the Feng P'ing-shan Library of Hong Kong University.

General Bibliography on Fiction Criticism and the Hsi-yu chi

Dudbridge, Glen. "The Hundred-Chapter *Hsi-yu chi* and Its Early Versions." *Asia Major*, n.s. 14. 2:141–91 (1969).

Koss, Nicholas. "The *Xiyouji* in Its Formative Stages: The Late Ming Editions." Ph.D. thesis, Indiana University, Bloomington, 1981.

Plaks, Andrew H. "Allegory in *Hsi-yu chi* and *Hung-lou meng*." In *Chinese Narrative: Critical and Theoretical Essays*, pp. 163–202.

Cheng Chen-to 鄭振鐸. "*Hsi-yu chi* ti yen-hua" 西遊記的演化. In *Chung-kuo wen-hsüeh yen-chiu* 中國文學研究. Hong Kong: Ku-wen shu-chü, 1972, pp. 263–299.

Chu I-hsüan 朱一玄, and Liu Yü-ch'en 劉毓忱, eds. *Hsi-yu chi tzu-liao hui-pien* 西遊記資料彙編. Cheng-chou: Chung-chou shu-hua she, 1983.

Liu Yin-po 劉陰伯. "*Hsi-yu chi* Ming-Ch'ing liang-tai ch'u-pan shih k'ao" 西遊記明清兩代出版史考. *Hua-tung shih-fan ta-hsüeh hsüeh-pao*, 1983. 3: 76–79.

Ōta Tatsuo 太田辰夫. "*Saiyūki* genryū kō" 西遊記源流考. In *Torii Hisayasu sensei kakō kinen ronbun shū: Chūgoku no gogen to bungaku* 鳥居久靖先生華甲紀念論文集:中国の語言と文学. Tenri-shi: Torii Hisayasu sensei kakōkinen kai, 1972, pp. 225–44.

———. "*Saiyūki no kenkyū* 西遊記の研究. Tokyo: Kenbun, 1984.

———. "Shin kanpon *Saiyūki* kō" 清刊本西遊記考. *Kobe gaidai ronsō* 22.4:1–19 (1971).

Torii Hisayasu 鳥居久靖. "*Tōkyō* shoken *Saiyūki* no shohon ni tsuite" 東京所見西遊記の諸本について. *Chūgoku koten bungaku zenshū geppō* 中国古典文学全集月報. Tokyo: Heibonsha, n.d., 17:1–4; 18:4–6; 19, 4–7.

Hung-lou meng

ABBREVIATED TITLE: Chih-yen chai 脂硯齋 manuscript copies. FULL TITLE: *Chih-yen chai ch'ung-p'ing Shih-t'ou chi* 脂硯齋重評石頭記 (Repeated Commentary on the *Story of the Stone* by Red Inkstone Studio). LENGTH: Extant manuscript copies vary as to how many chapters have survived, but all are based on an 80-chapter version of the novel or have copied the last forty chapters from another source. PUBLISHER: All private manuscript copies. DATE: The dated comments range from 1754 to 1784. PREFATORY MATERIAL: The so-called "Chia-hsü" 甲戌 (1754) copy has a "Fan-li" 凡例 (General Principles). Many of the items in it appear as chapter comments in other copies of the commentary. COMMENTARY: The comments appear in different form in the different extant copies but, taken together, they include prechapter, marginal, double- and single-column interlineal, and postchapter comments. Some are signed and dated and both black and red ink were used to record them. Chih-yen chai is the studio name of the most prominent of the commentators. The second most prominent group of comments is signed Chi-hu sou 畸笏叟. It is a subject of ongoing debate whether Chih-yen chai and Chi-hu sou are pen names of the same person or of two entirely different persons, although the latter opinion is predominant at this time. Various manuscripts also contain comments added later by persons removed from the original group of commentators, such as the later owners of the individual manuscripts. REMARKS: Some of the commentators were close friends of the author and participated in the composition and planning of the novel. AVAILABILITY: The following photo-reprints of various manuscripts are available: (1) "Chia-hsü" copy: *Ch'ien-lung chia-hsü pen Chih-yen chai ch'ung-p'ing Shih-t'ou chi* 乾隆甲戌本脂硯齋重評石頭記 (1754 Copy of the Repeated Commentary on the *Story of the Stone* from Red Inkstone Studio; Taipei: Commercial Press, 1961) and *Chih-yen chai chia-hsü ch'ao-yüeh tsai-p'ing Shih-t'ou chi* 脂硯齋甲戌 抄閱再評石頭記 (1754 Chih-yen chai Copied and Edited Version with Repeated Commentary of the *Story of the Stone*; Shanghai: Shang-hai ku-chi, 1985 reprint), (2) "Keng-ch'en" 庚辰 (1760) copy: *Chih-yen chai ch'ung-p'ing Shih-t'ou chi* (Peking: Wen-hsüeh ku-chi, 1955; Peking: Jen-min wen-hsüeh, 1974 reprint), (3) "Chi-mao" 己卯 (1759) copy: *Chih-yen chai ch'ung-p'ing Shih-t'ou chi* (Shanghai: Shang-hai ku-chi, 1980), (4) "Leningrad" copy: *Shih-t'ou chi* (Peking: Chung-hua shu-chü, 1986) and (5) *Ch'ien-lung ch'ao-pen pai-nien hui Hung-lou meng kao* 乾隆抄本百廿回紅樓夢稿 (The Ch'ien-lung 120-Chapter Manuscript Draft of the *Hung-lou meng*; Shanghai: Shang-hai ku-chi, 1984). The comments from the major extant copies, along with indications where the comments fall in the text of the novel, have been collected by Yü P'ing-po 俞平伯, ed., *Chih-yen chai Hung-lou meng chi-p'ing* 脂硯齋紅樓夢輯評 (Collected Chih-yen chai Comments on the *Hung-lou meng*; Shanghai: Shang-hai wen-i, first edition, 1954; Shanghai: Chung-hua shu-chü, revised edition, 1960) and Ch'en Ch'ing-hao 陳慶浩, ed., *Hsin-pien Shih-t'ou chi Chih-yen chai p'ing-yü chi-chiao* 新編石頭記脂硯齋評語輯校 (Hong Kong: New Asia Institute, first edition, 1972; Taipei: Lien-ching ch'u-pan she, revised edition, 1979; Peking: Yu-i ch'u-pan she, revised edition, 1987). The comments from the major manuscript copies are also available in *HLMTLHP*, pp. 97–515; the same editor has brought out a work titled *Hung-lou meng Chih-p'ing chiao-lu* 紅樓夢脂評校錄 (Collated Record of the Chih-yen chai comments on the *Hung-lou meng*; Tsinan: Ch'i Lu shu-she, 1986). For a transcription of the comments from the lost copy formerly owned by the Ching 靖 family, see the entry below under Mao Kuo-yao 毛國瑤. A complete collated version of all the Chih-yen chai comments and the textual variations in the different copies is planned for publication by Chung-hua shu-chü, Peking.

Chan Hing-ho (Ch'en Ch'ing-hao). *Le Honglou meng et les commentaires de Zhi-yanzhai*. Paris: College de France, 1982.

Liu, David Jason. "The Chih-yen Chai Commentary: An Analysis in the Perspectives of Western Theories of Literature." *Tamkang Review* 10. 4:471–94 (1980).

Wang, John C.Y. (Wang Ching-yü 王靖宇). "The *Chih-yen Chai* Commentary and the *Dream of the Red Chamber*: A Literary Study." In *Chinese Approaches to Literature*. Edited by Adele Rickett. Princeton: Princeton University Press, 1978, pp. 189–220.

Wu Shih-ch'ang. *On the Red Chamber Dream: A Critical Study of Two Annotated Manuscripts of the XVIIIth Century*. Oxford: Clarendon Press, 1961.

Chang Lan 章蘭. "Hu Shih t'an Chia-hsü pen" 胡適談甲戌本. *Hung-lou meng yen-chiu chi-k'an* 4:186 (1980).

Chang Min-ch'eng 張敏成. "Chi-hu sou chi Ts'ao Fu chih ch'u-cheng—fen-hsi i-tse Ching-pen p'i-yü" 畸笏叟即曹頫之初證—分析一則靖本批語. In *Wo tu Hung-lou meng*, pp. 205–10.

Chao Hsüeh-jui 趙學瑞. "Tui Chih-p'i 'so shu shen p'o' ti wo-chien" 對脂批索書甚迫的我見. *Hung-lou meng hsüeh-k'an*, 1980. 4:263–64.

Chao Kang 趙岡. "Chi-mao pen yü Keng-ch'en pen ti kuan-hsi" 己卯本與庚辰本的關係. *Hung-lou meng yen-chiu chi-k'an* 5:143–51 (1980).

———. "Chih-yen chai yü *Hung-lou meng*" 脂硯齋與紅樓夢. *Ta-lu tsa-chih* 20. 2:8–12, 20. 3:23–26, 20. 4:22–30 (1960). Reprinted in *Hai-wai hung-hsüeh lun-chi*, pp. 259–93.

———. "Lun *Ch'ien-lung ch'ao-pen pai-nien hui Hung-lou meng kao*" 論乾隆抄本百廿回紅樓夢稿. *Ta-lu tsa-chih* 28. 6:8–14 (1964). Reprinted in *Hai-wai Hung-hsüeh lun-chi*, pp. 361–76.

———. "P'ing Ch'en Ch'ing-hao chuan *Hsin-pien Hung-lou meng Chih-yen chai p'ing-yü chi-chiao*" 評陳慶浩撰新編紅樓夢脂硯齋評語輯校. *Ta-lu tsa-chih* 45. 3:54–57 (1972).

———. "T'an *Chia-hsü Chih-yen chai ch'ung-p'ing Shih-t'ou chi*" 談甲戌脂硯齋重評石頭記. *Tso-p'in* (Taipei) 2. 10:53–58 (1961).

———. "Ts'ung Ching Ying-k'un ts'ang ch'ao-pen *Hung-lou meng* t'an Hung-hsüeh k'ao-cheng ti hsin wen-t'i" 從靖應鵾藏抄本紅樓夢談紅學考證的新問題. *Ming-pao yüeh-k'an* 3. 2:2–7 (1968). Reprinted in *Hai-wai Hung-hsüeh lun-chi*, pp. 434–47.

Chao Ning 趙寧. "Shih 'Feng-chieh tien-hsi, Chih-yen chih-pi'" 釋鳳姐點戲脂硯執筆. *Hung-lou meng hsüeh-k'an*, 1980. 3:267–94.

Chao Wei-pang 趙衛邦. "*Hung-lou meng* san-ko chu-yao Chih-pen ti kuan-hsi" 紅樓夢三個主要脂本的關係. *Hung-lou meng hsüeh-k'an*, 1980. 3:267–94.

———. "Ts'ung Chih-yen chai liang-t'iao p'ing-yü k'an *Hung-lou meng* ti hsia pan-pu" 從脂硯齋兩條評語看紅樓夢的下半部. *Hung-lou meng yen-chiu chi-k'an* 3:303–12 (1980). Reprinted in *Hung-hsüeh san-shih nien lun-wen hsüan-pien*, vol. 3, pp. 388–99.

Ch'en Chao 陳詔. "Chien-se fa" 間色法. *I-shu shih-chieh* 藝術世界, 1982. 5:32 (*Hung-lou meng yen-chiu* reprint, 1982. 12:27).

Ch'en Ch'ing-hao 陳慶浩. "Ching-ta Chao Kang hsien-sheng p'ing *Hsin-pien Hung-lou meng Chih-yen chai p'ing-yü chi-chiao*" 敬答趙岡先生評新編紅樓夢脂硯齋評語輯校. *Hung-lou meng yen-chiu chuan-k'an* 10:71–91 (1973).

———. "*Hsin-pien Shih-t'ou chi Chih-yen chai p'ing-yü chi-chiao* tseng-ting pen tao-yen" 新編石頭記脂硯齋評語輯校增訂本導言. *Chung-wai wen-hsüeh* 14. 8:4–52 (pt. 1); 14. 9:4–52 (pt. 2; 1986).

———. "*Hung-lou meng* Chih-p'ing chih yen-chiu" 紅樓夢脂評之研究. *Hung-lou meng yen-chiu chuan-k'an* 5:1–74 (pt. 1); 6:24–66 (pt. 2; 1969).

———. "Lieh-ts'ang pen *Shih-t'ou chi* ch'u-t'an" 列藏本石頭記初探. *Chung-*

kuo ku-tien hsiao-shuo yen-chiu chuan-chi 1 : 157–214 (1979).

Ch'en Chung-ch'ih 陳仲笘. "T'an 'Chi-mao pen' *Chih-yen chai ch'ung-p'ing Shih-t'ou chi*" 談己卯本脂硯齋重評石頭記. *Wen-wu*, 1963. 3. Reprinted in *Hung-lou meng yen-chiu tzu-liao*, pp. 111–31 and in *Hung-hsüeh san-shih nien lun-wen hsüan-pien*, vol. 3, pp. 11–30.

Ch'en Hsi-chung 陳曦鐘. "Shuo 'chen yu shih-shih'—tu Chih-p'i sui-cha" 說真有是事—讀脂批隨札. *Pei-ching ta-hsüeh hsüeh-pao*, 1980. 5 : 85–86. Reprinted in *Hung-lou meng tzu-liao chi*, vol. 3, pp. 324–25 and in *Hung-hsüeh san-shih nien lun-wen hsüan-pien*, vol. 3, pp. 384–87.

Ch'en Hung 陳洪. "*Hung-lou meng* Chih-p'ing chung 'hu-lun yü' shuo ti li-lun i-i" 紅樓夢脂評中囫圇語說的理論意義. *T'ien-chin she-hui k'o-hsüeh*, 1984. 2 : 91–95, 69 (*Hung-lou meng yen-chiu* reprint, 1984. 3 : 123–28).

Ch'en Pao-ch'eng 陳包成. "T'an 'Chih-p'ing' ti Pao-yü kuan" 談脂評的寶玉觀. *Cheng-chou ta-hsüeh hsüeh-pao*, 1980. 1 : 78–83, 96.

Ch'en Po-liao 陳伯遼. "Tu *Ch'ien-lung chia-hsü Chih-yen chai ch'ung-p'ing Shih-t'ou chi* hou-chi" 讀乾隆甲戌脂硯齋重評石頭記後記. *Ch'ang-liu* 54. 1 : 22–27 (pt. 1); 54. 2 : 24–28 (pt. 2, 1976).

Chi Chih-yüeh 季稚躍. "*Chih-yen chai ch'ung-p'ing Shih-t'ou chi* (I-fu kuo-lu chi-mao pen) shang pu-fen chu-pi t'ien-kai wen-tzu shu Wu Yü-an k'ao" 脂硯齋重評石頭記 (怡府過錄己卯本) 上部分朱筆添改文字屬武裕庵考. *Hung-lou meng hsüeh-k'an*, 1983. 1 : 271–77.

Chiang Keng-yü 姜耕玉. "Ts'ao-she hui-hsien, k'ung-ku ch'uan-sheng" 草蛇灰線空谷傳聲. *Hung-lou meng hsüeh-k'an*, 1983. 3 : 99–121.

Chiang Wei-lu 蔣蔚廬. "Tui Chih-p'i *Shih-t'ou chi* t'i-pa, yin-chang chung jen-wu shih-chi ti hsin t'an-so" 對脂批石頭記題跋印章中人物事迹的新探索. *Hung-lou meng hsüeh-k'an*, 1982. 3 : 241–53.

Chiang Wei-t'an 蔣維錟. "Chih-yen chai tsu-nien yü *Shih-t'ou chi* ssu-p'ing" 脂硯齋卒年與石頭記四評. *Fu-chien shih-ta hsüeh-pao*, 1983. 2 : 66–69 (*Hung-lou meng yen-chiu* reprint, 1983. 11 : 72–75).

———. "Kuan-yü *Shih-t'ou chi* Lieh-ning ts'ang-pen ti nien-tai wen-t'i" 關於石頭記列寧藏本的年代問題. *Hung-lou meng hsüeh-k'an*, 1986. 3 : 263–78.

Chin Ming 金明. "Chih-p'ing wei shen-ma pei shan-ch'u" 脂評為甚麼被刪除. *Hung-lou meng yen-chiu chi-k'an* 4 : 328 (1980).

Chin Yang 金陽. "Ju-ho li-chieh 'chieh hsing-ch'in shih hsieh nan-hsün'" 如何理解借省親事寫南巡. *Hung-lou meng yen-chiu chi-k'an* 6 : 238 (1981).

Ching K'uan-jung 靖寬榮, and Wang Hui-p'ing 王惠萍. "'Ching-pen' so-i chi ch'i t'a" 靖本瑣憶及其他. *Wen-chiao tzu-liao chien-pao*, 1980. 8 : 14–22. Reprinted in *Hung-lou meng yen-chiu chi-k'an* 12 : 293–301 (1985).

Chou Chün-t'ao 周鈞韜. "Lun Chih-yen chai ti mei-ch'ou kuan" 論脂硯齋的美醜觀. *Ming-Ch'ing hsiao-shuo yen-chiu* 2 : 384–400 (1985).

Chou Hu-ch'ang 周祜昌. "Chih-yen hsien-sheng hen chi-to" 脂硯先生恨幾多. *Wen-hsien* 20 : 66–68 (1984).

———. "Meng-chüeh chu-jen hsü pen *Hung-lou meng* ti t'e-tien" 夢覺主人序本紅樓夢的特點. *Kuang-ming jih-pao*, 3/17/1963. Reprinted in *Hung-hsüeh san-shih nien lun-wen hsüan-pien*, vol. 3, pp. 181–93.

Chou Ju-ch'ang 周汝昌. "Chih-yen chai p'i" 脂硯齋批. In *Hung-lou meng hsin-*

cheng, pp. 833–940.

———. "Ching-pen ch'uan-wen lu" 靖本傳聞錄. In *Hung-lou meng hsin-cheng*, pp. 1050–66.

———. "Kuan-yü Chih-yen chai" 關於脂硯齋. *Wen-hui pao*, 8/28–29/1950.

———. "Meng-chüeh chu-jen hsü pen" 夢覺主人序本. In *Hung-lou meng hsin-cheng*, pp. 1024–36.

———. "Yang-chou Ching-shih ts'ang ch'ao-pen *Shih-t'ou chi* ti kai-k'uang" 揚州靖氏藏抄本石頭記的概況. In *Hung-lou meng yen-chiu tzu-liao*, pp. 251–63.

Chou Ju-ch'ang, and Chou Hu-ch'ang 周祜昌. *Shih-t'ou chi chien-chen* 石頭記鑒真. Peking: Shu-mu wen-hsien, 1985.

Chou Lin-sheng 周林生. "Tu *Shih-t'ou chi* Chih-p'i piao-tien i-te" 讀石頭記脂批標點一得. *Hsüeh-shu yen-chiu*, 1980. 5:81. Reprinted in *Hung-lou meng tzu-liao chi*, vol. 3, p. 297.

Chou Shao-liang 周紹良. "Tu *Chia-hsü pen Chih-yen chai ch'ung-p'ing Shih-t'ou chi* san-chi" 讀甲戌本脂硯齋重評石頭記散記. *Hung-lou meng yen-chiu chi-k'an* 3:225–33 (1980). Also in *Hung-lou meng pan-pen lun-ts'ung*, pp. 169–78.

Chou Ts'e-tsung 周策縱. "*Hung-lou meng* 'Fan-li' pu-i yü shih-i" 紅樓夢凡例補佚與釋疑. *Hung-lou meng hsüeh-k'an*, 1981. 1:246–58.

Chu Feng-yü 朱鳳玉. "*Hung-lou meng* Chih-yen chai p'ing-yü hsin-t'an" 紅樓夢脂硯齋評語新探. Master's thesis, Chinese Cultural Academy, Taipei, 1979.

Chu Nan-hsien 朱南銑. "Kuan-yü Chih-yen chai ti chen hsing-ming" 關於脂硯齋的真姓名. *Kuang-ming jih-pao*, 5/10/1962. Reprinted in *Hung-hsüeh san-shih nien lun-wen hsüan-pien*, vol. 3, pp. 238–41.

Feng Ch'i-yung 馮其庸. "Kuan-yü Chi-mao pen ti ying-yin wen-t'i chi ch'i t'a" 關於己卯本的影印問題及其他. *She-hui k'o-hsüeh chan-hsien*, 1981. 3:291–300. Reprinted in his *Meng-pien chi*, pp. 298–314.

———. "Lieh-ning-ko-le ts'ang ch'ao-pen *Shih-t'ou thi* yin-hsiang" 列寧格勒藏抄本石頭記印象. *Hung-lou meng hsüeh-k'an*, 1985. 3:5–19.

———. "Lun *Chih-yen chai ch'ung-p'ing Shih-t'ou chi* Chia-hsü pen 'Fan-li'" 論脂硯齋重評石頭記甲戌本凡例. *Hung-lou meng hsüeh-k'an*, 1980. 4:175–207. Reprinted in his *Meng-pien chi*, pp. 323–56.

———. *Lun Keng-ch'en pen* 論庚辰本. Shanghai: Shang-hai wen-i, 1978.

———. "Ying-yin *Chih-yen chai ch'ung-p'ing Shih-t'ou chi* chia-hsü pen shang pei Hu Shih shan-ch'ü ti chi-t'iao pa-wen" 影印脂硯齋重評石頭記甲戌本上被胡適刪去的幾條跋文. *Hung-lou meng hsüeh-k'an*, 1982. 3:344–46.

Feng Kuang-li 馮廣隸. "*Hung-lou meng* ti 'Fan-li' shih Ts'ao Hsüeh-ch'in hsieh ti" 紅樓夢的凡例是曹雪芹寫的. *Nan-k'ai ta-hsüeh hsüeh-pao*, 1976. 4:60–66.

Han Lien-ch'i 韓連琪. "Kuan-yü *Hung-lou meng* Chih-yen chai p'ing ti tso-che wen-t'i" 關於紅樓夢脂硯齋評的作者問題. In *Hung-lou meng yen-chiu lun-ts'ung*, pp. 259–77.

Hao Yen-lin 郝延霖. "Chih-p'ing 'tzu-chuan shuo' k'ao" 脂評自傳說考. *Hsüeh-shu yüeh-k'an*, 1982. 3:52–54.

———. "Chih-yen chai k'ao-pien" 脂硯齋考辨. *Hsin-chiang ta-hsüeh hsüeh-pao*, 1978. 1:37–47.

———. "Lun *Chih-p'ing* p'ing *Shih-t'ou chi* jen-wu hsing-hsiang ti su-tsao"

論脂評評石頭記人物形象的塑造. *Hung-lou meng hsüeh-k'an*, 1986. 1: 79–110.

———. "Lun Chih-p'ing p'ing *Shih-t'ou chi* ti hsing-wen pu-chü" 論脂評評 石頭記的行文布局. *Hung-lou meng hsüeh-k'an*, 1983. 4:260–93.

———. "Mo-lo kuei-tsu ti che-hsüeh—lun *Shih-t'ou chi* Chih-yen chai p'ing" 沒落貴族的哲學—論石頭記脂硯齋評. *Hsin-chiang ta-hsüeh hsüeh-pao*, 1979. 1–2:14–22.

———. "Tu-ch'uang ti i-shu fen-hsi—lun *Shih-t'ou chi* Chih-yen chai p'ing" 獨創的藝術分析—論石頭記脂硯齋評. *Hung-lou meng hsüeh-k'an*, 1981. 1:207–41. Reprinted in *Hung-hsüeh san-shih nien lun-wen hsüan-pien*, vol. 3, pp. 349–83.

Hsi-chung 曦鐘 (Ch'en Hsi-chung). "'Chin-ku wei yu chih i-jen'—Chih-yen chai lun Chia Pao-yü" 今古未有之一人—脂硯齋論賈寶玉. *Hung-lou meng yen-chiu chi-k'an*, 1980. 4:39–45.

———. "Shuo 'Yü i wang-ch'üeh'—tu Chih-p'i sui-cha" 說余已忘却—讀脂 批隨札. *Ch'iu-shih hsüeh-k'an*, 1981. 3:87–88. Reprinted in *Hung-lou meng tzu-liao chi*, vol. 4, pp. 363–64.

Hsü Chi-wen 徐繼文. "Chih-yen chai nai Chi-hu sou" 脂硯齋乃畸笏叟. *Kuang-chou shih-yüan hsüeh-pao* 廣州師院學報, 1987. 1:27–37 (*Hung-lou meng yen-chiu* reprint, 1987. 2:70–80).

Hsü Ch'ih 徐遲. "Ju-ho tui-tai Chih-yen chai" 如何對待脂硯齋. *Hua-ch'eng*, 1979. 2:236–39. Reprinted in *Hung-lou meng tzu-liao chi*, vol. 2, pp. 501–4 and in his *Hung-lou meng i-shu lun* 紅樓夢藝術論 (Shanghai: Shang-hai wen-i, 1980), pp. 131–37.

Hsü Kung-shih 徐恭時. "Chih-pen p'ing-che tzu-liao chi-lu" 脂本評者資料 輯錄. In *Hung-lou meng pan-pen lun-ts'ung*, pp. 200–220.

Hu Shih 胡適. "Pa Ch'ien-lung keng-ch'en pen *Chih-yen chai ch'ung-p'ing Shih-t'ou chi*" 跋乾隆庚辰本脂硯齋重評石頭記. *Hu Shih wen-ts'un* 胡適文存. Taipei: Yüan-tung, 1974, vol. 4, pp. 396–411. Reprinted in *Hu Shih*, pp. 118–27.

Hu Wen-pin 胡文彬. "*Hung-lou meng* Chih-p'i chung 'I hua i shih ju yu i' ti ch'u-ch'u" 紅樓夢脂批中一花一石如有意的出處. *Hsüeh-hsi yü ssu-k'ao* 學習與 思考, 1981. 6:54.

———. *Lieh-ts'ang pen Shih-t'ou chi kuan-k'uei* 列藏本石頭記管窺. Shanghai: Shang-hai ku-chi, 1987.

Huang Cheng 黃爭. "'Chi-mao pen shih Keng-ch'en pen ti ti-pen' pien-cheng" 己卯本是庚辰本的底本辨證. *Hung-lou meng hsüeh-k'an*, 1983. 3:289–96.

Huang Hsiao-yün 黃笑雲. "Chih-yen chi" 脂硯記. *Hung-lou meng yen-chiu chi-k'an* 1:261–62 (1979).

Huang Yeh 黃葉. "Shu Yüan-wei hsü pen *Hung-lou meng* hsiao-cha" 舒元煒 序本紅樓夢小札. *Hung-lou meng yen-chiu chi-k'an* 5:208 (1980).

Hung Tou 紅豆. "Yang Chi-chen ts'ang-pen *Hung-lou meng* erh, san shih" 楊繼振藏本紅樓夢二三事. *Hung-lou meng yen-chiu chi-k'an*, 1980. 5:240.

I-su 一粟 (Chou Shao-liang 周紹良 and Chu Nan-hsien 朱南銑). "Kuan-yü 'Sung-chai'—chien-t'an k'ao-cheng ti fang-fa yü mu-ti" 關於宋齋—兼談 考證的方法與目的. *Wen-hui pao*, 6/2/1962.

Itō Sōhei 伊藤漱平. "Kinnen hakken no Kōrōmu kenkyū shin shiryō—Nankin Seishi shozō kyū shōhon sonota ni tsuite" 近年発現の紅樓夢研究新資料—南京靖氏所藏旧抄本その他について. *Daian* 大安 12. 1 (1966).

———. "Shiken sai to Shiken sai hyōpon ni kan suru oboegaki" 脂硯斎と脂硯斎評本に関する覚書. *Jinbun kenkyū* 人文研究 12. 9:56–71 (1961); 13. 8:33–55 (1962); 14. 7:72–89 (1963); 15. 6:39–60 (1964); 17. 4:50–88 (1966).

Kan Chao-tuan 干朝端. "Chih-p'ing ti wen-i p'i-p'ing ssu-hsiang" 脂評的文藝批評思想. *Wu-han shih-yüan Han-k'ou fen-pu hsiao-k'an*, 1981. 1:48–53.

———. "Ying-kai ju-ho p'ing-chia Chih-yen chai" 應該如何評價脂硯齋. *Hung-lou meng hsüeh-k'an*, 1981. 4:157–62.

Kung P'eng-ch'eng 龔鵬程. "Ching-pen Chih-p'ing *Shih-t'ou chi* pien-wei lu" 靖本脂評石頭記辨偽錄. *Ch'eng-kung ta-hsüeh hsüeh-pao* 成功大學學報 17:15–26 (1982).

Kuo Yü-shih 郭豫適. "Kuan-yü 'Chih-p'ing' wen-t'i—lun ch'üan-p'an p'i-tao 'Chih-yen chai p'ing' chih pu-tang" 關於脂評問題—論全盤批倒脂硯齋評之不當. *Hua-tung shih-fan ta-hsüeh hsüeh-pao*, 1983. 6:32–39 (*Hung-lou meng yen-chiu* reprint, 1984. 1:113–21).

Li Hsi-fan 李希凡, and Lan Ling 藍翎. "Cheng-ch'üeh ku-chia *Hung-lou meng* chung 'Chih-yen chai p'ing' ti i-i" 正確估價紅樓夢中脂硯齋評的意義. *Jen-min jih-pao*, 1/20/1955.

Li Hsin 李昕. "Kuan-yü 'Keng-ch'en pen' ti ssu-shih hui i-t'iao Chih-p'i ti 'lai-yüan' ho li-chieh ti ch'ien-chien" 關於庚辰本的四十回一條脂批的來源和理解的淺見. *Hung-lou meng hsüeh-k'an*, 1981. 1:84–87.

Li Meng-sheng 李夢生. "Lun Chia-hsü pen 'Fan-li' ti tso-che chi hsieh-tso nien-tai" 論甲戌本凡例的作者及寫作年代. *Hung-lou meng yen-chiu chi-k'an* 10:373–93 (1983).

Li Pai-ch'un 李百春. "Chih-p'i pu k'o i-tu—t'ung 'Chih-p'i ho *Hung-lou meng* tso-che chih mi' ts'un-i" 脂批不可臆度—同脂批和紅樓夢作者之謎存疑. *Mu-tan chiang shih-yüan hsüeh-pao* 牡丹江師院學報, 1984. 2:58–63 (*Hung-lou meng yen-chiu* reprint, 1984. 4:116–22).

———. "Mo-chiang lao-seng k'an chiao-niang—yeh lun Chih-yen chai ch'i-jen" 莫將老僧看嬌娘—也論脂硯齋其人. *Ta-ch'ing shih-chuan hsüeh-pao* 大慶師專學報, 1984. 1:68–76.

Li Shao-ch'ing 李少青. "'Keng-ch'en pen' shih chü 'Chi-mao pen' kuo-lu ti ma?" 庚辰本是據已卯本過錄的嗎. In *Hung-lou meng yen-chiu lun-ts'ung*, pp. 244–59.

Li T'ung 李彤, and Liang Tso 梁左. "Chih-yen hsien-sheng hen chi-to" 脂硯先生恨幾多. *Hua-ch'eng*, 1980. 5:259–63.

Liang Tso 梁左, and Li T'ung 李彤. "'Ching-huan ch'ing-pang' tseng-shan pien—ts'ung Keng-ch'en pen ti liang-t'iao Chih-p'ing t'an-ch'i" 驚幻情榜增刪辨—從庚辰本的兩條脂評談起. *Hung-lou meng yen-chiu chi-k'an* 9: 295–310 (1982).

Lin Hsing-jen 林興仁. "Yü pu-t'ung, yü miao; yü ts'o hui-i, yü ch'i—ts'ung *Hung-lou meng* Chih-p'ing lun 'ssu pu-t'ung' hsiu-tz'u fang-shih ti ch'eng-li" 愈不通愈妙愈錯會意愈奇—從紅樓夢脂評論四不通修辭方式的成立. In

Hsiu-tz'u hsüeh lun-wen chi 修辭學論文集. Fu-chou: Fu-chien jen-min, 1984, pp. 409–22. Also in his *Hung-lou meng ti hsiu-tz'u i-shu*, pp. 206–23.

Liu Kuang-ting 劉廣定. "Chih-yen chai fei Ts'ao Yung i-fu-tzu k'ao" 脂硯齋非曹顒遺腹子考. *Lien-ho pao*, 4/28/1977. Reprinted in *T'ai-wan Hung-hsüeh lun-wen hsüan*, pp. 592–97.

Liu Meng-hsi 劉夢溪. "Lun Chih Ch'üan-pen *Shih-t'ou chi* ti 'Fan-li'" 論脂銓本石頭記的凡例. *Nan-k'ai ta-hsüeh hsüeh-pao*, 1977. 2:69–74. Reprinted in his *Hung-lou meng hsin-lun*, pp. 248–67.

———. "Lun *Hung-lou meng* tsao-ch'i ch'ao-pen ti hui-ch'ien shih ho hui-mo shih tui" 論紅樓夢早期抄本的回前詩和回末詩對. *Chung-hua wen-shih lun-ts'ung*, 1981. 3:31–60. Reprinted in his *Hung-lou meng hsin-lun*, pp. 200–247.

Liu Ts'un-jen 柳存仁. "Kuan-yü Su-lien ts'ang pa-shih hui ch'ao-pen *Hung-lou meng*" 關於蘇聯藏八十回抄本紅樓夢. *Hung-lou meng yen-chiu chuan-k'an* 10:1–52 (1973). Reprinted in *Hai-wai Hung-hsüeh lun-chi*, pp. 377–92.

Lu Hsing-chi 盧興基. "*Hung-lou meng* Chia-hsü pen 'Fan-li' hsi-cheng" 紅樓夢甲戌本凡例析證. *Hung-lou meng yen-chiu chi-k'an* 7:283–99 (1981).

Ma Li 馬力. "Kuan-yü Keng-ch'en pen *Shih-t'ou chi* ti ssu-shih erh hui hui-ch'ien ti i-t'iao Chih-p'ing" 關於庚辰本石頭記的四十二回回前的一條脂評. *Hung-lou meng hsüeh-k'an*, 1983. 3:273–88.

Mao Kuo-yao 毛國瑤. "Ching Ying-k'un ts'ang-pen *Hung-lou meng* fa-hsien ti ching-kuo—chien lun Ching-pen p'i-yü ti t'e-tien ho chung-yao hsing" 靖應鵾藏本紅樓夢發現的經過—兼論靖本批語的特點和重要性. *Hung-lou meng yen-chiu chi-k'an* 12:267–77 (1985).

———. "Tui Ching-ts'ang pen 'p'i-yü' ti chi-tien k'an-fa" 對靖藏本批語的幾點看法. *Wen-chiao tzu-liao chien-pao*, 1974. 8–9. Reprinted in *Hung-lou meng pan-pen lun-ts'ung*, pp. 318–28.

———, ed. "*Hung-lou meng* Ching-pen (Chih Ning-pen) p'i-yü" 紅樓夢靖本(脂寧本)批語. *Wen-chiao tzu-liao chien-pao*, 1974. 8–9. Reprinted in *Hung-lou meng yen-chiu tzu-liao*, pp. 291–313; *Hung-lou meng yen-chiu chi-k'an* 12:279–91 (1985); and *Hung-lou meng pan-pen lun-ts'ung*, pp. 301–17.

Mei Chieh 梅節 (Mei T'ing-hsiu 梅挺秀). "Lun Chi-mao pen *Shih-t'ou chi*" 論己卯本石頭記. *Chung-pao yüeh-k'an* 中報月刊 17:84–90; 18:82–88 (1981).

Mei T'ing-hsiu 梅挺秀. "Hsi 'Feng-chieh tien-hsi, Chih-yen chih-pi'" 析鳳姐點戲脂硯執筆. *Hung-lou meng hsüeh-k'an*, 1984. 4:229–40.

Menshikov, N.L., and Riftin, B.L. "Ch'ang-p'ien hsiao-shuo *Hung-lou meng* ti wu-ming ch'ao-pen" 長篇小說紅樓夢的無名抄本. Translated by Sung Ya 松厓. In *Hung-hsüeh shih-chieh*, pp. 244–60. Reprinted in *Hung-lou meng hsüeh-k'an*, 1986. 3:7–25. From the original in *Narody Azii I Afriki* 5:121–28 (1964).

Na Tsung-hsün 那宗訓. "Lun Chih-p'i (ch'u-kao)" 論脂批(初稿). In *Hung-lou meng t'an-so*, pp. 123–60.

———. "T'an Chia-hsü pen *Hung-lou meng*" 談甲戌本紅樓夢. *Ta-lu tsa-chih* 60. 3:33–39 (1980). Reprinted in *Hung-lou meng t'an-so*, pp. 35–46.

———. "T'an so-wei Ching-ts'ang pen *Shih-t'ou chi* ts'an-p'i" 談所謂靖藏本

石頭記殘批. *Ta-lu tsa-chih* 58. 5:43–45 (1979). Reprinted in *Hai-wai Hung-hsüeh lun-chi*, pp. 448–54 and in his *Hung-lou meng t'an-so*, pp. 161–68.

P'an Chung-kuei 潘重規. "Chia-hsü pen *Shih-t'ou chi* ho-lun" 甲戌本石頭記覈論. *Hsin-ya shu-yüan hsüeh-shu nien-k'an* 新亞書院學術年刊 14:171–205 (1972). Reprinted in *T'ai-wan Hung-hsüeh lun-wen hsüan*, pp. 398–434.

———. "*Hung-lou meng* Chih-p'ing chung ti chu-shih" 紅樓夢脂評中的注釋. *Chung-yang jih-pao*, 8/1/1974, p. 10.

———. "*Hung-lou meng* chiu ch'ao-pen chih-chien shu-lüeh" 紅樓夢舊抄本知見述略. *Shu-mu chi-k'an* 10. 1:17–32 (1976).

———. "*Hung-lou meng* ti 'Fan-li' " 紅樓夢的凡例. *Ch'ang-liu* 19. 1:2–4 (1959).

———. "Lieh-ning-ko-le ts'ang ch'ao-pen *Hung-lou meng* chung ti shuang-hang p'i" 列寧格勒藏抄本紅樓夢中的雙行批. *Hung-lou meng yen-chiu chuan-k'an* 12:66–72 (1976). Reprinted in *T'ai-wan Hung-hsüeh lun-wen hsüan*, pp. 709–16.

———. "Lieh-ning ko-le ts'ang ch'ao-pen *Hung-lou meng* k'ao-so" 列寧格勒藏抄本紅樓夢考索. *Ming-pao yüeh-k'an*, 1985. 3–5. Reprinted in *Hung-hsüeh shih-chieh*, pp. 261–96.

———. "Lun Lieh-ning-ko-le ts'ang pen *Hung-lou meng* ti p'i-yü" 論列寧格勒藏本紅樓夢的批語. *Chung-hua yüeh-pao* 中華月報 700:15–21 (1974). Reprinted in *T'ai-wan Hung-hsüeh lun-wen hsüan*, pp. 693–708.

———. "T'an *Ch'ien-lung ch'ao-pen pai nien hui Hung-lou meng kao*" 談乾隆抄本百廿回紅樓夢稿. *Ta-lu tsa-chih* 30. 2:1–11 (1965). Reprinted in *T'ai-wan Hung-hsüeh lun-wen hsüan*, pp. 446–63.

———. "Tu Lieh-ning-ko-le *Hung-lou meng* ch'ao-pen chi" 讀列寧格勒紅樓夢抄本記. *Ming-pao yüeh-k'an* 8. 11:38–46 (1973). Reprinted in *T'ai-wan Hung-hsüeh lun-wen hsüan*, pp. 479–99 and *Hung-lou meng pan-pen lun-ts'ung*, pp. 329–51.

P'an Ming-shen 潘銘燊 (Poon Ming-sun). "Chih-yen chai lun fu-pi" 脂硯齋論伏筆. Paper presented at the 1986 International *Hung-lou meng* Conference, Harbin, China.

P'an Shen 潘慎 et al. "*Chih-yen chai ch'ung-p'ing Shih-t'ou chi*—ch'üan-kai p'ang-kai yü-yen i-shu chü-yü" 脂硯齋重評石頭記—圈改旁改語言藝術舉隅. *Hsiu-tz'u hsüeh-hsi* 修辭學習, 1985. 1:59–60.

P'ang Ying 龐英. "Kuan-yü Su-lien k'o-hsüeh yüan tung-fang yen-chiu so Lieh-ning-ko-le fen-pu so-ts'ang *Hung-lou meng* kao" 關於蘇聯科學院東方研究所列寧格勒分部所藏紅樓夢稿. Translated by Wang Ch'ang-kung 王長恭. *Wen-chiao tzu-liao chien-pao*, 1982. 3–4:22–27.

Pao Tao 鮑蹈. "Chia-hsü pen shih i-ko chiao ch'ih ti pan-pen—chieh-shao Na Tsung-hsün ti k'an-fa" 甲戌本是一個較遲的版本—介紹那宗訓的看法. *Hung-lou meng yen-chiu chi-k'an* 7:86, 85 (1981).

P'i Shu-min 皮述民. "Chih-yen chai yü *Hung-lou meng* ti kuan-hsi" 脂硯齋與紅樓夢的關係. *Nan-yang ta-hsüeh hsüeh-pao* 7:37–43 (1973). Reprinted in *Hai-wai Hung-hsüeh lun-chi*, pp. 294–307 and in *Hung-lou meng k'ao-lun chi*, pp. 31–50.

———. "Pu-lun Chi-hu sou chi Ts'ao Fu shuo" 補論畸笏叟即曹頫說. *Nan-yang ta-hsüeh hsüeh-pao* 8–9:56–65 (1974–75). Reprinted in *Hai-wai Hung-hsüeh lun-chi*, pp. 308–24 and in *Hung-lou meng k'ao-lun chi*, pp. 71–94.

Shang Yu-p'ing 尚友萍. "Chi-hu p'i-yü 'chi san ssu fu' ti ssu-tzu shih yen-wen" 畸笏批語及三四副的四字是衍文. *Hung-lou meng hsüeh-k'an*, 1983. 3: 334–35.

Shih Hsin-sheng 石昕生, and Mao Kuo-yao 毛國瑤. "Ts'ao Hsüeh-ch'in, Chih-yen chai ho Fu-ch'a shih ti kuan-hsi" 曹雪芹脂硯齋和富察氏的關係. *Jen-wen tsa-chih*, 1982. 1:84–85 (*Hung-lou meng yen-chiu* reprint, 1982. 5:29–30). Reprint in *Hung-lou meng tzu-liao chi*, vol. 5, pp. 64–65.

Shih Yen 石燕. "P'an Chung-kuei chiao-ting cheng-li *Hung-lou meng kao*" 潘重規校定整理紅樓夢稿. *Hung-lou meng hsüeh-k'an*, 1982. 1:239–40.

Sun Hsün 孫遜. "Chih-p'ing so she-chi ti shih-chien kai-lun chi chia-chih" 脂評所涉及的時間概論及價值. *Shang-hai shih-fan hsüeh-yüan hsüeh-pao*, 1983. 1:73–77 (*Hung-lou meng yen-chiu* reprint, 1983. 3:73–77). Reprinted in *Ming-Ch'ing hsiao-shuo lun-kao*, pp. 300–308.

———. "'Chih-p'ing' ssu-hsiang i-shu chia-chih ch'ien-t'an" 脂評思想藝術價值淺談. *Hung-lou meng hsüeh-k'an*, 1980. 2:243–59. Reprinted in *Hung-lou meng yü Chin P'ing Mei*, pp. 227–46 and in *Hung-hsüeh san-shih nien lun-wen hsüan-pien*, pp. 332–48.

———. *Hung-lou meng Chih-p'ing ch'u-t'an* 紅樓夢脂評初探. Shanghai: Shang-hai ku-chi, 1981.

———. "Ts'ung Chih-p'ing k'an Hu Shih wei-hsin lun ti miu-wu" 從脂評看胡適唯心論的謬悞. In *Hung-lou meng yü Chin P'ing Mei*, pp. 247–65.

Tai Pu-fan 戴不凡. "Chi-hu sou chi Ts'ao Fu pien" 畸笏叟即曹頫辨. *Hung-lou meng yen-chiu chi-k'an* 1:223–59 (1979). Reprinted in *Hung-hsüeh san-shih nien lun-wen hsüan-pien*, pp. 290–331.

———. "Chih-p'i chung ti nü-hsing shih 'She-yüeh'" 脂批中的女性是麝月. *Hung-lou meng yen-chiu chi-k'an* 3:287–302 (1980).

———. "Shuo Chih-yen chai—Chih-p'i k'ao chih erh" 說脂硯齋—脂批考之二. *Hung-lou meng yen-chiu chi-k'an* 2:253–74 (1980). Reprinted in *Hung-hsüeh san-shih nien lun-wen hsüan-pien*, pp. 242–268.

T'ang Mao-sung 唐茂松. "Kuan-yü Chih Ching-pen *Hung-lou meng* p'i-yü ti chiao-cheng" 關於脂靖本紅樓夢批語的校正. *Wen-chiao tzu-liao chien-pao*, 1985. 1:129.

Teng Sui-fu 鄧遂夫. "Chih-p'i chiu-shih t'ieh-cheng—kuan-yü *Hung-lou meng* tso-che wen-t'i yü Tai Pu-fan t'ung-chih shang-ch'üeh" 脂批就是鐵證—關於紅樓夢作者問題與戴不凡同志商権. *Hung-lou meng hsüeh-k'an*, 1979. 2:209–35.

———. "*Hung-lou meng* kao-pen ti ch'ao-lu che pu-shih Chih-yen chai" 紅樓夢稿本的抄錄者不是脂硯齋. *Hung-lou meng hsüeh-k'an*, 1983. 4:294–318.

———. "Lun Chia-hsü pen 'Fan-li' yü *Hung-lou meng* shu-ming" 論甲戌本凡例與紅樓夢書名. *Hung-lou meng hsüeh-k'an*, 1986. 3:239–62.

———. "'Ssu-tzu' pien-wu—tu Chih-p'i hsiao-cha" 四字辨悞—讀脂批小札. *Hung-lou meng yen-chiu chi-k'an* 11:99–102 (1983).

Ting Kuang-hui 丁廣惠. "*Hung-lou meng* Chih-p'ing tso-che pien, ch'ien-p'ien" 紅樓夢脂評作者辨前篇. *Hsüeh-shu chiao-liu* 學術交流, 1987. 1:87–101.

Ts'ai I-chiang 蔡一江. "Chih-p'ing shuo Ts'ao Hsüeh-ch'in" 脂評說曹雪芹. *Wen-i pao*, 1979. 2:104–9. Reprinted in *Hung-lou meng tzu-liao chi*, vol. 2, pp. 458–63.

Tseng Yang-hua 曾揚華. "Lun 'Chih-p'i' ti chu-yao kung-hsien" 論脂批的主要貢獻. In *Chung-kuo ku-tai hsiao-shuo li-lun yen-chiu*, pp. 294–305.

Wan Pin-pin 萬彬彬. "'Fu-hsien' ti hsü-shu chi-ch'iao yü 'Chih-yen chai p'ing' chung so-shu *Hung-lou meng* chih ch'ing-chieh" 伏綫的敘述技巧與脂硯齋評中所述紅樓夢之情節. *Lien-ho pao*, 6/6/1980 (summary of a conference paper).

Wang Ch'ang-ting 王昌定. "Chih-p'ing yü *Hung-lou meng* hou ssu-shih hui" 脂評與紅樓夢後四十回. In *T'ien-chin she-hui k'o-hsüeh*, 1983. 2:80–86 (*Hung-lou meng yen-chiu* reprint, 1983. 5:69–75).

Wang Chih-ch'ing 汪稚青. "Tui 'Chia-hsü pen' Chih-p'ing *Shih-t'ou chi* shang P'u-shih t'i-pa chih i-chieh" 對甲戌本脂評石頭記上濮氏題跋之異解. *Hung-lou meng hsüeh-k'an*, 1984. 1:77–78.

Wang Ch'ing-hua 王慶華. "Chi-hu sou wei chien mo-hui ching-huan 'ch'ing-pang'" 畸笏叟未見末回警幻情榜. *Hung-lou meng hsüeh-k'an*, 1985. 3:198.

Wang Ching-yü 王靖宇. "Chih-yen chai p'ing ho *Hung-lou meng*" 脂硯齋評和紅樓夢. *Hung-lou meng yen-chiu chi-k'an* 6:333–49 (1981).

Wang Hui-p'ing 王惠萍, and Ching K'uan-jung 靖寬榮. "Ch'ien-t'an Ching-pen *Shih-t'ou chi* ti yüan-yüan chi ch'i t'a ch'ao-pen cheng-wen p'i-yü ti i-t'ung" 淺談靖本石頭記的淵源及其他抄本正文批語的異同. *Hung-lou meng hsüeh-k'an*, 1984. 2:274–89.

Wang Meng-pai 王孟白. "Lun Chih-p'ing shih-liu hui ts'an-pen *Shih-t'ou chi*" 論脂評十六回殘本石頭記. *Ha-erh-pin shih-yüan hsüeh-pao*, 1977. 4:103–14. Reprinted in *Hung-hsüeh lun-wen hsüan* 紅學論文選. Harbin: Ha-erh-pin shih-ta, 1986, pp. 307–29.

Wang Pen-jen 王本仁. "*Hung-lou meng* Chih ts'an-pen 'Fan-li' shih-t'an" 紅樓夢脂殘本凡例試談. *Ch'ing-hai shih-fan hsüeh-yüan hsüeh-pao* 青海師範學院學報, 1980. 3.

Wei Shao-ch'ang 魏紹昌. "Ching-pen *Shih-t'ou chi* ti ku-shih" 靖本石頭記的故事. *Hsin kuan-ch'a* 新觀察, 1982. 17:31–32 (*Hung-lou meng yen-chiu* reprint, 1982. 9:78–79). Reprinted in *Hung-lou meng tzu-liao chi*, vol. 5, pp. 337–38.

Wei T'an 魏潭. "'Chi-mao pen shih Keng-ch'en pen ti ti-pen' shuo chih-i" 己卯本是庚辰本的底本說質疑. *Hung-lou meng yen-chiu chi-k'an* 2:241–52 (1980).

Wei T'ung-hsien 魏同賢. "Ying-yin Chi-mao pen *Chih-yen chai ch'ung-p'ing Shih-t'ou chi* pien-chi shou-chi" 影印己卯本脂硯齋重評石頭記編輯手記. In *Wo tu Hung-lou meng*, pp. 238–59.

Wen Lei 文雷 (Hu Wen-pin 胡文彬 and Chou Lei 周雷). "Tu hsin fa-hsien ti Chih I-pen *Shih-t'ou chi* ts'an-chüan" 讀新發現的脂怡本石頭記殘卷. *Li-lun hsüeh-hsi* 理論學習, 1975. 3. Reprinted in *Hung-hsüeh ts'ung-t'an*, pp. 143–55.

Weng T'ung-wen 翁同文. "Man-t'an Chih-yen chai p'i-yü yin-shih" 漫談脂硯齋批語引詩. *Hung-lou meng yen-chiu chuan-k'an* 11:44–48 (1974). Reprinted in *T'ai-wan Hung-hsüeh lun-wen hsüan*, pp. 717–23.

———. "Pu lun Chih-yen chai wei Ts'ao Yung i-fu-tzu shuo" 補論脂硯齋為曹顒遺腹子說. *Ta-lu tsa-chih* 33. 1:6–14 (1966). Reprinted in *T'ai-wan Hung-hsüeh lun-wen hsüan*, pp. 598–618.

Wu Chih-hsün 吳智勛. "Ch'ien-p'ing Chao Kang hsien-sheng t'an Chih-p'ing pen *Shih-t'ou chi*" 淺評趙岡先生談脂評本石頭記. *Hung-lou meng yen-chiu chuan-k'an* 10:95–104 (1973).

Wu En-yü 吳恩裕. "Chih-p'i *Shih-t'ou chi* chung ti 'Sung-chai' shih shui?" 脂批石頭記中的宋齋是誰. *Wen-hui pao*, 3/28/1962.

———. "Hsien-ts'un Chi-mao pen *Shih-t'ou chi* hsin-t'an" 現存己卯本石頭記新探. In *Hung-lou meng pan-pen lun-ts'ung*, pp. 115–45. Reprinted in *Ts'ao Hsüeh-ch'in ts'ung-k'ao*, pp. 213–70.

———. "Tsao-ch'i ch'ao-pen *Shih-t'ou chi* p'i-yü shih-chieh" 早期抄本石頭記批語試解. In *Ts'ao Hsüeh-ch'in ts'ung-k'ao*, pp. 271–317.

———. "'Tu Chih-p'i *Shih-t'ou chi* sui-cha' tu-hou" 讀脂批石頭記隨札讀後. *Kuang-ming jih-pao*, 6/23/1962.

———. "Tu Ching-pen *Shih-t'ou chi* p'i-yü t'an Chih-yen chai, Chi-hu sou ho Ts'ao Hsüeh-ch'in" 讀靖本石頭記批語談脂硯齋畸笏叟和曹雪芹. In *Hung-lou meng pan-pen lun-ts'ung*, pp. 179–99.

Wu En-yü, and Feng Ch'i-yung 馮其庸. "'Chi-mao pen' *Shih-t'ou chi* san-shih pu-fen ti fa-hsien chi ch'i i-i" 己卯本石頭記散失部分的發現及其意義. *Kuang-ming jih-pao*, 3/24/1975. Reprinted in *Hung-hsüeh san-shih nien lun-wen hsüan-pien*, vol. 3, pp. 3–10 and in *Meng-pien chi*, pp. 315–22.

Wu Hsiao-ju 吳小如. "Tu 'Chih-p'i *Shih-t'ou chi* sui-cha erh-tse'" 讀脂批石頭記隨札二則. *Kuang-ming jih-pao*, 6/5/1962.

Wu Shih-ch'ang 吳世昌. "Chih-yen chai shih shui?" 脂硯齋是誰. *Kuang-ming jih-pao*, 4/14/1962. Reprinted in *Hung-hsüeh san-shih nien lun-wen hsüan-pien*, vol. 3, pp. 231–37.

———. "Lun *Chih-yen chai ch'ung-p'ing Shih-t'ou chi* (ch'i-shih pa hui pen) ti kou-ch'eng, nien-tai ho p'ing-yü" 論脂硯齋重評石頭記(七十八回本)的構成年代和評語. *Chung-hua wen-shih lun-ts'ung* 6:215–84 (1965). Reprinted in *Hung-lou meng yen-chiu tzu-liao*, pp. 29–97; in his *Hung-lou meng t'an-yüan wai-pien*, pp. 146–200; and in *Hung-hsüeh san-shih nien lun-wen hsüan-pien*, vol. 3, pp. 31–95.

———. "Tsai-lun Chih-yen chai yü Ts'ao-shih chia-shih" 再論脂硯齋與曹氏家世. *Kuang-ming jih-pao*, 8/9–11/1962. Reprinted in his *Hung-lou meng t'an-yüan wai-pien*, pp. 22–31.

———. "Ts'an-pen Chih-p'ing *Shih-t'ou chi* ti ti-pen chi ch'i nien-tai" 殘本脂評石頭記的底本及其年代. *Wen-hsüeh yen-chiu chi-k'an* 文學研究集刊, 1964. 1. Reprinted in *Hung-lou meng yen-chiu tzu-liao*, pp. 153–214 (revised), and in his *Hung-lou meng t'an-yüan wai-pien*, pp. 96–145.

Wu Yü-feng 吳玉峰. "Chih-yen chai shih shui?" 脂硯齋是誰. *Shao-kuan shih-chuan hsüeh-pao* 韶關師專學報, 1985. 1:47–57 (*Hung-lou meng yen-chiu* reprint, 1985. 2:65–75).

Yang Ch'uan-jung 楊傳容. "I-t'iao Ching-pen Chih-p'ing ti chiao-tu" 一條靖本脂評的校讀. *Hung-lou meng yen-chiu chi-k'an* 12:358, 357 (1985).

Yang Ch'uan-yung 楊傳鏞. "Chih-yen chai 'fan ssu-yüeh p'ing kuo' shih-chieh" 脂硯齋凡四閱評過試解. *Hung-lou meng yen-chiu chi-k'an* 6:367–72 (1981).

———. "*Hung-lou meng* ch'ao-pen shu-wen" 紅樓夢抄本述聞. *Wu-han shih-yüan Han-k'ou fen-yüan hsüeh-pao*, 1982. 2:61–65, 110.

———. "Kuan-yü ying-yin Chi-mao pen ti chu-pi kai-t'ien wen-tzu" 關於影印己卯本的朱筆改添文字. *Kuei-chou wen-shih ts'ung-k'an* 貴州文史叢刊, 1985. 4:105–11 (*Hung-lou meng yen-chiu* reprint, 1986. 1:72–78).

Yang Hsing-ying 楊星映. "Chih-yen chai lun jen-wu su-tsao kuan-k'uei" 脂硯齋論人物塑造管窺. *Hung-lou meng hsüeh-k'an*, 1982. 3:325–43.

Yang Kuang-han 楊光漢. "Chih-yen chai yü Chi-hu sou k'ao" 脂硯齋與畸笏叟考. *She-hui k'o-hsüeh yen-chiu*, 1980. 2:103–13. Reprinted in *Hung-hsüeh san-shih nien lun-wen hsüan-pien*, vol. 3, pp. 269–89.

———. "Keng-ch'en pen chi-t'iao p'i-p'ing chiao-shih" 庚辰本幾條批評校釋. *Hung-lou meng yen-chiu chi-k'an* 6:351–65 (1981).

———. "Kuan-yü 'Chia-hsü pen' 'Hao-liao ko chieh' ti ts'e-p'i" 關於甲戌本好了歌解的側批. *Hung-lou meng hsüeh-k'an*, 1980. 4:231–40.

Yang Yen-fu 楊延福. "Lüeh-t'an ku-chi ying-yin ti i-ko wen-t'i—hsin tu ying-yin *Chih-yen chai ch'ung-p'ing Shih-t'ou chi* Chi-mao pen" 略談古籍影印的一個問題—欣讀影印脂硯齋重評石頭記己卯本. *Wen-hui pao*, 6/8/1981.

Yeh Lang 葉朗. "Pu-yao ch'ing-i fou-ting Chih-yen chai ti kuan-hsi" 不要輕易否定脂硯齋的關係. *Hsüeh-shu yüeh-k'an*, 1980. 10:63–69.

Yen Hui-yün 顏慧雲. "Fu-kuei yü yü han-suan hua—'Chih-p'ing' i-shu lun shih-ling" 富貴語與寒酸話—脂評藝術論拾零. *Wen-hsüeh chih-shih* 文學知識, 1984. 2:28–29.

Yen Tung-yang 嚴東陽. "*Hung-lou meng* ti p'i-yü ho p'i-shu jen" 紅樓夢的批語和批書人. *Kuo-li pien-i kuan kuan-k'an* 國立編譯館館刊 1. 2:212–27. (1972). Reprinted in *T'ai-wan Hung-hsüeh lun-wen hsüan*, pp. 633–92.

———. "Ts'ung *Hung-lou meng* ti hsieh-tso ho p'ing-yüeh t'an Chih-yen chai p'ing ch'ao-pen" 從紅樓夢的寫作和評閱談脂硯齋評抄本. *Fan-kung* 反共 351 (1971).

Ying Pi-ch'eng 應必誠. "Kuan-yü *Shih-t'ou chi* Chi-mao pen ho Chi-mao pen ti ying-yin" 關於石頭記己卯本和己卯本的影印. *Chung-kuo she-hui k'o-hsüeh*, 1981. 2:187–204.

———. *Lun Shih-t'ou chi Keng-ch'en pen* 論石頭記庚辰本. Shanghai: Shang-hai ku-chi, 1983.

Yü P'ing-po 俞平伯. "Chi 'Hsi-k'uei shu-wu' *Shih-t'ou chi* chüan i ti p'i-yü" 記夕葵書屋石頭記卷一的批語. *Hung-lou meng yen-chiu chi-k'an* 1:205–21 (1979). Reprinted in *Hung-hsüeh san-shih nien lun-wen hsüan-pien*, vol. 3, pp. 400–416.

———. "Chih-yen chai p'ing *Shih-t'ou chi* ts'an-pen pa" 脂硯齋評石頭記殘本跋. In *Yen-chiao chi* 燕郊集. Shanghai: Liang-yu fu-hsing t'u-shu, 1936, pp. 206–8.

———. "Ying-yin *Chih-yen chai ch'ung-p'ing Shih-t'ou chi* shih-liu hui hou-chi" 影印脂硯齋重評石頭記十六回後記. *Chung-hua wen-shih lun-ts'ung* 1:299–

339 (1962). Reprinted in *Hung-hsüeh san-shih nien lun-wen hsüan-pien*, vol. 3, pp. 96–131.

————. "'Ying-yin *Chih-yen chai ch'ung-p'ing Shih-t'ou chi* shih-liu hui hou-chi' ti pu-ch'ung shuo-ming" 影印脂硯齋石頭記十六回後記的補充說明. *Chung-hua wen-shih lun-ts'ung* 3 : 294 (1963).

ABBREVIATED TITLE: Yu-cheng 有正 large- and small-character editions. FULL TITLE: *Yüan-pen Hung-lou meng* 原本紅樓夢 (Original Edition of the *Hung-lou meng*). LENGTH: 80 chapters. PUBLISHER: Yu-cheng shu-chü, Shanghai. Basically a photolithographic copy with changes of a late eighteenth-century manuscript version of the novel. DATE: 1912 (large-character edition), 1920 (small-character edition). PREFATORY MATERIAL: Ch'i Liao-sheng 戚蓼生 (1782 *chin-shih*) preface. The large-character edition contains an advertisement offering money for comments to be incorporated into the next printing. COMMENTARY: Prechapter, marginal, double-column interlineal, and postchapter comments. The marginal comments and some of the chapter comments represent new material. The bulk of the comments are by Chih-yen chai and his co-commentators but the dates and signatures appended to certain of the comments in other editions have been elided. DISTINGUISHING FEATURES: For chaps. 1–40 the large-character edition has marginal comments by the editor, Ti Pao-hsien 狄葆賢 (b. 1873), who is mostly concerned with comparing the text of this edition with printed ones already available. An advertisement for someone to provide comments for the remaining chapters run in the large-character version apparently brought results, because the small-character edition has marginal comments for the second forty chapters as well. REMARKS: One of the new chapter comments is signed with the pen name Li-sung hsüan 立松軒, and there is speculation that the chapter comments and some of the new interlineal comments in the related Meng wang-fu 蒙王府 (Mongolian Prince) manuscript copy of the novel are all by him. The first half of the manuscript copy that Ti Pao-hsien used as the base text for his photo-lithographic edition with minor changes was found in Shanghai in 1975. A related manuscript copy of the novel done in a different hand is held in the Nanking Library. AVAILABILITY: Photo-reprints of the large-character edition: *Ch'i Liao-sheng hsü pen Shih-t'ou chi* 戚蓼生序本石頭記 (Ch'i Liao-sheng Preface Edition of the *Story of the Stone*; Peking: Jen-min wen-hsüeh, 1973) and *Kuo-ch'u ch'ao-pen Yüan-pen Hung-lou meng* 國初抄本原本紅樓夢 (Manuscript Copy of the Original *Hung-lou meng* from the Early Republican Period; Taipei: Hsüeh-sheng shu-chü, 1976). Photo-reprint of the small-character edition: *Yu-cheng hsiao-tzu pen Hung-lou meng* 有正小字本紅樓夢 (Small-Character Edition of the *Hung-lou meng*; Taipei: I-wen yin-shu kuan, 1976). The preface and the non-marginal comments from these two editions are included in *HLMTLHP*, pp. 97–516. All of the comments are included in the two collections of Chih-yen chai comments by Yü P'ing-po and Ch'en Ch'ing-hao. The comments from the Meng wang-fu copy not repeated in other versions have been collected by Ch'en Yü-p'i 陳毓羆 and Liu Shih-te 劉世德, "Meng-ku wang-fu pen *Shih-t'ou chi* p'i-yü hsüan-chi" 蒙古王府本石頭記批語選輯, *Hung-lou meng yen-chiu chi-*

k'an 1:263–322 (1979) and "Chih Meng-pen *Shih t'ou chi* ts'e-p'i hsüan-chi" 脂蒙本石頭記側批選輯 (Selected Single-Column Interlineal Comments from the Mongolian Prince Copy of the Chih-yen chai Commentary on the *Story of the Stone*), in *Hung-lou meng yen-chiu tzu-liao* (see general bibliography below), pp. 275–90. A selection of Ti Pao-hsien's marginal comments can be found in the same collection, pp. 314–32. Some of the Meng wang-fu copy comments are also available in the Chou Hu-ch'ang 周祜昌 and Chou Ju-ch'ang 周汝昌 article cited below, and a photo-reprint of the entire copy, *Meng-ku wang-fu pen Shih-t'ou chi* 蒙古王府本石頭記 (Peking: Shu-mu wen-hsien, 1987) is now available.

Cheng Ch'ing-shan 鄭慶山. "Li-sung hsüan pen *Shih-t'ou chi* tsung-shuo" 立松軒本石頭記總說. *Pei-fang lun-ts'ung*, 1983. 1:41–48, 60 (*Hung-lou meng yen-chiu* reprint, 1983. 2:61–69).

———. "Li-sung hsüan p'i-yü ho *Shih-t'ou chi* san-lun" 立松軒批語和石頭記散論. *Ch'i-ch'i ha-erh shih-fan hsüeh-yüan hsüeh-pao*, 1982. 1:25–34 (*Hung-lou meng yen-chiu* reprint, 1982. 4:67–76).

———. "Meng-fu pen *Shih-t'ou chi* ti ts'e-p'i yü Li-sung hsüan" 蒙府本石頭記的側批與立松軒. *Hung-lou meng hsüeh-k'an*, 1983. 4:319–45.

———. "Shih-t'an Li-sung hsüan pen ti cheng-li che" 試談立松軒本的整理者. *K'o-shan shih-chuan hsüeh-pao* 克山師專學報, 1984. 1:53–58 (*Hung-lou meng yen-chiu* reprint, 1984. 2:111–16).

Cheng Ts'ang-shan 正蒼山 (Cheng Ch'ing-shan). "T'an Yu-cheng Ch'i-hsü pen *Shih-t'ou chi* ti p'i-yü" 談有正戚序本石頭記的批語. *Hung-lou meng yen-chiu chi-k'an* 8:277–304 (1982).

Chou Hu-ch'ang 周祜昌, and Chou Ju-ch'ang 周汝昌. "Ch'ing Meng-ku wang-fu pen *Shih-t'ou chi* mo-pi hang-ts'e p'i chi-lu" 清蒙古王府本石頭記墨筆行側批輯錄. In *Hung-lou meng pan-pen lun-ts'ung*, pp. 251–93.

Chou Ju-ch'ang 周汝昌. "Ch'i Liao-sheng k'ao" 戚蓼生考. In *Hung-lou meng hsin-cheng*, pp. 941–52.

———. "Ch'i Liao-sheng yü Ch'i-pen" 戚蓼生與戚本. In *Hung-lou meng hsin-cheng*, pp. 971–98.

———. "Ch'ing Meng-ku wang-fu pen" 清蒙古王府本. In *Hung-lou meng hsin-cheng*, pp. 999–1015.

Fang Hao 方豪. "*Kuo-ch'u ch'ao-pen Yüan-pen Hung-lou meng* pien-yen" 國初抄本原本紅樓夢弁言. *Shu-mu chi-k'an* 10. 1:76–80 (1976).

Hu Shih 胡適. "Pa Mao Tzu-shui ts'ang Yu-cheng shu-chü shih-yin ti Ch'i Liao-sheng hsü *Hung-lou meng* hsiao-tzu pen" 跋毛子水藏有正書局石印的戚蓼生序紅樓夢小字本. In *Hu Shih shou-kao* 胡適手稿. Taipei: Academia Sinica, 1970, vol. 9B, pp. 169–70. Reprinted in *Hu Shih*, pp. 153–54.

Kao Yang 高陽. "Hsi-chien 'Yu-cheng pen' *Hung-lou meng*—t'i-ch'u tz'u-pen 'tsung-p'ing' tso-che wei shui ti i-ko ch'u-pu chia-she" 喜見有正本紅樓夢—提出此本總評作者為誰的一個初步假設. *Shu-mu chi-k'an* 10. 2:168–70 (1976).

Lin Kuan-fu 林冠夫. "Lun *Shih-t'ou chi* Wang-fu pen yü Ch'i-hsü pen" 論石頭記王府本與戚序本. *Wen-i yen-chiu*, 1979. 2:110–25. Reprinted in *Hung-*

lou meng tzu-liao chi, vol. 2, pp. 464–79.

———. "Lun Wang-fu pen—*Hung-lou meng* pan-pen lun chih i" 論王府本—紅樓夢版本論之一. *Hung-lou meng hsüeh-k'an,* 1981. 1:177–206.

Liu Kuang-ting 劉廣定. "Ch'i-pen *Hung-lou meng* ti yüan-pen" 戚本紅樓夢的原本. *Shu-p'ing shu-mu* 73:31–32 (1979).

———. "Hsü-t'an Ch'i-pen *Hung-lou meng*" 續談戚本紅樓夢. *Shu-p'ing shu-mu* 86:118–20 (1980).

———. "T'an Ch'i-pen *Hung-lou meng*" 談戚本紅樓夢. *Shu-p'ing shu-mu* 70:28–30 (1979).

Mao Kuo-yao 毛國瑤. "T'an Nan-ching t'u-shu kuan ts'ang Ch'i-hsü pen *Hung-lou meng*" 談南京圖書館藏戚序本紅樓夢. In *Hung-lou meng pan-pen lun-ts'ung,* pp. 160–68.

Shang-hai shu-tien 上海書店. "Chiu-ch'ao Ch'i Liao-sheng hsü pen *Shih-t'ou chi* ti fa-hsien" 舊抄戚蓼生序本石頭記的發現. *Wen-wu,* 1976. 1:33–35.

Sung Ch'i 宋淇. "Ch'i-hsü Yu-cheng pen *Hung-lou meng* ti shih-mo" 戚序有正本紅樓夢的始末. *Ming-pao yüeh-k'an* 13. 1:51–57 (1978). Reprinted in *Hsiang-kang Hung-hsüeh lun-wen chi* 香港紅學論文集 (Tientsin: Pai-hua wen-i, 1982), pp. 305–21.

Wang San-ch'ing 王三慶. "Tsai-t'an *Kuo-ch'u ch'ao-pen Yüan-pen Hung-lou meng*" 再談國初抄本原本紅樓夢. *Ch'u-pan yü yen-chiu* 出版與研究 54:18–19 (1979). Reprinted in *T'ai-wan Hung-hsüeh lun-wen hsüan,* pp. 442–45.

———. "Ts'ung ying-yin ti *Kuo-ch'u ch'ao-pen Yüan-pen Hung-lou meng* t'an-ch'i" 從影印的國初抄本原本紅樓夢談起. *Shu-mu chi-k'an* 10. 3 (1976). Reprinted in *T'ai-wan Hung-hsüeh lun-wen hsüan,* pp. 435–41.

Wei Shao-ch'ang 魏紹昌. "Hsin fa-hsien ti 'Yu-cheng pen' *Hung-lou meng* ti-pen ch'ien-shuo" 新發現的有正本紅樓夢底本淺說. *Hung-lou meng hsüeh-k'an* 2:165–78 (1979). Reprinted in his *Hung-lou meng pan-pen hsiao-k'ao,* pp. 11–24 and in *Hung-hsüeh san-shih nien lun-wen hsüan-pien,* vol. 3, pp. 167–80. Also in *Hung-lou meng pan-pen lun-ts'ung,* pp. 146–59.

Wen Lei 文雷. "Ch'i-hsü Yu-cheng pen *Hung-lou meng* liu-ch'uan shih-mo hsin-cheng" 戚序有正本紅樓夢流傳始末新證. *Hung-lou meng hsüeh-k'an,* 1980. 2:270. Reprinted in *Hung-hsüeh ts'ung-t'an,* pp. 324–25.

Weng Chih-p'eng 翁志鵬. "Shih-lun *Shih-t'ou chi* Ch'i-p'ing ti Fo-chia ssu-hsiang" 試論石頭記戚評的佛家思想. *Hang-chou ta-hsüeh hsüeh-pao,* 1981. 4:76–83 (*Hung-lou meng yen-chiu* reprint, 1982. 1:71–78). Reprinted in *Hung-lou meng tzu-liao chi,* vol. 4, pp. 474–81.

Wu Yu-yüan 吳幼源. "Ch'i-pen *Hung-lou meng* Chih-yen chai i-shou t'i-shih ti chih-i" 戚本紅樓夢脂硯齋一首題詩的質疑. *An-hui shih-fan ta-hsüeh hsüeh-pao* 安徽師範大學學報, 1977. 5:93–96.

Yang Ch'uan-yung 楊傳鏞. "Wang-fu pen ts'e-p'i pu-shih Chih-p'ing" 王府本側批不是脂評. *Hung-lou meng hsüeh-k'an* 2:332–46 (1982).

ABBREVIATED TITLE: Sun Sung-fu 孫崧甫 commentary. FULL TITLE: *Sun Sung-fu hsien-sheng p'ing-tien Hung-lou meng* 孫崧甫先生評點紅樓夢 (*Hung-lou meng* with Commentary by Sun Sung-fu). LENGTH: 120 chapters. PUBLISHER: Single manuscript copy of the text of the novel with commentary. DATE: 1829. PRE-

FATORY MATERIAL: Sun Sung-fu preface (dated 1829), Ch'eng Wei-yüan 程偉元 (ca. 1745–1820) preface, and "*Hung-lou meng* pien-yen tsung-lun" 紅樓夢弁言總論 (Prefatory General Remarks) by Sun Sung-fu. COMMENTARY: Prechapter and double-column interlineal comments by Sun Sung-fu (style Hsin-ch'ing chü-shih 心情居士, 1785?–1866). AVAILABILITY: Single copy held by private family in Nan-t'ung, Kiangsu Province.

Liang Tso 梁左. "Sun Sung-fu ch'ao-p'ing pen *Hung-lou meng* chi-lüeh" 孫崧甫抄評本紅樓夢記略. *Hung-lou meng hsüeh-k'an*, 1983. 1:252–65.

ABBREVIATED TITLE: Tung-kuan ko 東觀閣 edition. FULL TITLE: *Hsin-tseng p'i-p'ing hsiu-hsiang Hung-lou meng* 新增批評繡像紅樓夢 (Illustrated *Hung-lou meng* with Newly Added Commentary). LENGTH: 120 chapters. PUBLISHER: Hui-wen t'ang 會文堂. DATE: 1830. PREFATORY MATERIAL: Tung-kuan ko chu-jen 東觀閣主人 (Owner of Tung-kuan ko) preface ("Chih" 識), Ch'eng Wei-yüan and Kao E 高鶚 (1788 *chin-shih*) prefaces. COMMENTARY: Single-column interlineal comments, unattributed. REMARKS: This is an 1830 reprint of the Tung-kuan ko edition (first printed 1811) with added commentary. AVAILABILITY: This edition is not the same as the Tung-kuan ko edition reprinted by Kuang-wen shu-chü in Taipei. There is an original copy in the Library of Congress, Washington, D.C.

Na Tsung-hsün 那宗訓. "Mei-kuo kuo-hui t'u-shu kuan so-ts'ang *Hung-lou meng* pan-pen chien-chi" 美國國會圖書館所藏紅樓夢版本簡記 *Ta-lu tsa-chih* 63. 1:37–41 (1981). Reprinted in *Hung-lou meng t'an-so*, pp. 169–76.

Yü P'ing-po 俞平伯. "Chi Chia-ch'ing chia-tzu pen p'ing-yü" 記嘉慶甲子本評語. In *Hung-lou meng yen-chiu ts'an-k'ao tzu-liao hsüan-chi*, vol. 2, pp. 147–61.

———. "Tsai-t'an Chia-ch'ing pen" 再談嘉慶本. In *Hung-lou meng yen-chiu ts'an-k'ao tzu-liao hsüan-chi*, vol. 2, pp. 164–68.

ABBREVIATED TITLE: San-jang t'ang 三讓堂 edition. FULL TITLE: *Hsiu-hsiang p'i-tien Hung-lou meng* 繡像批點紅樓夢 (Illustrated *Hung-lou meng* with Commentary). LENGTH: 120 chapters. PUBLISHERS: San-jang t'ang. Numerous later reprints. DATE: Around 1830. PREFATORY MATERIAL: Nothing new beyond the Tung-kuan ko edition. COMMENTARY: Single-column interlineal comments unattributed. REMARKS: This edition is basically the same as the Tung-kuan ko edition, but there are minor differences in the commentary. The illustrations are related to the T'eng-hua hsieh 藤花榭 edition. AVAILABILITY: A copy is held in the Library of Congress, Washington, D.C.

Na Tsung-hsün 那宗訓. "Mei-kuo Ha-fo Yen-ching ta-hsüeh t'u-shu kuan so-ts'ang *Hung-lou meng* pan-pen chien-chi" 美國哈佛燕京大學圖書館所藏紅樓夢版本簡記. In *Hung-lou meng t'an-so*, pp. 177–89.

———. "Mei-kuo kuo-hui t'u-shu kuan so-ts'ang *Hung-lou meng* pan-pen chien-chi" 美國國會圖書館所藏紅樓夢版本簡記. *Ta-lu tsa-chih* 63. 1:37–41 (1981). Reprinted in *Hung-lou meng t'an-so*, pp. 169–76.

ABBREVIATED TITLE: Wang Hsi-lien 王希廉 edition. FULL TITLE: *Hsin-p'ing hsiu-hsiang Hung-lou meng ch'üan-chuan* 新評繡像紅樓夢全傳 (Newly Commentated, Illustrated, Complete Edition of the *Hung-lou meng*). LENGTH: 120 chapters. PUBLISHER: Shuang-ch'ing hsien kuan 雙清仙館, Suchou. DATE: 1832. PREFATORY MATERIAL: Wang Hsi-lien (fl. 1832–1875, courtesy name Hsüeh-hsiang 雪香, style Hu-hua chu-jen 護花主人) preface, 1832; Ch'eng Wei-yüan preface; "*Hung-lou meng* lun-tsan" 紅樓夢論讚 (Evaluations of the Characters of the *Hung-lou meng*) and "*Hung-lou meng* wen-ta" 紅樓夢問答 (Questions and Answers on the *Hung-lou meng*) by T'u Ying 涂瀛 (style Tu-hua chu-jen 讀花主人); "Ta-kuan yüan t'u-shuo" 大觀園圖說 (Explanation of the Diagram of Grand Prospect Garden) by Huang Ts'ung 黃琮, first published 1826; "*Hung-lou meng* t'i-tz'u" 紅樓夢題詞 (Prefatory Poems on the *Hung-lou meng*) by Chou Ch'i 周琦; and "Tsung-p'ing" 總評 (General Comments) and "Yin-shih" 音釋 (Phonetic Glosses) by Wang Hsi-lien. COMMENTARY: Postchapter comments. DISTINGUISHING FEATURES: The prefatory material comes from many hands and belongs to many different, separate genres. REMARKS: In some editions the last half of Wang Hsi-lien's "Tsung-p'ing" is separated out and labeled "Chai-wu" 摘悮 (List of Errors). AVAILABILITY: Photo-reprint of 1832 edition: *Wang Hsi-lien p'ing-pen hsin-chüan ch'üan-pu hsiu-hsiang Hung-lou meng* 王希廉評本新鐫全部繡像紅樓夢 (Newly Cut, Completely Illustrated *Hung-lou meng* with Commentary by Wang Hsi-lien; Taipei: Kuang-wen shu-chü, 1977). The "Tsung-p'ing" and chapter comments were later published together without the text of the novel as *Shih-t'ou chi p'ing-tsan* 石頭記評讚 (Comments and Evaluations of the *Story of the Stone*; 1874) and also as *Hung-lou meng p'ing-tsan* 紅樓夢評讚 (Comments and Evaluations of the *Hung-lou meng*; 1876). All of the prefatory items except "Ta-kuan yüan t'u-shuo" can be found in *HLMC* and many are included in *HLMTLHP*, pp. 543–637.

Wang Ching-yü 王靖宇. "Chien-lun Wang Hsi-lien *Hung-lou meng* p'ing" 簡論王希廉紅樓夢評. In *Shou-chieh kuo-chi Hung-lou meng yen-t'ao hui lun-wen chi* 首屆國際紅樓夢研討會論文集. Edited by Chou Ts'e-tsung 周策縱. Hong Kong: Chinese University Press, 1983, pp. 1–5.

ABBREVIATED TITLE: Ch'en Ch'i-t'ai 陳其泰 commentary. FULL TITLE: *T'ung-hua feng ko p'ing Hung-lou meng* 桐花鳳閣評紅樓夢 (Commentary on the *Hung-lou meng* from T'ung-hua feng ko). LENGTH: 120 chapters. PUBLISHER: Unpublished manuscript copy of comments written onto a 1792 Ch'eng Wei-yüan printed copy of the novel. DATE: Commentary begun in 1816 and probably finished in the 1850–1860s. PREFATORY MATERIAL: "Tiao meng wen" 吊夢文 (Requiem for the *Hung-lou meng*) and a list of suggested changes in the chapter titles, and postface by Ch'en Ch'i-t'ai (1800–1864, style T'ung-hua feng ko chu-jen 桐花鳳閣主人). COMMENTARY: Marginal, single-column interlineal, and postchapter comments by Ch'en Ch'i-t'ai, plus a few comments by Hsü Po-fan 徐伯番. AVAILABILITY: The comments and prefatory material have been collected and edited by Liu Ts'ao-nan 劉操南, *T'ung-hua feng ko p'ing Hung-lou meng chi-lu* 桐花鳳閣評紅樓夢輯錄 (Edited and Collected Ch'en Ch'i-t'ai Commentary on the *Hung-lou meng*; Tientsin: T'ien-chin jen-min, 1981). This volume also has an introductory essay by Liu Ts'ao-nan. The chapter comments and some of the prefatory material are included in *HLMTLHP*, pp. 694–768.

Lin Hsing-jen 林興仁. "Shih chien-tien ch'u yü hsiu-tz'u—tu *T'ung-hua feng ko p'ing Hung-lou meng chi-lu*" 失檢點處與修辭—讀桐花鳳閣評紅樓夢輯錄. In his *Hung-lou meng ti hsiu-tz'u i-shu*, pp. 197–205.

Liu Ts'ao-nan 劉操南. "Ch'ing-tai Ch'en Ch'i-t'ai *T'ung-hua feng ko p'ing Hung-lou meng* hsü-lu" 清代陳其泰桐花鳳閣評紅樓夢叙錄. *Hang-chou ta-hsüeh hsüeh-pao*, 1978. 3.

———. "Ch'ing-tai Ch'en Ch'i-t'ai *T'ung-hua feng ko p'ing Hung-lou meng* k'ao-lüeh" 清代陳其泰桐花鳳閣評紅樓夢考略. In *Hung-lou meng yen-chiu lun-ts'ung*, pp. 287–309.

———. "T'i *T'ung-hua feng ko p'ing Hung-lou meng*" 題桐花鳳閣評紅樓夢. *Wen-chiao tzu-liao chien-pao*, 1983. 11:30–35.

Wang Ta-chin 王達津. "P'ing *T'ung-hua feng ko Hung-lou meng p'ing*" 評桐花鳳閣紅樓夢評. In *Chung-kuo ku-tai hsiao-shuo li-lun yen-chiu*, pp. 306–23. Also in his *Ku-tai wen-hsüeh li-lun yen-chiu lun-wen chi*, pp. 227–46.

Yen Pao-shan 嚴寶善. "'Ch'en Ch'i-t'ai p'ing *Hung-lou meng* hsü-lu' pu-cheng" 陳其泰評紅樓夢叙錄補證. *Hang-chou ta-hsüeh hsüeh-pao*, 1980. 2:51–52.

ABBREVIATED TITLE: Qasbuu (Ha-ssu-pao 哈斯寶) edition. FULL TITLE: *Hsin-i Hung-lou meng* 新譯紅樓夢 (The *Hung-lou meng* Newly Translated [From the Chinese into Mongolian]). This is a translation into Chinese of the Mongolian title, *Shine orchighŭlŭghsan Hung Leu Meng bichig*. LENGTH: 40 chapters. PUBLISHER: Exists only in manuscript copies transcribed at various times. DATE: A copy held in Ulan Bator supposedly has a preface dated 1819, but most scholars think the work was finished in 1847, the date of the preface in the version that has been published in Mongolian. PREFATORY MATERIAL: Preface (dated 1847), *tu-fa* essay, and "Tsung-lu" 總錄 (General Comments), all by Qasbuu (also transliterated as Khasbo, fl. 1819–1847, style Tan-mo-tzu 耽墨子, Mongolian name transliterated in Chinese as Ha-ssu-pao). COMMENTARY: Postchapter comments. DISTINGUISHING FEATURES: This is an abridged translation into Mongolian with commentary by Qasbuu. REMARKS: Qasbuu was greatly influenced by Chin Sheng-t'an and Chang Chu-p'o. AVAILABILITY: The chapter comments and prefatory material have been translated into Chinese by I Lin-chen 亦鄰真, *Hsin-i Hung-lou meng hui-p'i* 新譯紅樓夢回批 (Huhehot: Nei-meng-ku jen-min, 1979). This book also contains an introductory essay by the translator. The chapter comments (in Chinese) are also available in *Hung-lou meng yen-chiu tzu-liao*, pp. 333–84. The preface, chapter comments, and "Tsung-lu" are available (in Chinese) in *HLMTLHP*, pp. 768–833. Mongolian copies are held in the Inner Mongolian Provincial Library, University of Inner Mongolia Library, the Institute for the Study of Mongolian Language and History, and in Ulan Bator. A collated edition (Huhehot: Nei-meng-ku ta-hsüeh, 1975) and a photo-reprint (Huhehot: Nei-meng-ku jen-min, 1980), based on the original Mongolian manuscript copies, exist. The 1847 preface, the *tu-fa* essay, and selections from the chapter comments are translated by Charles R. Bawden (see the article listed below).

Bawden, Charles R. "The First Systematic Translation of *Hung-lou meng*: Qas-buu's Commented Mongolian Version." *Zentralasiatische Studien* 15:241–306 (1981).

Cheng Hsüan-chu 鄭宣祝. "Meng-Han wen-hua chiao-liu ti li-shih chien-cheng —p'ing Ha-ssu-pao *Hsin-i Hung-lou meng hui-p'i*" 蒙漢文化交流的歷史見證— 評哈斯寶新譯紅樓夢回批. *Nei-meng-ku ta-hsüeh hsüeh-pao*, 1975. 3.
———. "P'ing Ha-ssu-pao *Hsin-i Hung-lou meng hui-p'i*" 評哈斯寶新譯紅樓夢回批. *Nei-meng-ku ta-hsüeh hsüeh-pao*, 1974. 3:37–41.
Chou Shuang-li 周雙利 et al. "*Hung-lou meng* yü Meng-ku tsu ku-tien wen-hsüeh ti fa-chan" 紅樓夢與蒙古族古典文學的發展. *Nei-meng-ku she-hui k'o-hsüeh* 內蒙古社會科學, 1983. 4:78–83 (*Hung-lou meng yen-chiu* reprint, 1983. 9:3–8).
Hsing Li 邢莉. "*Hsin-i Hung-lou meng hui-p'i* ti ssu-hsiang chia-chih" 新譯紅樓夢回批的思想價值. *Min-tsu wen-hsüeh yen-chiu* 民族文學研究, 1985. 3:83–87.
———. "Meng-ku tsu Hung-hsüeh p'ing-tien chia Ha-ssu-pao ti hsiao-shuo li-lun" 蒙古族紅學評點家哈斯寶的小說理論. *Chung-yang min-tsu hsüeh-yüan hsüeh-pao*, 1984. 1:104–8.
Hu Wen-pin 胡文彬, and Chou Lei 周雷. "*Hsin-i Hung-lou meng hui-p'i*" 新譯紅樓夢回批. *Hung-lou meng hsüeh-k'an*, 1980. 3:218. Reprinted in *Hung-hsüeh ts'ung-t'an*, pp. 318–19.
I Lin-chen 亦鄰真, trans. "Ha-ssu-pao *Hsin-i Hung-lou meng* chai-lu" 哈斯寶新譯紅樓夢摘錄. *Nei-meng-ku ta-hsüeh hsüeh-pao*, 1974. 3:42–46; 1975. 3.
Ko-jih-le-t'u 格日勒圖. "Kuan-yü Ha-ssu-pao ti *Hsin-i Hung-lou meng* chi ch'i t'a" 關於哈斯寶的新譯紅樓夢及其他. *Nei-meng-ku ta-hsüeh hsüeh-pao*, 1976. 1.
Liang I-ju 梁一孺. "*Hsin-i Hung-lou meng*" 新譯紅樓夢. *Nei-meng-ku jih-pao* 內蒙古日報, 10/22/1983 (*Hung-lou meng yen-chiu* reprint, 1983. 10:78).
———. "Meng-ku wen pen *Hsin-i Hung-lou meng* p'ing-chieh" 蒙古文本新譯紅樓夢評介. *Hung-lou meng hsüeh-k'an* 2:197–208 (1979).
Liang I-ju, and Se-yin-pa-wei-erh 色音巴維爾. "Ha-ssu-pao ho t'a ti *Hsin-i Hung-lou meng*" 哈斯寶和他的新譯紅樓夢. *Kuang-ming jih-pao*, 11/26/1977.
Pao-yin-ho-hsi-ko 寶音賀希格. "Ha-ssu-pao *Hsin-i Hung-lou meng* nien-tai k'ao" 哈斯寶新譯紅樓夢年代考. *Nei-meng-ku ta-hsüeh hsüeh-pao*, 1978. 1:52–53.
Wang Chün-ling 王俊玲. "Ha-ssu-pao *Hsin-i Hung-lou meng hui-p'i* ch'u-t'an" 哈斯寶新譯紅樓夢回批初探. *Nei-meng-ku ta-hsüeh hsüeh-pao*, 1985. 3:47–56, 74 (*Hung-lou meng yen-chiu* reprint, 1985. 5:65–75).

ABBREVIATED TITLE: Manuscript copy of the Chang Hsin-chih 張新之 commentary. FULL TITLE: *Miao-fu hsüan p'ing Shih-t'ou chi* 妙復軒評石頭記 (Commentary on the *Story of the Stone* from Miao-fu Studio). This title does not appear in the copy in the Peking Library seen by the editor, but it is the title most commonly used by scholars. The only formal title in the Peking Library copy appears in Chang Hsin-chih's preface: *Miao-fu hsüan Shih-t'ou p'ing*. LENGTH: 120 chapters. PUBLISHER: The Peking Library copy is a manucript copy of the comments along with the quotation of the sections of the novel to which they refer. DATE: The commentary was completed in 1850. PREFATORY MATERIAL: Tzu-lang shan-jen 紫琅山人 (pseud.) preface, Yüan-hu Yüeh-ch'ih-tzu 鴛湖月痴子 (pseud.) preface (1851), Wu-kuei shan-jen 五桂山人 (pseud.), "*Miao-fu hsüan Shih-t'ou p'ing* tzu-chi" 妙復軒石頭評自記 (Preface by the Author) dated 1850, and "T'ai-p'ing hsien-jen *Hung-lou meng* tu-fa" 太平閑人紅樓夢讀法 (How to Read the *Hung-lou meng* by the Man of Leisure of the Great Peace). At the end of the last volume there are three poems by Chang Hsin-chih celebrating the completion of the commentary. COMMENTARY: Comments written after selected passages from the novel, plus postchapter comments, by Chang Hsin-chih (fl. 1828–1851, style T'ai-p'ing hsien-jen, studio name Miao-fu hsüan). REMARKS: Chang Hsin-chih's *tu-fa* essay and comments were reprinted in a variety of late Ch'ing editions of the novel, sometimes with rather severe textual variations. AVAILABILITY: A copy is held in the Peking Library, but it appears not to be the one mentioned by Liu Ch'üan-fu 劉銓福 as being bound in twelve large volumes (see introduction to chapter VII above). The prefatory material from the Peking Library copy is transcribed and reprinted in *HLMC* and *HLMTLHP*.

Plaks, Andrew H. "Late-Qing Confucian Interpretations of the *Honglou meng*: The Zhang Xinzhi Commentary." Paper presented at the 1986 International *Hung-lou meng* Conference, Harbin, China.

Chou Ju-ch'ang 周汝昌. "Liu Ch'üan-fu k'ao" 劉銓福考. In *Hung-lou meng hsin-cheng*, pp. 953–65.

Chuang Wei 莊葳. "Liu Ch'üan-fu ho Chao Ho-ch'ien" 劉銓福和趙和謙. *Chung-hua wen-shih lun-ts'ung* 8:414 (1978).

Fang Hao 方豪. "Tsai T'ai-wan wan-ch'eng ti *Miao-fu hsüan p'ing Shih-t'ou chi*" 在台灣完成的妙復軒評石頭記. *Chung-hua wen-hua fu-hsing yüeh-k'an* 中華文化復興月刊 2. 4:50–52 (1969). Also in his *Fang Hao liu-shih tzu-ting kao* 方豪六十自定稿. Taipei: Hsüeh-sheng shu-chü, 1969, pp. 1158–94.

Hao Yü 豪雨. "T'an *Hung-lou meng* ti Miao-fu hsüan p'ing pen" 談紅樓夢的妙復軒評本. *Hsin-min pao wan-k'an*, 3/20–22/1953.

Lin Wen-lung 林文龍. "Hsien-hua *Miao-fu hsüan p'ing Shih-t'ou chi*" 閑話妙復軒評石頭記. *T'ai-nan wen-hua* 台南文化 6:70–77 (1979).

TITLE: Liu Lü-fen 劉履芬 commentary. LENGTH: 120 chapters. PUBLISHER: Private copy of 1811 Tung-kuan ko edition with added manuscript comments. DATE: Two of the comments are dated to 1865 and 1871, respectively. PREFATORY MATERIAL: No new material. COMMENTARY: Marginal, bottom (*ti-p'i* 底批), and single-column interlineal comments written by Liu Lü-fen (1827–1879, courtesy name Yen-ch'ing 彥青). Additional comments are written in blank space under indented material (such as poetry). Both red and black ink used. Some of Wang Hsi-lien's comments have been transcribed onto this copy by Liu Lü-fen. AVAILABILITY: An edited collection of the comments has reportedly been published by Wang Wei-min 王衛民 as *Hung-lou meng Liu Lü-fen p'i-yü chi-lu* 紅樓夢 劉履芬批語輯錄 (Collected Comments on the *Hung-lou meng* by Liu Lü-fen; Peking: Shu-mu wen-hsien, n.d.).

Chou Ju-ch'ang 周汝昌. "*Hung-lou meng Liu Lü-fen p'i-yü chi-lu* hsü" 紅樓夢 劉履芬批語輯錄序. *Wen-hsien* 15:75–80 (1983).

Wang Wei-min 王衛民. "T'an Liu Lü-fen Tung-kuan ko p'i-yü" 談劉履芬 東觀閣批語. *Wen-hsien* 11:74–87 (1982) (*Hung-lou meng yen-chiu* reprint, 1982. 11:67–77).

ABBREVIATED TITLE: Sun T'ung-sheng 孫桐生 edition. FULL TITLE: *Miao-fu hsüan p'ing-pen hsiu-hsiang Shih-t'ou chi Hung-lou meng* 妙復軒評本綉像石頭記 紅樓夢 (Illustrated Miao-fu Studio Commentary Edition of the *Shih-t'ou chi/ Hung-lou meng*). LENGTH: 120 chapters. PUBLISHER: Wo-yün shan kuan 卧雲山館. DATE: 1881. PREFATORY MATERIAL: Ch'eng Wei-yüan preface, Sun T'ung-sheng preface (1873) and postface (1876), and Chang Hsin-chih's *tu-fa* essay minus the last three items. After the text of the novel are printed Chang Hsin-chih's poems commemorating the completion of the commentary and Sun T'ung-sheng's poems in response. COMMENTARY: Double-column interlineal and postchapter comments by Chang Hsin-chih, edited by Sun T'ung-sheng. REMARKS: This edition was edited by Sun T'ung-sheng (1852 *chin-shih*), who wrongly identified the commentator as T'ung Pu-nien 仝卜年. This version of the *tu-fa* essay omits the last three items and divides four of the previous items into two parts for a total of thirty-one items. Many of the comments are given in a form slightly different from that of the Peking Library manuscript copy, and some comments in the latter are completely omitted. AVAILABILITY: A microfilm of this edition courtesy of Professor Itō Sōhei of Tokyo University is available in the Gest Oriental Library, Princeton University. Some of the prefatory material peculiar to this edition is available in *HLMC* and *HLMTLHP*.

ABBREVIATED TITLE: "Chin-yü yüan" 金玉緣 editions. FULL TITLE: *Tseng-p'ing pu-hsiang ch'üan-t'u Chin-yü yüan* 增評補像全圖金玉緣 (The Affinity of Gold and Jade, Fully Illustrated, with Additional Comments and Illustrations). LENGTH: 120 chapters in 16 *chüan*. PUBLISHER: T'ung-wen shu-chü 同文書局, Shanghai. DATE: 1884. PREFATORY MATERIAL: Hua-yang hsien-i 華陽仙裔 (pseud.) preface (1884), "T'ai-p'ing hsien-jen tu-fa" 太平閑人讀法 (How to Read Essay by Chang Hsin-chih), preface and "Tsung-p'ing" by Wang Hsi-lien, a portion of Chu Lien's 諸聯 *Hung-lou p'ing-meng* 紅樓評夢 (Commentary on the Dream from the Red Chamber) entitled here "Ming-chai chu-jen tsung-p'ing" 明齋 主人總評 (General Remarks by the Owner of Ming Studio), "Ta-mei shan-min tsung-p'ing" 大某山民總評 (General Comments by Yao Hsieh) attributed to Yao Hsieh 姚燮 (1805–1864, style Ta-mei shan-min), T'u Ying's "*Hung-lou meng* lun-tsan" and "*Hung-lou meng* wen-ta" (here entitled "Huo-wen" 或問 [Someone Asked]), "Ta-kuan yüan ying-shih shih-erh yung" 大觀園影事十二咏 (Twelve Poems on Incidents in the Grand Prospect Garden; anonymous), prefatory poems by Chou Ch'i, phonetic glosses by Wang Hsi-lien, and "Ta-kuan yüan t'u-shuo." COMMENTARY: Double-column interlineal and postchapter comments by Chang Hsin-chih. His postchapter comments are followed by chapter comments by Wang Hsi-lien and Yao Hsieh. REMARKS: In later editions the date at the end of the Hua-yang hsien-i preface is set later and later and the preface itself is renamed "Ch'ung-k'an *Chin-yü yüan* hsü" 重刊金玉緣序 (Preface to the Reprinting of the Affinity of Gold and Jade). The "Tsung-p'ing" attributed to Yao Hsieh is not by him at all. Seventy-six of the eighty items there are copied with only minor changes from the notes appended to Chiang Ch'i's 姜祺 "*Hung-lou meng* shih" 紅樓夢詩 (Poems on the *Hung-lou meng*; quoted in *HLMC*, pp. 475–90). These notes, which might have been written by Wang T'ao 王韜 (1828–1897), were copied onto Yao Hsieh's personal copy of the novel, a transcribed version of which is held in the Chekiang Provincial Library, where they are properly identified. AVAILABILITY: Late Ch'ing reprints from this filiation are generally available but usually very fragile because of the poor quality of the paper used. A photo-reprint of a 1908 edition is available: *CYY*. In that edition the *tu-fa* essay and the phonetic glosses have been left out (even though they are listed in the table of contents), and a new piece entitled "P'ing-lun" 評論 (Comments) has been added. This new piece is actually just a selection from Hua-shih chu-jen's 話石主人 (pseud.) *Hung-lou meng pen-i yüeh-pien* 紅樓夢本義約編 (The Basic Meaning of the *Hung-lou meng*; for quoted section, see *HLMC*, pp. 182–83). A photo-reprint of an example of this type of edition will be published by Shang-hai ku-chi in the near future. Many of the separate pieces in this edition are reprinted in *HLMC* and *HLMTLHP*.

Chao Hsing-ken 趙杏根. "Yao Hsieh chu-shu k'ao" 姚燮著書考. *Chung-hua wen-shih lun-ts'ung*, 1985. 2:277–90.

Chia Shih 佳士. "Ta-mei shan-min" 大某山民. *Shih-chieh jih-pao* 世界日報, 12/29/1948.

Hung K'o-i 洪克夷. "Ta-mei shan-min chi ch'i *Hung-lou meng* p'ing" 大某山民及其紅樓評. *Hung-lou meng hsüeh-k'an*, 1984. 4:219–28.

ABBREVIATED TITLE: "Shih-t'ou chi" 石頭記 editions. FULL TITLE: *Tseng-p'ing pu-t'u Shih-t'ou chi* 增評補圖石頭記 (*Story of the Stone* with Added Commentary and Illustrations). LENGTH: 120 chapters. PUBLISHER: Kuang-pai-sung chai 廣百松齋, Shanghai. DATE: No later than 1886. PREFATORY MATERIAL: Ch'eng Wei-yüan preface, "T'ai-p'ing hsien-jen tu-fa, fu pu-i ting-wu" 太平閑人讀法附補遺訂悞 (*Tu-fa* Essay by T'ai-p'ing hsien-jen with Rectification of Lacunae and Errors Appended), "Tsung-p'ing" and "Chai-wu" by Wang Hsi-lien, "Tsung-p'ing" by "Yao Hsieh," T'u Ying's "Huo-wen" and "Tu-hua jen lun-tsan" (same as "*Hung-lou meng* lun-tsan"), Chou Ch'i's prefatory poems, "Ta-kuan yüan ying-shih shih-erh yung," and "Ta-kuan yüan t'u-shuo." COMMENTARY: Postchapter comments by Wang Hsi-lien and Yao Hsieh, in that order. This edition also has interlineal and marginal comments, many of which are by Yao Hsieh. All of the prefatory material except Yao Hsieh's "Tsung-p'ing" have marginal comments. REMARKS: Some of the marginal and interlineal comments are similar to Chang Hsin-chih interlineal comments. Although there are twenty-seven items in this version of the *tu-fa* essay, some of the items here are new, while others from the Sun T'ung-sheng version have been dropped. This version of the essay is clearly not based on the manuscript version because wherever Sun T'ung-sheng's version differs from the manuscript version the "Shih-t'ou chi" version follows the Sun T'ung-sheng version or later recensions of it. In both the text of the *tu-fa* essay and the Ch'eng Wei-yüan preface, the words "Hung-lou meng" have either been omitted or changed to "Shih-t'ou chi." A transcribed version of Yao Hsieh's commentary and notes on a Wang Hsi-lien edition of the novel is held in the Chekiang Provincial Library. As is the case with the "Tsung-p'ing" attributed to him in this and the "Chin-yü yüan" editions, some of the original material was merely collected by Yao Hsieh and is not by him. The transcribed copy also contains material not selected by Yao Hsieh but added onto the copy by the transcriber (probably Hsü Ch'uan-ching 徐傳經, style Hsi-hsin tz'u-k'o 惜馨詞客). Different colored inks and the particular placement on the page of the comments were used by the transcriber to separate the different materials, but materials from the different authors and texts have been indiscriminately copied into the printed Wang-Yao editions without regard to their provenance or authorship. The "pu-i" and "ting-wu" appended to the *tu-fa* essay, although not found in the transcribed copy of the Yao Hsieh commentary seen by the editor, refer to peculiarities of the text of the Wang Hsi-lien woodblock edition of the novel. Later editions, including the "Shih-t'ou chi" versions under discussion, do not have these peculiarities, therefore later reprints of the "Shih-t'ou chi" editions dropped first the text of those two items and then the reference to them in the title of the *tu-fa* essay. AVAILABILITY: There is a photo-reprint in the *Kuo-hsüeh chi-pen ts'ung-shu* 國學基本叢書 (Basic Sinological Collection; Taipei: Commercial Press, 1968 reprint), vols. 257–58. A later, slightly different version originally titled *Ching-chiao ch'üan-t'u ch'ien-yin p'ing-chu Chin-yü yüan* 精校全圖鉛印評注金玉緣 (Fully Illustrated, Finely Collated, Lead Type, Annotated and Commentated Affinity of Gold and Jade) with one extra prefatory item, Liu Chia-ming's 劉家銘 "Tsa-shuo" 雜說 (Miscellaneous Comments), is available in a photo-reprint: *Ching-p'i pu-t'u Ta-mei shan-min p'ing-pen Hung-lou meng* 精批補圖大某山民評本紅樓夢 (Commentary Edition of the *Hung-lou meng* by Yao Hsieh, Finely Commented on with Additional Illustrations; Taipei: Kuang-wen shu-chü, 1973).

TITLE: *Tu Hung-lou meng sui-pi* 讀紅樓夢隨筆 (Random Notes on Reading the *Hung-lou meng*). LENGTH: Only treats up to chap. 69. The commentary does not appear to be based on any presently extant recension of the novel. PUBLISHER: Private manuscript copy without the text of the novel. DATE: Probably completed in the later 1880s. PREFATORY MATERIAL: Prior to the comments on chap. 1, there is an untitled section of general comments. COMMENTARY: Chapter comments. REMARKS: Major sections of this commentary were later copied into

Hung Ch'iu-fan's 洪秋蕃 *Hung-lou meng chüeh-yin* 紅樓夢抉隱 (Hidden Meaning of the *Hung-lou meng* Revealed; Shanghai: Shang-hai t'u-shu, 1925). AVAILABILITY: Photo-reprint: *Tu Hung-lou meng sui-pi* 讀紅樓夢隨筆 (Ch'eng-tu: Pa-Shu shu-she, 1984).

Hu Pang-wei 胡邦煒. "*Tu Hung-lou meng sui-pi* ti fa-hsien chi ch'i i-i" 讀紅樓夢隨筆的發現及其意義. *T'ien-fu hsin-lun* 天府新論, 1985. 1:56ff. Reprinted in *Chung-kuo ku-tien hsiao-shuo i-shu ti ssu-k'ao*, pp. 177–98.

ABBREVIATED TITLE: Tieh-hsiang hsien-shih 蝶薌仙史 edition. FULL TITLE: *Tseng-p'ing chia-p'i Chin-yü yüan t'u-shuo* 增評加批金玉緣圖說 (Illustrated Explanations of the Affinity of Gold and Jade with Added Commentary). LENGTH: 120 chapters in 12 *chüan*. PUBLISHER: T'ung-yin hsüan 桐蔭軒, Shanghai. DATE: 1906. PREFATORY MATERIAL: Same as "Chin-yü yüan" editions. COMMENTARY: Besides Wang Hsi-lien's postchapter comments, double-column interlineal comments have been added by T'ieh-hsiang hsien-shih (pseud.). AVAILABILITY: There is a copy in the Peking Library.

TITLE: *Hung-lou meng so-yin* 紅樓夢索隱 (The Hidden Meaning of the *Hung-lou meng*). LENGTH: 120 chapters. PUBLISHER: Chung-hua shu-chü, Shanghai. DATE: 1916. PREFATORY MATERIAL: Preface and "Li-yen" 例言 (General Principles) by Wang Meng-juan 王夢阮 and Shen P'ing-an 沈瓶庵, and "*Hung-lou meng so-yin* t'i-yao" 紅樓夢索隱提要 (Abstract of the *Hung-lou meng so-yin*) by Wu-chen tao-jen 悟真道人 (pseud.). COMMENTARY: Interlineal comments and occasional interpolated essays. REMARKS: The novel is interpreted as being a disguised account of the relationship between the first Ch'ing emperor and one of his consorts. AVAILABILITY: Original edition and reprints commonly available. For instance: *Hung-lou meng so-yin* 紅樓夢索隱 (Taipei: Chung-hua shu-chü, 1964).

Sha Yü 沙予, and Wen Ch'üan 文銓. "'So-yin' chin-hsi t'an" 索隱今昔談. *Sui-pi* 隨筆 16:57–58 (1981). Reprinted in *Hung-lou meng tzu-liao chi*, vol. 4, pp. 217–18.
Teng Ch'ing-yu 鄧慶佑. "T'an *Hung-lou meng so-yin*" 談紅樓夢索隱. *Chi-ning shih-chuan hsüeh-pao*, 1984. 2:55–59 (*Hung-lou meng yen-chiu* reprint, 1984. 4:15–20).

TITLE: Wang Hsieh 王瀣 commentary. LENGTH: 120 chapters. PUBLISHER: Wang Hsieh's (1884–1944, courtesy name Po-hang 伯沆) commentary was copied by hand onto a Wang Hsi-lien edition copy of the novel. His copy was lacking the first *chüan* with the prefatory material, so he substituted the corresponding section of a 1905 Japanese typeset reprint of a "Shih-t'ou chi" edition. DATE: 1914–38. PREFATORY MATERIAL: No new material, but Wang Hsieh has added some comments to the printed prefatory material. COMMENTARY: Single-column interlineal, marginal, bottom (*ti-p'i* 底批), and postchapter comments.

DISTINGUISHING FEATURES: The bulk of the comments are written in the top and bottom margins of the pages. The commentary does not seem to have been written with publication in mind. The comments were written in five different time periods between 1914 and 1938 in five different colors of ink according to the time period each comment was recorded. REMARKS: According to tabulation by Chao Kuo-chang 趙國璋 and T'an Feng-liang 談鳳梁, there are over 12,000 separate comments in this commentary. AVAILABILITY: Parts of this material were first published in *Nan-ching wen-hsien* 南京文獻 21 (1948). Chao Kuo-chang and T'an Feng-liang, eds., *Wang Po-hang Hung-lou meng p'i-yü hui-lu* 王伯沆紅樓夢批語彙錄 (Collected Wang Hsieh Comments on the *Hung-lou meng*; Nan-t'ung: Chiang-su ku-chi, 1985) contains the text of the comments with enough quotation from the novel to allow the reader to find the appropriate place in the text. Selected comments were reproduced by the same editors as "*Hung-lou meng* Wang Hsieh p'i-yü hsüan-k'an" 紅樓夢王沆批語選刊, *Hung-lou meng yen-chiu chi-k'an* 5:257–89 (1980).

Chao Kuo-chang 趙國璋, and T'an Feng-liang 談鳳梁. "*Hung-lou meng* Wang Hsieh p'ing-pen kai-shu" 紅樓夢王沆評本概述. *Hung-lou meng yen-chiu chi-k'an* 5:241–55 (1980).

Selected Traditional Works on the Hung-lou meng

Yüeh Hung-lou meng sui-pi 閱紅樓夢隨筆 (Notes on Reading the *Hung-lou meng*), by Chou Ch'un 周春 (1729–1815), reprinted in *HLMC*, pp. 66–77. There is a photo-reprint (Shanghai: Chung-hua shu-chü, 1958) of a manuscript copy. Includes 1794 preface, "P'ing-li" 評例 (Principles of the Commentary), and "Yüeh-p'ing" 約評 (Brief Comments). The comments are randomly organized.

Hung-lou meng shuo-meng 紅樓夢說夢 (Dream Talk on the *Hung-lou meng*), by Erh-chih tao-jen 二知道人 (pseud.), printed edition 1812. Included in *HLMC*, pp. 83–103. Preface by Chu Fu 朱矞, poems and random comments.

Liu Shih-te 劉世德. "*Hung-lou meng shuo-meng* tso-che k'ao" 紅樓夢說夢作者考. *Hung-lou meng hsüeh-k'an*, 1981. 1:339–45.

Ch'ih-jen shuo-meng 痴人說夢 (The Idiot Discourses on a Dream), by T'iao-hsi yü-yin 苕溪漁隱 (pseud.), 1817 Huai-Hung lou 懷紅樓 edition.

Chou Shao-liang 周紹良. "*Ch'ih-jen shuo-meng* pa" 痴人說夢跋. *Hung-lou meng yen-chiu chi-k'an* 2:252 (1980).

Hung-lou meng ou-shuo 紅樓夢偶說 (Random Remarks on the *Hung-lou meng*), by Ts'ao-she chü-shih 草舍居士 (pseud.). The author's preface is dated 1821, but the first printing seems to date to 1876 and is by Lou-fu shan-fang chu-jen 簍復山房主人 (pseud.), who also edited and arranged the individual comments that make up this work. Portions are reprinted in *HLMC*, pp. 121–25, but a complete photocopy (publication information not indicated) is held in the Gest Oriental Library, Princeton University.

Hung-lou p'ing-meng 紅樓評夢 (Commentary on the Dream from the Red Chamber), by Chu Lien 諸聯 (b. 1765), 1821. Included in *HLMC* in abridged form, pp. 116–21.

Tu Hung-lou meng kang-ling 讀紅樓夢綱領 (An Outline for Reading the *Hung-lou meng*), by Yao Hsieh, author preface 1860. Not published until 1940 under the title *Hung-lou meng lei-so* 紅樓夢類索 (An Index to Categories of Things in the *Hung-lou meng*; Shanghai: Chu-lin shu-tien, 1940), edited by Wei Yu-fei 魏友棐 and Hung Ching-shan 洪荊山. Two sections of this work are reproduced in *HLMC*, pp. 164–75.

Chao Ching-shen 趙景深. "Yao Hsieh ti *Hung-lou meng lei-so*" 姚燮的紅樓夢類索. *Yü-chou feng i-k'an* 宇宙風乙刊, 3/16/1941. Reprinted in his *Chung-kuo hsiao-shuo ts'ung-k'ao* 中國小說叢考. Tsinan: Ch'i Lu shu-she, 1980, pp. 431–32.

Ch'en Nan-hsüan 陳南軒. "Chien-chieh *Hung-lou meng p'u* ho *Hung-lou meng lei-so*" 簡介紅樓夢譜和紅樓夢類索. *Tz'u-shu yen-chiu* 辭書研究, 1982. 4:163–65.

Kuo Yung 郭庸. "I-pen Ch'ing-tai ti chiu Hung-hsüeh chu-tso" 一本清代的舊紅學著作. *Shu-lin*, 1981. 1:50. Reprinted in *Hung-lou meng tzu-liao chi*, vol. 4, p. 52.

Tu Hung-lou meng tsa-chi 讀紅樓夢雜記 (Miscellaneous Notes on Reading the *Hung-lou meng*), by Chiang Shun-i 江順怡, privately published in Hangchou, 1869. Included in *HLMC*, pp. 205–10.

Hung-lou meng ou-p'ing 紅樓夢偶評 (Random Comments on the *Hung-lou meng*), by Chang Ch'i-hsin 張其信. Published in 1877 by the Pao-jen t'ang of Peking and included in abridged form in *HLMC*, pp. 214–18.

Hung-lou meng pen-i yüeh-pien 紅樓夢本義約編 (The Basic Meaning of the *Hung-lou meng*), by Hua-shih chu-jen 話石主人 (pseud.), 1878, and included in abridged form in *HLMC*, pp. 179–83.

Shih-t'ou i-shuo 石頭臆說 (My Thoughts on the *Story of the Stone*), by Chieh-an chü-shih 解盦居士 (pseud.), 1887 P'i-ling ching-she edition. Included in *HLMC*, pp. 184–97.

Meng-ch'ih shuo-meng 夢痴說夢 (Dream Talk from Dream-Crazy), by Meng-ch'ih hsüeh-jen 夢痴學人 (pseud.), Kuan k'o-shou chai, 1887. Included in abridged form in *HLMC*, pp. 218–27. Prefaces for the first and second halves of this work are dated 1871 and 1879. The writer uses Taoist and *I Ching* concepts in his interpretations.

Hung-lou meng fa-wei 紅樓夢發微 (Making Manifest the Subtlety of the *Hung-lou meng*), by Pien-shan ch'iao-tzu 弁山樵子 (pseud.), published in *Hsiang-yen tsa-chih* 香艷雜志, issues 11 and 12 (1916). Quoted in abridged form in *HLMC*, pp. 326–31. This work includes a fourteen-item *tu-fa* essay.

Shih-t'ou chi so-yin 石頭記索隱 (The Key to the *Story of the Stone*), by Ts'ai Yüan-p'ei 蔡元培 (1868–1940). First published in serial form in *Hsiao-shuo yüeh-pao* 小說月報 (Fiction Monthly) in 1916. There is a preface by the author for the sixth reprint. The novel is interpreted as anti-Manchu and concerned with twelve Ming dynasty literati who collaborated with the Ch'ing dynasty. An appendix by Ch'ien Ching-fang 錢靜方 and one by Meng Sen 孟森 refute other roman à clef interpretations of the novel.

Ts'ai Yüan-p'ei 蔡元培. "*Shih-t'ou chi so-yin* ti-liu pan tzu-hsü" 石頭記索隱第六版自序. In *Hung-lou meng yen-chiu ts'an-k'ao tzu-liao hsüan-chi*, vol. 3, pp. 34–38.

"Ts'ai Yüan-p'ei" 蔡元培. *Hung-lou meng hsüeh-k'an*, 1982. 2:190–94.

Chin-yü yüan ti wen-fa kuan 金玉緣的文法觀 (Rhetoric in the Affinity of Gold and Jade), by Chou Wo-t'ing 周斡庭, 1925. Published in two *chüan*. Incomplete copy (first *chüan* only) in Peking Library. This work consists of selections from the novel classified by type with comments appended.

General Bibliography on Fiction Criticism and the Hung-lou meng

Plaks, Andrew H. "Allegory in *Hsi-yu chi* and *Hung-lou meng*." In *Chinese Narrative: Critical and Theoretical Essays*, pp. 163–202.

A Ying 阿英 (Ch'ien Hsing-ts'un 錢杏邨). "*Hung-lou meng* shu-hua" 紅樓夢書話. In *Hsiao-shuo erh-t'an* 小說二談. Reprinted in *Hsiao-shuo hsien-t'an ssu-chung*, pp. 128–35.
———. "*Hung-lou meng* shu-lu" 紅樓夢書錄. In *Hsiao-shuo ssu-t'an* 小說四談. Reprinted in *Hsiao-shuo hsien-t'an ssu-chung*, pp. 1–103.
Chu I-hsüan 朱一玄, ed. *Hung-lou meng tzu-liao hui-pien* 紅樓夢資料彙編. Tien-tsin: Nan-k'ai ta-hsüeh, 1985.
Ch'un Hung 春紅. "*Hung-lou meng* shu-lu to-i chih erh" 紅樓夢書錄掇逸之二. *Hung-lou meng yen-chiu chi-k'an* 8:420, 419 (1982).
Han Chin-lien 韓進廉. *Hung-hsüeh shih kao* 紅學史稿. Shih-chia-chuang: Ho-pei jen-min, 1981.
Hsü Kung-shih 徐恭時. "*Hung-lou meng* pan-pen yu kuan jen-wu tzu-liao cha-chi" 紅樓夢版本有關人物資料札記. In *Hung-lou meng pan-pen lun-ts'ung*, pp. 221–50.
Hu Wen-pin 胡文彬. *Hung-lou meng hsü-lu* 紅樓夢叙錄. Ch'ang-ch'un: Chi-lin jen-min, 1980.
———. "*P'ing-pen Hung-lou meng* chih-chien so-lu" 評本紅樓夢知見瑣錄. *Wen-hsien* 3:172–76 (1980).
Hung-lou meng yen-chiu tzu-liao pien-chi tsu 紅樓夢研究資料編輯組. *Hung-lou meng yen-chiu tzu-liao* 紅樓夢研究資料. Peking: Pei-ching shih-ta, 1975.
I-su 一粟 (Chou Shao-liang 周紹良 and Chu Nan-hsien 朱南銑), ed. *Hung-lou meng chüan* 紅樓夢卷. Shanghai: Chung-hua shu-chü, 1963.
———. *Hung-lou meng shu-lu* 紅樓夢書錄. Shanghai; Ku-tien wen-hsüeh, 1958; Shanghai: Shang-hai ku-chi, revised edition, 1981.
Kuo Yü-shih 郭豫適. "*Hung-lou meng* p'ing-tien p'ai" 紅樓夢評點派. *Shang-hai shih-fan hsüeh-yüan hsüeh-pao*, 1979. 1:74–85. Reprinted in *Hung-lou meng yen-chiu chi-k'an* 4:71–99 (1980).

―――. *Hung-lou meng yen-chiu hsiao-shih kao* 紅樓夢研究小史稿. Shanghai: Shang-hai wen-i, 1980.

―――. "Ts'ung Hu Shih, Ts'ai Yüan-p'ei ti i-ch'ang cheng-lun tao So-yin p'ai ti chung kuei ch'iung-t'u―chien p'ing *Hung-lou meng* yen-chiu shih shang ti hou-ch'i So-yin p'ai" 從胡適蔡元培的一場爭論到索隱派的終歸窮途—兼評紅樓夢研究史上的後期索隱派. *Hung-lou meng yen-chiu chi-k'an* 4:71–98 (1980).

Liu Meng-hsi 劉夢溪. "*Hung-lou meng* ti pan-pen yen-pien ho Hung-hsüeh shih shang ti tou-cheng" 紅樓夢的版本演變和紅學史上的鬥爭. In his *Hung-lou meng hsin-lun*, pp. 268–85.

Shang Ta-hsiang 尙達翔, and Chin Yü-t'ien 金玉田. "Ch'ing-tai Hung-hsüeh lüeh-ying" 清代紅學掠影. *Cheng-chou ta-hsüeh hsüeh-pao*, 1981. 2:22–30. Reprinted in *Hung-hsüeh san-shih nien lun-wen hsüan-pien*, vol. 3, pp. 591–609.

Tai Pu-fan 戴不凡. "Pan-pen shih hsiao-lu" 版本史小錄. *Hung-lou meng yen-chiu chi-k'an* 4:255–69 (1980).

Tuan Ch'i-ming 段啟明. "'Chiu Hung-hsüeh' chung ti tien-hsing lun" 舊紅學中的典型論. *Hung-lou meng yen-chiu chi-k'an* 8:71–76 (1982).

Wei Shao-ch'ang 魏紹昌. *Hung-lou meng pan-pen hsiao-k'ao* 紅樓夢版本小考. Peking: Chung-kuo she-hui k'o-hsüeh, 1982.

Wen Lei 文雷 (Hu Wen-pin 胡文彬 and Chou Lei 周雷). "*Hung-lou meng* pan-pen ch'ien-t'an" 紅樓夢版本淺談. *Wen-wu*, 1974. 9:33–39. Reprinted in *Hung-lou meng pan-pen lun-ts'ung*, pp. 1–11; in *Hung-hsüeh ts'ung-t'an*, pp. 109–20; and in *Pan-pen*, pp. 586–96.

Yang Wei-chen 楊為珍, and Kuo Jung-kuang 郭榮光. *Hung-lou meng tz'u-tien* 紅樓夢辭典. Tsinan: Shan-tung wen-i, 1986.

Yü P'ing-po 俞平伯. "Tu *Hung-lou meng* sui-pi" 讀紅樓夢隨筆. *Ta-kung pao*, 1/1/1954 to 4/23/1954. Reprinted in *Hung-lou meng yen-chiu ts'an-k'ao tzu-liao hsüan-chi*, vol. 2, pp. 38–168.

List of Commentary Editions of Traditional Chinese Fiction Other than the Six Novels

This list is by no means complete. It is designed to bring attention to the most commonly available editions.

Ch'an-chen i-shih 禪真逸史. Various commentators. Tsinan: Ch'i Lu shu-she, 1986, typeset edition.

Ch'ang-yen tao 常言道. Hao-hao hsien-sheng 好好先生, comment. In *Ku-tai chung-p'ien hsiao-shuo san-chung* 古代中篇小說三種. Hangchou: Che-chiang ku-chi, 1986.

Chien-hsiao ko p'i-p'ing mi-pen ch'u-hsiang Sui-shih i-wen 劍嘯閣批評秘本出像隋史遺文. Yüan Yü-ling 袁于令, author and comment. Taipei: Yu-shih wen-hua, 1975, typeset edition chapter comments (marginal comments deleted).

Chih-nang ch'üan chi 智囊全集. Feng Meng-lung 馮夢龍, comment. Nanking: Chiang-su ku-chi, 1986.

Ching-hua yüan 鏡花緣. Tao-kuang edition (incomplete) held by Columbia University. See also *Ching-hui* … and *Hui-t'u.* …

Ching-hui ch'üan-t'u tsu-pen Ching-hua yüan 精繪全圖足本鏡花緣. Shanghai: Shang-hai ch'i-hsin shu-chü, 1924, chapter comments only.

Ch'ing-shih lei-lüeh 情史類略. Feng Meng-lung 馮夢龍, comment. Ch'ang-sha: Yüeh-lu shu-she, 1984, typeset edition.

Chu-ch'un yüan hsiao-shih 駐春園小史. San-yü t'ang 三餘堂 edition, 1783, microfiche in Van Gulik collection.

Feng-shen ch'üan-chieh 封神詮解. By Yü Ching 俞景. *Wen-lan hsüeh-pao chi-k'an* 文瀾學報季刊 2.3–4 (1931).

Feng-shen yen-i 封神演義. Chung Hsing 鍾惺 (attrib.), comment. Canton: Kuang-tung jen-min, 1980, typeset edition based on Ssu-hsüeh ts'ao-t'ang edition, also Shen-pao kuan ts'ung-shu chi edition.

Hsi-yu pu 西遊補, 1641, Tung Yüeh 董悅, comment. Peking: Wen-hsüeh ku-chi k'an-hsing she, 1955; Taipei: Shih-chieh shu-chü, 1962 photo-reprint. Typeset edition with chapter comments only, Shanghai: Shang-hai ku-chi, 1983. T'ien-mu shan-ch'iao 天目山樵 (Chang Wen-hu 張文虎) comment., in *Shuo-k'u* 說庫. Taipei: Hsin-hsing shu-chü, 1963 reprint.

Hsiang-chu Liao-chai chih-i t'u-yung 詳注聊齋志異圖詠. Lü Chan-en 呂湛恩, annot. Peking: Chung-kuo shu-tien, 1981, photo-reprint.

Hsiao-i Hsüeh Yüeh Mei 孝義雪月梅. Te-hsüeh t'ang 德學堂, 1775 preface. Comment. by Tung Meng-fen 董孟汾. See *Hsüeh Yüeh Mei chuan.*

Hsin-chüan Ch'en Mei-kung hsien-sheng p'i-p'ing Ch'un-ch'iu Lieh-kuo chih-chuan 新鐫陳眉公先生批評春秋列國志傳. Ch'en Chi-ju 陳繼儒, comment.

Tokyo: Yūmani shobō, 1983 photo-reprint in *Taiyaku Chūgoku rekishi shōsetsu senshū* 対訳中国歴史小説選集 series.

Hsin-chüan ch'üan-hsiang t'ung-su yen-i Sui Yang-ti yen-shih 新鐫全像通俗演義隋煬帝艷史. Jen-jui t'ang 人瑞堂 edition, "Fan-li," *chüan* comments by Pu-ching hsien-sheng 不經先生, copies held by Columbia and Stanford Universities. Later edition with interlineal comments, copy in Berkeley and Naikaku Bunko.

Hsin Chung-kuo wei-lai chi 新中國未來記. By Liang Ch'i-ch'ao 梁啟超, preface and chapter comments (chaps. 3–4) by author. In A-ying 阿英, ed., *Wan-Ch'ing wen-hsüeh ts'ung-ch'ao: hsiao-shuo i-chüan* 晚清文學叢鈔:小說一卷. Peking: Chung-hua shu-chü, 1960.

Hsin-hua ch'un-meng 新華春夢. Chang Ming-fei 張冥飛, comment. Mu-tan chiang: Hei-lung chiang Ch'ao-hsien min-tsu, 1985, typeset reprint.

Hsiu-hsiang Sui-T'ang yen-i 綉像隋唐演義. Peking: Chung-kuo shu-tien, 1986, reprint of Chung-yüan shu-chü edition, chapter comments but no "Fa-fan" or Lin Han 林瀚 preface.

Hsü Hsi-yu chi 續西遊記. Chen-fu chü-shih 真復居士, comment. Huai-yin: Chiang-su wen-i, 1986, typeset edition.

Hsüeh Yüeh Mei chuan 雪月梅傳. Tung Meng-fen 董孟汾, comment. Tsinan: Ch'i Lu shu-she, 1986). See also *Hsiao-i....*

Hua-yüeh hen 花月痕. Hui-wen t'ang 會文堂 edition, marginal and chapter comments by the author, Wei Hsui-jen 魏秀仁. Fu-chou: Fu-chien jen-min, 1981 reprint, chapter comments only.

Hui-t'u Ching-hua yüan 繪圖鏡花緣. Peking: Chung-kuo shu-tien, 1985, photo-reprint of 1888 Shanghai Tien-shih chai edition, chapter comments (probably incomplete) only.

Jou p'u-t'uan 肉蒲團. Chapter comments by the author, Li Yü 李漁, various editions.

Ku-chin hsiao 古今笑. Feng Meng-lung 馮夢龍, comment. Shih-chia-chuang: Ho-pei jen-min, 1985, typeset edition.

Lao Ts'an yu-chi 老殘遊記. Chapter comments by the author, Liu E 劉鶚. Tsinan: Ch'i Lu shu-she, 1981.

Liao-chai chih-i hui-chiao hui-chu hui-p'ing pen 聊齋誌異會校會注會評本. Edited by Chang Yu-ho 張友鶴. Shanghai: Chung-hua shu-chü, 1962. See also *Hsiang-chu....*

Lin Lan Hsiang 林蘭香. Chi-lü san-jen 寄旅散人, comment. Shenyang: Ch'un-feng wen-i, 1985, typeset edition.

Lung-t'u kung-an 龍圖公案. Li Chih 李贄 (attrib.), comment., copy in Columbia University.

Mei-p'i hsiang-chu Lao Ts'an yu-chi 眉批詳注老殘遊記. Leng-ning jen 冷凝人, comment. Taipei: Ho-p'an ch'u-pan she, 1979.

Nü-hsien wai-shih 女仙外史. Tientsin: Pai-hua wen-i, 1985, chapter comments by Liu T'ing-chi 劉庭璣 et al.

Pai-kuei chih 白圭志. Shenyang: Ch'un-feng wen-i, 1985, typeset reprint, chapter comments.

P'ai-an ching-ch'i 拍案驚奇. Hong Kong: Yu-lien ch'u-pan she, 1966, typeset edition, marginal, interlineal comments.

P'ing Shan Leng Yen 平山冷燕. Peking: Jen-min wen-hsüeh, 1983, chapter comments.

Shih-erh lou 十二樓. Shui-hsiang chi-chiu 睡鄉祭酒, comment. 1800 Hui-ch'eng t'ang 會成堂 copy in Columbia University. Typeset edition with post-chapter comments only, Peking: Jen-min wen-hsüeh, 1986.

Shui-hu hou-chuan 水滸後傳. Ts'ai Yüan-fang 蔡元放, comment. Taipei: T'ien-i ch'u-pan she, 1975 photo-reprint.

Sui-shih i-wen 隋史遺文. See *Chien-hsiao ko*. . . .

Sui-T'ang liang-ch'ao chih-chuan 隋唐兩朝志傳. Yang Shen 楊慎 (attrib.), comment. Photocopy in Columbia University.

Sui-T'ang yen-i 隋唐演義. See *Hsiu-hsiang*. . . .

Sui Yang-ti yen-shih 隋煬帝艷史. Taipei: T'ien-i ch'u-pan she, 1974, reprint of 1936 edition. See also *Hsin-chüan*. . . .

Tang-k'ou chih 蕩寇志. 1853, copy in University of Chicago.

T'ieh-hua hsien shih 鐵花仙史. Shenyang: Ch'un-feng wen-i, 1985, typeset edition, chapter comments.

Tou-p'eng hsien-hua 豆棚閑話. Peking: Jen-min wen-hsüeh, 1984, chapter comments by Tzu-jan k'uang-k'o 紫髯狂客. Also Taipei: Hsin wen-feng, 1982.

Ts'an-T'ang Wu-tai yen-i chuan 殘唐五代演義傳. Li Chih 李贄 (attrib.), comment. Copy in Columbia University. Also Peking: Pao-wen t'ang shu-tien, 1983 typeset edition, chapter comments.

Tung-Chou Lieh-kuo chih 東周列國志. Ts'ai Yüan-fang 蔡元放, comment. Peking: Chung-kuo shu-tien, 1986, photo-reprint of Tian-shih chai edition.

Wu-se shih 五色石. Shenyang: Ch'un-feng wen-i, 1985.

Yeh-sou p'u-yen 野叟曝言. 1881 P'i-ling Hui-chen lou 毘陵彙珍樓, copy in Hong Kong University.

Yü Ch'u hsin-chih 虞初新志. Shih-chia-chuang: Ho-pei jen-min, 1985, typeset reprint.

LIST OF CONTRIBUTORS

SHUEN-FU LIN took his B.A. at Tunghai University, Taiwan, and received his Ph.D. from Princeton University. He is Professor of Chinese Language and Literature at the University of Michigan, Ann Arbor. His publications in the field of traditional Chinese fiction include articles on the *Ju-lin wai-shih* and *Lao Ts'an yu-chi*. He has also published a book on the Sung Dynasty *tz'u* poet Chiang K'uei and recently coedited *The Vitality of the Lyric Voice: Shih Poetry from the Late Han to the T'ang* (Princeton University Press, 1987). He is currently engaged in research on the *Chuang Tzu*.

ANDREW H. PLAKS received his Ph.D. from Princeton University and is presently Professor of East Asian Studies at Princeton University. His many publications in the field of traditional Chinese fiction include *Archetype and Allegory in the Dream of the Red Chamber* (Princeton University Press, 1976) and *The Four Masterworks of the Ming Novel* (Princeton University Press, 1987). He is also the editor of *Chinese Narrative: Critical and Theoretical Essays* (Princeton University Press, 1977). He is currently engaged in work on a volume of translations from representative works of traditional criticism on the *Dream of the Red Chamber*.

DAVID L. ROLSTON received his Ph.D. from the University of Chicago. He has taught at the University of Chicago and is presently Assistant Professor in the Department of Asian Languages and Cultures at the University of Michigan. An article of his in Chinese, *"Lin Lan Hsiang yü Chin P'ing Mei"* appeared in *Wen-hsüeh i-ch'an* (1987.5) and *Ming-Ch'ing hsiao-shuo lun-ts'ung* 5 (1987).

DAVID T. ROY received his Ph.D. from Harvard University and has taught Chinese literature at Harvard and Princeton. He is presently Professor of Chinese Literature at the University of Chicago. He is the author of *Kuo Mo-jo: The Early Years* (Harvard University Press, 1971) and his articles on traditional Chinese fiction include "Chang Chu-p'o's Commentary on the *Chin P'ing Mei*" in *Chinese Narrative: Critical and Theoretical Essays*. He is currently engaged in a complete translation of the earliest extant edition of the *Chin P'ing Mei*.

JOHN C.Y. WANG received his Ph.D. from Cornell University. He has taught at the University of Iowa and the University of Michigan and is now Professor of Chinese at Stanford University. His numerous publications concerning traditional Chinese fiction criticism include *Chin Sheng-t'an* (Twayne, 1972) and articles on the Chih-yen chai and Wang Hsi-lien commentaries on the

Dream of the Red Chamber. He is currently completing a major work to be entitled *The Narrative Art of the Tso-chuan.*

ANTHONY C. YU received his Ph.D. from the University of Chicago, where he has taught religion and literature for the Divinity School and Chinese literature for the Department of East Asian Languages and Civilizations for the last twenty years. Currently he is Carl Darling Buck Professor of Humanities at the University of Chicago. He is the author and annotator of a complete translation of the *Hsi-yu chi, The Journey to the West* (University of Chicago Press, 1977–83) and his many publications include articles on that novel and the *Dream of the Red Chamber (Story of the Stone).*

INDEX

Index